HISTORY OF THE AMERICAN CINEMA

Volume 4

1926–1931

John Barrymore and Mary Astor in Don Juan *(Warner Bros., 1926).*

HISTORY OF THE AMERICAN CINEMA

CHARLES HARPOLE, GENERAL EDITOR

4
THE TALKIES:
AMERICAN CINEMA'S
TRANSITION TO
SOUND, 1926-1931

Donald Crafton

UNIVERSITY OF CALIFORNIA PRESS
Berkeley · Los Angeles · London

University of California Press
Berkeley and Los Angeles, California

University of California Press, Ltd.
London, England

First Paperback Printing 1999

Library of Congress Cataloging-in-Publication Data

Crafton, Donald.
    The talkies : American cinema's transition to sound, 1926–1931 /
    Donald Crafton.
        p.   cm.—(History of the American cinema ; v. 4)
    Includes bibliographical references and index.
    ISBN 0-520-22128-1 (alk. paper)
    1. Sound motion pictures—History.   I. Title.   II. Series.
PN1993.5.U6H55   1997 vol. 4
[PN1995.7]
791.43'0973—dc21   99-20221
                                                            CIP

Originally published by Charles Scribner's Sons, a division of Macmillan Library Reference.

A different version of chapter 20 appeared in Noël Carroll and David Bordwell, eds.,
Post-Theory: Reconstructing Film Studies (Madison: University of Wisconsin Press, 1996).

Printed in the United States of America
08   07   06   05   04   03   02   01   00   99
10   9   8   7   6   5   4   3   2   1

The paper used in this publication meets the minimum requirements of
ANSI/NISO Z39.48-1992 (R 1997) *(Permanence of Paper)*. ∞

Advisory Board

The Cinema History Project and the
History of the American Cinema
have been supported by grants from the
National Endowment for the Humanities and the
John and Mary R. Markle Foundation.

To Andy
Little Pal

Contents

Acknowledgments

Discussions with graduate students in my seminars at the University of Wisconsin inspired much of conceptual underpinnings of this work. Kevin Heffernan, Scott Higgins, Rodney Hill, Henry Jenkins, Moya Luckett, Tim Merritt, Michael Quinn, Sara Ross, Paul Seale, Greg Smith, Jeff Smith, Murray Smith, Vincent Suarez, Michael Walsh, and Rafael Vela contributed ideas (and term papers) about the coming of sound. In addition to their academic contributions, Teresa Becker, John Gerbig, and Heidi Kenaga also helped as research assistants.

The patient staffs of the dozen or so international archives I visited know that I appreciate their advice and generosity. Especially crucial were Ned Comstock, Bill Whittington, and Stuart Ng at the Warner Bros. Archives of the University of Southern California. Ruta Abolins, Ben Brewster, and Maxine Fleckner Ducey were invaluable informants at the Wisconsin Center for Film and Theater Research. Sheldon Hochheiser at the AT&T Archives graciously opened his corporate treasures for me. Richard May, at that time with Turner Entertainment, was a source of constant filmographic information in general, and read an early draft very closely. Jan-Christopher Horak shared his vast resources twice: first at the George Eastman House in Rochester, then at the Munich Film Museum.

Antonia Lant, Stephen Bottomore, Greg Linnell, and Tim Romano sent clippings and other imporant material my way. Special thanks to Carolyn Schaffer, who devoted an inordinate amount of time researching Frank Irby. Joseph Yranski lent not only his rare archival photographs and documents, but freely gave his intensive and extensive knowledge of the early sound era. His passion for the talkies is matched only by his affection for Colleen Moore. Selections from his magnificent collection grace these pages.

I am very grateful to my colleagues for their thoughtful readings of the manuscript and/or their valued suggestions: Lea Jacobs, Stephen Vaughn, Richard Koszarski, and Charles Wolfe. Ron Hutchinson, genial founder of the Vitaphone Project, pointed me toward important primary resources and updated the manuscript. Kristin Thompson and David Bordwell read different drafts of the manuscript and made copious corrections and suggestions, earning my heart-felt thanks. Rick Altman and his graduate seminar on sound at the University of Iowa provided welcome advice and a few reality-checks during their review of several chapters-in-progress. All through this project, I felt the special support and rapport of a community of gifted scholars.

The twin godfathers of this book are Charles Harpole, whose low-key but steady prodding was much needed, and Tino Balio, who first "pitched" *The Talkies* in my office on a snowy afternoon. See what you started?

Elise and Andy Crafton, not always willingly, devoted a chunk of their young lives to this book. Thanks, unsung collaborators. Susan Ohmer not only shared her astounding clipping file and library, she suggested many sources and ideas about theorizing audiences. Her constant encouragement made the author's chores more bearable. *Merci bien!*

1

Introduction:
The Uncertainty of Sound

*The serious problem of injecting sound into the now silent drama is in
the offing. What producers will do in this regard, of course, is an
unknown factor.*

MAURICE KANN, *Film Daily*, 2 APRIL 1928

Silent and Sound cinema. Few demarcations are so sharply drawn, so elegantly
opposed, so pristinely binary. In the movies, sound is either off or on. Everyday conversation, reference books, shelving in video stores, college film courses and their text-
books, film rental catalogs, and festivals are organized around this fundamental rift in
the history of the medium. Over the years the story of the transition from silence to talking has been retold so many times that it has become a kind of urban legend. Everyone
just knows it to be true. The components of the popular retelling of sound always represent it as a dividing line between the Old and New Hollywood. In no small part, this
is a matter of rhetorical convention. Sound divides the movies with the assuredness of
biblical duality. The emphasis often is on the effects of sound on individual actors—the
great lover whose career was wrecked by a squeaky voice. The transition was also
inevitable: sound was something that cinema lacked, and sooner or later it would have
to be added. Unfortunately, in the process, the Art of the Silent Film was destroyed. So
goes the legend.

An exemplary account representing the talkies as a sudden shift was written by the
music critic Deems Taylor (remembered as the narrator of Disney's FANTASIA [1940]):

> It was in the late summer [of 1927] that the blow fell. A new contraption had
> been peddled around the studios, a device for producing pictures that
> talked, by means of a wax recording of the actors' voices, synchronized with
> the film projector. But the well-established producers did not fall for any
> such newfangled nonsense; besides, the cost of wiring all the theaters for
> sound would be prohibitive. It remained for the comparatively obscure and
> financially worried Warner Brothers to take a chance on the new process,
> which they named Vitaphone. They hired Al Jolson, one of the most popu-
> lar musical stars of the day, selected a maudlin play entitled *The Jazz Singer*,
> and went to work. . . . *The Jazz Singer* [1927] out to be a box-office gold

mine that made over two million dollars for the Warners and set them on
their feet financially. It made a movie star out of Jolson. But above all, it
turned the film industry topsy-turvy and consigned the silent picture to the
scrap heap. (Deems Taylor, *A Pictorial History of the Movies* [New York:
Simon and Schuster, 1943], pp. 201–2)

Like so much of the writing about the conversion to sound, Taylor emphasizes its divi-
siveness. Before THE JAZZ SINGER, sound was only a dream; after the "revolution,"
Hollywood was rocked by the hasty conversion to "all-talking, all-singing, all-dancing."
This shattering of the past became the central motif—and the title—of Alexander
Walker's book:

There has been no revolution like it. It passed with such breakneck speed,
at such inflationary cost, with such ruthless self-interest, that a whole art
form was sundered and consigned to history almost before anyone could
count the cost in economic terms or guess the consequences in human
ones—and certainly before anyone could keep an adequate record of it.
There has never been such a lightning retooling of an entire industry—even
wartime emergencies were slower—nor such a wholesale transformation in
the shape and acceptance of new forms of mass entertainment. . . . The
shape and especially the sound of cinema movies today was decided during
those few years. Not in any cool-headed, rational fashion: but amidst unbelievable confusion, stupidity, accident, ambition and greed. (Alexander
Walker, *The Shattered Silents: How the Talkies Came to Stay* [New York:
William Morrow, 1979], p. vii)

A second component of the popular view of the coming of sound centers on the disruption of the lives of the stars. For most people, Hollywood and glamorous movie stars are
synonymous. When Hollywood represented the change to sound in the revered musical
SINGIN' IN THE RAIN (1952), directed by Gene Kelly and Stanley Donen, it produced a
wonderful piece of nostalgic entertainment that, on more than one occasion, has been
shown in film history classes as a kind of documentary. In fairness, the film may be
slightly more accurate than most Hollywood historical treatments. And rightly so, since
its producer, Arthur Freed, had, as they say, "been there, done that." As a young lyricist,
Freed was hired by Irving Thalberg at MGM in 1929. He wrote the words to, among a
hundred other songs, "Singin' in the Rain," featured in two early musicals. The 1952
production was a cinematic roman à clef layered by the writers Betty Comden and Adolf
Green with the patina of romance. Movie star Don (Kelly) reminisces for his fans at the
gala premiere of his latest vehicle, THE DANCING CAVALIER. His costar and rumored
fiancée, Lina (Jean Hagen), is strangely silent. Through a flashback, we see the "truth"
about the matinee idol. He and his partner Cosmo (Donald O'Connor) arrive in
Hollywood as vaudevillians and eke out a living playing mood music for the actors filming silent movie scenes. Don eventually becomes a John Gilbert–like screen lover, per-
petually cast with the Greta Garbo–like siren Lina. Cosmo becomes head of
Monumental Pictures' music department. In the middle of a filming session, the studio
head rushes in to halt the take. THE JAZZ SINGER is a hit; there will be no more silents.
Lina, we learn, is not only stupid and vindictive, she has a voice like a chain saw. But she
controls the studio's sound policy because of her all-powerful stardom. Meanwhile, Don

has fallen in love with Kathy Selden (Debbie Reynolds), a showgirl who is everything Lina is not. She is bright, spunky, and independent, has a golden voice, and can she dance! The sneak preview of Monumental's first all-talkie, THE DANCING CAVALIER, is disastrous. The audience hoots at Lina's diction, laughs at Don's passionate "I love you, I love you, I love you," and howls at the technical blunders, especially when the film and its record go out of synchronization. In an inspired all-night skull session (broken up by a song-and-dance number), Don, Cosmo, and Kathy decide to try naturalistic acting, jettison melodrama, and add music and dance. They also invent techniques which would be used in the talkies: voice-doubling and dubbing (Kathy will substitute her voice for Lina's) and pre-recorded playback. Lina finds out and threatens to block Kathy's career as a star in her own right, but when Don, Cosmo, and the studio head expose Lina as a fraud at the Chinese Theater, the coast is cleared for Don and Kathy's costardom in the movies, paralleling their union in private life.

In the best classical manner of the history film or the biopic, the film weaves a tapestry of fact, fantasy, and character development. It creates the illusion that, though the events happening before our eyes are fictional, the underlying factual basis is real. Thus, for the historian of the talkies, SINGIN' IN THE RAIN hovers in the distance as a ghost. It is the return of a repressed idea that the transition to sound was *really* about the division between Old and New Hollywood. The timing in the 1950s could hardly have been coincidental. The motion picture industry was recovering from a major economic realignment—the 1948 consent decrees which required the studios to divest themselves of the theater holdings they had acquired during the late 1920s. Hollywood was also alarmed by the growing popularity and affordability of television, so what better subject than a film about coping with the threat of new technology? As Hollywood had survived the earlier revolution, analogously, it could weather the onslaught of television. This is the story of sound told the way Hollywood wanted it told—a crisis with a happy ending. Of course, in SINGIN' IN THE RAIN there are no pesky trade unions, no Actors Equity strikes, no mention of William Fox's ruin, nor of a thousand lawsuits. . . .

The talkies succeeded silents because that's how nature is. Little seeds grow into oaks. The inevitability of sound as an organic metaphor pervades much popular writing. One of the most striking examples is in the aptly named *The Film Finds Its Tongue,* which describes how Sam Warner and a technician became fascinated with sound film by way of radio: "They spent hours poring over the mysteries of vacuum tubes, amplifiers, microphones, monitors, loud speakers. *They were scrutinizing the embryonic ganglia of the Talkies!*"[1] The image connotes an electrical device that will eventually grow into something simulating the human nervous system.

It is difficult to think of a more profound discrepancy between popular and academic discourse on a subject than that which currently exists with regard to movie sound. In the 1970s and 1980s, several historians began emphasizing film as an industrial *system* whose parts have specific relationships. When changes occur, they are harmonious. Instead of confusion and hotheadedness, analysts, led by Douglas Gomery, evaluated changing Hollywood as a macroeconomic structure and found deliberateness and rationality. The transition was driven by the dominant studios' need to respond to competition from the outsiders Warners and Fox. Their one-two punch of physical expansion and experimentation with sound threatened to disrupt the major studios' established oligopoly. The industry responded according to a classic paradigm consisting of three phases. "Invention" covers the development of the synch-sound apparatus up to 1925, when Warner Bros. became interested in exploiting it as Vitaphone. "Innovation" includes the period when Vitaphone, Fox, and the "Big Five" studios defined various ways of applying sound. This phase ended in 1928 when the majors decided together to commit themselves to sound. "Diffusion" was the coordinated dissemination of sound domestically and abroad according to mutually beneficial terms dictated by the studios. This phase also included the swift wiring of theaters. Gomery constantly emphasizes the majors' rational handling of the transition and concludes, "It was a gradual *evolution*, not a rapid revolution or panic. The majors did *not* rush into the production of talkies. They preplanned each step. . . . The changeover . . . was not chaotic, confused or filled with conjecture. In retrospect it was accomplished with little turmoil and saw all the majors *increase,* not lose, both profits and power."[2]

One of the lessons from recent research that informs this book is that the boundaries dividing Hollywood "before" and "after" sound were not so clear-cut. In fact, there is no unanticipated landmark event or watershed film which separates the golden age of silents from the modern age of the talkies. The transition was years in the making and in the finishing. While Warner Bros. played a crucial role in innovating sound, other corporations—Western Electric, RCA, De Forest Phonofilm, and Fox Films—were also spearheading the change. The central position of Jolson and THE JAZZ SINGER in Taylor's retelling is absolutely typical, but the claim that this movie was the genesis of sound cinema cannot withstand scrutiny. And the motion picture industry did not turn topsy-turvy because of the talkies. No studios closed on account of the coming of sound; most increased their profits. Many theaters did go out of business during the time of the changeover, but whether these closures can be ascribed solely to the talkies is doubtful. There were abundant outside economic factors (radio listening and automobile driving are two obvious ones). For those theaters that made the switch, 1929 and 1930 were record-setting years for film attendance. The Depression caused the studios to scale back and theaters to close. But by 1931 sound production had been standardized and projection practice was again routine.

This book emphasizes the longevity—not the suddenness—of the transition to sound. Instead of focusing on one personality, event, studio, or single strand of technological development, I address several interlaced aspects of film production, reception, and, to a lesser extent, distribution. The interpretations espoused by Taylor, Walker, and the "Freed unit" provide a good story, but like so many narratives of film history, they succeed by drastically simplifying and reshaping the subject according to preconceived notions. Competing readings have been sheared off. Making sound violently revolutionary displaces the hidden violence of the historical method that produced the illusion of a clean break with the past.

Like much of our general knowledge about Hollywood, the concept of a dividing line between antediluvian silent cinema and the *modern* talkies was coscripted by the industry and the media. RCA in particular—but the other manufacturers were complicit, too—advertised its technology as the avatar of a New Era. Sound film was associated with the "coming" (in the Messianic sense) of the next millennium. "It was the dawn of a new era in amusement," wrote Green about the advent. "In this year, 1929, the talkie is here, and here for the rest of the century."[3] With an eye already on the end of the 1990s, the promoters of sound represented their devices as a total break with the past, as represented not only by silent movies but by the whole universe of pre-electrical communication.

This book portrays the transition to sound as partly rational and partly confused. In this respect, my argument departs somewhat from the revisionist accounts, which stress the systematic nature of developments in film. (Is there such a thing as "surrevision-ism"?) While I do not object to the "big picture" approach, my own research slightly shifts the central issue. Certainly the studios had a strategy for change. They wished to hold their markets, remain competitive, and maximize profits. But the devil was in the details. They also had to reduce risk. It would be more accurate to argue that the studios *tried* to develop a proactive approach to the transition to sound but more often responded retroactively. They developed a coordinated master plan, then scrambled to contain the disruption of the talkies on an ad hoc basis.

Symptomatic of the newer academic treatment of sound is the rejection of history told as the exploits of business geniuses, or of individual stars, like Jolson. We now see these movers and shakers as cogs in the larger system. More attention is directed to film form and style. David Bordwell's short but persuasive chapter in *The Classical Hollywood Cinema* was a linchpin in his and his coauthors' argument that the sound transition epitomized Hollywood's limitless resiliency and capacity to absorb technical or economic challenges. Far from disrupting traditional practice, the talkies made it even more entrenched. "By 1933," Bordwell maintains, "shooting a sound film came to mean shooting a silent film with sound."[4] Preserving dialogue-film style reined in certain non-classical tendencies which sound introduced. Techniques were modified to make them more amenable to creating a talking simulacrum of what had been lost. The effort to contain sound was emblematic of the industry's need for production efficiency and equilibrium and is mirrored in the microcosm of film style. Again, I cannot disagree. Repeatedly, one finds Hollywood technicians conversing about the need to "return to silents" and, after 1930, making rather smug pronouncements that they had more or less accomplished that goal.

One element missing from these approaches is the film audience. A model proposed by Rick Altman includes viewers in the calculus. In his theorizing of early sound, the individual film is not a text but an "event" which he likens to "the pinhole at the center of an hourglass."[5] The two volumes of the glass represent the work of production and the process of reception. Traffic between the halves is two-way, with reception and production eventually feeding back into each other. This model avoids channeling films into preset textual meanings and analyzing them as lapidary works. Altman writes,

> Conceived as a series of events, cinema reveals rather than dissimulates its material existence. From the complexity of its financing and production to the diversity of its exhibition, cinema must be considered in terms of the material resources that it engages. From the standpoint of sound, this is of capital importance, for it removes cinema from the customary, purely visual definition. As a material product, cinema quickly reveals the location and nature of its sound track(s), the technology used to produce them, the apparatus necessary for reproduction, and the physical relationship between loudspeakers, spectators, and their physical surroundings. Such an approach encourages us to move past the imaginary space of the screen to the spaces and sounds with which cinema must compete—the kids in the front rows, the air conditioner hum, the lobby cash register, the competing sound track in the adjacent multiplex theater, passing traffic, and a hundred other sounds that are not part of the text as such, but constitute an important component of cinema's social materiality. (Rick Altman, ed., *Sound Theory/Sound Practice* [New York: Routledge, 1992], p. 6)

These manifold conditions of spectatorship would include the audience's attitudes and preferences. But these were not documented at the time. Of course, there are many people living who recall their first experiences attending sound films. Northeast Historic Film conducted a survey in 1990–1991 and asked, "Do you remember your first sound picture?" and, "What did you think about the change?" THE JAZZ SINGER, SONNY BOY (1929), SEVENTH HEAVEN (1927), and WINGS (1927) were mentioned. (The last two titles were released only with synchronized music.) Though most responses were limited to a word or two, every one of the thirty or so who answered gave the sound film a positive review. They "loved it" and described the change as "great," "more real," and "miraculous." Some of the memories were quite specific, especially concerning the emotions elicited by Jolson's films ("Strong men cried"). One person recalled the competition among theaters in her small town ("Whoever had sound got the most people"). Another described the experience of seeing and hearing a film in 1928: "The star was Conrad Nagel, and the 'talking' was of one *partial* duration—not for the whole picture. Spooky—hollow sounding voices—larger than life and ghostly! But fascinating."[6]
Oral histories and recollections are valuable testimonies about the impact of sound on specific individuals, but they are necessarily limited by the representative validity of their small sample size, lack of controls, and, of course, subjectivity due to inevitable loss and embroidery as memories become more distant. Any account of the film audience (the plurality and diversity of its components are understood) must be a compromise. Is the materiality of reception an attainable ideal? Or is it always a wild card?

My emphasis in this book is more on end-use than on production. There is, perhaps, one form of documentation, the exhibitors' trade news, which provides a roundabout clue to how audiences in general received the talkies. Whereas the foremost trade publication, *Variety,* tried to present a broad view of the entertainment field, its coverage was diversified among theatrical, vaudeville, and film production. *Moving Picture World* (which had merged with *Exhibitor's Herald*), *Harrison's Reports,* and *Film Daily,* however, addressed the concerns of theater managers. The last, a daily newspaper, cultivated links with exhibitors and responded to their concerns. Of course, it paraphrased studio press releases, just as the other trades did, but its editors also spoke up for the interests of its primary readership. Maurice "Red" Kann especially was an impassioned promoter of the sound film, believing it had the potential to bring entertainment to hitherto untapped audiences, and riches to his subscriber-exhibitors. *Film Daily's* reviewers gave (allegedly—I have not been able to dispute this) objective reactions to the current films. Unlike other journalists who attended special press previews, the paper made a big deal of going to the movies with "ordinary" folks (though, practically, its reviewers appear to have restricted themselves to the Broadway entertainment district). Unlike *Harrison's Reports,* a reviewing service that advised independent managers on the profitability of new releases, *Film Daily* was an outlet for wide-ranging issues affecting the business, protocol, and politics of showing movies. While its pages do not put us in the audience, they do give us a view of the coming of sound from the perspective of the exhibitor and his or her constituencies.

Audience involvement in film is far from systematic. I picture the industry as engaging with active but unpredictable consumers, trying to divine their entertainment desires. The films of this period are more like tests than texts. Rather than seeing Hollywood as a manufacturer planning for a rational changeover (the way Detroit retooled from one make of auto to the next), I prefer the analogy of the noisy bazaar. Eager customers were shouting for a new item, and the vendors were having difficulty

Movie crowd as a bazaar. Premiere of BULLDOG DRUMMOND *(United Artists),*
May 1929.

keeping up with demand. The crowd clamored for some articles (for example, the filmed revue) but quickly changed its mind, leaving the supplier overstocked. Other goods (gangster films with charismatic stars) were in short supply. Hollywood, like the canniest and most prosperous merchant in the bazaar, tried to hedge by covering all the positions, anticipating future demand, and trying to satisfy everyone (thus offering a great diversity of films and genres during the transition). It was probably audiences' tastes that pushed Hollywood, not to establish an alternate style of filmmaking, but to modify traditional silent practices.

Quickly the industry and film styles assimilated sound and settled down. But the way Hollywood achieved its goal of containing sound in 1931 was not at all what had been envisioned in the master plans of 1925–1929. Foremost, the introduction of sound set off or exacerbated various struggles for control over the new technology, film distribution, production and exhibition practice, social control of spoken language, and economic control of labor and the audience. Some of these contests ended definitively; others are still unresolved.

I also stress the effects of the international business depression on the changeover. After 1930 consumers could or would not spend their dwindling resources on the movies the way they did in the twenties. Though the pressure of standardization was always present in Hollywood, it was hard times—that is, lost admission revenue—that definitively forced the industry to limit its diverse, hedging approach to technology.

Producers abandoned technical experiments (like widescreen and 3-D), adopted industrywide technical norms, concentrated on moneymaking genres, and decided on a uniform foreign distribution strategy. The economic contraction blunted the struggle for control by forcing Hollywood further into noncompetition and product uniformity.

The transition to sound cinema was not the paroxysm which the industry itself and popular writers describe, but it was a complicated and messy business, owing in no small part to the vicissitudes of mass audiences. In this account, I try to preserve the tentativeness and uncertainty of the events, and the complexity of the industrial and cultural relations. In many ways, this history of these struggles for dominance is more engaging than the romantic version in SINGIN' IN THE RAIN. There are tales of brilliant but eccentric inventors, naked corporate avarice, stars ruined and restored, the race against competitors to wire theaters, violent labor strife, international cultural imperialism, the climax of the Crash, and the denouement of the Depression. But there are also a lot of loose ends and unknown factors in this story. At the time when sound was introduced, it was not clear whether it was important or whether it would be permanent. The steps necessary to implement it and what its place in the theater program should be were still open questions.

What you are about to read is organized as discussions of the negotiations and struggles for power over this new technology. I have not structured the book as a strict linear narrative (although chronology has been preserved as much as possible in each discussion for clarity), but as chapters with overlapping temporal frames. The progression, then, is not from one constituent phase of evolution to the next (link to link), but rather from general issues to more specific ones. Part 1 introduces the electrical aura in which film sound was first surrounded. In Part 2, I focus on how producers incorporated sound in particular films during the three release seasons of the transition, from mid-1928 through the spring of 1931. Part 3 examines particular aspects of the popular reception of the talkies. My history, perhaps archly, closes where many accounts of film sound begin—with a case study of THE JAZZ SINGER.

But first, here is a chronology which will provide the temporal context for these discussions.

American Cinema's Transition to Sound: An Overview

Metaphorically speaking, sound did not arrive in town all at once like an express train. It came gradually, in little crates, over a period of more than ten years. Some shipments came unsolicited, many came "on approval," and some left the factory but never arrived at their destination. In other words, the concept of synchronizing music, noises ("effects"), and speech did not take producers by surprise in the late 1920s. True, there was a shortage of equipment, and physically installing it in theaters required putting in overtime. This bottleneck was caused by everyone converting at once after the studios decided that the box-office response was strong enough to justify the investment. This was no revolution; it was an ordinary supply problem. It had come about because one supplier, Western Electric, and one studio, Warner Bros. (through its Vitaphone subsidiary), had tried to be the technology's gatekeepers.

When the first films began appearing, the uniqueness of sound was sufficient to bring in the public. *Photoplay,* for example, urged readers to check out THE FAMILY PICNIC

(1928) precisely because it turned everyday noises into novelty: "The reel proves that natural lines, without any attempt to be literary or dramatic, are effective just because they are natural. And ordinary noises—a stalled engine or the honking of horns—are funny because they are so completely true to life. So see this picture, just as a novelty and just to find out what Movietone can do."[7] But soon the box office favored certain types of sound films and punished others. Moviegoers judged the talkies, stars, and stories according to their own standards. More than one commentator characterized the public as "shopping around." The times tested the most successful studio heads' talent for second-guessing audiences and learning from mistakes. Trial and error describes these first sound productions: the part-talkie, the courtroom drama, the musical revue, the vaudeville comedy, the Metropolitan Opera, and the Western were attempts by Hollywood to determine what kind of sound film the public really wanted.

THE 1920s

It was always known that Edison's film laboratory had experimented with linking the motion picture film to the phonograph. Serious demonstrations of workable systems by various inventors had been made at least since 1906. None had succeeded. But after World War I there was a great boom in electrical research and a new attitude toward technology: increasingly researchers linked applications across a broad network rather than continue to "perfect" individual devices along a single trajectory. A representative of Electrical Research Products, Inc. (ERPI), the company responsible for furnishing sound equipment to the studios and installing reproducing devices in theaters, observed in 1929 that "the 'talkie' as we know it did not descend from the attempts of the early inventors to produce talking motion pictures; it came down through a number of other sciences and devices, and owes almost nothing to the earlier attempts in the talkie art."[8] These parallel areas of research included public address, phonography, telephony, radio, and miscellaneous electrical devices (like electromagnets). Many of these apparatuses continued (and still continue) to evolve in directions that had nothing to do with cinema. But some applications were adapted for the movies.

Most efforts to synchronize sound and image either did not make it out of the lab or failed to win approval because they did not work. The illusion that a voice is emanating from a person on-screen is very fragile. The tolerance is less than one frame of projection time, a standard difficult to maintain for the duration of a ten-minute reel. For twenty years most inventors tinkered with phonograph discs as the sound medium, but a few were working with the expedient of photographically recording on film (either on a separate strip of film or as a track exposed next to the pictures).

As important as synchronization was, amplifying the recorded sound to fill a 1920s movie palace was an even greater challenge. This technology was held in the grip of RCA and Western Electric, which, in 1926, cross-licensed each other's amplification patents. Using state-of-the-art vacuum tube amplifiers, movie sound, whether recorded on disc or film, could boom into the auditorium of the biggest Bijou. The trick was to control that power, a task for which acoustic engineering, a new specialty, was created.

In the twenties few in the workshops and corporate research labs dreamed of "revolutionizing" silent Hollywood by making commercial movies talk. More typically, the inventors extended existing electrical systems. They used moving pictures to stake their claims on developing communication media, especially telephone and the hot area, radio. Thus, during the period of concentrated development in the mid-1920s, the electronics pioneer Lee de Forest saw sound cinema as an area into which he could expand his rights to exploit the vacuum tube. At the same time, the executives of Western Electric (the manufacturing branch of AT&T) and, later, RCA (controlled by AT&T's rivals General Electric and Westinghouse) were seeking more diversity for their existing sound-recording patents. The leaders looked to the movies.

In 1925 there were no takers in the film industry for Western Electric's working sound movie system. Even the Warner brothers, soon to become talking-picture pioneers, approached the sound device hesitantly. At first they vaguely saw it as an adjunct to their fledgling radio business, then as a gimmick to spice up silent film programs, then as a money-saving (and union-busting) alternative to the pit orchestra in small towns. Instead of innovating toward a specific goal, the manufacturers of the equipment had no concrete application in mind, and the movie company was not certain which of several directions to take. The scheme settled on was to circulate silent features with "canned" musical accompaniment, along with filmed performances by name entertainers from the New York stage, opera, and high-class vaudeville. These were replacements for the live "presentation acts" of the big picture palaces.

Film consumers were aware of these acoustic experiments because the competing manufacturers were eager to associate their sound film equipment with progressive science. There were articles in mass-circulated magazines and "popular science" journals that represented sound film as an electrical marvel and an inevitable stage of civilization. AT&T promoted movie sound as an improvement on the telephone; General Electric pushed it as an extension of radio. Did these strategies create an aura of electrical wonder and mystification, or were they efforts to exploit the populace's existing predisposition to sanction electrical engineering as modern? Probably *both* conditions prevailed. During the late 1920s, a climate of acceptance was nurtured by fast-breaking developments in electronic (what was then called thermionic) technology. The public was curious and appreciative and welcomed the talkies as a new form of *electrical* entertainment.

Though the Warner Bros.' decision to invest millions in Western Electric's apparatus appears risky in retrospect, the initiative coincided with a go-go period of corporate expansion. We all know about the bull market in stocks in the 1920s. From 1920 through 1929, equities averaged an annual return of 13.86 percent, almost twice that of the previous two decades. But less well known is the rally in bonds. The market returned an average annual yield of 8.16 percent for the decade, compared to .97 percent annually for the period 1900–1919. This increase indicated a demand for corporate debt of unprecedented magnitude.[9] Like other businesses, movie companies were borrowing heavily to finance growth on many fronts (including mergers to acquire and build studio facilities, theater outlets purchased in bulk, and positions in broadcasting). Though the Warners' venture in *sound* was unusual, highly leveraged diversification and expansion were standard business practices. It is true that the Warner brothers were gamblers, but they rolled the dice under the watchful eye of Wall Street financiers who carefully calculated the potential risks and rewards.

1926

Warner Bros. was hopeful that Western Electric's sound system (and the prestige of being associated with AT&T) would yield immediate payback if the public response to its sound experiments was favorable. The company formed the Vitaphone partnership with Western Electric in April with the dual purpose of producing and distributing sound films and sublicensing recorders to the other Hollywood studios. An unreleased big-budget silent feature, DON JUAN, was retrofitted with a score and loosely synchronized sound effects. The plan was to construct an all-sound film program which would generate public excitement as a media event in its own right and attract the investment of Hollywood's Big Five companies.

While these preparations were being made, Fox Film, another second-tier producer, bought the rights to a sound-on-film system which had been developed by Theodore Case in de Forest's laboratory. Chief executive William Fox had an even less well defined mission for sound; for the time being, he would do whatever Warners did. His investment initially was speculative—a bet that, if sound took off, he would have a part in it.

The DON JUAN show premiered in August 1926 and surpassed all expectations as a box-office hit and a critical success. A second synchronized feature, THE BETTER 'OLE, opened in October. Again attendance was good and critics raved. The short subjects were especially well received. George Jessel re-created his stage routine, and Al Jolson, on film, addressed the audience and sang. For the first time, Warner Bros. publicity began to hint that the Vitaphone system would be used for regular speech and singing in a feature, in addition to canned music. Around this time an idea congealed and was readily absorbed by the public: sound film technology could do for theater and vaudeville what radio and the telephone were doing. It could transmit performances from the entertainment capital, New York, to local theaters. The popular press enthused about the new sound shorts, willingly suspending disbelief and writing as though the performances were unfolding in the space of the theater. Perhaps self-serving, the film producers cultivated a democratic ideology to rationalize sound. Warners, Fox, and RCA (just beginning to exploit GE's film patents) also suggested that the sound film was a simulacrum of an in-person appearance (a premonition of the "Is it live or is it Memorex?" advertising campaign of the 1990s). I call this effect "virtual Broadway." The end-user, like his or her counterpart in modern virtual reality games, imagined that new technology could envelope the viewer in believable real space and time.

Other executives, William Fox and Paramount's Adolph Zukor, did take an interest in Vitaphone—not to take out petty sublicenses but to buy the company. The Vitaphone officers, however, held out for big stakes. In December 1926, the major studios agreed informally to act as one on the sound issue. They would boycott Vitaphone, encourage RCA to develop its competing device, and squelch internal competition by all promising to license the same system. The plan might strike us as illegal collusion and restraint of trade, but in the 1920s it was condoned as associationism, the practice of businesses banding together to share knowledge, limit competition, and combine their resources for greater economic power.

1927

William Fox would not wait. In January he signed with Western Electric and cross-licensed the patents he controlled in order to continue developing his system, which he called Movietone. Fox needed access to amplifiers, the phone company's manufacturing capability, and its installation expertise. His New York studio competed directly with Vitaphone, producing a series of filmed vaudeville shorts and silent features with added synchronized music tracks. Sound-on-film Movietone was much more mobile than the Vitaphone disc system. Fox pressed this advantage by filming outdoors. Scenes of marching West Point cadets and, especially, of Charles Lindbergh's historic transatlantic flight takeoff were greeted with keen public interest. Fox's staff thought of a new use for sound: tying it to the existing newsreel as an extra bonus. The earliest sound newsreels resembled radio. There were addresses by public figures and scenes which exploited synch-sound for its own sake. Live-recorded sound gave the impression of "being-there-ness" to the news.

AT&T realized that it had made a tactical mistake in giving Warner Bros. broad licensing rights. It created the Western Electric subsidiary Electrical Research Products, Inc., in January 1927. The Vitaphone corporation was forced to reorganize. This tactic enabled the major producers to begin negotiating directly with the manufacturer for sound rights. In February they formalized their wait-and-see agreement for one year.

Meanwhile, Warners was trying to book its sound films into as many theaters as possible, but with limited success. ERPI was charging exorbitant rates. The manufacturing and installation of equipment were far behind schedule. But the box-office appeal of the Vitaphone films also seemed to be lagging. Warners hoped to rejuvenate interest by buying the rights to a popular melodrama, *The Jazz Singer.* Al Jolson, America's most popular recording star, stepped into the title role at the last minute. For a few brief moments, this film, shot as a traditional silent and scored with a typical Vitaphone orchestral track, crackles into direct sound as Jolson's character, for instance, talks to his mother and sings some hit songs. Contrary to myth, the movie THE JAZZ SINGER was not a smash at the Broadway premiere, and it did not by itself convince the other producers to "consign the silent film to the scrap heap." The film demonstrated forcefully, though, the importance of star voices in the sound film, the appeal of popular music, and the potential rewards for adding dialogue and singing to otherwise silent films. Warners, buoyed by the response to Vitaphone and a three-picture contract with Jolson, stepped up its sound film production schedule.

RCA, taking advantage of its year of grace to perfect its sound-on-film system, now called Photophone, began demonstrations in the summer of 1927—well before Jolson's big film premiere. RCA, though, was trailing far behind Western Electric in manufacturing capability. ERPI also gained a big advantage over RCA by setting up a music clearance bureau for its future clients. As the one-year producers' moratorium neared its end and Paramount wanted to convert its huge theater chain to sound as soon as possible to block Warners' and Fox's progress, it became clear to RCA that ERPI would win. Fallback strategies were activated.

The feature films of 1927, and many of the shorts, were conceived of as silents with sound added. Even newsreels celebrated the medium's newfound acoustic ability by emphasizing synchronous sound effects. Throughout the book I use the critical term *foregrounding* (and sometimes *Variety's* jargon *spotting*) to mean accentuating the unique or novel properties of a medium. For the Vitaphone features, sound was treated as an add-on or enhancement of the ordinary film. This concept mirrored the technological conditions of making sound prints because the sound track was literally sold separately as an option.

1928

Decades of historical accounts notwithstanding, the sound film revolution did not commence with the premiere of THE JAZZ SINGER, Fox's prestige sound film SUNRISE (1927), or the Movietone Newsreel. Initial audience response was not wholeheartedly in favor of sound, and the Vitaphone features—THE FIRST AUTO, for instance—were not unqualified box-office hits. The films as a group did well in some regions but not in others. There was resistance from exhibitors, and from areas with strong unions. Sometimes silent versions made more money than sound prints. Nevertheless, the major studios signed with ERPI in May, committing them to Western Electric when, and if, they went talkie. Collectively, they were at first ambivalent. Paramount was ardent about launching sound production, while MGM laid back to see whether the public response would justify the expense. The other big studios (United Artists, First National), the minors, and the independents arrayed themselves at various places along the enthusiasm spectrum. But signing made good business sense; the studios were poised to add sound to their regular lineup if that was what the public wanted, or not, if that was what exhibitors wanted. Pathé, controlled by Joseph P. Kennedy, who had entered into a joint venture to develop sound theaters with RCA, was the only studio to commit to Photophone production.

The films of 1928 were frequently re-releases of silents with music and effects, or part-talkies. The latter were films with a reel or two of dialogue added, often as a finale (much like the way in which Technicolor reels were used at the time). This practice is consistent with the conceptualization of sound as an extra flourish. It also reveals fiscal conservatism. The studios tried to anticipate the outcome of the audible cinema trend by hedging, that is, by continuing their silent production practices while adapting to new techniques. Producers pledged allegiance to the exhibitor who chose not to convert to sound. Most continued to supply silent prints with intertitles into the early thirties. Many commentators, including those within the industry, envisioned separate production of silent and sound material. Certain types of movies (for example, slapstick comedy) were better left silent, while other types, especially theatrical adaptations, would benefit from the sound "treatment." Some envisioned separate venues for sound films, as later happened with Cinerama theaters. These hedging plans encountered two economic realities: redundancy was too wasteful to continue producing dual versions, and patronage of silent films dropped whenever competing talkies were available.

Warner Bros. widened its substantial lead in sound production in 1928 while continuing to make dual versions and part-talkies. In September the studio bought First National and committed to all-sound production but nevertheless continued to derive most of its income from rentals of silent versions. Warners also pursued a strategy of adapting successful plays as part of the virtual Broadway concept. Part-talking films like GLORIOUS BETSY and THE LION AND THE MOUSE impressed reviewers, but some began to complain that the dialogue parts were a distraction because they reminded the viewer that the sound was "mechanical." The surprise hits were THE LIGHTS OF NEW YORK, an ultra-low-budget production released in the summer of 1928 (usually the dead season), and THE TERROR, which drew capacity crowds for weeks. The allure? Gangster characters speaking argot in the former, and, in the latter, an all-talking mystery movie which foregrounded vocal cues to solve the whodunit. That sound *in some form* was here to stay was apparent after Al Jolson's second feature, THE SINGING FOOL, was released in September. Though a weak actor, Jolson milked the bathetic story of losing a child for all it was worth and elicited tears from genuinely moved audiences. The other studios added or upgraded their sound capabilities and revised their production schedules to include all-talking features. In the fall they were prepared to satisfy what now appeared to be a continuing demand for "talkers."

The all-talking film was not just an extended part-talkie. In addition to using dialogue as a special effect or an add-on, directors used it to tell a story in the traditional Hollywood style. Speaking actors developed more personality and psychological character depth. The voice, as Jolson proved, was an important ingredient in star appeal. By late in the year, studio heads were testing their actors' voices to determine whether they would be suitable for the talkies. As a shortcut, they were also hiring Broadway directors, writers, composers, and, of course, actors from the legitimate stage.

In the nation's theaters, filmed amusements substituted for presentation acts in all except the deluxe metropolitan houses, thereby achieving one of the producers' original goals. They could exploit the obvious canned vaudeville productions, but the producers' need for more shorts on the evening program created a market as well for animated cartoons with synchronized sound. This demand gave Walt Disney his big break, and other studios (MGM, Universal, Van Beuren, Fleischer, and Warner Bros.) were also picking up the ball. The result of eliminating the live acts was greater standardization of the cinema program as national distributors wrested power from local managers.

1929

Some of the films of early 1929 were substandard movies hastily cobbled together to meet the unexpectedly strong demand for talkies. Many of the clichés of the early sound cinema (including those in SINGIN' IN THE RAIN) apply to films made during this period: long static takes, badly written dialogue, voices not quite in control, poor-quality recording, and a speaking style with slow cadence and emphasis on "enunciated" tones, which the microphone was supposed to favor. But it was also a time of experimentation and concerted efforts by studio technicians, directors, and sound engineers to make the new technology work. The goal was greater comprehension of dialogue. This was accomplished by better mikes, mechanical improvements (for example, microphone placement during recording, loudspeaker placement, and continuing volume adjustment during projection), and changes in the actors' vocal performance.

Certain types of dramas were selected to "spot" talking. Thus, the first major cycle of the new cinema was the trial film, which replaced much of the action with expository dialogue. Frequently this was an adaptation of a theater success (like THE BELLAMY TRIAL [1929]). The other imported cycle was the musical, with its performances integrated into a backstage plot (as in THE BROADWAY MELODY [1929]) or transposed intact (I use the term *encapsulated*) from stage revue antecedents (for example, THE SHOW OF SHOWS [1929]). One side effect of the musical craze was to provide employment opportunities for African Americans on the screen. The films exploited blacks as gifted but one-dimensional performers. Or they became character actors, usually cast in demeaning plantation stereotypes. Equally disturbing to modern audiences, but everyday movie fare during this period, are the numerous films in which whites, made up in blackface, impersonated African Americans. The talkies revivified this remnant of a moribund minstrel heritage. Other ethnic groups were represented, usually also as caricatures, in early sound films. One group, the Yiddish-speaking enclave of New York City, did find its voice briefly during the period and made several dozen movies. These productions took advantage of cinema's dialogue capabilities to tap a niche market in a non-mainstream culture.

Reneging on their pledges of the year before to continue making silents, one studio after another announced all-sound product for the 1929–1930 season. Merger mania continued to grow. William Fox took over (temporarily, it turned out) Loew's, the parent of MGM, and the British Gaumont theater chain. Paramount expanded its Publix theaters, and Warner Bros. and United Artists made futile efforts to join together.

Fan magazines caught the talkie bug and used sound to construct narratives suggesting that readers could vicariously share their favorite stars' triumphs or hardships during the transition. They implied that fans might even have some degree of control over performers' fates. The movie voice went through distinct phases of representation in popular writing. At first it was an embellishment to the star's already-known personality. Fans and critics responded to the voice as if it were "disembodied," an entity apart from the speaker. This notion enabled critics to judge whether an actor's voice was "appropriate" for his or her appearance. Much of the anxiety over vocal quality was a thinly disguised fear of technology's power to transform it. "Mike fright" tended to dissipate as critics began to emphasize naturalness rather than "elocution." The reproduction of the voice greatly improved as a result of better recording techniques (for example, increased use of mike booms) and other refinements which increased the signal-to-noise ratio on the sound track. Cameras and sound-recording gear became more mobile, and filming outdoors in remote locations became practical. Filmmakers at first had to overcome the immobility of the cameras, which, because of their noisy mechanism, were kept inside soundproof cabinets. To circumvent the static mise-en-scène which resulted, directors used multiple cameras. That is, for each take up to a half-dozen views were shot at the same time from different angles and distances. The resulting footage was edited together to produce the rhythmic changes in scale to which audiences were accustomed in silent films. The static phase of the talkies proved to be very transitory.

The studios' conversion to sound was matched by exhibitors' rapid wiring of their theaters. Those chains affiliated with studios, about 15 percent of all the theaters, were obligated to install Western Electric equipment and to show only films licensed by ERPI. At the end of 1928, however, Western Electric conceded that its Movietone and RCA's optical sound tracks were interchangeable. Many of the independently owned theaters began installing the cheaper RCA Photophone reproducing systems. Unless they were economically strapped, theater owners had no choice but to convert to some brand of sound system because otherwise the affiliated chains would take away their business. Although the national chains were a numerical minority, they set the pace in the most important markets. As a result, at the time of the stock market crash in October 1929, out-of-the-way theaters and those servicing poor neighborhoods were the only ones still waiting for amplification. The transformation of American movie houses from almost all silent to almost all sound therefore took about a year and a half. Owing primarily to sound, the studio system had become a huge tentacular structure with interests in publishing, music, and electric companies. The film manufacturers also became internationally diversified.

The film industry complained about the many millions of dollars it took to finance this conversion, but in reality the changeover was funded by borrowing against mushrooming profits. Audiences flocked to the movies in 1929, making it one of the best years in Hollywood history. Union leaders pointed out that this prosperity was in contrast to the thousands of musicians, crew members, extras, and specialty workers laid off during the transition to sound. Actors Equity, the New York–based union, tried to organize the Hollywood performers, but a strike called for July was ineffectual. Many of the workers' demands, however, were addressed in later negotiations with producers. When the market crashed, some of the wind was knocked out of the business's sails, but many predicted that movies would never lose their popularity. During 1929 the studios had invested in infrastructure, expanded their theater holdings, diversified into other entertainment fields, and dabbled in technological innovation (besides sound, variable screen shapes and stereoscopic imagery). The onset of the Depression forced the industry to concentrate on the basics.

1930

By mid-1930 the film industry was in a severe recession from which it did not emerge for about four years. Hollywood went into retrenchment. The ramifications for sound were that shooting schedules and techniques had to be made as efficient as possible. With silent-running cameras, lightweight cranes and booms, and improved lighting and record-ing materials, the expensive practice of multi-camera filming was phased out. Distributors circulated fewer silent versions to small houses. ERPI stopped wiring theaters which were judged to be economically unstable, leaving them to RCA and small entrepreneurs. The studios, except for Paramount and Warners, closed their New York production facilities. Many theaters affiliated with the producers were sold off to raise cash.

Attendance fell. Exhibitors reacted by lowering ticket prices and inaugurating the various come-ons which now have become part of Depression-era nostalgia: bank night (the winning ticket stub collected a jackpot), door prizes, giveaways of dishes and other items, and blonde night (they got in free—when accompanied by a paying escort). Theaters hosted fan clubs and special matinees for kids. The wildly popular Mickey Mouse clubs are a good example of one way a theater could make money from activities ancillary to the actual projection of films. Independent theater owners complained that the studios were engaged in unfair trade practices, and eventually (but not soon enough to provide any economic relief) the courts agreed. Sound enabled the studios to dictate terms to independent theater owners—for example, basing rental on a sliding percent-age of the gate instead of the prior practice of charging a flat fee. Small owners had lit-tle means of resistance. Some theaters closed their doors and tried alternative amusement enterprises, like miniature golf.

American producers, ERPI, and RCA took advantage of the recession in Europe to get an early lead in licensing Continental studios and wiring theaters. In 1929, however, the German conglomerate Tobis Klangfilm won significant patent decisions which raised unexpected legal obstacles and slowed the Yankees' takeover. Hollywood fretted, meanwhile, about the best way to distribute films overseas. Millions were allocated to establishing a shadow production system whereby American films were remade in mul-tiple languages, either in the States or in European film factories.

The sound track called attention to its existence less stridently. Critics praised films which integrated ambient sounds and music into the background. These "inaudible" effects were not necessarily attended to but lent subtlety and verisimilitude to scenes. The sound effects which might stand out as artificial were narrativized, that is, incorpo-rated into the story. A judge's echoing pronouncement in MGM's THE VOICE OF THE CITY (1929) commands our attention because of its strangeness but remains "natural" because he is speaking from a great distance behind a door. I use the term *containment*, which is more or less the opposite of foregrounding. Filmmakers began incorporating passages of silence. These sections were different from the silence of the part-talkie because they used the absence of dialogue for dramatic contrast. Various formal devices implicated the filmgoer, such as learning plot twists by overhearing a supposedly secret conversation, thus transforming eavesdropping into a narrative device. As filmmakers gained more control over the stages of recording and reproduction, they learned to handle them in more complex and subtle ways. I call this careful orchestration of effects the "modulated sound track."

Audiences' preferences changed. Hollywood learned that hard times seemed to increase the appetite for "topical" films, not for musicals, which had been the industry wisdom. Organized crime was making headlines and became grist for the early Warners gangster pictures. "Realist" films like APPLAUSE (1929), THE BIG HOUSE (1930), ANNA CHRISTIE (1930), and MIN AND BILL (1930) provided glimpses of the gritty lives of marginalized people and contrast with the escapist fare generally associated with Depression-era entertainment. The musical film slid into disfavor in 1930, presumably because audiences were sated with the emphasis on "all-singing, all-dancing" superabundance at the expense of narrative. Ernst Lubitsch's exceptional adaptations of European comic operettas, which integrated music and song with romantic stories and appealing stars, did excel at the box office.

Social realism, the risqué language of Broadway, "modern" subjects (as in THE WILD PARTY [1929]), and suggestive poses and innuendo in film advertising were addressed in the Production Code of 1930. Written and administered by Will Hays's Motion Picture Producers and Distributors of America (MPPDA), the Code was an effort to block state and federal censorship by creating guidelines for regulating film expression, especially the use of the voice. Secondarily, through self-censorship the industry used sound as an excuse to maintain the power to distribute its product without external interference by local censors. Sound had stimulated some boards to demand extensive changes which entailed recutting, reshooting, and preparing multiple versions for different regions. Hollywood would save millions by having to make only one set of prints for the national market.

1931

Charles Chaplin released THE CIRCUS in January 1928, just as the industry was dallying with the possibility of sound. The world's most popular performer saw immediately that the talkies would force him to come to terms with his Little Tramp character. The role had evolved from English music hall and French boulevard comedy prototypes and was, Chaplin believed, essentially pantomimic and therefore silent. Chaplin was also chary of his pronounced British accent, which he feared would work against the universality of the character (and perhaps disappoint fans who imagined him speaking in their own regional voice). Though the sound issue was not the only reason, his next release, CITY LIGHTS, was delayed until January 1931. In the intervening years, Chaplin mounted an attack against the talkies. During the long publicity buildup, he was pictured as an aesthetic purist holding out for the principles of the silents, and then as an artist martyred by the talkies. Neither was completely accurate. The reception of CITY LIGHTS laid to rest permanently any possibility of an alternative silent cinema, an idea which Chaplin had bruited about in 1929. If anything, it confirmed his silent-comic genius while symbolically ending the era of silent production. Equally important was the success of European imports, especially THE BLUE ANGEL (1930), BLACKMAIL (1929), and LE MILLION (1931), because these films demonstrated that sound could be used evocatively and creatively.

The Depression convinced producers (if indeed they needed much pressure in this direction) that their films must appeal to "mass" rather than "class." In other words,

Hollywood felt that it could not afford to produce films aimed at narrow markets. Highbrow projects, such as operettas and melodramas from the New York stage, were scaled back. Sound became standardized, assimilated, and blended into the mass-produced merchandise of the Hollywood bazaar. As the decade of the thirties began, sound was no longer a special effect or a symbol of scientific progress. The Depression dashed that utopian flummery.

What had begun as an experiment to establish a separate minor branch of film practice to be marketed to small theaters had ended up altering fundamentally some aspects of the whole Hollywood system. The developments were unexpected, but not enormously disruptive. The adoption of sound technology set off reverberations in distribution, exhibition, and the general attitude toward the movies, but the major film companies responded rapidly to adjust to their consumers' mass acceptance of dialogue films. Production practices were altered. Studio heads began looking for reliable means of determining audience preferences. The environment inside theaters was transformed, not simply because sounds were coming from the screen, but because the patrons' behavior and attitudes were also changing.

But some things were not affected. The cinema remained primarily a storytelling medium. The film style of the previous fifteen years changed little. And the basic appeal of the movies was the same. Whether a 1920s silent, a 1930s talkie, or SINGIN' IN THE RAIN, the movies still gave audiences what they expected: an engaging story with action, romance, comedy, and adventure. Apparently for most audiences, hearing the winsome heroes and despicable villains speak their parts was a welcome improvement on a good thing, not the end of a golden age.

PART 1

A New Era in
Electrical Entertainment

*We wonder—is this the only business in the world that needlessly
burns electric lights in broad daylight?*

MAURICE KANN, 1928

There are no simple technologies. Even the tools and materials used to make inventions are themselves objects and processes with histories. Peter Wollen, for instance, has observed that film and sound editing were transformed by the seemingly insignificant introduction of Scotch brand transparent tape.[1] Now tape editing has replaced the cement film splicer. The "sound apparatus" embraced by Hollywood in the late 1920s was not a simple machine, but a many-faceted assortment of equipment and applications, not all of which worked in harmony.[2] To refine the point a bit more: none of the competing sound systems in the 1920s was simply an autonomous device (like a newly invented lens). Rather, theatrical sound was a new configuration of many existing electrical applications, most of which had not been developed for use in Hollywood movies at all.

Furthermore, the function of this equipment was not controlled by a course set by any one individual, inventor, or corporation but was competed for by those with vested interests and the financial clout to assert themselves. Consumers had been exposed to efforts to make the movies "talk" for several years before THE JAZZ SINGER (1927) and had rejected them because they did not work. The experiments had failed to create the illusion of naturalism which the exhibitors had promised. Synchronization between word and image was not maintained, the sound was unpleasant, and the content of the recorded material was uninteresting. At the same time, consumers seemed willing to believe that the talkies *might* work. This belief was encouraged by publicity which, cap-

Alice White, "Incandescent with 'It,'" embodies the electrical spirit in BROADWAY BABIES *(First National, 1929).*

italizing on past achievements of science, promoted talking pictures as "a new era in entertainment." Nearly all popular accounts of the new sound systems of the 1920s emphasized their global connection to technology, not the details of their material substructure. For instance, the modern alloys used in microphone construction and Eastman's improvements in film emulsion were extremely important in improving motion picture sound. Yet these contributions were seldom mentioned in popular texts about sound, nor were they promoted by movie studios. In contrast, authors constantly emphasized the talking cinema's connection, often dubious, to electrically derived technologies. There was a reason for this.

By the time of the commercially successful releases by Warner Bros. (Vitaphone) and Fox (Movietone), the fundamental developments had been in place in the laboratories of inventors, university professors, and electrical conglomerates for several years. Manufacturers had to "sell" talking cinema, not only to movie producers, whose executives for the most part were loathe to change, but also to consumers, whose tastes and moviegoing habits were notoriously unpredictable. For these groups, there was one common meeting ground: the talkies made sense when they were considered as a new form of *electrical* entertainment. Warner Bros.' director, Roy Del Ruth, looked to cinema's scientific origins as the promise of vast technological change: "The talking device . . . marks another step forward in modern science and its perfection is the most marvelous accomplishment since the discovery of electricity by Benjamin Franklin. . . . Its value to posterity will prove more far-reaching to civilization than the perfection of aeronautics, I dare say."[3] MGM's general manager, Louis B. Mayer, loquaciously, though characteristically inscrutably, agreed that the future belonged to science—and therefore to sound: "Electrical science, new advances in the technique of screen drama and screen literature and discoveries that have opened the way for the screen to appeal to two of the human senses, as heretofore only one, have enfolded for the future strides so enormous that to contemplate them is almost staggering to the imagination."[4]

We do not know specifically what motivated early audiences to go to the talkies. In general, we do not know what they thought about the movies, science, or any other subject. One definition of private life is that it is precisely that part of people's thought and routine behavior that is not open to public scrutiny. It is evident, though, that a spirited battle surrounded the introduction of sound cinema and attempted to align the technology with existing properties controlled by large electric corporations. Prospective audiences were bombarded with competing claims about the origins of the talkies. But in fact, the electric companies had an easy task because the public formed its own impression about the nature of the new motion picture entertainment. Science was often considered progressive in the 1920s, and anything associated with electricity tended to generate awe and respect, as it combined intellectual complexity, the promise of a better future, and the risk of mishandling. The talkies were readily plugged into this popularly constructed circuit that connected new developments in transportation (electric trains and elevators), communication (telephone and radio), and labor-saving and leisure-time appliances (the phonograph). Like other electrical technologies, the sound film was on the cusp of modernity. More specifically, it was the newest application of electrical science, thermionics, which was proffered to explain the "origins" of the talkies and to create an aura of modernity and inevitability. This was the name for the far-flung applications based on the vacuum tube, which include the modern sound cinema.

The corporations which vied to control the rights to thermionic devices did so on two fronts. Behind the scenes, their work took the form of labyrinthine litigation, negotiation, and old-fashioned back-stabbing. Up front, they waged a public relations war to link the popular comprehension of these products to other technological domains that were less disputed. The aggressiveness with which the phone company and the radio cartel fought for the bragging rights to the talkies implies an actively selective public. As consumers of "popular science," people had their own ideas about technology.

The diverse blend of technologies from which the talkies profited were not destined to come together as cinema sound but were the product of the strong "pull" of electric companies vying for control of public opinion. The popular press, however, found it more compelling to dramatize the talkies as continuing scientific progress and the avatar of a new millennium.

2

Electric Affinities

Often the best way to understand a new technology is to compare it to an older one already understood. Frequently when writers in the late 1920s introduced the talkies, the simile of choice was the automobile. George Klee used the car to illustrate his point that the talkies were still in an embryonic stage: "The talking film may by no means be compared to the present film in the same way as the electric engine to the steam locomotive or the airplane to the automobile."[1] On the subject of the part-dialogue film, "it was as if Henry Ford had tried to ease into production on his new car by sending out his old model with a new gearshift, promising a complete model in a few months."[2] Jesse Lasky of Paramount also used the car as a paradigm: "It would be foolish to pretend that the talking picture has attained its ultimate excellence. Nothing has. But it is here to stay—as substantial a product of our progress as the motor car or the airplane."[3]

Perhaps the most striking object lesson about technology is contained in the film that Warner Bros. produced in 1927 to showcase its Vitaphone sound system, THE FIRST AUTO. It was written and supervised by Darryl Zanuck, the production manager responsible for guiding the studio's features into the uncharted realm of sound. The plot, as though symbolizing his concerns, is a parable that addresses the cultural stress introduced during a critical moment when a new technology—the automobile—makes its forerunner obsolete. There is one sequence of pure spectacle: a parade of antique vehicles shows the modern auto of 1927 "morphing" out of its earlier form as the horseless carriage. The unmistakable metaphor is that the Vitaphone, like the auto, will transform our old way of life, silent film.

Once installation of sound systems began in 1928, most of the writers in the popular press of the day—but not all—presumed that the talkies were destined to become universally accepted. This was based on technological determinism, the conviction that the essence of something new originates from the sequence of technological innovations that produced it. Many popular film commentators in the 1920s saw the perfected talkies as an inevitable outgrowth of modern science—a predestined consequence of other communication technologies. The film historian Terry Ramsaye was the boldest in tracing the origins of the talkies back to the roots of cinema. The coming of sound had been preordained when Edison invented the phonograph: "Critics are still dubious, and some of the old masters of the movies are secretly skeptical, but the buying millions have made the decision. Mr. Edison's primary and original project of the motion picture as an accessory to the phonograph has arrived, like the newsboy who became president, in triumph."[4] Another typical statement was, "It won't be long now until everybody through-

Radio Pictures advertisement, February 1929.

out the country will be seeing and hearing great artists that hitherto have been merely phantoms or phonographic records to them; and every audience, even the remotest, will hear pictures accompanied by the greatest symphonic and band music in the world."⁵ Myron M. Stearns agreed: "Already the handwriting is on the wall. Five minutes of any 'all talker,' no matter how poor the story may be, will show you how quickly the audience accepts the new convention of sound. . . . One year, two years, three years, and, it seems safe to predict, the silent movie of yesterday and today, except in out-of-the-way corners and Little Theaters, will be no more." By 1929, people interested in film could read, "you may like them or lump them, but [sound pictures] are here to stay"; and, "'See, hear and touch' will probably be our next miracle."⁶ Articles like these suggest that the commentators regarded the transition to sound as an unstoppable technological force.

Wireless radio broadcasting provided another model for understanding the inevitability of sound cinema. Some authors suggested that sound in pictures could be achieved by "marrying" radio and film. Silent cinema, John Butler argued in 1922, had been handicapped by its lack of sound:

> This industry, while already a giant in size and accomplishment, has been permitted only half expression, only half development. But with the radio to act as its tongue, its handicapping lack of speech will be removed.
>
> That industry is, of course, the movies. Speechless, it has perfected the art of visual expression to a degree that has won it the unqualified respect and affection of the entire human race. . . .
>
> Through all its progress its sponsors have mourned its handicaps; have irked under the inevitable burden of its muteness. Now they are eagerly awaiting the hour when the stifling hand of silence is lifted. They are certain that hour is coming, borne on the wings of the radio. (John H. Butler, "Radio to Make Movies Talk," *Illustrated World*, July 1922, p. 673)

Alert readers already knew of considerable research in this field being conducted at General Electric. This was the well-publicized Pallophotophone, developed by Charles A. Hoxie. This device recorded sound on motion picture film stock, but not as movie entertainment. It was for radio broadcasting. "The transmission of 'canned music' and voices over the radio is by no means new," wrote a journalist in 1922. "In fact, it is little short of being a bore, but the record of the pallophotophone can not be compared to the phonograph."⁷ Potential applications included the making of talking movies, but that was only one use among many—for example, the scientific study of the voice. *Scientific American* added that the device could also be used to broadcast playbacks of a speech simultaneously on multiple stations.⁸

When Western Electric became publicly involved in exploiting sound pictures, AT&T's advertising encouraged the public to view the telephone as the ancestor of the talkies. The phone for decades had been promoted as a device embodying progressive technology. Writers readily agreed; for instance: "The instruments that have made the dumb drama articulate are really not so difficult of comprehension as most people think; that is, if you understand the simple principle of the telephone—which you probably don't. . . . All speakies, of whatsoever name or design, begin with a telephone."⁹ *World's Work* made the telephonic link specific in its thumbnail film history:

> The man who invented the telephone is primarily responsible. When he sent
> spoken words over metal strand the last folks he could have been thinking of
> were the careless herds who mill around the playhouse lobbies. Yet the
> moment he created the telephone diaphragm he made possible the talkie. . . .
> Exploitation of one scientific process never contents keen minds cloistered in
> laboratories. Each discovery must pay by-product dividends. (Robert E.
> MacAlarney, "The Noise Movie Revolution," *World's Work*, April 1929, p. 48)

For many, the talkies were envisioned only as a way station to a device that would
broadcast image and sound together. One of the most influential critics, Robert E.
Sherwood, assumed that the talkies would usher in television and noted cynically that
Hollywood had become an electrical "'subsidiary,' like the electric toaster industry, or
the vacuum tube industry. It will be part of that vast and superbly organized scheme by
which entertainment is to be delivered, free of charge, to the multitude."[10] The prolific
and widely admired arts critic Gilbert Seldes was one who saw a link between the technology of the past and that of the future. Movies and TV would vie for complete audiovisual illusionism:

> [W]ithin another year we shall probably have the simple and comparatively
> inexpensive mechanisms, now being perfected, which will throw on a small
> screen set up beside the home radio set a moving picture projected from a
> central broadcasting station; it is only a matter of time before this televisual
> entertainment is extended so that it, too, will have speech and sound in per-
> fect synchronization. . . . In its competition with television, the talkie will
> presently have the aid of three-dimensional films and of color. (Gilbert
> Seldes, "Talkies' Progress," *Harper's*, September 1929, pp. 454, 460)

Two decades later, Seldes would write a respected history of television.[11]

The movie czar Will Hays, president of the Motion Picture Producers and Distributors Association (MPPDA), reflected Hollywood's interest in television when he
painted a picture of a new Hollywood dominated by scientists, not scenarists:

> The motion-picture industry today has become a veritable laboratory of the
> research scientist, the engineer, the chemist and the inventor. Heretofore it
> has been popularly regarded as the workshop of the author and the scenario
> writer, of directors, artists and producers. Today dramatics, mechanics,
> music, chemistry and electricity have joined forces to advance cinematic
> progress. Even television is within the scope of such progress. (Will Hays,
> "The Cinema of Tomorrow," *Ladies' Home Journal*, July 1930, p. 51)

But others objected to the idea of a transformed cinema. A significant dissenter from the
euphoric view that the talkies were the next stage of radio and a stepping-stone to TV
was D. W. Griffith. The pioneer of narrative cinema still, in 1924, claimed a cachet as a
spokesperson for film art. In his vision of the future, he saw radio and the motion picture going separate ways, pronouncing emphatically that, "when a century has passed,
all thought of our so-called speaking pictures will have been abandoned. It will never be
possible to synchronize the voice with the pictures. This is true because the very nature
of the films forgoes not only the necessity for but the propriety of the spoken voice."[12]

Instead, he foresaw "symphonic orchestras of greater proportions than we now dream." This view expressed that of the minority who felt that the technology bringing the voice betrayed cinema's essence as a visual or "pantomimic" (silent theatrical) art. As late as 1929, when many theaters had already converted to sound, there were still diametrically opposed opinions about the technological inevitability of the talkies. Welford Beaton, outspoken editor of the *Film Spectator*, wrote:

> It is the fact that the present age is becoming overcanned. We stood for the phonograph and the radio, but talking pictures carry the thing just a little too far. Now we are promised television and a third screen dimension, depth added to height and width. As a toy, television will amuse for a time, and it may be put to some practical uses, but we never are going to be entertained by hearing Jack Barrymore read Hamlet to us from one of our living-room walls. (Welford Beaton, "A Real Tail on a Bronze Bull," *Saturday Evening Post*, 21 September 1929, p. 140)[13]

There were, however, few such complaints that the talkies had overmechanized society. Most popular writers, trying to understand the new mode of film, recast it as an industrial revolution—something new, yet determined by what had come before. The success of the old technological advances—the auto, phonographs, telephones, radio, electrical science—forecast the inevitability of the newest ones, the talkies and 3-D color television.

Electricity and Thermionics

The zesty fast-paced era of the 1920s known as the Jazz Age could just as readily be called the Thermionic Age. Admittedly, it is easy to see why this label never caught on. It does not exactly lilt off the tongue, and few know what the term means anymore. Thermionics is the branch of physics concerned with the electrical effects produced by heated metals in a vacuum. In the twenties, everyone was aware that the jazz in the air and on phonograph discs was heard thanks to newly developed vacuum tubes (or valves, in British usage). (*Thermionics* was a predecessor to the word *electronics*, which was coined in the 1920s but not used widely until after the invention of the transistor in 1947.) The advances in telephone transmission, public address amplification, medical imaging, electric lighting, and other electrified devices contributing to the swirl of modern life could be traced to the commercialization of vacuum tubes. Sound cinema, too, was one further application of thermionics. The equipment that movie moguls installed in their studios and exhibitors in their theaters relied on the fundamental underlying technology of vacuum tube devices.

The idea of using electricity to work communication magic and improve life became an organizing motif of everyday life early in the twentieth century. Consumers enjoyed electrical appliances made possible by war spin-off technology, mass-production, increasing middle-class affluence, and government subsidy of electric service. During the first stages of sound transition, movie critics and consumers emphasized the talkies' utopian and scientific potential.[14] Film sound was part of the brave new world of electronic gadgets. To some extent, Vitaphone, which could be construed to mean "living telephone," was just another kind of appliance, but one to be enjoyed by a consuming community rather than privately in the home.

That movie sound evolved from electricity and vacuum tubes was uncontested as far as the public was concerned. What was at stake for the corporations that controlled the technology was to convince consumers that sound belonged to a particular manufacturing group and that the group enjoyed a "natural" claim to exploit sound. (Note that the manufacturers derived their money only indirectly from the ticket-buying public; their direct consumers were the studio- and theater-owning clients.) As a selling point, the equipment manufacturers promoted their own time-tested expertise in the technologies from which sound cinema allegedly descended, telephone, radio, and the phonograph. Public demonstrations of equipment, planted articles in trade journals, and unacknowledged collaborations with authors in mass-circulation magazines aimed to cement in the minds of the public and exhibitors a perceived affinity with this or that electrical ancestor. Modern-day marketers call this capturing "mindshare."

The name Electrical Research Products, Inc. (ERPI), which AT&T created in 1927 for its sound system marketing unit, was well chosen. From the beginning, movies had been perceived and promoted as having an electrical mystique. Theaters a couple of decades earlier had appellations like "Electric Kinema." Film exhibition in the 1920s retained its association with light and electrical energy. Movie stars still had their names "in lights," that is, in a thousand bulbs on marquees. Powerful searchlights illuminated premieres and theater grand openings. Inside the picture palace, one filed past radiant displays of lobby cards and posters, past the bright concession stands, and into the auditorium where the walls and ceiling were washed in auroras. Spotlights highlighted the color and texture of the curtain. The gaudy Wurlitzer organ glowed. Though we do not think about the cinema's roots in electricity these days, in 1926 the connection was not taken for granted. Certainly the near-religious awe of the electric lightbulb had long since dissipated, but the science that developed from it, thermionics, still hummed with those connotations. AT&T and its subsidiary Western Electric, as well as General Electric and RCA, had similar interests in advertising the talkies as the product of electrical science. These corporations had research departments which required constant product innovations. That movie sound was being supplied by major corporations with familiar corporate names sanctioned the talkies as a serious and respectable enterprise. If electrical engineers, a new and esteemed profession, were devoting their labors to making the movies talk, then this spectacle must be legitimate science. It was readily conceivable that talking pictures someday might be as ubiquitous as lightbulbs, radios, and telephones.

For a good specific illustration of the awe of electricity, the priestly mantle of the electrician, and electricity's association with sound, we can look at the technical manual *Handbook of Projection,* written in 1929. F. H. Richardson exhorted his readers, who were practicing and aspiring projectionists, to learn about electricity because film sound was really nothing more than electric current. He prided himself on his up-to-date knowledge of the present state of electrical science:

> In this work I shall adopt the latest theory of electric action, which holds that what we term electric current consists of minute particles of negatively charged electricity called "Electrons." . . . I am not proposing to take part in any argument as to whether this theory is right or wrong. I merely am telling you it is now the theory accepted by scientists, hence we shall use it in this work. . . . The acceptance of the new theory is very recent.

Rainbow Super-Tubes advertisement, March 1927.

Richardson did not mince words. He promoted the talkies as a scientific wonder which should inspire reverence in any projectionist.

> The marvelous results attained in perfection of sound in synchronization with motion as applied to motion pictures is literally an outstanding monument to the genius of mankind, and particularly it is a monument to those scientists and engineers who have, by years of hard work devoted to tremendously difficult research, with perseverance almost unbelievable, made it all possible. (F. H. Richardson, *Handbook of Projection: The Blue Book of Projection,* vol. 3, rev. [New York: Chalmers, 1930], pp. iv, v)

Science was constant progress and an amelioration of the human condition. It was through electricity that the talkies were linked to the industrialized universe: "This simple principle, or method of obtaining force and motion by electrical means, is utilized in some form in all the electric motors in the world, from those that drive fans and dentists' drills to those that propel battleships and haul the transcontinental trains over the Rocky Mountains." Richardson also told his projectionists that their knowledge would give them an intellectual advantage over the ordinary populace, which was not as well informed about the electrical foundation of the talkies. "Remember," he advised, "that we are dealing with the action of light and electricity, both of which are enormously rapid—more rapid than can be understood or conceived by the untrained mind."[15]

One of the most portentous applications of electricity resulted from harnessing the electrons streaming from a filament heated in a vacuum. The theory of electrons that Richardson mentioned had been first published in 1902 and was the basis for continuing research into thermionics in the major electrical research labs. In 1906 the independent inventor Lee de Forest[16] patented a three-electrode thermionic vacuum tube, the triode, which he called the Audion. Diode and triode vacuum tubes could be used to send and detect radio signals, amplify telephone current, turn alternating into direct current and vice versa. Because the movie sound system utilized many vacuum tubes, the talkies were readily perceived to be a branch of thermionics, along with telegraphy, the telephone, wireless radio (called radio telephony in the early twenties), and X-ray imaging. Movie sound was not differentiated as a freestanding technology.

The special knowledge that Richardson claimed to be imparting was certainly intended to empower the projectionists, to dignify their social status, and to impress the boss. In the age of "scientific masculinity," it might also have enhanced their self-image as men.[17] Projectionists were represented as skilled technicians, not just simple machine attendants. We can probably assume that Richardson's belief in electricity as a powerful branch of knowledge was shared not only by his readers but by many ordinary people. The promoters of sound cinema wished to align themselves with this preexisting faith in electricity. So when the first Radio Pictures film, STREET GIRL (1929), premiered, newspaper ads announced a "New Era in Electrical Entertainment."[18] As Richardson had advised the projectionists to associate themselves with electricity, so RKO was suggesting that audiences, by patronizing this film, were actively participating in reshaping the coming age.

Among the thermionic devices for the talkies were rectifiers, diodes which convert alternating current to the direct current needed to power electronic circuits. Rectifiers were also crucial for controlling the motors kept synchronous by the tuned circuits in the cameras, sound recorders, and projectors. Amplifiers based on triodes were used to step up the weak electrical currents from microphones and from the sound-reproducing sources in the projection booths.

Researchers at the AT&T laboratories in New York were fashioning multi-filament tubes for amplifying extremely weak electrical signals. These tubes enabled stepped-up current to travel along telephone lines or to drive loudspeakers. AT&T recognized the potential of de Forest's Audion and paid nearly $400,000 for his patents.[19] Western Electric encouraged internal competition to find ways to exploit the device. The significant ones included using it as a "repeater" to relay phone messages, establishing a "radiophone" service, and making it the heart of a public address system.

Engineers elsewhere rushed to find new uses for the triode. Tests at the General Electric labs in Schenectady, New York, aimed to produce a high-frequency alternating current generator for radio transmission, X-ray devices, and the high-efficiency gas-filled incandescent lamp, an unanticipated by-product. At Westinghouse, the vacuum tube was used as a signal detector, amplifier, and oscillator for radio. De Forest worked on developing an airplane-to-ground transmitter. Of these numerous applications, the fastest-growing use for thermionics was decidedly in radio communication.

As a wartime measure, the government banned civilian radio from 1917 to 1919. It was nonetheless a period of intense corporate development, completely subsidized by the government. The wireless receivers and transmitters of the U.S. Signal Corps and the navy utilized more than half a million tubes made by Western Electric. After the war, de Forest and the Marconi Company joined forces to market Golden VT receiving tubes, which for a brief time were the only ones legally available to the public. Still, in general, on the eve of the introduction of commercial sound film, AT&T, GE, and RCA completely controlled the thermionic industry.[20]

The development of thermionics coincided with several relevant changes in American business practice. Major corporations established engineering centers (later called departments of research and development) where "pure" research took place. Bell Laboratories, for example, grew out of the Western Electric Engineering Department. The second change was diversification. General Electric went from producing mainly lightbulbs and electrical transmission apparatus to making consumer products such as ranges, refrigerators, and vacuum cleaners.[21] Not only did research lead to production, it became a commodity in its own right as the major corporations competed with each other to fund inventing, hire promising scientists, promote diversified electric products, and corner the market on seminal patents to further develop, sell, or pool. "Rational" competition and the sharing of information through trade organizations helped lessen the effect of competing claims to similar research. Cross-licensing, negotiating manufacturing domains and sales territories, and establishing noninterference zones in research were intended to replace the cutthroat competition and wasteful litigation which had marked earlier corporate science. Heavy industry was fueled by government investment and contracts well after the wartime exigencies had passed.

Bell Laboratories charged ahead, exploring every conceivable use for vacuum tubes. Telephone researchers claimed as their fiefdom the entire domain of sound. AT&T executive William Peck Banning recalled that "scientific progress had brought visions of new fields in which the tube function was basic. Tube development in the telephone laboratories was inseparable from the development of communications facilities. Whatever pertained to sound—its creation, amplification, transmission, and reproduction—was of course constantly explored by telephone scientists."[22] Gerald Tyne has also described the single-minded approach of the Western Electric Engineering Department after the war:

"The . . . step-by-step innovations illustrate the teamwork of engineers. Each step was the culmination of attention to multitudinous details of construction and materials, meticulous measurements, and exhaustive performance testing."[23] To achieve diversification, Bell Laboratories initiated a policy of distinguishing between research designed for telephone use and research destined for so-called non-associate use, that is, for commercial products not directly related to the telephone industry. One of these was electrical sound recording.

The form of thermionics which most consumers knew was the radio tube. These were available from numerous distributors—legitimate and bootleg—but most bore the RCA trademark. In 1922, five hundred private-sector stations were licensed and demand for home receiving sets was so brisk that RCA, Westinghouse, Western Electric, and the many unlicensed independents had trouble maintaining the supply of tubes.[24] Despite fierce disputes between the radio and telephone groups, there were also truces which divvied up research territories—wireless and phonography for RCA, and "wire" communication for AT&T. In the realm of thermionics, the radio and telephone groups had partially resolved their competitive differences by exchanging basic patents to various tube designs and applications. This cross-licensing was crucial for the talkies because studios and theaters depended on a steady supply of powerful amplification tubes.

PHOTOEMISSIVE CELLS

Whether disc-based or photographically based, all successful motion-picture recording and reproduction systems used electrical amplification. But photographic systems—that is, sound-on-film—additionally required thermionic photoelectric cells. Recording sound on film depends on a highly controllable light source. Photoemissive cells, among many experimental uses, were gradually adapted for recording this kind of sound track. These gas-filled vacuum tubes transform the electric current produced by microphones into a pulsating light source which exposes photographic film stock in proportion to the intensity of the original sound. General Electric scientists working between 1911 and 1913 discovered that filling these tubes with heavy gases such as argon caused them to give off light when charged.[25] Lee de Forest, probably influenced by this research, made a light cell he called Photion, using a gas-filled tube.[26] De Forest tried to adapt the instrument for recording sound on a photographic negative. The glowing light exposed the moving film, but the results were not very good. He then learned of an improved light emitter developed by Theodore Case and his collaborator Earl I. Sponable in which a quartz tube containing an oxide-coated wire, a metal plate, and helium gas glowed proportionately to the voltage supplied. Case had named his invention Aeo, the acronym for alkaline earth oxide. Unlike the filament of an ordinary lightbulb or the Photion, the Aeo light's short glow decay made possible more accurate recordings of higher sound frequencies. These tubes could be installed inside a camera to record picture and sound simultaneously (single-system) or inside a separate "sound camera," which could be synchronized with the picture camera (double-system). When the moving film stock was exposed by the pulsating intensity of the light, the result was a "variable density" photographic sound track.[27] On 23 July 1926, after Case had broken with de Forest, he teamed up with the movie magnate William Fox to exploit the Aeo light in what would be called the Fox-Case Movietone system. The tube was replaced in 1929 by the Western Electric light valve (a nonthermionic device discussed later).

Variable-density optical sound track (from Richardson, Handbook of Projection, *1930).*

Working at the same time as de Forest and Case, but with the goal of transmitting images by radio, Vladimir Kosma Zworykin at Westinghouse produced a cell with a cesium-magnesium cathode which converted light into electrical current.[28] These vacuum photoemissive cells produced a much faster response than even the Aeo. Their extremely rapid fluctuations made possible high-quality reproduction of music and speech.

PHOTOCONDUCTIVE CELLS

Photoconductive cells are also known as photoresistors and are used for playing back photographic sound tracks during projection. The tubes are coated with a light-sensitive rare earth, originally selenium. The electrical resistance varies according to the intensity of light striking the coating. Sound is reproduced by passing the film's optical sound track past a constant-intensity beam of light from a small lamp as the filmstrip moves through the projector. The degree of light-and-dark exposure on the film's track blocks the beam to a greater or lesser extent, causing the light to strike the photoelectric cell with varying intensity. The cell's resistance pulsates according to the amount of light hitting it. The resulting modulated current is relayed to the amplifier.

Case had developed a working sound-on-film system in 1917, based on a photoemissive cell he called Thalofide. It was used during the war for sending wireless signals.[29] De Forest was also interested in these cells in the teens, but as components in film-phonographs, a new application for his Audion amplifier, not to reproduce motion picture sound.[30] Beginning in 1918, he began developing an alternative to the disc phonograph, the basic principle of which he found to be "fundamentally & hopelessly imperfect." He wrote in his 1919 journal: "*Light,* photography, selenium or photo-cell, the Audion (always the Audion!) and sounding board, or the reproducing bulb or flame—these are the elements which can capture and release music in all its beauty."

His device was to be called Photophone, but he did not envision motion picture uses until he began collaborating with Case in July 1921. The De Forest Phonofilm Corporation was formed in November 1922, with Theodore Case's Aeo in the camera and Lee de Forest's Thalofide cell in the projector.[31]

The public knew and understood this research only to a limited extent. It was technically complex, but the manufacturers and researchers also wished to control the release of information. Rather than learning specifics, readers were told in general terms about how the many possible applications of thermionics improved life. The electric companies were rushing to develop more than just talking motion pictures. AT&T, for example, was at least as interested in improving transatlantic cable service as it was in cinema. The major corporations did not target any one sector; they were intent upon spinning off as many *combinations of devices* as possible in order to increase usage and maximize licensing profits.

The talkies had to use various thermionic devices, so the public took for granted their electrical nature. It was up to the manufacturers to convince people that the sound motion picture was a *specific* appliance. This issue boiled down to whether talking cinema was more like telephone or radio (with some influence from the phonograph).

The Telephone

A Senate committee in 1921 declared the phone company a "natural monopoly" and relaxed antitrust laws. Between 1921 and 1934, the Bell System bought 223 independent phone companies. By the mid-1920s, the government-supported AT&T telephone monopoly, with its Bell research juggernaut and its Western Electric manufacturing plants, was the vertically integrated kingpin of electrically assisted verbal communication. The fast pace of improvements in phone service, including spectacular milestones such as transcontinental and intercontinental hookups, made it easy to believe that a communications utopia was just over the horizon. The U.S. census showed a rapid increase in the number of phone-equipped households after World War I; by 1929 subscriptions peaked at about 40 percent of the population.[32]

On many pragmatic levels, the telephone had become fundamental to the American household. It was a domesticated scientific instrument. John Brooks has concluded, "People assimilated national telephony into their minds as if into their bodies—as if it were the result of a new step in human evolution that increased the range of their voices to the limits of the national map."[33] Chatting on the 'phone (or eavesdropping on a party line) became a leisure-time activity. Despite their success at wiring residences, telephone executives were alarmed that the sale of radio sets was increasing much faster than new telephone subscriptions. Almost as many households owned radios as had telephones. AT&T worried—with reason—that this competing device would soon outpace phone receivers. Administrators instituted a mandate for Bell researchers and salesmen to devise "new and additional uses" for the telephone.[34] The film sound experiments were part of this drive. From 1927 through 1930, when Western Electric was promoting the talkies, its advertising pushed the idea that sound cinema was inseparable from the telephone. The popular press obligingly relayed the news that the talkies were telephonic communication.

Because the telephone made it possible to converse "close up" at great distances, it was also one-half of the nineteenth-century fantasy of the "far-sight far-sound" machine.

Billboard advertising Don Juan, *Times Square, 1926.*

The talking cinema could be readily imagined as the other half, supplying the distant vision to go along with the voice. The audience at the first Vitaphone program, for example, could regard the film of Will Hays addressing them as a long-distance communication—with moving visual accompaniment. The title cards and programs—even billboard advertising—reminded moviegoers that Vitaphone was "presented" by Western Electric. Warners distributed an eight-page brochure at screenings that claimed, "In the Vitaphone, Science has provided a means for the synchronization of motion pictures with reproduced sound, with a degree of perfection never before attained." The three "major scientific research developments" which made it possible were: an electrical system of registration, a remarkable electrical device which reproduced the sound waves, and an adaptation of the public address system. The last amplified sound "by means of properly located loud speaking telephones." And a specially constructed telephone supposedly ensured correct volume and naturalness for music.[35]

Early talkies exploited the phone's prominence in everyday modern life by incorporating it as a prop residing in the background or foregrounded, for example, when we eavesdrop on the conversations in Cohen on the Telephone and The Lights of New York (1928). In George Jessel's 1926 Vitaphone short, his routine is interrupted by a call from "Mama." Vitaphone and Fox Movietone Newsreel speeches were not "live"; nevertheless, they were somehow "telephonic" in the way the performers' and celebrities' natural voices created the impression of intimate physical presence while speaking from a great distance.

The technology of sound pictures, as the phone company aggressively demonstrated, was built upon underlying telephonic devices. The two designs which related directly to sound cinematography were the mike and the loudspeaker.

Western Electric had constantly sponsored research to enhance the clarity and volume of its sound transmitters. The greatest improvement was a flat frequency-response microphone invented by Edward C. Wente.[36] It was originally produced for wireless military communication. The so-called condenser transmitter (later referred to as a capacitor microphone) became the standard in public address, in broadcasting, and in

*Greta Garbo and director Clarence Brown contemplate the Western Electric con-
denser transmitter on the set of* Anna Christie, *1930. The cup-size microphone is
attached to the long preamplifier by a swivel.*

Hollywood. The current from these mikes was so weak that it had to be preamplified by tubes on the unit which were housed in a salami-shaped case. The name for this device evolved gradually from "transmitter" to "microphone"—little telephone.[37] Western Electric's microphone revolutionized the phonograph industry and was fundamental to the film sound system that eventually became Vitaphone. Mechanical microphones favored loud noises; now soft sounds and high frequencies could be reproduced on records. These improvements benefited movie acoustics as well. There was a physical advantage. The microphone's wire connection, unlike the morning-glory horn of mechanical recording, was flexible and could be located at some distance from the recording apparatus. For instance, microphones were hidden around movie sets, concealed in bushes, and suspended from booms.

AT&T was also publicizing improvements in the sound reproducing part of the telephone. What we now call public address systems were developed in the early 1920s as "loud-speaking telephones." The company envisioned a technology which would transmit speeches and announcements to assemblies. It conducted a prototype demonstration in 1921 at which President Harding spoke at Arlington National Cemetery and was heard by outdoor crowds in New York and San Francisco through Western Electric horns via AT&T long lines.[38] Final adjustments were still being made at the time of the Vitaphone premiere of DON JUAN in 1926. Meanwhile, RCA was designing speakers intended to fit inside compact radio cases. These transmitted vibrations by a vibrating cone of stiff cardboard, were cheaper to manufacture, and produced less harsh sounds than Western Electric's horns. Giant versions were made for theatrical installations.

Hollywood was an avid consumer of public address systems. Jack Warner described their use during the filming of NOAH'S ARK (1929):

> A telephonic network, connected with loud speakers, was strung from the director's platform to various points, so that assistants and players were always within hearing of any command. In order that every camera and every player should start together in the mass scenes, a siren whose shriek could be heard for a half mile around was used to signal the start and termination of the scene. (J. L. Warner, "Facts from the Studio about *Noah's Ark*," souvenir program, 1927, Yranski Collection)

Technicians in the 1920s distinguished between the electrical and acoustic components of sound reproducers. The Western Electric sound receiver was functionally similar to (and named after) its telephone receiver. It consisted of an aluminum diaphragm in a metal chamber, and a wire-wound driving coil which required its own twelve-volt power source, usually a wet-cell battery. The current from the amplifier caused the diaphragm to vibrate. The acoustic component was the horn, looped or "folded" to fit into more compact spaces. The horns were quite large and, to provide needed amplification with minimal distortion, were deployed in a bank of five—three above and two flanking the screen.[39]

The whole Western Electric system was often referred to generically as "telephonic."[40] *Scientific American* summed up the situation in a description of Movietone:

> In the new process, aside from [Fox's] own patents, such as for example, the Aeo tube, certain telephonic apparatus is necessary. This embraces the use of such devices as amplifiers, microphones, and loud-speakers, both in recording and reproducing. Wherever telephonic apparatus is employed the

devices of the Western Electric Company are used. These are the instruments which were acquired by Vitaphone under an exclusive license from Western Electric, and the use of which by Movietone is covered by an agreement between the Fox-Case Corporation and the Vitaphone Corporation. (A. P. Peck, "Sounds Recorded on 'Movie' Film," *Scientific American*, September 1927, p. 236)

Vitaphone, "presented by Western Electric," was supposed to reinforce the idea that both the talkies and the telephone were intimately connected industries.

Radio

David Sarnoff, in a June 1927 speech, pointed out that *radio* "has quickened every industry with which it has come into contact." The general manager of RCA dismissed the primacy of the telephone in the new communications. Instead, he claimed that thermionics was the foundation technology:

> The greatest achievements of the phonograph industry, in recording as well as in reproduction, have come from the electrical arts associated in the development of radio. Transcontinental telephonic service was made possible largely by the vacuum tube. The new transatlantic telephone service rests upon radio communications. And now the latest of the electrical arts has come to solve the problem of synchronizing the spoken word with the moving picture. (David Sarnoff, "A Look at Television's Future," address before the Chicago Association of Commerce, 8 June 1927, reprinted in Sarnoff, *Looking Ahead: The Papers of David Sarnoff* [New York: McGraw-Hill, 1968], p. 90)

Sarnoff's vision of a utopia centered on radio—we shall call it "Radiopolis"—must have seemed feasible at the time. As the 1900 generation became thirty-somethings, the "wireless" had changed from a scientific curiosity to a wartime communications boon, to a hugely popular news and entertainment medium. Although AT&T and RCA envisioned radio as a commercial medium from the beginning (selling advertising, promoting consumer tie-ins, encouraging audience patronage and consumption), it was a fragmented business throughout much of the twenties, reflecting, in Julie D'Acci's words, "heterogeneity, localness, and struggle over financing and control."[41] While we often think of radio as preceding the talkies as a cultural force, in fact, it did not consolidate as an industry until competing broadcast networks began to be organized around 1926—in other words, concurrent with, not before, the dissemination of the talkies. Much of the programming before the 1930s consisted of "anonymous musicians playing nostalgic or semiclassical songs."[42] The same might describe a program of early Vitaphone shorts. It was not radio's improvement in the laboratory, but its availability as easy-to-operate sets in homes (and even automobiles), via broadcast "chains" (networks) supported by advertising revenue, that enabled radio to enter American life at such a phenomenal rate between 1927 and 1933. And of course, there was the illusion that it was "free." Manufacturers like RCA would want to encourage a belief that the talkies would be as powerful an entertainment force as radio.

General Electric, Westinghouse, and AT&T had organized the Radio Corporation of America (RCA) as a government-encouraged monopoly sanctioned to regularize radio and to avoid the "monotonous litigation" of patent wars.[43] A secondary intention was to thwart a "foreign" competitor, the British-owned American Marconi Corporation, and an economic competitor, de Forest. James Hijiya explains the arrangement succinctly:

> In October 1919 the General Electric Co. bought control of American Marconi Co. and turned Marconi's assets over to a new firm, the Radio Corporation of America, with which GE exchanged all patent rights. In July 1920 RCA negotiated a cross-licensing agreement with AT&T, which previously had purchased rights to de Forest's triodes; and in June 1921 the Westinghouse Electric Co. also signed the agreement. Under this arrangement AT&T gave RCA the right to manufacture triodes; RCA gave the right to GE and Westinghouse; GE and Westinghouse made the triodes, put them into radios, and sold the radios to RCA; RCA sold the radios to the public; and nobody had to buy anything from the Radio Telephone & Telegraph Co. of Lee de Forest. (James A. Hijiya, *Lee de Forest and the Fatherhood of Radio* [Bethlehem, Pa.: Lehigh University Press, 1992], p. 95)

As radio consumption took off, AT&T announced its plans to enter the broadcasting business. Though unsure in which direction the venture might take it, the president of the company, Harry Bates Thayer, was "preparing to furnish this broadcasting service to such an extent as may meet the commercial demands of the public."[44] AT&T, leaving no potentially profitable diversification untried, interpreted the 1919 RCA agreement as giving it the exclusive right to charge for airtime. The next year, station WEAF atop Western Electric's Long Lines Building in Manhattan was selling time by the fifteen-minute segment. The company gradually realized that its radio fortune did not lie in broadcasting but rather in its monopoly of high-quality telephone lines. It effectively controlled the transmission of signals linking broadcasters who wished to go beyond their local range. As it had previously done in the thermionics industry, and as it would later do in the film industry, AT&T took a stance which was both competitive and cooperative. Independent radio broadcasters had to choose between sending signals to their affiliates by way of obsolete Western Union telegraph lines or leasing AT&T's long-distance network at exorbitant prices. In 1924, when an arbiter appeared ready to rescind AT&T's monopolistic line-leasing services, the company stated that it would reopen negotiations with the Radio Group and would license any station on reasonable terms. Brooks has observed that this strategy was analogous to the company's position in earlier cases in which its monopoly was challenged.[45] Later, when the company's film sound monopoly was challenged, AT&T followed a similar pattern of slow capitulation.

In 1925 AT&T's new president, Walter Gifford, set about streamlining the company. Among the subsidiaries he divested was the radio business. On 1 November 1926, for $1 million, AT&T sold to RCA its broadcasting licenses, a promise to supply wire services to the newly created National Broadcasting Company (NBC), and an option to purchase WEAF. Gifford announced sanguinely, "The objective of a broadcasting station was quite different from that of a telephone system."[46] It was not that simple; it was understood that Western Electric would continue to supply radio equipment and to monopolize line services in exchange for refraining from broadcasting. NBC would lease only AT&T long lines. In an arrangement that would characterize 1920s big business, both sides won by dividing power along negotiated channels of control, rather than per-petuating competitive infrastructures. Furthermore, AT&T's decision to divest one entertainment subsidiary coincided with its embarking on another venture: the movies.

There was great public confusion about the technical relationship between film and radio, even among professionals. Richardson rather huffily told the readers of his pro-jection manual, "This is not a radio book. It is a sound-in-synchronization-with-motion book, and while there is of course a considerable similarity, in a general way, between film and radio, still the fields are wholly separate and their problems for the most part entirely different."[47] While today it is difficult to see any similarity between radio and movies, evidently in the late 1920s the dividing line was not so sharp. This impression comes from the writers of explanatory articles who doubted the ability of lay consumers to fathom the technical complexity of talking pictures. In addition to pointing out how sound films derived from the telephone, they would also typically use radio terms. Movietone, for example, works because "vacuum tubes somewhat like those you have in your radio receiver do the amplifying." A trade editor explained: "The radio tube, such as is found in the ordinary home receiving set, figures prominently in the development [of talking machines]: It is through this medium that most of these devices secure their amplification which, of course, controls the volume necessary to make them suitable for theater use."[48] Michele Hilmes has written about the mystique of radio:

> It is hard for those of us living in the latter half of the twentieth century to comprehend the fantastic, almost magical qualities attributed to the idea of radio waves in its first decades. Earliest responses to the coming era of "wire-less" communication combined head-shaking mysticism with ecstatic predic-tions of a new utopia. The presentation of radio as a mysterious technology, a wonder machine calling up voices from the void, allowed technological bedazzlement to overshadow potential social and economic implications, even among those assigned to the task of harnessing and regulating this new phenomenon. (Michele Hilmes, *Hollywood and Broadcasting: From Radio to Cable* [Urbana: University of Illinois Press, 1990], p. 9)

Playing up the talkies as radio capitalized on its aura of mystification, scientific com-plexity, and cutting-edge technology. A good example is the "advanced" radio depicted in Mysterious Island (MGM, 1929). Constructed of what appear to be neon spokes, Tinkertoys, and quite a few boiling beakers, it can maintain communication with distant submarines. It is a creation of a scientist's lab, chock-full of electrical devices anticipat-ing Dr. Frankenstein's a few years later.

Actual experiments in movie-radio hybridization had begun in earnest during 1922. Butler's musings were typical. He foresaw the addition of sound to film "borne on the wings of radio":

> The large city theater or ball ground, the moving-picture film, the phono-graph record—all are limited in distribution. The distribution by film and record is great: almost limitless, but not quite. Distribution by radio *is* lim-itless. . . . The radio people, the movie people and the artists themselves have confidence in the future of this work. (Butler, "Radio to Make Movies Talk," p. 677)

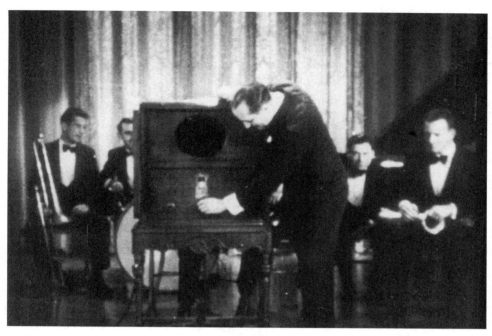

Public fascination with radio was a plot device in WEARY RIVER *(First National, 1929).*

He described experiments by Frank Bacon, who was attempting to broadcast the sounds of the plays *Molly Darling* and *Lilies of the Field* in synchronization with film images. Harry J. Powers, Jr., also presented "radio talking pictures" in which actors spoke their lines while watching a film. Their voices were broadcast to remote theaters where the film was projected.[49]

Radiophone further linked wireless and movies. This 1922 device relayed broadcasts to movie houses where patrons could listen to concert music before the film began. Then there was Radio Film, "making it possible to show a picture in a hundred theaters with an explanatory lecture coming through from a single transmitting station."[50] It played in 1923 at Hugo Riesenfeld's New York theaters.

Two experiments in 1925 tested this idea on a larger scale. On 25 August, Fritz Lang's film SIEGFRIED (1923) was screened at the Century Theater in New York City with a score by Riesenfeld. By arrangement with UFA (the German studio) and RCA's station WJY, the score was broadcast to an audience of five hundred at the Briarcliff Lodge, thirty-five miles away. Technically the results were poor; reception was interrupted several times by static. But the audience and industry representatives were impressed. Joe Fliesler of UFA said that other experiments would follow and that screenings at distant Paramount theaters might be synchronized with music performed at the Paramount in New York. A *Film Daily* editor prophesied this was an important milestone for small houses: "There is but one way that this development can come—through radio. Such marvelous strides have been made that even this seemingly impossible innovation may occur. At all events do not be surprised if—and when—it happens."[51]

Simultaneously, MGM and station KFI were trying a similar experiment in Los Angeles with the cooperation of fourteen theaters in the West Coast chain. This was the brainchild of the younger brother of the movie star Norma Shearer, Douglas Shearer, who was visiting her in Hollywood. The "master film," a promotional short for A Slave of Fashion (1925), with Norma and Lew Cody, was projected at the station while the stars spoke along with their screen images. Picture and sound never quite came together, and Douglas found a job in the Warner Bros. prop department.[52]

These experiments combining moving images and broadcast sound were technological dead ends, combining a previously recorded medium with a live one. But the fact that they were attempted suggests that some, perhaps many, people thought that movies' and radio's combination was a certainty.

Movie theaters themselves were the sites of much broadcast entertainment. Most of the larger ones had already installed public address systems, frequently obtained from Western Electric, and hooking up radio to the output was a logical step. Samuel "Roxy" Rothapfel's programs had been heard live from Broadway's Capitol Theater since November 1922. By 1924 many major theaters sponsored programs, had musical programs broadcast from their stages, and/or housed local radio stations in their buildings.[53]

There was mixed opinion among exhibitors about whether radio hurt or helped business. Many felt that their shows benefited from radio's indirect advertising. Harold B. Franklin, at the time with the Famous Players chain, instructed managers of Paramount theaters to exploit tie-ins with local radio programs. He emphasized the social advantage of theatrical radio: "It is also important to remember that the theater serves as a sort of community house where the neighbors meet and exchange greetings. Mrs. Smith still wants to get out to see Mrs. Jones and the radio does not serve to bring about those meetings." Others, like William Brandt, chair of the New York Motion Picture Theater Owners association, saw radio as "a serious competitor of the motion picture theater and [it] will prove more menacing each day as the radio itself improves." Hugo Riesenfeld felt that radio was competition for bad films, but not for good ones. The U.S. Treasury Department, which tallied admissions based on the excise tax on tickets, reported that attendance in 1923 had increased over the same period in 1922, showing no negative radio influence at all.[54]

Harry Warner, one of the founding Warner brothers, was an early advocate of commercial radio. He proposed that the film industry build its own stations under the auspices of the MPPDA. He reasoned:

> Programs could be devised to be broadcast before and after show hours, tending to create interest in all meritorious pictures being released or playing at that time. Nights could be assigned to various companies calling attention to their releases and advising where they were playing in that particular locality. Artists could talk into the microphone and reach directly millions of people who have seen them on the screen, but never came in contact with them personally or heard their voices. (*Film Daily*, 3 April 1925, p. 8)

The prototype was Warner Bros.' own station KFWB in Hollywood, which had just begun broadcasting in March 1925. The following year its WBPI began providing similar programming from its studios in the Warners' Theatre on Broadway.

Paramount–Famous Players–Lasky attempted to set up its own national network to advertise current releases. Adolph Zukor's idea, announced in May 1927, was to pro-

MGM Telemovies advertisement, December 1927.

duce dramatizations of first-run Paramount films and sell advertising airtime to compete with RCA-owned NBC. Despite several attempts by Zukor, including buying a half-interest in the Columbia Broadcasting System (CBS), the scheme never became fully operational.

Loew's and its subsidiary MGM also announced a sixty-station $1–3 million network that would depend upon negotiating a contract for a national land hookup via AT&T lines. The proposal called for broadcasting theater acts from New York and was to begin in February 1928.[55] As an experiment, MGM arranged to air LOVE (1927), starring Greta Garbo and John Gilbert, from the Embassy Theater. In a seemingly strange choice, the radio sports announcer Ted Husing gave listeners a "ringside" description of the events on-screen, while the regular orchestra played in the background. This so-called Telemovie was broadcast on a national hookup on 20 December 1927.[56] Meanwhile, Universal, First National, and Fox contracted with various stations to broadcast programs plugging their films and their stars. But direct ownership of a national radio network by a studio failed to materialize.

Many factors dampened the studios' desire to become involved with radio. One venture in particular was perceived as a warning sign. On 29 March 1928, United Artists arranged a special broadcast on *The Dodge Brothers Hour.* Fifty-five stations signed up for home transmissions, but UA's real interest was in exploring theatrical possibilities. The most prestigious theater to broadcast the show was the Fifth Avenue Playhouse in New York. For the program, Norma Talmadge, Charlie Chaplin, Douglas Fairbanks, D. W. Griffith, John Barrymore, and Dolores Del Rio gave recitations before the mike.[57] Gloria Swanson refused to appear, ostensibly "in fairness to exhibitors whose investments deserve protection." In addition to the huge anticipated audience (50 million, or 5.4 persons per radio set), what was new about this "big broadcast" was that it took place during prime movie hours—9:00–10:00 P.M. EST. Theater owners protested loudly long before the broadcast date. The pressure was so great that UA's president, Joseph Schenck, promised, even before the show, that the event would not be repeated.[58]

Characteristically, *Film Daily* sided with exhibitors. In an editorial entitled "What to Do About Radio," Red Kann, the outspoken editor, observed: "The use of film personalities over the air is a practice which creates sharp differences of opinion. The preponderance of argument is against it. Yet nobody knows whether subsequent business increases proportionately or not and there is no need to play with a dangerous experiment. . . . The answer is to stay off the air during show time."[59] Another obstacle was the musicians' union. Several exhibitors who had planned to tie up said they were prevented because of contracts which restricted remote broadcasts in their theaters.[60]

The actual program was a disaster. As with the SIEGFRIED transmission, bad weather caused severe static in New York State. But theater audiences objected to the "commercials" for Dodge cars. At the Fifth Avenue Playhouse, patrons booed, hissed, and yelled, "Take it off!" for twenty minutes until the management was forced to comply. When the furor subsided, there was no clear determination as to whether the competing program actually affected box-office receipts. Also unclear was the effect on movie fans. Some were said to be disillusioned "because of the transition from silent to speaking performances on the part of the stars," while others saw the hookup as an opportunity to thrill to their screen idols' seldom-heard voices.[61]

While the "big broadcast" probably made film executives question whether radio was worth the effort, it did not hinder expansion. Warners relocated its station KFWB to the new Warner Theatre in Los Angeles. Paramount built KNX, which, operating with five thousand watts, became the fourth most powerful station in the country.[62]

One more fling for theatrical radio occurred on election night, 6 November 1928. Realizing that most of their patrons would stay home to listen to election results, many theaters arranged special programs mixing entertainment and live news coverage of Herbert Hoover's victory in an effort to cash in on what otherwise would have been a slow night.[63]

Despite the attraction of radio for the film industry, there was never any question of domination; many more stations were owned by newspaper companies than by studios. The relation between film and broadcasting extended the reciprocity which had grown between movies and journalism. Motion picture advertising could be counted on as steady revenue for the stations, while radio programming could provide vast publicity for the film companies. The producers found it sufficient to sponsor programs—for instance, Warners' *Vitaphone Jubilee* on CBS—without having to buy the whole network.

Radio and movies were mingling in other ways less visible to the public. Hilmes observes that "just as the factors that would later dominate commercial broadcasting entered the scene through the back door, so to speak, unnoticed at first and unremarked, so the involvement of the film industry in radio grew slowly but steadily through the early years, reaching a peak in 1927."[64] Throughout the decade, government regulators attempted to rein in the runaway entertainment media, with little success. In February 1927, Congress passed the Radio Act and established the Federal Radio Commission (FRC) to allocate frequencies and to formulate policy. Paramount's monopolistic practices already were being attacked by the Federal Trade Commission, and the FRC cooperated to quash the film industry's efforts to enter radio by way of the boardroom.

Learning about its competitors' work, AT&T, which was embarking on its WEAF broadcasting experiment, sought to capitalize on its own sound-film recording expertise. A revealing internal document shows precisely how the AT&T complex created spin-off technologies to enhance product diversity. On 12 December 1923, W. E. Harkness of AT&T wrote a letter to the Western Electric vice president Frank Jewett, referring to some demonstrations of motion picture sound recordings that had been given for record companies. Harkness pointed out that "it seems to us there may be a marked advantage in our having some privileges or rights in the commercial aspect of the sound-recording and reproducing devices. It would be of benefit to us in connection with our radio and wired programs to be able to record certain speeches or musical numbers for future use."[65] So within AT&T, early on, there was cross-fertilization between divisions to co-develop the same technology so that it could be utilized for both film and radio.

There was another potential "marked advantage." At the time of the memo, AT&T still controlled the transmission of radio over its phone lines, forcing the Radio Group to seek alternatives. One experiment involved shortwave relays of broadcasts; another idea was for super-power transmitters to blanket the nation. High-quality recordings on long-playing discs could sidestep AT&T's costly lines. Programs could be recorded, then distributed cheaply (though not "live") by sending out discs—a "chainless chain." The *Amos 'n' Andy Show,* produced at WGN in Chicago and distributed nationally on disc in 1928, is an example. AT&T obviously had a strong interest in staking a preemptive claim to this process and eventually did develop a radio transcription product that ERPI marketed to broadcasters at the same time it was selling theatrical sound systems to the movies.[66]

Rick Altman has argued that the 1926 Vitaphone program shown with DON JUAN was conceived as a simulated radio broadcast. Specifically, Warners imitated a program spon-

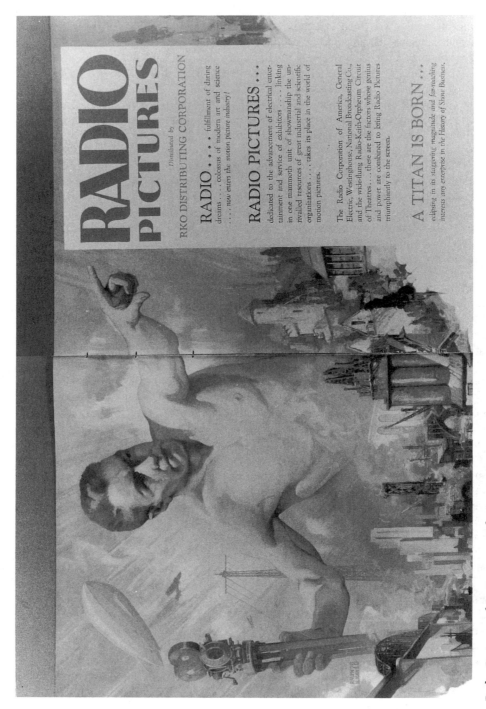

Radio Pictures advertisement, February 1929.

sored by the Victor record company on WEAF starring the tenor John McCormack. "It is thus no surprise," Altman claims,

> that Warners should model their first variety film program on Victor's successful radio program, right down to their signing of John McCormack. Although McCormack eventually did not appear in the opening Vitaphone program, Warners' advance announcement of the new process leaves no doubt about their intention of recreating Victor's radio show: "At phenomenally small cost," explained Albert Warner, "the unquestionably planned and perfected radio music program will begin a new era for moving picture patrons throughout the country." (Rick Altman, "Introduction: Sound/History," in *Sound Theory/Sound Practice* [New York: Routledge, 1992], pp. 119–20)

The intention was probably not to trick people into thinking that they were watching radio-plus-pictures, but to tap into the audience's awareness of radio's program format. Indeed, the *New York Times* credited radio with building a "sound-receptive audience," thus preparing people for the talkies. "The spread of radio broadcasting had," the author reported, "familiarized the general public with dramatic dialogue and high-grade music to a far greater extent than ever before."[67] RCA's studio subsidiary, RKO, in 1929, emphasized its electronic pedigree by naming its production unit Radio Pictures. RKO's strategy, quite simply, was to present the transition to sound as the next phase of civilization. The advertisement painted by Ralph Iligan depicted a classical "Titan." The giant reaches across an allegorical landscape, embracing a motion picture camera in his right hand (curiously, a hand-cranked one) and pointing, Michelangelo-esque, toward the "Radio" in the film company's new logo. The landscape on the right side is Mediterranean and classically bucolic; on the left it displays highlights of technological modernity: the steel bridge, an electrical transmission tower, airplanes, a dirigible, and a white skyscraper complex that looks remarkably like the future Rockefeller Center, home of the "Titan," David Sarnoff. The text specifically invokes the electrical ambience of broadcasting:

> RADIO . . . fulfillment of daring dreams . . . colossus of modern art and science . . . *now enters the motion picture industry!* RADIO PICTURES . . . dedicated to the advancement of electrical entertainment and service of exhibitors . . . linking in one mammoth unit of showmanship the unrivaled resources of great industrial and scientific organizations . . . takes its place in the world of motion pictures. (*Film Daily*, 5 February 1929, pp. 10–11)

Of course, in this public relations world of the future (anachronistically pictured as linked to the ancient past), communication and entertainment take place over the ether. The Titans of Radiopolis will not use telephones in their wireless utopia.

Television

Television in the 1920s was a subcategory of radio because it was considered to be a direct and inevitable improvement upon wireless transmission of sound. The president

Harold Bauer, accompanist for Efrem Zimbalist, in their 1926 Vitaphone short. Radio plus pictures?

of the Society of Motion Picture Engineers (SMPE) predicted as early as 1922 that television would soon be perfected.[68] That TV was "in the air," both in laboratories and in the popular imagination, was confirmed by F. H. Robinson in 1924:

> There is a close association between the kinema and radio, obvious when one realizes that light waves and wireless waves travel through the same medium— ether. A definite link has now been established between these two types of waves. It is called television, and far from being the "dream of the future" is an established fact. (F. H. Robinson, "The Radio Kinema," *Kinematograph Weekly*, quoted in "Radio Pictures," *Film Daily*, 14 April 1924, p. 1)

Unlike motion picture sound, for which competing working models were in place, television was still more a fantasy than a laboratory reality. There were many widely publicized experiments. C. Francis Jenkins, who had been a motion picture pioneer in the Edison laboratory, was, in the 1920s, the most prominent American independent investigator of "radio pictures," as he called his version of TV. In April 1925, he succeeded in sending an image from one building to another on a radio frequency. According to the *Film Daily* reporter, "In this small room the witnesses observed on a small screen a fairly good reproduction of the picture. They report that there was considerable flickering, just as there was in the early moving pictures." Thus, TV was described as a parallel to the movies at a primitive stage in their development.[69]

Though John Logie Baird in England and Jenkins claimed to be already transmitting moving images, AT&T expressed skepticism in public. In private, its engineers were also working hard to develop television. Though they had succeeding in sending still photographs over AT&T's long lines, the engineers proclaimed that *moving* images could never be relayed by phone or wireless: "The prospect of shooting prizefight pictures from the ringside to radio audiences, or of transmitting synchronized pictures with opera or other entertainment, was said [by AT&T] to be simply nil."[70]

By 1927, however, AT&T was ready to go public with a demonstration of long-distance television. Secretary of Commerce Herbert Hoover, in Washington, talked with Gifford of AT&T, in New York, via television. The images were not broadcast but sent over phone lines at the rate of eighteen frames per second. *Film Daily* reported that the image on the two-by-three-foot screen was unsatisfactory. Nevertheless, the transmission was successful because, "in this experiment time and space were eliminated." Another part of the show was a blackface skit by the performer A. Dolan called the "first vaudeville act to go on the air as a talking picture." This demonstration, and the phone company's press release, reveal that AT&T's initial conception of television was to "illustrate" two-way long-distance telephone conversation (still an AT&T preoccupation). A secondary function was to present current events and entertainment in formats indistinguishable from the Movietone Newsreel and the Vitaphone short. The difference was that television would be "live":

> Officials of [AT&T] state that the commercial future of the invention lies in public entertainment by way of super-news reels flashed before audiences at the moment of occurrence, as well as dramatic and musical acts carried over the ether waves in sound and picture at the instant they take place at the studio. Telephone company officials say that years of further experimentation are ahead in order to develop its possibilities. (*Film Daily*, 10 April 1927, pp. 1, 12)

Bell Telephone Lab's successful experiments influenced the Federal Radio Commission to set aside broadcast channels for experimental television transmission.[71] Meanwhile, General Electric had its own sound-picture transmitter, called the Kenographone. Thomas Edison was said to have seen his face and heard his voice on the system.[72]

The dominant technology being innovated was mechanical television, using spinning disks or some variant to scan the image. Only a few inventors explored electronic scanning, the fundamental method of modern television imaging. Philo T. Farnsworth, a precocious inventor from Utah, developed the thermionic applications from cathode ray tube research. His many inventions included an "image dissector" for capturing the picture, and—seminal for broadcast video—the "electron multiplier" for amplifying it. His company, Television, Inc., was formed on 27 March 1929. Using film clips of Mickey Mouse in "Steamboat Willie," the Dempsey-Tunney knockout, and the Pickford-Fairbanks film THE TAMING OF THE SHREW (1929), Farnsworth demonstrated his system to representatives of RKO, Fox theaters, and others. David Sarnoff, who had already hired Vladimir Zworykin from Westinghouse to head RCA's research laboratory, offered to buy out the inventor for $100,000.[73] Farnsworth refused, later sued RCA for infringing his patents, and won.[74]

While all of the Big Five movie producers, Paramount in particular, were intrigued by the possibility of theatrical television, the trade press usually downplayed the potential of TV. Lee de Forest said cautiously, "Television, I believe, must continue to be extremely intricate, and must be built and operated at great cost until new discoveries are made in the field of physics." *Film Daily* was skeptical, editorializing, "Radio pic-

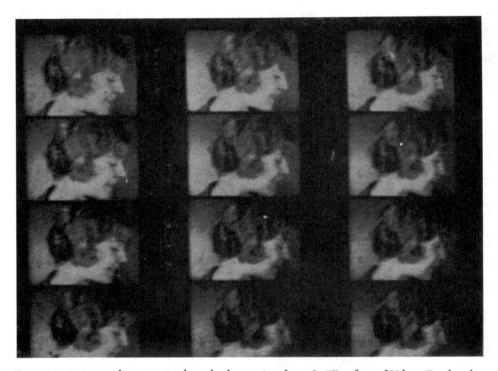

Experiment in sending movies by telephone, April 1928. "Ten feet of Vilma Banky shot in Chicago yesterday were transmitted to New York via the wires of A. T. and T."

tures still are in the embryonic stage, with little possibility seen that they will become practical for a considerable period of time, if ever," and even more candidly, "All this talk about motion pictures by radio in the home and color by television is the veriest bunk." Government regulators were the biggest obstacle to active ownership of television by the film industry. Nevertheless, NBC (which was related to RKO) and CBS (which was still half-owned by Paramount) obtained Federal Radio Commission licenses to experiment with TV in 1931.[75]

To the general public, of course, imaginary constructions of television had been common for a long time. Television was a futuristic fantasy, like movies in sound, color, and maybe 3-D. The realization of radio and talking movies suddenly gave the idea of TV fresh currency. It was easy for someone like Sarnoff to conceptualize television as a hybrid product. After RCA had given a public demonstration of large-screen television at the RKO-Proctor Fifty-eighth Street Theater in New York in 1930, he commented:

> With great motion-picture theaters forming huge centers of entertainment, with neighborhood picture houses in every city, with radio and the "movies" at every crossroad, it might seem at first thought an extraordinary effort of the imagination to envisage virtually millions of "little theaters" added to the constellation of entertainment made possible by radio, talking pictures, and the modern phonograph. And yet the progress of the electrical arts inevitably points in this direction. A separate theater for every home, although the stage may be only a cabinet and the curtain a screen—that, I believe, is the distinct promise of this era of electrical entertainment. (Quoted in *New York Times*, 13 July 1930, reprinted in Sarnoff, *Looking Ahead*, pp. 91–92)[76]

While Sarnoff was looking ahead to TV, he was also looking around at the phonograph business and trying to convince the RCA board of directors to buy the biggest company, Victor Talking Machines.

Phonography

In terms of sheer numbers of customers exposed to new sound technology, the talking cinema was less significant than the introduction of cheap, but high-quality, home sound reproducers—the phonograph. Though "wax" (shellac, later vinyl) disc recording did not lose its market dominance until the 1980s, it was challenged by alternative systems throughout the twenties, including recording on film and magnetic recording.

OPTICAL SOUND RECORDING

Recording sound on moving photographic film stock has been traced to the turn of the twentieth century.[77] One of the earliest inventors to link photographed sound with moving pictures was Eugene Lauste. He had worked with W. K. L. Dickson in Edison's lab, then with the American Mutoscope and Biograph Company before pursuing his research in his native England. In 1911 he came back to the United States and demonstrated a working prototype for a system that recorded sound on film. The coincidence of the timing of his visit with the renewal of interest in sound film at the Edison lab and by Case and de Forest is noteworthy. Lauste made another foray in 1918 and succeeded in interesting Charlie Chaplin. He wrote, "The idea which has already accomplished, is to photograph pictures and sounds simultaneously on the same film, and in one operation, and reproduce same without any contact on the film, or the use of a gramophone or phonograph. The sounds is absolutely clear, no scratching whatever or distortion in the voice or music, I am certain that you will be very surprise to hear it." Chaplin replied with a request for more details, but strangely, Lauste seems not to have replied.[78]

Another sound-recording pioneer was Joseph Tykocinski-Tykociner, the first professor of electrical engineering at the University of Illinois. The Polish-born radio technician had been a friend of Zworykin back in Russia before emigrating to the United States after the 1917 Revolution. Tykociner projected a successful composite picture and sound print at the American Institute of Electrical Engineers conference in Urbana on 9 June 1922. Several reels of this film restored by Joseph Aiken in 1957 were found to be "feeble," with uneven speed, but otherwise functional. Tykociner had the advantage of access to an improved photoelectric cell which used a mercury vapor bulb for the light emitter and a telephone transmitter for the sound input.[79] The result was a variable-density sound track.

The prototype of Lee de Forest's sound system was the film-phonograph he called Photophone. The invention, intended to be a superior music reproducer, was demonstrated successfully in January 1920. But old paradigms die hard; rather than using a motion picture strip, de Forest recorded on a spinning photographic plate. The Photophone was a sort of photographic gramophone.[80]

The developments with the farthest-reaching results, however, were taking place in the fiercely competitive environment of the major research laboratories. Hoxie, at the General Electric research labs in Schenectady, began working on ways to record radio transmissions on photographic film during World War I. Between 1917 and 1920, GE manufactured his visual photographic recorder under contract to the U.S. Navy. This device exposed high-speed incoming wireless code onto film for later analysis. It evolved into Hoxie's sound-on-film recorder and playback system, which he called the Pallophotophone (meaning "shaking light sound"). It was derived from the oscilloscope, a device for measuring electrical waves that had been in use since 1893. The Pallophotophone used a tiny mirror cemented onto a movable diaphragm which vibrated when connected to a microphone. Light beamed on it reflected onto the moving filmstrip, exposing a wavy line that tracked the acoustic frequencies of the source. It was demonstrated on 6 October 1921. GE foresaw two applications: for playing back delayed radio broadcasts, and for mastering phonograph records. In 1922 a test broadcast was made over company-owned station WGY. Listeners were invited to mail in comments if they heard anything different about the announcer's voice. Many respondents felt that his voice (pre-recorded on film, unbeknownst to them) was more distinct than usual.[81] *Scientific American* drafted a list of potential uses:

> It appears very likely that such [transcribing] applications of the photographic recording of sounds will become quite common in the future, and that lectures and important speeches may be simultaneously broadcasted from several radio stations. This system has a definite application in recording speeches, songs and other sounds for future generations. Its application to the theater is, of course, obvious. ("Pictures That Talk," *Scientific American*, January 1923, p. 71)

Presumably the last sentence referred to broadcasting plays; making motion pictures with recorded sounds was *not* obvious. But GE was definitely interested in talking pictures. On 2 April 1923, Hoxie connected his equipment to a Simplex projector for a demonstration to company executives. But by this time, De Forest Phonofilm's lack of success was becoming evident. Instead of pursuing the film option, GE promoted the device as a way to record musical performances on film which could be re-recorded onto phonograph discs. In 1925, to compete with the Western Electric Orthophonic (electric) recording process in use by Victor and Columbia, the Brunswick-Balke-Collender Company took out a license to use the Hoxie optical sound system for making its Light Ray recording masters.[82]

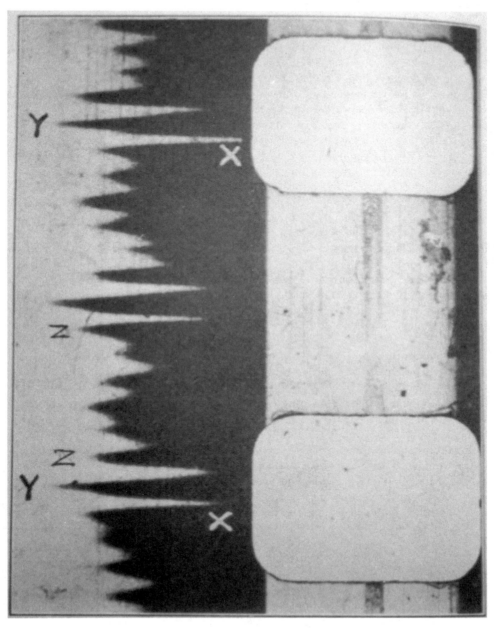

Variable-area optical sound track (from Richardson, Handbook of Projection, *1930).*

Meanwhile, Western Electric was proceeding in its typically organized fashion. Two research teams were assembled by Assistant Chief Engineer Edward B. Craft. One was under the direction of Wente (who had developed the condenser microphone), and the other was led by Joseph Maxfield. Wente's group studied sound-on-film. His team adapted a device formerly called a string galvanometer, which Lauste had invented at GE. (Cross-licensing gave Western Electric the rights to it.) This device was a light modulator, or light valve, as they called it. Two ribbons of metal foil repelled each other when electrically charged, forming a thin slit through which the light beam could pass. The opening varied according to the strength of the signal, so when light struck the moving film, an exposure was made that produced a "variable-area" (rather than a variable-density) sound track.[83] Western Electric began making sound-on-film tests in 1923. It was double-system recording; that is, picture and sound were recorded in separate cameras synchronized via two selsyn motors. Eventually this light valve became the standard in the Western Electric recording system. By 1923, however, many factors, primarily the company's expertise in disc recording, contributed to Western Electric's decision to pursue sound-on-disc, rather than optical sound, for its film sound system.

Though proponents of each of these optical reproduction systems claimed superiority, to the average auditor in the theater it probably made little difference how the sounds were made. Kellogg, an engineer, recalled, "During the earlier years of commercial sound, the advantage seemed to be on the side of [variable-] area for music but [variable-] density for speech intelligibility. With both at their best there was little to choose in clarity of speech reproduction, but the density system seemed able to take more abuse without too serious loss of articulation."[84] All systems had difficulty reproducing the highest frequencies of speech, resulting in the infamous "s" problem. Actors speaking sibilants were perceived to be making "f" or "th" sounds, owing to recording distortion.

Essential for the recording and reproduction of sound on film is a transport for moving the emulsion past the exposing beam at a constant rate. This was accomplished by stretching the film across a heavy flywheel that evened out the jerks caused by the starting and stopping of the film during each frame's recording/projection. Simple as it seems, the mechanical flywheel concept was claimed as proprietary by many international inventors and litigated well into the 1930s.

Regardless of how the film was exposed, all these methods were played back the same way, by an exciter lamp and photoconductive cell combination. Light from a small lamp passing through either a variable-density or variable-area track produced electrical currents which reproduced the original sound. The amplification circuits and vacuum tubes were controlled by RCA's patents and licenses.

Electromagnetic Recording

Visitors to the 1900 Exposition Universelle in Paris might have heard a scientific marvel, the Telegraphone. The invention of the Danish telephone engineer Valdemar Poulsen, it recorded and played back fluctuating magnetic fields on a fast-moving wire. His application was a dictation machine, which was marketed in the United States by the American Telegraphone Company. Lee de Forest worked briefly with some entrepreneurs around 1913 on an abortive attempt to apply a similar wire-recording system to film. When it failed to materialize, little effort was made to incorporate magnetic sound into the movies for about forty years.[85] (Poulsen also obtained patents which, in the 1930s, gave him and his assignees valid claims on optical sound projection.)

Disc Recording

These optical and electromagnetic recording techniques aspired to improve upon the acoustical-mechanical phonograph, which had changed little since Edison's and Emile Berliner's nineteenth-century models. There were countless efforts to synchronize phonographic cylinders and discs with movies right from the beginning.

Those same 1900 visitors to the Paris Exposition, if not already sated by science-as-entertainment, could savor the demonstration which took place at the Phono-Cinéma Théâtre. Paul Decauville opened the attraction in April. Films and cylinder recordings of the stars Sarah Bernhardt, Coquelin Cadet, and Victor Maurel (an important baritone interpreter of Verdi) were roughly synchronized. Because of competition from other cinemas, lack of a varied program, and audiovisual problems, the theater closed after only two months without having made back the cost of its construction.[86] Probably the most technically successful early system, based on viewing restored prints, was the Chronophone. This had been a passion of Léon Gaumont, founder of France's second-largest film studio. Gaumont dreamed that sound films would help him command a larger share of the American market, and in 1907 he opened a production branch in Flushing, New York, with Herbert Blaché and his wife Alice Guy Blaché in charge of operations. The Chronophone went through several developmental stages, ending in a version which was exhibited regularly at the huge Gaumont Palace theater in Paris and, in June 1913, at the Thirty-ninth Street Theater in New York. Gaumont used a compressed-air amplifier called the Elgéphone and a turntable which was connected to the projector by cables. Synchronization was maintained by wiring the projector and phonograph motors in series on the same direct-current circuit. Typical subjects included vaudeville sketches and songs by popular music hall artists—for example, Mayol.[87]

The most notorious film-phonograph combination, at least in terms of its effect on developments in the 1920s, was the Kinetophone, designed by the Edison laboratory. This was a system that recorded onto and played back from an oversize cylinder. It used a mechanical amplifier based on the type that had been used aboard ships for communicating between decks. Unlike the Chronophone, the projector for the Kinetophone was driven by the phonograph, not the other way around. The connection was made via belt pulleys. Though well received at its New York vaudeville premiere, subsequent runs were unsuccessfully synchronized and the sound was shrill; some audiences booed the presentation. Peck, in 1927, recalled one show, perhaps involving the Kinetophone:

> It was about 14 years ago that the writer sat in a small motion-picture auditorium, eagerly awaiting the presentation of a "talking movie." Finally the picture flashed on the screen, and a few seconds after one of the characters had started to move his lips in the introductory phrases, his first words issued from a phonograph situated on the stage near the screen! Someone had blundered and as a result, all through the production, the voices were always a few paces behind the actions of the characters. Nor was that the only trouble. The speed of the phonograph had not been carefully regulated, and as

Phono-Cinéma-Théâtre poster, c. 1900.

Questions indiscrètes *(Gaumont Chronophone, c. 1906), with Mayol.*

the action continued, the voices fell more and more in arrears. Next, the motor spring became weak and it was necessary to wind it up, with the usual accompanying noise. To cap the climax, the voices continued to be reproduced for several seconds after the picture was finished. (A. P. Peck, "Giving a Voice to Motion Pictures," *Scientific American,* June 1927, p. 378)[88]

The Kinetophone limped on until 1915, a failure frequently cited by studio heads in the next decade when approached by others promoting movie sound systems. On 9 December 1914, the Kinetophone lab was destroyed by fire and Edison abandoned the project.[89] The elderly Thomas Edison said that he had sold the rights to a foreign entrepreneur:

> We took the voice on a phonograph record, and arranged the talking machine so that it could be operated from the projection room of the theater. The phonograph was placed down in front of the screen, and it worked fine.
>
> I had hardly set the machine to working, when a Japanese man nearly went crazy over it. He asked what I would take for the invention. I really did not think much of it, and thought that $2,000 or $3,000 would have been a pretty fair price. Before I could make a price, however, he up and offers me $50,000 for the rights. Did I give them to him? Certainly I did. As soon as I caught my breath after the jolt. (*Film Daily,* 4 March 1927, pp. 1, 2)

Of the attempts made in the early twenties, the most attention-getting was Orlando Kellum's Talking Pictures, not because of any particular technical distinction, but because it was used in conjunction with a big premiere of a famous director's film: D. W. Griffith's DREAM STREET (1921). By profession a tailor, Kellum had seen Edison's Kinetophone, and he borrowed $1,500 from a relative of his maid to finance an improved version. He founded the Kellum Talking Picture Company in 1916. The May 1921 program was to be his big break. It consisted of a short song, a monologue in "Negro dialect" by Irving S. Cobb, and a prologue spoken by Griffith in which he praised Kellum's "marvelous and accurate" machine. A selection of standard phonograph records and one specially composed song sung by Richard Grace accompanied the film. Those present complained of the loud needle noise. Talking movies, one reviewer reacted, "will do more to drive audiences out of motion picture theaters than bring them in." The gimmick was discarded after a few performances, but Kellum continued promoting his process in Canada and England. He enthused in 1925: "There is still one great equation to be added: color! I am working on that now. If I can perfect it—and I think I can—the theater, concert hall, and lecture rostrum will be revolutionized indeed."[90]

At the time when Wente's team was working on sound-on-film, the AT&T team led by Joseph Maxfield was improving sound-on-disc, in both recording and reproduction. The earliest public demonstration was in Woolsey Hall on the Yale campus on 2 October 1922. E. B. Craft projected a silent instructional film, AUDION, accompanied by a somewhat synchronized lecture on how amplifiers work, to 2,475 members of the American Association of Electrical Engineers. According to Gleason Archer, "Western Electric thus scored a triumph over its rival [GE], but a triumph somewhat marred by the fact that the movie and talkie failed to synchronize. It was not a case of two hearts that beat as one but two hearts that pulsated separately."[91] Using capacitors and linked drive shafts, stroboscopic lights, and wow-and-flutter meters on the recording and projection equipment, Maxwell's team would greatly improve the synchronization but never totally overcome the problem. Maxfield and his collaborator H. C. Harrison utilized the latest developments in microphones and amplification to produce electromagnetic recordings with increased sensitivity, frequency response, and signal-to-noise ratio. Their paper "Methods of High-Quality Recording" also addressed room tone, wax cutting, and horn design. These experiments led, in 1925, to the mass production of electrically recorded discs which were playable on the new Orthophonic machines made by the Victor Talking Machine Company and the Vivatonal brand made by the Columbia Phonograph Company, both under license from Western Electric.[92] These phonographs brought high-quality music to millions of new listeners. The first generation of home Orthophonic players had electric turntables, but they reproduced sound through acoustic horns, not electrical amplification.[93] Though in demand by broadcasters, electric machines did not dominate the home market until the mid-1930s, when they were frequently combined with a radio receiver in the same cabinet. Electronic amplification was essential for filling a huge space like a 1920s movie palace with the full, rich sounds of the singing human voice or a symphony orchestra. Western Electric's Vitaphone sound-on-disc combination did the job very well. Richard Koszarski has astutely observed, "Few of the Vitaphone first-nighters [in 1926] had ever heard an electrically recorded and reproduced phonograph record, and none had ever experienced theater-quality sound. What impressed them was not just the synchronization (which would always prove a problem) but also the clarity, range, and sheer volume produced by electrical amplification."[94]

The Vitaphone disk was 16 inches in diameter and played at 33 1/3 rpm. The stylus tracked from the center outward.

Just as talking cinema might be thought of as long-distance telephone or radio with pictures, it was not difficult to imagine it as phonograph records with pictures. Performers, whether recorded by de Forest's Phonofilm, Fox's Movietone, or Warners' Vitaphone, often were supplementing their musical or vocal renditions with their synchronized image. Frequently the recording company to which the performer was under contract was identified in the title, which facilitated the consumer's purchase of his or her records. No doubt it was the hope of publicity and extra sales of their recordings that prompted many performers to visit the studios and face the mike.

The Western Electric sound-on-disc system, which would become Vitaphone, may have achieved perfect synchrony in the laboratory, but in the field—that is, in the nation's theaters—the picture-sound match was frequently off a bit, owing to the inevitable slippage in the mechanical link between turntable and projector head. This small lapse between the "flapping" of the lips and the hearing of the voice militated against the illusion of naturalism. Additionally, the telltale needle-scratching in the background was always audible and must have reminded viewers that Vitaphonic recording was a product of the phonograph industry. (Both these defects are greatly exaggerated in SINGIN' IN THE RAIN.) It may also be that the early propensity to record a wide range of musical material (from opera to ukulele performances) was, among other things, a proud demonstration by the Western Electric technicians of the hitherto impossible recording range of Vitaphone, their enhanced phonograph. Warner Bros. ads extolled the quality that made it worthwhile: "The high character of Warner Bros. Singing, Talking Technicolor Productions demand the utmost in Sound Recording and Reproduction. Vitaphone Discs supply just that."[95]

Other Technologies

Enabling the efficient production and exhibition of the talkies required the coordination of many more industries and technologies. For example, specialized photographic processes were required. Eastman Kodak, in 1927, set up a dedicated lab under the direction of Otto Sandvik for research and development of sound film emulsions. The lab introduced fine-grain panchromatic emulsions, tinted release-print stock for sound prints, and new processes for developing negatives. Incandescent lighting, already becoming the industry standard, was adopted after 1928. Many of the other technologies deployed are not normally considered part of "film history." For example, cantilever engineering, a wartime product of bridge architecture and aviation, was used for manufacturing lightweight mobile cranes and booms to swiftly and silently maneuver cameras, lights, and microphones about the film set. The necessity to suppress ambient noise in enclosed soundproof sets and in movie theaters spurred improvements in quiet-running fans and air conditioning. The rapid development of industrial magnets during the early 1920s had important ancillary applications in the transformers and cones in horns and dynamic speakers, as well as the galvanometers in light valves.

These factors may have been necessary for sound to be innovated, but none alone was a sufficient determinant to explain where motion pictures with sound "came from." These multipurpose technologies were developed for other uses and would have been applied with or without the coming of sound. What happened was that the electrical companies and the studios, with the support of the popular press, created a *climate of acceptance* for sound cinema. This was done primarily by creating a discourse which aligned the talkies with the already powerful myths of scientific progress and technological determinism. For a while, it was enough to know that sound films were electrical, or that they ran on vacuum tubes. The editor of an important fan magazine said it pithily in 1928: "This is an electrical age, the radio and the wireless prove it. And before five years have elapsed the movies will all be talkies, the sound effects and dialogue being transmitted through electricity. All of the big picture houses in the cities are now being wired to carry the *juice* which spells sound and dialogue."[96] Lee de Forest also wrapped the talkies in the mantle of electricity: "Today [1929] the talking motion picture has shunted aside the silent screen. Tomorrow—who knows to what uses it will be put for entertainment and education? Its development and the development of so many things that make for comfort and progress in living depend upon how well scientists become acquainted with that master force so commonly called electricity."[97]

It was also in the manufacturers' interest to cultivate the idea that the talkies were inevitable. Sarnoff, the most outspoken, explicitly attributed the development of sound to modernism. He worked hard to capitalize on the public's millenarian anticipation, a feeling that the twentieth century would be a turning point in civilization. But the technology of film sound was not foisted upon a passive public. Since the industrial boom that followed World War I, the notion that American society was entering a new technological epoch was pervasive. The valorization of technology was embodied in the phrase "New Era," which one heard everywhere in the twenties. It was applied to everything from politics to stock-picking theories, to product brand names. The rhetoric surrounding the early sound film attempted to link the technical medley that comprised Photophone, Vitaphone, Movietone, and the others with new-millennium optimism and faith in industrial progress.

Significantly, few commentators, if any, saw sound as a natural outgrowth of silent cinema production practice. On the contrary, the talkies were something new, part of the electrifying spirit of the twenties. Sound film's alleged origins in thermionics made it essentially *different* from the classical Hollywood cinema. As a result, no one knew which form the new medium would take. It might resemble Broadway theater or vaudeville, a phonograph or radio with pictures, or it could substitute for a live orchestra. The one thing that hardly anyone anticipated was a quick, smooth continuity between silent and sound movie production.

The tenor Giovanni Martinelli sings "Vesti la Giubba" from the opera I Pagliacci *by Leoncavallo (Vitaphone short, 1926).*

3

Virtual Broadway, Virtual Orchestra: De Forest and Vitaphone

Talking pictures are perfected, says Dr. Lee De Forest. So is castor oil.
JAMES QUIRK, *Photoplay,* MARCH 1924

Once a new technology enters public usage, it is susceptible to being co-opted for any number of new purposes—many of which the creators did not foresee. The sound film emerged as an exhibition phenomenon several years preceding 1927, the generally accepted date for the "birth of the talkies." When the recording and reproducing apparatuses moved out of the laboratories and into theaters, few if any inventors or promoters thought that the sound film would take over Hollywood to transform the silent feature into the all-talking, all-singing phenomenon that would become popular around 1929. Rather, the sound film was perceived as a novelty. The mainstream industry, as Quirk suggested with scatological innuendo, regarded the sound film as an irritation. The problem for the filmmakers was, without any extant models, how were they to merchandise this new kind of film to the public? They relied on what they knew. The resulting films blended the most popular ingredients of the current entertainment mix of vaudeville, live musical accompaniment for silent films, lectures, public address, and radio. Filmmakers capitalized on cinema's capability to suggest a *virtual* presence, an imagined being-there, in order to bring performer and auditor together in the space of the filmed performance. Broadway, the "Street of Streets," was coming soon to the local theater.

Lee de Forest and Phonofilm: Virtual Broadway

The Audion tube had brought Lee de Forest fame and fortune. His name was synonymous with the pioneering spirit of early radio. But in the early 1920s he became fanatical about talking pictures. Although previous accounts have dismissed him as an eccentric personality and a failed entrepreneur—and he was both—de Forest's Phonofilm venture was influential as a catalyst for other developers and for establishing a model for early sound film forms.

An impulsive opportunist, de Forest had a scheme to take advantage of the German economic depression by moving there and hiring cheap research assistants. He arrived in Berlin in October 1921 with his current project, the film-gramophone idea. In Europe film sound had been developing rapidly. At the time of de Forest's visit, a team of three inventors were already showing sound-on-film shorts produced by Josef Engl, Hans Vogt, and Joseph Massolle at the Alhambra theater in Berlin. The voice synchronization was perfect, but reports said that the tonal quality needed "improvement."

The details of de Forest's contact with the three inventors are unknown, but he referred to their screenings in his press releases. Eventually their research resulted in the Tri-Ergon sound-on-film process, which would become the chief European rival to the American sound systems. When de Forest learned of it, Tri-Ergon had already had a checkered career. The inventors had applied for patents in Germany, England, Austria, and France in 1919. Germany and England had rejected their work as too unoriginal for a patent, and the patents granted in Austria and France were later nullified. In 1921 they applied for a U.S. patent. It is possible that this is how de Forest learned of the process. (In a 1932 lawsuit against ERPI, American Tri-Ergon demonstrated that its patent application preceded de Forest's by three months.) In April 1922, de Forest announced to the film trade in a dispatch from Germany that he had perfected his new Phonofilm, a system for recording synchronized voice onto film. He expected to market it soon.[1]

De Forest returned from Europe in September, characteristically full of energy and optimism. He described his Phonofilm experiments to the *New York Times.* The device, as he then pictured it, was "a method of recording voices, accurately synchronized on film, that eventually may be broadcast." In other words, de Forest expected radio transcription to be the primary use for his device, not theatrical sound films, as with the Tri-Ergon process. In this early phase, he apparently did not intend to record images on the film stock. For example, he proposed using sound cameras to record courtroom and congressional proceedings for delayed broadcasts. Soon, though, Phonofilm had the look and feel of the original Tri-Ergon films. De Forest told *Radio Broadcast* in December that his method was superior to the Germans' process and illustrated his remarks with a filmstrip showing himself and his voice track.[2] Although at this time de Forest seems to have been concentrating on wireless applications for Phonofilm, he had started thinking of its ramifications for commercial motion pictures. He indicated that the silent feature was unlikely to change. "Ordinarily," he said, "the film picture of today would not be greatly benefitted by the addition of the voices of the actors." Instead, he predicted an alternative film form evidently inspired by New York variety shows and the European music hall. Phonofilm would display the talents of star performers: "An entirely new class or type of moving picture play will be evolved for the Phonofilm. Actors and actresses who can speak as well as look pretty and make funny faces will be in demand." De Forest was not proposing a change in the fundamental structure of Hollywood and its star system; rather, he wanted to supply self-contained filmed acts to add to the standard movie bill. De Forest's efforts to promote Phonofilm to the major film producers failed dismally. William Fox especially annoyed him when he would not even grant an interview. For this and for personal reasons (de Forest was anti-Semitic), the inventor cultivated a dislike for Fox.[3]

Though producers were blasé, the adventurous exhibitor Hugo Riesenfeld, who was interested in theatrical radio, backed de Forest's experiments. This support enabled the inventor to lease the old Talmadge film studio on East Forty-eighth Street.[4] In April 1923, de Forest said he was ready to begin releasing Phonofilm subjects on a weekly schedule. The inventor was quick to point out that the system would not compete with silent features, and that there would be only very limited "talking":

> The "phono-film" is adapted primarily for the reproduction of musical, vaudeville numbers and solos. It is not De Forest's idea that the ordinary pantomine [*sic*] drama is adapted to the "phono-film," but he expects scenario writers to write stories around the acoustic idea to work in the voice and music to the greatest possible advantage. De Forest points out that his invention opens the way to scenics carrying their own music, played by first class orchestras and comedies, and animated cartoons with bright lines and patter. (*Film Daily*, 7 April 1923, pp. 1–2)

An inaugural program opened at Riesenfeld's Rivoli on 15 April and featured the Broadway headliners Weber and Fields, Sissle and Blake, Eddie Cantor, Eva Puck and Sammy White, Phil Baker, and Conchita Piquir. The journalists present emphasized the novelty but had harsh words for the sound quality. The reviewer for the *New York Times* reported that the sound of THE GAVOTTE (1923) was scratchy. He was surprised that, "while one could hear the instruments being played for the dancers, one could not hear the slightest sound of a footfall. Hence it seemed as if the dancers were performing in rubber shoes. One also expected to hear the swish of the silken skirts of the woman, but all that issued forth were the strains of musical instruments." He condescendingly admitted that the sounds of THE SERENADE (1923) were at least as good as an "old time phonograph." The synchronization, however, was maintained perfectly throughout.[5]

Tepid reviews did not dissuade de Forest. To finance production, he boldly sold all his shares in his radio business, the De Forest Company. In June 1923, he announced that nationally distributed releases would be available in September. Each weekly reel was to consist of three to five numbers, including dances, songs, monologues, dialogues, and "here and there an ambitious ensemble." In a strategy reminiscent of early cinema showmanship (when theater managers exercised complete control of the movie program), de Forest encouraged exhibitors to cut up the numbers and distribute them throughout the evening to create "what amounts to a vaudeville show for the price of film." Again, showmen were more interested than Hollywood. Florenz Ziegfeld was said to have expressed a desire to have an entire program of the Ziegfeld Follies "Phonofilmed."[6]

De Forest Phonofilms, Inc., was formed in February 1924, with Lee de Forest as president. Theodore Case was a partner, and Earl Sponable an employee. The production plans were augmented to include a variety of genres: "dramas, comedies, condensed versions of famous operas, scenics in which nature's sounds, such as the singing of birds, roaring of animals, dashing of waves, will be brought out, news pictures, vaudeville acts and comic cartoons with the character's words actually spoken instead of being printed." J. Searle Dawley was chosen to direct more productions.[7]

De Forest ambitiously produced ABRAHAM LINCOLN (1924), a two-reel film (that is, about twenty-four minutes) adapted from a stage play by John Drinkwater and directed by Dawley. Its Phonofilm highlights were some campfire songs and Frank McGlynn (in the title role) delivering the Gettysburg Address. Again, critics applauded the synchronization and panned the tonal quality: "The sound is so vastly less realistic than the pictures themselves that it can scarcely carry conviction" (*New York Herald*); "rather crudely done" (*Times Square Daily*); "in its present stage the 'Phonofilm' is not likely to be taken up by those who are producing on a large scale" (*New York Times*). The *Times* reviewer also criticized the directionality of the sound reproduction, hearing the voices come from the corner of the screen, not from the actor. *Film Daily* commended the picture as "the best of the talking films yet seen," but its reviewer also had reservations about the acoustics. "One is always aware," he complained, "that the voice comes from a record of some sort."[8]

De Forest at last garnered some favorable publicity for MEMORIES OF LINCOLN (1924), a four-minute film in which ninety-year-old Chauncey Depew reminisced about his personal experiences with the U.S. president. The content was so captivating that reviews overlooked the noisy sound reproduction. "Amazing," said the *Herald*. "It was easy to imagine, after the film had run awhile, it was Mr. Depew himself sitting there in the theater and talking of Lincoln as he knew him in quiet conversational tones." While the *Times* reviewer was still bothered by the loudspeaker placement at the sides of the screen, he admitted, "There are moments when one loses sight of this defect by the sheer interest one feels in what the speaker utters."[9] Both comments reveal the listeners' willingness to ignore the mechanical obstacles in order to indulge a complete acoustic illusion and a desire to be "tricked" into thinking that the screen presence was real.

The 1924 presidential election was a three-way race, and Phonofilm gave each candidate the opportunity to speak before the camera in MAJOR ISSUES OF THE CAMPAIGN (1924). In what some might now consider to be a foreshadowing of contemporary media coverage of politics, the speakers' vocal styles captured more attention than the substance of their remarks. The differences in their forensic qualities were noted with detailed curiosity:

> All three read from their party platforms, first [John W.] Davis, whose voice, incidentally, does not reproduce as well as either the President's or Senator La Follette's. Davis speaks in an easy, unhesitating style though he varies his expression but little. Senator [Robert M.] La Follette is more vigorous and while at times he slurs syllables, it is usually easy to understand what he says. The President's [Calvin C. Coolidge] speech was delivered in his usual slow, decisive fashion with that unmistakable New England twang. He hesitated occasionally. An attentive audience will not find it difficult to understand the speakers. (*Film Daily*, 5 October 1924, p. 10)

At least thirty theaters showed the campaign film. Also in 1924, de Forest synchronized a music sound track for THE COVERED WAGON (1923) and SIEGFRIED (1923). He made LOVE'S OLD SWEET SONG (1924, a two-reel dramatic playlet with Una Merkel) and, in 1925, shot a reel using an experimental color process. He combined music and animation in a series of Max Fleischer's "bouncing ball" sing-along cartoons.[10]

De Forest claimed to have sold the Phonofilm system to an additional fifty theaters. Many of these were not permanent installations but were sold to showmen who moved from theater to theater. The Phonofilm was highlighted as an entertainment form in its own right, recalling the programs of Lyman Howe and other early traveling entrepreneurs.[11] These shows had twin selling points: the technical marvel of sound-on-film ("$10,000 Reward paid to any person who finds a phonograph") and virtual Broadway ("the most dazzling cast of stars ever assembled"). The income permitted de Forest to hire John Meehan as production head and James Elliot as his business manager.

De Forest Phonofilm advertisement, 1924.

Together they aggressively tried to market the system to theaters and vaudeville houses. Still, no big chains showed any interest.[12]

The company needed more capital for its expansion plans, even though shares of De Forest Phonofilm stock had climbed from $20 to $100.[13] De Forest Phonofilm, Ltd., was formed in Toronto in November 1924. In terms of numbers of theaters, this branch was potentially much more significant than de Forest's American market because it could give him access to the 250 theaters in the Canadian Famous Players chain.[14] This proved to be the apogee of the Phonofilm company. In December, de Forest floated $22 million of new stock. The company said it would use the funds to finance its plan to film entire musical revues and to launch foreign production.[15] The state of New York intervened and canceled the stock issue because of Phonofilm's shaky financial base and de Forest's reputation as a wheeler-dealer. Calvin Coolidge became enraged when he learned that Phonofilm salesmen were showing his campaign film to sell stock, and he ordered the Justice Department to investigate. (Charges were never filed.) In September 1925, the innovator Theodore Case quit De Forest Phonofilm, taking with him de Forest's license to use his patents. Sponable also left the organization.

Earl Sponable had been secretly shopping the Case system around before the breakup. He had made presentations to Western Electric and General Electric in 1925, but the engineers of both corporations decided that the process did not add anything to their existing patent coverage. Case, in July 1926, agreed to sell his rights controlling sound-on-film recording and playback to de Forest's old nemesis, William Fox. On 20 September they formed the Fox-Case Corporation, and Sponable was hired as head of research.

Even if de Forest had possessed extraordinary acumen, his pockets simply were not deep enough and he was out of touch with the big changes occurring in the U.S. film industry. Production and exhibition were concentrated in a few controlling companies. The "Big Three" were Paramount, Loew's (which owned MGM), and First National; the "Little Five" were Fox, Universal, Producers Distributing Corporation (PDC), Film Booking Office (FBO), and Warner Bros. The theater chains of Loew's, Stanley, Balaban and Katz, and others had grown in the twenties, modeled on the retail chain store concept. Unaffiliated theater alliances, mostly family-run, were consolidating their holdings to become national competitors. Only a few independent metropolitan exhibitors—like Riesenfeld in New York—or regional movie chains, vaudeville houses, and temporary venues were available. Unlike the major studios, which could pledge future income and real estate holdings for collateral and margin loans, de Forest had a record of dubious dealing and bankruptcy.

A look, however, at his Phonofilm productions confirms that he was attracted to fascinating personalities. William E. Waddell, Phonofilm's general manager, noted the various levels of audience appeal in the programs. Some of the subjects filmed included Governor Al Smith making a speech and singing, George Jessel doing a monologue, and De Wolf Hopper reading "Casey at the Bat." Eddie Cantor sang songs and recited from his play *Kid Boots*. Waddell pointed out that this was a big hit at the Rivoli and Rialto Theaters, around the corner from the Selwyn, where Cantor was performing live. Cantor convinced his friend Sophie Tucker to make a recording, but the deal fell through when de Forest could not pay her cash in advance.[16]

Also appealing was the range of entertainment made possible: "it runs the gamut from grand-opera to slap-stick." Waddell reassured exhibitors who might have in mind "failures of the past" (that is, Edison's and Kellum's) that "Phonofilm is a veritable talking film." The greatest allure, though, was in de Forest's own celebrity and his association with radio. Although de Forest was no longer connected with the manufacturing company that bore his name, Waddell noted that his label still appeared on many thousands of radio sets:

> The name of "DeForest" is known to every radio fan and they are all anxious to see and hear his latest creation, "Radio Talking Pictures."
>
> Two questions the exhibitor might ask himself are "How many radio fans are there in my audience?" and "Would they care to see and hear the great stars of opera, musical comedy and vaudeville?" (*Film Daily,* 15 March 1925, p. 27)

This attempt to associate Phonofilm with radio reveals much about the characteristics of the sound film as an entertainment form and defines virtual Broadway. The *subject* was to be stage amusement of the light, popular variety—speeches, lectures, and two-reel excerpts (musical or dramatic) from revues. The *medium* was analogous to radio. Like radio, Phonofilm would beam entertainers from the New York stage into the local auditorium—not into listeners' homes obviously, but into their community movie theater. De Forest's directors had a penchant for recording famous personalities speaking directly to the audience or reading their published works, much like the radio interview. The Phonofilm interest in topical subjects was similar in practice to broadcast journalism.

De Forest thought of the *function* of Phonofilm as an augmentation of, not a replacement for, the Hollywood feature. We can say that his design was program-driven, not feature-driven. That is, he wished to sell exhibitors short items to enhance the value of "an evening's entertainment," not compete head-on with the major film producers or restructure what we now call the classical Hollywood cinema.

Chronically underfunded and mismanaged, Phonofilm became insolvent in 1926. There are several reasons for de Forest's failure. Phonofilm was acoustically limited because the inventor did not have legal access to thermionic circuitry controlled by AT&T and RCA, neither of which was likely to negotiate with him. But the Phonofilm system was functionally identical to Case's Fox Movietone system of 1927 and the Powers Cinephone of 1928—which were technically and commercially satisfactory—so the explanation is not purely mechanical inferiority. De Forest's exhibitor-oriented approach was badly timed, for it came when the large chains were putting pressure on the independent theater owners, reducing expenses by consolidating their buying power, and making the programs more uniform. Novelties supplied by freelance producers like de Forest would have increasing difficulty finding exposure as the decade of the twenties advanced.

De Forest made two contributions to the coming of sound. As he struggled to get exhibitors interested in his enterprise, his highly visible work must have been a goad to the sound research teams at Western Electric and General Electric. De Forest's experiments in radio, then in film, were only possible because in his 1912 negotiations with AT&T he had retained the right to develop new applications for the Audion. Throughout the twenties, the inventor's loud boasting about his accomplishments was a thorn in the side of the corporate giant's research department (and kept the legal department busy, too). At General Electric, management's decision to take Hoxie's talking film device, the Pallophotophone, out of mothballs was definitely prompted by de Forest's shows. His highly public campaign for film sound must have been a challenge that could not be ignored by corporations staking their claims on all things acoustic.

Second, the Phonofilm program concept became a model for the talking-picture format that was passed on intact to the other early sound film producers—Vitaphone and Fox—when they entered the market. Indeed, many of Vitaphone's performers and Movietone's celebrities had appeared previously before de Forest's camera. The realization of the special value of the speaking and performing star would later prove to be an essential component of the talkies. This conception of sound cinema as virtual Broadway—New York stage material and radio-like delivery—proved to be far longer lasting than the Phonofilm system itself.

Warner Bros. and Vitaphone: The Virtual Orchestra

Western Electric's sound-on-disc and sound-on-film recording and playback systems were both working in late 1924, but AT&T chose to commercialize the disc method. The engineer Joseph P. Maxfield provided an explanation. He recalled in 1946 that

> the reason sound-on-disc recording was chosen for early production experiments was because the wax disc industry had many years of experience in making each record perfect for reproduction of sound. On the other hand, there was the danger, if not the certainty, that sound-on-film recording, processed by the rule-of-thumb methods then in vogue in the commercial film laboratories, would yield uncertain results. (*Film Daily*, 6 August 1946, p. 16)

Aside from tonal quality, the issue was also one of control. Western Electric opted to keep film sound out of the hands of the film labs, where they had little expertise, and in the hands of its acoustic engineers, an industry they dominated because of extensive prior research and existing business arrangements with record companies.

Western Electric's salesmen fared no better than de Forest's in getting the attention of Hollywood. In 1924 Famous Players–Lasky, Loew's, and First National all said "no thanks." On 27 May 1925, an outside promoter, Walter J. Rich, signed a memorandum with Western Electric acquiring the rights to market the system for nine months.[17] At about the same time, Nathan Levinson of Western Electric, the engineer who had supervised the installation of equipment in the Warner radio stations, told Sam Warner of the exhibition of talking pictures he had seen at the Bell Laboratories in New York. Sam, with difficulty, won over the other Warner brothers and, just as importantly, their financial manager, the investment banker Waddill Catchings of Goldman, Sachs and Company. On 25 June 1925, Rich and Warner Bros. created a joint venture to explore sound film production. Far from being nearly bankrupt—a persistent myth—Catchings and Warners were engaged in a strategic plan of aggressive expansion to increase theater holdings, consolidate distribution, and diversify into broadcasting. The sound experiment was an acceptable risk as part of a highly leveraged design to catch up with the Big Three studios. It was also a cost-cutting play, since it would eliminate orchestras and presentation acts in the newly acquired movie houses. This plan was consistent with the speculative economic climate in other growth industries of the mid-1920s. The policy also meant investing in a big-name actor, John Barrymore, and a director, Ernst

Lubitsch. The Vitaphone deal was one of several tactics designed to elevate the small outfit to the status of a film major.

In September 1925, Warners began refitting its newly acquired (but very old) Vitagraph studio at 1400 Locust Avenue in Flatbush, Brooklyn, to produce sound films. Meanwhile, there was a change of command at Western Electric, and John E. Otterson became the general manager. He was keenly interested in Rich's film venture and took over negotiations. On 20 April 1926, a fifty-seven-page contract was signed between Western Electric and the new Vitaphone company, which had been incorporated with Rich as president and Warner Bros. as the majority shareholder and provider of capital. Western Electric granted to Vitaphone the exclusive right to use the recording apparatus for its own films, to sublicense other producers, and to sublicense the reproduction equipment in theaters.

To secure talent for its sound movies, Vitaphone signed license agreements with Victor Talking Machine, the Metropolitan Opera, and (later) the Brunswick-Balke-Collender record company for the rights to record their contract artists. Brunswick-Balke-Collender's exclusive roster included a wide range of entertainment, from the popular Al Jolson to the high-class New York Philharmonic.[18]

Naturally Warners wished to show off its star John Barrymore of the "royal family of Broadway." The early twenties was the zenith of Barrymore's stage career, and he was basking in the success of *Hamlet* in New York and London. He had also dabbled in the movies since 1913. Jack Warner signed him for BEAU BRUMMELL (1924) and subsequently for a three-picture contract which paid him $76,000 each, plus perquisites. This was far better than he was receiving for stage work.[19] In September 1925, Warners hired the director Alan Crosland on a long-term contract and announced that his first feature would be DON JUAN, starring Barrymore. The film was shot in the traditional silent method and was receiving the finishing touches in January 1926, with its release set for February.[20] With the success of the preliminary experiments and test screenings, at the last minute it was decided to give the feature Vitaphone accompaniment.

Upon the signing of the Vitaphone contract in April, Warner Bros. declared that the company and Western Electric had a "New Musical Device." This first announcement, which does not mention Vitaphone by name, reflects a distinct effort to mold the reception of sound in the mind of exhibitors and the public. First, it couches the new development in technology: "Scientific developments which may revolutionize the presentation of films in the largest as well as the smallest theaters have just been perfected by the Western Electric Co., and Warner Bros." There was great emphasis on the electrical nature of the recording, amplification, and sound reproducer mechanisms. Second, an identification with big-time corporate experimentation was established: "[Sound films] are the result of years of research in the Bell Telephone, American Telephone and Telegraph Co., and Western Electric laboratories." This claim differentiated the Western Electric system from rival music synchronization systems, such as de Forest's. Third, the system's main advantage was called its "naturalness," without further elaboration. Fourth, Vitaphone's founders insisted, as de Forest had done, that it would be used only for music:

> The invention is in no sense a "talking picture" but a method whereby a film can be accompanied by the music cue and other musical and vocal numbers given by means of what is now known as the recording machine, for want of a better name. The invention is expected to bring to audiences in every cor-

ner of the world music of the symphony orchestra and the vocal entertainment of the operatic, vaudeville and theatrical fields. (*Film Daily*, 26 April
1926, pp. 1, 6)

As with Phonofilm, Vitaphone was intended to supplement the regular film program. It
would replace the orchestra, but not the traditional silent feature. Sam Warner arranged
the Broadway premiere for the new Warners' Theatre (formerly the Piccadilly).[21] In
addition to the musically accompanied feature, DON JUAN, he announced a prologue,
two sketches, and a musical comedy routine. The music would be provided by a ninety-
piece orchestra. Originally the opening was set for 1 July 1926, but there were numerous delays, in part because Wente and other AT&T technicians were redesigning their
speaker horns for the Warners' theater.[22]

By May the Warners strategy was taking shape. In addition to the twenty-six regular features it had already announced for the 1926–1927 season, it was adding nine
specials. All would have recorded sound tracks available. DON JUAN and MANON
LESCAUT were to be John Barrymore vehicles; Syd Chaplin (Charlie's half-brother)
would have three films, including THE BETTER 'OLE; the films BLACK IVORY and
NOAH'S ARK did not yet have directors or players assigned. Warners' star director
Lubitsch would make two pictures. Again the company stressed that "they are not to
be misconstrued as talking pictures as the new recording machine . . . perfectly syn-
chronizes music with the film."[23]

Perhaps the most ambitious component of the program was Warners' intention to
produce sound prologues, that is, musical short subjects, for each of the twenty-six regular features in the 1926–1927 season. Both Sam and Albert Warner repeated the
refrain that the "smallest hamlets" would be able to have first-class presentations and
music. Albert believed that within five years this would be the industry standard: "The
public will demand not only bigger and better productions but will also demand proper
musical accompaniment, suitable for their particular production. The public is being
educated to the finer things in music, through the radio and other mediums."[24]

The marketing plan now called for DON JUAN to have a Broadway premiere on 22
July, followed by road-show engagements in Chicago, Boston, and Los Angeles. This
accelerated schedule coincided with Warners' announcement in its annual report that
the company was taking a $1.3 million charge for the cost of expanding its national dis-
tribution through the purchase of the Vitagraph Company in April 1925. DON JUAN and
THE BETTER 'OLE cost $1.5 million to complete. In addition, the cost of Vitaphone
experimentation had been written off the books. The biggest expense, though, had nothing to do with the Vitaphone project: the charge for the selling expenses of unplayed
silent film contracts.[25]

The summer months were busy ones. The defunct Manhattan Opera House was
leased and converted to a makeshift soundstage. More artists were signed up to be
Vitaphoned; the Metropolitan Opera stars Giovanni Martinelli, Anna Case, and Marion
Talley were among the most impressive.[26] And there were sneak previews of Vitaphone,
for example, before the Wisconsin Telephone Association at the Strand Theater in
Madison. The three short subjects shown there were "loud, clear, and perfectly distinct."
The anonymous trade reporter ventured that, "where in the past directors have been
content to portray emotion through gesture and action, they must now add the spoken
word which may mean a revolution in production, and a new type of star." So even
before the premiere of DON JUAN (which was not previewed in Madison because the

Filming the "La Fiesta" soprano solo; Anna Case is accompanied by the Cansinos and the Metropolitan Opera Chorus (Vitaphone short) on the stage of the Manhattan Opera House, July 1926.

score was still being recorded at the Manhattan Opera House under Sam Warner's supervision), critical reaction to Vitaphone had zeroed in on the speaking star as the most intriguing aspect of the new system. The canned music that the company tried to focus attention on was of little interest.[27]

Warners tried to prepare exhibitors and audiences for the new system on the eve of its introduction. Its press release, "What the Vitaphone Promises," reveals more of its strategy for selling sound. The constant refrain, which was echoed by Will Hays and popular journalists during 1926–1928, was that sound would greatly multiply the geographic and cultural contacts with the performing arts. In addition to the "New Era" millennial rhetoric surrounding these scientific devices, the creators and promoters of Vitaphone also made an appeal to "democracy" in their description of the new system. It was film's destiny to disseminate oral and aural culture to the masses. A redundant phrase that recurs—and belies the hand of an originating Warners publicist—is "small hamlet." The press readily picked up on the democracy angle. The *New York Times* observed in a glowing editorial: "The most obvious fact is that this invention in its various forms will enable the smaller communities to participate to a greater degree than even the radio permits in the cultural advantages that have been possible in the past only in places of large population."[28] In its 1926 brochure, the company promised to make available orchestras and opera and theater stars to "every corner of the world. . . . It is now possible for every performance in a motion picture theatre to have a full orchestral accompaniment to the picture, regardless of the size of the house. . . . There can be no question of the boon that Vitaphone will be to the music-lovers who live in the out of the way hamlets."[29]

At first, these statements seem like a populist discourse, since they invoke a plan for decentralizing culture and making it accessible to geographically dispersed consumers. The strategy was clearly imitating telephone company advertising, which proclaimed that phone service was uniting the country. But the culture proposed to be spread by Vitaphone *was not film.* Sound cinema was to be a medium, not an art in its own right. The models for the new sound cinema were opera, classical music, light drama, and Broadway vaudeville entertainment, with its characteristic melting-pot flavor of New York ethnicity. Though calling for democracy, the producers were advocating the spread of what they regarded as elite culture to an underclass and to non–New Yorkers. Whether this "democratic" motif in the promotion of sound was a bald publicity department creation on the part of Warners or Hays's MPPDA is difficult to say. Many of the actual Vitaphone shorts were jazzy instrumental numbers or plebeian hokum. It is likely that the published appeals to high culture reflected competition for a narrow but powerful segment of the entertainment market—upper-middle-class New Yorkers who seldom attended movies or listened to popular entertainment on radio, but who patronized the Metropolitan Opera and Broadway revues. Not only was it desirable to attract the disposable income of this leisure class, it was important to benefit from their goodwill and potential power as bankers, shareholders, influences on local censorship, and arbiters of taste. The aesthetic and democratic rhetoric also distracted from the lowbrow interests plainly visible in many Vitaphone productions. In DON JUAN, for instance, shifting attention to the New York Philharmonic diverted moralists from the licentious plot and the semi-clad chorus girls who graced the sets.

The Warners formulation closely resembles the de Forest virtual-Broadway model for short film production. But Vitaphone was also designed to be applied to features—as a virtual orchestra. That is, it would replace the actual orchestra in the pit. Again, this was pitched by the producers as an advantage for small towns. Not only would nationally recognized orchestras supplant the local piano player and snare drummer, but the music would always be appropriate to the mood on the screen, timed to match the action, and reliably executed. Not mentioned in these promotions was the all-too-apparent downside: musicians would lose their jobs, the music sounded "canned," and the intangible pleasure derived from a live performance would be gone.

The virtual orchestra would also keep the voice in its place—behind the music. Although Warners had emphatically banished talking features only months before, "What the Vitaphone Promises" tentatively opened the door. "If its scope extends to the vocal reproduction of entire pictures," the publicist wrote, "casts will be selected not only for their 'silent drama' ability, but by their voice ability as well." Many of the first-generation Vitaphone features would have vocal parts, but either in a musical context or as a dramatic "special effect." The shout of "Bob" by the father in THE FIRST AUTO, the screaming earthquake victims of OLD SAN FRANCISCO (1927), and the dialogue in THE JAZZ SINGER are examples of how the voice is subordinated to the musical part of the sound track. The shorts seemed to abide by separate rules and tolerated a few lines of spontaneous speech now and then.

Like the ideal orchestra and conductor who could accompany any film that came from the distributor, Vitaphone was also advertised as being adaptable. According to its original formulation, theater managers could spice up the program by renting from a library of shorts. They could also revive old films by presenting them with a new musical sound track.

This is accomplished by projecting the picture in the usual way and recording the music, as previously cued, in synchronism with the projection instead of in synchronism with the photographing. Any picture which has ever been produced can be orchestrated and synchronized. The Vitaphone corporation has in mind the assembling of a library which will embrace the best in various fields of endeavor such as music, vaudeville and musical comedy. Exhibitors will rent the process as now they do the films. (*Film Daily*, 27 June 1926, p. 29)

PRESENTATION ACTS

Another merchandising point of the original Vitaphone concept was that the virtual orchestra would substitute for the "presentations" which had become popular in big-city movie theaters. The target market for Vitaphone was the midsize theater with a 500–1,000 capacity—that is, too small to afford big-time live entertainment, but big enough to afford the cost of installing sound. The use of presentations, an important trend in exhibition practice, was growing steadily in large cities in 1926 and 1927. For years films had been preceded by live prologues such as tap dance numbers, choral ensemble, singers, comedians, or an organ recital. But to compete with other movie palaces and with live shows, exhibitors began to stage increasingly elaborate entertainments that, by 1927, imitated revues at Broadway vaudeville houses. Headliners such as Ben Bernie and his orchestra, Burns and Allen, George Jessel, and Eddie Cantor would show up for a ten-minute performance before the movie. Orchestras swelled from eight to eighty pieces. The length of the presentation approached two hours, during a period when the typical Hollywood feature was about sixty-five minutes long. Usually, but not always, there was an attempt to tie in the presentation acts with the theme or mood of the feature. With their economies of scale, the chain theaters, especially Publix, were able to mount extravagant traveling shows to tour with the films.[30]

While these expensive presentations were popular with audiences, among producers and some exhibitors a strong reaction set in against them (see chapter 11). Smaller exhibitors could not compete with large houses in nearby big cities. Producers and even film directors spoke out against the performances as distractions. John Ford, as president of the Motion Picture Directors' Association, objected on the grounds that live actors detracted from the filmed ones:

> Usually the players are $35 to $50-a-week players who would not be doing that sort of thing if they were capable of greater enterprise. . . . They come before an audience and attempt a characterization not knowing what it is all about. It detracts from the screen players' delineations in that it gives the wrong impression before the audience has an opportunity to see the picture.
>
> This is an angle of presentations that is disheartening to the motion picture director, who has spent weeks, sometimes months, carefully selecting his cast—after he has literally combed the list of available talent in his efforts to choose actors he feels capable of interpreting the parts intrusted to them to the best of their ability, by advice and encouragement.
>
> It is one thing to make a feature picture and another thing to have it crippled by a presentation. (*Film Daily*, 12 June 1927, p. 47)

Ford noted that D. W. Griffith never allowed presentations with his films. Mood could be established sufficiently by a musical overture and a theme song.[31]

Warner Bros. saw the presentation fad as a double opportunity. The exhibitor who wanted one could have it, but filmed, not live. "The small exhibitor," Warners pointed out, "cannot afford to hire 'name' acts or put on elaborate prologue numbers." And the showman who wanted to get rid of the expense of the presentation could substitute much cheaper Vitaphone "virtual" versions.[32] From the producers' point of view, filmed presentations could help drive away the live competitors.

The presentation act craze partly explains the interest in theatrical radio in the mid-1920s. If music could be piped in electronically, the live part of the program eventually could be replaced. Vitaphone's virtual orchestra should be seen as parallel to the efforts by Paramount and MGM to use radio for disseminating sound nationally from a central source. Vitaphone was supposed to augment moving pictures the same way but used mass-produced standard discs instead of the airwaves. De Forest's concept of developing a library of interchangeable entertainment units from which the exhibitor could pick and choose also influenced Warners' idea of establishing a rental library of musical shorts. If implemented, the result would mimic a radio broadcast, but radio itself was also borrowing from vaudeville and from the movie presentation. It was not a question of who was influencing whom (a chicken-and-egg proposition, to be sure) but of the malleability of the borders of popular entertainment during this period. No medium could corner the market on singers, ventriloquists, monologists, tap dancers, and a horde of quipping comedians.[33]

Warners' advertisement for Vitaphone visualized the virtual orchestra in a drawing that showed the word *Vitaphone* literally spanning the Hudson River to connect Broadway's theaters to the mainland. "*Vitaphone* obliterates the miles that used to separate you from the Street of Streets, and brings Broadway to you. From the world's great stages, *Vitaphone* is transplanting the most celebrated singing, dancing, and dramatic stars and 'acts' to the screens of thousands of theatres."[34]

The Vitaphone Premiere

Don Juan finally opened on 6 August 1926. Tickets were $10 (standard for a Broadway premiere, and mostly distributed gratis); afterwards the admission was scaled down to between $1 and $5. The Warner publicity machine worked overtime to turn out purple prose predictions: "Like the rumblings of a coming storm, word-of-mouth comment comes low and slowly, but gathering power as it sweeps onward, it carries like lightning to the far corners of the world. Such will be the praise for 'Vitaphone!'"[35]

At least on opening night, it looked like the prophecy would be fulfilled. *Film Daily* said, "Repeated and prolonged applause indicated that both the Vitaphone and the picture thrilled the audience which filled the house. That the Vitaphone marks a new era in entertainment was the opinion generally expressed in the lobby."[36]

The program had the look and feel of the typical movie presentation, as well as a radio revue. There was a speech, operatic numbers, a monologue, a novelty skit, an orchestral number, then the feature. "Red" Kann, the *Film Daily* editor, described the opening night audience's response. They were attentive to Will Hays, president of the MPPDA. They applauded Mischa Elman and Josef Bonime's rendition of Dvořák's "Humoresque," Efrem Zimbalist and Harold Bauer's "Kreutzer Sonata" by Beethoven, and Anna Case in "La Fiesta." However, neither soprano Marion Talley nor the Russian

Harry Warner, Will H. Hays, Walter Rich, and Sam Warner on Hays's Vitaphone remarks set, 1926.

Peasants in "An Evening on the Don" was well received; the former "did not make the impression it should have, possibly owing to Miss Talley's inexperience," and the latter was not liked because the "group singing did not register effectively." The most enthusiastic applause was given to Roy Smeck, playing banjo, ukulele, and guitar in "His Pastimes," and—the big hit—Giovanni Martinelli singing a selection from *I Pagliacci*. "None of the famous tenor's personality and tone was lost by the Vitaphone interpretation," Kann reported. "Storms of applause and cheers greeted the rendition."[37]

The general press agreed that Talley's singing was a disappointment. There were synch problems; the *Evening World* said that her voice was a few seconds in arrears of her facial expression. Richard Barrios observes that Talley, the eighteen-year-old "Kansas City Canary," suffered from more than technical problems: "Striking while the iron was hot, Warners filmed her in the role of her Met debut, Gilda in *Rigoletto*. Unfortunately, an artistic immaturity that was obvious enough onstage at the Met was magnified on film, and more than any other part of the program, the Talley segment drew heavy critical fire." She was also victimized by blatantly sexist comments that described her as physically unattractive. *Photoplay* wrote: "As for her face, the producers made the mistake of allowing the camera to come too close. . . . Long-shots—and good, long ones—were just invented for that girl."[38]

Giovanni Martinelli's *I Pagliacci* created a sensation. For the *Times* correspondent, the tenor's filmed image was an effigy of the real person: "Those who first heard and saw the pierrot of 'Pagliacci' in the person of the moving likeness of the living Martinelli fill a great hall with the vibrant sound which moved the audience as the presence of the

Marion Talley singing "Caro Nome" from the opera Rigoletto *(Vitaphone short, 1926).*

singer could not have done more effectually, perhaps not as affectingly, were present as at the performance of a seeming miracle in which the tongue of the dumb image was made to sing." Barrios argues that "this single three-and-a-half-minute performance . . . was crucial to the successful entry of sound film. In a very real way Martinelli was the first musical film star, demonstrating more than a year before THE JAZZ SINGER the power resulting from the meeting of amplified voice and projected image."[39]

For many, like the *Times* reporter, it was not simply the content or the star quality of these recordings, it was the *presence* of the subject that was much of the allure. Speaking of Will Hays's address, Fitzhugh Green wrote:

> The phenomenon was like watching a man flying without wings. It was uncanny. . . . His was a short speech; when it was done and he stood there, people found themselves clapping, unconsciously. As if he heard them, he bowed. He seemed to be present, and yet he did not seem to be present. No wonder a scientist the next day called it: "the nearest thing to a resurrection." (Fitzhugh Green, *The Film Finds Its Tongue* [New York: Putnam's, 1929], pp. 11–12)

After the intermission, DON JUAN was presented, with its score arranged by Major Edward Bowes, David Mendoza, and William Axt. Henry Hadley conducted the New York Philharmonic. The *Film Daily* reviewer also experienced this uncanny sensation of presence/absence: "By closing one's eyes a person could easily imagine that the musicians were 'down front.'" The only ominous moments came near the end of the feature when the film and music stopped briefly several times. Blame was laid on "the nervousness of the operator when switching reels and not attributable to any mechanical defects."[40] Kann reported a strong response to Barrymore, who, he opined, was simply the greatest living actor. Much of the critical reaction to the Vitaphone system itself, perhaps reflecting the influence of the studio's advance publicity and Will Hays's

The overture "Tannhäuser" by Richard Wagner, played by the New York Philharmonic Orchestra (Vitaphone short, 1926).

John Barrymore and Montague Love in Don Juan *(Warner Bros., 1926).*

recorded statement, stressed the *musical* nature of the system and the permanence of the recordings:

> The motion picture [Hays stated] is a most potent factor in the development of a national appreciation of good music. That service will now be extended as the Vitaphone shall carry symphony orchestras to the town halls of the hamlets. It has been said that the art of the vocalist and instrumentalist is ephemeral, that he creates but for the moment. Now neither the artist nor his art will ever wholly die. (*Film Daily,* 8 August 1926, p. 1)

Speaking editorially, Kann predicted that more attention to musical accompaniment would have to be paid while films were still in production. He also felt that for music the potentialities were tremendous: "Mediocre music supplanted by the best in the rank and file of the nation's theaters truly makes a rosy picture. Dance and song numbers, vocal selections, violin solos, jazz bands in synchronized form sold on a weekly basis to offset the competition created for the little fellow by presentations at big theaters—that too, is a potential Utopia for the average exhibitor." Mouthing Warners' line, he foresaw Vitaphone headed for the small and midsize theaters:

> It seems beyond human conception that the smallest theater in the smallest hamlet of this country can exhibit Don Juan with an orchestral accompaniment of 107 men in the New York Philharmonic Orchestra. It will be not to

the de luxe theater that the Vitaphone will prove a boon. The relatively few houses of this type will look upon the process as a novelty. It is not to be expected that the Vitaphone will replace orchestras at theaters like the Capitol, New York, or the Uptown, Chicago. . . . The tremendous influence of good music is now brought to the very lobby of every theater in America. (*Film Daily,* 8 August 1926, p. 3)

Every one of New York's twelve major newspapers reviewed the opening, most enthusiastically. "The greatest sensation of the decade next to radio," expressed the *New York Evening Journal.* The sound quality, however, was characterized by several reviewers as "mechanical" or "metallic." The *Sun* reporter suggested that this effect disappeared after the listener became accustomed: "[Vitaphone] boasts of a minimum of 'mechanical' finish. After the first half hour of hearing it you may shut your eyes and easily imagine that Will Hays is talking to you from the stage, or that Martinelli is singing to you. When you first hear Vitaphone, though, you realize that it is a reproducing mechanism that is operating. The personal, or human, touch is absent." The *Telegram* described the sound as "strong and with a mighty metallic ring," while the *New Yorker* found lacking "the snap, or edge, of real acoustics." The synchronization was hailed by all ("uncanny" said the *Times*). Several papers felt that Vitaphone was not yet perfect, but that it would soon be a "wonder of the world."[41] Lilian W. Brennan noted that Vitaphone could provide managers with an alternative to presentations:

> The Vitaphone is a step in a new direction and it should do much for the exhibition end of the business. Presensations [*sic*] through the use of the Vitaphone, should become simplified. It will create a desire for the better things in entertainment and subsequently bring about an ambition for the better grade of picture. If the invention fulfills the hopes of its sponsors, it cannot but achieve startling results. It is claimed that it will be within the reach of exhibitors generally; and for those who find it impracticable at present to offer the type of presentation found in the larger theaters, Vitaphone is certain to fill a want. (*Film Daily,* 16 August 1926, p. 7)

Although the Warner Bros. press release reiterated that Vitaphone would be used only for music, it also confirmed that "its use in producing 'talking pictures' is considered the next logical development," an idea rephrased by Mordaunt Hall in the *New York Times* a week later.[42]

In contrast to the generally favorable reviews of the shorts, DON JUAN received decidedly mixed notices. Barrymore's athletic performance was compared to Douglas Fairbanks, and some found him to be stiff. There were many jokes about the hero's never-ending kissing. The story was described as failing to make sense, idiotic, a frantic absurd melodrama, childish, devoid of intelligence, and on and on.[43] Margot Peters has commented that the film was "more joyfully panned by New York critics than any movie in recent memory." In an effort to improve it, after the premiere Warners cut the film from twelve to ten reels and reedited the ending.[44] The novelty of synchronized sword clashes and rousing music remained the principal attraction. In any event, the Warner brothers were crying all the way to the bank—DON JUAN's net profit at the Warners' theater was nearly $20,000 per week.[45]

Warner Bros. stock leaped on the Monday after the premiere. Vitaphone's president, Walter Rich, prognosticated that 1927 earnings could be $3.5 million (versus the previous year's loss), and that projection caused a big run-up on the New York exchange. During a bullish summer, Warner Bros. was the most sought after film stock on the market. Three weeks after the premiere, its value had already doubled.[46] Vitaphone's success triggered rumors that Warner Bros. was a takeover target. In October, Adolph Zukor made overtures for a friendly merger, offering outlets in the Publix theater chain in exchange for control of Vitaphone. Harry Warner denied that the deal existed, explaining that talks were under way about Vitaphone installations in Publix theaters and that Warner Bros. was not for sale. Other sources said that Zukor refused to pay Warners' high price tag.[47] Besides the previously announced specials Noah's Ark and Black Ivory, all twenty-six regular features on the 1926–1927 schedule would also have Vitaphone sound available (in addition to the regular silent versions). In other words, less than three weeks after the premiere of Don Juan, Warner Bros. had committed itself to an all-Vitaphone policy.[48]

The successful screening initiated a change of marketing strategy. Instead of roadshow tours, as announced, Warners would show the film only in pre-release extended runs in a few major markets—first Atlantic City, then Chicago and St. Louis. This change may have been due to a wish to stall the national release pending installation of Vitaphone equipment. In Los Angeles, for example, no theaters were ready to run the sound program, so Don Juan opened at Grauman's Egyptian theater as a conventional silent.

The sound version of Don Juan and the Vitaphone program opened in Los Angeles and Boston on 1 November. As in New York, critics approved, though technical infelicities remained. The *Los Angeles Express* said that "the Vitaphone is not perfect. Illusion is not complete." The *Boston Globe* wrote, "It would be too much to claim that the Vitaphone recording is always absolutely perfect musically. There are still occasional defects of tone quality and of clarity in the reproduction, as is the case with all mechanical devices." "Muddy and diffuse at times," observed the *Boston Herald*. The *Transcript* compared the Vitaphone score to a live performance: "The music (during the showing of Don Juan) is for the most part suavely and resonantly projected; there are no awkward breaks, no snatching for cues, no arbitrary alterations in tempo as a conductor tries to catch up with, or slow down for, a change in celluloid tempo never quite gauged in advance." Unlike those in New York, Boston audiences "were not deeply stirred."[49] In Los Angeles, though, excitement ran high. Harvey E. Gausman, *Film Daily*'s correspondent, wrote:

> It is not exaggeration to say that Vitaphone has amazed the Coast, for the reception which greeted the premiere of the device, is being echoed in the conversations around the studios. Directors and players are wondering just what the advent of Vitaphone will mean to the production branch of the industry, which crowded the theater at the $5.50 show to see the new development. (*Film Daily*, 29 October 1926, p. 9)

The next step was to find and wire movie houses in which to show the Barrymore blockbuster. Harry Warner embarked on a cross-country trip to lease theaters; a circuit of fifty to showcase Vitaphone was his goal. A debut in London was also contemplated. On Broadway, in addition to its own theater, Warners leased the Colony in September and the Selwyn, a legitimate theater which was converted to sound. It was also reported that

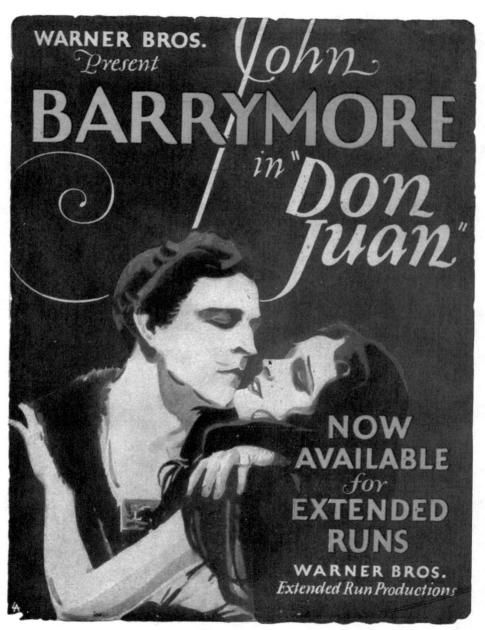

Don Juan *extended-run poster, February 1927.*

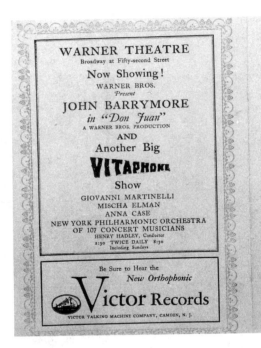

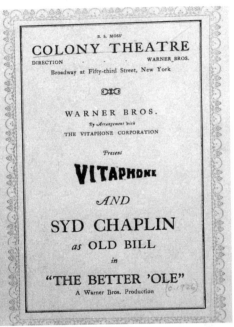

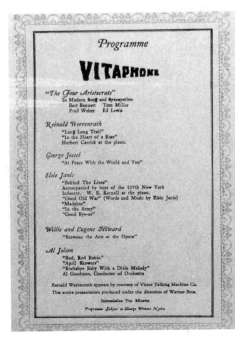

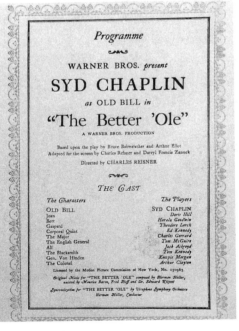

The Better 'Ole *program, Colony Theater, New York, 1926.*

the West Coast Pantages circuit, always in competition with the Keith-Albee chain, was ready to enlist Vitaphone in its offensive.[50] When interviewed by the *Wall Street News,* Warner Bros. executives anticipated that 1926–1927 earnings would exceed $5 million, and they expected to be running Vitaphone shorts and the two completed features in "every big city in the country" by January 1927.[51]

On 7 October 1926, the second Vitaphone feature, THE BETTER 'OLE, opened at the Colony in New York. Syd Chaplin played Old Bill in Captain Bruce Bairnsfather's World War I comedy. Recently restored prints reveal Chaplin's portrayal of the character to be fresh and funny. The silent feature with a synchronized orchestra was not promoted as intensely as Barrymore's Vitaphone epic, but in some ways this premiere was even more significant than the first one. For one thing, Vitaphone definitely had the attention of film people. Kann wrote, "The second debut of this device at the Colony theater embodied elements of box-office appeal that exhibitors cannot disregard. . . . The potentialities of the Vitaphone might well stagger the imagination. The Warners have in their hands an instrument which can be made to mean much for this industry." The audience was packed with invited executives, exhibitors, and personalities, including Will Hays, Adolph Zukor, Walter Wanger, and de Forest.[52]

Syd Chaplin was almost universally liked, and his slapstick talents carried the feature.[53] The *Evening World* thought that THE BETTER 'OLE would be good for a long run even without the Vitaphone. Critical opinion about the sound quality was still mixed. The *New York American* praised the synchronization for never missing "the fraction of an inch," but the *Daily Mirror* reported that, "unlike the Vitaphone apparatus at Warners theater, that of the Colony last evening was quite scratchy and incoherent at times."[54]

Again there was a long program of entertainment shorts. The audience expressed its satisfaction with applause, as if watching live performances. And such performances. The shorts featured the cream of vaudeville. Willie and Eugene Howard were veterans of the Palace and the Winter Garden and were currently (1926–1929) featured in George White's *Scandals.* The Howards were noted for their "Hebrew humor," their rapid-fire patter, and their comic impersonations of rival performers, including ironically, George Jessel and Al Jolson. They recorded one of their classic routines, BETWEEN THE ACTS AT THE OPERA (1926).[55] There was great cheering for George Jessel performing a trademark monologue, "Hello, Mama," wherein he talked to his mother on the telephone. He was "natural and pleasing." In his later years, Jessel's TV fame came primarily from being put down by the likes of Sid Caesar and Jack Paar. However, in the mid-1920s he was one of New York's most prominent stars of vaudeville and music revues. Since September 1925, he was identified primarily with the lead in Samson Raphaelson's play *The Jazz Singer.* Jessel performed the part of Jackie Robin on stage more than one thousand times. It was Al Jolson, though, who provided the showstopper in THE BETTER 'OLE program.

Contemporary commentators marveled at Jolson's ability to enthrall audiences. Could this charisma be captured on film? Star of musical comedies and blackface minstrel songs, "the King of Cork" was by far the most popular entertainer of the twenties. He was rehearsing for his musical play *Big Boy* when the Warners approached him. For his one-reel performance, which was recorded on 7 September 1926, he received $25,000. He appeared in his customary blackface makeup and sang his big hits "Red, Red Robin," "April Showers," and "Rock-a-bye Baby with a Dixie Melody." *Film Daily* reported, "His renditions were remarkable for their clarity and appeal. The personality which brought Jolson fame on the stage evidenced itself from the screen in no uncertain manner." Jolson also ad-libbed a few lines in a relaxed, casual voice. Kann was struck by how the Vitaphone conveyed instantly Jessel's sensitive voice and Jolson's charm:

> Just as motion pictures have developed personalities peculiar to the art, just as the radio has created its stellar attractions, so will the Vitaphone. It is not stretching the imagination to predict that when Vitaphone reaches a maximum and regular distribution, the public will seize upon favorite performers and, by popular demand, build them just as the drawing cards in pictures have been developed.
>
> This was amply demonstrated last night by Al Jolson and George Jessel. By the cleverness of their performance and the appeal of their personalities, they made an instantaneous impression on the audience. To what extent their vogue might extend if seen and heard regularly over the Vitaphone, no one can conjecture. (*Film Daily*, 8 October 1926, pp. 1, 2)

Kann thought that THE BETTER 'OLE was good, too ("one of the funniest ever made"), but he also sensed that the appeal of Jessel and, especially, Jolson was something new and surpassed even radio's potential.[56]

As part of its strategy to penetrate the market as quickly as possible, the Vitaphone Corporation announced in October that it would license the system to any and all producers and exhibitors "of standing." Vitaphone's original arrangement with Western Electric put the burden on the film company to sell the system to other studios. The response to Vitaphone's new ecumenical licensing policy was not overwhelming. Nevertheless, Famous Players commissioned a Vitaphone score for OLD IRONSIDES (1926) when it opened at the Rivoli on Broadway. This may have been a test made when Zukor and Warner Bros. were negotiating their merger. There were no Vitaphone short subjects on the bill, and OLD IRONSIDES would prove to be the only title by another studio with a Vitaphone sound track.[57] Meanwhile, a Dow Jones news wire report (denied by all studios) reported that Warners was ready to sell up to 50 percent of Vitaphone to a combine consisting of Famous Players, First National, MGM, United Artists, and PDC. To prepare for the expected onslaught of orders, the company started to build a new studio in New York and opened distribution centers in New York, Chicago, and Los Angeles.[58]

By mid-November, Harry Warner claimed to have fifty Vitaphone projector units ready to install by January and one hundred subjects ready to show. These would be distributed in the same manner as silent films, but the installation fee and the rental would be determined by the individual theater's circumstances. Things moved slower than predicted; by the end of December, Warners said that twenty Vitaphone installations had been made in eight cities. Even this claim was misleading, however, because Warners rented out the equipment as well as the films. It was also installing "on approval." Although Vitaphone may have been installed twenty times, it actually was playing in only four cities on 30 December: New York, Los Angeles, Chicago, and Detroit.[59]

As 1926 drew to a close, DON JUAN and THE BETTER 'OLE were approaching the magic gross receipts figure of $1 million each. But these figures included income from silent versions of the films. Warners needed profits from its existing contracts in unwired houses—that is, almost all houses. Because of block booking and blind bidding, exhibitors had an obligation to show these films whether or not they purchased Vitaphone. A disturbing trend (from Warners' perspective) emerged. In many houses, the silent prints made more money than the audio versions. While the sonorized DON JUAN and THE BETTER 'OLE were doing great business on Broadway, the films lost money and were pulled from screens in Boston and St. Louis. No trend emerged during this early period: "Vitaphone failed and succeeded; it had long runs and closed within a week. Most exhibitors waited, hoping to learn more before deciding."[60] These circumstances show that audience factors were having an influence. Local variables such as advertising content, competing shows, and the degree of interest in stars like Barrymore, Jessel, and Jolson must have contributed to the inconsistent results. Also, if the theater's presentation acts and live orchestras were particularly good, the "virtual" ones might have suffered by comparison.

Other Talkies

Besides Fox, whose efforts to capitalize on Case's and de Forest's research were contemporaneous with Vitaphone's premieres, numerous Vitaphone imitators were encouraged by Warners' Broadway success. Among the most widely marketed competing systems were Orchestraphone, Magnola, Symphonium, Vict-o-phone, Vocafilm, and Bristolphone.[61] Almost all were disc-based technology, designed to play back nonsynchronously from a library of licensed records. Most were doomed because of lack of access to the synchronization and amplification patents of the Western Electric and radio groups, and because Warner Bros. had already acquired the most important music licenses. Vocafilm failed at its press debut and never recovered from this technical disaster. One promising contender was Bristolphone. In October the Bristol Machine Works in Waterbury, Connecticut, was experimenting with a talking film device. William Bristol, though a dogged businessman, faced many of the same distribution problems that de Forest encountered. The American film industry had the power to shut out anyone it chose from production and to limit distribution and exhibition.[62]

Of the majors, at least Paramount and Universal explored the idea of imitating Fox in developing their own in-house sound systems. Paramount's Jesse Lasky assigned the task to the special effects technician Roy Pomeroy, while Carl Laemmle at Universal was exploring a device invented by Allen Canton. It used high-speed oscillating lights to record and play back sound on film without distortion. The output was powerful enough not to require an intermediate amplifier, and the new speakers avoided "the nasal or metallic sound common to present type of loud speakers."[63] It was apparent that an industry standard would be preferable to proliferating incompatible systems. On 8 November 1926, Famous Players, MGM, United Artists, and PDC renewed their previously rumored offer to purchase a 50 percent interest in Vitaphone. Again Warners declined.[64] Instead, Warners decided against maintaining its own circuit of sound houses and, in December, offered to lease the Vitaphone system to other theater chains. This was intolerable to the Hollywood majors, who agreed to keep up a united front and secure sound on their own terms.

Although 1926 was the "year of Vitaphone," the percentage of all moviegoers who actually witnessed the new attraction was small. Warner Bros. sound films had played only in a few large cities at road-show prices (five to ten times the regular admission charge).

Wherever they ran, audiences noted the illusion of physical presence that talking gave the screen characters. This experience of virtual presence was replayed a few years later when sound films were introduced to the home market. DeVry's Ciné-Tone 16-mm system, for example, advertised: "Your favorite actor or musician sounds forth from the loud-speaker as natural as life, and simultaneously on the screen appear the characters, who merge the sound and action into one organic whole—the perfect entertainment."[65] DON JUAN attracted as much attention as a Barrymore vehicle with risqué love scenes as it did as a sound film; THE BETTER 'OLE capitalized on the Chaplin name and a popular literary source. Both films were also widespread successes as silent releases. In his New Year's look into the future, Red Kann predicted that 1927 would be the greatest year in history for the film industry. But he made no mention of the coming of sound.[66]

It was the synchronized shorts which attracted the most critical praise. At the very least, they were interesting technical novelties which affirmed the progress of electric communication. The Vitaphone program seemed to combine the socially defined qualities of the telephone, the phonograph, radio, and television. It transported Broadway to the hometown via technology. Vitaphone connected public taste to popular science. The entertainment format (vaudeville, the musical revue, theater) implicitly appealed to a pre-formed audience which should have been a receptive market. This target was not Variety's hicks in the sticks, but sophisticated middle-class urbanites accustomed to high-priced live entertainment at nightclubs, roof gardens, and movie palaces. The experiments with "canned" versions of their stage favorites via Phonofilm, combined with the popularity of the pre-film presentation, suggested to entrepreneurs like Sam Warner and William Fox, who had disdained sound for years, that the time had come for a major investment.

In 1926 "sound film" usually meant music, not speech. Although many reports describe the tonal quality of Phonofilm and Vitaphone as screechy, scratchy, and metallic, staking out music and the theatrical revue format made the new technique non-threatening to the Hollywood establishment. The initial Vitaphone concept was an exhibition process and was specifically advertised as not affecting traditional filmmaking. Warners, itself a studio that provided primarily silent features, understood that Hollywood had no incentive to change its stable system of production. Producers foresaw union headaches (with on- and offscreen personnel), technical uncertainty (which meant investment of capital), and the need to make films in totally new ways. Perhaps most seriously, the whole star system would be disrupted.

Providing canned entertainment shorts to flesh out a program and replacing the orchestra with a recorded sound track made sense economically; making "speaking dramas" as features did not. But the initial reception was not what Vitaphone had expected. The way audiences were responding to the talking appearances of Jolson, Jessel, and other big-name attractions proved that seeing and hearing stars sing and speak was just what people wanted in a sound film. Kann was prescient when he predicted that the public would "seize" performers and "build" them according to its, not film companies', desires. It did not take long for the public to redefine virtual Broadway on its own terms, forcing a melding of star cultures. The radio celebrity, the vaudeville performer, the opera diva, the wisecracking comic—all would be auditioned as performance models for the new talkies. As a result, Hollywood soon left behind the virtual orchestra and got over its fear of talking.

4

Fox-Case, Movietone, and the Talking Newsreel

Nowhere is there a better illustration of the "trying on" of forms for the talkies than William Fox's development of Movietone. First, however, the shoals of de Forest's legal challenges had to be navigated. In 1926 Lee de Forest knew of Western Electric's work in sound cinema. Nevertheless, he experienced "a shock, like a blow," when he first saw Warner Bros.' big Times Square billboard announcing Vitaphone while en route to his Forty-second Street office.[1] It is an indication of de Forest's failure to find a wide market for his system that there were no comparisons to Phonofilm in the flow of critical ink describing the gala 1926 Vitaphone premiere. One exception was Roy Chartier, who pointed out that the difference between Vitaphone and Phonofilm lay in showmanship, not acoustic superiority:

> Whether the Vitaphone is any better in its voice reproduction and synchronization than the De Forest Phonofilm, is left open to dispute. The only conceivable difference between the two is that Vitaphone has been launched on a more elaborate scale, with Metropolitan Opera and concert stars singing before it instead of the vaudeville artistes De Forest has used thus far. (Roy Chartier, "Whether the Vitaphone Is Any Better?," *Billboard*, 14 August 1926, quoted in Barrios, *A Song in the Dark*, p. 25).

Meanwhile, the trade publicity surrounding the impending launch of Vitaphone coincided with Case and Sponable's approaches to William Fox, who previously had been completely uninterested. Fox purchased the Case sound-on-film device in 1926, but it seems he had no preconception of what to do with it. The studio informally subsidized some tests during the summer, shot in Fox Film's New York office. One of these was immortal footage of Gus Visor singing "Ma, He's Makin' Eyes at Me," punctuated by loud quacks from the trained duck under his arm.[2] The content suggests that Fox was mimicking the Phonofilm program concept and that, like Vitaphone producers, Fox producers were looking over the same vaudeville rosters de Forest had previously scoured.

The new company, Fox-Case, was announced in July 1926. Fox's vice president in charge of newsreels, Courtland Smith, had conducted the negotiations, but there was no

Fox Movietone News crew on assignment, ca. 1929. The microphone is behind the dog on left.

mention of applying sound to news films.[3] Instead, as with Vitaphone, the aim was to provide a canned "presentation," and there was no consideration of "talking" features. But as was happening at the Vitaphone studio, some irrepressible stars insisted on ad-libbing. Harry Lauder, who recorded for Fox-Case on 25 October, stopped in mid-song to announce, "This is a test," presumably to prevent unauthorized exploitation of his performance. The vaudeville monologist Chic Sale, a specialist in "outhouse" humor, filmed his country-bumpkin routine, THEY'RE COMING TO GET ME (1926). The big score, however, came when Fox signed a genuine star who would provide high-class appeal: Raquel Meller, a Spanish-born soprano who, in the 1920s, was the toast of the London Hippodrome and the Paris Olympia. In 1926 she had just arrived in the States for an extended vaudeville tour.[4]

In contrast to Warner Bros.' high-profile publicity, William Fox tried to soft-pedal his experiments. The *Wall Street News* reported that Fox Film had a sound device under development, "but the nature of its functioning and operation is being kept a secret."[5] One reason for discretion was fear of de Forest's well-known litigious tendency. Predictably, upon reading the Fox press release, de Forest promptly sued. Wishing to prevent de Forest from causing trouble, in September 1926, Fox paid him $100,000 for an option to buy Phonofilm for $2.4 million. Behind the scenes, Fox was actually buying time. The legal situation was tangled; Western Electric and GE had already decided that Case's work added nothing to their sound-on-film patent pool. Fox's legal staff investigated de Forest's claim that he, not Case, owned the patents. Fox was also leery of the uncomfortable similarity between the Case–de Forest system and the German Tri-Ergon system. After deciding that Case's patents would stand, Fox let the de Forest option expire, infuriating the inventor, who thought he had a sure thing. Years later, in a lawsuit against Western Electric and ERPI, de Forest claimed that the defendants had conspired to falsely convince Fox that he did not own the patents he was attempting to sell.[6] Though his advisers recommended against purchasing Tri-Ergon, William Fox paid $60,000 for a 90 percent stake in the American rights for himself (not for Fox Film), an action which would have important ramifications.[7]

Fox did not try to monopolize sound or to challenge corporate colossi. His approach was to forge bonds with as many competitors as possible to ensure that, regardless of which side won, he would be on it. Buying rights and forming license pools were strategies to cover all the bases and to prevent any future closeout. But Fox was also addressing a crucial lack. The Case system still had inadequate electronic amplification. Fox first approached RCA to obtain a license to use its amplification system. Owen Young, General Electric's chief executive, was amenable, but the request attracted David Sarnoff's curiosity. On a hunch, Sarnoff blocked Fox's request for a license in order to explore movie sound as a commercial operation for RCA. In October 1926, Fox, the music conglomerate Brunswick-Balke-Collender, General Electric, and RCA began negotiating to form an RCA-like consortium in response to Western Electric and Warner Bros.' unexpected success with Vitaphone. Forming an interlocking directorate by electing an RCA officer to the Fox board was to be part of the deal. The new process the group would promote was GE's Pallophotophone, though initial press releases incorrectly identified it as a disc system.[8] But Fox's participation in this venture with the Radio Group was short-lived. He then turned to John Otterson at Western Electric. Otterson had grown impatient with his Warner Bros. partners, whom he regarded as bad businessmen, and was looking for a way to diminish their power when Fox knocked on the door. On 31 December 1926, Fox secured a sublicense from Vitaphone (against the wishes of Warners) to use Western Electric's equipment. In exchange, the patents owned by Fox-Case were cross-licensed with Western Electric, effective 5 January 1927. William Fox was now in the sound business.[9] Commentators saw this not as competition but as the opposite. "Movietone and Vitaphone have wedded and once again all is quiet along the Potomac. Where previously a commercial tilt of no mean proportions threatened, you find a complete and most amicable accord."[10] As in thermionics, and as in radio, all the major patents were now linked together through the AT&T, GE, Westinghouse, and RCA alliance. Once again, de Forest was thrown out of the contest.

De Forest Phonofilm wasted no time in alleging that the Pallophotophone device was infringing on its patents, specifically, the use of a narrow slit for masking the exposure area on the film.[11] The Fox option to control Phonofilm expired unexercised in November 1926, and de Forest reinstated his original infringement suit against Fox, Case, et al., vowing again to prosecute every offender.[12] De Forest demanded $2 million.[13] But William Fox countersued. Claiming that de Forest had misrepresented the patent situation in the 1926 option arrangement, Fox now demanded the return of the $100,000 he had paid.[14] Fox later dropped the claim and paid de Forest $60,000 in an out-of-court settlement.[15]

Phonofilm, meanwhile, was still producing short movies. In December 1926, it appeared that the British branch had scored a coup. The cantankerous George Bernard Shaw had agreed to appear before de Forest's camera. The playwright had refused to visit the United States in person because "the mere mobbing I would receive wherever I went would kill me in no time."[16] Shaw would soon make his film debut—but on Fox Movietone, not on Phonofilm.

By April 1927, de Forest's company was reaching for Vitaphone's scraps, offering very low-cost installations in the $2,500–4,000 range. Small houses—for example, the Detroit Theater of the U-B chain in Cleveland—were targeted. But only six projectors were installed, all in New England.[17] De Forest reported (hyperbolically) that three companies were dickering for rights to use Phonofilm. One wanted the production rights, and two—Keith-Albee (represented by J. J. Murdock) and an unnamed company—wanted the exhibition rights. De Forest got a boost when his sound film of Lindbergh's receptions in Washington and New York was booked into several theaters. Powel Crosley, Jr. (owner of the large Crosley Radio Company) made a deal to manufacture and deliver one hundred Phonofilm systems. Through a chaotic series of business maneuvers, Crosley had become president of the De Forest Radio Company, which de Forest had sold in 1923. Pat Powers, a veteran film entrepreneur and hustler, was another investor. The equipment would be distributed on a states' rights basis (that is, licensed to show the films in exclusive territories).[18]

De Forest's precarious finances and the scent of potential profits in sound made the company a likely target for a takeover. Pat Powers made a hostile proxy bid for Phonofilm in June 1927. De Forest found a "white knight" to refinance the ailing company's debt and keep the company out of the hands of Powers. Undeterred, Powers hired William Garrity, a former de Forest technician, and began marketing a cloned system under a new name—Cinephone.

Next, de Forest mounted a European assault. He and his assistant Eugene Moehring spent April 1927 touring England, Spain, and France. Desperate for capital, in September, de Forest demonstrated Phonofilm in London. The Lindbergh footage was extremely popular and played (they claimed) in forty-five theaters there. In December 1927, de Forest sold Phonofilm to I. W. Schlesinger.[19] He was a financier whose South African trust, the International Variety and Theater Agency, had formed British International Pictures (BIP) in December 1926.[20] During 1927–1928, he was trying to buy up the smaller British theater circuits and no doubt saw Phonofilm as a competitive advantage against the imminent introduction of Vitaphone in England. The sale marked the end of de Forest's career as a movie producer, but his litigation against Fox, Powers Cinephone, and other British, Canadian, and American "infringers" went on for several years. In 1928 Crosley's "new" De Forest Radio Company went bankrupt—again.[21]

Phonofilm production did not move to South Africa but stayed in England. British Phonofilm had been producing shorts for domestic consumption at the Clapham studios since 1924. Schlesinger and Harold Holt made plans to use BIP's Wembley studio for Phonofilm shorts to accompany BIP features and anticipated taking over American production soon. Exhibitors were told at first that Phonofilm would "concentrate on topical subjects," that is, become a newsreel. Later Schlesinger announced he would be exporting films of American entertainers to South Africa, "where there is a great demand for the work of popular American actors, singers and musicians, and where the reproduction of Broadway attractions will be welcomed." He was also trying to induce British-born Hollywood actors to return to England.[22] Phonofilm was reorganized as British Talking Pictures. It had produced 50,000 feet of talking film by then and offered to lease its Phonofilm equipment to any producer.[23] Phonofilm also premiered in Argentina, where the promoter Edward Ricci licensed the Argentine-American Corporation, purchased equipment to outfit a recording studio, and ordered theater apparatus.[24] In the United States, on 31 August 1928, Max Schlesinger formed General Talking Pictures, Inc., to handle equipment distribution. Another subsidiary, American Sound Film Productions, began making sound shorts in New York City. Like other small manufacturers, Phonofilm targeted the exhibitor of modest means who was looking for a readily available cheap system.[25]

In exchange for his remaining patent claims, Lee de Forest remained active in Schlesinger's Phonofilm as chief engineer. Few changes were made, since the system now conformed to Western Electric sound-on-film standards.[26] In 1929 the Junior De Forest Phonofilm system for houses of under-750 capacity became available at a bargain rate of $4,975, payable over ten years. The New York City sound studio was refurbished to handle the anticipated increase in orders. Meanwhile, the lawsuits continued. General Talking Pictures sued a Philadelphia exhibitor, claiming the Powers Cinephone infringed three De Forest patents.[27]

Movietone's Synchronized Shorts and Features

Its January 1927 cross-licensing agreement with Vitaphone benefited Fox. Its acquisition of exhibition licenses and Western Electric equipment for all its theaters provided an incentive for Fox to increase sound production. The new line of Movietone films was demonstrated to the trade in New York on 24 February 1927 (and placed on the market the next day). Production began at the rate of four short subjects a week. Fox also planned to make "regular dramatic features" at a West Coast studio which would be built in the near future. Already one feature (which turned out to be a reissue of WHAT PRICE GLORY? [1926]) was being synchronized. The features would contain no dialogue. The reporters attending Fox's press showing saw some of Case's tests as "Studies in Movietone" (not intended for release), the monologues by Chic Sale, and the numbers by Raquel Meller that had been recorded in 1926. They also toured the specially constructed Fox-Case studios at 460 West Fifty-fourth Street and saw the radio entertainer Billy Day at work on a new series of comedy shorts.[28] There were two stages, each entirely enclosed within a foot-thick double wall of "patented material of cellular texture." The press observed a production in progress. There were two directors: one on the stage, and a "vocal director" who sat in an adjacent room and monitored the recordings by "telephonic apparatus." Movietone's initial version was single-system, that is, the sound was recorded in the camera on the same strip of film being photographed, not in a separate sound-recording camera (double-system).[29]

Fox needed a showcase theater in which to promote its new venture. The lavish new Roxy (on the northeast corner of Fiftieth Street and Seventh Avenue) was a public corporation financed by more than nine thousand small stockholders and presided over by Samuel "Roxy" Rothapfel. William Fox was negotiating to buy the theater even before its construction was completed; he paid $12 million for it. It seated 6,200 patrons and was decorated with gilt plaster statues and "renaissance" murals. When it opened on 11 March 1927, it was equipped with projectors for showing Vitaphone discs and Movietone optical tracks. According to the publicity brochures, the sound installation was tagged for presentations, "with selections by individual artists featured on the program it is understood." In other words, the shorts would take their place on the program along with the live acrobats and vaudeville crooners.[30]

In June 1927, the Fox Varieties unit was consolidated with the newsreel, under the supervision of Truman Talley. The Phonofilm and Vitaphone shorts were clearly the model for Movietone's recorded acts. Gertrude Lawrence, star of *Oh Kay*, sang some numbers, which premiered with SEVENTH HEAVEN at the Harris on 21 January.[31] Fox feature specials were being issued with Movietone scores and sound effects. WHAT PRICE GLORY?, the big 1926 silent hit, was re-released with a sound track. SEVENTH HEAVEN, which had played in Los Angeles and on Broadway in May as a silent, reopened at the Roxy in September with a Movietone score arranged by Erno Rapee. It was also performed with a live chorus. The first original Fox feature to premiere with Movietone was SUNRISE (1927), F. W. Murnau's somber "song of two humans."[32] The score is an appropriate pastiche of popular classics, but it is also laced with moody tones reflecting the composer's apprenticeship with Gustav Mahler. In one famous scene in which the husband comes to his senses and cries out for his wife in a storm, his voice is simulated by two long held notes on the French horn.

In a *New York Times* interview, William Fox predicted that in five years no producer would think of making silent pictures. To underscore his point, he announced that Fox-Case was meeting with Western Electric in an effort to lower the cost of Movietone installation from $16,000 to $2,000. By the end of September, all Fox-owned theaters had Movietone operating.[33]

Things looked promising. The premiere of SUNRISE at Fox's newest theater, the Times Square at 653 Eighth Avenue, was glittering. The Movietone recording of Mussolini and the parade of his Fascist regiments was an excuse for inviting Italian consulate officials; in honor of director Murnau, German officials were invited; Catholic representatives were on hand to hear the Movietoned Vatican boy choir. Kann said that Murnau's direction was "one of the finest accomplishments in production—not only for this year but for all years." He felt that the sound was better than Vitaphone: "In tonal range and quality, Movietone has demonstrated its superiority in the field of synchronized sound and action films." The New York critical establishment by and large agreed, adding praise for George O'Brien and twenty-year-old Janet Gaynor. The Artists Guild awarded SUNRISE its blue ribbon for best picture of the year. Although the box office during its New York run was disappointing, the film was a big hit in Los Angeles, where, allegedly, "producing organizations have issued instructions to their director and technical staffs to view the picture with a view of absorbing some of the angles that are catching the popular fancy." Again, Fox voiced optimism. Movietone, he told the press, will "enhance silent films with meritorious music. Features, comedies, newsreels—all are slated for the same treatment."[34] The conventions of the virtual orchestra were being codified, as delineated by John Ford regarding MOTHER MACHREE (1928):

> There is a wealth of [musical] material from which to draw. There is the song, itself—"Mother Machree." The earlier sequences are laid in Ireland, along the sea-coast. This, alone, presents a veritable mine of Irish folk-songs, heart-stirring with their tuneful melodies and their fascinating romance.
>
> And, as the action shifts to America, with the swiftly-moving activities into which the whole case is plunged, there is ample opportunity to further enhance the character values in the new environment through what I like to think of as the "folk-songs" of our own country—as well as the unforgettable war-time ballads and marching songs. (John Ford, "Thematic Presentations, A Wish for the Future," *Film Daily*, 12 June 1927, p. 47)

A recurring theme song and variations on it would create something like the operatic leitmotif to identify character, establish moods, and even telegraph narrative information (for example, mnemonically recalling an earlier scene). The score would be more of a compilation than an original composition, except for a theme song which would be especially written for the film and would have at least one complete vocal performance. Sheet music with colorful illustrations based on the film would be available in the lobby. There were also songs which the audience would recognize. These would either be popular tunes owned or licensed from Fox's publishing affiliates, primarily De Sylva, Brown and Henderson, or Red Star Music, or tunes from the public domain. These melodies could move to the foreground to establish character or comment on the action. Otherwise, they were strung together by background music, similar to operatic underscoring. There were few passages without music, except during a caesura—stopping the sound suddenly for emphasis. The synchronized tracks of the Fox films attempted to create the virtual orchestra, just like the early Vitaphone features. A director like Ford could thus control music-image juxtaposition and establish the proper mood. Without a sound track, these elements could not be monitored once a silent film went into wide release.

John Ford's FOUR SONS, released in February 1928 (nationally in September), fits this mold precisely. The theme song, "Little Mother," was written by Erno Rapee and sung by Harold van Duzee. The original score was by Carli Elinor. S. L. Rothapfel arranged the musical selections. For local color, there was a "folk" selection consisting of Tyrolean yodeling rendered by the "Roxy Male Quartette." Since FOUR SONS performed extremely well, there was little incentive to change the formula.[35]

FAZIL, released in New York in June 1928 (nationally in September), was directed by Howard Hawks, still regarded as a minor director. The film did not play well. But critics found something new to say about sound: it could actually help a mediocre film. The *New York Daily News* liked the music better than the story, saying, "The Movietone accompaniment is a great help to this picture, which certainly needs something to enliven the action."[36]

Fox did not seriously explore alternatives to plain musical synchronization until November 1927. The studio allotted several million dollars for "a series of experiments to determine the commercial value of talking pictures." This highly tentative decision to go talkie, made in the wake of THE JAZZ SINGER, shows the influence of Jolson's part-talking hit. But even without Warners' stimulus, it is likely that Fox's own dialogue shorts produced throughout 1927 had planted the notion—as Vitaphone's shorts had done at that studio—that dramatic talking sequences were feasible. The next features of its ace directors, Murnau, Frank Borzage, Raoul Walsh, and Ford, would have talking sequences. However, Fox proceeded with extraordinary caution. The resulting films

> will be released only when and if the Movietone sequences are successful. If not, the Movietone sequences will be scrapped, and further experiments undertaken, before the Movietone picture is presented as a practical commercial proposition. The Movietone will be made to stress dramatic situations, where the use of synchronized action and sound is especially important. (*Film Daily,* 23 November 1927, p. 1)

The first Fox film released specifically designed to be Movietoned with dialogue was announced as BLOSSOM TIME, in December, to be directed by Walsh.[37]

Movietone Newsreels

An unexpected reaction to a new film changed the course of sound production. Fox, on 20 April at the brand new Roxy, ran a midnight sneak preview of an experimental sound film depicting West Point cadets. The post commander gave a short speech, followed by long takes of the drill and a procession. The audience responded with thunderous applause. The footage was added to the regular Roxy program on 29 April.[38] Fox's vice president and general manager, Winfield R. Sheehan, was inspired by the enthusiastic response and immediately began exploring the possibilities of talking newsreels.

The newsreel had been an essential component of the standard movie program for more than a decade. But by 1927 the market was glutted. The Fox News Service was far behind the leader, Pathé. Sheehan saw immediately that adding sound would give his company's product a singular advantage, since the only other studio with sound capability, Warners, had no newsreel. Recent improvements in the Western Electric microphone and the stability of sound-on-film recording (unlike the delicate Vitaphone discs) had made it practical to record sound outdoors. Sheehan instituted a new policy of stationing camera and sound crews around the country and in Europe to record newsworthy events and "world figures in action and sound." Fox News officials saw that a transformation in the newsreel was about to take place.[39]

As with features, the idea of an all-talking newsreel was slow to take hold. Truman Talley, director of Fox News, said that his newsreel would "talk" only "when it has something to say." He continued: "Whenever anything occurs that can be photographed which will be more interesting and entertaining when accompanied by sound we will spare no effort to see that it is done. We are working and planning for many things and the time is not far distant when every issue of Fox News will have one or more subjects with sound accompaniment."[40]

On 20 April 1927, Charles Pettijohn, general counsel for the Hays Office and head of the Film Boards of Trade, was meeting with Benito Mussolini. He suggested that the dictator sit for a filming, and Mussolini, a longtime film buff, readily agreed. Il Duce liked the result so much that he "is having a talking film prepared that will show his daily activities." Mussolini reportedly said, "Let me speak through [the newsreel] in twenty cities in Italy once a week and I need no other power." This film would enable him to appear in public with no threat of assassination. The Movietone newsreel premiered with SUNRISE on 23 September 1927 and featured Mussolini speaking "a message of friendship" in Italian and English.[41]

Some of Fox's subjects were not as eager, and the camera operators became precursors of paparazzi. Allegedly, King Gustav of Sweden was filmed without permission. The police arrested the Movietone crew lurking on Newcastle Bridge to shoot King George.[42]

These newsreels had a powerful impact on exhibitors. The president of the Interstate Amusement theaters, for instance, had seen a demonstration of Movietone in New York and signed with Fox on the spot. He explained, "One of the great problems which the progressive exhibitor has to face is how he can increase his patronage. I believe that Movietone, especially the plans which call for its extensive use in Fox News, will have a definite effect in that direction."[43]

Newsreels caught one of the most captivating phenomena of the twentieth century, Charles Lindbergh's solo transatlantic flight. This event had important repercussions for the sound film. The Lone Eagle's departure from Roosevelt Field, Long Island, on 20 May 1927, was filmed by Movietone News (as well as by the Phonofilm crew) and

George Bernard Shaw's Fox Movietone News appearance, 1927.

screened before an amazed and jubilant crowd at the Roxy that same evening. Lindbergh landed at Le Bourget Airport, Paris, on 21 May, thirty-three and a half hours later, where he was greeted by frenzied journalists. But the Movietone crew had not yet arrived. Nevertheless, Fox News was first with the scoop. It filmed "radio stills"—wirephotos transmitted from Paris on Western Electric equipment—and included them in its 25 May newsreel, along with Movietone footage of the "hop off" from New York. Speaking editorially, Red Kann noted that movie newsreels were becoming as aggressive as their newspaper brethren. Hearst's International News, Kinograms, Pathé News, and Paramount News all vied to show footage of the landing. "'Get it on the street first' has been changed to 'Get it on the screen first,' . . . Watch the scramble when the steamer carrying the film reaches New York."[44] The novelty of sound made Fox's coverage the toast of the town wherever it was shown. But there was competition. The De Forest Phonofilm version of the takeoff and Lindbergh's gala return opened at the Capitol in New York on 12 June. Fox News ran its footage of Lindbergh's Washington, D.C., reception and New York ticker-tape parade at the Roxy for several weeks, beginning 14 June.[45] The fantastic offers that Rothapfel and the big vaudeville chains all made to Lindbergh for a personal appearance easily would have exceeded $1 million had he accepted them. The major film studios offered him parts in features, all of which he declined. "Colonel Lindbergh will have none of the talking newsreels," it was reported. "His business is flying, not speaking, and the newsreel men—who recorded his speaking image without his permission at his Washington homecoming—say that his friends advised him that this shot was not worthy of a great hero and that he should avoid the microphone."[46] Lindbergh's natural reticence and his resistance to film exploitation made the Movietone recording of his returning remarks all the more in demand. Awe of technology, hero worship, patriotism, and Lindbergh's charismatic American rugged individualism came together in a formative moment for the newsreel. He also made an impact on the animated cartoon. Walt Disney, searching for a personality model for his new character's first film, made Mickey Mouse a caricature of Lindy in PLANE CRAZY (1928).[47]

Another indirect result of Lindbergh's flight affected film distribution and exhibition. The rush to deliver the reels to the various regional exchanges as rapidly as possible necessitated using aircraft. Thereafter the major newsreel producers routinely chartered planes to fly prints between distant key cities. Aviation technology therefore helped the newsreel capture some of the marvelous immediacy of radio.

Sheehan went full-speed ahead with the talking concept. The first program of all-sound newsreels, which included shots of the Yale-Army football game, ran at the Roxy during the week of 1 November. Rothapfel's patrons burst "into a frenzy of cheering and for the moment you weren't sitting in a theater at all but in the bowl at New Haven. It wasn't just a picture, but the game itself." (Football and other sporting events were also popular radio fare.) Kann praised THE ROMANCE OF THE IRON HORSE (1927), an educational film on the history of locomotives, and also applauded the combined sights and sounds of the Yale-Army game. The only thing missing was color—"Someday you'll find that in all newsreels too."[48]

On 4 December 1927, Fox Movietone Newsreel Number One was released, with weekly releases planned thereafter. Kann predicted that "when the record of accomplishment for 1927 is written, the Movietone newsreel, by every right, will be found making a formidable bid for first honours."[49] Conscious of the historical (and publicity) value of the endeavor, William Fox offered to place films in the National Archives.[50] Sound motion pictures, he predicted, would become important in the "social, educational, political fabric of the nation." Fox understood that his arrangement with Western Electric was for exclusive rights to sound newsreels, but he was willing to sublicense Movietone news production to competitive organizations if the price was right. Winfield Sheehan predicted 30,000 Movietone installations around the world by 1930. They would have to move quickly: by the end of 1927, Western Electric reported that there were 150 Movietone installations and 100 back orders. ERPI (which installed Movietone as well as Vitaphone) was setting its 1928 installation goal at two a day.[51]

Fox Movietone enjoyed the talking newsreel field exclusively for nearly a year. Its popularity soared, owing not only to the intrinsic interest in current events but to the attraction of direct-recorded sound and speech. During this period there was also a subtle change in how "the news" was constructed in these films. In early Movietones, the camera crew was a passive observer, one witness among many at various public events. Football games, public addresses, and political rallies would have occurred with or without the cameras. But as awareness of the newsreel's power and popularity increased, the camera structured events. Appearances by Mussolini in 1927 and Shaw in 1928 illustrate this trend. When earlier films had contained direct addresses to the movie audience—for example, de Forest's "interviews" with presidential candidates—they showed the subjects delivering prepared statements as though speaking from a public podium. If the speakers acknowledged the camera's presence at all, they seemed discomfited by it. The new Movietones, on the other hand, set up the scenes to allow the subjects' public personalities to come through. The public showed a particular fascination for Shaw's film. He came across as an amiable, crotchety, audacious, eccentric English gentleman. "That white whiskered lad," said Variety, "is some bimbo."[52] The Shavian wit was in full force. One highlight of his monologue is an impersonation of Mussolini, or to be more accurate, of the Movietone recording of Mussolini. Shaw's newsreel was not something that occurred spontaneously, but an event set up by him and the crew. As the film begins, he ambles down a gravel path and feigns surprise at meeting the film audience. He looks directly into the camera and greets us in second-person. But he lampoons this carefully contrived illusion by saying, "Good evening, or good day, if this is a matinee showing." Offscreen, Shaw took sound film seriously and was interested in making a talking version of his play *St. Joan*.[53] Most Movietone newsreels did not acknowledge the artificiality of the event with such reflexive force, but crews were quickly becoming more proactive in managing not only the appearance of their stories but their content. The newsreel camera was no passive fly on the wall. Gerald J. Baldasty's comments on the commercialization of news in nineteenth-century journalism apply here as well:

> Autonomy from government, increased readership, and lower per capita costs are clearly the benefits of commercialization in the newspaper. But there are trade-offs. Commercialization imposes the imperative that newspapers must entertain their readers. When entertainment is paramount, difficult issues or current events that are not inherently interesting or entertaining may well get short shrift. (Gerald J. Baldasty, *The Commercialization of News in the Nineteenth Century* [Madison: University of Wisconsin Press, 1992], p. 9)

Fox's diversity was enhanced immeasurably by its European coverage. The newsreel shown in April 1928 on the program accompanying STREET ANGEL demonstrates the newsreel's rapid shift to what we call now "soft" or even "tabloid" news. It presented both ends of the conversation initiating AT&T telephone service between New York and Paris (hardly an accidental choice of subject!); stunts in a swimming pool; Winnie Lightner singing jazz numbers; scenes from the rehearsal of the Moulin Rouge stage show in Paris; and the British king and queen attending the opening of the new Lloyd's building in London.

The extraordinary variety in Fox's coverage was made possible by the fleet of nineteen Movietone trucks already on the road, and another eleven were being equipped. By October 1928, less than a year after its official beginning, there were two all-sound editions of the newsreel each week.[54] Fox attempted to block Paramount and MGM from producing sound newsreels. William Fox thought that he had received the exclusive right to make newsreels and educational and political films from Western Electric in exchange for his Case and Tri-Ergon patents.[55] Whether this tactic delayed competition from the other ERPI licensees is unknown. Fox, however, had no leverage against the RCA group. In June, Photophone began marketing a sound truck similar to Movietone's for recording in the field. Pathé Sound News began using it in November. In 1929, despite announced plans for sound newsreels by Paramount, Kinograms, and International, the pacesetters Fox and Pathé (now a distant second) had widened their already impressive lead. Movietone went to a four-a-week release schedule. After Fox merged with Loew's in March 1929, the silent MGM newsreel was absorbed to create the MGM Movietone News. In September 1929, the MGM Hearst Metrotone News was ready, appearing twice weekly. Exhibitors could choose either disc or optical sound.[56]

The public's appetite for topical newsreels was enormous. Of the Big Five studios, only Warners never had a newsreel. Paramount, in January 1930, was issuing three sound editions a week and one silent version. By May all the major producers had discontinued their silents.[57]

Movietone did news better than radio did. Government regulations restrained the networks from competing with newspapers. (Hence there were no radio "reporters" during this period; they were required to call themselves "news commentators," which remains part of the vernacular.) This unanticipated journalistic advantage created a powerful social and economic niche for the talking newsreel. Furthermore, the first sound newsreels were constructed to foreground the impression of being-there-ness. Their outdoor settings recorded with omnidirectional microphones created transportive pictures and placed the viewer-listener "in" the Yale Bowl or brought Lindbergh "inside" the local theater for his speech. Mussolini's filmed likeness stood in for his vulnerable real being. In this sense, the newsreel was very similar to the concept of virtual Broadway, intended to collapse the space between subject and consumer.

From the exhibitor's point of view, the sound newsreel was a welcome variation to the program. It provided a sought-after service for delivering the news ("soft news" though it may have been) and a way to build audiences. Its varied subjects—sports coverage and fashions, for example—appealed to different sectors of the market.

Only a year after joining with Theodore Case to challenge Vitaphone, Fox's productions had undergone noticeable changes. Some were the result of competitive pressure—keeping up with the Warners. Other changes derived from the portable attributes of the technology of sound-on-film recording. As a consequence, the Fox output migrated from the virtual orchestra and the revue short (in the de Forest and Vitaphone tradition) to the sound newsreel. It might seem incongruous that one of the first studios to have dialogue capability persisted in extolling the virtual orchestra concept for its feature releases. Fox's reluctance to switch to an all-talking format illustrates that the industry needed models as well as the requisite technology. Though in retrospect it might seem "natural" to move from the virtual orchestra to dialogue films (especially after THE JAZZ SINGER), the path was not so clear to the filmmakers of 1927–1928.

5

Enticing the Audience:
Warner Bros. and Vitaphone

The decision to add Movietone and Vitaphone to the product lines of Fox and Warners in 1927 was viewed as a curio (like color and stereoscopy) which might boost
a program. Synchronized sound could also save money for theaters by replacing presentation acts and orchestras with "electrical" facsimiles. Winfield Sheehan and Harry
Warner expected these short films to succeed in small towns but not necessarily in big
cities, where the simulacra would compete with the real thing. An audience's first exposure to a sound film might have been in one of four forms in 1927: a synchronized musical score added to a feature; a talking short, with music and patter recorded by opera,
vaudeville, and radio personalities; the synch sound newsreel; or sound prevue trailers.
The idea of a normal feature film with spoken dialogue was considered a possibility but
not taken seriously. Thomas Edison, though out of touch with the industry, spoke a common prejudice:

> No, I don't think the talking moving picture will ever be successful in the
> United States. Americans prefer silent drama. They are accustomed to the
> moving picture as it is and they will never get enthusiastic over any voices
> being mingled in. Yes, there will be a novelty to it for a little while, but the
> glitter will soon wear off and the movie fans will cry for silence or a little
> orchestra music.
>
> I believe the experiments will prove highly successful. I am certain that
> voices can be reproduced to fit in just the right place with the play on the
> screen, but the American people do not want it and will not welcome it. We
> are wasting our time in going on with the project. (*Film Daily,* 4 March
> 1927, pp. 1, 2)

This vote of no confidence by the patriarch of electrical science came as a blow. (Terry
Ramsaye's recently published *A Million and One Nights* had been dedicated to and
included a frontispiece portrait of "the Wizard.") Harry Warner reacted, pointing out
that Vitaphones were already operating in fifty theaters and being installed at the rate of
five per week. Fox also objected to this most famous of all scientists dismissing his venture. He dispatched a crew to Edison's West Orange lab to project some Movietone tests

Patsy Ruth Miller and Barney Oldfield in THE FIRST AUTO *(Warner Bros., 1927).*

and to shoot footage of the inventor. Edison listened to the selections and, his serious hearing impairment notwithstanding, revised his opinion and called the talkies a "distinct advance."[1]

Harry Warner wrote to stockholders in January 1927, alerting them to the cost of their company's major commitment to Vitaphone. Since August 1926, he reported, the firm had invested $1.57 million in the process, and the fall quarter would show a $100,000 loss. Despite the initial public interest in Vitaphone, Warners found the enthusiasm difficult to sustain. At year-end 1926, Warners had planned to install 350 machines during the coming year. But because installations by Western Electric were running four months behind, that estimate was soon lowered to 300. In March 1927, Walter J. Rich, president of Vitaphone, reported that there were still only 51 machines in use.[2] Aside from equipment back orders, the spring of 1927 saw a definite loss of momentum for Vitaphone as a feature producer. The music-synched films had done well on Broadway and set records at their 100-performance marks (one barometer used to measure box-office success). DON JUAN grossed $790,000 during its 36-week run at the Warners'. But in the spring and summer of 1927, some theater owners were removing the system. For example, in Jacksonville, DON JUAN performed well, but THE BETTER 'OLE was a flop. The Kentucky Theater in Lexington stopped showing Vitaphone features and played the shorts only on the Monday-through-Thursday off-days. Throughout the summer, the system was pulled from larger cities as well. The Metropolitan in Washington, D.C., canceled Vitaphone in June. The shows were discontinued at the important Mark Strand in Brooklyn. It lasted three months in Atlanta, where it "failed to measure up to expecta-

Darryl F. Zanuck, 1927.

tions. It did not catch popular fancy" and was permitted to "die quietly"—a choice, probably unintended, pun.[3] Warner Bros. clearly needed two things: smash programs which
would bring enthusiastic audiences back to sound films, and more wired theaters.

The Big Five studios watched this activity intently and worked behind the scenes to
position themselves to deal with sound in case their competitors' experiments showed
signs of making money. Their voluntary detachment from competition in sound gave
Warners a potential advantage if the studio could act quickly enough. The studio
responded by upgrading Warner production facilities and rethinking the content of the
Vitaphone programs. In February 1927, at a cost of $1.6 million, Warners rebuilt the old
Hollywood Vitagraph studio, 4151 Prospect Avenue at Talmadge (now the site of ABC-
TV Center), to create the most up-to-date sound facility. Darryl Francis Zanuck, head
of the writing department, was promoted to Jack Warner's assistant. He continued to
write scenarios in addition to supervising most productions.

Warner Bros. signed a new ERPI agreement on 4 August 1927. Walter Rich was
bought out, and Vitaphone became a wholly owned Warner subsidiary. The brand name
Vitaphone, which formerly designated the recording and reproducing mechanism,
henceforth would be the trademark for a line of sound films. The equipment would now
be called by a new name, Western Electric Sound Projector System. Warners' aspiration
to be a monopoly licensor was destroyed in one fell swoop. The studio's new agreement
with ERPI was nonexclusive. Fox and Warner Bros. studios and their affiliated theaters
used the same recording, amplification, and reproducing equipment (though Fox had no
interest in cutting sound tracks on disc). This arrangement had a major impact on exhibition: Vitaphone- and Movietone-licensed houses now shared reciprocal rights to run
all Warners and Fox sound films, greatly increasing the amount of available material. For
Warners, it put Vitaphone films into the chain of forty-five theaters which Fox owned or
had an interest in, including his West Coast (Wesco) group, the Roxy, and other flagship
Broadway theaters. Western Electric would supply on a first-priority basis a projection
system which could play both discs and Movietone optical tracks.[4]

Warners' revenue came from a "seat tax," from an installation royalty, and from
increased rental rates. Theaters paid Vitaphone 10¢ per seat per week whenever the
equipment was used. Averaging around $200 for each show, Warner Bros. expected to
supplement its regular film rental by $45,000 per week. Theaters agreed to play
Vitaphone films forty weeks per year. Because there was no reliable way to check attendance, the seat royalty was constant regardless of the size of the audience. Thus, if patronage was poor, the theater, not Vitaphone, took the loss. This was an onerous arrangement
for smaller houses because the Vitaphone films were drawing spotty crowds.

It may have been the fault of the films. John Barrymore's vehicle Manon Lascaut
was now retitled When a Man Loves (1927). When the music-synchronized movie
opened at the Selwyn on 3 February, it was received without enthusiasm, except for
Barrymore, who was called "a splendid romantic figure. Oh, how the women will fall for
him in his resplendent costumes." Dolores Costello was "a lovely creature and a capable
actress." But Alan Crosland's direction was found to be heavy-handed. The New York
Daily News said that, "without the Vitaphone program [of shorts] that goes with it, it
assuredly would not be a so-called special." Variety, on the contrary, found the shorts to
be "a pretty severe experience," owing not only to the sound quality but to the loss of
the aura of a live performance: "[T]he mere knowledge that the entertainment is a
reproduction has the effect of erecting an altogether imaginary feeling of mechanical
flatness, such as one gets from a player piano."[5]

OLD SAN FRANCISCO *(Warner Bros., 1927), with So-Jin, Anna May Wong, and Kamiyama.*

THE FIRST AUTO, which opened at the Colony on 27 June 1927, was said to have been "muffed." *Film Daily* thought that the parts intended to be serious were actually the funniest and complained that the real-life racer Barney Oldfield, billed as a featured player, was barely visible in a cameo. Other reviews noted the morbid irony of the death of the star Charles Emmett Mack while driving to the Warner lot. OLD SAN FRANCISCO was disparaged as an "elaborate meller [melodrama] with hoke laid on thick. Padded but has big moments. Hardly a Special. . . . The earthquake comes as the climax, with the Vitaphone accompaniment utilized to provide shrieks, wails and moans as the city tumbles in ruins." Mordaunt Hall of the *New York Times* wrote that the Vitaphone shorts were "infinitely more sane and far more interesting than the principal film subject."[6]

Perhaps as a way to elevate its cultural status and reach new audiences, Warners added more highbrow material to its programs. Syd Chaplin's next feature, THE MISSING LINK (1927), was to be accompanied by a thirty-minute version of the opera *Carmen*, with Giovanni Martinelli and Jeanne Gordon. Martinelli, the Met star who had been so popular in the first Vitaphone program, signed a three-year contract to make a series of operatic adaptations. Harry Warner was also making arrangements with the Shubert organization for *The Student Prince, Iolanthe,* and *The Pirates of Penzance.* The *New York Times* saw this development as a benefit for the art:

> Hardly an opera in the world is self-supporting. The sound film may unlock
> sources of revenue that may relieve American millionaires and European

Joe E. Brown in "Twinkle, Twinkle" (a.k.a. In the Movies; *Vitaphone short, 1927).*

governments of the necessity of paying deficits out of their pockets and trea-
suries. Possibly moving picture organizations will maintain their own operatic companies for the sole purpose of presenting Wagner and Puccini
simultaneously in a hundred theaters at a low price and with a magnificence
never approached by the State-supported operas of Europe. (Quoted in
Film Daily, 13 February 1927, p. 4)

The *Times'* speculation was consistent with the emerging consensus that the sound film
would grow as a branch off the main trunk of the Hollywood film. Carmen (1927)
appeared as one of the opening-night attractions at the Roxy, where it was presented as
a mixed-media event accompanied live by the Metropolitan Opera House chorus and
ballet.[7]

Opera's presence in the Vitaphone programs soon declined. The shift toward popular music probably reflects both increased awareness of the public's musical tastes and
the availability of popular compositions made available by Warners' negotiations with
publishers. Charles Wolfe also points out that this change was temporary and related to
the move of Vitaphone filming to the new Hollywood studio, to which the Met singers
were reluctant to travel. The decision to resume filming in Brooklyn in 1928 was influenced by Warners' desire to retain grand opera in its repertoire of shorts. The distribution of the Vitaphone shorts, which exhibitors booked individually from the whole
catalog rather than in preconstituted programs, made it possible to tailor programs to
local tastes. Wolfe observes that "the divide between opera and 'popular' music appears
less a function of class stratification than of urban-regional boundaries."[8]

Warner Bros. exploited Vitaphone to rival MGM's famous constellation of stars.

The commitment to opera was "balanced" by a broad spectrum of performers. As de Forest had done, Warners looked to the stars of the New York stage to bring back audiences. Contracts were signed with Joe E. Brown, Bernardo De Pace, mandolin player, and Sissle and Blake, identified as "colored entertainers."[9] Reviewing the Vitaphone shorts at the Colony Theatre, Charles Hynes remarked, "All in all, it looks as if Vita has at last struck its stride in turning out a program of variety to strike the popular appeal."[10] Vaudeville managers understandably saw these and other contracts as raids. The Keith-Albee office counterattacked by banning Vitaphone headliners from vaudeville engagements. Like radio, the talkies were perceived as an encroachment on live entertainment. Sam Warner pressed his advantage:

> [U]nless a sensible attitude is taken by vaudeville, it will be the sufferer, not Vitaphone, as we can give well known artists a yearly contract for as much salary as any vaudeville circuit can afford to pay, and they can work all seasons without leaving New York or Los Angeles. In that way, instead of the vaudeville circuits "blacklisting" Vitaphone, Vitaphone will be in position to engage artists exclusively for its own purposes. (*Film Daily*, 23 March 1927, pp. 1, 6)

His belligerence was no doubt underscored by his knowledge that Albee's J. J. Murdock was part of an effort to take over Vitaphone and was also negotiating with de Forest and RCA for Albee's own sound deal. In April 1927, the vaudeville chain merged with Pathé, PDC, and Orpheum, so its interdiction against film performances was quickly forgotten.

THE JAZZ SINGER

When patrons read the program they received at the screening of THE BETTER 'OLE, they had the pleasant surprise of learning that George Jessel had been signed to reprise his starring role in the Broadway hit *The Jazz Singer.* From its inception, the film was planned to be something special. Warners had purchased the motion picture rights to Samson Raphaelson's play for Ernst Lubitsch to direct as a silent in 1926, but he had left for MGM. So the project fell to Crosland. Throughout the spring, looking for ways to generate popular interest, Harry Warner repeated his promise that the company would be experimenting with talking features for the 1927–1928 season. Accordingly, Warners announced that this would "be the first picture into which Vitaphone will be introduced for dramatic effect." Jessel would be recording Mammy (minstrel) songs and a synagogue service.[11]

In the spring of 1927 the press reported that the Jessel picture was in trouble. The entertainer said that "his Vitaphone contract for this stage play *The Jazz Singer* does not have anything about singing, and therefore added compensation for his vocal talents should be provided." *Variety* printed an unsubstantiated story that Jessel also objected to making the film with the non-Jewish Alan Crosland, Eugenie Besserer (who played Jack Robin's mother), and Warner Oland (his father).[12]

Warners did not search far for a replacement. The trades reported in May that Al Jolson would be the new "jazz singer." Though it has been suggested that the substitution was premeditated, this seems unlikely because advance publicity materials featuring Jessel already had been circulated. For Jolson, it was a once-in-a-lifetime casting opportunity. The entertainer, who sang jazzed-up minstrel numbers in blackface, was at the height of his phenomenal popularity. Anticipating the later stardom of crooners and rock stars, Jolson electrified audiences with the vitality and sex appeal of his songs and gestures, which owed much to African-American sources. In September he had grossed $57,286 for a one-week personal appearance at the Metropolitan Theater in Los Angeles. The crowds were so wild that Jolson gave three extra performances without pay. His songs in the 1926 Vitaphone short, A PLANTATION ACT, had amply demonstrated the singer's celluloid appeal. And having auditioned the competitors Jessel and Jolson together on the same Vitaphone program and compared audience reactions certainly must have made the Warners imagine how nice it would be to sign Al.

Jolson filmed the silent scenes in June and the eight sound sequences in August 1927 at the Hollywood Vitaphone studio. Though the myth is that Jolson spontaneously blurted out his famous speaking part, all summer Crosland had been telling the press that THE JAZZ SINGER would have some talking. "They are planning to use dialogue in certain scenes of this production—dialogue with musical accompaniment."[13] The film opened on 6 October 1927. Warners set the Broadway premiere on the day before Yom Kippur as a show business flourish, since the film's plot centers on that holiday.

The story of this legendary film is one of generational conflict and atonement. A prologue shows young Jakie Rabinowitz (Bobby Gordon) singing ragtime renditions of "My Gal Sal" and "Waiting for the Robert E. Lee" in a Lower East Side saloon. His father (Oland), a cantor at the synagogue, catches him, they argue over his profane singing, and Jakie leaves home. The story jumps ten years and "Jack Robin" is now eking out a living as a jazz singer. He finds success, partly through the influence of a talented vaudeville performer, Mary Dale (May McAvoy). He and Mary are scheduled to appear together in a big Broadway show. Jack goes to visit his mother, Sara Rabinowitz (Besserer), and performs "Blue Skies" for her. Cantor Rabinowitz enters unexpectedly, yells "Stop!" and makes Jack leave. Opening night of the show falls on Yom Kippur, but the cantor has not recovered from his shock and cannot sing. Jack answers his mother's appeal to come visit and is so moved by his father's suffering and the call of his own reawakened religion that he sings the Kol Nidre in his father's place. The cantor dies, but his lifelong dream of hearing his son sing the ancient hymn has been fulfilled. In an epilogue, Jack appears onstage at the Winter Garden theater and sings "Mammy" to his mother in the audience.

In the screenplay, there was considerable room for improvisation owing to the lack of precedents for writing a part-talking film. There was a note for one scene that read: "The rendition of the song will have to be governed entirely by the Vitaphone routine decided upon. The scenes herewith are only those necessary to carrying on the story."[14] Crosland allowed the ebullient Jolson to ad-lib lines. In an early scene, Jack performs "Toot, Toot, Tootsie" in Coffee Dan's club. When it is over, Jolson exclaims, "Wait a minute! Wait a minute! You ain't heard nothin' yet." These lines, among the most famous in film history, are also among the most misrepresented. First, Jolson does not say them to Besserer aloud in the later scene, as is widely believed; rather, that line is repeated in a conventional silent intertitle: "Mama—You ain't heard nothing yet." Second, though the lines do not appear to have been scripted, they were planned for deliberately and calculated to spark recognition and applause from his fans in the audience, since "You ain't heard nothin' yet" was the signature tag line Jolson always repeated during his stage act. The vaudeville tradition of the tag line is comparable to George Jessel's "So help me," Bugs Bunny's "What's up, Doc," and Rodney Dangerfield's "I get no respect." Walker, noting that no reviewer commented on this allegedly historic utterance, offers: "They might have commented if it *hadn't* been in the film!"[15]

Who knows who inspired these ad-libbed sequences? Sam Warner was said to have been impressed by Jolson's unscripted lines in the Coffee Dan sequence and suggested that the writer, Alfred A. Cohn, think up some dialogue on the spot. Jolson told a fan magazine that the whole thing was his idea: "Everybody on the set was crying when I got through."[16] Darryl Zanuck recalled:

> I was on the set when they were rehearsing the parts where Jolson sings to his mother. We were all standing around waiting for the music to be played. Suddenly it dawned on me, why don't they have a conversation? The mike was on! I said, "Why doesn't Jolson turn to his mother and say, 'Mama, I wanna sing a song for you.'" Then the guy turned the sound machine on early. (Mel Gussow, *Don't Say Yes Until I Finish Talking: A Biography of Darryl F. Zanuck* [Garden City, N.Y.: Doubleday, 1971], p. 41)

While so many wished to take credit for this inspiration, it is important to keep it in perspective; there had been precedents for such scenes in Vitaphone shorts, including Jolson's own.

Unlike the premiere of Don Juan, there was little advance publicity for The Jazz Singer, and little response (enthusiastic or otherwise) in the daily reviews. In the trade papers, the premiere was overshadowed by the sudden death of Sam Warner, at age forty, the previous day. He had died in Los Angeles of pneumonia while recovering from surgery for a sinus infection. The surviving Warner brothers had rushed to California, thus missing opening night.[17]

Reviewers acclaimed Jolson's singing but panned his acting style. Robert Sherwood, usually a stickler for quality acting, wrote in *Life* that he would trade all of Hollywood's super-spectacles "for one instant of any ham song that Al cares to put on." Hall commented in the *Times* on the thunderous applause for Jolson, and the "effectiveness" of Vitaphone, but demurred, "The dialogue is not so effective." As he had done with the shorts, he also criticized the sound quality, or rather, its lack of "presence": "There are also times when one would expect the Vitaphoned portions to be either more subdued or stopped as the camera swings to other scenes. The voice is usually just the same whether the image of the singer is close to the camera or quite far away." "The Jazz Singer," according to *Exhibitors Herald*, "is scarcely a motion picture. It should be more properly labeled an enlarged Vitaphone record of Al Jolson in half a dozen songs." *Film Daily* observed that the movie rode on Jolson's coattails, but that sound would boost the film's box-office potential: "With Vitaphone accompaniment an immense entertainment. Without it an attraction anyway because of Jolson's drawing power. . . . Jolson's reputation is sufficient to stamp The Jazz Singer as a money-maker. It steps into the class of top-notchers, however with the Vitaphone accompaniment."[18] Within months the film would make a great sum for Warners, but at the time it was not the biggest hit of the season. Barrios notes, "Some tickets [to the premiere], in fact, were still available on the morning of October 6, even with the announcement that Jolson would attend." Nor was there any heralding in the trade press of how Hollywood was "revolutionized."[19] The film was represented as a triumph for Jolson, and for Warners in hiring him, but not for talking cinema. Nevertheless, the message was clear to small exhibitors outside of New York. Though the price of wiring for Vitaphone was exorbitant, the prospect of having Al Jolson "play" in the local theater made it a surefire investment.

Warners, of course, had a head start on the big studios. Its executives were still deliberating in early 1928 while Vitaphone was making profits. Accounts of THE JAZZ SINGER's huge success usually date the film's Broadway premiere as the starting point of the rush to sound. It is more likely that it was the national opening of the sound version in January 1928 that helped convince producers to settle the sound issue and sign with ERPI quickly. Frances Goldwyn (wife of Samuel) recounted the story of Hollywood executives sitting in silence after the Los Angeles trade preview. Instead of applause, there was "terror in all their faces."[20] They were said to have been disconcerted by reports from theater managers that audiences were flocking to the Warners talkie instead of their silent films. According to existing studio records, THE JAZZ SINGER, throughout 1931, earned around $2 million for Warners. This figure includes substantial revenue from the silent version and the 1931 re-release, so the amount attributable to the sound release would have been considerably less. These were not staggering grosses by then-current Hollywood standards, so one questions the immediate impact the film might have had on movie moguls. However, because the negative-cost (that is, the cost of completing the film) was only $422,000, Warners was rewarded with a strong return on investment.[21]

The success of the film throughout 1928 reflected popular demand to see and hear Jolson, certainly. It was also the result of a shrewd marketing plan devised by Warners' sales manager, Sam Morris. When a house became wired, Jolson's film was usually the first screening. Audiences came for the novelty and proven drawing power of this by-then famous film. And to make certain that as many people as possible had the opportunity to see the film, a special clause in Warners' Vitaphone exhibition contract virtually guaranteed long runs. Theaters had to book THE JAZZ SINGER for full rather than split weeks. Instead of the traditional flat rental fee, Warners took a percentage of the gate. A sliding scale meant that the exhibitor's take increased the longer the film was held over. The signing of this contract by the greater New York Fox circuit was regarded as a headline-making precedent.[22] The silent film practice of renting for a flat fee eventually was replaced by this new escalating percentage-of-the-gross arrangement. On 24 March 1928, THE JAZZ SINGER was playing in 235 theaters, a "day and date" record for any film, Warners claimed.[23] (However, the announcement glossed over the fact that most of these screenings were of the silent version.) It was a combination of THE JAZZ SINGER's popularity and the augmented revenue from Warners' expanding theater chain that propelled the company's earnings 500 percent ahead of 1927. In three years, Warner Bros. stock rose from $21 to $132 per share.[24] Small wonder that the majors were sitting up and taking notice.

Warner Bros.' annual winter production hiatus ended 15 March 1928, and a new policy took effect. On the East Coast, the Brooklyn Vitagraph studio reopened with new emphasis on one-reel musical comedies and two-reel "playlets," directed by Bryan Foy.[25] The latter were adaptations of stage properties. Feature work was concentrated on the West Coast, with Darryl Zanuck in charge. He resumed filming NOAH'S ARK, with Michael Curtiz directing and starring Dolores Costello and George O'Brien, who had been borrowed from Fox. Conceived of as a true blockbuster, Curtiz labored through the summer with thirty assistant directors and five thousand extras.[26]

The studio's policy of attracting audiences by signing the biggest stars continued, with Fanny Brice set to make a Vitaphone feature. Brice was as big a vaudeville draw as Jolson, famous for her Yiddish and working-class humor. Her tag line was, "I've been poor and I've been rich. Rich is better!" Warners boasted, "No longer do Belasco, Ziegfeld and Albee hold a monopoly on her services." MY MAN (1928), titled after her signature song, was directed by Archie Mayo. Jolson was signed up for his next feature,

Though billed as "Warner Bros. Supreme Triumph," posters for the national release of The Jazz Singer *did not highlight Vitaphone.*

which would be THE SINGING FOOL (1928). Myrna Loy and Conrad Nagel were "elevated to stardom" from the ranks of contract players. John Barrymore, who had defected to United Artists in 1927, was now bargaining to return to Warners to make his first talking film. THE DESERT SONG (1929), the first Broadway musical to be Vitaphoned in its entirety, was planned as a road-show special. "It is expected to be the most pretentious musical film the Warners have ever attempted." (*Pretentious,* meaning "distinguished," was a positive adjective in the 1920s.) The producer of the operetta, Lillian Albertson, sued Warners over the rights. The studio said it was not worried, but the production was put on hold.[27]

The Vitaphone shorts in general were garnering good reviews, but the ones riding the crest of the jazz craze were the most popular. STORIES IN SONG (1928) showed off Adele Rowland's voice to advantage. A Broadway fixture in the early twenties, she was in the midst of an attempted comeback at the Palace Vaudeville Theater. She performed some of her specialty "'story songs,' often with a Pollyanna-type theme."[28] Another "jazz" selection was XAVIER CUGAT AND HIS GIGOLOS (1928), a "satisfactory 'Talkie.'" Though the sound reproduction was good, "when shown at the Warner theater in New York [it] was somewhat hard on the eardrums because of the volume. Would have been more effective if toned down." *Film Daily* called ABE LYMAN AND HIS ORCHESTRA (1928) a "corking fine number" that testified to "the appeal that a first class jazz band has for the average audience."[29] Sophie Tucker signed with Vitaphone in September. She claimed to have invented stage jazz, performing in blackface at all the big-time New York houses and nightclubs. At the time of the Warner short, she was starring in a revue which included, among other songs, a parody of the Jolson hit "Bye, Bye, Blackbird," which she sang as "Bye, Bye, Greenberg."[30] These performers were the established troupers of Broadway. The surviving shorts chronicle the dissemination of African-American and Caribbean music forms given their distinctive New York–Jewish inflection.

On 14 March 1928, TENDERLOIN replaced THE JAZZ SINGER at the Warners' Theatre. The feature was directed by Curtiz and featured Conrad Nagel and Dolores Costello. Unlike the Jolson film, whose brief talking sequences were embedded in the story, TENDERLOIN was shot as a silent with four dialogue sequences lasting a bit less than fifteen minutes added after the fact. TENDERLOIN enjoyed a long profitable run in New York, further convincing those who had not yet signed with ERPI that they might miss the talkie boat with further delays. Written by Zanuck under the pseudonym Melville Crossman, the melodrama is a prototype for the later Warners gangster films, with rain-slicked streets and the iconography of urban seediness. Costello is a nightclub dancer caught between the law and the underworld until rescued by Nagel. The film was also a learning experience for Warners. The surviving discs for the film reproduce the actors' voices satisfactorily, including Costello's. Reportedly, however, audiences laughed at Costello because the Vitaphone system recorded her speech as a lisp. Her line—allegedly rendered "Merthy, merthy, have you no thithter of your own?"—has become almost as legendary as Jolson's catchphrase. Even without the sibilance, however, her performance, as Barrios points out, is awkward and she seems unable to combine speech and gesture for the camera.[31]

Harry and Jack Warner announced that all thirty-four films in the 1928–1929 season would be Vitaphoned. This decision supposedly was based on a survey showing strong audience preferences for sound over silent versions. (The latter would still be produced). A $200,000 studio expansion plan was inaugurated to accommodate the increased workload. In October work started on a fifth sound stage on the Los Angeles lot.[32]

Dolores Costello and Conrad Nagel in Glorious Betsy *(Warner Bros., 1928)*

The fate of the old Vitagraph studio in Brooklyn shows Warners' difficulty in trying to second-guess the audience. In June, after operating for only a few months, it was abandoned as an active stage and converted into a distribution center for Vitaphone equipment. Warners stated that "the making of this type of picture is being concentrated on the [West] Coast." In August 1928, however, demand had increased to such a level that the company allocated $500,000 for refurbishing the Brooklyn stages.[33]

Glorious Betsy opened simultaneously in the New York and Los Angeles Warners' theaters on 26 April 1928. This part-talking film directed by Crosland tells the story of the romance between Jerome Bonaparte and Betsy Patterson (Nagel and Costello). William C. DeMille, who attended, recalled the audience's thrill when Nagel spoke his first line of dialogue, but also his own disappointment in the sound quality:

> Poor Dolores Costello's excellent voice came out at times as a deep rich bari-tone, while Conrad Nagel thundered in a sub-human bass, like immortal love declaiming through the Holland Tunnel. When they whispered together confidentially, the resulting sounds took me back to the old wood-shed of my boyhood where the hired man wielded a mean saw. (Quoted in Alexander Walker, *The Shattered Silents: How the Talkies Came to Stay* [New York: William Morrow, 1979], p. 57)

Its writing, direction, and acting, however, received rave trade reviews:

> This latest Warner effort marks a rather important something in the advance-
> ment of pictures. It offered proof that the use of sound to augment dramatic
> and entertainment values is no mistake when used properly. And in this
> instance, the spoken dialogue was sensible, effective and often stirring. . . .
> The synchronization and spoken sequences are handled with a nicety which
> indicates that the Warners are getting a firmer hold on and a better under-
> standing of how far to go with the injection of sound into the no longer silent
> drama.
>
> It appeared that no attempt was entered upon to force spoken lines
> where they did not logically have a right. Therefore, when the characters did
> talk, the conversation fits in satisfactorily with the action and actually
> advances the development of the story. (*Film Daily*, 27 April 1928, p. 1)

These comments by Kann defending the use of dialogue *when appropriate* reveal an
aesthetic underlying the partial use of dialogue in Warners' 1928 productions. These features were perceived as properly using speech as a special effect, not as an integral part
of the mise-en-scène.

THE LION AND THE MOUSE premiered at the new Warner Bros. Theatre (6433 Hollywood Boulevard) on 21 May and contained more than 50 percent dialogue. Again,
reviewers praised the voice of the male lead, Lionel Barrymore, and complained about
that of the female star, May McAvoy. The *Los Angeles Examiner* stated, "Without the
Vitaphone, [it] would be mediocre entertainment. With the Vitaphone it becomes something of an innovation." The New York papers responded similarly. The *Daily News* felt
that the novelty of the spoken dialogue was more interesting than the picture. The
Evening World said the film was "both a startling demonstration of the possibilities of
talking movies and a horrible example of the things which might happen if this new toy
is not kept within complete control. And, as it happens, the horrible example sort of outweighs the other." In New York there were problems with reproduction: "Once or twice
the mechanics of the Vitaphone failed [Barrymore], sometimes making his voice a little
too resonant and on other occasions giving him more than a suggestion of a lisp." The
independent critic Welford Beaton totally disagreed. He thought that silent pictures
henceforth "will be as dead as the dodo."[34] *Film Daily*'s reviewer criticized the studio's
silent version for neglectfully cutting out too much of the plot and losing the talking version's dramatic effectiveness:

> If Warners had built this as a straightaway picture with punch and drama,
> the addition of sound would have made *The Lion and the Mouse* stand out
> as an extraordinary attraction. But they didn't. . . . The punch scene where
> Barrymore realizes money isn't everything and where he practically regen-
> erates himself is not shown at all. This robs the picture of its principal moti-
> vation and makes the result weak. (*Film Daily*, 24 June 1928, p. 5)

In other words, if the studio is going to release dual versions, the one going to silent
houses should be able to stand on its own.

Despite these decidedly mixed reviews, Warner executives were delighted with the
response to the dialogue sequences, as measured by the box office. In June their enthusiasm was reflected, first, when Warners stood by its promise that all pictures in the
1928–1929 season would have not just musical scores but talking sequences, too. Harry

The Lights of New York *(Warner Bros., 1928). "Take him for a ride."*

Warner said he now believed that the public's attitude toward dialogue justified the use of this "more elaborate effect." Second, THE LIGHTS OF NEW YORK was completed, "marking the first time that dialogue has been used throughout the picture." At fifty-seven minutes, this all-talker was just barely a feature, having grown out of a two-reel playlet called "The Roaring Twenties." The opening was at New York's Mark Strand on 6 July.[35]

Despite *Variety's* pan—"This 100 percent talkie is 100 percent crude"—THE LIGHTS OF NEW YORK was a box-office smash. The film cost $23,000 to make and took in $1 million.[36] Its silly story about a pair of barbers who become ensnared in big-city crime, its awkward acting and vocal rendition of hackneyed lines, and its obvious placement of the mike inside props, have earned it a reputation as the quintessential bad early talkie.[37] But overlooked are the genuinely interesting voices of some of the characters. While Wheeler Oakman's unintentionally hilarious "Take him for a ride" has become a classic golden turkey line, Eugene Pallette's gravelly baritone is diverting and, indeed, launched him on a long and productive career in the sound cinema. The Warners press kit emphasized the sound technique's novelty and intimated that it could bring the milieu of New York to moviegoers who might be unfamiliar with the big city: "There is the country girl working in a fashionable night club and this gives a great chance for showing, through Vitaphone, the entertainment given in these places. This is one of the best things for which the Vitaphone is responsible."[38] Hall again criticized the "s" distortion, observing that it was more pronounced in speech than in music and singing. The self-consciousness of the actors bothered him. They "do not seem able to forget even momentarily that not only their faces but their voices as well are being taken for posterity."[39]

Kann again offered to the producers some candid suggestions from the perspective of the consumer. Noticing laughter in the audience during the sentimental ending, he said that THE LIGHTS OF NEW YORK "proves all over again that the most rigid care must be exercised in the selection of words given the characters to speak." He praised the filmmakers' use of "masked microphones." This is the technique (made infamous by its send-up decades later in SINGIN' IN THE RAIN) of camouflaging the mikes as telephone receivers, hiding them in vases, and painting them to match the wall coverings. He noted approvingly that characters could now be heard when they turned away from the camera. Some players' voices worked well; however, some did not. The lack of action and the dependence on rehearsed stage lines bothered him: "We question most seriously the advisability of this [theater] method." He also criticized the sound editing of LIGHTS OF NEW YORK: "A something in sound pictures which is best likened to the fade-out in silent pictures is needed. . . . There the jumps between spoken sequences are abrupt and land harshly on the ear. The flexibility of the fadeout applied to sound in some manner will do the trick."[40] (About six months later, D. W. Griffith claimed to have invented the "first sound fade-out" in LADY OF THE PAVEMENTS [1929].)[41] Like Kann, the New York critics thought that THE LIGHTS OF NEW YORK was a bad film redeemed as an acoustic experiment. According to the *Sun*, it might even prove to be "a turning point in motion picture history." Reviews and the heat and rain in New York notwithstanding, business for THE LIGHTS OF NEW YORK was "phenomenal." It grossed $50,000 during its first week.[42]

In Los Angeles critics were more positive than in New York, but flaws were found with the slow story and hammy acting. Many of the reviews referred to the sound reproduction and acoustics. In particular, the distortion of "s" sounds was annoying. The *Los Angeles Express* commented on the volume level at the Warners' theater screening:

"Consonants still bother the recording technicians, and the hair-line between volume and naturalness seems to have them stumped." *Motion Picture* magazine also remarked on the distortion and linked it to the actors' manner of speaking: "The dialogue is marred by the apparent inability to record 's' sounds, and by the monotonous sameness of the masculine voices." Unlike Kann, this reviewer did not perceive the masked microphone as any improvement in the recording technique. "It is difficult to say which of several characters is speaking—it is thus far impossible to have the actors speak with their backs to the camera and the recording device."[43]

THE TERROR was advertised as the first "titleless" all-talking film, and truly it was a 100 percent talker; even the opening credits were spoken. The director, Roy Del Ruth, attempted some creative uses of sound—for example, signaling the villain's approach by offscreen footsteps, heard increasing in volume (an effect inspired perhaps by radio plays). It also had a specially arranged score by Louis Silvers that, unfortunately, sometimes drowned out May McAvoy's light voice and contributed the false impression that she, too, had a lisp. (Did people think that Warners hired only lisping actors?) When its run began in August, Kann went out on a limb: *The Terror* easily becomes the best talking picture so far made." He generously said that May McAvoy's voice via the Vitaphone was improving. What of the problem of showing the film in unwired houses? An all-talkie could not simply have intertitles inserted to make the silent version. Warners instead shot two films simultaneously, one with dialogue, one without.[44] This immediately so-called dual-version policy became the standard practice at Warners and elsewhere.

Critics liked the "100 percent all-talking" experiment, and some even liked the story, which was a clever thriller adapted from a 1927 hit London play by Edgar Wallace. Edward Everett Horton registered well, but "his gesticulations are a bit too Broadwayish," commented the *Daily News*. There were many complaints that the dialogue retarded the action, that the acting was bad, and that there was too much talk. McAvoy's voice, in particular, according to these less sympathetic reviewers, either lisped or "overloaded the machinery."[45]

Warner Bros. reported a profit of over $2 million for the fiscal year ending in August 1928. The astonishing turnaround was "attributable entirely to sound." Financial analysts reported that "[t]he last quarter of the 1928 year rolled up a profit of $920,894, a phenomenal figure and a most striking indication of the exhibitor demand for sound pictures such as *The Jazz Singer, Glorious Betsy, Lion and the Mouse, The Terror.*"[46]

Vitaphone Trailers

The sound film at Warners during this early period was a chameleon-like thing, changing and transforming to give a huge audience what it wanted. Warners took advantage of an opportunity that had evolved within the film program to address viewers directly: the prevue trailer. The many trailers the studio produced to entice viewers into its Vitaphone presentations are a neglected aspect of the studio's output.

The silent film trailer was a staid affair, often giving just the actors' names and a few descriptive phrases. Sometimes production stills or star portraits would be included. If the film was produced by Columbia, Film Booking Office, First National, Fox, MGM, Paramount, Pathé, United Artists, Universal, Warner Bros., or one of several independent producers, then the National Screen Service (NSS) held the exclusive right to make trailers using scenes from the studio's negatives. Founded in 1919, NSS was licensed by pro-

John Miljan introduces Al Jolson and Eugenie Besserer in the JAZZ SINGER *trailer, 1927.*

ducers to distribute lobby cards, stills, and posters as well as to make trailers. Not surprisingly, because NSS had no sound production facilities, Warner Bros. also made the first talking trailers. Well before the premiere program in October 1926, Warners was already profiting from having stars pitch films in their own voices. Press releases claimed that the studio's two biggest stars were appearing in sound trailers: Rin Tin Tin, the beloved German shepherd dog, and John Barrymore in a trailer for DON JUAN. For many actors and fans alike, these cameos were their first exposure to sound. Sam Morris, in charge of sales, announced that because trailers were so successful they would be adopted as a standard product and supplied for all Warner pictures "at actual cost basis." In 1930 Warners set up its own permanent trailer production unit, with Lou Lusty in charge. The trailers were marketed along with the features through the studio's exchanges.[47]

The sound film made possible this new style of advertising, which attempted to "sell" films to the public by emphasizing talking stars and sound itself as desirable commodities. These mini-films dispensed teasing dabs of the real product as a free sample.

The prevue that Warners prepared for THE JAZZ SINGER shows that the studio already had adopted a definite strategy for its advertising. The trailer was shot on 11 November 1927, at the Vitaphone Brooklyn studio. The director was Herman Heller, assisted by F. M. Long. It consists of a speech by the character actor John Miljan, clips from THE JAZZ SINGER, and documentary footage shot at the film's premiere. Though Miljan's talk lasts only a few minutes, the shoot required four hours (3:00–8:00 P.M., assuming a one-hour dinner break). There must have been a lot of setting up and adjusting going on. The trailer was made to advertise the second-run opening of Jolson's film at the Criterion theater on Broadway, and it was distributed nationally to advertise the general release of the film in key cities on New Year's Day 1928. The Vitaphone production records for this trailer describe the action: "Miljan enters from behind curtains" and appears before a "draped curtain set." He is framed from a low angle, the slightly tilted-up perspective simulating the audience's view from a little below the screen. The draped background blends into the curtained-off proscenium surrounding the screen in the movie house, creating the illusion that Miljan is standing on the theater's stage.

Miljan, whose demeanor is rather nervous, looks directly into the camera and begins addressing the audience. His voice seems rather high-pitched, and his eyes dart back and forth across cue cards as he reads them, seemingly without benefit of rehearsal. Two cameras record the scene simultaneously, one for the long shot, and one for inserted medium shots—standard procedure at Vitaphone. "He says he is making the first living Vitaphone announcement," the synopsis continues. "He then tells of the picture 'The Jazz Singer.'" Actually, he mainly lauds Al Jolson as a great star, quipping, "Mama, how that blackbird can warble!"

"He tells of the opening of 'The Jazz Singer' in New York City." Here the trailer shows throngs of fans milling outside the Warners' Theatre at the October 1927 premiere. Miljan, in voice-over, spots various celebrities as though he is watching the footage with the audience for the first time.

The one thing viewers were *not* given during THE JAZZ SINGER trailer was the opportunity to hear Al Jolson sing or speak. There are some teasing glimpses of him applying his cork makeup, but no talking. For that one would have to pay. Synch dialogue is provided "free" in the form of Miljan's address, but the real magnet, Al Jolson's voice, is withheld.

As the first Vitaphone shorts entered wide distribution, the problem of applause became acute. Because Warners was trying to re-create a virtual live performance, the directors instructed performers to imagine that the film audience was responding. When the tenor Beniamino Gigli, for instance, sang three numbers in CAVALLERIA RUSTICANA (1927), he perplexed some viewers by returning to take deep bows as though acknowledging applause.[48] If there was only a smattering of clapping customers, presumably the rest of the audience would squirm in uncomfortable silence. Warners, anxious to strengthen the perception that talking film was a kind of transmitted vaudeville, encouraged audience participation as though at a live show. To this aim, in June 1927, the studio commissioned a custom trailer from the National Screen Service: "The trailer contains special announcements at the end of a talking film, inviting patrons to applaud."[49]

In addition to trying to shape the response to its films, the studio quickly realized that trailers might be used for two-way communication with an audience. In this early stage of the transition, Warner Bros. was uncertain which genres would be most appropriate for sound treatment. On 13 January 1928, it filmed a general Vitaphone trailer for the purpose of eliciting audience preferences.[50] Conrad Nagel, then Warners' leading vocal celebrity, looked into the camera and made the plea:

> Ladies and Gentlemen:
> I have been asked by Warner Bros. and by the management of this theatre here to say just a word about the Vitaphone and to ask your assistance in creating programs for your own enjoyment. Most of you, no doubt, have already heard the Vitaphone and all of you have certainly heard about it. Vitaphone is the realization of the dream that has been before the motion picture industry since the making of the first camera, the day the silent drama would find its voice.
> Vitaphone has made spoken film drama possible.
> You will see pictures here accompanied by the Vitaphone symphony Orchestra of seventy-five pieces. In the prologue numbers you will see and hear such artists as Al Jolson, Marion Talley, Willie and Eugene Howard, Martinelli, Shuman-Heink, Irene Rich, Clyde Cook, Hobart Bosworth, Mitchell Lewis, Bessie Love, and in fact, the leading stage and screen talent of the country.
> So you see, whatever kind of entertainment you prefer, Vitaphone is prepared to give to you. The management of this theatre is particularly anxious to know just what your wishes are. As you witness the Vitaphone programs in the future, why not form the habit of showing your preference for certain numbers by applause after each number is finished. In this way, by the volume of applause, your theatre manager will have a very good idea as to whether you prefer a certain type of operatic number, a musical act, a comedy sketch or perhaps a dramatic playlet.
> Your opinions in turn will be passed on to the Warner Brothers Studios in Hollywood where Vitaphone numbers are made, to serve as a guide to planning your future entertainment. Vitaphone is opening a new era in theatre history. Given your cooperation and assistance, it will open other undreamed-of sources of happiness and entertainment. (Vitaphone trailer no. 2430, continuity, Warner Bros. Archives [WBA])

Audience feedback was hard to come by, so this request for direct response was valuable research for the studio. For its participation, the consumer was promised future entertainment better tailored to his or her tastes.

Vitaphone trailers clearly aimed to shape reception and to create anticipation for the coming feature. They quickly fell into a pattern, in effect creating a new film genre. A master of ceremonies—usually a costar or supporting member of the cast, always male—would appear in a proscenium and introduce another character or two. The discursive mode was a visual and narrative tease, spoken in second-person with eye-camera contact. The audience was presented with a few clips from the film and shots of the players, who might or might not be making a speaking appearance. Usually the star's "presence" was withheld as part of the come-on. Here is the dialogue continuity for THE LION AND THE MOUSE trailer spoken by William Collier, Jr., on 27 January 1928:

> Hello Everybody—
>
> My purpose here is to tell you about a picture coming to this theatre—a picture which will become one of the milestones of movie history—the first spoken film drama.
>
> That picture is the Warner Brothers picturization of one of the most powerful American stage plays, "The Lion and the Mouse."
>
> You've all marveled at the Vitaphone prologues, short sketches, the famous opera and stage stars and the symphony orchestra accompaniments. But in "The Lion and the Mouse" you will see for the first time a big dramatic film with spoken dialogue just as its [sic] done in a stage play.
>
> It's the biggest thing that ever hit the movies. Don't you think you'd like to hear the living voices of May McAvoy, Lionel Barrymore and Alec Francis? Of course, I speak too—but now you're hearing me.
>
> Just try to imagine a great drama like "The Lion and the Mouse," with the players in the big dramatic scenes speaking their lines as well as acting them.
>
> Here is a story of the clash of powerful wills. And no doubt you recall the unforgettable characters of this stirring play. Here we are—
>
> (1st cuts)
>
> Lionel Barrymore gives his most forceful characterization as the lion of industry and finance—Ready Money Ryder. Incidentally, he's a great fellow. And May McAvoy, the timid mouse who twists the lion's tail is simply immense. This was May's first experience in speaking lines and when she discovered how her voice sounded on the Vitaphone she got a wallop out of it as you'll get. And you ought to see how impressive she is in the big dramatic scenes—take a peep:
>
> (2nd cuts)
>
> Of course everybody loves Alec Francis. After seeing him as May's father, the kindly old Judge crushed by this Ready-Money man for giving an honest decision, I hope you'll have a little affection left for me. I play Ryder's son— in love with Miss McAvoy. Would you like to see the lovers together?—
>
> (3rd cuts)
>
> "The Lion and the Mouse" is the greatest dramatic work of America's great dramatist, Charles Klein. It was directed for the screen by Lloyd Bacon.
>
> And now, ladies and gentlemen. I hope you'll see and hear this play when it comes to the screen with the wonderful effects that Vitaphone can give it. I thank you. (Trailer for THE LION AND THE MOUSE, no. 2350, continuity, WBA)

This trailer, typically, invites the moviegoer to experience the feature film as though it were a live dramatic event transposed to the screen via Vitaphone's neutral translation. The film experience, Collier promises, will be just as good as attending the Broadway production. This trailer also illustrates how important stars' voices were in selling the movie. Giving glimpses of them but reserving their speech lured the patron back to the theater. The trailer is also a prospectus, outlining the genre, plot, and some key dramatic themes and conflicts. And, of course, it was mainly selling sound—with sound.

The trailer for TENDERLOIN, narrated by Nagel, was filmed in February 1928:

> Ladies and Gentlemen:
> I am going to impose on your good nature long enough to tell you a few things about a new picture that is coming soon—"Tenderloin."
> Perhaps you've heard about it and are looking forward to it already. It is one of the first great features put out by Warner Brothers to be presented with lines spoken on the Vitaphone.
> I don't have to tell you what Vitaphone is—the whole world's been talking about it since "Don Juan," "Old San Francisco," "The Jazz Singer," and "The Lion and the Mouse." But you will notice that each successing [*sic*] picture brings an advancement in the adaptation of Vitaphone to film drama. "Tenderloin" is a further step in this development.
> The star of "Tenderloin" is—well, you'll recognize her on sight—(a wistful close-up of Miss Costello)
> Dolores Costello—one of the most beautiful and gifted actresses on the screen as well as one of the most popular. And in "Tenderloin" for the first time you will not only see Miss Costello but you will hear her speak in several dramatic situations in the picture.
> "Tenderloin" is a gripping, tense crook melodrama, full of dramatic situations and colorful with the sinister light of the New York underworld background. It is the poignant love tale of a girl and boy tangled in the scheming meshes of a band of crooks and struggling frenziedly to escape. Miss Costello has the role of a dancing girl in a Bowery dive and the boy friend is played by the modest individual you see before you.—(Insert 2)
> Now don't get the impression that "Tenderloin" is all romance—although there is a lot of it in the picture. There's action in it—plenty of action. Take a look at this—
> (Insert scenes—fight—flood—etc)
> That should prove that "Tenderloin" is a picture you don't want to miss. It is one of Dolores Costello's best vehicles, and she is seen to rare advantage.
> I hope all of you will see, hear and [illegible] "Tenderloin."
> I thank you. (Trailer for TENDERLOIN no. 2420, continuity, WBA)

When Warners publicized Al Jolson in THE SINGING FOOL, the company took the unusual step of commissioning the National Screen Service to prepare a special nine-minute prevue. *Film Daily* reviewed the advance trailer as though it were a regular short:

> Al Jolson plugging his own picture is sufficient of a novelty to make this trailer better entertainment than the average short talker. Al walks on smok-

ing a cigar, and launches into a friendly chat about himself, his public and the coming attraction. He proves himself a good salesman, and by the time he walks off it's a cinch that the theater owner has his publicity work half finished for him. (*Film Daily,* 2 September 1928, p. 9)

The scant evidence we have of the reception of these trailers confirms that they were regarded as novel attractions in their own right. The reviewer for the *Detroit News* commented, "One of the most striking features of the Madison [theater] program is a 'trailer' advertising the coming Vitaphone film, THE LION AND THE MOUSE. Buster Collier comes right out and gives volume to some laudatory remarks concerning the production and easily adds his name to the list of those whose vocal chords [*sic*] are certain to be reckoned with when the talking pictures become the rage."[51] THE TERROR trailer invited the audience to participate in a game of whodunit. Alec Francis "makes a short speech. Then he introduces each actor or actress in turn. They all assert they are not 'The Terror.'"[52] Herbert Cruikshank, in his *Motion Picture* column, praised the trailer for THE TERROR as "one of the most interesting developments in the use of Vitaphone."

> These "Coming Next Week" reels are called trailers. Warner has introduced the talking trailer. For instance, in telling of their film, *The Terror,* which has both sound and dialogue, Alec Francis, who plays one of the characters, appears on the screen and talks about the show. Later he introduces the entire cast, each member of which says something about the film. (Herbert Cruikshank, "Soundings," *Motion Picture,* November 1928, pp. 66–67)

All of these trailers employ direct address, establishing an imaginary link to the audience. Nagel attempts to create the impression of physical contact in real time and pretends to acknowledge the response of a theatrical audience. The short films also exploit the fan-oriented appeal of seeing stars in their "natural" state, that is, outside of their performing roles. Importantly, this included speaking in their natural voice, as opposed to the stage voice prevalent in 1928–1929, a dialect adapted from the "sophisticated" New York stage. Nick Lucks's remarks, though scripted, reveal the attempt to project an offhand, self-effacing picture personality:

> I suppose you wonder what I do [in GOLD DIGGERS OF BROADWAY, 1929]? Well, I'll let you hear one of the songs I sing. [Sings "Tip Toe Through the Tulips"]
> These are only a few of the many songs I sing in the picture. I haven't time now to sing them all. These songs were especially written for this production, and I must admit they are all good.[53] However, if you don't like me in this picture, I hope you will like the songs. Thank you! (GOLD DIGGERS OF BROADWAY trailer, continuity, WBA)

The trailer for SHE COULDN'T SAY NO (1930) staged a fight between two characters. Chester Morris runs in and calms the audience:

> Wait a minute! Wait a minute! Now don't be alarmed folks. They'll have this argument settled by the time the picture plays this theatre and don't forget the title—SHE COULDN'T SAY NO. . . . And when it does play this theatre, you

Ad-Vance Talking Trailer advertisement, May 1929.

will not only see a wonderful picture, but you will hear wild Winnie Lightner, the original gold digger of Broadway at her best. (She Couldn't Say No trailer, continuity, box 1077, WBA)

Like the fan magazines, some of these trailers attribute sophisticated knowledge about show business to the moviegoers. Milton Sills, introducing Ben Bard in Love and the Devil (1929), assumed that the audience had seen his live performances as well as his filmed ones: "Ben Bard, whom you have seen in many screen impersonations and whose work you doubtless know in musical comedy and vaudeville, plays the part of the Italian tenor."[54] Similarly, it was acknowledged that a primary enticement was hearing a star's voice for the first time. Thus, in advertising Lilies of the Field (1929), the announcer began: "Particular attention is always attached to a screen star's all-talking production, so it is with great pleasure that I bring you the news of Miss Corinne Griffith's one hundred percent dialogue picture for First National Vitaphone, Lilies of the Field."[55]

The talking trailer, at least for the period 1926–1930, became an entertainment in its own right, not simply a pendant to the feature. The freshness of hearing stars speaking made audiences sit up and take notice. On the assumption that they had paid their admission to see the feature program, the trailer seemed to be gratis, an extra value. Having characters look you in the eye and speak directly from the screen was a startling departure from the "invisible fourth wall" theatrical aesthetic of the classical Hollywood cinema.

The radio emcee was a contemporary model for the direct address and interlocutory function of the Vitaphone trailers. The on-screen character who is both a narrative agent and a salesman resembles the announcer. In a typical late-twenties variety show or dramatic program, he (rarely she) would introduce the characters, intervene with information to move the plot forward, and suggest that the listener try a brand of soap flakes or toothpaste. Similarly, the masters of ceremonies in these trailers occupy a position between Hollywood and the consumer. Alexander Gray sounded very much like a radio pitchman in his trailer for No, No, Nanette (1929): "I am sure that you will all want to return to this theatre and see the picture in its entirety. It is a comedy, so don't come expecting to cry. Most of the music is new, but you will hear 'Tea for Two' and 'I Want to be Happy.'"[56] The announcers' status fluctuates between the image of "the star," a creation of celluloid illusion, and "the management," the spokesperson for the creators of Vitaphone.

The prevue is analogous to a free peek behind the curtain at a sideshow. Of course, prevues of coming attractions were advertising. But Hollywood had cleverly hit upon the technique of disguising product promotion as entertainment. Audiences cheerfully enjoyed films that sold films.

Like the carnival barker, the radio announcer, or the star speaking as a personal testimonial, the goal of these first talking trailers was to enhance sound as a thrilling novelty in its own right, to tease the fan with the promised future appearance of the speaking star, and to entice the customer to return for the "coming attraction."

6

Battle of the Giants: ERPI and RCA Consolidate Sound

We could no longer ignore the handwriting that was gradually appearing on the wall with a plainly audible screech of the slate pencil.
JESSE LASKY, WITH DON WELDON, *I Blow My Own Horn*, 1957

The Creation of ERPI

It is unlikely that cinema sound would have become established as an international norm without some dominant organization taking charge and setting an agenda. That company would need manufacturing capability, deep financial reserves, and a large workforce for sales, installation, and service. Warner Bros., Inc., was *not* that kind of organization. Prior to its Vitaphone experiments, the company was a supplier of low-budget "programmer" pictures, many featuring Rin Tin Tin. Its only human star was John Barrymore, and its one prestige director was Lubitsch. Yet Warners' powerful contract enabled it to control the dissemination of Western Electric's sound system. Indeed, the fact that this small operation was able to negotiate such favorable terms in April 1926 suggests that John E. Otterson's predecessors in the electrical behemoth did not regard Warners' film sound experiments as much more than a short-term field test.

Probably no one was more surprised by the success of Vitaphone than executives at Western Electric. After the unexpected triumph of DON JUAN, Otterson was convinced that Walter J. Rich and the Warners were more interested in putting Vitaphone into their own theaters than in making Western Electric products available to the largest possible market. The studio was using its exclusive access to Vitaphone to establish a commanding lead in sound. In an internal memo, Otterson told his superiors that the Vitaphone management was "incompetent and unsatisfactory" in its dealings with the studios.[1] Certainly, compared to AT&T's squadrons of representatives, Warner Bros.' sales staff must have seemed like ineffectual bumblers. Western Electric learned a few things about the sound movie business during the industry's reaction to Vitaphone in late 1926. There had been a change in fundamental conditions: the moguls who had dis-

Vitaphone advertisement, 1929.

dained sound were now ready to commit to it as a supplement to their existing programs. They began searching for ways to pool their corporate power. Meanwhile, RCA, which in theory was positioned as well as Western Electric to dominate sound, was making its move.

These were probably some of the considerations that led Western Electric to form the new division, Electrical Research Products, Inc., in January 1927. Its equity was held entirely by Western Electric. The offices were at 250 West Fifty-seventh Street. Otterson, of course, was president. With one thousand employees, it became the fastest-growing component of the Bell System. Its mission was to manage Western Electric's nontelephone products, services, and licensing. The sales staff marketed broadcast equipment, managed the transatlantic cable, and promoted devices for hard-of-hearing people. ERPI's fundamental enterprise, though, was installing and servicing sound motion picture systems.

One immediate effect was standardizing the cost of installing Vitaphone. Previously installation had been negotiated on a house-by-house basis. In February 1927, installation was set at $12,000, payable to Western Electric, not Warners. Like telephones in homes and businesses, the equipment remained the property of Western Electric, which had the right to reclaim it after five years.[2]

Otterson was in a dilemma. Since Vitaphone's 1926 agreement gave Warners exclusive sublicensing rights, ERPI could not initiate service without the studio's assent. But no other studio would apply for a license if Warners had the power to accept or reject it. Western Electric's way out of this catch-22 was to threaten to sue Vitaphone for *its* breach of the contract. This was alleged to have occurred when Vitaphone declined to license William Fox for Movietone, except under duress from Otterson. ERPI claimed that it was at liberty to bargain with the other producers. Waddill Catchings advised the Warners to renegotiate the contract rather than face a long court battle. In May 1927, Otterson got his revised agreement. The Big Five producers would be dealing only with Western Electric, not with a rival producer.[3]

The Five-Cornered Agreement

Owen D. Young, vice president of General Electric (with David Sarnoff, head of its RCA subsidiary), and Adolph Zukor, president of Paramount Famous–Lasky (and Jesse L. Lasky, his vice president), were the architects of the film industry's 1926 coordinated response to the introduction of Vitaphone. Aware of the Western Electric system and the Fox-Case system, they were investigating sound film as a possible expansion of RCA's phonographic and thermionic interests. This application might capitalize on GE's languishing film patents and forestall Western Electric's advance into a new area after having just exited broadcasting. Young had already acquired considerable experience in dealing with corporate giants and was a partisan of business associationism. In his previous negotiations (for example, for the distribution of RCA radio tubes), it had been his strategy to arrange mutually beneficial alliances when the more desirable goal of complete monopolization was not feasible.

Knowing of the studios' reluctance to subordinate themselves to Warner Bros., Young tried to seize the opportunity to interest the industry in the GE sound-on-film device. Twice, in October and December 1926, Young put together behind-the-scenes cabals to block Vitaphone's exclusive access. Fox had walked out of the first meeting. Young set up the second one in Palm Beach, Florida, to which he brought representatives from Famous

Players–Lasky, MGM, Universal, Producers Distributing Company (PDC), Fox, and Film Booking Office (FBO). Theater people representing the Shubert and Albee organizations were also present. E. F. Albee later breached confidentiality and reported that Young was promoting a merger of the RCA and Western Electric talking film systems. The entertainment giants would restructure Vitaphone to make sound equipment available to producers and exhibitors on their own terms. Young's idea seems to have been a replay of the formation of the RCA holding company a decade before. Zukor, however, convinced the other members that this plan would not work, and the meeting broke up.

Adolph Zukor had reason to know that the Young plan would not succeed because he himself had just failed to put together a similar deal with Vitaphone. He was still bitter. Harry Warner and his financial chief Catchings had approached Zukor around the time of the DON JUAN premiere in August. They reached a tentative agreement whereby Famous Players–Lasky and Warner Bros. would buy out Walter Rich and jointly operate Vitaphone as a canned presentation-act service. By November 1926, however, the deal had soured. Zukor told Western Electric that he would only deal in unison with the other major producers. Besides, Young's overtures were now being heard loud and clear. RCA's newly acquired access to Western Electric's amplification patents gave sound-on-film a new luster, and the industry representatives decided they should take a look. At a December 1926 meeting convened by Zukor after the Palm Beach conference concluded, the producers gave Sarnoff a chance to prove the merits of the GE sound device and to formulate an offer which would compete with Otterson's. The Big Five producers reconvened to adopt an all-for-one agreement on 17 February 1927.[4]

The plan, called the "Five-Cornered Agreement" by *Film Daily*, united Loew's (MGM), First National, Famous Players–Lasky (which, on 29 March 1927, changed its name to Paramount Famous Lasky Corporation), Universal, and PDC. (Fox had already signed with ERPI, and FBO was committed to RCA, so neither participated in the deliberations.) Each company appointed one member to a producers committee charged with achieving a solution to the various problems of sound. The membership was top-heavy with personnel from Paramount, whose general manager in charge of distribution, Sidney R. Kent, chaired the committee. Louis Swarts of the Paramount legal staff was a member. Roy J. Pomeroy, head of the special effects department, chaired the technical subcommittee. The producers pooled their economic power to force the Radio and Telephone Groups to compete with each other for the prize of the talkies. The actual text of the agreement, of course, was not so blunt. It highlighted issues of compatibility and stressed the public benefits of cooperation:

> Inasmuch as most or all of the systems now on the market are in an experimental stage and further development should follow the line tending toward standardization of devices to keep the market open to all, the five film companies will appoint a committee that will determine upon the system or systems best adapted for standardization in the motion picture industry. This committee will employ scientific experts and consult with governmental authorities and will make comprehensive experiments with all devices now or hereafter made available. (*Film Daily*, 23 February 1927, p. 5)

Other producers were cordially invited to send representatives (but none did). The moratorium was to last one year, so in theory the potential disruption that the sound film threatened had been contained.

In March 1927, there began a high-stakes competition as ERPI demonstrated its two Western Electric systems (Vitaphone and Movietone) in New York, and General Electric showed off the RCA Photophone (its eventual name) in Schenectady.

The producers' one-year moratorium was a boon to ERPI. "The most difficult part of the job," as Otterson described it retrospectively, was "that of selling a revolutionary idea to an established successful industry."[5] The agreement enabled Otterson to put together a package so sweet that no one could think of going with RCA. The American Society of Composers, Authors, and Publishers (ASCAP) was insisting on royalties for the music heard in movies. Otterson saw that a central organization could best handle the licensing chores. He followed the precedent set by AT&T in 1925 when ASCAP accepted a blanket fee in lieu of paying for the individual compositions played on station WEAF. ERPI paid $1 million to the society for film rights retroactive to DON JUAN and agreed to take out performance licenses for songs used in future Movietone and Vitaphone recordings. ERPI really had no choice since, in 1926, 11,000 exhibitors had taken out ASCAP licenses which would have prevented them from playing unauthorized sound tracks.[6] In December 1927, ERPI worked out an arrangement whereby E. C. Mills, "acting as agent and trustee for practically all of the music publishers in the United States," licensed music rights for motion pictures. In lieu of royalties to ASCAP and other performance rights societies, exhibitors paid ERPI a seat tax. The organization then negotiated a rate with the music societies. Though the music clearance office required a large staff, its operating expenses were absorbed into ERPI's overhead. By 1930, fifty-two British and ninety-seven Continental publishers also sublicensed through ERPI, bringing the number of compositions available to moviemakers to well over one million.[7]

During the wait-and-see period of 1927, ERPI engineers were installing Movietone and Vitaphone equipment for Fox and Warners and gaining valuable field experience. The pace was slow, at first taking up to six weeks to wire a single theater. The major studios' hesitation gave Western Electric time to gear up for high-capacity production and to iron out the remaining glitches in the system, of which there were several, even after the premiere of THE JAZZ SINGER. For instance, the development team requested additional funds after overspending its $15,000 budget, citing "numerous difficulties" with the theatrical amplifiers, including noisy tubes and a persistent AC hum.[8]

ERPI Gets a Head Start

In January 1928, Pomeroy's technical committee determined that three systems were acceptable: General Electric–RCA sound-on-film, Western Electric sound-on-disc, and Western Electric sound-on-film. The so-called Five-Cornered Committee disbanded in February and left producers and exhibitors to decide which system to use. From ERPI and RCA's view, there were two objectives. One was to win over the producers, the other was to convert the biggest theaters. ERPI won the battle for the moguls. The producers' financial backers felt more secure (or more prestige) being associated with the corporate giant AT&T. ERPI, emulating Western Electric practice, promised extensive on-site consulting and product support. Its established Western Electric equipment-manufacturing plant in Hawthorne, Illinois, was already grinding out recording and projection machines around the clock. A bet on ERPI was a hedge: whether disc or photographic recording won out, the producers would be covered. By the end of May, a beaming Otterson could report that Paramount, Loew's, United Artists, First National, Hal Roach, and Keith-Albee-Orpheum had signed ERPI licenses for the Western Electric system and would all use the name Movietone. Christie Studios signed in June, Universal in July, and Columbia, after a trial period, joined in September, bringing ten producers into ERPI's fold.[9]

The twenty-seven-page ERPI contract was designed to cover both production and exhibition. It was careful to prevent any of the sound technology from interfering with AT&T's telephone or radio business. An exception was made for experiments such as MGM's "Telemovies." The studios could make records to accompany other studios' product, as well as sublicense other producers according to defined conditions. Any sound patents owned or developed by the licensee, or any in-house improvements (perhaps anticipating tinkerers like Sponable at Fox and Pomeroy at Paramount), would have to be shared with ERPI. Producers' royalties were on a variable scale but were basically set at $500 per 10 minutes of running time, with a minimum of $50,000 per year. All licensees were entitled to the same rates. The studios were responsible for the living expenses of the ERPI consulting engineers during their visits to service the equipment. There was a long section on contingencies and indemnities in case patent lawsuits disrupted service. The agreement ran through the year 1944. Foreign royalties and music rights were addressed separately.[10]

While ERPI was the logical choice for producers, on the exhibition front the selection was not so clear. Managers of the affiliated chains installed what the home office told them to install: Vitaphone discs, often with the Movietone optical sound option. This left the minor chains and the independent theater owners to make the dreaded decision of whether or not to convert to sound, and which system to install.

It seems that Western Electric was slow in realizing the scope of the demand for sound equipment. In an internal memo from February 1927, a manager estimated that "the yearly demand [for theater amplifiers] will be approximately 200."[11] This estimate proved to be accurate for 1927, but as a long-term forecast, it was grossly inadequate. In April 1928, even before the major theater chains had signed with ERPI, Warners was already complaining that the installers were far behind schedule. Vitaphone tried to push ERPI into speeding up installations by invoking the binding arbitration clause in its contract.[12] Almost four hundred shorts and fifty features were available to rent, but in July 1928 only about four hundred theaters were projecting sound pictures, although twice that number of independent exhibitors had signed ERPI contracts. Western Electric enlarged its Hawthorne facility to handle the increased load. By August the plant had one thousand workers on twenty-four-hour shifts, but orders had fallen six months behind.[13] By the end of 1928, more than one thousand ERPI systems had been installed. The number would have been larger had Western Electric been able to keep up with demand.

Fox's Movietone equipment was also behind schedule, but William Fox chose to stay out of the fracas. One reason for his uninvolvement became clear when his vice president Winfield Sheehan told a *Los Angeles Times* interviewer that ERPI deals were already enriching the company. He explained that Fox Film and Fox Theaters controlled 50 percent of the Fox-Case Corporation, which owned the rights to Movietone and received royalties for all Western Electric installations in theaters and studios.[14]

The studios were adjusting rapidly to sound. By the end of 1928, one hundred disc recorders and sixty sound-on-film recorders were in operation.[15] Western Electric responded to complaints from producers using discs that other studios using the optical system had an unfair advantage when filming outdoors. ERPI introduced portable disc-recording units housed in two-ton vans similar to those used by Movietone News. The so-called Kearny Trucks, named after the New Jersey town where they were manufactured, made it possible to record anywhere there were roads.[16] ERPI's policy was to supply all licensees on an equal footing, thereby diminishing competition among users to maximize the diffusion of Western Electric products.

With the major and smaller studios alike announcing their plans to produce talkies, the largest exhibitors signing up, and Western Electric wallowing in back orders, it became clear to *all* theater owners that staying unwired was a greater risk than installing sound. Will Hays assured them that, unlike the earlier crazes,

> there is no doubt about [sound's] future. It will be universally adopted—that is, it will be used universally to the extent that it is used. Sound will be dramatized when such dramatization adds to the total dramatic value of the picture. Great new interest will be created, probably great new audiences. (*Film Daily*, 21 June 1928, pp. 1, 3)

Hays's statement about the drama of sound is gobbledygook, but his near-guarantee of "new audiences" made the investment seem like a sure thing.

The Beginnings of RCA Photophone

The creation of ERPI galvanized General Electric. Hoxie's Pallophotophone, dormant at the laboratories for a couple of years, was revived as the Kinegraphone. The sound-on-film system was demonstrated to the scientific press on 30 January 1927 in Schenectady, and to the film trade in New York at the Rivoli on 11 February. Hoxie's original system had been improved by adding Western Electric microphones and amplifiers (available because of 1926 RCA-AT&T cross-licenses) and by RCA's proprietary Hewlett loudspeakers, which used dynamic cones. GE began a campaign to show off the system's advantages to the studios. Its research laboratories emphasized that there would be minimal disruption to existing production techniques. This claim is not surprising because, in the spring of 1927, Photophone was being described as a system for post-synchronizing music to silent prints, mimicking the Vitaphone virtual orchestra:

> Development of this field requires no change in the technique of making the original film. After the original picture film has been made and titled, the accompanying music is played by a concert orchestra and is recorded on a film. The picture and sound are then printed on one film in the proper time relation. . . . The community picture house, accustomed to having a piano, or piano and violin, will be able to have the same music as the metropolitan theater. ("Talking Motion Pictures," *Scientific Monthly*, March 1927, pp. 286–89)

Perhaps acknowledging de Forest's interview films (and anticipating Movietone subjects), the prospectus also hypothesized a talking newsreel: "Not only will it be possible to show important persons, but they can talk to the audience, and visiting notables can extend their

greeting." The anonymous author admitted that "at this early date it is not possible to define the fields in which this new type of talking motion pictures will be of use."[17]

RCA commenced to market its reproduction equipment but lagged far behind Western Electric in manufacturing it. President James Harbord was able to announce on 14 September 1927 only that the system was "almost ready." He described the device as 1920s radio-with-pictures:

> In furnishing good music to the scattered motion picture theaters of the country, many of which still depend on a solitary pianist, it would seem that radio were destined to repeat there the service it now renders to millions of homes.
>
> The new system, employing the technique of radio reproduction, brings nearer the day also of the "talking movie" news picture, when current personalities will not only be shown on the screen, but will be heard by the audience as they are being interviewed by a movie reporter; the picture of an important event will be accompanied by all the stirring sounds that emanate from a great mass of people; the parade thrown on the canvas will bring the music of the bands and the cheering of the spectators. The system would have great educational value. (*Film Daily,* 15 September 1927, p. 6)

GE claimed that Pathé, First National, MGM, and United Artists were interested in jointly financing the General Electric–RCA system. It was decided that rights to the device, still referred to as the Kinegraphone or the Pallophotophone, would be sold to the highest bidder. For demonstration purposes, two reels of FLESH AND THE DEVIL (MGM, 1927) were given a synchronous score.

Owen Young was successful in keeping RCA in contention during the Big Five's 1927 system trials. He and Sarnoff must have felt that they had a powerful ally in Adolph Zukor, who was already experimenting with GE sound equipment. In April 1927, the trade press assumed that because of Paramount's influence, the Five-Cornered Committee would select RCA.[18]

General Electric technicians began working with Roy Pomeroy to make two special versions of WINGS (1927) with music and sound effects—propellers and plane roars. The technically sophisticated Pomeroy had developed two of his own sound systems at

Paramount. One used cued discs. The film opened to great acclaim on 12 August 1927 at the Criterion in New York and at the Erlanger in Chicago. "Each time an airplane hurtled in flames to the earth there was a doleful hooting behind the screen," reported Mordaunt Hall. "When the aviators are about to take-off and the propellers are set in motion, the sound of whirring motors makes these stretches all the more vivid."[19] The other system was Pomeroy's modification of the Pallophotophone; it read the optical track from a separate filmstrip as it was projected on a second interlocked machine. The sound-on-film device was utilized for the early 1928 road shows of WINGS. RCA provided the amplification and dynamic cone speakers for both systems. This system was less satisfactory. If the picture and sound films lost synch, it was difficult to restore. A break in either would raise havoc with a show.

In March 1928, after the wait-and-see agreement had expired but before the major studios signed with ERPI en masse, Jesse Lasky announced that Paramount was entering the sound field "in the greatest possible way." Zukor made an informal agreement with RCA and announced that the "Pomeroy Device" would be widely used, perhaps to make a talking newsreel. The equipment arrived in Hollywood for testing in mid-April. All twenty-five films in the upcoming 1928–1929 season would have synchronized tracks using this "Paramount-Tone" system. Victor Schertzinger was hired to arrange the scores. For his efforts, Pomeroy's six-year contract was renewed.[20]

The consensus of the Five-Cornered Committee had moved rapidly to Western Electric. The members acknowledged that the GE system was less cumbersome than Western Electric's, its synchronization was better, and RCA's financial terms were more favorable. But reports of bad sound and the frequent breakdowns plaguing the WINGS road show worked against RCA. ERPI had the corporate and financial clout of the telephone company behind it. The country was covered with a corps of 450 field engineers, and ERPI's operations in Europe and Asia were established. Plus, ERPI offered more than technical assistance. It cleared music rights and established projectionist training centers, for example. Perhaps most important, ERPI was wiring a theater a day, whereas RCA Photophone was still a creature of the laboratory. The technical sub-committee attended a side-by-side demonstration in Pomeroy's Hollywood lab, and a week later the Big Five chose not to mandate either ERPI or RCA. In a remarkable about-face, Paramount abandoned RCA and joined the other large studios in signing an ERPI license on 11 May. Zukor cited two factors influencing his decision. One was the availability of Victor Talking Machine music rights for accompaniment. Although RCA was known to be trying to purchase Victor, the major recording company had already signed a music licensing agreement with ERPI that would survive an RCA buyout. Zukor also took into account Western Electric's ability to produce machines and to wire theaters in quantity, since Paramount's extensive chain of Publix theaters would require sound projection without delay. The fact that ERPI was not endorsed exclusively suggests that the committee wished to keep its relations amicable with both these corporate giants.

David Sarnoff was ready for this. When the committee members sided with ERPI, he and Young put their contingency plans into operation. RCA Photophone was incorporated in March 1928, with ownership split 50–30–20 percent among RCA, GE, and Westinghouse. Sarnoff was president. But all the while the Five-Cornered Committee was deliberating, Sarnoff had been dealing with some powerful banking and securities interests represented by a Bostonian whose business acumen matched his own.

Robertson-Cole Studios, 780 Gower Street, Hollywood, late 1920s.

Enter Joe Kennedy

This major player was Joseph Patrick Kennedy (father of John F. Kennedy). He had been president of a bank (Columbia Trust) at age twenty-five, a shipbuilding tycoon, an importer, and a stock speculator. Recently his attention had turned to the movies. Operating a string of New England theaters convinced him that the big profits were being made by producers and distributors, not by exhibitors. Kennedy, said to disdain Hollywood's businessmen as "pants pressers," determined to buy into this burgeoning enterprise. In February 1926, he put together a partnership to purchase a small Hollywood studio, Robertson-Cole, and its New York distributor, Film Booking Office (FBO). Kennedy easily refinanced the operation, put FBO on solid footing, and furnished a weekly schedule of low-budget features, mostly Westerns, to small-town cinemas. For his vice president in charge of production, he hired William LeBaron, a seasoned Famous Players–Lasky associate producer. LeBaron was the image of the suave New York producer. Educated at the University of Chicago and New York University, LeBaron began his film career at Hearst's Cosmopolitan Productions. He had risen to general director when the company merged with Goldwyn in 1924. LeBaron did not wish to move to California at that time and joined Famous Players–Lasky. He had been in charge of the Paramount Long Island studio's feature production unit until it was closed in a downsizing move in March 1927. Kennedy enlisted his services and sent him to Hollywood to become vice president and general manager of FBO.[21]

Sarnoff, trying to divert the tide which was turning toward Western Electric's sound system, approached Kennedy in October 1927 to sway FBO into the RCA camp. Photophone bought a $500,000 stake in FBO, about 11 percent of the stock. Harbord

William LeBaron, 1929.

of RCA and Young of GE joined the FBO board of directors. On 6 January 1928, RCA and FBO jointly announced that the GE device was ready to be sublicensed to the film industry. Kennedy issued an optimistic statement:

> I have been vitally interested in the development of sound reproduction in conjunction with motion pictures ever since the first experiments along that line, and have watched with eager interest, every phase of the progress that has been made toward that end. Long ago, I was convinced that the so-called "talking movie" was only the first small step.
>
> The devices developed by the G.E. and the methods perfected by their engineers open the door to a development which is actually staggering in its possibilities, and I am happy indeed that FBO will be able to bring them to the industry. (*Film Daily,* 5 January 1928, pp. 1, 8)

Among the advantages of the Kinegraphone (Photophone) was that it could record either on the film taking the picture or on a separate film—the process now called double-system recording. "The two recorders can also be mounted separately and the sound and picture film negatives made as individual units, such an arrangement being preferable when the camera is being shifted constantly."[22]

The availability of the device was delayed until 6 April. Rather than sublicensing through FBO, producers and exhibitors would deal with the newly created RCA Photophone subsidiary. Subverting ERPI, the new combine promised to supply films to all exhibitors, regardless of the kind of equipment installed. Sarnoff also identified a potentially lucrative nontheatrical market which Western Electric had neglected. Since the Photophone equipment was relatively compact, RCA targeted schools and churches and developed a library of sound films for institutional and home use.[23]

National theaters were essential for competing with the majors, but when Sarnoff and Kennedy began talking in 1927, Kennedy had only a few houses to offer. During the formation of their alliance, though, a separate chain of events was unfolding in the vaudeville business. The Keith-Albee circuit merged with the Orpheum theater group to form KAO. The mover behind the deal was John "J. J." Murdock, a ruthless businessman and aggressive point man for his employer. Murdock had been involved in film since almost the turn of the century.[24] In June 1927, Murdock acquired on behalf of the KAO chain the Pathé film studio and the Producers Distributing Corporation. Pathé, one of the original movie companies, had become a rather stagnant distributor. The PDC studio was on the former Ince lot in Culver City and was controlled by its principal shareholder, Cecil B. DeMille. In February 1928, Murdock made himself president of Pathé and engaged his old friend Joe Kennedy to consolidate the two small filmmaking concerns. Though Kennedy was an "unpaid" special adviser, KAO invested $1 million in his FBO to interlock the organizations.

One of Kennedy's first tasks was to oversee Pathé's merger with PDC. This was not difficult, since a friend of Kennedy's, the copper baron Jeremiah Milbank, was a shareholder in both. Having made his movie millions financing The King of Kings (1927), he was ready to take his profits. But Kennedy had to placate the assertive DeMille, who was threatening to join United Artists if his demands were not met. A mutually beneficial reorganization was reached after six months of negotiations. PDC was subsumed, DeMille became a Pathé producer with a seat on its board of directors, and Murdock and Kennedy ended up in control of the enlarged Pathé Exchange.

But Kennedy already had a studio. For him (and for RCA) the most valuable asset in the merger was the Keith-Albee-Orpheum vaudeville houses, which could be converted to sound. Murdock sold out Albee by secretly transferring his KAO stock options to Kennedy. Milbank put together a syndicate which included Lehman Brothers, Chase National Bank, and other backers. Together they made a generous offer to Albee that, unbeknownst to the aging theater magnate, would deprive him of his voting majority. Kennedy installed himself as president of KAO in May 1928 and launched a reorganization. One historic change was the top-billing of films on the programs of the venerable vaudeville circuit.

Kennedy, with Sarnoff behind him, pushed sound. In January 1928, LeBaron supervised the dismantling and shipment of the GE lab studio from Schenectady to the FBO lot in Hollywood. A second studio was set up in the New York City RCA headquarters. Meanwhile, the GE and Westinghouse plants were said to be producing sound reproduction equipment in great quantities. The trademark Pathé rooster had its crow recorded in June. DeMille's KING OF KINGS and his last PDC/Pathé film, THE GODLESS GIRL (1928), both originally silent, were scheduled for national release on the 1928–1929 program with symphonic and choral scores recorded by RCA. Anticipating bad reviews of the latter, Pathé held up the New York release until April 1929 and added two talking scenes at the end, which everyone thought were gratuitous. As for DeMille, he quit Pathé and joined MGM as an independent producer.[25]

A major film studio also needed big stars, and FBO had produced mainly low-budget Westerns with two cowboy heroes. Tom Mix had been picked up when Fox did not renew his contract. Fred Thomson (husband of the screenwriter Frances Marion) was just as popular and admired for his daring stunt work. In 1928 he left FBO for Paramount and, unfortunately, contracted a fatal case of pneumonia. During this period Kennedy was associated with Gloria Swanson, one of the most admired stars of the silent era, who also had a reputation as a savvy business person. They had met in November 1927, and at first their relationship was strictly professional. He was a silent partner in Gloria Productions and set up her company on the FBO lot. But the two quickly became romantically involved. Swanson would seem to have been a logical candidate for the company's big star. Indeed, in February it was reported:

> Gloria Swanson, who is transferring production activity to the FBO lot, is being sought to appear in a picture to be made with Kinegraphone, [the] talking film device sponsored by the Radio Corp. of America, General Electric and Westinghouse. These three firms recently acquired an interest in FBO.
>
> William LeBaron, FBO production head, is expected to return [to Los Angeles] tomorrow, prepared to begin production of talking pictures. Some time ago it was reported that he was to supervise Gloria's next picture. (*Film Daily,* 1 February 1928, p. 3)

Swanson, however, was still bound by a distribution contract with United Artists and was therefore unable to participate in RCA's expansion. Kennedy did finance the production of this film, QUEEN KELLY (1929), but not for FBO (see chapter 12).

Sarnoff was looking for stars in the musical heavens. In January 1929, RCA purchased Victor's manufacturing and recording plant in Camden, New Jersey, its music contracts, and its extensive list of performers who would become valuable for both talking pictures and Sarnoff's National Broadcasting Company radio programs. Television's future need for talent was cited specifically as a further justification for the acquisition.[26]

Following the lead of the majors, FBO instituted sound production in New York to capitalize on local celebrities. The first Photophone part-dialogue film was THE PERFECT CRIME, which premiered 17 June 1928 and opened at the Rivoli on 4 August. Directed as a silent by Bert Glennon and starring Clive Brook, the sound version was touted by Sarnoff as proof that Western Electric's and RCA's systems were interchangeable, a claim immediately denied by ERPI's John Otterson. Most critics trashed the film. There were damaging reports that its synchronization was way off. This is puzzling. The film may have been shown with the sound on a separate optical track which had gone out of synch (as was the case with the WINGS road-show prints and with Photophone versions of LILAC TIME). Another possibility is that the dialogue had been improperly dubbed over the original silently shot footage. Neither FBO nor Pathé was capable of shooting live dialogue until about August, when the Photophone equipment became operational in the studios. On 22 August 1928, Kennedy signed Photophone licenses and set up a lab called Sound Studios, Inc., within the Manhattan Studios (124th Street and Park Avenue). Sarnoff acquired music licenses from the Music Publishers Protective Association (MPPA). The facility was under the direction of Robert T. Kane, a former First National and Paramount producer. (It was Kane who had introduced Swanson to Kennedy.)[27]

For three months in 1928, Kennedy, the forty-year-old financier-turned-mogul, even took charge of First National. Founded as a consortium of theater owners, it had started a production branch to compete with the major studios. Now it was being torn apart from within by powerful competing theater chains, of which Stanley was the largest. Westco, owned by William Fox, had one-third of the shares in First National. Other franchisees included Balaban and Katz, Skouras Brothers, Saenger, and KAO. The First National board wished to hire Kennedy to reorganize the company as he had done with Pathé. One of his first moves, which stunned the industry, was to attempt to renege on First National's commitment to the Western Electric system and switch to Photophone. This was after the synchronization of LILAC TIME using Firnatone, its proprietary disc system manufactured by Victor, had already begun. Kennedy pointed out that no contract had actually been signed with ERPI. After this, and realizing that Kennedy intended to merge their company with the Pathé group, the directors of the First National board became hostile and declined to ratify his appointment. On 14 July 1928, First National rebuffed Kennedy by forcing him to sign with ERPI. The trade was stunned again. Kann editorialized:

> Here Kennedy has RCA and General Electric as partners in FBO and yet, First National, one of Joe's "specially advised" companies signs with Western Electric for sound. Nobody would have believed it. But it was all decided the day Kennedy left for the Coast. A number of fellows traveled up to Harmon [north of New York City] with him and when the arguments cleared away, it was all set for F.N. to go Western Electric. (*Film Daily*, 22 July 1928, pp. 1, 28)

The loss of the First National franchise was a blow to RCA and contributed to the deterioration of relations between Kennedy and Sarnoff. Kann observed that Kennedy's inability to deliver First National's theaters would have no permanent effect on RCA: "If you think [Sarnoff's] outfit, backed as it is by millions, is going to allow W.E. to walk away with the sound picture field, you need some straightening out. So watch Sarnoff. He's clever."[28] Shortly thereafter, RCA balked at Kennedy's proposal to build a $1 million studio in Manhattan. This was but one bone of contention in a power struggle between two stubborn individuals.

Kennedy told his recalcitrant board of directors at First National that he would resign if he did not get the complete control he wanted. He first flexed his muscles by announcing a 40 percent cut in overhead. Then he refused to renew Richard A. Rowland's contract, which expired 2 August 1928. Rowland had been in charge of production at First National since 1921. Kennedy also fired twenty-five other executives and placed LeBaron (already heading production at FBO and Pathé) in command of First National. One draconian plan was to dismantle Pathé's Culver City facility (formerly DeMille's) and relocate it in First National's Burbank studios, which would be converted for sound production. He was planning a huge merger that would have combined all the Kennedy interests with the Stanley theater chain and Warner Bros. But the First National board, which was advised by Waddill Catchings (who also represented Warners), voted against him. Despite these internecine feuds, when Kennedy's contract was finally signed, the board of directors gave him free reign for five years, $150,000 annual salary, and an option to buy 25 percent of First National's stock.[29]

On 17 August, a week after signing his five-year contract, Kennedy announced he was quitting First National. When Kennedy licensed Photophone for FBO and Pathé on 22 August, he also secretly sold RCA an option to buy the controlling interest in FBO. Then he departed on a five-week transatlantic vacation.[30]

Emboldened by First National's resistance to Kennedy, the KAO board of directors showed mutinous tendencies as well. They declared that his contract, which was set to expire on 1 December 1928, would not be renewed unless efficiency and morale improved. Kennedy seemed to be wearying and extracting himself from the film business. During a radio address on 30 September 1928, he said:

> The day has gone when the intelligent public we seek as permanent customers will tolerate a hodge-podge of poor plots and pretty faces. They want substance to stories and real acting. Perhaps the time will come when television will carry the best of entertainment into the home. I don't know. . . . But one thing I do know, and everybody who has any business in the amusement business should know—that sophistication is on the increase, and that prizes in the form of profits only go the way of producers who bet their brains and money in the long run on popular intelligence. (*Film Daily*, 3 October, 1928, p. 4)

In October, while Warners was reportedly attempting a hostile takeover of Kennedy's Keith-Albee-Orpheum and the shareholders were complaining of his drastic cuts, Kennedy sold his stock in KAO and FBO to RCA. In addition to the appreciated value of the shares, he received $150,000 from RCA for his services as a facilitator. He resigned from both companies (but stayed as head of Pathé). A later audit would reveal that KAO-FBO had lost $1,064,278 during the eight months ending 31 August 1928. But after less than three years in the film business, Kennedy was some $5 million richer. By 23 October, Sarnoff had at his command KAO and its 200 theaters, the Hollywood production facilities of FBO and Pathé, the potentially lucrative RCA Photophone system, and the licenses, research staff, technological prowess, and corporate clout of RCA.

The new holding company, Radio-Keith-Orpheum, was formed on 21 November 1928. Sarnoff was RKO's first chairman. In January 1929, he completed his purchase of the Victor Talking Machine Company, placing RCA in a position not only to dominate the radio-phonograph industry but either to go head to head with Western Electric in talkie production or to collude with them on noncompetitive strategies. Kann predicted the latter. No protracted battle would take place. "Here is significant indication that Western Electric and RCA have no thought of open tussles insofar as sound is concerned. They will be competitors quite naturally, but that friendly cooperation is to mark their efforts may be taken for granted."[31]

Sarnoff selected a site in New York on Sixth Avenue and Twenty-fourth Street for RKO's new Photophone sound stage. RCA had already taken out a master music performance license with ASCAP. The industry was surprised when RKO won the bidding war for *Rio Rita*, a Harry Tierney operetta which Ziegfeld had turned into the biggest Broadway hit of 1927.[32]

At the end of 1928, Western Electric ruled the nation's sound film supply. The ERPI-signed studios had announced plans for 156 features and 712 shorts using the Western Electric system. RCA, by comparison, had 16 features and an insignificant number of shorts in production. Its most important client was the independent producer Tiffany-Stahl. All other systems combined had about two dozen features in the works. In theaters, the Photophone equipment promised in April began trickling in around November. Customers complained frequently that it did not work well.

RCA also announced that it planned to market a disc system which would sell for about one-third the price of Photophone. The machine obviously was intended to play Vitaphone records in addition to disc copies of RKO sound tracks. Though exhibitors could play these discs physically, could they play them legally? It appeared that reproducing Western Electric sound tracks on RCA players would violate the exclusivity clauses of ERPI's contracts with studios and exhibitors.

The Interchangeability Dispute

Sarnoff, beaten out of the production end by ERPI, concentrated on Otterson's weak area, expensive theater installation. RCA played a trump card: the Photophone system could project any optical track, and the company would gladly sell it to any exhibitor at a price substantially below ERPI's Movietone equipment. RCA initiated an ambitious advertising campaign pitched toward exhibitors who had not committed to any sound system. The goal was to convince them that Photophone was not only technically and legally interchangeable, it was intrinsically a superior system because of its connection to radio science. The advertisements declared that, "in the entertainment field, *Science* has always blazed the trail." Radio engineers were responsible for the system's acoustic excellence: "Much of the effectiveness of 'talking' pictures is dependent upon the skill exercised in the placing of the microphones. The Radio Group's vast experience in such work as the result of its broadcasting activities will be utilized in the production of all films."[33] Tonal fidelity was said to exceed Western Electric's, thanks to the variable-area track, which was implied to be better than the variable-density track. RCA used cone loudspeakers rather than horns, supposedly for a flatter frequency response. Photophone never lost synch because it did not require a phonograph. RCA claimed that the prints were more durable. The sound track was more permanent than records.

Projectors were more easily modified. The prints provided "full-sized" pictures. This last benefit was obtained by optical-printing the full-frame negative onto the release print, creating a wide frame line that slightly reduced the picture size. This made room for the sound track while preserving the original aspect ratio. Finally, RCA said that projectionists could service the equipment themselves, saving the theater the expense of the mandatory ERPI service contract. Underlying these bold claims, though, was the reality that Westinghouse, where the equipment was to be manufactured, was not yet ready to begin production on a commercial basis. An ad in June 1928 acknowledged that production was behind demand, but RCA tried to assure exhibitors, "You can afford to wait."[34]

Otterson countered Sarnoff's claims about interchangeability: "We have had no occasion to either try other types of sound films on our projectors or to adapt our own records and films to use on other machines. Why should we?"[35] ERPI exerted control over exhibition through its leases with exhibitors and its license contracts with producers. But the ambiguity in the "quality" argument began to backfire as RCA, Pacent, Bristolphone, and other competitors claimed that their systems met or exceeded Western Electric's standards. Otterson issued a statement on 26 June acknowledging that the exhibitor physically could run other films on Western Electric equipment, but the "responsibility would of course be his own and not that of the manufacturer or the equipment."[36]

In fact, at the time the two optical systems, RCA Photophone and Western Electric Movietone, were similar, because of the cross-licensed patents, but not absolutely identical, owing to their ancestry in different labs. The width of the sound tracks on the prints was slightly different. Kann aired the exhibitor's lament that the compatibility issue must be resolved: "Why not? When you buy a Radiola, you don't have to use RCA tubes, do you? If you prefer a Brunswick talking machine, what is to prevent your using Victor records? Or any one of several gases in your car? The results may not be alike, it is true, but that, after all, is a consumer's, not a manufacturer's, problem."[37]

One significant—and at the time puzzling—test was the initial Broadway screening of the re-released synchronized sound version of The King of Kings. Scheduled to open at the Rivoli on 8 July 1928, the Pathé print had what the engineers called a "loud" track, 100 mils wide (a mil is one thousandth of an inch). The Rivoli was a Western Electric house, and the projectors were calibrated for an 80-mil sound track, producing distorted audio. Western Electric sent engineers, who were able to replace the pickup just before show time. ERPI hastily stated that "this was done at the request of officers of the Radio Corp. and is not to be construed as a precedent as to its future policy under like conditions."[38] Why was this assistance given to a competitor? Later FCC testimony revealed that Sarnoff and Otterson were discussing an agreement that would have ended their direct competition. It resulted in a letter allowing RCA-produced films to be exhibited on ERPI equipment—as in the King of Kings case—but no other concessions. Anticipating a future alliance, ERPI did not mount a strenuous defense of the interchangeability clause after July 1928, and RCA's lawyers determined that its equipment could be used for recording by other studios.[39]

In order to solve the mechanical problem, RCA changed the dimensions of the Photophone sound track and projector slit to match the Western Electric 80-mil width. While Otterson was out of the country in August, Sarnoff conducted a trade demonstration at the Astor Theater and announced with fanfare that Western Electric films had been proven projectable on Photophone equipment. Afterward the interchangeability issue became more of a legal concern for exhibitors than a technical question.

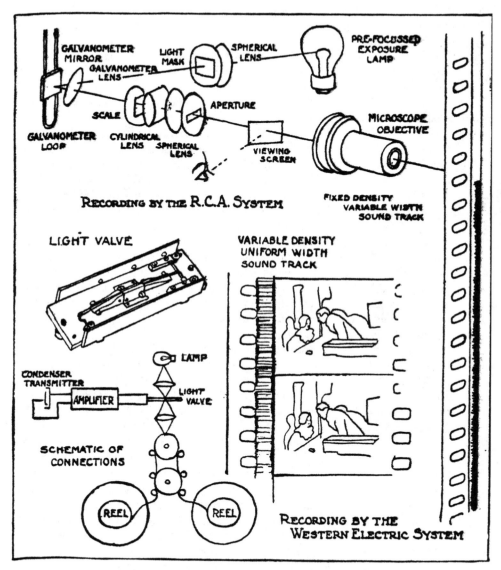

Two types of optical sound tracks (from Krows, Talking Pictures, *1930)*

In acquiring their ERPI licenses, producers agreed that they would not allow their sound tracks to be reproduced on non-ERPI equipment. The wording of the particular clause was couched in a "quality" argument:

> Licensee recognizes the highly technical nature of the said methods, systems and equipments, and of the art of recording and reproducing sound for the purposes herein contemplated, and that the production of sound records under the licenses herein granted and the reproduction of sound from such records by the use of equipment or with methods and systems other than those prescribed by [ERPI], may produce results of such inferior quality as to seriously impair the prestige and business reputation of the parties hereto, and also that uses of said equipments otherwise than as herein licensed may involve infringement of patent rights of third parties. Therefore, in order to secure and insure the proper production of sound records made hereunder and the proper reproduction of sound from such records to the satisfaction of the parties hereto, Licensee agrees that it will use the recording equipment to be leased to it by [ERPI] as herein provided, pursuant to the methods and systems and in the manner prescribed by [ERPI] from time to time, and that it will distribute sound records made hereunder only for use with, on, or in connection with, reproducing equipment which operates properly, reliably and efficiently to reproduce sound from sound records made hereunder, with adequate volume and of quality equal to that obtained by the use of equipment supplied by [ERPI]. (Recording License Agreement, p. 5)

The company's right to rule whether the quality of another system matched its own was a veto power which it used to keep other manufacturers' films and equipment out of its licensed theaters.

ERPI's tolerance was tested by a theater owner who showed LILAC TIME (First National, 1928, released with Vitaphone discs) on a Bristolphone disc system in Hagerstown, Pennsylvania. Distributors who balked at delivering prints and discs of LILAC TIME to non–Western Electric theaters in Detroit and Madison, Wisconsin, were sued by newly aggressive theater owners. Producers and the regional exchanges were also upset with the inconsistent enforcement of the ERPI interchangeability clause. In October, MGM and First National became the first majors to announce that they would rent their pictures to non–Western Electric houses unless the quality of the sound system was unacceptable. With his major licensees forcing his hand, Otterson conceded in a 23 October statement that other systems were mechanically interchangeable and that ERPI would not interfere as long as the equipment was of high quality. Independent exhibitors, who, in Kann's words, had been "floundering in a sea of uncertainty," now were free to order sound equipment from almost any manufacturer without jeopardizing their access to major studio releases. On 28 December 1928, Otterson issued a statement to ERPI's producer-licensees that, though persisting with the quality argument, basically told them to furnish product to anyone. "If other manufacturers can build and sell equipment as good as ours for less money, and it is equipment that does not infringe our patents," he wrote, "they deserve the business and will get it."[40] Two months later, Red Kann could observe that the "interchangeability issue" had moss growing on it.[41]

Disc versus Optical Sound

With compatibility between optical systems assured, the changeover from disc to sound-on-film was very rapid. Until mid-1928, most sound films were recorded and played back on ERPI disc systems. The second half of 1928 and the beginning of 1929 was a time of transition. Most studios switched to sound-on-film registration, but in theaters playback was mainly on disc. By the end of 1930, however, the majority of theaters projected Movietone, Photophone, or an off-brand optical sound track. A decreasing but sufficient number of exhibitors continued to order sound tracks on discs. What caused this turnaround, and why did some theaters resist the change? Standardization may explain the industry's motives. Producers wished to consolidate a redundant manufacturing operation. It may also be the case that they made a deliberate effort to drive discs out of the exhibition market.

In the first months of 1929, the most important distributors, Paramount, MGM and United Artists, announced that they would discontinue disc releases. Recording the primary sound track on disc was a practice that, except at Warners and First National, had failed to catch on in Hollywood. Nevertheless, most studios, including the ones which had always recorded optical sound tracks (Fox, Pathé, and RKO), supplied disc versions of all their sound-on-film releases.

The film producers claimed that their motive was to eliminate the competitors' poor-quality reproduction as a service to exhibitors and the public. (This strategy mimicked the telephone company's "quality" argument put forth to justify its monopoly.) Sidney Kent at Paramount led the charge against discs. Surface noise and scratches, he said, inevitably crept into disc recordings. The records were physically bulky, hard to handle, and broke easily. The average one was good for no more than twenty runs.[42] Kent also stated that optical sound had better tonal quality (a vague claim which many disputed). Pat Powers, promoting his own Cinephone optical system, was quick to characterize discs as uneconomical, especially because multiple shipments of backups were necessary. Optical sound prints were easily repairable, unlike prints for disc systems, which required "patches," "injecting ugly flashes" into the picture. (Powers was referring to the blank frames which had to be inserted in a projection print in order to maintain synchronization with the disc if the print had been damaged.) A director at Tiffany-Stahl, Al Ray, disliked the aural properties of discs. "Nothing can be more annoying than the scraping of a needle on a record," he asserted. "This is always heard when using the disc method of recording." Marty Cohen, his film editor, liked optical because there were "no jumping or screechy tones." Carl Laemmle, Jr., at Universal noted that optical sound avoided the possibility of the exchange shipping the wrong discs with the film. The Fox director Charles Klein (a former assistant of de Forest) claimed that the notorious lisping and other diction problems were handled best by film recording.[43]

Directors were enthusiastic about the flexibility to be gained in double-system recording, in which the sound track and the picture were photographed on separate synchronized filmstrips. Fred Niblo, MGM's star director who was currently at work on REDEMPTION (1930), explained his preference:

> The chief advantage is that the sound track and the film of pictorial action both receive proper development. With Movietone, one or the other must be favored in the developing process. With the double film track, each

receives most careful attention. THE BROADWAY MELODY, for instance, utilizes this film recording.

The Disc process is easiest to synchronize because facilities for reproducing are more advanced. The principle follows closely that of phonograph recording. Most trailers utilize the Vitaphone disc for their short subjects. The disc has limitations technically, in being unable to record the very low or high sounds that can be clearly discerned on synchronized film, with its greater register. (*Film Daily*, 18 June 1929, p. 3)

The veteran exhibitor Barney Balaban disputed the quality claim for optical but nevertheless gave a pragmatic reason for choosing it: "While at the present time it is our experience that sound-on-disc gives better tonal results, we find sound-on-film to be so much more simple and convenient to handle that we feel it is much to be preferred."[44]

Only Warner Bros./First National said they would continue recording and distributing Vitaphone discs exclusively. Albert Warner responded to Paramount's optical-only test by saying that his company was still sold on discs. Warner lieutenants lined up to agree with their generals. The Vitaphone vice president George Quigley prudently said he was more worried about keeping up with the demand for installation. Darryl Zanuck, though his claims were rather dubious, positively raved about disc, "the only system which permits music to be synchronized beneath dialogue, thereby allowing the symphony orchestra to play a score throughout a picture." He felt that the phonographic technique gave a more accurate reproduction of voice and sound effects and generated less surface noise. "I sincerely believe," Zanuck testified, "that all companies will ultimately release their talking pictures on discs."[45] A 1929 ad emphatically assured theater owners,

> Warner Bros. will continue to supply their productions exclusively on discs. Experience and research have conclusively proven the superiority of Discs over any other method of sound recording. Our confidence in Disc recording has been further confirmed with the excellent results obtained in connection with the increased use of Technicolor. Until engineering science has evolved some better system, we shall continue to record all of our productions exclusively on Discs. (*Film Daily*, 31 October 1929, p. 12)

But even Warners had to admit that optical sound was editable. At some time around 1930 its engineers began transferring disc recordings to optical for editing, then rerecording the final track back to disc for release. In 1931 Warner Bros. stopped recording on disc, though it continued to release sound tracks transferred to that format.[46]

The partisans of optical sound claimed that their system sounded better, but the quality argument did not hold up. The Western Electric disc was the state of the art in phonographic reproduction. Merritt Crawford, an electrical engineer and sound specialist, wrote, "[S]ound-on-film is certainly not superior to sound-on-disc in tone quality, while in photographic values it is, on the average, much inferior. . . . The chief arguments against the disc are not based on its sound reproducing quality, but on the material of which the disc is made." He predicted that the discs of the future would be made of metal.[47] Neither the disc nor the optical system was perfect, and there was no impartial verdict in the trade press on the acoustic merits of one or the other. For present-day researchers, listening to modern restorations of disc recordings reveals them to be less noisy than early optical sound, with a limited but pleasing frequency range. Optical prints invariably have a loud background hiss but seem to reproduce high frequencies more accurately. These, however, are subjective opinions that do not (and cannot) take into account the effects of the extensive electronic re-mastering that the restoration and transfer process usually entails. Furthermore, even if we were to compare playbacks on original equipment, we would not resolve the question satisfactorily, for we cannot duplicate the acoustics of, say, the Rivoli's optical versus the Warners' disc installations, and contemporary accounts noted significant variations in reproduction from theater to theater.

The motives of the producers in discontinuing disc were more likely to have been economic than aesthetic. We might speculate that some of the anti-disc sentiment was orchestrated by ERPI against Warner Bros., which, after all, was openly backing Pacent, a competing disc system (discussed in chapter 8). For the distributors, circulating a second sound track added an extra overhead expense. Most important, the cheap unlicensed systems with bad reproduction were almost all disc-based and installed in unaffiliated theaters. The ERPI-licensed producers and movie chains must have realized the obvious competitive advantage to be gained from squeezing rival discs out of the marketplace. Making film sound optical-only was one way to accomplish this objective.

The campaign against disc systems by the major producers, if it existed—and the question is still open—was not immediately successful. Without giving any reasons, Paramount decided to end its experimental discontinuation of discs and, in May 1929, went back to releasing sound tracks in both formats. By the end of the year, MGM and UA had also brought back discs.[48] One reason was Vitaphone's huge hardware advantage. At the start of the sound conversion, Movietone had been treated as an optional accessory. So every house wired by ERPI before 1929 had the basic disc system. Many had dual components, but none had optical-only. The studios conceded that some discs would always be used and continued to support disc and optical sound. MGM in 1930, for instance, was still making dual-purpose prints. In addition to its optical Movietone tracks, it had edge-numbering for disc synchronization. Labs included instructions and stern warnings to projectionists on print leaders.[49] Even RCA recognized the importance of the market for discs. In late 1931, the company introduced its new twelve-inch Vitrolac shellac disc. It weighed only four ounces, compared with the twenty-four-ounce Vitaphone record.[50]

Sound-on-film became the standard for large theaters through a combination of factors: the concerted efforts by ERPI and the studios, market forces of supply and demand, and the optical format's projection convenience. Small exhibitors were loathe to abandon their investment, so disc playback lingered on. But these houses were in the nation's backwaters. At the 1930 SMPE convention, a paper on disc versus film recording "failed to awake any warm discussion."[51] Respondents to a survey in August 1930 revealed that half the theaters in the country no longer were equipped to use disc recordings, but in New York City only 4 percent of the theaters played discs.[52] Though the majors obviously wished to do away with disc sound, servicing the silent houses continued as long as the rental return justified the cost of maintaining this separate system of sound distribution.[53]

As late as 1931, 5,000 theaters were equipped for disc accompaniment only. In March 1932, there were 3,500 theaters which could not project optical sound.[54] Long after ERPI's disc recorders had been mothballed by the studios, many of its durable playback units remained in service.

Challenges to ERPI

ERPI's one-thousandth installation occurred at the Lucas Theater in Savannah, Georgia, on 24 December 1928. Impressive though this was, the competition was expanding much faster. Sound was still an urban phenomenon; three-quarters of the most important theaters in big cities had been wired by the end of 1928 (although they constituted only 5 percent of the total U.S. theater census).

Many independent theater owners were eager to acquire licenses after the studios announced sound production, but they did not like the terms of ERPI's agreement. Midwest exhibitors gathered in Des Moines to lament the plight of the small showman. Despite the initial rhetoric about the sound film's spreading of "democracy," few theaters in towns with population less than 25,000 could afford to invest in ERPI equipment. Showing the films was expensive. The rental fee for sound prints tended to be double that of silent films. Discs had to be purchased outright. Then there was the ERPI service charge and mandatory service contract. The small exhibitor's only option was to hold out until competition brought lower prices, better terms, and alternative equipment. The owners sensed—correctly, as it turned out—that the small chains and the independents were in for a rough time. Abram Myers, immediately after becoming head of the Allied States Association theater owners' trade group in January 1929, sought relief for exhibitors (and indirectly producers) by asking the Justice Department to outlaw agreements that restricted Western Electric–recorded product to approved machines. This was a direct attack on ERPI's recording and exhibition license agreement. Myers claimed that the situation was no different from the government's suit against the Motion Picture Patents Company in the early days of the industry.[55]

Not only were theater owners mad at ERPI, but RCA also threatened to sue Western Electric for violating the Sherman Antitrust Act. Sarnoff complained to the Department of Justice that the exhibition contract restrained RCA's trade. At some time during 1928, Western Electric's share of the exhibition market slipped to below 50 percent. Photophone and "gray market" sound systems ate further into ERPI's market share. Western Electric responded by advertising a standard price tag—$5,500 for a disc or optical playback system, $7,000 for both. The service charge was also reduced.

With demand exceeding supply, the remaining 95 percent of unwired theaters was fertile territory for ERPI's competitors. Many of these small-company outfits simply patched a phonograph into the theater's public address system to play nonsynchronous background music. The synchronous devices were knockoffs geared to play the unique Vitaphone format: a 16-inch-diameter disc which rotated counterclockwise at 33 1/3 rpm. Only three competing systems (Cinephone, Phonofilm, and Sonograph) were sound-on-film.[56] W. Drake, an ERPI executive, identified these "icicles" as his corporation's biggest challenge:

> It is competition. As with every other successful enterprise, there have been a large number of imitators (icicles as they call them in the motion picture business) who have entered the field looking for easy money. . . .
>
> They have brought about a condition that is disturbing not so much from our own viewpoint as from their effect on the public's response to talking pictures. As far as we know there is not a single bootleg equipment giving satisfactory reproduction in theatres. (*Erpigram*, 20 June 1929, pp. 1, 4)

TO THE PRODUCER

POWERS

CINEPHONE

ONLY EXPERIENCE
CAN PRODUCE QUALITY

THE ORIGINAL PIONEERS IN THIS NEW ART OF THE DIRECT PHOTOGRAPHY OF SOUND ARE EITHER IN THE POWERS ORGANIZATION OR ARE ASSOCIATED WITH IT.

As a result THE POWERS CINEPHONE EQUIPMENT CORPORATION can record and reproduce sound with greater accuracy than those who are only now gaining their first experience.

To this organization, skilled in sound recording, Mr. Powers brings the vital factor of long years of experience and the highest technique in the Motion Picture Art.

This combination eminently qualifies the Powers organization to apply sound to motion picture negatives either during or after the filming of the picture.

NEGATIVES ARE NOT INJURED	THE SOUND LINE DOES NOT DESTROY A PORTION OF THE PICTURE	INTERCHANGEABLE WITH OTHER LEADING METHODS OF SOUND PHOTOGRAPHY IN REPRODUCTION	ABSOLUTE SYNCHRONIZATION IS ASSURED

INQUIRIES FROM PRODUCERS
ARE NOW SOLICITED

THE POWERS CINEPHONE EQUIPMENT CORP.

POWERS BUILDING
723 7TH AVE., N. Y. CITY

"A GREAT NEW ART IN THE MAKING"

Powers Cinephone advertisement.

In April 1929, ERPI began an expensive public relations campaign to reach eight million readers of numerous mass-circulated magazines. The high quality of Western Electric sound was stressed in an effort to convince consumers that any other sound was inferior. The public, it was probably hoped, would pressure exhibitors to remove their "icicle" equipment. The pitch emphasized the scientific origins of the talkies: "Sound Pictures—a product of the Telephone," one ad read. Another claimed that "Science, art and business, working shoulder to shoulder have accomplished [sound motion pictures]." The rapid progress of the talkies was cited, appealing to those who might have been turned off by attending an earlier screening. The wonderful technicians of Bell Laboratories had cured the talkies of their "lisp." Engineers studied pitch and timbre, and "the results of these investigations are the basis for the design of all Western Electric equipment. . . . We have mastered the 'S' in Sound Reproduction."[57]

Western Electric also embarked on a campaign to improve its image within the industry. ERPI formed a Department of Educational Talking Pictures and distributed films made to order by outside producers. Its first release was BUSINESS IN GREAT WATERS (1928), a five-reeler about the transatlantic cable. This publicity tactic paralleled and reinforced other AT&T strategies emphasizing the telephone as a public service, not just a corporate monopoly. Telephone advertising campaigns stressed its social value, its contribution to building communities, and its role in personal safety. ERPI's ads similarly not only generated goodwill among film people and consumers but enhanced the image of Western Electric. Claude Fischer has argued that the public service activities and advertising were part of an effort to combat the telephone's "shortage of charisma." He notes, "In the late 1920s AT&T leaders worried . . . that the rate [of telephone service] adoption was not great enough, because more American families were buying cars, electricity, and radios than were buying telephone service."[58] Again, ERPI patterned its activities on those of its corporate parent, using advertising to counteract its own imminent loss of competitive "charisma."

Western Electric provided free program material to exhibitors and provided audiences with what might today be called "edutainment" or "infotainment." Two examples from 1929 were WHAT MAKES THE FILM TALK, a silent to be projected before the house was wired, and FINDING HIS VOICE, to be played with a first talker. The films contained schematic explanations written by C. W. Barrell, head of the Western Electric Motion Picture Bureau. They were produced by Max Fleischer and animated at the Carpenter-Goldman studio. After a weeklong run at the Capitol, the manager reported that "Broadway patrons are intensely interested in seeing and hearing how films get their voice."[59]

Western Electric Makes Silence Silent

ERPI stopped trying to control the exhibition of talking cinema and instead built on its advantage in the production sector. The chief activities of the company in 1930–1931 were helping Hollywood establish foreign-language production and exhibition, adding new product lines to supplement its diminishing share of the theater trade, specializing in acoustic consulting, expanding into nontheatrical markets, and introducing noise-reduction recording techniques.

Producers in 1930 were preoccupied with the "foreign problem," that is, how to show their films in non-English-speaking markets. ERPI would have to be instrumental, so

Otterson's attentions were focused increasingly on international adaptation. Milestone theater installations were achieved. The five-thousandth ERPI system was put into the Lyceum Theatre in Belfast, Ireland; the six-thousandth at the Comœdia in Marseilles, France. Western Electric devices were installed in forty countries and on two steamships.

ERPI continued to diversify its product offerings. Otterson put his vice president, J. J. Lyng, in charge of domestic affairs. One innovation was individual headsets to aid the hearing-impaired. In August 1929, the Paramount in Brooklyn became the first theater to install them.[60] They were distributed nationally beginning in 1930. The company introduced a new screen called Ortho-Krome, claimed to transmit sound and reflect light better. It diversified its broadcasting apparatus and test-marketed a new line of rubber-coated wire. A big seller was the Western Electric radio "superimposing" (dubbing) system, which added sound effects from a record library (applause, for example) to live broadcast material. Fifty-six stations leased the system. ERPI also operated an "electrical transcription" service which sent out disc recordings of *The Chevrolet Chronicles* (to mention one program) to 122 stations.[61]

In addition to creating new products, the company also emphasized service. An acoustic consulting department was created in 1929 and augmented in September 1930. A former Yale engineer, S. K. Wolf, was in charge. The unit consulted with industrialists, architects, and managers of arenas and theaters outside the motion picture business. Wolf garnered favorable publicity when he took his analyzing equipment into noisy urban environments such as the New York subway. This activity exploited the company's close ties to Bell Laboratories and reinforced the association between sound technology and the telephone. ERPI (recalling AT&T's social uplift publicity) emphasized its contribution to the common good: "It is a matter of . . . possessing knowledge and making it of practical value for the first time." The acoustics consultants went into seventy-five theaters a week with their reflectors and echo-detectors, advising managers on how to improve their sound systems. In a typical study, "Articulation Test for Sound Houses," Wolf reported that movies were aspiring to match the normal speech comprehension rate of 96 percent, as measured by the "curve of conversational efficiency" developed by Dr. Fletcher of Bell Laboratories. The engineers were trying to quantify the variables of volume, extraneous noise, and excessive reverberation. The engineer's mission was to foreground speech and desired sounds and to suppress the background. By increasing the ratio of signal to noise, the film could be played at lower volume, generating less distortion. The consultants' theater surveys no doubt improved the effectiveness of ERPI's equipment, but they also redistributed a certain amount of exhibition control, taking it away from the theater management and giving it to Western Electric.[62] The company's momentum suffered a setback in August 1930 when J. J. Lyng died while attempting to save his sister from drowning.[63]

Each sound transport, whether disc or optical, had its own distinctive background noise. Phonograph records had scratches and needle scrape. Variable-density optical (Western Electric) had continual hiss. Variable-area (RCA) had ticks and pops. The acoustic superiority of sound-on-film took a decided step forward on 8 December 1930 when ERPI introduced the Western Electric New Process Noiseless Recording System. This involved "flashing" the raw film stock with low-intensity light to alter its photographic density. Also, recorders were equipped with a newly designed light valve. ERPI Vice President H. M. Knox described the improvement as a response to consumer demand:

> Motion picture audiences are well aware of the hissing or scratching sound which becomes audible as soon as the sound apparatus is turned on. In other

Now
SOUND PICTURES
for the Hard-of-Hearing!

THAT you may bring even more patrons to your box office, Electrical Research Products makes available sound picture apparatus for the hard-of-hearing.

Approximately 15,000,000 people in this country have defective hearing, which means that almost one seventh of those in your community are so affected. The equipment to attract your share of these people to *your* box office — and to give them full enjoyment of the show — is now ready for installation as a part of your standard Western Electric Sound System.

This equipment is further proof that it pays to choose Western Electric. With this system you are assured the benefits of every new development in sound reproduction apparatus.

Good Will and Profits!

Advertisement for Western Electric's device for hearing-impaired moviegoers, December 1929.

words, during the silent introductory title of a picture everything is quiet. Just before the recorded portions of the film start listeners are warned of the coming sound by the scraping ground noise coming from the screen. While in good recording this ground noise is not particularly offensive, it nevertheless means that any whispers or low level sounds must be raised artificially to a relatively high volume if not masked by the noise of the system itself. During normal dialogue or music the presence of the ground noise fades to relative unimportance and, of course, during loud dialogue or heavy passages of music it is completely covered up. It is therefore a question of making "silence" silent.

. . . It is now possible to record the lowest whispers in thrilling silence. Fortunately this innovation comes at a time when audiences are demanding more realistic sound and at a time when producers are using less dialogue and more silence. To be effective the silence must be complete. During dramatic periods the expression will soon be true that "it was so quiet that one could hear a pin fall"—even in a talking picture theatre. (H. M. Knox, "Great Advance in Recording," *Erpigram,* 15 December 1930, p. 8)

THE RIGHT TO LOVE (Paramount, 1930) was the first film released employing the new technique. *Film Daily* found that the system produced the "finest quality sound to date. . . . [It] adds greatly to the qualities of the dialogue." Jesse Lasky predicted that it would soon be in use by all major producers. The director Richard Wallace found ways to foreground his new quiet-recording capability: "[A] light breeze stirring the trees can be observed in the picture and the resulting rustle of the leaves distinctly heard from the screen. Here is naturalness which under the old method of recording would have been utterly impossible." One bit of fallout was that "talking pictures have become so quiet that system noises as well as sounds in the booth or auditorium that formerly went unnoticed may now become annoying." In other words, the ambient sound in the theater distracted the viewer's attention. Most theaters followed the precedent of one in Iron Mountain, Michigan, supposedly the first to deaden projector noise by covering the booth's openings with optically ground glass. Mordaunt Hall felt that, "because of the background of silence, the players' voices are more life-like than ever." But, hard to please, he added, "The quiet may seem at times too noticeable, but this is only because one has become accustomed to hearing the intrusive mechanical undertones." The introduction of noise-reduction recording made it possible for critics like Hall to demand using sound in ways which alternated between dialogue and silence, yet without calling attention to the manipulation of the sound track.[64]

In November 1931, ERPI received an Academy award for noiseless recording.[65] (It would receive four other sound-related technical awards from the Academy from 1931 to 1935.) Not only did noiseless recording help to hide the mechanical basis of reproduction, it further hastened the end of disc playback because the technique was applicable only to optical sound. RCA developed its own system simultaneously, and by 1931 its licensees, RKO, Pathé, Educational, Tiffany, Mack Sennett, Tec-Art, and Standard Cinema, were using noiseless recording.[66]

Though the motion picture industry weathered the first year of the Depression, theater revenues (and consequently ERPI's income) began to dwindle. In 1930 Western Electric's sales of theater equipment were down 12 percent from 1929. But in his year-end statement, Otterson glossed over the nation's economic problems and once again invoked the quality argument. He blamed bad (meaning non–Western Electric) sound for his company's woes: "At least a third of the American public doesn't know how good talking pictures really are because five thousand poorly equipped theaters have sent them away dissatisfied, and they don't come back for more."[67]

ERPI continued to look for new product outlets. In April 1931, it began selling a Western Electric 16-mm sound projection system to the general public. This utilized the single-perforation film stock which Eastman Kodak had introduced in 1929, and it competed with RCA's system, which had already begun to dominate this market. Nontheatrical talkies were popular with institutional and home users, but exhibitors saw them as a menace to their business. Though ERPI itself had no announced plans to manufacture nontheatrical films for the projector, the major studios had for years been releasing 16-mm silent prints for home screening, and naturally they would switch to sound. On behalf of theater owners, *Film Daily's* publisher, Jack Alicoate, lambasted ERPI for its nontheatrical campaign:

> [ERPI] leased, sold or otherwise bargained with the aforesaid [film] industry for plenty-plus of equipment at boo-koo jack, thereby, we presume, making for itself a most satisfactory profit. . . . We now find this ERPI–Western Electric combine practically closing the window as far as this industry is concerned and reorganizing its forces and shock troops for a powerful offensive on the non-theatrical front. Installations in Hotels, Clubs, Churches, Schools, Colleges, Institutions, etc. is the objective. . . . Would this hurt the legitimate picture business? Answer it yourself, for we haven't the heart. (*Film Daily*, 13 April 1931, p. 1)

While the nontheatrical market provided ERPI with new income, the identification of the company as a competitor, not a partner, must have further strained its relations with exhibitors. Sound continued to spread, but ERPI's presence in theaters declined.

The Conversion Continues

According to Film Boards of Trade statistics, in the spring of 1931 there were 21,739 motion picture theaters in the United States. Of these, the overwhelming majority (19,304) were independently owned and operated houses. Eleven percent (2,435) were affiliated with film studios. Sixty-two percent (13,000-plus) of the nation's theaters had converted to sound.

Table 6.1
WIRED THEATERS IN THE UNITED STATES, 1926–1931

As of Dec. 31:	1926	1927	1928	1929	1930	1931
By ERPI	12	157	1,046	3,157	4,922	5,537
By other	NA[a]	NA	3,000[b]	4,843	8,284	8,343
Total	12	157	4,046	8,000	13,206	13,880

a. Not available.   b. An estimate.

SOURCE: *Erpigram*, 1 January 1930, p. 1; *Film Daily*, 20 February 1931, p. 12; John Douglas Gomery, *The Coming of Sound to the American Cinema* (Ph.D. dissertation, University of Wisconsin, 1975), pp. 269–70. These sources vary slightly.

Table 6.1 shows that ERPI did not participate proportionately in the rapid rise of wired houses; its momentum stalled after its five-thousandth theater mark. Other reproducing systems, mostly but not entirely RCA Photophone, made inroads in ERPI's territory. If we assume that the majority of the ERPI-serviced theaters were studio affiliates, the table suggests that very few independents were choosing the Western Electric system. Not only was Photophone more affordable, but the apparatus was also owned by the theater. There were no burdensome service contracts. The equipment occupied less space in the booth and behind the screen. Both Western Electric and RCA continued improving theater sound, considered to be the weak link in acoustic reproduction. Combinations of dynamic cones and horns reproduced both music and speech with high quality. One result of these innovations, though, was that the two systems became slightly less compatible when one type of recording was played on the other's speakers. The SMPE proposed a standard in 1934 to resolve the problem.[68]

The slowdown in ERPI theater installations was not only the result of competition. The high-end market of giant picture palaces had been saturated. Acknowledging the increasingly severe effects of the Depression, ERPI did an about-face. Rather than competing for the remaining share, a strategic decision was made not to place equipment in small movie theaters.

> Approximately 65 per cent of sound installation propositions considered by the electrics [that is, Western Electric and ERPI] are understood being rejected on the grounds of bad risks. As practically every large house in the country is now wired, theaters at present seeking devices are almost exclusively small revenue producers. Rather than chance the possibility of being forced to take over the houses of uncertain accounts, the electrics are refusing to make numerous deals. (*Film Daily*, 29 March 1931, p. 1)

Western Electric estimated that it might take four years to wire the remaining silent houses, but this task would require a workforce whose costs would not be sustained by low-return theaters. The Depression trend was toward drastic layoffs, not increasing staff. So ERPI let RCA and the competitors take their chances with the leftover exhibitors. *Film Daily* reported that "the smaller sound equipment companies . . . are doing a thriving business among this class of houses."[69]

One of the signs of the company's diminished control was the effort to represent its high-quality service as a desirable commodity rather than a burden imposed upon an unwilling exhibitor. ERPI tried to change its image from that of primarily a provider of equipment to that of a source of "scientific" service. The ads to the trade portrayed the ERPI factory representative as a businessman dressed in a sharp suit. The electronic schematic of the amplifier was shown to be so complex that the lay person (or your ordinary projectionist) could not possibly decipher it.

Much of the organization's activities were spent defending its patents. Western Electric's backing gave ERPI practically unlimited resources to protect its rights and to mount lengthy defenses against infringers. So the litigation was never-ending. Eventually, twenty-two actions sought $175 million from ERPI. By 1938 the majority had been settled out of court.[70] Among the most significant lawsuits was *General Talking Pictures v. Stanley* (1930). *Film Daily* pointed out the significance:

Diagram of a Western Electric
Sound System Circuit

knows his way through this intricate circuit

*. . . that's why he is able to protect you
against Poor Sound, Breakdowns, Program Interruptions and Lost Patronage!*

Trained to Bell System standards of maintenance, the ERPI man can render this service more economically and efficiently than anyone else.

Backed by 50 years of voice transmission experience, the Western Electric Sound System is the finest equipment you can buy. Yet even the finest equipment needs regular, painstaking and expert inspection and service.

By keeping your Western Electric Sound System operating at peak performance for the life of your contract, the ERPI Service Engineer helps you earn dividends on your investment!

Northern Electric in Canada
Distributed by
Electrical Research Products Inc.
250 West 57th Street, New York

ERPI service man as executive and technical savant. Western Electric advertisement,
August 1931.

Although the action proper is against Stanley Co. of America, charging infringement of De Forest sound patents, it constitutes a test of Western Electric's position in the sound apparatus field. What the outcome will be is strictly a matter of judicial opinion. If General Talking Pictures [GTP] get the decision it means a radical shakeup in the situation affecting every phase of the business. (*Film Daily*, 1 July 1930, pp. 1–6)

Western Electric and ERPI won three counts and lost one to GTP; Western Electric immediately appealed the latter. On the strength of its partial victory, GTP sued RCA, RKO, Powers Cinephone, and Fox-Case. In May 1938, the federal district court ruled that ERPI's patent pool was legal, and that General Talking Pictures had to pay back-royalties. The U.S. Supreme Court reaffirmed the decision in November 1938.[71]

"Threats arrived regularly, on the average of one per month from 1928 until 1932, from a variety of firms," Gomery reports. In 1932 Sarnoff sued ERPI for antitrust activities. This set off a three-year Justice Department investigation of AT&T and ERPI. Separately, the Stanley theaters (on behalf of parent Warner Bros.) sued ERPI to eliminate the weekly service charge, arguing that the equipment was actually sold and not leased. The complaint cited several abuses. The service personnel were accused of condemning parts unnecessarily, installing overpriced replacements which the licensee was obliged to accept, and then reselling the used parts to other theaters. The plaintiffs asked the court to nullify all ERPI agreements since inception and to require the company either to accept for return all Western Electric apparatus or to reimburse the theaters $30 million. Duovac Radio Corporation and General Talking Pictures joined the suit in November 1932. The Danish producer Nordisk sued Paramount in November 1932, claiming infringement of its Peterson and Poulsen photoelectric cell patents. This led to a boycott, negotiations, and a settlement that paid the Danes royalties through 1935.[72]

ERPI's and the industry's biggest scare came from William Fox. Though he no longer controlled his original companies, he was still president of American Tri-Ergon. Unexpectedly, he found himself holding trump cards. The U.S. Patent Office granted Tri-Ergon's request for a patent on the standard double-printing process whereby the sound track is exposed on the edge of the film in a separate pass through the printer. Then the federal district court upheld the Tri-Ergon patent on a photoelectric cell, previously denied by the patent office. Fox wasted no time suing Paramount (and by extension, the industry). He also sued an RCA licensee for violating the Tri-Ergon flywheel patent, the crucial device that enabled the film to flow smoothly past the sound-recording beam. At the time, fifteen New York houses and distributors were showing or circulating German dialogue films recorded on the Tri-Ergon system. He sued them, too.[73]

ERPI and RCA pooled legal forces to defend against Fox. When the controversy reached the Supreme Court in 1934, the justices dealt a blow to the industry by declining to hear the cases. The victorious Fox immediately sued the other seven majors. Meanwhile, RCA's staff was scouring the files and discovered an application made in 1921 and granted in 1931 that anticipated the edge-recording technique. Without precedent, the Court vacated its earlier decision, heard the cases, and in March 1935 overturned the lower courts' decisions. Fox was allowed to collect royalties on his valid patents, but nothing like the tens of millions in fees that Hollywood would have owed him and American Tri-Ergon had the decision gone the other way.[74]

ERPI's clout with the studios almost vanished. For example, to make up for declining revenue, the company became very aggressive about collecting royalties, exploiting the

AMERICAN TRI-ERGON CORPORATION
10 WEST 47th STREET
NEW YORK CITY

WILLIAM FOX
President

Notice to the Sound Picture Industry

$\mathcal{P}$RESENT DAY sound pictures utilizing photographic film sound records are essentially dependent upon several early and important inventions of Messrs. Engl, Vogt, and Massolle. These inventors are German scientists who did pioneer work in this field, and were the first to produce and publicly exhibit successful film sound records.

The attention of the sound picture industry is directed to the following U. S. patents covering certain of these inventions now owned by American Tri-Ergon Corporation.

1. *Patent No. 1,713,726, Vogt, et al., granted May 21, 1929. This is the patent popularly known as the "flywheel patent" and it relates to certain methods and apparatus for uniformly moving the sound record film under the control of inertia, either in recording or reproducing machines utilizing sound controlled light in translating the sound to or from the film. This patent also relates to the photoelectric cell when used with such reproducing apparatus, as is now the general practice.*

2. *Patent No. 1,825,598, Vogt, et al., granted September 29, 1931. This patent relates to the process for producing combined sound and picture film by photographing the sound and pictures on separate films so that they may be developed separately, and then printing both records side by side on a single film. This process, as you know, is very extensively used in the industry. This patent was recently granted after prolonged litigation on priority with Dr. Lee De Forest, in which the Court affirmed the Patent Office decisions in our favor.*

Attention is invited to the patents themselves for a fuller understanding of their scope.

Applications for other early and important inventions are still pending.

Producers, exhibitors, and manufacturers utilizing any of the inventions of said patents are hereby notified and warned that they will be held liable for all profits made or damages arising from their infringements of said patents.

Infringement suits have recently been instituted under these patents against representative concerns in the industry. Further suits will be brought, if necessary, against infringing film producers and theatre operators and against manufacturers of infringing apparatus, for the purpose of restraining all unlicensed use of these inventions.

Licenses under these patents may be acquired under proper conditions. The object of this notice is to acquaint the industry with the situation in order that further liability for unlicensed use of the inventions may be avoided.

AMERICAN TRI-ERGON CORPORATION

American Tri-Ergon's notice to the trade, 27 November 1931.

vagueness of the 1928 license agreement. When ERPI tried to impose taxes on silent versions and foreign remakes as though they were new productions and claimed that trailers should be assessed as short subjects, producers refused to pay. The studios were generally successful in winning concessions. The much-maligned service and inspection requirements were eliminated in 1933. As a result, in 1935, ERPI's service department lost money for the first time.[75] The arbitration hearings between ERPI and Warner Bros. that had begun in 1928 resumed in September 1931 and led to an out-of-court settlement on 6 June 1934. ERPI agreed to pay Warners $4 million in cash and $2.1 million in credits.[76]

When the Depression deepened, ERPI found itself in the production business. It took over Christie Film Company and the Educational Pictures studios in 1933 when they could not pay their license fees. The studio also offered loans to back independent production through a New York subsidiary, Exhibitors Reliance Corporation. In three years it financed 33 features and 207 shorts. ERPI's dabbling in production ended after 1936, when it lost $1 million.

John Otterson resigned in June 1935. Most of the major studios switched to RCA Photophone. Symbolically, perhaps, Warners converted its Burbank sound stages to the RCA system in 1936, a move that left only Paramount, MGM, and United Artists still signed with ERPI. Western Electric deactivated the company in 1937, although its patent and contract royalties continued to flow in.[77]

RKO Radio Pictures

Sarnoff sailed to Paris in February 1929, ostensibly to oversee the "'invasion' of Europe by RCA-Photophone." It was rumored he was signing an agreement with Tobis, purveyors of sound equipment in most of Europe. In actuality, Owen Young had asked him to assist as confidential adviser on the German War Reparations Committee. Sarnoff's suggestions for restructuring Germany's crippling debt were effective, though subsequent historians have minimized the Young Plan's impact. The aim was, of course, to improve the country's economic situation; no one suggested that strengthening a potential market for American radios and films might have been a small consideration.[78]

RKO Productions, in February, adopted a new trade name, Radio Pictures, and a corporate logo with suggestive flying bolts of electricity. The studio made its films in Hollywood on the former FBO lot at 780 North Gower Street at Melrose (absorbed since into Desilu and Paramount) and distributed them out of New York. Kennedy's former studio head, William LeBaron, stayed on as vice president in charge of production, assisted by Lee Marcus as studio manager.

The most important order of business for LeBaron was consolidating Radio Pictures production on the West Coast, part of a $5 million expansion program. A new sound stage was built, and the two existing stages were revamped. A separate building was designed for housing the RCA Photophone recording equipment and the special effects and music departments. By March two complete Photophone installations were working.[79] During its first year, the studio turned out mostly low-budget musicals. The first films released on the Radio Pictures label were SYNCOPATION (1929), a musical directed by Bert Glennon that highlighted the radio personality Morton Downey and featured Fred Waring and the Pennsylvanians, and STREET GIRL (1929), directed by Wesley Ruggles and starring Betty Compson. It opened at the Globe Theater in New York on 30 July 1929 and was a well-received light musical comedy.[80]

In New York, RCA Photophone built the Gramercy Studios (between Twenty-fourth and Twenty-fifth Streets off Lexington Avenue) in February 1929. All recording equipment was state of the art, in wheeled sound-proof booths. But when production moved west, and with only two talking features slated to be shot in New York for the 1929–1930 season, the new studios suddenly became surplus property. Photophone rented the facility to low-budget independent producers. Prudence Pictures, for example, filmed THE TALK OF HOLLYWOOD (1929) there, starring Nat Carr. The studios also used Gramercy as a lab to test George K. Spoor's stereoscopic experiments.[81]

Most RKO business during 1929 was wheeling and dealing to grab market share. RCA Photophone cut its prices for theater installations in May to underbid ERPI (and to respond to the competition of Pacent and other low-end systems). RCA courted independents by making special arrangements with the little Tiffany-Stahl studio in August 1929: if a manager booked one of the Tiffany-Stahl blocks of twenty-six films, RCA would wire the theater for $2,995. The idea flashed, and 2,460 theaters had signed up by February 1930.[82]

Sarnoff joined forces with Paramount to engineer (unsuccessfully) a takeover of the Pantages theater chain. Meanwhile, when the powerful stock manipulator Mike Meehan

RCA Gramercy Studios, New York, 1929.

tried to put together a syndicate to buy Kennedy's Pathé stock, Sarnoff let it be known that he would block it; the effort fell apart in June. Sarnoff wanted the studio for himself and resumed talks with Kennedy.

At the end of its first year of operation, twenty-one of RKO's thirty releases had produced profits. In a short time, Sarnoff's holding company had become a diversified entertainment force, and RKO became the fifth member of the new "Big Five."[83] Film, of course, was only part of Sarnoff's growing empire. While RKO was prospering, RCA entered into an agreement with General Motors to combine two of the most exciting developments of the twentieth century into one apparatus: the car radio. Investors loved it. From March 1928 through September 1929, the price of RCA stock shot up 600 percent.[84] John Sedgwick's statistical analysis of RKO income shows that the 1929 releases RIO RITA, STREET GIRL, THE VAGABOND LOVER (directed by Marshall Nielan and starring the popular crooner Rudy Vallee), and, in 1930, THE CUCKOOS (directed by Paul Sloane, starring the team of Bert Wheeler and Robert Woolsey) provided RKO with the best return on investment that the company earned during its entire history (see appendix 1).

RCA's executives were intent on diversifying their installations and anticipated that 40 percent of their future sales would be to nontheatrical businesses. A 16-mm projector was introduced in 1930.[85] RCA's experience and connections as purveyors of tubes

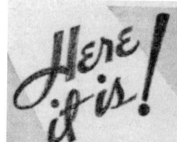

RCA PHOTOPHONE
All A.C. Operated
Special Size Equipment for
500 SEAT THEATRES
Lease Price
$1600⁰⁰

RCA PHOTOPHONE SPECIAL SIZE EQUIPMENT for theatres of 500 SEATING CAPAC-
ITY and under is now ready! Designed and built to meet the requirements of the
smallest theatres . . . compact . . . simple in operation and offered at a price that
makes it the salvation of hundreds of houses that heretofore have remained
dark or unprofitable with silent pictures or with unsatisfactory sound equipment.

COMPLETE A-C OPERATION

No Batteries . . . No Motor Generators . . .
Direct Connection with the A-C Power Line
. . . making operation extremely simple.
Built for small projection rooms.

DESIGNED FOR SMALL THEATRES

Adapted to Simplex, Powers and Kaplan
Projectors, operates with 110 volt, 60 cycle
and 50 cycle, and 115 volt, D-C Power
supply. (Powers and D-C equipments at a
slightly higher cost.)

AN ENGINEERING TRIUMPH!

At Last! The small theatre is given the same
opportunity as the super de-luxe house. With
confidence the small theatre owner can
proudly advertise his RCA PHOTOPHONE
SPECIAL SIZE EQUIPMENT, knowing that the
box-office attractions of the major studios
will be presented with the fidelity of tone
and perfection that characterizes RCA
PHOTOPHONE performance.

$100.00 DOWN, $25.00 A WEEK!

On the Lease plan, this RCA PHOTO-
PHONE SPECIAL SIZE EQUIPMENT may
be installed on deferred payments as
low as $25.00 per week which includes
lease and finance charges, insurance
and REGULAR SERVICE during the payment term. *It takes but a very few extra
admissions to pay for it and deliver a
profit from the first day of operation.*
For further information communicate with
nearest branch office or direct to

Commercial Department
RCA PHOTOPHONE, INC.
411 Fifth Avenue   •   New York City
A Radio Corporation of America Subsidiary
15 Branches in Principal Cities of United States and
authorized Distributers in Foreign Countries.

THE EMBLEM OF **RCA** PERFECT SOUND
PHOTOPHONE
INC
SOUND EQUIPMENT

Photophone's cut-rate campaign for small theaters, 1931.

and radios helped the company win federal contracts. There were 283 Photophone installations in 1930, for example, for the U.S. Navy.[86] Sarnoff cited the company's anticipation of a big rise in sales of home reproducing equipment (motion pictures, radios, and phonographs) as a rationale for merging RCA Victor and RCA Photophone.[87] RCA's AC current projector, aimed at institutions and small theaters, was a success. These products and their accompanying marketing strategies paid off. While ERPI's installations lagged, the business of RCA Photophone was up 200 percent in 1931 over the same period in 1930. Foreign expansion accounted for much of the new business.[88]

After a tumultuous collaboration followed by their breakup, Sarnoff's and Kennedy's ventures led them away from direct participation in the movie business. Their activities demonstrate how unexpected combinations of forces helped derail the Western Electric monopoly. The opposition between the Titan Sarnoff and the Olympian ERPI continued, but there was no battle royal. Instead, they divided the riches. The profits were vast enough to share.

If Laemmle had his Universal City and Fox had his Movietone City, should not Sarnoff have his "Radio City?" On 27 October 1929, he unveiled blueprints for a new corporate headquarters in a "giant Fifth Avenue amusement enterprise" in what would become Rockefeller Center. Under construction between 1931 and 1933, the seventy-story RCA skyscraper anchored the fourteen buildings comprised by the original plan.[89] The scheme called for the gleaming modern complex to accommodate twenty-seven radio and television broadcasting studios—a veritable radiopolis. The Metropolitan Opera would relocate into the complex. RKO would lease and operate four big theaters, including "one seating 7,000 and devoted to a new conception of variety entertainment." This, of course, was the germ of Radio City Music Hall.[90]

Though neither ERPI nor RCA Photophone achieved the dominance it sought, the ten years of competition and complicity between them facilitated the changeover to sound. Western Electric and RCA provided capital, competed to improve technology, and enabled moviegoers to become avid consumers of the talkies.

It was in RCA/ERPI's best interests to disseminate its products and services widely to all studios and theaters. It is unlikely that the talkies would have become universal had one film studio held all the power or if there had been two or three incompatible systems. By agreeing (reluctantly) to share the field between them (and later with Tobis Klangfilm in Europe), the companies made a calculated decision to exchange monopoly power—which would be expensive to attain and risky to hold—for defined competition. As would happen decades later with giant computer corporations, this strategy ultimately resulted in lost control as the technology multiplied beyond the oversight of any one company. Unchecked competition led to the demise of ERPI—but not, of course, of Western Electric. Film sound, because of this productive competition, became consolidated at a corporate stratum above the studio level. It helped unify the industry and standardize the product. As a result, the talkies changed from a special package of goods and services to one common trait shared by all movies. In 1927 synchronized sound was something extraordinary; by 1931 it had become generic. The film without speech, such as CITY LIGHTS, was the novelty.

7

The Big Hedge: Hollywood's Defensive Strategies

Talk may help the ballyhoo. It does not enhance the entertainment and is so palpably unnecessary that laymen are apt to sense this even if lacking the trade knowledge to define the flaws.

Variety, 3 APRIL 1929, ON THE DIALOGUE
SEQUENCES IN THE GODLESS GIRL

The "coming of sound" meant different things to the production and exhibition ends of the industry. Although the pace of equipment installation varied considerably with each studio, the main producers had the capability of releasing dialogue films by the end of 1928. The wiring of theaters, however, took longer. The point at which 50 percent of theaters were projecting synchronized sound did not occur until sometime in 1930. This discrepancy meant that for a while Hollywood was faced with the need to supply two sets of prints to silent and sound-equipped cinemas. Such an arrangement may strike us in looking back as wasteful or as a temporary solution until the transition was complete. But this may not be the case. It appears that industry insiders initially thought that Hollywood would make both sound and silent films, that some cinemas might not be converted, and that some films would retain long sections in which dialogue would be given in conventional intertitles. For a while in 1928 and 1929, sound cinema might have branched off and coexisted with traditional filmmaking.

The industry's uniform adoption of Western Electric and/or compatible RCA sound systems and the slackening of competition between those manufacturers eased anxiety about the technology. But it did nothing to answer questions about what went before the camera. Several options presented themselves. Should all films have sound, or only "specials?" What should be the balance in a film between synchronized music and talking? Should silent film be kept alive in case some theaters refused to convert, or in case the talking fad fizzled? Would silent and sound production develop along separate lines, the former staying with certain material, like comedy, while the latter adapted theater and stage musicals? The public statements by producers reveal that they were considering all these options. Meanwhile, they had neither clear-cut answers nor definite plans for sound motion pictures.

Voting Dry and Drinking Wet

Sound epitomized what businessmen hate most: uncertainty. William deMille declared, "We are face to face with a marvelous opportunity or tremendous catastrophe."[1] Harry Carr wrote in the *Los Angeles Times:* "What impresses me about the talkies is that no one knows what they are all about. Are they to be stage plays plastered onto a screen with all the stage dialogue? Or are they to be motion pictures with an occasional outburst into conversation? Or just a slamming door or the moo of a cow or the tick of a clock for punctuation?"[2] Sound transformed more than one mogul into a hypocrite. Producers, in order to reassure lovers of silent films, actors, unions, and small-town and foreign exhibitors, said publicly that the conversion would be gradual and controlled, and that there would always be silent movies.

Cecil B. DeMille equivocated, saying, "Talking pictures are here to stay, but they will not replace entirely the silent pictures. Two years from now I would not hazard a guess as to which will be the more popular."[3] Even William LeBaron of RKO, whose company made only talking films, did not think that sound would replace silents. Rather, sound film would "strengthen" them, presumably by reinforcing their silent values (perhaps in the hybrid part-talkie form).[4] Mordaunt Hall, in the *New York Times,* summed up the consensus: "It is by no means expected that the giving of a voice to the animated shadow figures will supplant silent film stories."[5]

Opponents of talkies within the industry were plentiful. Joseph Schenck of United Artists expressed the industry's cant: "Talking pictures will never displace the silent drama from its supremacy, or affect the appeal of motion pictures with synchronized music and special sound effects." United Artists would "use the sound device on those pictures to which sound is adaptable."[6] The director Sam Taylor was explicit: "The talking picture is not a rival of the silent picture. . . . The silent screen play of today is too big and fine a medium of dramatic expression to fear its destruction."[7] Fred Niblo, the admired MGM director, sounded his own warning, advising against tinkering with the silent film just because the talker was drawing a huge clientele. Among other things, he disliked the acoustic properties of film sound: "A good voice in a talking picture will be a canned voice, nevertheless."[8]

Lillian Gish was fearful that the cinema's past would be forgotten. "Whatever the public may feel about movies as they used to be before the sound innovations," she insisted,

> in the silent movies we achieved certain beautiful things. I mean that there were moments of beauty in pantomime and beauty in photography. Much of what we did was poor, but if the silent movies had had more time to develop, we might have made a really great and individual art in them. For myself, I still cling to the thought of creating those moments of beauty in pantomime. (*Film Daily,* 29 September 1929, p. 10)

While the silent cinema had achieved artistic status in its own right, the German theater producer and film director Max Reinhardt contended that sound film was a doomed stepchild to theater: "Talking pictures, bringing to the screen stage plays, almost in their entirety, with dialogue, tend to make this independent art a subsidiary of the theater and really make it only a substitute for the theater instead of an art in itself. Talking pictures, in their relationship to the stage, seem to me like reproductions of paintings."[9] Soviet filmmaker Sergei M. Eisenstein, recently hired and then fired by Paramount, offered an uncompromising critique of the soundtrack: "I consider the so-called 'all-talkie,' the film with conversation from beginning to end, nothing but rotten trash. The sound part of the American and German films is a luxury, an element that has just happened to be added to them, but which has nothing to do with the films themselves."[10]

Pat Powers, even while extolling the virtues of his Cinephone system, concluded, "The reaction to one hundred per cent talking pictures is problematical. Talking throughout the entire picture has a tendency to retard the action and it will probably be only a matter of time before the public will discard the novelty (as boresome) for something more enduring."[11] Many representatives felt, as did Herbert Brenon, one of the most popular directors, that adding voices to sound films doomed them. His argument, which was put forth time and again during the transition period, was that cinema had its own artistic essence. Applying literary or theatrical techniques would corrupt it. He maintained that "the production of motion pictures is a distinct art, having a basic formula—the presentation of stories in the form of pictures that move." Words, "whether injected in subtitles or in the rather metallic synchronization of the talking machine, are an anachronism and . . . the attempt to imitate the vocal exposition of the stage is a straddle of two horses at once, with the inevitable fall between them a foregone conclusion." Sound was a violation of the "purity" of the silent film because "the ideal picture is one that tells its story in a complete visual manner." Aside from its intrusion into a visual world, Brenon also hated the acoustic quality of the voice, which invariably reminded the viewer of the apparatus behind the screen. He identified this as "the impossibility of excluding a consciousness of the machine in any reproduction of the human voice." In case his theoretical objections were insufficient, Brenon also advanced an "efficiency" argument: "[A] situation on the silent screen can be convincingly registered in two minutes while the 'talking film' would take approximately six times as long."[12]

The decision to go to sound was made in the upper echelons of the Hollywood organizations. Many middle-rank managers and directors went along hesitantly. Monta Bell, at Paramount, is a good example of the prevailing notion that talking and film were antithetical, and that sound had to be administered in small doses:

> [Its] value lies in its discriminate usage . . . but I am afraid that our producers are rushing forward sheep-like and embracing "sound" as the panacea for all their ills. . . . Pictures give us a medium whereby we could put intimate stories in big theaters—the closeup allowing us to make our characters intimate. But not so with sound. . . . Basically, I believe it to be wrong for dialogues. Our writers will become lazy. It will be so easy to sit two characters down and let them talk instead of devising ingenious means for getting over points with pictorial action as we do now. . . . For effects and occasional high spot speeches, yes. For entire pictures—well as far as I am concerned, silence is golden. (*Film Daily*, 15 July 1928, p. 4)

Surprisingly, two weeks later Bell was appointed supervisor of all sound production at Paramount's Long Island facility. A year later, in a remarkable interview, the fan magazine columnist Herbert Cruikshank caught one of the most vociferous talkie-haters in the industry in this sublimely awkward inconsistency. Bell remained outspoken about the sound film's lack of merit. Yet, in the fall of 1929, he probably oversaw more talking film production than anyone else. When pressed, he defended his hypocrisy by distinguishing between his opinion and his work, prompting Cruikshank to conclude, "Of course, this is a personal—a very personal—opinion. Akin to those of the gentlemen who vote dry and drink wet."[13] Cruikshank's sly analogy between the national duplicity of Prohibition and the corporate attitude toward sound in Hollywood was apropos. Bell's attitude was emblematic of the industry's two-faced pronouncements. Kann presciently saw through the studios' rhetoric: "The industry unquestionably is concentrating the full force of its efforts on sound. Arguments to the contrary are not supported by the facts. This is, of course, a reflection of public demand and, if so, as we have no doubt it is, the conclusion is that the big money will continue to be found in sound films."[14] As producer-actor Gloria Swanson put it, "It's all very well to talk of art and artistic ideals. We all have artistic ideals to some extent. But when you think of the millions and millions that are tied up in motion picture productions, you must remember that there's got to be a return on that money."[15]

The major producers responded to this mixed prospectus for sound by means of the classic strategy for managing multiple risks: hedging. If it is impossible to guess whether scenario A, B, or C will play out, cover them all. This practice narrowed the odds of being shut out of competition, but it also lowered potential rewards. Hedging wastes some resources to save others; the perfect hedge produces neither a net gain nor a loss. Translated into practical terms, this meant that the safest route for producers would be to convert to sound as quickly as possible to satisfy public demand for talkies, while perpetuating existing (that is, silent) patterns of production.

The producers hedged in at least three ways: they redid successful films from the past as sound movies; they instituted dual-release policies, that is, they continued to make silent films (then silent versions of sound films); and they released films which combined silent technique and style with moments of dialogue, creating a new film form—the part-talkie.

Remakes and "Goat Glands"

One expedient for making a sound film was to recycle former silent box-office hits as newly made talkies. Warner Bros. redid THE GREEN GODDESS (1930) and THE GOLD DIGGERS (as GOLD DIGGERS OF BROADWAY, 1929). First National's successes THE ISLE OF LOST SHIPS (1929) was revived as a sound remake. Paramount chose GROUNDS FOR DIVORCE. REDEMPTION (1930) and ANNA CHRISTIE (1930) raised Irving Thalberg's hope for second-time success at MGM. Universal joined the remake bandwagon with a new version of the studio's all-time top moneymaker, THE PHANTOM OF THE OPERA (1930). For this film, members of the cast of the 1925 original reassembled, including Mary Philbin. Lon Chaney refused to participate because he was holding out for a huge speaking bonus at MGM; it is unlikely that Thalberg would have lent him to Universal anyway. In order to be able to reuse Chaney's performance, the studio interpolated new dialogue footage into the old silent film.[16]

Often films which had been completed (and sometimes released) as silents were retrofitted with music, sound effects, and perhaps a little post-dubbed dialogue. The majority of 1928 sound films fell into this category; THE KING OF KINGS (the nationally distributed version of the 1927 silent), THE GODLESS GIRL, and WHITE SHADOWS IN THE SOUTH SEAS are examples. The skeptical press disparagingly referred to these as "goat glands." This slang term derived from outrageous cures for impotency practiced in the

1920s, including restorative elixirs, tonics, and surgical procedures. It implied that producers were trying to put some new life into their old films. Paul Fejos's LONESOME (1928), for example, had been previously released as a silent film, then reissued with a scene wherein Glenn Tryon and Barbara Kent exchange some banal lines in bland voices about the color of their fantasy dream house. Critics disliked it. As usual, Gilbert Seldes's explanation for the aesthetic failure of goat glands was astute: "Inartistic as they are, these old [silent] pictures have a certain relation between their parts and this relation is completely destroyed when 'appropriate sounds' are applied."[17]

Dual Versions

The statements made by many in Hollywood implied that talkies would eventually coexist with traditional movies. *Film Daily*'s Kann implored producers on behalf of his exhibitor readership not to abandon the silent film: "It must be plugged, sold, exploited, merchandised as never before. It must be saved for the economic welfare of the entire industry."[18]

Nicholas M. Schenck, president of Loew's and MGM, suggested that sound might be applied according to story needs:

> I believe they [silents] will continue to be a very positive factor in motion picture production. . . . My personal opinion is that the silent film will never be eliminated, since certain stories are naturally suited for silent treatment and must be completely rearranged to serve as dialogue vehicles. . . . Most of the stars at the M-G-M studio seem to feel that the silent picture will remain for certain types of stories. (20 May 1929, p. 7)

Louis B. Mayer told distributors and exhibitors at the annual sales convention that the studio was going to "make a determined play for silent business." The 1929–1930 MGM season was scheduled to have sixteen silents, forty talkies, and seven synchronized releases.[19] MGM's strategy, attributed to Thalberg, was to let the other studios perfect the technology, then enter later to avoid the trial and expense of initial experimentation. Kann thought that such patience would be rewarded:

> Reflect for a moment on the upheaval talking pictures caused in this industry during 1928. Time was when the producer who had next season's product finished and on the shelf awaiting release was the fellow who walked away with much of the choice playing time. Last year, this selfsame individual was the one who developed the largest and most headachy of headaches. Such is the course of this business, sensitive as it is to innovations and the ever-changing mind of the public. (*Film Daily*, 6 January 1929, p. 1)

Paramount had been enthusiastic about sound for at least a year, but no one there foresaw all-talking production. Jesse Lasky believed in 1928 that the sound movie would

> travel two different and well-defined roads. There will be the all-dialogue picture, which will utilize the best features of stage and screen technique and which will be radically different from anything we know at present. . . .

> The second course of the cinema will concern itself with productions devoid of dialogue, but with their drama heightened by a thoughtful use of the emphasis of sound. (*Film Daily*, 2 September 1928, p. 6)

He also said that Adolph Zukor was of a similar opinion: "It is obvious that the talking picture has its definite place in the films scheme. But this does not mean that the silent picture is doomed. On the contrary, it will remain the backbone of the industry's commercial security."[20] Even in late 1929 Paramount's B. P. Schulberg balked at completely ruling out *all* silent production: "Sound is going to be our business for a long time. We are not going back to the silent screen ever except for occasional pictures." Sidney Kent, the general manager, echoed the boss: "It is probable that this silent demand will never reach zero, even in this country. There will always be some unwired houses. There may be theater clienteles in certain spots that may actually prefer silent to sound pictures."[21] At RKO, all films were shot as talkers. Nevertheless, President Joseph Schnitzer said that the silent picture would continue to be the basic production. Lee Marcus, his studio manager, said that ten of RKO's thirty pictures would have silent versions.

Carl Laemmle, president of Universal Pictures, addressed his customers, many of whom frequented rural theaters that were having difficulty affording to convert to sound. "No picture must stand upon the novelty of sound and dialogue. . . . All the sound in the world will not take the place of the four cardinal principles of the motion picture, namely, story, direction, action and photography."[22] Laemmle advertised his commitment to silents as a sign of support for the small theater by taking an oath that Universal would never stop making the old kind of films. "I am not one of those who believes that talking pictures sound the doom of silent pictures," he said.

> If the scenarists and directors in our business rise to the occasion as I thoroughly believe they will, the outlook for silent pictures seems to me an extremely bright and profitable one. The play's the thing, whether it is presented silently or with talk and music. The novelty of pictures which offer talking has now [1929] partly worn off. . . . This company is going to continue to make its pictures both silent and sound. And we are going to do that whether any other producer does it or not. (*Film Daily*, 20 May 1929, pp. 6–7)

His vice president, R. H. Cochrane, told how this primarily silent policy translated into practice: "Universal pictures are selected first with the idea of making a good silent picture, after which it is tested as to its qualities as a sound picture."[23]

Even the industry sound leaders, Warners and Fox, continued the dual-release policy. Warners had signed 4,283 silent film accounts for 1928–1929, mostly in towns with populations under 10,000. So it was obligated to provide silent product to these theaters, including trackless prints of talking successes like THE SINGING FOOL. After Winfield Sheehan announced in March 1929 that Fox would make no more silent films, he did an about-face in August and returned the studio to a "dual-dual" policy, that is, silent and talking versions of all films, and disc and optical sound tracks for all talking films.[24]

These policies were symptomatic of the industry's way of dealing with sound. The public's enthusiasm showed no sign of abating. So it was necessary to increase the proportion of talkie to silent releases to meet exhibitors' demands and the pressure of competition from other studios. Yet significant revenue still came from silent shows.

Furthermore, quite a few executives thought that sound was a fad. "Debate over permanency of the talkers continues at the studios," reported *Film Daily*. "Despite the fact that talkers are rolling up big grosses, there are many who believe that only the novelty is putting them over, with their vogue to pass after it wears off. A year's test, based on box office figures, is needed to settle the argument, they say. Meanwhile, studios are working twenty-four hours a day, turning out talkers."[25]

The decisive period proved to be when Hollywood was selling the 1929–1930 season to independent exhibitors. Examining the release statistics highlights the change that was taking place. In the final quarter of the 1928–1929 season (that is, the period ending in April 1929), of the 200 films that actually had been released, more than half (114) were silent-only. But at this critical moment, the proportion of *proposed* releases was very different. The scorecard looked like this: The studios announced 504 films. Less than 10 percent (43) were to be "pure" silents (that is, without sound analogues) compared to more than half in the season just ended. Small independent producers planned most of these. Among the larger studios, only Universal, abiding by Laemmle's promise, announced any silents (with eight). But the transition taking place here was not to the sound film exclusively. The vast majority—360 titles, or 72 percent of the releases— would be dual versions. The number of sound films without silent counterparts proposed for 1929–1930, though greater than before, was still expected to be only about 20 percent of the program. Universal, Pathé, Columbia, United Artists, and First National planned complete silent coverage for their talkies. Of Warners' 35 releases, 30 would have silent versions. Paramount would issue 28 talkers with 13 silent versions. (INTERFERENCE [1928], for example, which Roy Pomeroy directed as an all-dialogue feature, was made as a silent by Lothar Mendes.) Two-thirds of MGM's 50 releases would have silent covers. Clearly, it would have been against Hollywood's economic interest to junk silent cinema, and the producers had no intention of doing so.

Though it is easy to look back at the heyday of the dual version (roughly 1928 through mid-1930) and see it as a transitional stage, this view is not quite accurate. For a while many in the Hollywood establishment envisioned a permanent state of coexistence in which silent and sound production would reach a state of balanced equilibrium. At the time they signed with ERPI early in 1928, few expected that sound would predominate. It might not even be permanent. Therefore the dual-version policy was to be a diversification to satisfy a specific market demand. It was a new venture, not an interim stage. A year later, however, the talkies were becoming ubiquitous, and Hollywood was changing its mind.

Part-Talkies

The General Electric engineer Edward Kellogg was unusually frank about his early attitude toward the talkies:

> Many, even of the most enthusiastic advocates of the sound-picture development, were not convinced that the chief function of the synchronized sound would be to give speech to the actors in plays. The art of telling stories with pantomime only (with the help of occasional titles) had been so highly developed, that giving the actors voices seemed hardly necessary, although readily possible. . . .

As one who shared in this misjudgment, I would like to suggest to readers that it is difficult today to divest oneself of the benefit of hindsight. At
that time, the principal examples of sound pictures we had seen were
demonstration films, very interesting to us sound engineers working on the
project, but scarcely having entertainment value. None of us had seen a talking motion picture with a good story, and picture and script well designed
for the purpose. (Edward W. Kellogg, "History of Sound Motion Pictures,"
part 2, *JSMPTE*, July 1955, in Raymond Fielding, ed., *A Technological
History of Motion Pictures and Television* [Berkeley: University of California
Press, 1967], p. 186)

Judging from the surviving films, it is reasonable to think that Kellogg's prejudice against
the screen voice was shared by many filmmakers. During 1927–1929 one film form,
part-talkies, retained the vaunted narrative techniques and cinematic style of the silent
film while also entertaining the curious with the novelty of sound. These movies used
synchronized musical accompaniment throughout most of their length, punctuated by
occasional dialogue sequences.

Part-talkies had an economic rationale. If the dialogue parts were nonessential, they
could be cut out and replaced with explanatory titles to make the silent version service-
able at minimum cost. It now, of course, seems bizarre that silent versions of films like
The Jazz Singer, My Man, The Singing Fool, and Show Boat would circulate, but
they did and were even somewhat successful. Yet if one conceives of sound as an embellishment to a silent film, then the part-dialogue format makes sense. It would preserve
the silent film as an ideal, while exploiting the crowd-pleasing novelty of talking. A good
example is MGM's Mysterious Island (1929). Lionel Barrymore explains his subma-
rine project in the first reel but then is not "heard" from again. This was sufficient to bill
the film as a Barrymore talker. Similarly, Show Boat, released in July 1929, was originally shot silent. It was distributed with a few reels of dialogue, so it was really a goat
gland. Nevertheless, Universal billed it as "100% Talking Singing Dancing Thrilling."[26]

Viewing these surviving films suggests that dialogue was not applied gratuitously but
was used systematically to add interest and excitement to the stories. Many employed
speech as a "thrill" to surprise the moviegoer. Warner Bros.' The First Auto (1927)
used the voice as an interjection. Like all part-talkies, the film has a carefully synchronized sound track which closely matches the mood and action. Conventional dialogue
intertitles convey the "speeches." When the race between the auto and the horse com-
mences, however, something unexpected happens. The starter shouts "Go!" and we hear
as well as see him say it. But then "Go!" also appears in an intertitle. The same redundant effect is created later when the father shouts "Bob!" to his son. We are startled to
hear his voice in addition to having the word supplied on the traditional title card.

Old San Francisco (1927) saves its vocalizing for the climactic earthquake scene.
We hear the rumble and crash as building collapse, the sound of explosions, lip-synched
screams, and people shouting "Run!" and "Help!" The Divine Lady (1928–1929) was
billed as a part-dialogue film by First National, but it should have been accurately
labeled "part-singing" because there is no genuine recorded dialogue. When Emma
Hamilton (Corinne Griffith) visits the Vauxhall fair, she surprises the crowd (and the
film audience) by breaking into song. Though her singing voice is foregrounded, the film
denies her the possibility of a speaking voice, resulting in some fascinating inconsisten-
cies. For example, Griffith is singing loud and clear, but when she entreats the crowd to

Hank Armstrong (Russell Simpson) shouts to his son Bob in THE FIRST AUTO *(Warner Bros., 1927).*

THE DIVINE LADY (*First National, 1929*). *Corinne Griffith's singing voice does not change with the cut to a closer view.*

join her, or later when she sings and performs at the harp for Horatio Nelson (Victor Varconi), her nonsinging speech is conveyed in mute dialogue titles.

NOAH'S ARK (1929) has several talking sequences. Perhaps to avoid the jolt of the interjected voice, the film introduces talking gradually. For instance, one scene is identified as an "interval" in World War I; it is also an interval of talking in an otherwise synchronized sound film. First we see shots of the inside of the French bistro and hear soldiers singing their drinking song, but the voices do not come from any particular actor. Then an African American soldier who is shooting craps "blows" audibly on his dice. Next comes a scene in which a dancer (Myrna Loy) speaks to Mary (Dolores Costello) and the stage manager claps his hands (showing off Vitaphone's synchrony). We also hear the villain Nickoloff (Noah Beery) speak. His unguenous voice identifies him as a lecherous opportunist. When the speaking parts conclude, the film reverts to its predominantly silent narration, with the essential information presented as titles.

There is no question that, at least at Warner Bros., the part-talking pattern of these films was intentional, despite the huge financial success of the studio's all-talking feature THE LIGHTS OF NEW YORK, released in July 1928. In December 1928, Jack Warner confidently told *Variety* that he had determined the best acoustic proportion in a film to be 75 percent talking to 25 percent silent.[27] The Warner Proportion, as we might call it, shows that talking was still regarded as an "extra added attraction" to be measured out

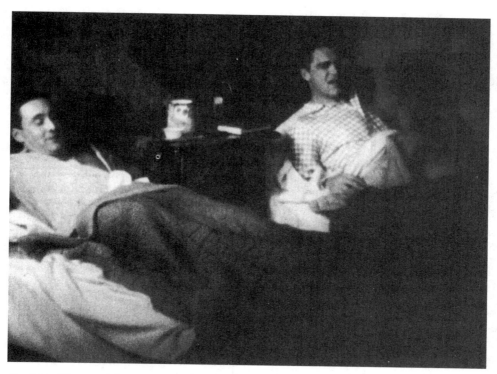

Paul McAllister and George O'Brien banter (awkwardly) in a NOAH'S ARK *dialogue sequence (Warner Bros., 1929).*

and controlled by producers. The Warner vice president Albert Warner, as late as May 1929, expressed his belief in the future of the part-talkie: "For a long time to come pictures will be produced with part sound, song and music, and part silent."[28]

Some other examples of part-talkies released in 1928–1929 are: Warner Bros.' THE SINGING FOOL, GLORIOUS BETSY, THE LION AND THE MOUSE, and TENDERLOIN; MGM's ALIAS JIMMY VALENTINE and LADY OF CHANCE; First National's THE BARKER; Paramount's BEGGARS OF LIFE and VARSITY; UA's LADY OF THE PAVEMENTS; Fox's MOTHER KNOWS BEST; and Pathé's SHADY LADY and SHOW FOLKS.[29]

PART-TALKIES FLOP

By and large, reviewers reacted negatively to the fluctuation of synchronized music and talking in films like THE LION AND THE MOUSE. The *Evening World* said that the film was "both a startling demonstration of the possibilities of talking movies and a horrible example of the things which might happen if this new toy is not kept within complete control. And, as it happens, the horrible example sort of outweighs the other." Hall wrote, "It is . . . a mistake to have silent sequences and then to hear a character who has been silent suddenly boom forth in speech." He believed that the practice drew attention to "the mechanical phase of the production." The reviewer for the *Los Angeles Times* wrote,

"The alternation of voice and silent sequences results in odd shifts of technique that are a bit difficult to become accustomed to. The long dialogues also cut into the physical action, causing in the ending particularly developments for which there is insufficient foundation."[30] This complaint centered on the change in tempo in editing rhythm; "action" and "dialogue" were incompatible. The unexpected shift to communicating plot information verbally rather than visually also upset the *L.A. Times* reporter. The filmgoer became aware of an intrusion into the narration by the "mechanical" aspect of film sound. Hall singled out the intrusiveness of sound in GIVE AND TAKE (Universal, 1928): "In the talking passages . . . there are many spots where the long silences cause one to feel that the people in the story are waiting for the sound wizards to unlock their tongues."[31]

In another synchronized attempt, Paramount's LOVES OF AN ACTRESS (1928), the silent star Pola Negri fared no better. Critics claimed that the sound track was too loud and the effects too abundant.[32] The *Times'* Hall felt that the film "demonstrates ad absurdum the potentialities of synchronization. The varied noises taking part in the action of the picture range from the squealing effect when a baby is shown crying through sundry barnyard effects early one morning to vocal selections. An orchestra in the pit would have been better."[33] Lupe Velez suffered the same merciless critique. Her acting was a bit too bravura in WOLF SONG (Paramount, 1929): "Lupe Velez [is] attractive, but sings between her teeth and heaves her chest like a tired acrobat in 'passionate' love scenes. . . . [She] grabs her mandolin and 'sings' a half dozen times with little provocation. When the film sags, Lupe sings—and the film sags more. Audience laughed at her love making, with chest exercises."[34] *The New York Sun* called Paul Leni's THE LAST WARNING (1929) "a curious and rather dull hodgepodge of bad talking sequences and unrelated silent ones." "Too many outbursts of shrieking, merely to prove the effects of the audible screen, to cause any spine chilling," said the *Times.*[35]

Kann, after seeing TENDERLOIN, summed up the perplexity that this use of sound caused for producers, exhibitors, and audiences alike:

> Exactly what the place [of spoken lines] is and how important it is to fit into the whole scheme nobody understands at this time, because it is an entirely new medium of dramatic expression insofar as motion pictures are concerned. Are the dramatic sequences to be long? Or are they to be short? How often will they fit into the feature without defeating the illusion, undefinable as it often is, that one gets from silent motion pictures? These are questions of moment. (*Film Daily*, 18 March 1928, pp. 1, 3)

The case of TENDERLOIN illustrates that audiences had some limited power to change film content. It was a goat gland, shot silent with four dialogue sequences lasting less than fifteen minutes added later. Kann thought that "the innovation suffered because of the utter banality of the words put into the mouths of the characters." Two days later he took the unusual step of returning to the theater. He reported that, "the second spoken sequence [with Mitchell Lewis] has been cut out. Replaced with Vitaphoned music and the picture is helped. It is still apparent that the injection of dramatic dialogue is a task which the industry will have to familiarize itself [with] before this entirely new element can be mastered."[36]

Not only was there a critical reaction against the part-talkie, but consumers wanted a clarification of the audio status of films in advertising. Sam Katz, the Publix executive who reported to Paramount, announced that owing to customer demand, all films shown thenceforth would be specifically labeled part-talking, all-talking, or synchronized. He declared, "People expect dialogue in all pictures billed as sound films."[37] *Film Daily* saw this trend as the beginning of the end for the part-talkie: "What you can count on for next season [1929–1930] is this: the picture that starts to talk will gab all the way. In betweens are out."[38]

As was the case with the dual-version policy, the part-dialogue feature might seem like a transitional step. Again, this impression is misleading. These films did not replace silents, nor were they replaced by all-talkies; they were contemporaneous with both formats. It seems likely that the producers of these features conceived of them as autonomous products, not as a stepping-stone toward a more advanced form. This conception is consistent with the underlying assumption that sound was a supplement to the movie, not an integral part of it. Eisenstein's observation that sound "was an element that just happened to be added," like widescreen or Technicolor, was perceptive, as usual.

Because of consumer preferences for all-dialogue films, the part-talkie became rare, then disappeared after 1929. Around 1930 the majors phased out silent versions, satisfied to let Poverty Row independents service the few remaining unwired markets. Thus, the transition to all-talking sound was gradual, neither an overnight revolution nor an inevitability.

Remakes, goat glands, dual versions, and part-talkies were to some extent responses to a specific economic problem. Sound-reproducing equipment was not uniformly installed in theaters. The studios needed to maintain a supply of silents until smaller houses had a chance to be wired. It was expected, and "rational," for the industry to continue to serve competing markets. But these film practices also reflect the inherent conservatism of dominant corporations. They resisted change, but when it was forced upon them by the marketplace (consumers and competitors), they attempted to stay in control by limiting technology. These containment efforts are reflected in film style and aesthetics as films were metered to take advantage of sound, but in "doses."

Producers hedged to maintain their silent film markets while incorporating sound as an added value for audiences in more populated locations. During the vogue of the part-talkie, many in Hollywood envisioned the development of a separate branch of filmmaking practice. Hedging strategies would preserve the traditional silent form, albeit with synchronized music effects. From the producers' vantage point, the development of the talkies could have stopped at the stage of the dual version or the part-talkie. There was no technical reason why silent filmmaking could not have proceeded alongside the talkies, just as executives for a brief period had assumed that it would. Or why the "dramatic" and "pantomime" (talking and silent) parts of films could have remained distinct. The pressure was external, from audiences.

The unique look and feel of the part-talkie reflected the novelty of synchronized recorded sound in 1927–1928. But after about two years traditional Hollywood cinema was reaffirmed. Films like THE BROADWAY MELODY, THE COCOANUTS, and THE VIRGINIAN in 1929, and LITTLE CAESAR, WHOOPEE!, and ANNA CHRISTIE in 1930, demonstrated the viability of sound techniques which were subordinate to the needs of narration and supported star values. These films modified traditional genres, often by partially transposing stage sources. They retained the narrative and stylistic norms which viewers expected of silent film: highly comprehensible linear narratives, character-driven plots, rhythmic editing, and fluid camera work. The use of sound in these later films added a new dimension to the film experience, acoustic verisimilitude. The actor's vocal performance takes place within a believable diegetic world. "Natural" sounds, such as background ambience and special effects (foghorns in MIN AND BILL, mooing cows in THE VIRGINIAN), create the illusion that dialogue is part of the recorded world, not something artificially added to it. This facilitates the viewer's imaginary participation in the unfolding narrative, psychological investment in the fate of the characters, and feeling of participating in the construction of the story. This aesthetic is different from that of the part-talkie. Those earlier films highlighted sound and played with the possibilities of surprising, even shocking the spectator with it.

The part-talkie, proposed by Hollywood but abandoned when the artistic and entertainment possibilities of the integrated sound film started to be realized, *could* have taken cinema in a different direction. Sound films might have coexisted with silent production and would have been screened in separate theaters, as Cinerama was in the 1960s and Omnimax and Imax are now. Certain genres, like society dramas, would have been given the sound "treatment," while others, notably slapstick comedy, would have remained "pantomime." This would have been the *real* revolution, had it occurred.

Of course, the all-dialogue form prevailed. Asked in 1929 for a public statement on the future of the silent film, Adolph Zukor pronounced it "doomed by the advent of sound." He added, "We already know from the reaction of the public that [sound] not only is an immense asset artistically, but also from the box-office standpoint." Eight other industry leaders participating in a trade roundtable said basically the same thing: there was no future for the silent picture in the United States.[39] The hedge, which both bought time for Hollywood producers and explored ways of using sound, was over.

Instead, traditional Hollywood standards were retained. Al Lichtman, the vice president and general manager for distribution at United Artists, expressed this sentiment:

> From now on it does not matter whether a picture is silent, with sound, all talking, part-talking or singing. It has to entertain the audience by telling a story effectively. . . .
>
> You can't very well admire electrical apparatus, year after year, when you go to the theater in order to be stirred and entertained. When people become unconscious of the mechanical equipment that reproduces the voice it will be better for the total illusion that must be maintained. (*Film Daily,* 16 December 1928, p. 11)

Lichtman and many others rejected the treatment of sound as an add-on because it destroyed the illusion of a fictional world in which the spectator could imaginatively enter for a while. The classical "suspension of disbelief" was hindered by these intrusive aural moments. Integrated approaches which treated sound and picture as a whole became the new ideal. The director King Vidor proclaimed a vision of a new art which exemplified this attitude toward sound:

> It becomes apparent that sound pictures, as we know them, partake less of the artistic qualities which characterize silent pictures. All the pantomimic art which had taken the silent picture twenty years to develop was cast aside in the grand rush and enthusiasm to achieve the spoken word. When a co-ordination between the two media is accomplished—that is, when sound and pantomime are united to create an impressionistic whole—then we will

have a new art which will be neither the stage, nor the silent or talking pictures as we know them today. It will be a painting with photographic quality and yet retaining the impressionistic inspiration of the painting. (*Film Daily,* 24 February 1930, p. 6)

Vidor's prescription for a film form that would meld image and sound into a unified whole spoke for the "new" approach to sound that prevailed after 1930. In retrospect, the goat glands, dual versions, and part-talkies seem transitional—patches to hold cinema together until it "found its voice." But at the time of their production, they were serious experiments with a new filmmaking practice.

Figure 8.1

FRANK S. IRBY, "THE SOUND-PICTURE INDUSTRY OF THE WORLD"

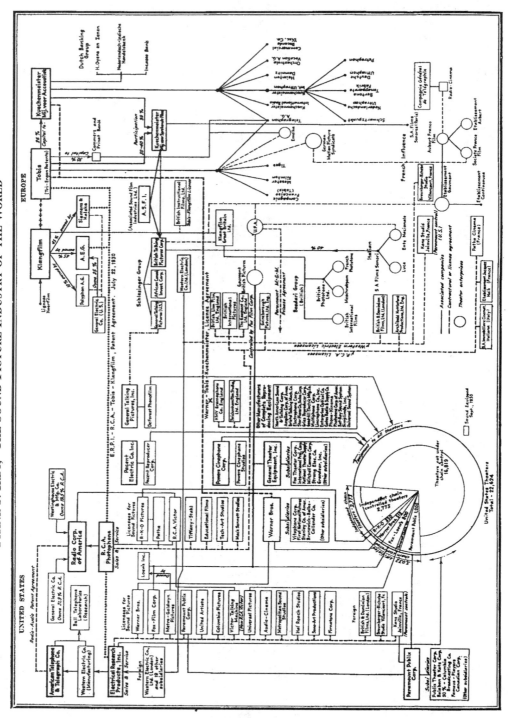

SOURCE: From *Electronics*, July 1930.

8

Boom to Bust

Try Wall Street. That's headquarters for suckers.
BANKER IN *On with the Show*, RELEASED IN JUNE 1929

The transition to sound straddled a watershed in American economic history. The rush to expand business by heavy borrowing and investing created unprecedented growth. Boom times gave the film industry the money for expansion. The collapse of the banking system in 1929–1930 and the onset of the Depression years tested the mettle of the most sophisticated managers. Most industries were affected; many businesses failed. Motion pictures were no different. During the early 1930s all the studios went through varying degrees of reorganization and retrenchment, and several entered involuntary receivership. The coming of sound and the change in Hollywood's fortunes after the Crash of 1929 are inextricably linked. This chapter will give only brief before-and-after snapshots of Hollywood's transition within a growing, then shrinking, economy and discuss the part that sound played in those changes.

As Hollywood capitalized to install sound, build up-to-date stages, and expand its picture-palace outlets, its own way of doing business was influenced by external big business practices. Whether this trend affected the production of specific films is debatable; what is more likely is that it introduced the principles of accountability, efficiency, and "scientific management" that business leaders were espousing in the 1920s. An infusion of executives from power companies contributed to the vague notion that movies were a kind of public utility, like gas, water, and electricity. Like many good businessmen, movie leaders looked to Washington for aid in improving profits. But the national expansion needed to convert to sound, and the resulting restraint of trade also led the industry closer to infracting the antitrust laws. Though the industry tried to maintain the appearance of being depression-proof, in fact the stock market crash hit Hollywood hard, if somewhat later than it hit most other businesses. Retrenchment entailed closing unprofitable theaters, stripping away nonessential distribution services, and streamlining the Hollywood product by confining it to generic categories.

In 1930, the editor of *Electronics* magazine, Franklin S. Irby, attempted to express graphically the complexity of the motion-picture industry by means of a remarkable organizational chart (figure 8.1). It illustrates the new post-sound, post-Crash business environment. Octopus-like, the film industry had spread across nations and other businesses. This complex of interlocking corporate relations was the result of aggressive acquisition and defensive position-taking triggered by sound and unexpected shifts in the economic circumstances of movie consumers.

1928–1929: Bullish in Hollywood

The furor over sound peaked in 1928. Maurice Kann observed that "all signs of reason seem to have been abandoned in the stampede toward sound which now prevails. Such rapidity of decision, marked as it is by a lack of complete analysis, is a sorry enough condition for the trade to face."[1] In its synopsis of 1928, *Film Daily Year Book* reported the difficulty that theaters experienced in keeping up with the change:

> July was proving a heyday for the wired houses, and conversely, the unwired ones were fighting with their backs to the wall. With all attention being centered on sound films, unwired houses were hard hit. Silent films were not being given proper attention, from several standpoints, notably exploitation. Frenzied efforts were being made to provide a synchronizer within reach of the little fellow's pocketbook. Many exhibitors were installing non-synchronous equipment, figuring mechanical music and sound effects would put over their shows, but their patrons were demanding talkers. Uncertainty and confusion were the result. (*Film Daily Year Book 1929*, p. 499)

As business conservatives, the Big Five producers expected to track demand without overinvesting in hardware. Taking a lesson from factory management techniques, the studios aimed to rationalize production. Examples might be the stringent divisions of labor that managers instituted in the late 1920s, or the detailed budget analysis and accounting procedures used by all the producers. The models for these operations were borrowed from chain stores—whose outlets were thought to be analogous to movie theaters—and from electric utilities, perhaps because they too "distributed" an intangible product to the masses, and because their investments were also sensitive to interest rates. Balio and Gomery have shown, however, that rationalization was more of an ideal than a reality, and that good business practices in other industries did not always work in Hollywood.[2] Changes in management, the effects of the Depression on the studios' gross revenues, exhibitor resistance, and especially the fickle taste of the audience—going wild for one cycle of films, then suddenly switching to another—all tended to make the movie business unpredictable. To cope with sound, the producers had to find ways to integrate it into the existing institutional framework, expanding just enough to hold the box-office line, but not too much.

The Washington Connection

Because film was an important growth industry, and because of its glamour and cultural cachet, the film moguls found friends in politics and the Republican White House. Calvin Coolidge was invited to appear in several talking newsreels, the most famous of which was Fox's Movietone record of Lindbergh's reception in Washington. After Herbert Hoover was elected in November 1928, things looked even rosier for the movie moguls. Hoover had been secretary of commerce since 1921, sitting on Harding's cabinet beside Will H. Hays, who had been postmaster general. Hoover had been keenly interested in radio and the movies and was receptive to the industry's needs. When Hays left the cabinet to head the Motion Picture Producers and Distributors Association (MPPDA), he worked with the Commerce Department to establish a special motion picture division.

Hoover was philosophically disposed toward cooperation among businesses and encouraged the associationist movement that typified American capitalism in the twenties.[3] This idea encouraged businesses to band together to regulate competition and share the market in the name of efficiency and limiting "wasteful" competition. Associationism was part of a pervasive philosophy of business, exemplified by a shift away from agrarian values and individual enterprise and toward social association. The historians Thomas C. Cochran and William Miller note that "American business, under the leadership of international corporations, interstate trade associations, national chambers of commerce, and 'booster' organizations, had already become much more cooperative than competitive, much more social than individualistic." Hoover's FTC had become "a research organization to discover ways in which business managers could cooperate more successfully. The Federal Trade Commission had originally been formed to check violations of the Clayton Antitrust Act. Under business pressures it became an instrument for rationalizing such violations."[4] The task of enforcing antitrust laws fell to the Justice Department, which administered them selectively, subject to all kinds of political influence.

The explosive expansion of the film industry in 1927–1929 was set against this background. Easy money flowed into the studios from consumers financing their leisure time on revolving credit plans and from brokers, banks, and big corporations eager to issue initial public offerings of movie company stock, float bonds, and give outright loans secured by the ever-growing chains of theaters and the rapidly appreciating land beneath them. The studios were awash with cash, credit, real estate, and stock equity. Studios were able to rebuild their physical plant for making films and to bid for movie chains in which to show them. The expense of sound conversion was immense, but so was the payoff. Will Hays reported to the U.S. Chamber of Commerce that it cost 22.5 percent more to run the film business in 1929 than it did in 1928. Even with this extra overhead, film company profits for the fiscal year ending 30 September surpassed those for 1928 by a wide margin; the *Wall Street News* attributed these returns to talking pictures.[5] Kann compared the consolidations and huge gains for the big chain theaters to Woolworth's stores, which had a similar rise in profits of 25–125 percent over the same period in 1928.[6] These profits funded the studios' ventures into experimental technologies, like color, widescreen, television, and, of course, sound.

Herbert Hoover's nomination, acceptance, and inauguration were media events. In Washington, in January 1929, broadcasters jostled with five sound newsreel trucks. President Hoover displayed a revitalized interest in motion pictures, and the film industry responded warmly, eager to reap federal favors. Hoover's friend Louis B. Mayer had introduced the president to William Randolph Hearst and the California clique after the 1924 election and chaired the Republican Party in California. Mayer exemplified the 1920s businessman-lobbyist.

> Since America's economy had become dependent to a large extent upon new consumers' goods industries and the success of these industries depended upon good public relations, it is not surprising that businessmen sought increasing social control. And since their "prosperity" won for them the confidence of a large part of the population, they became more than ever before the fountainheads of American ideas and the arbiters of

American morality. (Thomas C. Cochran and William Miller, *The Age of Enterprise: A Social History of Industrial America* [New York: Macmillan, 1942; reprint, New York: Harper & Row, 1961], p. 324)

Mayer was among the first guests to stay in the White House and had the president's ear when Fox took over Loew's, Mayer's parent company. It has been assumed (though not proven) that the Justice Department suit against Fox was in recognition of Mayer's loyalty.

On 9 May 1929, the White House screening room was wired for sound. Hoover asked Hays to select and install the apparatus. (He chose Western Electric.) *Film Daily* reported (a bit coyly perhaps?) that "both the President and Mrs. Hoover are very fond of pictures, but have seen few other than newsreels, which are shown two nights a week." Fox's THE VALIANT (1928), starring Paul Muni, became in June the first talkie feature screened in the White House. Exhibitors also played the Washington game. Coolidge's FTC chair, Abram F. Myers, became the new head of the Allied States Association, a powerful exhibitors' organization. It represented the independents and rivaled the Motion Picture Theater Owners of America (MPTOA), which represented the affiliated chains.[7] His connections in the Department of Justice transformed Allied States into a powerful check against the studio oligopoly.[8]

Producers and exhibitors had good reasons to cultivate federal commendation. The mergers and acquisitions of the late 1920s, made in part out of a desire to corner the sound market, had triggered investigations into Hollywood's monopolies and marketing schemes. Hoover's new attorney general, William DeWitt Mitchell, in an American Bar Association speech, vowed to enforce the antitrust laws. He singled out his predecessor's lackadaisical attitude toward Hollywood for attack. Specifically, he began investigating Fox and Warner Bros. for possible violations of the Clayton Antitrust Act. (Fox would pay the consequences in 1931, but the Warners suit was dismissed in 1934.)[9] Mitchell's offensive coincided with the post-Crash downturn in the economy, so the era of merger mania dried up anyway for lack of capital.

COOPERATIVE STRATEGIES

One way to cope with risk is to share it. The various self-protective associations worked well to defuse whatever threat sound may have represented. David Bordwell has shown how the producers banded together to exploit mutually their combined power to resist trade unionization, cosponsor research on incandescent lighting, and utilize the Producers-Technicians Committee of the Academy of Motion Picture Arts and Sciences (AMPAS) to carry out research and standardize practices. Discourses about "art" and "quality" (and events like awards ceremonies) enhanced the public's perception of the social and aesthetic value of Hollywood's products.[10] One could add as associationist examples the Five-Cornered Agreement, the creation of the Central Casting Corporation, the studios' support of ERPI's music-licensing department, and reciprocal agreements by competing distributors to book each other's films into their chains. Such arrangements were not magnanimous expressions of brotherhood, of course. They were founded on hardheaded business practices intended to limit the access of independents to the benefits of oligopoly. The coming of sound was precisely the kind of rocking of the boat that strategic planning and cooperative action were designed to control. The industry in general used the "threat" of sound to centralize and solidify its academy, its associations, and its distribution practices.

The Academy grew more assertive. In 1930 AMPAS used funds donated by the MPPDA to pursue its technical research through activities such as "sound schools." The first one was attended by 550 film workers. Sharing production secrets disseminated knowledge, but it also forwarded the goals of the Academy by standardizing the product and softening any competitive edge that one company might gain in technology.[11] Members of guild organizations—for example, the American Society of Cinematographers (incorporated in 1919)—as well as independent workers, writers, composers, and technicians migrated freely and shared knowledge among studios.

The Hays Office lobbied strongly and successfully on behalf of its members. The organization is best known for its Code of Ethics on Production and Advertising, which the industry adopted in December 1930. But the office was effective in many other

"Charging that the Fox West Coast Theatres constitute an arrogant monopoly which seeks to stifle the endeavor of motion picture artists and producers, these world famous personalities of the United Artists organization have announced they, if necessary, will show their pictures in tents, armories and halls, but in the future will not show them in the theatres of the Fox West Coast 'trust'. (Left to right) Al Jolson, Mary Pickford, in one of the costumes she wears in her latest picture, KIKI, Ronald Colman, Gloria Swanson, Douglas Fairbanks, Joseph M. Schenck, president and chairman of the board of the United Artists Corporation; Charley [sic] Chaplin, Samuel Goldwyn, Eddie Cantor." (Original UA caption, 1930)

HOOVER PROSPERITY!

Guaranteed in the motion picture industry by "THE BROADWAY MELODY," the Talking, Singing, Dancing Wonder Drama; WILLARD MACK'S "THE VOICE OF THE CITY," 100 per cent TALKING, *also silent version;* "THE DUKE STEPS OUT" (Haines, Crawford) "THE FLYING FLEET" (Novarro) "ALIAS JIMMY VALENTINE" William Haines' $2 Astor TALKING Hit; "THE BELLAMY TRIAL," The $2 Embassy TALKING Success; "WILD ORCHIDS" (Garbo) "A WOMAN OF AFFAIRS" (Gilbert-Garbo) and many more great Metro-Goldwyn-Mayer Pictures.

MGM rides the coattails of "Hoover Prosperity" in March 1929.

ways. Will Hays, for instance, presided over the Paris conference on world sound patents. And he helped in little ways, as when he petitioned the Interstate Commerce Commission to lower express shipping rates on movie discs. In May 1930, the producers united behind the MPPDA to declare a moratorium on widescreen systems until a uniform standard could be adopted, replaying their approach to sound three years earlier.[12] Hays maintained cordial relations with the Academy as well as the Association of Motion Picture Producers (AMPP) (founded in 1924). The latter group sought to improve public relations, but it also owned the important Central Casting Corporation, which placed extras in the films of all producers.[13]

The exhibition sector had its own associations and its share of collusive practices. Publix and Warner Bros., for example, declared that they would stop buying houses in each other's territory and would show and promote each other's product. Warners and First National films were booked reciprocally into the Fox and Loew's circuits. Universal, which had shed most of its theaters, booked its features into RKO's first-run houses and the Warner-Stanley chain. United Artists ran its films in all Warner Bros., Publix, and Loew's theaters. The Columbia lineup would play in Warner Bros. houses. Of course, cooperation had its limits. The compatibility issue was briefly resuscitated when Warners insisted that all films have disc recordings to play in its chains, even if that required making a new sound track.[14] It quickly backed down. Another dissonant note sounded when Joseph Schenck discontinued showing United Artists pictures in Fox West Coast theaters because of a dispute over rental fees.[15] The artists said they would rather show their films in tents and armories than in Wesco theaters. But aside from these exceptions, the noncompetitive exhibition arrangements are a good example of how the majors attempted to maximize profits for all through cooperation, while making it more difficult for independents to play on a level field.[16]

The Justice Department continued to target these and similar cooperative strategies. Slowly small cracks appeared in the motion picture industry's monopoly. For example, in November 1930, the Supreme Court upheld a judgment against the Hays Office, the Film Boards of Trade, and ten distributors, finding that part of the studios' standard exhibition contract violated the Sherman Antitrust Act.[17]

The End of the "New Era"

Wall Street, according to *Variety's* historic headline, laid an egg on 29 October. Until then, the year 1929 had been one long boom. In February a commentator noted that "interest in the stock market, which the public is going in for heavily these days is seen as a contributing factor in the strong box office draw being shown by THE WOLF OF WALL STREET [1929]."[18] In "Vast Movie Crowds Key to Prosperity," the *New York Times* reported long lines at theaters in August, usually the dead month. The writer surmised that, in addition to the presentation acts, air cooling, and "audible film," it was "increased national prosperity" that undoubtedly attracted crowds.[19] These articles reflect the prevailing sense of affluence. Although paychecks were low, Americans could collateralize to borrow cash, which could be used for such things as stock-picking on margin, taking the family to the movies, and generally making whoopee (having fun). John Kenneth Galbraith, however, in his classic study of the Crash, maintains that "the long accepted explanation that credit was easy and so people were impelled to borrow money to buy common stocks on margin is obviously nonsense." He attributes the sudden decline in value in part to psychological factors. "Far more important than rate of interest and the supply of credit is the mood. Speculation on a large scale requires a pervasive sense of confidence and optimism and conviction that ordinary people were meant to be rich."[20] Recent analysts have attributed complex causes to the Crash. According to Ned Davis, the 1921–1929 mega-bull run happened when "basically, a revolution in industry caused dramatic productivity gains and therefore booming earnings, thus capturing the fancy of the public investor."[21] Perhaps the mushrooming picture palaces—temples of opulence and conspicuous consumption—and the rapid diffusion of technologically sophisticated distractions, such as the talkies, contributed to the feeling that the New Era really was here to stay.

Margin calls and forced selling dissipated the dream and led to the market meltdowns of 24 and 29 October. The public's infatuation with stock speculation ended abruptly. Jack Alicoate wrote that three out of every five businessmen in the film industry had been hurt. But he also viewed the Crash as a temporary slowdown. Merger talks and financing might be delayed. He pointed out confidently that the movie industry had suffered fewer losses than most big industries, including transportation, oil, steel, chain stores, and utilities.[22] This was optimistic. Although it has been reported that motion pictures were not immediately hurt in the downturn, a look at the ticker shows otherwise. After the Crash, the *New York Times* industrial index fell from a September high of 469.49 to 220.95 in the November trough, down about 53 percent. Film-related stocks seemed to have fared only scarcely better—and several did quite a bit worse.

Table 8.1
Selected Film-Related Stocks

	9 *September 1929*	13 *November 1929*	*Percentage down*
Amer. Tel. & Tel.	304.00	197.25	35.1
Eastman Kodak	214.75	153.00	28.8
General Electric	396.25	168.13	57.6
RCA	101.00	28.00	72.30
Fox Film	97.13	54.75	43.60
Fox Theaters	28.00	11.88	57.6
Loew's	62.50	36.00	42.40
Paramount Famous–Lasky	72.00	41.50	42.4
Pathé Exchange	10.50	4.13	60.1
RKO	36.13	14.50	59.90
Universal Pictures	20.00	8.50	57.5
Warner Bros.	60.50	30.25	50.0

Source: *Film Daily* financial tables; Frederick Lewis Allen, *Only Yesterday* (1931; reprint, New York: Harper & Row, 1964), p. 280. United Artists, which traded over-the-counter, on 3 September 1929 was asking 10, bid 5; on 13 November no trades were listed in *Film Daily*.

Analysts urged calm, predicting the market would bounce back. The motion picture trade also looked for silver linings as film stocks tracked the broad market's descent. Alicoate declared immediately that the market was on an even keel. "Hard times and even panics do not affect desire of American public for clean amusement at cheap prices. This fact alone makes picture stocks of our big established companies as fine an investment as can be had." The next month he wrote, "One thing is certain, this so-called slowing up of business has not hurt this industry and is not likely to."[23] Will Hays assured the U.S. Chamber of Commerce that employment and wages would be even higher than the banner year of 1929 and predicted "still further substantial increase in the attendance."[24]

Meanwhile, New York's mayor, James J. Walker, did his bit. The morning after Black Tuesday, his office telephoned the city's theater managers. Would they please show optimistic pictures as a "means to counteract the depression caused by the crash?"[25] Soon "depression" would take on new meaning.

The Depression Bogey

The Standard Statistics Company confirmed that even with the fourth-quarter shock, 1929 had been one of the best years ever for motion pictures. Profits increased 160.6 percent over 1928. Standard also reported that the three groups with increased profits in the last quarter of 1929 were films, electrical equipment, and food products. The analysts continued, "The average depreciation in motion picture stocks was less than the decrease in such basic industries as foods, automobiles, motor equipment, rubber, leather, chain stores, mail order and others. The 1929 market crash undoubtedly killed what might have been a bull movement in film stocks as a result of the sensational success of talkers." The first quarter of 1930 showed an aggregate increase of 85.4 percent by the six top theater and film companies—compared to an 18.5 percent drop by the index of 306 industrial companies (the forerunner of the Standard & Poor's 500 index). Thus, the amusement business headed their list of "depression-proof" industries.[26]

The advisers of Engerleider & Company assured investors that the movie business was not likely to suffer from the general recession. They repeated a familiar palliative: "The motion-picture-going habit is so deeply rooted in the American public that even in times of business depression theater attendance is little affected." The stock analysts at Theodore Prince & Company also declared that the film industry was now a safe investment and rated motion picture stocks a buy. This optimism was buoyed by company profit reports for 1929. Paramount's were 78 percent higher than in 1928. RCA made $2 million instead of losing money.[27]

The *Wall Street Journal* was not too bothered by reports of an attendance decline, which was more than usual for the season but did not foretell a drastic decrease:

> Movies are an American habit and now that more people than ever have been drawn to the picture houses by sound, any sharp falling off in attendance is unlikely. . . . Sound has enabled the film producers to offer better amusement in the form of Broadway talent heretofore unavailable to the great mass of the public.
>
> . . . While the advent of sound pictures entailed large initial capital expense for soundstages and equipment of theaters, the actual cost of making sound films is no larger than that of silent films and is probably less in many cases. A picture with dialogue must be more carefully planned and there is no filming of expensive scenes to be eliminated later. Also much more work is done in the studios where organization is better instead of on location where daily expenses for maintaining a large company is [*sic*] enormous. (*Film Daily*, 9 June 1930, p. 6)

But even as this was being written, owners were reporting big drops in theater patronage. Nevertheless, Jack Alicoate philosophized:

> The lowest ebb is the turn of the tide. Sane economists and close business observers agree that we are at or about the little junction called the "Turning Point" and from now on the business road should be smoother. Soon business will be booming again and the cares of today will be forgotten in the progress of tomorrow. Clean wholesome amusement is as necessary to the world as food and clothing. (*Film Daily*, 15 July 1930, p. 1)

One symbolic event stoked Alicoate's optimism. Warner Bros.' greater expansion expenses and falling revenue had raised doubts about whether it would suspend its quarterly dividend. When it was paid, there was a sigh of relief. "With attendance upward bound, good profits are just ahead for well-governed film companies. This little business may have its recessions and its occasional difficulties, like any other industry, but it is quick to rebound."[28]

Film executives unanimously agreed, at least in the presence of reporters. The slump was over, and it had been mild. Many promulgated a Darwinist view that strong films would drive the weaker ones from the theaters. Al Lichtman, vice president and general manager of United Artists, said,

> Economics can't be blamed for inferior pictures, and the only pessimists are those with duds on their hands. . . . All this talk of depression really

means nothing in the face of genuinely entertaining attractions. It seems to me that weak stories, lacking in punch and originality, have been at the bottom of our depression, that not enough care has been taken in preparing the picture before the cameras start turning. (*Film Daily*, 3 September 1930, p. 11; 28 August 1930, p. 1)

Cecil B. DeMille, filmmaker turned dilettante economist, also spoke out:

Let me say a word about "depressions." From Squaw Man [1914] to [The] Squaw Man [1931] I have seen about four of the gloomy periods we are now undergoing. Out of them all I have gained just one central thought and that is "depressions" are bad on bad pictures; but they never really affect good entertainment. In bad times people seek relaxation more energetically than in days of prosperity, but they shop more for their shows. You can't satisfy them with bunk. You must deliver the goods in entertainment, and if you do, good pictures have always broken records in even the worst of "panics." (Cecil B. DeMille, "Squawman," *Hollywood Reporter*, December 1930, quoted in Tichi Wilkerson and Marcia Borie, *The Hollywood Reporter: The Golden Years* [New York: Arlington House, 1984], pp. 28–29)

The people at Fox subscribed to the view that the Depression was caused by consumers not spending enough. Movietone released a short to stimulate recovery. Its little parable showed a Mr. Courage telling Mr. Fear to spend an extra dollar a week. A narrator "urges the public to shake off the fear and overcaution that is mostly to blame for the depression."[29]

Sam Katz tried a psychological tactic and issued orders to his Publix personnel to join in a war against the "depression bogey." He declared, "Theaters are directed to see that a note of joy, happiness and optimism is injected into all parts of every program and advertising." Alicoate applauded: "'Bad times' often are nothing more than bad mental conditions, gloomy exaggerations of natural cycles in affairs. Putting the public mind in a healthy state by filling it with cheer and assurance is one of the surest methods of promoting 'good times.'"[30]

Despite these salutary words, the reality of economics crept in. One indicator was the increasing number of thieves who went after movie box offices. A particularly bold bandit took $11,000 from the till of the Broadway Paramount. But 250 other New York vicinity theaters had nothing to steal. Even as rampant closures swept the East, distributors were optimistic that "aggregate patronage" would not be affected. By late May, 700 houses had gone out of business in the metropolitan area. The theater owners' association put the best face on it. It was just as well that these "junk" theaters had been weeded out.[31]

Nine Chicago silent houses closed owing to competition with sound theaters. "Chief among the houses that have gone dark," *Film Daily* reported, "are the Monogram, Indiana and Vendome, in the Negro district, where serious unemployment has been a contributing factor." By June 1930, thirty-one more Chicago houses had closed.

Audiences would not or could not pay two dollars a ticket for "road shows" anymore, and everyday "popular prices" were lowered, at first to a maximum of fifty cents. Alicoate doubted that this was a healthy trend and pointed to radio set manufacturing as a cautionary example for exhibitors:

"Should prices be reduced?" Here is a mooted question that seems to be raging in many sections of the country. . . . Last year the radio folks were forced to slash prices right and left as the result of overproduction. The result was that they could hardly give sets away. Keep your attractions up to a standard and your admission price will take care of itself. (*Film Daily,* 15 July 1930, p. 1)

By December the price-cutting was being described as an epidemic. Thirty-five-cent admissions were not uncommon. Lower ticket prices led to even more austere retrenchment. Katz ordered "rock bottom" cost-cutting for the Publix chain. Following suit, Fox West Coast banned all billboard advertising and slashed the remaining advertising budget by 10 percent.[32]

One economizing measure was to drop male ushers for female usherettes because the girls worked cheaper. "The current crop of prospective usherettes is exceptionally large, owing to depression in nearly all fields of commercial activity, and the girls are willing to work for from 20 to 30 percent less than boys," laconically reported *Film Daily.*[33]

Producers embarked on retrenchment by closing the few remaining New York studios. Pathé, for example, abandoned East Coast production after completing the January 1930 schedule. Only the Metropolitan Sound Studios in Fort Lee (which serviced independents), Paramount in Astoria, and Warners' Vitaphone studio in Flatbush remained committed to New York shooting. The studios' need for Broadway-based musicals and short playlets justified the policy.[34]

On the West Coast, Fox consolidated by closing its old studio at Sunset Boulevard and Western Avenue and moved to its new Movietone City lot. Warners also relocated most of its Sunset Boulevard operations to Burbank, leasing out its former space to independents. (One tenant was Leon Schlesinger, whose cartoon series Warners distributed. The animators nicknamed the premises at 1123 North Bronson Avenue "Termite Terrace.") In October the ever-optimistic *Film Daily* saw these moves as another turning point: "Film industry companies have completed their retrenchment movements, with shakeups and cutting of forces and salaries at an end. . . . The industry will no doubt be enabled to make rapid and broad strides toward that talked-about era of new prosperity."[35]

One strategy to aid producers and exhibitors was surreptitious, anticipating what is now called product placement. In RKO's DANGER LIGHTS (1930), a new-model RCA-Victor phonograph was displayed prominently in close-up for thirty seconds in the party scene. As a cross tie-in, Victor gave a free phonograph and ten records to each RKO house that played the film, while RCA dealers plugged the show with displays in their stores. Though no money changed hands, the practice skirted the MPPDA policy that discouraged direct advertising in films. Citing verbal allusions to cigarette brands and highly visible billboards placed in movie backgrounds, in November the producers ordered a ban on all name-brand product references. They claimed that the practice amounted to free advertising and competed with their own efforts to initiate paid advertising in the guise of industrial shorts. They had another reason, however, for discouraging advertising—audience intolerance. Trailers for products were frequently greeted with catcalls by viewers. It was reported that a "commercial film" shown at the Strand prompted at least thirty people to walk out. "Many others were heard suppressing something in the nature of a groan. New Yorkers, at least, don't seem to care for commercial advertising as part of their screen bill-of-fare." In November the Fox circuit banned all advertising within its theaters. Since 1928 (the inception of the CBS network), radio had

Product placement: sheet music published by companies owned by Warner Bros. is prominent in Success *(Vitaphone short, 1931, with Jack Haley);* The Gigolo Racket *(Vitaphone, 1931) plugs a Warner Movie.*

been rapidly transformed into a sponsor-subsidized form; providing ostensibly advertising-free entertainment was part of the film industry's attempt to differentiate itself from radio by cultivating an aura of quality and public service.[36]

Sound Effects: Studio Strategies

The following account shows how the major studios dealt with the need to adapt hastily to sound production, then to cope with the changing external demands of the Depression. The trends before the Crash were: changes in the infrastructure, acquisition of music rights, technological competition, and building up production in New York and Hollywood. After 1930 the studios cut back budgets, downsized, and focused on turning out product that would add to the bottom line.

WARNER BROS./FIRST NATIONAL

Warner Bros. matched its technological innovation with a voracious appetite for theaters. Based on the cash flow from Vitaphone, the financial guru Waddill Catchings encountered little difficulty raising money on the promise of even greater future earnings. In September 1928, he put together a deal to acquire the 270-theater Stanley chain. In another lightning move, Warners acquired the St. Louis Skouras chain and appointed Spyros Skouras head of the suddenly huge Warner theater empire.[37] Warners also gained Stanley's controlling interest in First National.

First National was the earliest of the major filmmakers to commit publicly to a sound system. President Clifford Hawley announced in April 1928 that the company would adopt a system called Firnatone. Having no sound facilities or expertise of its own, First National had hired the Victor Talking Machine Company, which had cross-licensed its music rights in exchange for ERPI's recording license agreement, thus permitting Victor to enter the movie sound-track business as a freelance provider. Licensed from Western Electric and installed by ERPI, Firnatone was a disc recording system identical in every respect except its name to Vitaphone. ERPI and Victor technicians traveled to the Burbank studios to decide which First National properties would be most amenable to the Firnatone treatment.[38] They determined that LA TOSCA was the most promising project and started planning a talking version with Billie Dove. But executives felt otherwise. Hawley wanted Colleen Moore's next production, LILAC TIME, to premiere with dialogue, but Moore, on the advice of her husband, manager, and First National producer John McCormick, vetoed the idea. Nathaniel Shilkret recorded the music in June at the Victor studios in Camden, New Jersey, while a crew visited the Philadelphia Navy Yard to record the sounds of planes and machine guns.[39] But Joseph Kennedy took over First National, Hawley was out, and so was his sound system. When the film premiered at the Carthay Circle in Los Angeles with a Photophone track, it was not successful. The effects were judged by the *Herald* to be "not entirely in hand." The *Los Angeles Times* agreed: "Photophone, with which LILAC TIME is synchronized, was not effective at all times last night. Certain sequences produced an almost deafening roar, even taking it for granted that seven aeroplanes combined can stir up quite a lot of racket."[40] For its general release, this and all other First National films were distributed with discs.

Kennedy had not been able to pull the organization together, and his ruthless cost-cutting had devastated morale. Two weeks after he quit as First National's financial con-

First National/Vitaphone studios, Burbank, 1929.

sultant, Warners paid $3.8 million for a controlling interest in the franchise.[41] The deal gave Warner Bros. a place at the table with the other big producers, distributors, and exhibitors. It also gained the extensive First National production facility in Burbank, California, which was built beginning in 1922.[42] Although still legally autonomous, Warners and First National studios thenceforth functioned as one, with Jack Warner in charge.

The two companies' foreign offices were merged in January 1929. The stages on the Burbank lot were completely refurbished, giving First National all-dialogue production capacity by March. Previously, sound films made at Burbank were recorded by sending the signal over telephone lines to Vitaphone equipment at the Sunset Boulevard lot. After the October stock market crash put William Fox, a minority partner in First National, in desperate straits, Warners bought out his 36 percent. According to the terms of purchase, the First National brand had to continue to be used. It was a good deal for Warners. The worldwide First National exchange allowed Warners to compete with the big distributors. And the studio acquired significant performer contracts, for example, those of Richard Barthelmess, Douglas Fairbanks, Jr., Loretta Young, Billie Dove, and Constance Bennett.

The studio's strong balance sheet led to more bold expansion moves. In January, Warners bought M. Witmark and Sons, a major music publisher. That summer it picked up Dreyfus, Harms, and five others to form the Music Publishers Holding Company. This move was a carefully strategized plan to control all of its own film music, and perhaps that of other producers as well. It was also a salvo aimed at ERPI. The agreement with the Music Publishers Protective Association (MPPA) that enabled ERPI to sublicense compositions was about to expire. Instead of having to pay royalties through ERPI, Warners could now simply buy the publishers. The music historians Russell Sanjek and David Sanjek conclude that "Warner Brothers' purchase of the Witmark business and the impending deal to buy all of the Dreyfus music holdings clearly indicated that they intended to pull the MPPA down." When the ERPI contract expired, instead of dealing with a cartel of publishers, film companies would have to deal with a Warner subsidiary.[43] In 1930, Warners bought Brunswick-Balke-Collender, a diversified music, phonograph, and entertainment company, for $11 million. The package included radio and phonograph patents as well as record-manufacturing plants and recording studios around the world. The plan enabled Warner Bros. to press its own records, effecting savings for both its Vitaphone operation and its consumer music libraries. The deal did not include the Brunswick bowling and billiard equipment business. Although Harry Warner later said this omission was a mistake, it made sense at the time, indicating the company's desire to restrict its diversification to the field of "electrical" entertainment.[44]

Controlling music was essential in 1928–1929 because musicals and talkies were almost synonymous. The studio clearly believed that monopolizing access to music was a way to dominate film sound. In Burbank the composers physically displaced the writers—a move that clearly indicated music was in the air:

> In a big office building on the First National/Vitaphone lot the song-writers under contract to that company have taken up their abode. Formerly the building housed only scenarists and "gag men." Now it is filled with the sound of pianos, saxophones, voices raised in song and the tap-tapping of clog dancers. It is musical headquarters. From morning to night songs are written and tried out and the dialogue scenes for "talkies" are rehearsed

within these walls. (SMILING IRISH EYES souvenir program, 1929, Yranski Collection)

A look at the 1 February 1929 contract that Jack Warner signed with the composer Gus Edwards (who was working for MGM) reveals how important owning one's own music was. "If I Came Back to You and Said I'm Sorry" was written exclusively for THE GAMBLERS (1929). Warner Bros. reserved all motion picture rights, and the studio was careful to limit further film use of its new song:

> It is definitely understood, however, that no royalty whatsoever shall be payable to you upon any other form of reproduction of such song, either words or music, except upon such sheet music, and in particular, no royalties whatsoever shall be payable upon any reproduction thereof by records, sound or discs used in connection with the Vitaphone or other instrument for the synchronization of sound with pictures which may be provided with such method of reproduction. We shall in all cases be entitled to the free and exclusive use without payment of any royalty whatsoever for Vitaphone or other synchronized method of projection or other motion picture purposes, including the use of title, words, music or any portion or portions thereof. (Agreements file 1080a, Warner Bros. Collection, University of Southern California)

But Edwards's terms were potentially very lucrative for him. He received a $1,500 advance, one cent per copy from all sheet music sales (which could be substantial), and 22 percent of Warners' share of radio broadcast or phonograph record income.

The Warners' spending spree continued through the first quarter of 1929 when the brothers tried to merge with United Artists in a deal masterminded by UA's head, Joseph Schenck. Chaplin was the first of the "Artists" to balk, saying that he would rather bid out his films than relinquish control. The proposal died in May when Pickford, Fairbanks, and finally the Warner brothers themselves could not stand to give up autonomy.[45]

Warners rehabbed the Hollywood Vitagraph studio and added a new soundstage in Flatbush, Brooklyn. Here production of Vitaphone shorts under Bryan Foy's supervision continued at a brisk clip—more than one hundred in the first quarter of 1929.[46]

Mastering other technologies, analogous to controlling music publishing, was another competitive strategy. The management of Warner Bros. thought that color held the same promise as sound. The search was on throughout 1929 for a pleasing yet practical system. In February, Jack Warner announced that six color features would employ a process developed by Lee Fargue, a French inventor. This arrangement evidently did not work out, for shortly thereafter Warners signed a contract with Technicolor for fifty-six color and sound pictures (on the Warner Bros. and First National labels) to be made over the next two years. ON WITH THE SHOW (1929) would be first, then SALLY (1929).[47]

Technicolor had established a lead in the color business. Like sound, color was considered a special "treatment" to be reserved for scenes of spectacle and pageantry, or used expressively, as in Paramount's REDSKIN (1928). Here black-and-white footage and color alternated for dramatic effect, distinguishing the monochrome East from the colorful West. A newly developed process had reduced the cost of color prints (though they were still four times higher than black-and-white) and improved their durability. Although this option did not apply to disc users, the new prints were now capable of car-

SALLY (*First National, 1929) souvenir program.*

rying a silver optical sound track. Technicolor's two-color process reproduced only in shades of blue-green and orange-red. In August 1929, a new Hollywood plant doubled the company's capacity. Warners clearly wished that its expensive alliance with Technicolor would give it another competitive edge on the industry, as sound had done.

Chafing at its perceived abuse by ERPI—suits and countersuits were still wending through the courts—Warner Bros. bought the Nakken Patents Corporation to acquire that company's basic patents in sound-on-film, television, and a process for the "transmission of pictures and facsimile messages by wire and radio."[48] Warner Bros. also openly backed an alternative sound reproduction system developed by Louis Gerard Pacent, a radio engineer. Although it too used discs, in many ways the Pacent system was superior to Vitaphone. For instance, it used no batteries, a relief from the troublesome wet cells that powered the Western Electric horns. Pacent said that its dynamic speakers with tuned baffles gave better distribution of sound. The amplifier used two channels (monaural) for superior reproduction, and one could serve as a backup if the other failed. Finally, the $2,500–3,500 price, based on a house's size, handily beat ERPI. Warner sales agents were reported to be actively pushing the system. Vitaphone issued a carefully worded statement on compatibility:

> [Vitaphone] will require reproduction of its product by means of equipment which operates properly, reliably and efficiently to reproduce the same with adequate volume and quality equal to that obtained by the use of equipment supplied by Electrical Research Products, Inc. Where such satisfactory equipment is installed, The Vitaphone Corporation will, subject to its regular sales policies and then existing commitments, enter into negotiations with the exhibitor for its product. (*Film Daily*, 8 February 1929, p. 9)

This assured theaters that they could play Vitaphone discs on other systems—such as Pacent's—if Vitaphone approved. The orders came in, and Pacent started manufacturing 250 machines per month.

Not unexpectedly, AT&T, Western Electric, and ERPI sued Pacent for infringing on eight patents granted between 1915 and 1924. Separately, Western Electric sued the Stanley Company (as part of Warners) for installing encroaching Pacent systems. Ordinarily, just the threat of an ERPI lawsuit was sufficient to make alleged infringers capitulate, but Louis Pacent was in the extraordinary position of having Warners' backing. His lawyers won a dismissal on a technicality, but John Otterson doggedly refiled. The suit was dismissed again and appealed again until, in 1932, ERPI won.[49]

Despite gobbling up theaters and music publishers, investing in speculative technologies, and indirectly challenging the supremacy of AT&T and RCA in theater sound, Warners was still flush. At the end of its 1929 fiscal year, net profits for all operations were up a breathtaking 744 percent over 1928. The rental data summarized by H. Mark Glancy (see appendix 1) reveal what an extraordinary year the 1928–1929 season was for the studio: "In this early sound period Warner Bros. had broken away from its 'poverty row' image and emerged as an industry leader. One measure of its success can be seen in the fact that the average earnings figure for 1928–1929 ($973,000 [per feature]) was well above that of MGM ($808,000)."[50]

The year 1930 was, economically, a peak for Warner Bros. With assets of more than $230 million, it now ranked as one of the Big Five. Yet the Depression took a quick and heavy toll, and the studio would not be financially secure again for nearly twenty years.[51]

Warners began the year on a roll, with many ambitious plans. By February all Warner-Stanley houses were showing only sound films. Warners again affirmed its commitment to color production and announced it would begin shooting widescreen Vitascope films on 65-mm stock. Jack Warner had started an extensive renovation of the Sunset lot, the forty-acre Warner Ranch backlot, and a tripling of the Burbank studio plant to an aggregate floor space of one and a half million square feet. An upgraded Vitaphone studio in Brooklyn, under the supervision of Murray Roth, was capable of finishing six shorts a week. (Bryan Foy was transferred to Burbank in January to make features, replaced in Brooklyn by Herman Raymaker.)[52]

While the serious decline in revenue that began in the summer of 1930 hit Warners hard, the seeds of the studio's unmaking had been planted in its highly leveraged acquisitions and internal expansion. The debt had stretched the balance sheet thin. Furthermore, Warner Bros. had invested heavily in the musical and operetta genres. The audience spurned these films in 1930, but the notes, interest payments on bonds, and mortgage payments kept coming. Earnings for the first quarter of 1930 were $1.67 million, down 55 percent from the first quarter of 1929. In August, Harry Warner initiated extensive retrenchment and refinanced short-term debt by floating new stock. After he resisted a shareholder group which charged mismanagement and sued to put the company in receivership, the stock issue raised $17 million in capital, enabling Warner Bros. to show a net 1930 profit of $7 million.[53]

Instead of cutting back on quantity and increasing production value, the studio seemed to do just the opposite. Production was stepped up, and Jack Warner moved his executive offices to Burbank. Both East and West Coast studios continued to work at full speed all spring with eight productions per week. The Brooklyn Vitaphone facility was operating at full capacity: it set a new record by filming twenty shorts at a time in November 1930.[54] The following year the Brooklyn studio was expanded. Space for six writers was added, and Warners acquired land next to the studio for future development.[55]

Warners made two important changes. The original sixteen-inch discs were replaced by lighter twelve-inch recordings, made possible by narrower grooves. And the company conceded the increasing use of optical sound. The six First National and three Warner Bros. films currently in release and all of the fall 1930–1931 season would be available with sound either on film or on disc. THE DAWN PATROL (1930) and SALLY (1930) were among the First National films to be distributed in both sound formats.[56]

Retrenchment made greater production efficiency mandatory. Before sound, the Warner and First National units normally had a fall layoff so that workers would not have to be paid. When Darryl Zanuck became general manager in 1931, the studio switched to a twelve-month schedule, eliminating the usual hiatus.[57] This change was also supposed to improve quality. Under the new system, directors were to spend twelve to fourteen weeks on each script. A maximum of four films would be in production at once. The most significant change at Warners, though, was the elimination of the banks of multiple cameras shooting scenes simultaneously. Jack Warner emphasized that more preparation, with less shooting, was replacing what he called "the old mass method."[58]

Warners suffered huge losses throughout the 1930s but refused to go into receivership. Instead, theaters and nonproduction assets were shed, budgets and salaries were cut, and loans were refinanced. Meanwhile, the studio produced some of the most popular films of the decade.

Fox Movietone City, as seen in October 1928 and June 1929.

FOX MOVIETONE

William Fox engineered the most astonishing merger of the period. Propelled by gross annual receipts of $135 million, he edged out Warners to buy Loew's theater chain and its MGM studio subsidiary in February 1929. Corporate assets swelled to eight hundred theaters, worth around $225 million. (In addition to the Roxy in New York, the company also owned Grauman's Chinese on Hollywood Boulevard.) Fox confidently boasted that by the end of 1929 he would have one million movie seats. This was an empire built on talking; on 24 March 1929, the studio announced that it had made its last silent film.[59] Fox ceased making vaudeville shorts and discontinued all New York production except for the newsreel. Though a hit with theaters and audiences, the enormous setup charge for Fox Movietone News generated a $3 million loss between 1926 and 1931.[60] Work on features and shorts was concentrated at Movietone City in Westwood (in what now includes Century City). The complex grew at a tremendous rate. During the summer of 1929, thirteen new buildings costing $2 million sprawled across forty acres of the hundred-acre Fox Hills lot between Pico and Santa Monica Boulevard. Two 325- by 200-foot stages connected by sound cables were built in October 1929.

Fox was also a player in the musical craze and, to achieve its competitive edge, bought a substantial interest in the De Sylva, Brown, and Henderson firm, composers of numerous popular songs and Broadway show tunes.[61] Four of their revues were running simultaneously on Broadway in 1929, and they had written the mega-hit "Sonny Boy" for Warners' SINGING FOOL. The three Tin Pan Alley songsmiths packed up for Hollywood to write musical comedies, the first of which was SUNNY SIDE UP (1929).[62] Fox also acquired an interest in the American Broadcasting System. In addition to music revenue, radio broadcasting would exploit Fox movies and plug Fox theaters. The models were RKO's synergistic relationship to NBC and Paramount's to CBS.[63] Not content with his thousand domestic theaters, Fox added another three hundred when he bought the Gaumont British chain.

William Fox's plans for acquiring one million movie seats and conquering Hollywood unraveled precipitously on 17 July 1929. While driving in Old Westbury, Long Island, he was seriously injured and the chauffeur was killed when his Rolls Royce overturned avoiding a collision. Though the doctors promised a complete recovery, it proved to be slow. Insiders felt that some of the mogul's zeal and shrewd judgment dissipated after the accident.[64]

When the stock market crashed, so did William Fox's empire. He had put the MGM deal together on a $15 million loan from AT&T that would be due in the spring. He owed $6 million in notes for Gaumont. Then in November 1929, the Justice Department sued Fox for creating an illegal monopoly. The financial paroxysms continued through the first quarter of 1930. Wall Street watched as Fox lined up new debt to underwrite the old with "hourly rumors, mostly unfounded, drifting up and down the big street."[65] The extent of Fox's wheeling and dealing is suggested by the length of the list of motion picture transactions he submitted to the U.S. district court—forty pages. Though complex, the crux of the problem was that $45 million in loans was due within sixty days. "The present heavy debt was incurred primarily in the acquisition of the English Gaumont circuit of theaters and in assisting Fox Theaters Corp. to acquire a substantial block of common stock of Loew's, Inc., both of which acquisitions the board of directors believes will prove to be profitable," wrote Fox's board to their shareholders. "Failure to effect such refunding before the decline in market values of securities last autumn is the immediate cause of the corporation's financial embarrassment."[66]

The fight for these assets pitted two powerful banking alliances against each other. Fox's coalition consisted of Bank of America/Blair & Company, Lehman Brothers, and Dillon, Read & Company. The Fox plan secured refinancing and stipulated that William Fox would resign from all his companies. Opposing the reorganization plan were the former Fox allies John Otterson (representing Western Electric/ERPI) and Harold Stuart (of Halsey, Stuart & Company). The stockholders at the annual meeting voted in favor of the Fox (Bank of America) plan. William Fox responded, "The winning of the present fight again prevents the entrance into the field of a monopoly which the telephone company was trying to establish in talking pictures as a result of certain patents they own." His optimism was misplaced. The bankruptcy court subsequently gave control to Otterson and Stuart. On 31 March, proceedings on the Fox matters were taking place in a U.S. circuit court of appeals, U.S. district court, New York state court, and the New York State Supreme Court, and pending in Brooklyn Supreme Court. Twenty-two attorneys were counted at one hearing.[67]

Fox settled in April 1930 by selling all his stock to a syndicate headed by General Theaters Equipment Company. Harley L. Clarke became the studio's new president. Educated at the University of Michigan and a young electric utilities capitalist, Clarke was a far cry from the founder. The deal was financed through a consortium—AT&T, Bank of America, Halsey, Stuart & Company, Lehman Brothers, and Dillon, Read & Company—with the provision that Fox and his board resign. Winfield Sheehan had spoken out against William Fox and his proposition, favoring Western Electric. As a result, he continued as vice president and general manager of the studio. Sheehan told the press, "The war is over and we're back in the amusement business." By the end of the year, facing losses and veering toward receivership, Fox sold back ten New York houses to independent exhibitors.[68]

Business did go on at Fox throughout the turmoil. Early in 1930 the studio was confident that the musical would continue forever and hired twenty-four songwriters and composers. Countering Warners' move to color, Sheehan laid plans for building a $1 million Fox color plant in Hollywood. In February the studio expected to make three negatives for each film in the 1930–1931 season: Grandeur widescreen, standard Movietone, and standard silent. The studio budgeted $20 million for feature production. Work was scheduled to begin on eight new soundstages at Movietone City. Among the big names contracted were the composers George and Ira Gershwin, the cartoonist Rube Goldberg, and Joseph Urban, a designer and architect.[69] In retrospect, this expenditure looks extravagant for the times. But in early 1930 revenue was still pouring in from the vast theater chain. As the Depression deepened, Clarke's Fox Film Corporation would sink.

The suits against Fox Film Corporation, Fox Theaters, and William Fox charging violation of the Clayton Antitrust Act ended in 1931 when the U.S. district court ruled that the takeover of Loew's had been illegal. The court ordered Fox Film to divest all of its remaining interest in Loew's and MGM. Fox Film Corporation lost $4.2 million in 1931, in contrast to its $10 million profit in 1930. Though William Fox was no longer associated with his companies, he was personally sued by the managers of Fox Film and Fox Theaters for manipulating stock and would eventually serve time in prison for bribing a jury.[70]

Harley L. Clarke, president of Fox Film and Theaters, 1930.

PARAMOUNT

Adolph Zukor brought Paramount's sound whiz Roy Pomeroy east in 1928 to reopen the dormant studio in Astoria, Long Island. Throughout the summer and fall he worked with Western Electric engineers to retrofit the big stage for sound production. Zukor made it clear that Astoria would be used for "certain types of stories that can best be made here in the East on account of the availability of a particular type of talent," in other words, Broadway performers. The "regular" schedule, as opposed to the eastern "stage unit" productions, would remain in Hollywood for both sound and silent production. The first Long Island sound "channel" (the term designating the recording unit) was put into operation on 16 July 1928. Production started one month later on an Eddie Cantor short. In October the first talking feature started up—THE LETTER, with Jeanne Eagels (released 1929).

In December the Astoria plant was enlarged.[71] Pomeroy was named head of sound production, and the trades reported feelers about Paramount's starting a joint talking-picture department with MGM and United Artists.[72] Paramount, despite having ERPI facilities to do all its own synchronization, farmed out Erich von Stroheim's THE WEDDING MARCH (1928) to Pat Powers, who recorded its musical track on his Cinephone system. This is not surprising, since Powers had financed the film as an independent producer.[73]

The year 1929 got off to a disastrous start when Paramount's newest Hollywood soundstage burned to the ground on 16 January. It had been Western Electric's most ambitious production installation, with four stages under one roof and eight separate recording systems. Jesse Lasky downplayed the setback. All production, he said, would be transferred to the other Gower Street stages and to Long Island. The need to keep the recording laboratory separate from the shooting stage had saved it. Cables were trenched from it to the undamaged stages, and ERPI dispatched four Kearny sound trucks from Philadelphia to provide emergency recording service.[74]

While other studios were beating a strategic retreat from New York, Paramount continued to shoot feature-length talkies there, sometimes up to three simultaneously. Second and third sound channels were added in January and February 1929. By September, Paramount's Long Island studio had expanded 25 percent.[75]

Paramount was no slouch in the music division either; indeed, it claimed to have the largest music department. For a while it boasted of the services of the nation's most popular composer, Irving Berlin, who wrote music for THE COCOANUTS. The studio's coup was hiring the Broadway director Rouben Mamoulian, who had staged *Porgy* and *Wings over Europe* for the Theater Guild. In June he started APPLAUSE, starring Helen Morgan, at Astoria.[76]

Paramount continued to be the studio most actively exploiting radio as a publicity medium for its talkies. In February 1929, there was a "Big National Tie-up" between the studio and Philco, the radio manufacturer. Paramount hired billboards, distributed autographed star photos, took out magazine ads, sponsored rotogravure newspaper sections, and made available ad mats for local papers. In June 1929, the studio executed a stock tender exchange for a 50 percent interest in the Columbia Broadcasting System so that similar radio tie-ups could be expanded and regularized.[77]

Challenged, perhaps, by the Fox-Loew's combination, Paramount attempted a friendly merger with Warner Bros. in September 1929; it would have created the largest entertainment conglomerate ever. Attorney General Mitchell's threat to sue put an end to the proposed "Paramount-Vitaphone Corporation."[78]

Billboards from the Philco-Paramount radio tie-up, 1930.

Having the largest and farthest-flung theater chain, Paramount needed a steady stream of quality film. The company's seriousness in maintaining production at Astoria was confirmed when its prize director, Ernst Lubitsch, was appointed to the position of supervising director of the eastern Paramount studios.[79] Dorothy Arzner, basking in the success of her Ruth Chatterton melodramas, was transferred east to direct Claudette Colbert and Fredric March in HONOR AMONG LOVERS (1930).[80]

On the West Coast, Paramount was evaluating its programming strategies. Like the other majors, the studio signed with Technicolor for shorts and some features. It sponsored a 56-mm widescreen process called Magnafilm.[81] Analogous to Zanuck's decision to focus on topicals, B. P. Schulberg and his new general manager of West Coast production, David O. Selznick, were reported to be "going after the kiddie market." TOM SAWYER (1930), With Jackie Coogan and Mitzi Green, was the first of a proposed series of juvenile releases. "Paramount's mighty magnet to bring back the kids!" it was hoped.[82]

The magnet lost its charge quickly, drained by the Publix theaters' drop in attendance. A finance committee headed by the Lehman Brothers executive John Hertz (who later founded the car rental agency) was formed in November 1931 to steer the company back to solvency—without success.

MGM

In June 1928 (the day after Warners' announcement that all its films would have talking sequences and well after Paramount had started shooting all-talking features), Nicholas Schenck conceded that MGM would also incorporate Movietone effects into "many" of its pictures. As he wrote, a 7,000-square-foot enclosure was being built on vibrationless pilings with soundproofed walls. The Culver City installation was supervised by Western Electric, Victor Talking Machine engineers, and Professor Verne Knudsen of the University of Southern California, one of five academic sound consultants hired by MGM. Sound would also be used for the independent films distributed by MGM: its own Movietone Newsreel (produced by Hearst) and the Hal Roach comedies (including Our Gang and Laurel and Hardy). The studio also leased the Cosmopolitan Studios in New York (127th Street at 2nd Avenue). Eddie Albert and other entertainers signed contracts to make Vitaphone-like musical shorts there.[83]

Schenck criticized the industry for its hasty conversion. Perhaps thinking of his own studio's questionable success in its first goat gland attempt, WHITE SHADOWS IN THE SOUTH SEAS, he said,

> The novelty of sound has upset all reason. Sound has been applied indiscriminately whether it belonged or not. Everywhere the cry is for "talkies" regardless of subject matter. Certain properties lend themselves to dialogue, but they are not many and there you have the root of the trouble. Hysteria on the part of exhibitors who envision fortunes accruing through sound has reached the studios via sales departments and the pressure from the field. (*Film Daily*, 20 December 1928, p. 1)

He vowed to continue proceeding slowly. Schenck's statement acknowledges that the demand for sound, and for dialogue in particular, was coming from "hysterical" consumers (voiced through exhibitors) and was not being pushed on a passive public by the major producers. Moving at a stately pace, MGM's last silent film was THE KISS, directed by Jacques Feyder and starring Garbo, released with disc-synchronized music in December 1929.

Despite the resistance of Schenck and Irving Thalberg, the grosses from MGM's sound films could not be ignored. Glancy (appendix 1) notes that WHITE SHADOWS IN THE SOUTH SEAS and ALIAS JIMMY VALENTINE, despite their weak star value, earned excellent returns in the 1928–1929 season. The draw of sound was confirmed with the tremendous success of THE BROADWAY MELODY, MGM's first all-talker, which opened in February 1929.

When it did convert, MGM did so in a big way. The facilities, state-of-the-art Western Electric, were installed under the supervision of Douglas Shearer, working under a new screen credit, "recording engineer." By the end of 1929 the Culver City facility had a preview theater seating 1,500 and the industry's largest soundstage, capable of shooting twelve scenes simultaneously. Amid the new quarters was a music building dedicated "for the sole use of composers and music writers, and here the largest musical library on the coast is now established. Under the leadership of such men as Arthur Lange, famous composer, and Dr. William Axt, former musical director of the Capitol Theatre, New York, each new story is studied with a view to preparing the proper musical setting."[84] The arrangers could avail themselves of MGM's new acquisition, the Robbins Music Company, which the studio bought in October 1930. Though its changeover to sound production was slow, from the point of view of the consumer, the company was advanced. In fact, Loew's chain of theaters was among the first to be fully wired.[85]

After Fox's sudden hostile takeover of the studio's parent company, there was a brief period of uncertainty. Nicholas Schenck had not informed Louis B. Mayer or Irving Thalberg about the pending Loew's sale, so there was a lingering rift in the company management. But William Fox was not only preoccupied with theater acquisition, not filmmaking, but recuperating from his auto accident after July 1929, so with Mayer and Thalberg still in charge, the schedule proceeded as planned.

MGM continued its cautious transition to sound, producing a smaller percentage of box-office hits than it was accustomed to but nevertheless doing good business. The studio's investments in sound were more modest than those of the other big producers. It spent about $1 million expanding its two new soundstages. It also dabbled in color production and in the widescreen process called Realife, which was photographed with Mitchell Grandeur cameras borrowed from parent company Fox. A comparison of the profits noted in the Mannix ledger to Loew's balance sheet reveals the extent to which theater revenues contributed to the overall operation of this Big Five company. For 1930, MGM's film rentals produced a profit of $5.94 million; Loew's total profit was $14.6 million. If these figures are reliable, they show that MGM film rentals made up only about 40 percent of the company's revenue.[86]

Loew's scaled back to cope with the post-Crash economy but was able to reorganize effectively in order to avoid receivership. Gomery points out that MGM never failed to make a profit even in the leanest years.[87] Strong returns on its sound films, which capitalized on the stellar Garbo, Chaney, and, surprisingly, Marie Dressler, kept the company going.

RKO-PATHÉ

RKO's big hits of 1929–1930 brought in cash. Unlike ERPI, which did not produce or distribute films, RCA Photophone could promise independent owners access to RKO product at favorable terms in exchange for installing its system. The number of theaters owned outright by RKO increased to 180.

Despite the market crash the previous October, the year 1930 began auspiciously with the opening of another soundstage—500 by 150 feet and seven stories high—on the Hollywood lot. William LeBaron announced yet another $2 million addition in March. RKO purchased a 500-acre ranch for shooting exteriors. In New York the Radio–Victor Gramercy Studios were refurbished.[88]

RKO's scramble for market share continued. In January 1930, the company installed Spoor-Berggren widescreen equipment in RKO theaters. "Stereoscopic" versions of DIXIANA (1930), a big-budget musical with Wheeler and Woolsey to be filmed completely in Technicolor, and DANGER LIGHTS (1930), a railroad melodrama, were announced in February. The RCA sound engineers would use their new dish-shaped concentrator microphone.[89] It seems that management was still cultivating the aura of technological progress.

In July 1930, Paramount stopped playing its films in RKO's houses. This caused a shortage of product, which had to be replenished because of contractual obligations to theater owners. RKO was forced to look for another production branch. The obvious choice was Pathé, over which Sarnoff and Joseph P. Kennedy had haggled for two years. In addition to interlocking directorates, Pathé and RKO were the only producers using RCA Photophone. Now Pathé was in financial trouble, but it held several resources. In addition to its distribution exchanges and its program of features, shorts, and Aesop's Fables cartoons, Pathé could also bring its profitable newsreel to RKO.[90]

Kennedy had been elected Pathé's chairman of the board in May 1929.[91] In light of his early interest in sound, it is not surprising that Pathé, in spite of its size and Poverty Row status, paced the other studios in converting to all-talking production. The release schedule was slow, with only two Pathé talkies completed by April. The studio announced that Pathéchrome, a French process, was to be introduced in its films—and perhaps it was, but it could not compete with Technicolor.[92]

Pathé's chronic lack of stardom continued to be a problem. William Boyd was a rugged leading man, inherited from DeMille's silents. His all-talking debut, THE FLYING FOOL (1929), was a low-budget programmer. *Film Daily* recognized the actor's fine comedy sense, saying it was Boyd's best work to date.[93] He would find fame after 1935 when he became the quintessential matinee cowboy, Hopalong Cassidy.

Pathé also suffered a fire, this time with tragic consequences. On 10 December 1929, eleven workers were killed and twenty were injured in the soundstage leased from the Manhattan Studios. A spark from an arc light ignited the soundproofing that lined the walls. Indirectly, this incident contributed to moving sound production out of New York. The New York City fire chief gave sound studios three days to remove all the cotton batting used to dampen echoes in the recording areas. The edict also affected the many theaters that were using this material to improve the acoustics in their auditoriums. Some small houses claimed they would have to close because they could not afford to remodel.[94]

Kennedy and Sarnoff were working on a Pathé-RKO merger at the time of the fire. The talks had fallen through, but Kennedy left the door open by saying that the failure "does not mean that [Pathé] may always steer away from affiliations." In March 1930, he resigned from the RKO board of directors and retired from actively managing both Pathé and Gloria Pictures. He announced that he would resume his former association with the investment banker Elisha Walker. United Artists quickly reminded him that he was under

Publicity for THE FLYING FOOL *(Pathé, 1929).*

contract to produce two more Swanson pictures in addition to What a Widow! (1930), her second talkie, then being completed. Despite his professed indifference, Pathé stockholders reelected Kennedy chairman of the board of Pathé at the June 1930 meeting.[95]

RKO, unlike Pathé, ended the fiscal year 1930 in good shape, with a profit of $3.4 million and assets of $117.8 million.[96] Such a balance sheet enabled Sarnoff and Kennedy to settle on a price. Pathé stockholders met to vote in January 1931 either to accept a payment of $5 million cash and notes from RKO or to place the company in receivership. The payment was accepted, but a group of seventy-five angry stockholders accused Kennedy of selling them out for his personal enrichment. They felt the company was worth at least $1 million more. At the next Pathé shareholders meeting—"the main session was generally hectic and frequently out of control"—Kennedy defended himself against charges that the sale to RKO had been put through quietly. He disclosed that Pathé had been offered to Howard Hughes, United Artists, and Paramount but that no one was interested. Kennedy denied that he had made $18 million on the FBO-RKO deal and that he would make a similar amount on the RKO-Pathé deal, although he held about 70 percent of Pathé's preferred stock. When the brouhaha subsided, RKO took control of Pathé's assets on 31 January 1931. Hiram Brown, the RKO head, said the companies would remain separate.[97]

The downturn in theater-going affected RKO during the late spring of 1930, just as the studio was gearing up for its fall production season. Revenue fell, and paying for the overpriced theater chains drained RKO's reserves. The big scale-back began. First, LeBaron announced that for the 1930–1931 season the company was canceling its plans for all-color films. Also, no more silent prints would be made. The elaborate special cinematography plans for Dixiana were abandoned, and color was downscaled to two reels in the "Mardi Gras" finale. Instead of maintaining the Gramercy studio, RKO bought a stake in the Van Beuren Corporation, the producer of Paul Terry's cartoons and a specialist in short subjects. Amédée J. Van Beuren retained control of his own company and took over RKO's East Coast production in October.[98]

Of RKO's thirty-four films released in the 1930–1931 season, nineteen lost money. The biggest loser in 1930 was Dixiana, which went into the red $300,000.[99] Bebe Daniels did not recapture her Rio Rita (1929) charm and was further hindered by a lugubrious leading man, Everett Marshall. Danger Lights, RKO's once-promising and technically innovative feature, received a blasé reception. "With the clang of bells and the din of locomotive whistles, this feature starts out at express speed only to slow down to a local after its first few minutes. It's the old stuff with hardly a modern touch."[100]

Sarnoff hired David O. Selznick after he quit Paramount in the summer of 1931. Selznick's job was to "take over both [RKO and Pathé] studios and to merge them."[101] With profits disappearing, Sarnoff replaced Hiram Brown with NBC's president, Merlin Hall Aylesworth, who, like Brown, was a former utilities executive. In November 1931, RCA Photophone forced a reorganization of RKO. When it was over, RCA's stock interest in RKO had increased from 22 to 60 percent. The deal triggered a Senate investigation in December.[102]

RKO entered receivership in January 1933 and did not emerge for seven years, though it continued to release films. Throughout the thirties, RKO lost money on its big-budget features. But, as Sedgwick concludes, RKO's average- and low-budget pictures tended to be more profitable than its "A" product, thus seeming to "support the contemporary perception of RKO as a 'programmer's studio.'"[103]

UNITED ARTISTS

The unique structure of United Artists probably retarded its entry into sound. Founded in 1919 as a partnership to release the films of its independent producer-filmmakers, notably D. W. Griffith, Douglas Fairbanks, Mary Pickford, and Charles Chaplin, UA was not a studio per se.[104] When Joseph Schenck, as chair of the board of directors, signed with ERPI in May 1928, he bound UA's producers to using the Western Electric system, if and when they chose to make sound films. Being wealthy and popular stars, the "Artists" could afford to move slowly, and they did. Al Lichtman, the executive in charge of distribution, said in July that the company would make silent and synchronized musical versions of its films, but that there were no plans to record the voices of Chaplin, Pickford, Norma Talmadge, Dolores Del Rio, or Douglas Fairbanks.[105]

Lichtman was echoing the views of the original partners, as well as Joseph Schenck, whose aversion to the talkies rivaled that of his brother Nicholas at MGM. Even during the sound stampede in the summer of 1928, Joe Schenck was predicting that the fad would last only four or five months. "We are not going to make talking pictures. We have not shown any talking pictures, and I am not going to show any until I am convinced that the public want them." He liked the Movietone "topicals," but as for features, "the danger is that the public may be poisoned by the 'talkies.'" He declared, "Dialogue in films destroys their sincerity, and the unreality of mechanical voices will mean early death for the talkers."[106] Schenck's views were shared by Charles Chaplin, then in the throes of beginning CITY LIGHTS.

Schenck's and Chaplin's antagonistic views concerning sound were not held by all. Samuel Goldwyn, another partner releasing through UA, announced several sound films as soon as the ERPI license had been signed. The first of these was supposed to have been THE AWAKENING (1928), starring Vilma Banky. Goldwyn convinced Schenck to build what was claimed to be Hollywood's largest soundstage on the UA lot at 1041 North Formosa at Santa Monica Boulevard. (Later it was called the Samuel Goldwyn Studios). It was 225 by 132 feet by 73 feet high, "large enough to accommodate outdoor sets." Anticipating simultaneous multi-camera shooting, there was space for ten camera booths and scores of mikes. But what was the motivation for including in the design "a permanent theater with a pipe organ to be used for opera atmosphere?" Evidently the executives thought there would be a future need for silent accompaniment. Goldwyn commissioned Hugo Riesenfeld to write the score, while the director Victor Fleming and the scenarist Carey Wilson set about creating "speaking effects." THE AWAKENING was slow to arise, snoozed until November, then was tucked in again until 28 December. These postponements became a pattern at UA. Banky and Ronald Colman in TWO LOVERS and Colman's THE RESCUE were also announced in May. The former, which turned out to be the first United Artists sound film (with synchronized music), was released 12 August 1928. Colman's solo film, planned with dialogue but released only synchronized, was not ready until January 1929.

While ranting against talking, Schenck, who as head of Art Cinema was also a producer, was entering the sound field himself by releasing TEMPEST (a John Barrymore film that had run silent on Broadway) for national distribution with a music track. The synchronized version premiered at the Paramount on 18 August 1928.[107]

Douglas Fairbanks announced in June 1928 his intention to Movietone his next film. He cautiously told a reporter, "Perhaps dialogue in films has come to stay, and perhaps it hasn't. But there's a hundred thousand dollars of my money going into that soundproof stage out there."[108] His ambivalence is emblematic of Hollywood's hedging strategy. Mary Pickford settled on COQUETTE (1929), a 1927 Broadway hit, for her talking debut.

Just as it previously had owned no major production facility, UA also owned no extensive theater chains. But this fact is misleading. The brothers Joseph and Nicholas Schenck arranged deals with the Big Five that ensured outlets for UA films in return for not competing in national exhibition.[109] In 1930 there were nine United Artists releases, a record. But after expenses, the bottom line barely showed a profit ($400,000).[110]

Balio has shown that during the 1928–1932 period at United Artists, it was Samuel Goldwyn and Schenck, as head of Art Cinema, and not the original founding partners, who were the most prolific producers.[111] Since the partners acted as individual business entities, the effects of the Depression affected each differently. But United Artists never regained the economic clout it had enjoyed before sound came.

COLUMBIA

The brothers Jack and Harry Cohn and their partner Joseph Brandt had been gradually consolidating their reserves since incorporating as Columbia Pictures in 1924. In March 1929, the company went public to finance its sound conversion and to acquire capital to buy up some small short-subject production companies, augmenting an area in which it already specialized. Going public also enabled the fledgling company to upgrade the lot at 1438 Gower Street at Sunset, in the area that was deprecated as "Gower Gulch" and "Poverty Row."[112] The "Columbia lady" logo was associated as much with shorts as it was with Capra's features. Distributing Disney's enormously popular Mickey Mouse and "Silly Symphonies" provided a windfall to the Cohns.

The studio was elected to membership in the Motion Picture Producers and Distributors of America in 1929, an event that symbolized its new privileged status. On its 1930 balance sheet Columbia had only $5.8 million in assets, yet it eked out a $1 million profit. Since the Crash had caught Columbia with little debt and it owned no theaters, it was affected minimally by the first years of the Depression.[113]

UNIVERSAL

While the majors signed with ERPI in May 1928, Universal held out, claiming that it was still experimenting with its own sound device, to be called Uniphone. This may have been a mere bargaining chip, for Universal continued to dicker with ERPI.

The largest of the "Little Three" (with Columbia and United Artists), Universal's financial position was too precarious to participate fully in the sound upgrade. While Carl Laemmle made a grand show of siding with the little exhibitor, his company's lack of major theater chains and its specialization in "oaters" (Westerns) prevented it from tapping the urban first-run market. He had to be content with small-town venues, where the theaters were called "shooting galleries" by the trades.

To raise cash, Universal sold off the relatively few theaters it owned. Carl Laemmle, Jr.'s promotion to studio head in 1929 (supposedly as a twenty-first-birthday present) coincided with the studio's tardy embrace of sound and a new high-quality production policy. Laemmle produced at least one enduring work, ALL QUIET ON THE WESTERN FRONT (1930). *Variety*'s Sime wrote

Carl Laemmle, Jr., general manager of Universal Studios, 1929.

> U[niversal] has turned out a talker picture that may live forever as a picture of the four-year war, and did so commercially, but to whom is due the rose for daring to make such a picture as this, with that commercialism in mind? If that person were young Carl Laemmle, who produced this film, then the kid is there with nerve, for he has done on that nerve perhaps something no other producer in the film industry would have cared or dared to chance. (*Variety,* 7 May 1930)

The bloated budgets quickly drove the studio into the red. Universal lost $2,048,000 in 1930, compared to a $491,000 profit in 1929.[114] The surprise 1931 hits DRACULA and FRANKENSTEIN began a horror cycle that helped pull Universal through.

INDEPENDENT PRODUCERS

Before sound, numerous independent producers existed on the margins of the film industry. Tiffany Pictures (begun in 1921), Mascot (started by Nat Levine in 1927), and Monogram (founded by W. Ray Johnston in 1929) were perhaps the best-known companies. The coming of sound did not at first severely limit these independents, as is usually thought. Paul Seale's research shows that a combination of factors actually lifted Poverty Row production in 1928–1929. Indeed, *Variety* reported an eight-year production high (342 features for 1928–1929). A complex symbiotic relationship developed wherein the "indies" provided product to fill out theatrical programs (as a weekday show or as half a double bill) and the major producers and exhibitors gave exposure and sometimes distribution to some independents in an effort to control competition. The large distributor tolerated certain small producers while others were shut out. From the exhibitors' view, the increased need for cheap double features played a role. From the producers' perspective, the excess capacity of Hollywood soundstages available for leasing, the availability of good actors willing to work for modest pay, and the generally low overhead in this kind of production encouraged these upstart companies.

This was the cut-rate sound domain prowled by De Forest Phonofilm, Bristolphone, and dozens of other providers of generic sound-recording systems. The equipment was cheap, but the expertise to operate it was frequently nonexistent. For those who could afford to, signing with RCA Photophone or Powers Cinephone or renting ERPI-licensed studios on a daily or weekly basis were options. There were many such studios to choose from: Metropolitan (operated by Pathé after 1928), FBO (then RKO), United Artists, Universal, and even MGM were happy to let out their stages during downtime. Some took advantage of a "bootleg sound price war in Hollywood with rates dropping to as low as $150 per day." Several independents followed the majors to New York, shooting their films there in one of ten independently operated sound studios.[115] These companies tried to carve out a niche, often in Westerns, drawing-room plays, mystery thrillers, or serials.

For the suppliers of quality product who were unaffiliated with a big studio, the coming of sound required that they shoot outdoors and rent studio space for interiors from one of the sound "horse barns" set up expressly for the purpose. Some of these soundstages, like Tec-Art (5360 Melrose Avenue), rivaled the larger facilities. Mimicking the majors, several indies set up cooperative distribution schemes. Their financing came not from banks but from credit advanced by processing labs grateful for the extra business. For talent, there were always actors looking for work in Hollywood, and because talkies tended to have smaller casts, better-quality performers were available for the independents.

Raytone (Rayart before sound came) switched to the talkies by renting space at Studio City in Los Angeles, Mack Sennett's independent operation. It was also based in Fort Lee, New Jersey, and entered the backstage musical derby in September 1929 with HOWDY BROADWAY! A diversified company, it also controlled Continental Pictures and Syndicate Pictures in Los Angeles, both of which made silent Westerns.[116]

One of the most ambitious independents was Sono Art Productions (shooting at Metropolitan Sound Studios). The company got off to a good start with a series of low-budget Westerns and all-talking musicals starring (and sometimes cowritten by) the radio personality Eddie Dowling. His THE RAINBOW MAN (1929) did so well in New York that Paramount took over its distribution. Dowling's film BLAZE O'GLORY (1929) was not as successful. After a disastrous preview, it was withdrawn and recut. Sono Art was also a states-rights distributor and made a deal with James Cruze to sell THE GREAT GABBO (1929). Though heavily promoted, the story of Erich von Stroheim as a mad ventriloquist, a horror film married to a backstage musical, was not successful. The film is usually regarded as the nadir of Cruze's and Stroheim's careers. In 1930 Sono Art distributed RENO, with Ruth Roland, who was a star of serials. Through its affiliate Sono Art-Worldwide, the distributor had a deal with British International Pictures that let it introduce Hitchcock's BLACKMAIL to American audiences in October 1929.[117]

The Poverty Row studios continued to supply product to diversify urban programs and to substitute their product for expensive films from the majors in economically marginal areas. Mascot's 1930 lineup suggests the range of material: a new Rin Tin Tin serial; "The Lone Defender" (a Tom Tyler Western serial); and "King of the Wild" (a wild animal serial). Tiffany-Stahl booked its features in nearly 2,500 theaters but was hurt by the lack of a profitable distribution network. Seale concludes, "Though certainly a few companies folded, most notably Tiffany-Stahl, the costly innovation of sound was hardly the only determinant of their failures."

The macramé of connections and kickbacks diagrammed in *Electronics* (figure 8.1) illustrates how sound transformed Hollywood into a multinational entertainment network. These are not branches growing according to a systematic master plan, but intertwined tendrils of several fast-growing vines spreading according to opportunity and means. The chart is an image of the robust gains made by these companies during the twenties by their simultaneously competitive and collusive strategies. It also represents the tenuousness of the connections, many of which would soon be realigned in the early Depression years.

Equity analysts, motion picture analysts, and people chatting at drugstore soda fountains just after the Crash agreed that the movies would be scarcely affected by the reversal of the economy. About six months later they had quickly lost their conviction that the film business was Depression-proof. During 1931 amusement stocks declined 75 percent. Among the hardest hit was General Theaters Equipment, the controller of Fox. Its convertible preferred stock dropped 98 percent, and the common lost 87 percent of its value. Fox itself was down 90 percent. Warner Bros. was down 87 percent, Paramount 83 percent, and Loew's 58 percent. The only gainer was a slight bump in Universal's preferred issue.[118] Executives' heads rolled, and the industry was in turmoil. Hollywood changed its ways of doing business. Producers had to return to budgets that were scaled to rental income, not to the availability of credit. Hoover-era laissez-faire approaches, including turning a blind eye to monopolies, could no longer be counted on. Feature production for the majors in 1930–1931 dropped to a fifteen-year low.[119] Industry insiders said that business was 40 percent below normal.[120] Still, the bottom was not plumbed. The drop in business did not reverse until 1932 or 1933.

How did the Depression affect sound? The primary installations of recording and projection facilities had been completed before the profits started running out, so the hardware was in place before hard times set in. Dropping attendance foretold lost income, so Hollywood began cutting back whenever possible (sometimes involuntarily, at the hands of hired managers, or by stockholders armed with court orders). The typical studio response included backing a few big prestige pictures or blockbusters while reducing the number of films released and slashing budgets. The studios curtailed investment in novelties such as widescreen and color and streamlined production practices. By late 1930 the techniques of dialogue production had been assimilated into standard practices. Wasteful practices like multi-camera shooting were abandoned. The Academy and the SMPE quickly adopted standards to eliminate incompatibility. Earlier schemes calling for dual versions of silent films were abandoned. The studios could not afford a shotgun approach to distribution (for example, sending comedies and Westerns to small towns, opera and "class" theatrical adaptations to the cities). Hollywood wanted to make only one kind of film—the profitable kind.

The Depression changed exhibition. When the distributors did not make profits on silent versions, the studios stopped making silent prints. When a theater could not play silents, the owner had to go into debt to convert to sound. If the theater could not make its payments, ERPI or RCA would place a lien on it and, usually, it would go out of business. The result was fewer theaters, concentrated in centers of capital, that is, affluent urban neighborhoods.

Perfectly consonant with the call for an integrated style in which neither speech nor music stood out as a special effect, the films of the early thirties subsumed sound in a "natural" way which supported action. Genres, or cycles, as they were then called, also helped Hollywood cope. Shooting films that resembled their successful predecessors cut costs by applying tried-and-true practices to similar material. Once the techniques were learned that enabled one to, let us say, light a set or adjust the sound for one kind of film, generalizing this knowledge to the next was easy—and saved money. Audiences, too, relied on generic descriptions of films in advertising and conversation.

The social effects of the Depression exerted an intangible influence on the stars and stories. The popular ingenue, sheik, and flapper images of the late twenties fell out of favor. Masculine men and worldly women became the movie fashion. Often their toughness and glamour were expressed as much through their vocal stylings as through their appearance or acting gestures. Though escapist stories never faded out completely, many more films of the early Depression years were topical. Hollywood movies were seldom overtly political—and the industry's executives had little to gain and everything to lose by a serious critique of government policy. But their audiences' economic plight was reflected in stories of individuals forced into desperate acts, whether men flirting with gangsterdom or women making moral compromises in order to get ahead. Not that many moviegoers were actually in these situations. But the knowledge that hard times could cause even the mighty and the pure to fall was part of the allure of the cinema of hard times.

9

Labor Troubles

Hollywood during the twenties successfully resisted the trend that was growing in large eastern cities toward unionization and the closed shop. There were a few labor groups. The carpenters and electricians had formed a bargaining unit; photographers and projectionists were represented by the International Alliance of Theatrical Stage Employees (IATSE, the "IA"); the musicians were represented primarily by the American Federation of Musicians (AFM); the screenwriters had formed their guild. Equity (the Actors Equity Association) had tried for years to organize movie personnel to secure the rights enjoyed by their Broadway counterparts. Despite taking credit for pressuring Paramount and the other studios to rescind an across-the-board 10 percent salary reduction enacted in 1927, Equity was unable to win the trust of movie stars. They were suspicious of the theater organization and apparently felt they had more to risk than to gain by union activity.[1]

The Studio Basic Agreement between nine producers and five unions was signed in November 1926. It was another example of Hollywood associationism; the studios appointed a committee to represent their common interests. Louis B. Mayer attempted to counter the unions' power by championing the organization which would become, in 1927, the Academy of Motion Picture Arts and Sciences. It provided a mechanism for arbitrating disputes among the studios, producers, directors, actors, and writers but would ultimately remain accountable to the leaders of the industry. The inspiration for this company union, which is how it was widely viewed, was probably the "industrial union" sponsored by General Electric. Owen D. Young formed his company union in December 1926, provoked by "different and often competing craft unions."[2]

While the Five-Cornered Agreement postponed the effects of recorded sound on Hollywood labor, it became apparent that if the sound film were to become widespread, it would have far-reaching effects on those who performed on the stage and those who played in the pit. The first consequences of sound for the labor force were not in the studios but in the theater dressing rooms, orchestras, and projection booths.

Presentation Performers and Projectionists

Stage artistes' notorious lack of job security was evident when theaters began replacing presentations and prologues with sound films. Their jobs simply disappeared.

Vitaphone, however, was good for projectionists in the short run. Operators could ask for helpers and higher pay because of the additional burden of handling discs, the responsibility of keeping them in synch and riding the volume level during the show, and the electrical and engineering expertise that sound systems entailed. Their union, the IA, also found itself with much greater power, because without a projectionist, the show couldn't go on. A dispute in Minneapolis was settled by giving the State Theater projectionists $150 each per week and adding a second operator to each shift (although the union had demanded three-person crews).[3]

Inevitably, there was competition for these plum jobs, leading to jurisdictional disagreements among unions. In New York, for example, the premiere of LILAC TIME at the Central Theater was disrupted by an argument between the electricians, the projectionists, and the IATSE stage employees. The theater projected the print accompanied by an orchestra.[4]

Musicians

One motive for using recorded sound as a virtual orchestra was to replace the real one. Many musicians' contracts with exhibitors expired annually on 31 August, and *Film Daily* warned in 1927 that "rumblings of impending differences between theater owners and organized labor continue to be heard throughout the nation."[5] The autumn was filled with negotiations. In St. Louis the musicians in Skouras's Grand Central demanded pay during the run of Vitaphone shows. The prior year had set a precedent: they had received their full salaries for seven weeks of idle time.[6] This was the beginning of a lengthy struggle which would become violent in 1928.

The musicians were picketing the Idlewild Theater in East St. Louis, and other workers were refusing to cross the picket line. In February someone bombed the theater, and the police blamed the labor activists. The strike was called off in March when the Skouras brothers agreed to stop laying off orchestras wholesale. In the Grand Central, Skouras retained seven musicians who played for two or three minutes between films but received a week's pay, "although that house is now devoted exclusively to the showing of Vitaphone features."[7] The musicians who had been laid off during the run of OLD SAN FRANCISCO were reassigned to orchestras in other city theaters. Those remaining players received weekly pay for performing about ninety seconds during each show.[8] The cost of these extravagances to the theaters was minimal compared to the savings achieved by the mass layoffs.

Soon the pickets reappeared. The St. Louis branch of the American Federation of Musicians was unusually visible (and audible). Utilizing some of the talkies' technology, they hired public-address sound trucks and visited local radio broadcasts to protest the Skourases' practices. In July several picketers were arrested during a scuffle with the police over "littering." The union, to gain public support, staged an outdoor concert "to demonstrate the difference between 'natural music' and mechanical music."[9] All the while, film studios seemed intent on pushing the theater orchestra toward obsolescence. Fox and Warners, for example, included reel/discs of "entrance," "overture," and "exit" music to be played before and after the feature, with the curtain closed.

During the summer of 1928 there were musician strikes in Des Moines and Omaha. Players asked ninety dollars to perform on sound film programs (up from the usual sixty

The AFM's 1931 campaign—fighting mechanical reproduction with the promise of live music escapism.

dollars). John Danz, the manager of the United Artists Theater in Seattle, closed the house rather than honor a demand by the musicians for a fifteen-piece orchestra. The theater had offered to carry eight. Tensions mounted, and three of Danz's theaters were dynamited.[10] In Chicago there was a three-day general strike in September, with seven hundred musicians picketing.[11]

Talkies were the main topic on the agenda of the 1928 national convention of the AFM, held in Louisville. The members resolved to draw up a plan of action and a model national contract inspired by featherbedding concessions obtained from the record and broadcast industries. In Chicago the union had sixteen microphones removed from orchestras that had been making theatrical broadcasts. It stipulated that a second orchestra of equivalent size would have to sit silent in the receiving theater during each radio broadcast.[12] This strategy became the one adopted against the "encroachment" of sound films. Members were assessed additional dues to form a legal-action war chest.[13]

They would have liked the agreement drafted by the Associated Musicians of Greater New York, local 802. Its punitive demands, modeled on broadcasting precedents, increased the fees which musicians would get during the screening of a sound film to two hundred dollars per musician for the regular five-and-a-half-day workweek. However, that agreement contained no stipulation that the players would actually have to perform during sound movie engagements. The International Musicians Union drafted bylaws giving theater musicians control over the installation and operation of all theater sound equipment.[14]

Joseph N. Weber, president of the AFM, invited Actors Equity to join the cause. Equity's executive secretary, Frank Gillmore, agreed that if the talkies succeeded, "why may not even Broadway be greatly deprived of legitimate drama?" William Green, president of the American Federation of Labor, testifying before a Senate committee, said that sound had thrown large numbers of musicians out of work. "Men who are artists, who have given their lives to their art, have begun to find they are losing out." One exception to the general opposition to sound was the Los Angeles union, which stood to benefit from the formation of radio and motion picture studio orchestras. Edward W. Smith of the local said, "Talking pictures, like other mechanical devices, eventually will prove a boon to musicians."[15]

Musicians must have realized that they were in a poor bargaining position. By August 1928, when the AFM had renegotiated half of its three hundred contracts, most musicians and theater owners had agreed to continue at the current scale, but with smaller orchestras. Weber said that the impact was not as bad as had been anticipated; only about 350 jobs in his union were lost nationally. The St. Louis musicians abandoned their proposed higher salary schedule and instead tolerated a pay cut of thirteen dollars per week. The new contract settled for five players per theater and was valid only for one year. The great majority of small-town musicians, however, did not belong to a union. Many players found employment elsewhere, but by the end of 1928 as many as twenty-six hundred theater musicians were looking for work.[16]

During 1929 the plight of theater musicians worsened. Several hundred attempted to march in New York to protest the cutbacks, but the police refused to issue a parade permit. The sponsor, the Musical Mutual Protective Union, claimed thirty-five thousand unemployed. The AFM put the number more conservatively at three thousand, with two hundred out of work in New York City. There were a few outbursts of protest: San Francisco stagehands walked out in a sympathy strike for musicians. The AFM, at its convention in Denver, adopted another resolution against canned music. The militant St.

Louis musicians settled their long dispute in December for a few face-saving concessions. Unrelenting, major theaters (for example, the United Artists in Chicago) dropped the orchestra to become "straight sound" houses.[17]

Movie Actors

Actors Equity had mixed feelings about the talkies. On the one hand, there would be employment opportunities for many out-of-work players, laid off because of Broadway's severe late-1920s decline. On the other hand, current film actors without stage experience would suffer. Executive Secretary Frank Gillmore's 1928 annual report predicted hard times for movie actors without good voices:

> I wonder if some of the truly beautiful creatures which float across the screen today will be quite as successful when they have to speak the lines of a long part. To do this their voices must be carefully modulated without a trace of accent except when the characterization calls for it. Some of us of the legitimate have been told we don't possess screen faces. I wonder how many in the future will suffer from the accusation of being minus screen voices? (quoted in *Film Daily,* 26 July 1928, p. 1)

Equity favored the method already being tried at Fox: using two directors, one from the movies, and one from the stage who would be more sensitive to thespians' talents and traditions. When the inevitable artistic differences arose, they would be resolved by professional arbitrators. To compensate for the additional rehearsals required for the talkies, Equity campaigned for payment for the time required to read scripts and rehearse, in addition to acting before the cameras.[18]

An examination of a typical contract clearly reveals the source of actors' complaints. Pasted onto Carroll Nye's "Standard Form Artist's Contract" for THE SQUALL (1929) was a rider sanctioning the Academy as a company union: "Accepted by the Producers and Actors branches and approved by the Academy of Motion Pictures Arts and Sciences." Among the provisions granted to the producer were the rights to record and reproduce the artist's voice in any form, and to schedule any number of retakes without further compensation.[19] Actors could also be called to film trailers and do sound tests without pay.

Were producers using the talkies as an excuse to cut actors' salaries and weed out troublesome players? Frank Gillmore thought so and used the transition to sound to renew his group's perennial campaign to establish a closed shop in Hollywood, as it had on Broadway. Since most of the newcomers brought in for the talkies (twenty-eight hundred, according to Equity) were already members, and the abuses were so rife, it seemed like an ideal time for a strong union drive.[20]

Without having to pay overtime, the only obstacle to round-the-clock film production was the stamina of stars and staff. Otherwise, the studios were unrestrained. "Recently conditions in the studios, as far as the actors are concerned, have been going from bad to worse," Gillmore claimed. "Many of the producers have been working their people unconscionable hours and keeping it up day after day." Many stars—for example, George Lewis—described this period in their career as physically grueling. For TONIGHT AT TWELVE (1929) he recalled working all night "just to get it out on the market as a talkie." Bessie Love later recounted the working conditions on the set of The Broadway Melody:

> At the time we had no unions, and we were worked all hours. They were really terrible; to get the film out before anybody else could beat them to it, we worked day and night. The film had a four-week shooting schedule, and we would have to be on the set ready and made-up to shoot at 9 A.M. and we wouldn't finish until about 9 or 10 at night. (John Kobal, *Gotta Sing, Gotta Dance* [London: Hamlyn, 1971], p. 39)

Among Equity's demands were a closed shop (that is, Equity members could not work with non-Equity actors), a forty-eight-hour week, and extra pay for retakes and trailers. Actors' consent would be required to use voice doubles.[21] Furthermore, "members should insist upon being paid from the time the actor is assigned the part until the completion of the actual taking of the picture."[22] In mid-June 1929, Equity called for a slowdown and threatened a general strike.[23] Although Gillmore claimed the job action had recruited an additional one thousand sign-ups, Cecil B. DeMille, who was then president of the Association of Motion Picture Producers, said there was no shortage of Equity and non-Equity actors for the talkies. Ten weeks into the slowdown he declared that Hollywood production had reached its highest peak and that all danger of an Equity strike was over.[24]

The main weakness of the Equity drive was that few of the important stars supported it. Some, such as Ethel Barrymore, John Gilbert, and Conrad Nagel (chairman of the Los Angeles Equity chapter), criticized Gillmore and spoke out against the strike. Nagel moved over to the Academy to chair the actors' committee there. Gilbert, alluding to his voice lessons, stated, "My principal worry at the moment is to conquer the new difficult and exacting technique which has entered my business. I should hate to have my desire to improve my work disturbed by any concentrated move on the part of the Actors' Equity of which I am a member. Should such a move take place, I feel my sense of loyalty to the men who have assisted me so greatly would direct my course of action."[25]

The Equity failure to organize Hollywood actors resulted in loss of status and members. Many demands—for example, twelve-hour breaks between calls—were eventually accepted, but under the auspices of the Academy of Motion Picture Arts and Sciences. In January 1930, a group of non-Equity actors began informal meetings with producers to revise the players' 1927 Standard Working Agreement. Jack Alicoate wrote, "The battle of Hollywood has been fought and won. Who it was won by nobody knows but all admit that Equity was slightly damaged in the melee. At any rate, everybody, including producers, actors, writers, directors and even Equity, seems happy." Equity offered to reinstate the 200–300 members who had been suspended during the 1929 campaign, but only eleven applied to take advantage of the amnesty offer.[26]

Conditions were bad for salaried actors, but for the occasional workers who outnumbered them it was much worse—if they were employed at all. Central Casting, the producers' cooperative, reported that sound had cut deeply into the ranks of extras in 1928. As a group, it earned $333,000 less than in 1927. Producers of talkies tended to hire small casts, and their films had fewer crowd scenes.[27] Thirteen thousand fewer extras were used in 1929, and 1930 shaped up as even worse. By 1930, Central Casting had 17,541 aspirants registered, 10,000 of whom were women. But there was work only for 800 per day, at a daily wage of $9.13.[28]

The Depression

Actors joined the millions of unemployed during the Depression. Alicoate felt that the talkies exacerbated the economic hardship:

> Actors, good ones, are as plentiful as sand in the Sahara. . . . Before sound, the situation was bad enough. Now it is appalling. . . . In several popular eating places the waitresses, collectively are better looking than an average Broadway chorus. Keep away from Hollywood. And that goes for directors, writers, actors and technicians. It is no place for hopers. . . . And these are all experienced people who know their business. (*Film Daily*, 20 October 1930, pp. 1–2)

What Alicoate was describing was, of course, a microcosm of what was going on all around America in October 1930: too few jobs for too many people. Many of these "hopers" were contemplating moving to Hollywood to better their fortunes.

The movie business contributed to unemployment. Teenage ushers and concession-stand workers were let go. RKO adopted a unique strategy of rehiring two hundred of its laid-off employees to use as house-checkers—counting the audience to verify the attendance for films being rented on a percentage-of-the-gate basis. Union projectionists, although few ever touched discs anymore, coasted on their earlier contracts. When these agreements began expiring in August 1930, many operators lost their featherbedded projection booths. In New York they accepted a 25 percent pay cut over two years.[29] Altogether, the exhibition industry saved $18.7 million in labor costs by furloughing stagehands and projectionists or cutting their pay. Owners cited as justification "the decrease and practical abandonment of sound-on-disc." Upgraded equipment meant that projection was becoming a more routinized, less skilled (and therefore worse-paying) occupation. By April 1931, the studios had adopted standard release prints with uniform sound levels, so they discontinued circulating the cue sheets which had advised projectionists about fader settings. Breakdowns and projection failure were less frequent. The aura of electrical expertise surrounding the man in the booth threading the projectors was rapidly dimming.[30]

Musicians were done in by the Depression. Weber of the AFM said that the whole film music industry in 1930 consisted of about 250 Hollywood studio players. He estimated that since the advent of the talkies, musicians' income had decreased $20 million. In naive desperation, the union started a Music Defense League to sway public opinion and convince independent theater managers to retain or reinstate the orchestra.[31] The U.S. Bureau of Labor Statistics reported in 1931 that "the introduction of sound in the motion-picture theaters . . . has proved to be the most revolutionary development in the recent history of the industry." Projectionists were felt to have been greatly aided, but about 50 percent of musicians had been displaced. "The only compensating factor in the amusement industry, so far as the employment of musicians is concerned," the report continued, "is the increased employment of musicians for radio broadcasting purposes."[32]

Carl Dreher, writing for the *Cinematographic Annual* in March 1930, took the unusual step of warning would-be sound technicians that there were fewer than one thousand sound jobs in Hollywood—and they were all filled. He concluded:

> It may be conceded that many of the men who are now knocking at the gates
> are just as good as those who are inside, but the ins are in, and the mortality
> among them is not sufficiently high to justify extravagant hopes on the part of
> the waiters in ante-rooms. . . . In short, sound must echo the warnings issued
> from time to time in the older branches of the industry against blind ventures
> in the direction of Hollywood, where neither the climate nor the scenery nor
> the presence of the national heroes and heroines can compensate for the lack
> of a personal income. (*Cinematographic Annual,* 1930, pp. 345–46)

Parenthetically, it should be noted that *Film Daily,* the source of much of the above
information, may not be an objective source in its labor reporting. Its readership consisted of the exhibitors who were the targets of many of these job actions. Though the
unions geared up for a battle over who would ultimately control public access to movie
sound—electricians or stagehands, theater musicians or owners, actors or moguls—in
the end the economic rug was pulled out from everyone. In 1933 the National Recovery
Act would step in and organize Hollywood according to externally imposed political
guidelines.

10

Inaudible Technology: The Trail of the Lonesome Mike

> We maintain sound has a place in the pictures of tomorrow. Producers
> have to learn what that place is.
>
> MAURICE KANN, *Film Daily*, 1 APRIL 1928

> We have unlimited variety in a motion picture. Unity is the quality
> desired, the thing to strive for, as no motion picture can qualify as a
> meritorious work of art without it.
>
> JOHN F. SEITZ, *Cinematographic Annual* 1930

For decades the myth was that Hollywood was in a state of equilibrium that the coming of sound disrupted. In John Seitz's thinking, sound had introduced potentially divisive "variety" and now it was necessary to restore "unity." Unquestionably, sound had caused decisive changes in the way films were produced. Throughout the twenties Hollywood had achieved efficiency, predictability, and sustained economic success by developing standard practices which were applied to acting, storytelling, photography, editing, and so on. The film industry's task was threefold: to develop strategies which would maintain the high level of attendance and entice new moviegoers to become regular consumers; to find efficient ways to incorporate the talkies into existing patterns of production with a minimum of economic disruption; and to ascertain and respond to audience selectivity. Only if all of these conditions could be satisfied would the talkies become a viable new film form.

Sound Infrastructure and **Mise-en-Scène**

Infrastructure refers to those fundamentals of production which are normally hidden from moviegoers, and *mise-en-scène* is the term for everything the camera lens reveals. Of course, they are two sides of the same coin. In chapter 7 we saw how the studios proceeded tentatively during 1928. Sound was treated as a novelty, not as a transition to a permanent form. Public support for sound cinema encouraged (and financed) investment in equipment, physical plant, and exhibition sites; by the time the 1929–1930 season began, those investments had pushed Hollywood past the point of no return. The

Paramount crew filming DANGEROUS PARADISE *(1930) on location in Catalina. On the barge there are three blimped cameras, a record cutter for wax playback disks (below camera 567), and a reflector for sunshine fill-in. Director William Wellman sits behind the reflector; the script girl is to its right. The Western Electric microphone is on a portable boom.*

studios rapidly abandoned silent production (although silent distribution continued for some time) as they sought to revise standards of production and norms of audio expression in films. Some of the infrastructural changes which took place included switching to a new kind of film stock, trying out new artificial light sources, and establishing sound-related practices.

While at first the newfound sonic capability was flaunted in *mise-en-scène*, Hollywood rapidly changed course to restrain and modulate acoustic effects. This practice was in response to audiences who made it clear that sound would be acceptable in features only if it did not interfere too much with the traditional storytelling movie. A few critics and consumers mourned the passing of silents, but the American public, commentators, and the majority of trade editors cheered the studios on with the rallying cry of Progress. Kann exhorted,

> We draw attention to the indisputable fact that almost every new dialogue picture denotes an advance over its predecessor. Perfection, of course, is still among the unachieved. The technique is new, the medium of sound unknown. It will take time. But we have an abiding faith in the ingenuity and the ability of the creative element in production that the problem will be surmounted. (*Film Daily*, 29 January 1929, p. 1)

In less than two years, Hollywood decided on uniform practices which allowed it to achieve something like the "classicism" of the silent period. Trade organizations, engineers, technicians, and industry suppliers pressed forward with unabashed confidence in scientific advancement. They worked quickly to streamline practices—offsetting variety by a return to unity, in John Seitz's terms—and getting down to the business of making popular films.

LIGHTS

Many aspects of the industry's transition to sound involved processes and procedures which the public neither detected nor found interesting. Lighting in cinematography is all-important yet unnoticed (as sound would become) except in special-effects circumstances. Indoor lighting for silent movies was a mixture of arc light, produced by creating a DC spark between a carbon and a steel rod, and Cooper-Hewitts mercury vapor light, which were arranged in banks of tubes and whose light resembled that of modern streetlights. During the transition to sound Hollywood changed to incandescent lights. Traditionally this infrastructural change has been linked to the need for noise reduction on the set because the arcs gave off a "fizz" or "sizzle," and the Cooper-Hewitts' transformers hummed. Technicians were fond of saying that "arc lamps cannot be used because their sputtering interferes." In reality, though, these problems could be surmounted by applying a "choke coil" capacitor to arcs and by moving the Cooper-Hewitts' transformer. The carbon ash and the bluish light these units gave off were more serious obstacles than their acoustic problems.[1] At the time of THE JAZZ SINGER's release, an article in *Film Daily* was already carrying a headline, "Carbon Lamp Seen as Doomed." So the change was under way before the conversion to sound began. Indeed, some studios, such as Paramount, Pathé, and Sennett, converted to incandescence before they installed sound.[2]

As they had done with sound, the studios banded together to maximize the potential of incandescent light and to negotiate in unison with manufacturers. During 1927 and 1928 the American Society of Cinematographers, the Society of Motion Picture Engineers, and the Academy conducted what became known as the "Mazda tests" (after the brand name of the General Electric lamps).[3] There were compelling pragmatic and aesthetic reasons for preferring incandescents, but the determining factor was that they consumed at least one-third less electricity than arcs or Cooper-Hewitts. Jack Warner announced that, as a direct result of the tests, he would convert to incandescents. By the time Jolson began shooting THE SINGING FOOL in June 1928, Warner Bros. was using only "inkies."[4] They were adopted by most major studios early in 1929. Bordwell has maintained that "the Mazda tests were a turning point in the history of Hollywood technology," not because noiseless incandescent lighting made sound recording possible, but because the tests were another instance of associationism—the studios cooperating to face a mutual problem.[5] The tests also substantiated Hollywood's ongoing infatuation with engineering and "scientific" solutions.

Mazda lights had advantages and disadvantages for sound recording. Obviously, they were silent. They could be brought in close, and their illumination could be manipulated to create a wide range of lighting effects (soft, harsh, patterned, etc.). Their intensity could be faded up or down. But they also produced intense heat, which was hard on the actors, and they taxed soundstage air-cooling systems, which in turn produced noise.

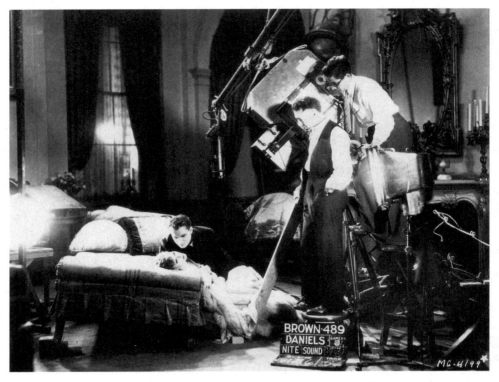

Greta Garbo and Gavin Gordon in a torrid scene in ROMANCE *(MGM, 1930) made hotter by incandescent lights. Note Mazdas behind bed, in window, behind camera, and on wall (turned off). Clarence Brown (vest) directs; William Daniels is the cinematographer.*

FILM STOCK

At the same time that incandescents were being introduced, the traditional black-and-white orthochromatic film emulsion, sensitive to wavelengths at the blue end of the spectrum, was being phased out by panchromatic emulsions, which recorded a wider frequency of light waves. (Thus, the new stock was better suited to the wider spectrum of light emitted by Mazdas.) Like the switch to inkies, this transition occurred while the talkies were being created. Salt contends that all the studios had adopted pan film by 1927. Certainly by 1928, Du Pont's and Kodak's improved formulas had become the industry standards. Eastman Kodak Supersensitive Panchromatic, a high-speed film (for that time) that became available in February 1931, was used primarily for newsreel and night photography. RKO-Pathé, however, switched to this stock exclusively for all its productions because sets could be lit with less electricity.[6] The industry's conversion to these picture-taking emulsions was independent of sound.

Obviously, because Vitaphone played the sound track from a disc, the type of film used for shooting or for release prints was irrelevant. For sound-on-film, however, the emulsion was crucial. Single-system recording (recording the picture and the sound on the same film inside the camera) presented problems. The image and the sound tracks had different developing requirements, so the result was a compromise. After early 1929 sin-gle-system was used primarily for newsreels, as in Fox-Case Movietone, and for location work. For double-system recording, the picture track and the sound track were processed separately for optimal results, then printed together to make a "married" release print. Eastman and Du Pont devised specialized films for recording sound tracks. These were orthochromatic with the very fine grain required to reduce background hiss.

Eastman Type 1507 negative for sound recording was marketed in 1928 and made specifically for variable-density tracks. In March 1929, Du Pont introduced two sound-recording stocks, Type VA and Type VD, for variable-area and -density. These competed with Eastman Reprotone. Eastman Type 1359 became accepted by the industry as the standard in 1932 for variable-density sound.[7] One reason Warner Bros. held out longer than other studios in converting to optical sound was because its wax blanks were much cheaper than the negative stocks for optical sound. The savings, said one executive, amounted to many thousands of dollars annually for the studio.[8] As competition increased and the price of raw stock declined, Warners had less incentive to stay with discs.

Bell vice president Edward B. Craft (center, with bow tie) introduces Vitaphone in
THE VOICE FROM THE SCREEN *(Warner Bros./Bell Labs, 1926), a short presented
before the New York Electrical Society. The camera is in its soundproof booth (with
the door removed for the demonstration). Six numbered microphones hang from the
ceiling. On the left, the mike mixing table and the wax record cutter for playback
(behind standing man) are visible. To the right is the set for a Vitaphone short,* WITT
AND BERG, *illuminated with "inkies." A bank of Cooper-Hewitt tubes hangs above
Craft and the unidentified director of the short.*

Tony's mother (uncredited) and Tony (William Collier, Jr.) in Little Caesar *(First National, 1930).*

Camera Design and Sound Abatement

The standard studio camera of the 1920s, manufactured by Bell and Howell, was prized by cinematographers for its rock-steady image. However, the mechanism that made it a great silent camera, a steel registration pin, also made it useless for sound recording because of its loud clattering noise. A competing camera made by the Mitchell Company became the new standard. As early as 1927 the Warner Bros. cinematographer Hal Mohr had patented a way to render a Mitchell camera "noiseless." He used it to shoot Bitter Apples.[9] The basic modifications involved replacing the external steel-spring tension belts on the film magazine with leather belts. (These equalizers took up slack as the stock ran through the camera.) The silent-standard four-hundred-foot roll of film was replaced by a thousand-foot magazine, which made it possible to record a full projection reel in one take, lasting up to ten minutes. Inside, fiber composition gears supplanted the metal ones.

Nevertheless, the sensitive and omnidirectional Western Electric capacitor mike still managed to pick up the slightest whir, making it necessary to isolate the source of the racket, the camera, inside a soundproof booth. The famous "icebox" was unwieldy, though not as absolutely static as legend has it. Mounted on wheels, it could be pushed around the soundstage with its cables dragging. The opening (covered with optically ground glass to reduce refraction) was wide enough to facilitate short pans and reframing movements. It was also possible to use the booth outdoors; for Hell's Heroes

Filming Madge Bellamy (impersonating Harry Lauder) in Mother Knows Best
*(Fox, 1928). The Movietone camera was not initially blimped; the Fox crew covered it
with heavy horse blankets to dampen the noise.*

(1930) William Wyler mounted one on tracks for moving shots on location in Death
Valley. Directional microphones operating out of mobile sound trucks made transporting the icebox outdoors unnecessary.

The studio camera booth contained a speaker monitor so that the one or two camera
operators inside could hear the playback as well as communicate with the sound engineers by intercom. To compensate for the increased distance from the actors, lenses of
longer focal length were used.[10] This practice resulted in decreased depth of field (a
shallow plane of focus), which is clearly visible in films from 1927 to 1930. Sharply
focused foreground figures stand out against blurred backgrounds. Some filmmakers
tried to explore shallow depth of field creatively, as Mervyn Roy did in Little Caesar
(1930). Tony, in a tender scene, is convinced by his mother to confess his crimes. As she
walks away from the camera crying, she is allowed to go out of focus, suggesting her son's
teary vision of her.

Each studio had its own tinkerers who devised ways to liberate the camera from the
booth. Fox had its horse blankets. The Warner Bros. blimp, though constructed of
resilient material, weighed thirty-seven pounds.[11] The MGM prototype was a lightweight housing containing a fibrous filler that fit snugly over the Mitchell body yet

On the set of SUNNY *(Warner Bros., 1930), left to right: unknown, Marilyn Miller, Theodore Kosloff (dance director), William A. Seiter (director), Jack Kramer (?), Florenz Ziegfeld (impresario). Three blimped cameras are on rubber-wheeled dollies, and a fourth is on the rear platform. Mikes hang from the ceiling.*

allowed focusing access to the viewfinder. In March 1931, AMPAS charged a committee with the task of achieving uniform camera silence.[12]

Once the camera quieted down, it could be placed on heavy-duty tripods, dollies, "Rotoambulators" (a combination dolly and crane), or giant cranes (as in BROADWAY [1929]). The myth that the talkies were stage-bound single-take affairs may apply to some of the earliest examples, like De Forest Phonofilms, but is dispelled simply by looking at the films of 1929–1930. Most contain at least a few very fluid moments. Salt concludes that

> if one makes a rough addition of all the cases, one finds that in fact there was remarkably little discontinuity in the use of camera movement across the transition to sound in Hollywood. . . . The use of the mobile camera in their early sound films by such second and third rank talents as Eddie Sutherland (THE SATURDAY NIGHT KID [1929]) and Paul Sloane (HEARTS IN DIXIE [1929]) attests to the vigour with which a burgeoning fashion could be pursued in the face of technical obstacles. (Barry Salt, *Film Style and Technology: History and Analysis* [London: Starword, 1983], p. 229)

ASPECT RATIO

Disk recording had no effect on the film image, so the Vitaphone picture filled all the area on the film stock between the sprockets, as in silent prints. The image had an aspect ratio (the proportion of height to width) of three by four (usually expressed as 1:1.33). With Movietone sound-on-film, the strip occupied by the sound track was borrowed from the picture area, resulting in an almost-square aspect ratio (1:1.15). The director Paul Fejos, for one, noted that the "use of sound changes the proportion of the screen slightly," but he felt that the square had more creative potential. "This change is an improvement over the old style and gives greater flexibility."[13] But producers, directors, and cinematographers were not totally in charge of the shape of the image. John Aalberg, an RKO-RCA technical consultant, observed in 1930 that theater owners, "for artistic reasons," had insisted on continuing to show optical-track films with three-by-four-proportioned aperture plates in the projector, even though doing so cut off 10 percent of the picture height. To compensate, cameramen had begun to frame their shots with more head room. Consequently, the sound engineer had to raise the microphone higher, away from the actor, in order to keep it out of the frame. Finally, in 1932, the industry adopted the "Academy ratio" with an aspect of 1:1.37 (close to three by four). This was achieved by adding a "hard matte"—black strips at the top and bottom of the frame on the film stock—thus conforming the sound-film image to the proportion that projectionists had been using for years.[14]

The Grandeur process, developed by Earl Sponable, debuted in September 1929 and was the most successful of several widescreen formats introduced during the period. Grandeur recorded and projected the image on 70-mm film stock in a very wide rectangular aspect ratio of 1:2.13. William Fox financed this venture by forming a partnership with Harley L. Clarke, the Chicago utilities magnate who also owned General Theaters Equipment Company (and soon would replace Fox as the chief executive). Fox and General bought an interest in the Mitchell Company to manufacture and control access to the special cameras. A 70-mm Super-Simplex projector was made by the International Projector Corporation to Fox specifications. Besides the expansion of the image, Grandeur also markedly improved the standard sound delivery system. It used a quarter-inch optical track, three times wider than the 80-mil track on 35-mm film. *Film Daily* observed that the extra area greatly reduced noise, "a troublesome matter with talking pictures at present."[15]

The experiment cost William Fox $2 million. Grandeur looked and sounded great (as restored prints of THE BIG TRAIL [1930] show). Other studios prepared to join the widescreen fad. Within weeks, MGM debuted its Realife process (for BILLY THE KID [1930]), and Warners unveiled its 65-mm Vitascope format (for KISMET [1930]). Both used discs for the sound track in order to take advantage of the full width of the film stock for the picture. RKO used the Spoor-Berggren Natural Vision system, which recorded on 63.5-mm stock and played the sound back on a separate film track. When Spoor shot *Lady Fingers* at the Gramercy Studios he placed his huge static camera eighty feet from the stage. The action was also filmed by regular cameras fifty feet from the stage. The film recorded the musical revue in one continuous take. Though advertising and press releases suggested that Natural Vision was a stereoscopic process, Belton claims that this was just publicity hype. Mordaunt Hall, however, often mentioned the "illusion of depth and distance" afforded by all these widescreen processes. He complained that in DANGER LIGHTS "while the persons occupying the centre of the

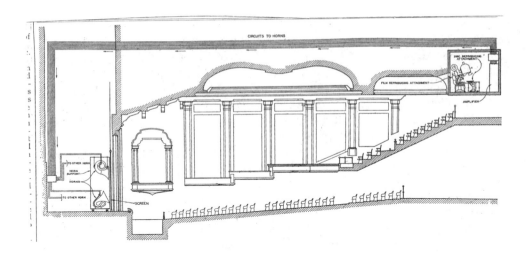

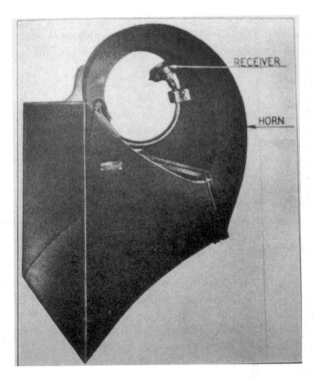

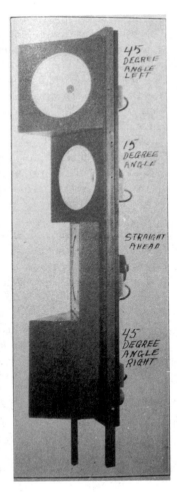

*Typical Western Electric installation showing
upper and lower horn banks behind the screen,
1928. Western Electric horn ca. 1929. RCA
dynamic cone installation tower for distributing
sound evenly from behind the screen, 1930.*

stage are in focus others in the background seem more out of focus than usual." He also noted that the widescreen image created a jarring effect when edited, a complaint to be heard about CinemaScope a quarter century later.[16]

Fox's move was widely regarded as a power play designed to force another major change onto an industry still trying to cope with sound. John Belton has speculated that, "through his sound patents, Fox hoped to secure a hold over sound film production, reducing other studios to the status of his licensees. The successful innovation of Grandeur could have resulted in the displacement of 35mm technology as the dominant mode of production, distribution, and exhibition and would have given him a similar control over image technology."[17] Ostensibly to agree on industry standards (but also to thwart Fox), the Academy declared a moratorium on widescreen in 1931.

SCREENS

Sound brought changes to the most visible yet least noticed aspect of the movie experience, the projection screen. Where should the loudspeakers be placed? The General Electric engineer Edward Kellogg recalled, "Our sense of the direction from which sounds come is too keen for us to be fooled by loudspeakers placed alongside or above the screen. Sound must come from directly behind the screen to give a good illusion. This is one of the lessons that was learned early." Though Phonofilm and the earliest Vitaphone experimented with placing speakers down in front of the screen to simulate the absent orchestra, this practice was fleeting. Kellogg attributed the invention of the 1927 sound-transmitting screen to Earl Sponable. The basic problem was resolving the screen's two incompatible functions—reflecting light and transmitting sound. A compromise was reached by perforating the material. The more holes there are in a screen, the more sound comes through undistorted, but the less light is reflected. The SMPE determined that perforating 4–5 percent of the surface area was optimal. In 1928 the higher-reflecting Cinevox screen appeared. The Vocalite Sound Screen ("porous but not perforated") was also "chemically correct for colored pictures." Da-Lite marketed an "eggshell" screen with a slightly yellow color to offset the bluish beam of the arc light in the projector.[18] ERPI also touted its "official" Ortho-Krome screens for both color and sound rendition.

SOUND RECORDING

The years 1927–1931 saw a steady increase in the proportion of signal-to-noise on the sound track and in theatrical reproduction. (That is, the sounds became louder and the silent passages became quieter.) This increase corresponded to a change in the fundamental conception of movie sound, away from producing a faithful recording of the filmed event to constructing a noise- and distraction-free sound track which assigned priorities to the voice and other sounds.

The transition occurred in roughly three stages. At first the main concern was external noise abatement: isolating the camera, constructing airtight studio buildings, filming outside of the city or at night, and warding off loud aircraft. These concerns were raised not only by the properties of the Western Electric mike but by its placement high above the actors to keep it out of camera range. The soundstage itself was part of the noise reduction system. The major studios built specially engineered spaces designed to isolate the interior from the noisy city streets outside. They also contained the mixing booth for the recordist. Usually the recording apparatus was in a separate room or even a sep-

arate building, connected to the stage by umbilical cables. ERPI supervised some construction, but the studios also engaged consultants such as Professor Knudsen of USC.
At least one new firm, the Austin Company, thrived as specialists in "acoustic science"
and designed soundstages for MGM and Columbia.[19]

It was gradually realized that some speech clarity could be lost because a trailing
voice or muffled tone consistent with the illusionistic space of the shot or justified by the
narrative could be tolerated. Thus, the barely audible conversations of the cowboys in
THE VIRGINIAN and the clanging background noises in DANGER LIGHTS are interpreted
by the viewer as convincing environmental sounds, not as errors in recording.

In the early 1930s advances in film stock, microphones, and new tactics for placing
mikes enabled technicians to isolate the voice from its background and to dub in effects,
rather than mixing them live during the take. The sound track came to be seen more as
an ensemble constructed in post-production rather than as a record of an acoustic performance. Putting it another way, the early aesthetic of the sound film as a transmitter
of virtual events gave way to a view of sound as an edited entity, parallel to (but seldom
matching in complexity) the image track.

SYNCHING TO PLAYBACK

A crucial change in sound recording occurred when studios began to film action which
matched a previously recorded sound track. The first playback session, according to lore,
was improvised during the shooting of the "Wedding of the Painted Doll" number in THE
BROADWAY MELODY (1929). When Thalberg ordered retakes, the sound technician
Douglas Shearer convinced him to reshoot while the dancers accompanied a playback of
the already satisfactory disc. The dancers kept to the beat. Not only did this allow for more
camera and performer mobility, it enabled control over the recording of the sound since
the music could be registered under optimal conditions in a separate studio. Actually, this
was a throwback to the earliest sound films, for example, the Gaumont Chronophone lip-
synching and dancing to prerecorded sound became standard for musical numbers.[20]

Playback also enabled crews to dispense with offscreen orchestras and to shoot musical numbers outdoors. Thus, in RIO RITA (1929) the singers and choreographed chorus
lines perform with orchestral accompaniment on the desert location, just as if they were
on a soundstage. Scenes requiring close views of singers, however, were difficult to lip-
synch. Eddie Cantor recalled, "My one problem was the novelty of recording songs in
advance, then appearing before the camera in costume and make-up, and mouthing the
words to a playback."[21] In WHOOPEE! (1930) we see a modification of the playback system. In the "Making Whoopee" number, Cantor seems to have been first recorded going
through his routine live. The camera pans to keep him framed in a medium close shot.
We can tell he is not lip-synching to a playback because he flubs the word *telephone* and
claps his hands without losing the sound track. This recording, then, became the source
for the playback record during the dancing and chorus shots, which are in long-shot, in
which a slight loss of lip-synch is not detectable. So the solution was to combine a live
close-up master shot, which shows him singing in synch, with long shots showing him
dancing (and doing a flip) synched to a playback of the sound from the master shot.

The unlinking of the microphone from the live event opened the door to unlimited
intervention in the construction of the music track. It was only a short time until the
whole sound track was susceptible to "sweetening"—improving (or creating) an otherwise nonexistent acoustic environment.

NOISE REDUCTION

Some strategies for improving the signal-to-noise ratio were straightforwardly pragmatic: diminish the noise and boost the signal. In response to pilots' fondness for Hollywood and Burbank airstrips, studios asked "aviators from nearby airdromes . . . to fly high when passing over studios, because noise of their motors penetrate sound proof stages." The studios optimistically painted signs on their soundstage roofs and hoisted red flags during shooting.[22] To silence pedestrian traffic, the producers adapted radio's "on air" sign and furnished stages with red lights on the door of the camera booth and around the set to warn would-be noisemakers.[23]

Normally, to boost the signal, one simply tried to move the mike as close as possible to the speaker, perhaps hiding it in a prop on the set. But a strong voice presented a particular difficulty: the only way to prevent such a voice from overloading a capacitor mike and causing distortion was to move it back. This was how Lawrence Tibbett was recorded for THE ROGUE SONG (1930). "The sound boys finally finished up with the mikes 15 feet back, the orchestra anchored, everybody grabbing hold of something, and [the director Lionel] Barrymore dictating, 'Fire when ready, Larry.'"[24] This technique had the side effects of increasing the pickup of ambient noise and heightening scale-matching problems by making the singer sound distant if the camera was not also pulled back.

Lawrence Tibbett, stripped and lashed to find the right mood for his scene, blasts the mike during a recording session for THE ROGUE SONG *(MGM, 1930). This recording would be played back on the set for lip-synch during subsequent filming.*

The weak link in sound reproduction was still at the consumer end, in exhibition. In May 1931, J. I. Crabtree, president of the SMPE, told the group that radio music sound was now superior to theater sound. The aptly named Progress Committee in October reported that some improvement in sound was observed in the better type of theater (that is, the studio-affiliated chains), but that there was no noticeable improvement in sound reproduction in general. One persistent problem was that vacuum tubes introduced a "frying" noise into the theater's sound system if not properly maintained.[25] With the lessening of ERPI's influence, the studios had little control over the sound quality in theaters they did not own.

MICROPHONE

The acoustic engineers' challenge was to curb the microphone's hunger for all sounds and to make mikes more portable. The standard Western Electric condenser microphones required frequent ERPI service and were cursed with a propensity to register equally all sounds from any direction. In an early effort to limit its omnidirectionality, Carl Dreher, an RKO engineer, developed what he called the beam microphone—it kept "extraneous noises out of the beam." For this reason, it was also called a concentrator microphone.[26] Dreher's cumbersome but effective product used a parabolic reflector dish about three feet across to gather sounds from one source and focus them on the pickup. The studio's widely publicized application of his parabolic mike was in DANGER LIGHTS, released in late 1930. Listening closely to the sound track, one can hear the technique foregrounded in the many outdoor scenes set with trains nearby. Their background sounds create atmosphere, and yet the conversations are still intelligible. The dialogue reproduction, however, sounds muddled, and the voices seem farther away than the actors. William LeBaron proclaimed that microphones were now as mobile as cameras and that outdoor locales, abandoned since the advent of sound, would return to favor.[27]

The parabolic mike was made obsolete (for ordinary use anyway) when RCA released its ribbon microphone in January 1931.[28] Later referred to as a velocity microphone (and still later as a cardioid mike), this microphone consisted of a thin metallic ribbon which generated a minute voltage when moved by air vibrations. This current was thermionically amplified and gave very good reproduction, with two added advantages. Clarity was increased because it did not pick up reverberation, and it was directional. The ribbon moved only front-to-back, so it recorded nothing coming in from the side (or from the back when the casing was in place). This directionality produced its distinctive heart-shaped pickup pattern. As long as the mike was aimed away from the camera (which was blimped as well), camera noise was a thing of the past. Dreher began using ribbon mikes on all RKO pictures in the summer of 1931 and praised them for eliminating "move-ins" (resetting the mike for each shot), thus helping to keep the sound level on the track at a uniform level.[29]

Western Electric also introduced a new concept, the electrodynamic transmitter (later called the dynamic coil mike). The characteristic "salami" preamplifier formerly attached to the condenser pickup could now be as far as two hundred feet away, thereby making it easier to hide the mike on set, put it in a mobile unit, or swish it around on a boom. ERPI boasted that since the electrodynamic transmitter was less affected by dust and moisture, it was no longer necessary to store the mike in a desiccator jar when not in use(!). Though D. W. Griffith used this "super-selective type microphone" to record THE STRUGGLE (1931), the dynamic coil did not come into widespread use in Hollywood, as Salt points out, until late in the 1930s.[30]

SOUND EDITING

Much of the film editing technology and many of the filmmaking divisions of labor still in use were devised to cope with sound. The picture editors were generally the ones who cut the sound tracks, effectively doubling the time it took to edit a film. Not surprisingly, sound was treated as an analogue to the picture, with similar names for similar effects (dissolve, straight-cut, etc.). King Vidor recalled the rigors of editing HALLELUJAH! (1929) without any new equipment:

> I rigged a push-button control from the projection room theater to a flashing lamp in the projection booth. The operator was instructed to make a grease pencil mark on the moving film when the light flashed signaling the onset of [a] line of dialogue. Afterwards the editor and I would go to the cutting room and try to synchronize the two tracks.
>
> When we would return to the theater to view the sequence with sound, we would invariably find that the synchronization was two to six feet off—the result of the time it took for me to press the button and the operator to reach into the mechanism of the projector with the marking pencil. (Vidor, *King Vidor on Film Making* [New York: David McKay Company, 1972], p. 15)

Paramount, under Roy Pomeroy, was probably the first studio to have a designated team of sound editors. Andy Newman and Merrill White there were credited with developing new devices to edit the picture and sound tracks separately.[31] John Aalberg, at RKO, invented an attachment for the Moviola viewing machine for cutting picture and sound. Analogous to the visual match-action cut, "the instrument enables the cutter to literally 'cut a word in half' with little difficulty."[32] Lodge Cunningham, a Christie sound engineer, was among several proud editors who laid claim to making first sound lap dissolve (in DIVORCE MADE EASY [1929]). Using this technique, voices in one sequence faded out while those in the next faded in, merging perfectly, it was said, with no "dupings of scenes."

Manufacturers quickly supplied the field with suitable equipment to streamline the editing chores. The Neumade Synchronizer went on the market in August 1930. Its sprocketed hubs fixed to a single shaft transported image and sound tracks together in locked synch for easy editing. Eastman and Du Pont's edge-numbered stock also helped editors keep frames aligned.[33] Even film splicing had to be modified. A straight-cut sound splice made a loud pop unless each cut was obscured. Editors advised using specially formulated "blooping ink" or, better yet, a piece of black film. Eastman stepped in with its sound film patches for blooping in 1931.[34]

Let us also mention Pat Bernard at RKO, the "most photographed man in talking pictures." He was the "marker" (later the "clapper boy"). "His duties consist of marking each scene by clapping blocks of wood together, giving the camera and microphone time to record the action, as each scene is taken during production."[35] By matching the sound of the clack on the optical track with the moment of contact in the picture, the editor could establish perfect synch.

A Vitaphone set in 1928 showing two suspended mikes.

Dubbing

Though associated mainly with foreign-language adaptation, there was little new or remarkable about dubbing, a term derived from phonograph work. It referred to the practice of combining sections from previous records to make a new composite. An ERPI engineer wrote that "the need for dubbing was anticipated. In fact, it was considered as a simple application of already developed processes."[36] In The Jazz Singer, Warners used the technique to edit Cantor Rosenblatt's performance of the Kol Nidre, which Jolson then lip-synched to a playback (predating the "Wedding of the Painted Doll" incident). The surviving Vitaphone "Re-recording notes" contain an annotation for this disc: "2204—Cantor Rosenblatt. Instead of being used in its entirety, a portion of the record was duped onto 2214 record along with the musical score. The record as such is therefore not being used."[37] This notation indicates that disc-to-disc dubbing was in use as early as 1927. Two years later the cinematographer William Stull confirmed that the technique was still in use. He wrote that, while Vitaphone discs could not be cut, "it is possible to 'play off' any given scene from one record to another, which gives the process a certain degree of flexibility in editing, or assembling the finished picture."[38] In actual practice, though, it was difficult to "edit" discs with any precision by re-recording, and the drop-off in quality was sharp. Later Warners edited optical sound and then transferred it to make master discs.

Dubbing with optical sound was also unsatisfactory in the early stages because each generation of printing added another layer of background noise. Undaunted, Pathé News experimented with a "sound double exposure" in 1928. The second issue of the newsreel contained scenes of a memorial parade superimposed over a French battle-field. Simultaneously, the sound track played a distant trumpet over a recitation of "In Flanders Fields."[39]

The ERPI engineer K. F. Morgan defined the various dubbing-related terms current in 1930: *scoring* (adding music to a picture with dialogue or sound effects); *synchronizing* (adding new sound effects or dialogue to a sound picture); and *re-recording* (transferring one or more film or disc records to a new film or disc by the electrical process originally used). He reported extensive use of synchronizing and scoring. Distinctive street sounds, water, revolvers, and so on, were routinely synchronized after the shooting was completed. "Libraries" of sound effects (obviously based on radio precedents) were readily available for re-recording. Special amplifiers had been designed to compensate for the loss of high frequencies and distortion of lows inherent in the re-recording process. Morgan even claimed that defects in the original recording, like "tubbiness," might be improved artificially during re-recording.[40] George Lewin of Paramount told an SMPE conference that, in addition to utilizing dubbing for "the faking of dialogue for foreign versions of domestic pictures," routine re-recording could also equalize volume levels from scene to scene. As re-recording became a universal practice, it took control of monitoring the gain away from the local projectionist.[41]

MUSIC SCORING

J. P. Maxfield, of Bell Labs, divided film music into pre- and post-scoring. Pre-scoring referred to recording music in a studio and playing it back on the set. He argued that it was best limited to incidental music, marching, and so on. Consistent with his scale-matching approach to the sound track, he argued that music used in this way had to match the "acoustic tone" of the scene. There were specific times when pre-scoring should not be employed: "It is difficult to pre-score a song in which the singer appears in a close-up or semi-close-up in the picture, since it has been found that the singer pays more attention to keeping in synchronism with the record than to acting. It is, therefore, preferable under these conditions to make a direct synchronous take"—that is, recording the singing and music together live (as in the WHOOPEE! example above). Post-scoring was "the addition of music and occasionally dialogue to a scene which has already been photographed." Here, too, he insisted that care be taken to match the acoustic to the visual space of the shot. Post-scoring would soon become the universal method of making music and singing sequences.[42]

BOOM

Boom devices for supporting the microphone seem to have spontaneously come into use as soon as microphones were light enough to lift on the end of a shaft of some sort. Gloria Swanson recalled:

> In 1925 when Henri [de la Falaise, her husband] and I arrived in New York from Paris, Lee De Forest asked us to do a talking segment as a stunt for a presentation at the Lambs Club. He got Allan Dwan and Tommy Meighan and Henri and me into a little studio in Manhattan and had us talk to one another while a cameraman photographed us and another technician waved a microphone around on a pole. We all sounded terrible; none of us could

believe our own voices. (Gloria Swanson, *Swanson on Swanson* [New York: Random House, 1980], p. 359)

The MGM writer Samuel Marx attributed the innovation to Lionel Barrymore, who "came to the [MGM] studio [in New York] and began to direct sound tests of the new players. Inhibited by the stationary microphones, he tied one to the end of a fishing pole, then moved with it, holding it above the heads of the players. Barrymore's innovation led to the contrivance of a boom-stick which became standard equipment, and movies began to move again." Bosley Crowther attributed the innovation to Louis B. Mayer's assistant Eddie Mannix, who improvised "an apparatus on the order of an old-fashioned well sweep on which to swing the microphone." Dorothy Arzner at Paramount has also been identified as the inventor.[43]

While many claimed credit, E. C. Richardson, of the Mole-Richardson Company, sketched in a 1930 paper for the SMPE a plausible scenario:

> As the sets became larger it became necessary to use a plurality of microphones and to fade from one circuit to another as the actors moved about. This operation of fading from one microphone to another contributed to errors in recording which while excusable a year ago would be highly criticized today.
>
> To obviate the use of plural microphones several devices were used. For instance, a microphone was sometimes suspended from the ceiling by means of a cord and moved about with a long pole, an operation quite obviously called "fishing." Some studios had their prop departments construct supporting arms or booms which would facilitate the quick placement of microphones. Most of these pieces of equipment were hurriedly made and crudely constructed and none too satisfactory in their operation.
>
> [MGM is using a boom which] consists of a substantial base supporting a vertical column which in turn supports a lever arm having an adjustable portion which can be extended or retracted at will by operating a cable drum by means of a crank from the floor. The under-balanced portion of the boom and the weight of the microphone are counterbalanced by a fixed counterweight and the boom is operated upon its vertical and transverse axis by an operating lever. (*Film Daily*, 7 May 1930, p. 6)

This is a description, not surprisingly, of the Mole-Richardson standard boom introduced in 1930. It also had a cable-operated swivel to enable the operator to point the diaphragm directly at the speaker and change positions during shooting. In 1932 the Jenkins and Adair Company introduced a cleverly designed portable boom with a telescoping tube. Its case, when filled with sand or water, became the counterweight.[44]

The boom and the new directional microphones improved the signal by placing the recording device closer to the source, the speaker's mouth. In one sense, the boom was too successful because it reduced not only unwanted background noise but desired sounds from the environment as well (including "room tone"); the latter thus had to be recorded separately and dubbed back in during post-production.

The silencing of the camera and the introduction of directional mikes combined with this simple tool to produce high-quality vocal recording. But like other film technology, the boom did not instantly replace its predecessors. A still from SMILING IRISH EYES (1929) reminds us that the boom was available to be used wherever needed. Yet SHOW

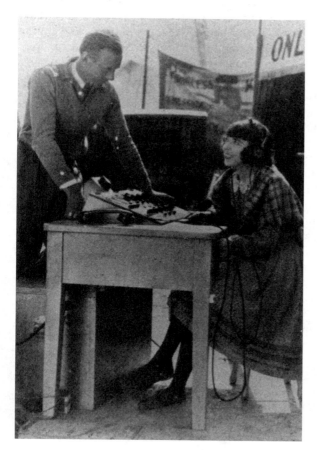

Colleen Moore demonstrates on-location sound recording to her fans. The boom holds the preamplifier, while the transmitter dangles. The sound technician Calvin Applegate explains the mixing table (SMILING IRISH EYES souvenir program, 1929).

GIRL IN HOLLYWOOD (1930) discloses in its studio shots that the mikes were still hanging from the soundstage rafters. The studio scenes in FREE AND EASY (1930) show the mike on a boom in some shots and slung from the ceiling by wires in others. Obviously these mike placement methods coexisted. Sound-recording directors shared knowledge and dipped into their pool of techniques as needed.

One salient feature of the Hollywood legend is the representation of the boom as the device that tamed the microphone's lack of control. Part of the allure of the story is the resourcefulness of technicians who applied tools from pretechnical society (brooms, fishing poles, well sweeps, etc.) to a new technology.

MULTIPLE-CAMERA CINEMATOGRAPHY AND *MISE-EN-SCÈNE*

In order to add rhythmic editing and motion to their films, the studios resorted to an expensive and film-wasting technique, multiple-camera cinematography. Using more than one camera to film a scene was nothing new. Events which could not be easily restaged, like fights and stunts, and footage shot for export processing—the "foreign neg"—had been filmed with several cameras for years. But for routine work in the silent days the filmmakers preferred the *multiple-take* method. They lined up each shot, custom-lit it, photographed it, then moved the camera to reframe from another angle at a different distance. The actors had to repeat their performance each time, trying to replicate their movements.[45] This system produced views which could then be edited together to produce the characteristic long-shot/medium-shot/close-up analytic cutting pattern of the classic silent film. Warner Bros. and Vitaphone wanted to maintain some semblance of this time-tested, audience-grabbing style of filmmaking. They were hamstrung, however, by their sound technology. The Vitaphone booths were too bulky to facilitate quick setups and retakes.

The *multiple-camera* method made it possible to keep the late-twenties pattern of analytic cutting intact. The cinematographer Lee Garmes explained how it worked:

> We had six cameras on every scene. One camera would be on a long shot and then there would be two cameras spaced on the right and two or three on the left. Each camera was getting a different size picture. If the scene ran a minute, two or maybe three minutes, they had the film to go with the record. So the needle would go around and do that two minute scene or whatever it was and they had it covered with six cameras. They felt that had to be done because we were in the hands of the sound department. Of course, photography went right out of the window. There wasn't any photography. It was just horrible. (David Prince et al., "Lee Garmes, A.S.C.: An Interview," *Wide Angle* 1, no. 3 [1976]: p. 74)

This practice was a major departure from the multiple-take system of silent film production.[46] Instead of repeating lines read by the director (or simply improvising), actors in the first talkies were expected to memorize a whole day's shooting, much as theater actors do. Many comments about silent film actors' "stupidity" were probably references to their resistance to memorizing large chunks of script. Of course, with multiple cameras rolling, retaking to repair a blown line would ruin a lot of film. The fear of a director's wrath when retakes were needed must have been more intimidating to actors than the famous "mike fright," especially among those without stage experience. To avoid having to do expensive retakes, the dialogue director rehearsed scenes thoroughly before shooting. In one extreme case, Alan Dwan devoted seventy-two hours to filming a complete dress rehearsal of WHAT A WIDOW!, with Gloria Swanson, "so that analysis and revision may be afforded prior to filming the actual picture."[47] Such theater-like rehearsals had been rare in Hollywood, perhaps because the Studio Basic Agreement between actors and producers provided compensation only for time spent before the cameras. Until a new contract was negotiated, actors had to report for rehearsal on their own time—another reason stars resisted the talkies!

To accommodate movement on the set, the director of photography had to devise a lighting scheme which would keep the set uniformly lit for all the action in the sequence. Even E. B. DuPar, the head cameraman for Vitaphone, complained about having to light three to five angles at the same time.[48] The heat of the incandescents, magnified by the need to turn off noisy fans and air conditioning during shooting, produced a sweltering environment that roasted camera operators in their booths and made stars' makeup run.

Like the cinematographer trying to anticipate all the lighting problems, the sound technicians had to anticipate the actors' movements. As with multiple-camera lighting, mike placement had ramifications for the viewer's comprehension of screen space. Should the sound "follow" the camera as it changed angle and distance? Mordaunt Hall complained about ON TRIAL (1928) that "there are giant heads, four or five feet high, that speak with the same volume as those in the long shots. Not that one anticipates or wants stentorian tones, but it might be an improvement to have as few close-ups as possible." Concerning MY MAN (1928), he found it a pity that the director "does not keep his camera on Miss Brice while she is entertaining a gathering, for when Mr. Mayo turns his camera on the throng listening to Miss Brice, the voice still comes from the centre of the screen. Miss Brice's vocal efforts also are just as resonant when her back is turned to the camera."[49] Rick Altman has detailed the theoretical debate between those sound technicians who thought that screen voices should be maintained at a fixed level and those who advocated that the voices vary according to viewers' implied distance from the speaking source.[50] The former view, which Altman calls the unified body theory, was put forward by technicians working for RKO (Carl Dreher, John L. Cass). The latter position, called scale-matching, was taken by the followers of the Bell Labs scientist Joseph P. Maxfield.

Those who argued for conceiving the sound track as a simulation of human perception (the unified body) noted that we hear continuously, without sounds "jumping around." To achieve this effect of spatial continuity, multiple microphones had to be used. It was necessary to suspend several mikes above the "hot spots" and to follow the motion by pulling the mikes with ropes or fading between inputs in the mixing booth. The rule was to provide one mike for each camera position: if the camera moved, the mike moved, and only one mike at a time should be activated. "The insistence on this requirement on one of the early pictures," Maxfield scoffed, "led some humorist to call this technic 'The Trail of the Lonesome Mike.'"[51]

Maxfield's alternative approach was designed to achieve scale-matching. The scene was set up with only one microphone near the camera and in line with the subject. The recording level varied according to the distance of the speaker from the camera. If an actor faced away from the camera, or moved toward it, his or her voice diminished on the sound track, as it would be perceived to do by anyone present on the set. One of the jobs of the sound technician, according to Maxfield's view, was to intervene to adjust the recording operation to produce the most intelligible speech, even if it meant cheating or faking environmental "fidelity." (Telephone engineers routinely manipulated sound to prioritize speech.)

Each theory had its convincing arguments. The unified body approach ideally produced maximum dialogue clarity because the sound mixer could use the closest microphone. Scale-matching produced a more convincing illusion of integrated visual and acoustic space but sacrificed intelligibility when the speaker was too far from the mike. James Lastra has pointed out that in both these conceptions of the film, the listener is a static auditor in the best seat in a theater. This "fidelity-based" model was more suited to phonograph recording or broadcasting than to cinematography. Furthermore, these were theoretical positions. In actual filmmaking practice, there was a clash between electric company sound technicians, with their sonic representation ideals, and Hollywood craftsmen, who had a different sort of spectator ideal. The filmmakers wanted to restore the "mobile" spectator of the silent cinema.[52]

It is difficult to find a pure example of concrete applications of either approach, and the films which might illustrate them do not correspond to the expected RCA (unified body) versus Western Electric (scale-matching) opposition. The studio that clung most rigidly to multiple-miking was not RKO, as we would predict, but Warner Bros. Its ERPI-outfitted stages in Burbank and Brooklyn contained many banks of microphones suspended from the ceiling. And one of the best examples of scale-matching is in an RKO film, The Vagabond Lover (1929). When the camera is close, the voices boom; when it is at a distance, the voices are weak. In everyday work, the image and sound space of the early talkies seldom matched this closely.[53] Altman analyzed Applause (1929) and found that a scene would be

> shot with a single microphone, while two cameras are churning out images of different scales. Once edited together, the two simultaneous camera takes produce a scene typical of the period. Perhaps it is fitting to remark here that the term editing, entirely appropriate for the images, is less so for the sound, since the sound take used is apparently continuous and uncut. In fact, it would be perfectly correct to say that the contemporary practice of using a single microphone system synchronized to two or three cameras fairly begged early editors to use a continuous sound track as the bench mark to which they edited the various images. (Rick Altman, "Sound Space," in Rick Altman, ed., *Sound Theory/Sound Practice* (New York: Routledge, 1992), p. 51)

Multiple-camera work changed the space of the silent film. With the traditional multiple-take method, props could be moved and actors repositioned to achieve the desired spatial composition (as in the overhead shots of Garbo in The Kiss [1929]). No such cheating was possible with the multiple-camera method because extreme angles would reveal the other cameras. To compensate, one camera was frequently positioned to give a high-angle view (as in On with the Show [1929]). But the space was not fragmented, as it often was in silents.

The number of cameras used depended on the complexity of the scene and on whether silent and export versions were being shot. Some simple Vitaphone shorts and trailers used only two (long-shot and medium-shot at an angle), while as late as 1932 Paramount was still on occasion using up to ten. A shot in Showgirl in Hollywood

SHOW GIRL IN HOLLYWOOD (*First National, 1930*). *Vitaphone technicians monitor the cutting of disks.*

(1930) shows the sound engineers scrutinizing the record-cutting machines while a take apparently using six camera booths is in progress. One mobile camera might pan or track to follow the action. The goal was to furnish the film editor with complete coverage of the scene from one wide view—the so-called master shot—and a sufficient number of angles and focal lengths from which to fashion a smoothly cut sequence adhering to the established principles of continuity (observing the 180-degree rule, no jump cuts, etc.). The filmstrips could be combined in any way desired as long as frames were neither lost nor added; loss of synch would have resulted. Because match-on-action cuts helped mask the edit, and since laying the synced strips of film side by side and cutting anywhere would produce a match-cut automatically, this kind of transition was common.[54] Editors also developed tricks such as laying a word over a cut to further "soften" the edit.[55]

The result of this method was a simulacrum of the late-twenties Hollywood silent editing that is so close it often takes frame-by-frame viewing and listening with headphones to detect whether multiple-camera cinematography was used. Doing so reveals that the technique was widespread, but not ubiquitous. It lasted at Warners/First National officially until 1931, when disc recording was abandoned. But at other studios directors and cinematographers resisted the awkward procedure. Paramount practiced it intermittently. In THE LOVE PARADE (1929), Lubitsch seems to have used extensive multi-camera shooting in some scenes and a single camera in others. MGM used it much less than other producers; its filmmakers usually limited themselves to filming two angles at a time. MGM films (and those of other studios as well) often combined multiple-camera and multiple-take methods. For example, in UNTAMED (1929), one scene takes place on a three-room set. It uses a combination of a tracking shot, multiple cameras, and inserts of a shot–reverse shot conversation made with a single camera. In THE BISHOP MURDER CASE (1930), it is easy to identify inserted close-ups because the background sounds change with each cut (an example of scale-matching). Three cameras were used in the interrogation scene—one for the master shot, one oblique from the right, and one from a high overhead angle. However, a scene shot around a dinner table, which would have been tricky to stage without revealing multiple cameras, was made the traditional way with one camera and multiple takes. Because of not only the expense but the complaints from directors and cinematographers, the studios gradually reinstituted the old multiple-take system.[56] Lee Garmes, for example, claimed that he was able to convince Jack Warner to let him shoot DISRAELI (1929) with one camera (although he may be remembering a later film).[57]

While the multiple-camera system seemed unwieldy and restrictive to technicians, for a while the end justified the means. The final result on the screen matched the prevailing silent-film convention for a naturalistic representation. The sound track was headed in a parallel direction. In order to make a convincing illusion of natural sounds, highly artificial and labor-intensive means were required. While such manipulation did a disservice to "authenticity," in fact no one was really interested in a truly authentic representation of the one-shot static camera variety. That it was electrical wizardry that produced the illusion of presence (as it did in phonography, the radio, and the telephone) gave the technicians license to reassemble image and sound in a synthesis which was more "real," by audience standards, than what had been recorded.

The film industry at the end of the 1920s was not resting on some static plateau of technological stability, waiting to be disrupted by something like the coming of sound. On the contrary, experimentation with talkies was only one of several technological changes already under way. Roland Barthes, meditating on the technology of reproduction, noted a historical paradox: "The more technology develops the diffusion of information (and notably of images), the more it provides the means of masking the constructed meaning under the appearance of the given meaning."[58] This certainly describes the efforts by filmmakers, producers, and equipment manufacturers who, in deciding how to hold in check the potentially disruptive technology of synch-sound dialogue, opted for "masking" it as "natural" or "realistic," rather than exploit its possibilities as a new kind of expressive filmmaking. In its first years, sound was most successful when it "stood out" from the image. Its electrical nature and its startling synchronism with the image were selling points. But after the conversion was complete, the emphasis changed and technology was diverted to making sound "invisible," exactly as editing, lighting, framing, camera movement, and the other arrows in Hollywood's quiver had been sharpened to create an unobtrusive illusionism. The sound track progressively was isolated from the image track to eliminate the inherent randomness of the natural world.

Paradoxically, the copy of the acoustic environment was inauthentic. Lastra has mentioned that around 1931 sound technicians settled on a planar system for sound. Voice, music, and sound effects were recorded on different filmstrips and then mixed together in just the right proportion. Furthermore, they were ordered into a hierarchy of foreground and background sounds.[59] Sound technology moved progressively toward limiting randomness by isolating (or fabricating) individual elements and constructing the scene according, not to what it originally sounded like, but to what it should sound like.

Much as different types of emulsions, filters, and development processes had evolved to control the chemical process of photography, acoustic technology was channeled toward the structured arrangement of sounds on the track.

Lee de Forest, when asked to rank the most prominent inventions related to the talkies, produced an interesting list: automatic volume controls, which played back the sound track at a constant level; the silent splicing device (probably referring to blooping tape); the baffle board enclosure for microphones, which extended their low-frequency range; talking-picture paint specially formulated to reduce echo on sets and in theaters; and lightweight cameras.[60] These diverse and otherwise superfluous inventions are linked by their contribution to one major function: reducing some sounds (noise) while amplifying others.

Audiences and producers agreed that sound was becoming more realistic. "Realism," which has always been trotted out to justify new technology, can mean many different things.[61] Sound certainly connoted a sense of "being-there-ness" in the public's imagination. Long before the theorist André Bazin elaborated his notion of "total cinema," filmmakers were linking sound with color and stereoscopic movies. "The demand for color photography," wrote Seitz, "increased to an almost unbelievable extent after the advent of sound and is steadily increasing. No doubt the incongruity of black and white images speaking lines and singing songs like living beings created a demand for a greater illusion of reality. This color photography helps to supply." Roy Pomeroy was already at work on a stereophonic sound system in 1928.[62]

Whether owing to the economic constraints of 1930–1932, the inherent conservatism of corporations, or simply a general will to resist change both in Hollywood and in the theaters on Main Street, sound was treated as something to be domesticated rather than spotlighted in its own right. A few voices, mainly influenced by European attitudes, called for radical acoustic experiments, but these theorists (like Eisenstein, who also appealed for a square screen) were not taken seriously in the United States. De Forest's list of recent achievements in the talkies might have been challenged in its details but not in its overall intent: overcoming Hollywood's horror of noise (defined as any sonic element not under the control of engineers). Certainly there were experiments that went against the grain—in short subjects, isolated moments in features, animated cartoons—but these were not mainstream trends.

The path of least resistance for producers would have been to continue treating sound as a highlighted add-on. Instead, they rejected sound cinema's alternative acoustic properties. The result was that, according to Barthes's model, when the studios adopted sound technology they devoted their efforts at first to exhibiting it, then to making it disappear. The major technologies (and the minor ones de Forest mentioned) were called to action in order to facilitate this process. The result was that by around 1931 an ideal of an acoustically and pictorially unified cinema was more or less achieved—paradoxically, through the radical means of multi-camera work and planar sound tracks. It may even be that this ideal of unity strengthened the narrative component of classical cinema: a more engaging (one might say enchanting) story would draw the moviegoer's attention away from the mechanical distraction of the early reproduction apparatus. Technology was pushed to give audiences what they desired: to hear stars act out stories with "natural" voices against an appropriate background—"unheard" music, "inaudible" environmental sounds, and "noiseless" silence.

11

Exhibition:
Talkies Change the Bijou

Prologue is dead! On with THE SHOW OF SHOWS.
FROM THE FILM "PROLOGUE" TO THE SHOW OF SHOWS, 1929

For exhibitors and for audiences, the coming of sound and the coming of hard times after 1930 caused permanent changes in the institution of moviegoing. In retrospect, it seems as though filmgoers abandoned with few regrets a cherished form of entertainment, the silent cinema. "This is one of the great mysteries of this part of film history," Alan Williams has aptly observed. "Why, with no previous indications of dissatisfaction, did audiences suddenly embrace the talkies, acting as if they had been dissatisfied with 'silent' cinema for a long time?"[1] Perhaps the shift to sound films seems mysterious because it has been assumed that producers were pressing their wares on a passive public resistant to change. A look at exhibition during the transition will demonstrate the impact of audiences' selectivity as a factor precipitating the changeover.[2]

The Demise of Prologue Presentations

The case of the live prologue (see chapter 3) is a good example of how the film industry responded to consumers' heterogeneous tastes. Exhibitors initially had embraced the presentation as a way to establish their autonomy from producers and to differentiate their shows from competing theaters. A popular act could compensate for a bad film which, because of block booking, the exhibitor was obliged to run. The large film companies were also indirectly responsible for the rise of this form of stage entertainment because after the success of independent exhibitors, they had sponsored prologues in their own theater chains and organized vaudeville-like touring circuits. These live performances were quite successful, but producers and exhibitors alike began to regard them as a Pandora's box. Robert Sisk characterized the practice as opening the door to the talkies:

> So there has grown up what is known as the presentation act in the big film houses. . . . When the great Publix theatres were ready to open, they found that the films wouldn't keep them filled. So they too let out a call for stage stars: "Hey, Paul—come on down and play for us!"

THE SHOW OF SHOWS *(Warner Bros., 1929)*. *"Prologue," personified by Monte Blue, is sentenced to death by Tully Marshall.*

Mr. Whiteman, ever willing to oblige, drew $9,500 weekly for his orchestra. He was billed as being of more importance than the film feature. Sophie Tucker, another eminent star, sang in the picture houses. John Philip Sousa's band played; Gertrude Ederle swam. All of this cost a great deal of money. The picture became subsidiary. A big stage act saved a bad film. Soon the two became inseparable. . . .

Then the talking pictures came along. (Robert F. Sisk, "The Movies Try to Talk," *American Mercury,* August 1928, p. 492)

When the Strand on Broadway installed Vitaphone, the management retained a few live acts to extend the program to its accustomed two hours. The critic Jack Harrower thought that "the general impression seemed to be that there was too much screen, and there was a noticeable lack of comedy to which all Broadway audiences have long since been educated. Looks as if they will have to work in some good short comedy Vitaphone stuff if they are going to make the new policy a success."[3] These comments suggest that at least some customers had started attending theaters as much to see the stage material as to see the picture, and that on occasion they preferred the former to the latter. Though vaudeville was declining, the prologue challenged Hollywood's domination of theaters. It was an annoying form of competition which canned performances could easily make obsolete. The raison d'être of "virtual Broadway" was to move the performance off the stage and onto the screen. Sid Grauman, of the Chinese theater in Hollywood, speculated in June 1928 that sound equipment would eliminate prologues within two years. Kann, right from the start, pegged the rapid sound conversion as a reaction to exhibitors who were "pyramiding the presentation craze." He acknowledged that many forthcoming sound films would be bad, "but most of them will be far better than the vaudeville junk that trips over the boards of de luxe theaters all over the country today."[4]

Hollywood mounted an all-out attack against this enemy in the theater. United Artists' Joseph Schenck said, "Good pictures never needed acrobats or spangles in the past."[5] Jesse Lasky, who had toured vaudeville before entering the movies, and whose company (Paramount) owned the Publix theaters, peppered his critique with a bit of history:

> Prologues were introduced by exhibitors who felt that properly to show a picture they first had to put on a stage act which through dialogue and music, would create the proper atmospheric setting. This always struck me as being rather silly. Any well made picture carries its own atmosphere, put into the picture at the studio. It seems absurd that, after a studio has spent thousands of dollars on a production, the house manager of a theater, with his necessarily limited resources, should feel obliged to stage a brief act to interpret the picture to the audience. It would be just as sensible to expect the house manager of a legitimate theater on Broadway to stage a prologue to, say, [the plays] *The Trial of Mary Dugan* or *The Racket*. (*Film Daily*, 4 January 1928, pp. 3–4)

He declared that the film must always be the main attraction at a movie theater and that stage acts, if used at all, must not subordinate the picture.

From the producers' vantage in 1929, prologues had become anathema, in part because they diverted potential film rental revenue to theaters and performers. Many theater owners were also turning against presentations. Live performances required high overhead, including maintaining a union orchestra. Hollywood devised specific strategies to kill off prologues. Distributors adopted the fee system based on attendance (a percentage of the gate) to replace the flat rental charge (which formerly left any surplus to the exhibitor, who could use it to pay his vaudevillians). The virtual Broadway concept supplied theaters with name entertainment that surpassed in spectacle and quality anything that a local exhibitor could book. Relatively cheap film rentals undercut live performers' salaries. As sound became established, audiences were eager to hear famous comedians like Eddie Cantor, with whom they were familiar from radio. They preferred watching a filmed Ziegfeld revue to sitting through twenty minutes of anonymous local hoofers on the stage. The beginning of the end of live prologues came in April 1929 when Sam Katz began replacing them with "selected short subjects" in Publix houses.[6]

Merger mania and the coming of sound hastened the decline of local exhibitors' power, though in sheer numbers they were always the majority. As vestiges of the old showman tradition, they had exercised considerable influence on what audiences saw. By controlling the content and the length of the program, they could respond to the tastes of the community.

The virtual Broadway in the early sound films was crafted to "poach" from entertainments which were enjoying success as stage acts and radio performances. Exhibitors had been profiting by presenting these live attractions, but not Hollywood. The studios corrected this imbalance by producing filmed facsimiles of the star performances that audiences wanted to experience. It may even be that the superabundance of early Hollywood musicals was in part an effort to make the live stage show pale by comparison. By using sound the producers were able to take charge of the structure as well as the content of the film program.

The Talkies Spread Wide and Thin

Hollywood converted to sound quickly, but for Americans living outside of big cities, the "Golden Age of Silents" dragged on while they waited for their local theaters to be wired. In the summer of 1929 *Film Daily* conducted a thorough census of movie theaters. The snapshot was especially timely since it caught the apex of the pre-Crash motion picture economy. It also shows how misleading the notion is that conversion to talking pictures happened overnight.

The number of theaters wired for sound had reached 5,251 on 1 July 1929, a year and a half after Hollywood's decision to sign with ERPI and RCA. This figure represented a bit less than one-quarter of all U.S. movie theaters. To no one's surprise, most of the cinemas were concentrated in the six cities with populations over one million.

Table 11.1
**NUMBER OF WIRED THEATERS IN THE
SIX LARGEST U.S. CITIES, JULY 1929**

City	Wired Theaters
New York	500
Philadelphia	125
Chicago	120
Los Angeles	87
Detroit	85
Cleveland	35

SOURCE: *Film Daily*, 8 August 1929, p. 10.

Table 11.1 shows that while Hollywood was the capital of production, New York was by far the film consumption capital. Almost 10 percent of all the nation's talking cinemas were within its boroughs. ERPI confirmed that "scarcely a theatre north of 42nd Street is not equipped for the showing of sound pictures."[7]

But the statistics also revealed that while most wired theaters were in metropolises, the dispersal of sound among other cities was also significant. As Table 11.2 shows, talkies were playing in numerous towns smaller than 100,000.

Table 11.2
DISTRIBUTION OF THEATERS BY POPULATION, JULY 1929

Population of City	Number of Wired Theaters	Percentage of All U.S. Theaters
Over 1,000,000	952	18
500,000–999,999	278	5
250,000–499,999	348	7
100,000–249,999	348	7
Under 100,000	3,288	63

SOURCE: *Film Daily*, 8 August 1929, p. 10.

The project's statistician, James P. Cunningham, was impressed by the penetration of the talkies into smaller towns. He concluded:

> While naturally, the development has been more pronounced in the larger cities, the wiring of houses has not been confined to the large centers of population, many small towns being included in the line-up. These grade down to towns of but a few hundred population, the survey shows. Another interesting fact brought out is the unusual large number of small theaters which are wired. In many cases, houses that have capacities as low as 200 are fully equipped to show sound pictures. (*Film Daily*, 8 August 1929, p. 10)

In midsize cities like Madison, Wisconsin (population 47,600), wiring had already reached the second and third tiers of the smaller theaters, such as the Majestic (745 seats), which had converted on 10 July. The figures do not include Canada, which, it was also reported, had 135 (14.5 percent) of its 930 theaters wired.[8]

Sound exhibition not only had permeated every size of town but was also dispersed geographically. Cunningham found no exchange territory where sound was not being presented (see table 11.3).

Table 11.3

Distribution by Territory, July 1929

Exchange Territory	Percentage of All Wired Theaters
Midwest	34
North Atlantic	26
Southeast	11
Pacific	11
Southwest	9
New England	6
Mountain	3

Source: *Film Daily*, 1 September 1929, pp. 17–53.

Even the sparsely populated mountain states had a few wired houses. Sound picture shows were especially widespread in the Midwest. The data suggest that, although theater saturation was very thin outside of urban centers, the talkies were distributed across wide geographical distances. Yet attendance was high—probably the result of a mobile population having access to automobiles.

To put the facts in another light, sound films were *within driving distance* for most middle-class people by the end of 1929. This fact illuminates an important change observable in the subjects of early talkies. Prior to mid-1929, most consumers saw films in big theaters in big eastern cities, so it is not surprising that these movies, even those made in California, reflected New York culture. Among the subjects were Broadway musicals, adaptations of legitimate theater, vaudeville, and revues, especially those with ethnic appeal. The data show, however, that in 1929 the situation was changing. The national audience was becoming vast. Moviegoers' tastes and expectations in general had always differed from those of the urban minority. The result was that, as the demographics for talkies shifted from an urban to a national basis, producers altered the content of the films to make them less culturally specific to New York and more like the genres that had been popular as silents. The virtual Broadway revue, opera, the sophisticated drama, and ethnic comedian comedy had to be rethought. Westerns, action films, slapstick comedies, and small-town stories (of the type Colleen Moore had starred in) were introduced into the sound-film lineup to respond to the growing diversity of consumers.

Before the poll, *Film Daily* had criticized the industry and ERPI for neglecting rural exhibitors. Red Kann reminded Hollywood that Will Hays, William Fox, and the promoters of Vitaphone had promised that "small towns were to be benefited principally. Until now, however, this has been so much hot air, and the only noises that the little fellow has heard have been his own squawks, punctuated with not a few groans." He recalled that talking pictures originally had been sold to replace presentations and thereby aid the small exhibitor. But "the subsequent stampede did everything but that. The result was that the de luxe theaters, fortified by the producer-ownership and massed buying power, captured the balm designed for the little man." After the poll, Kann was optimistic that "the balance is now slowly but steadily swinging the other way." He proclaimed that the first stage of talking pictures, with exhibition concentrated in large eastern cities, was over.[9]

The survey revealed that the 75 percent of theaters remaining unwired were in very thinly populated and/or economically depressed areas. These were owned by individual proprietors outside the control of the studios or the big chains. Hollywood had a conflict of interest. As producers and distributors, the studios relied on these small-time independents for substantial revenue. Executives (hedging, as we have seen) pledged to stand by them and keep them supplied with silent product. But as chain owners, the motion picture companies saw that one way to diminish competitive risk to their own theaters was for the studios to convert as rapidly as possible to a product which many theaters could not use, and to satisfy consumer demand for something the competitors could not supply—sound films. Whether the majors organized such a campaign to use sound as a means of gaining control over small exhibitors is unknown. But what happened is that Kann's rosy scenario of talking films saturating every nook and cranny of the country did not materialize. The silent exhibitor was forced to choose between being driven out by competitors, selling the theater to a chain, or converting to sound (probably with borrowed money). Many of the smallest theaters simply shut their doors. During a two-week period in March 1929—well before the October Crash—313 theaters closed. In the small towns surrounding Battle Creek, Michigan, patrons deserted their local movie houses for the talkies. "Good roads, enabling farmers and others to go to cities to attend sound theaters, are among the factors injuring the small town."[10]

The trade journals were full of discouraging news for the independents. The famous theater architect John Eberson pointed out that purchasing sound equipment was only the initial expense in a conversion. Ideally the owner ripped out the insides of the theater and rebuilt from the floor up. Items like new upholstered chairs were needed to absorb echoes. Silent air conditioning had to be installed.[11] Albert Warner did not mince words about the recourse available to the "little guy" who hesitated to convert. "In the interim unwired houses will be compelled to play whatever type of picture is placed on the market. If the bulk of the market is composed of sound pictures, the exhibitor will have to run them minus the sound."[12] This Machiavellian prediction suggests that producers and distributors knew full well that many of these marginal cinemas would go under when the supply of silent prints was cut off.

The talkies were welcomed by large exhibitors after it became apparent that customers would support those who invested in sound and punish those who did not. There was considerable resistance to the talkies, however, from small theater owners. The Allied States Association president, Abram Myers, publicized the bleak conditions for independents. Many out-of-the-way managers complained of bad sound tracks, bad pictures, high overhead, and no customers for silents. Sound prints cost more than silent ones, and "there just isn't that much more money." They griped that Vitaphone engaged in unfair business practices. In fact, Warners relied on commissioned salesmen in a manner similar to the use of "pluggers" in the phonograph and music industries. Exhibitors protested that Warners did not have a standard sales contract and let its representatives charge as much as the market would bear. They sold sound-track discs separately "from $7.50 to what ever the salesman can get." The conceptualization of sound as an optional accessory to the film fostered these dubious practices. The owners proposed boycotts of talkies and considered forming an alternative silent-film distribution combine.[13]

Exhibitors also disliked block booking, blind bidding, and having to sign forward contracts for features that were never delivered ("vaporware" is today's term for such promised software). One owner sued RKO. Realizing that millions were at stake, the studio brought in the celebrated attorney Louis Nizer, who was kept on retainer by the New York Film Board of Trade. He convinced the federal arbitrator that the producers were not liable for these phantom movies.[14]

Thomas Soriero, manager of the Rochester Theater, represented many exhibitors who doubted the value of the talkie investment: "Sound pictures have not been entirely a success, owing to so many inferior ones on the market. Large expenditures for the cost of installations have been necessary, and, as well, the pictures themselves are more costly." He pointed out that most small owners were glad they had not switched too soon, since only recently had the quality of sound films improved and their costs been lowered.[15]

It is unlikely that any tears were shed in Hollywood or Manhattan over the plight of these businessmen. Sound, or more precisely, the mass audience's demand for sound, had put the majors in the driver's seat. Small independents rightly felt that talking films were being used by studios to force them to buy something they could not afford. "It is my belief," Soriero concluded, "that a great mistake has been made on the part of the producers in not fully acquainting themselves with the exhibiting end of the show business."[16]

The Tom Thumb Menace

There was, however, one thing theaters could do that scared Hollywood—stop showing films. *Film Daily*'s survey of theaters indicated that despite the buying binge of the preceding years, the six producer-owned chains still controlled less than 20 percent of U.S. houses. Publix (Paramount) operated 1,500, Fox 900, Warner Bros. 850, RKO 250, and Loew's owned 200 theaters. Universal still had 100 theaters but was trying to sell them. Revenues for these big houses remained fairly constant throughout the spring of 1930. But in the summer the industry entered recession and the smaller independents began closing. New theater construction went down 60 percent from 1929. When the entrepreneur B. S. Moss announced that he might purchase some independent houses to start a new chain, he received 150 offers from theater owners eager to sell their property.[17]

Falling attendance was by far the exhibitors' number-one problem. They tried many ways to entice their customers back to the theaters, beginning with dusting off their old ballyhoo publicity techniques. Among the most spectacular were probably the aerial

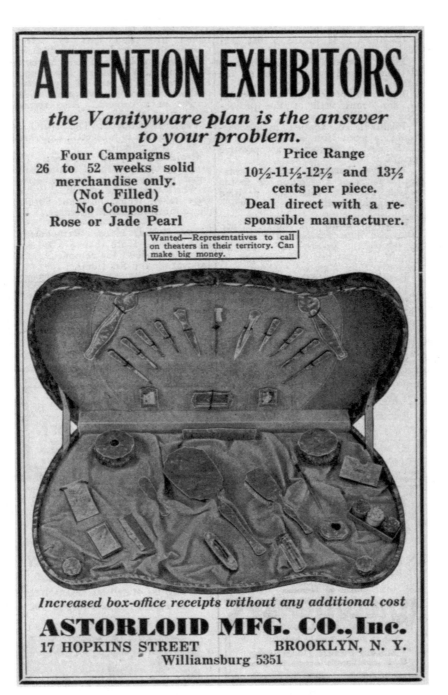

The Vanityware plan—moviegoers collected a "free" piece each week to complete a set.

flyovers advertising THE DAWN PATROL (1930). Theaters playing the film could book a small squadron of planes provided by the Curtis Wright Flying Service. Other practices included adding matinees, midnight screenings, and Thursday night previews at which the new Friday feature could be seen for free following the regular show. Gift nights at which patrons received door prizes became popular again. Come-ons like dish night and vanity night were successful because the customer had to return regularly to complete the set, which was given out one piece a week. Everyone knew that these lures were at best a temporary salve. "Free lunch, free refreshments, free cigarettes, and various other gratuitous offerings are now being held out by some theaters as special inducements to draw patronage," Alicoate caviled. "Whether the bait is bringing any results worth mentioning, the records do not yet show. . . . If the show is poor, even the side offer of a free turkey dinner will not bring very many." The U.S. Post Office maintained that such gimmicks were lotteries and that therefore the postcards advertising them were illegal to mail.[18]

One novelty was theatrical television. The Lincoln Pavilion Park in Chicago was one of the first theaters to broadcast TV. The theater sent a program out over the airwaves to ten theaters, but only four were able to pick up clear images. In New York, Alicoate attended an AT&T press demonstration of television and was able to see his assistant in a studio a few miles away. "The effect was uncanny," he enthused. "Television is here. Not one shadow of a doubt about it. . . . It would be suicide for the big minds of this great industry to close their eyes to television and its unlimited possibilities." Alicoate must have known that Harry Warner and Adolph Zukor were investigating television, and that David Sarnoff was already heavily invested in TV research and development. First National, Universal, and probably the other majors had been routinely inserting clauses into their literary property contracts that gave them television rights. In June the Federal Communications Commission (its name—significantly—changed from the Radio Commission) designated five 100-kilocycle bands of the frequency spectrum for television transmission.[19]

Mickey Mouse clubs began at the Fox Modjeska Theater in Milwaukee as a "kid stunt on the Disney-Columbia cartoons." The gimmick proved to be a powerful force in cultivating return audiences. The children gathered on Saturdays to sing the club theme song, "Minnie's Yoo Hoo," to watch cartoons, serials, and low-budget films, and to buy concessions. The Columbia press release explained the success of the club: "Like their dads, the average youth likes to be identified with social organizations, and the latest Mickey Mouse stunt is a darb to satisfy that yen. It is a membership card in the local club, a green card with a red imprinted number, that makes it look official and important."[20] The clubs grew explosively. In March 1931, Walt Disney took over Howard Hughes's former Caddo offices at 1540 Broadway to administer them. It was claimed that more than three million kids belonged to the six hundred Mickey Mouse clubs. Disney and NBC talked about a club radio program.[21]

Another method of attracting moviegoers was to upgrade the auditorium and its sound system. The trade press put theater owners on notice that "Bad Sound—is synchronized murder":

> When in place of ordinary even projection you have a constant rain storm on the screen and instead of pleasing voices and tuneful melody you get from the loud speaker a symphony of squeaks, scratches and air pockets, the effect upon the customer regarding his future and continued patronage is

Mickey Mouse Club advertisement, 1931.

apt to be most discouraging for the exhibitor. . . . In former days an old print was bad enough but under the new order of things bad sound from either print or records is nothing short of synchronized murder. (*Film Daily,* 2 January 1930, p. 1)

While these sentiments echo the ERPI sales pitch, there is evidence that acoustics could indeed be pretty bad. The SMPE heard reports that the "marvelous realism" heard in Broadway theaters had room for much improvement outside of town. Clarence Brown, the MGM director, felt that 75 percent of the sound's quality was lost by the time the film was shown in theaters.[22] One independent observer thought that

the actual talking picture is at present an utter failure. The picture with synchronized music is better, but no one with an appreciation of tone can say that even this branch of the synchronised production is successful. In spite of all the claims of perfect reproduction, the fact remains that the quality of the sound is inferior to that of the radio or of the better grade phonograph. However, as there is every reason to believe that American science can overcome this defect, it is one which should not enter into this discussion. (Herbert McKay, "Home-'Talkies,'" *Photo-Era,* January 1929, p. 55)

But even on Broadway reproduction was not perfect. When WHAT A WIDOW! (1930) played at the Rialto, "the utterances of the players were more often than not quite indistinct, and when Miss Swanson sang poor synchronization added to the faulty tonal quality." The Metropolitan soprano Grace Moore sang in A LADY'S MORALS (1930) at the Capitol, but "the sound reproduction was so poor that it spoiled a climactic song and also caused the dialogue to be so muffled that it seemed as though one's ears were filled with cotton."[23]

One solution was to buy new improved equipment, especially if the installation was two years old or bootlegged. Several showcase theaters revived the discontinued system of running the optical track separately on an interlocked sound reproducer. MGM equipped the Astor on Broadway with such a double system for its two-dollar shows. The film was free from the intermittent motion required for the image, so there was supposed to be less wow and flutter.[24]

The Earl Carroll Theater in New York hired an "attaché" who sat in the audience and monitored the show's volume.[25] ERPI urged this practice as an ideal. Some movie houses instituted theater-style rehearsals—for the projectionists. *Film Daily's* technical columnist described the procedure:

The projectionist cannot accurately judge the volume of sound in the theater. Rehearsals enable the theater management to determine fairly well the proper volume adjustment for each scene. Too often audiences suffer from monotony by listening to sound, the volume of which is either too loud or too soft. To obtain the correct effect it is necessary to maintain the volume at a level which is most natural for each subject. A close-up should be somewhat louder than a long-shot, and the voice of a single person should not be louder than the cries of a mob. (*Film Daily,* 19 October 1930, p. 7)

The local operator had the responsibility of ensuring that the level of sound matched the visual scale of each shot.

The necessity to "ride" the volume was caused by the varying levels of gain on the sound track (film or disc). (Modern reprints and some archival restorations of films from the period routinely eliminate the high variations in the originals by electronic equalization of the scene-to-scene changes in gain.) Obviously the solution was to equalize the output by adjusting the sound track in the recording lab, not by depending on the ears of the nation's projectionists. But before 1931 "timing" the sound track for level output by re-recording it had the objectionable side effect of introducing even more background hiss and scratching. Until noiseless recording improved the signal-to-noise ratio and made re-recording feasible, the best solution was to control the sound in the projection booth and to place the responsibility on the projectionist, who frequently could not hear the results of his adjustments. It is likely that only the most dedicated operator rehearsed or monitored the sound very meticulously. It was not until 1938 that the industry agreed on a standard for audio output.

The simplest way to improve sound reproduction was to turn the volume down. "The ground or surface noises that are part of the talking picture, as the phonograph needle's scratching is part of the talking machine, is emphasized by volume. This is especially true where there are many silent stretches in the picture. Lower volume, on the other hand, tends to obliterate these noises." Loudness was still the most frequently heard complaint. Fans complained of headaches. One auditor in Arizona claimed to have been deafened by a trip to the movies. The problem was so serious that the New York City Board of Health amended its sanitary code to require theater owners to tone down their movie speakers or remove them. Engineers advised projectionists to start the volume low and fade up. Otherwise, "sensitivity is deadened, with the result that the listener is satisfied with the volume before it has actually been diminished to a level that should be used."[26] Joe Weil of the Universal theater chain laid the blame on management. In 90 percent of the complaints about sound, "the real trouble can be laid to lack of proper supervision of the sound reproduction by the manager of the theater. . . . The manager must monitor the show and telephone the projectionist when adjustments are required."[27] Kann claimed to have seen "secret figures proving what bad business rotten talkers are doing."[28] He told anecdotes (possibly apocryphal) to show that poor-quality sound was no longer tolerated:

> One night last week, an audience in a New York neighborhood theater walked out. Couldn't stand such rotten sound. Recently, a distinguished star's first talker had a nice New York opening. Everything there but the sound. Then there was a certain picture, handicapped to begin with because it was terrible, that had an unfortunate premiere not long ago. The reproducer squawked against performing. What a night that was! All over the land, bad sound is driving dollars away from theaters, many of them never to return. . . . The public demands a good show and doesn't give a hoot in L what troubles have to be waded through to give it. (*Film Daily*, 1 July 1929, p. 1)

Jack Alicoate picked up the fight in an editorial against "the universally bad reproduction of sound and dialogue in the small and medium-sized houses." He said that "the main reason for poor or spotty reproduction is cheap, bootleg or home-made equipment. Close behind comes lack of intelligent inspection, tardy replacement of worn parts and the employment of cheap and untrained operators."[29]

In addition to upgrading the sound system, another strategy for boosting attendance was to improve the decor and ambience of the auditorium. Loew's theaters, for instance, removed sheet-music stalls from the lobbies. "A wise move, it seems, this eliminating of the music stand which in many instances has impaired the beauty and attractiveness of numerous de luxe houses," Alicoate editorialized. "The hawking of pop corn and music may be within the bounds of etiquette in small theaters but it's out of place in the modern up-to-the-minute Picture Palace."[30] Exhibitors who might have considered trying this would have found themselves in the difficult situation of having to sacrifice a few dollars of needed ancillary income to pay for "class." Most continued to sell concessions.

The talkies made theaters cooler in summer. In the old days many theaters closed in July and August because of the heat and humidity. This practice changed in the late twenties when "refrigerated air" became a selling point. The coming of sound necessitated acoustic control inside the theater, leading to the end of opened doors and noisy ventilation fans. Quiet air conditioning not only improved the noise level but enabled theaters to remain open year-round. This increased the demand for more movies, led to the cancellation of the traditional winter recess in Hollywood, and opened the door for more independent product.

One telling change in film-going behavior not usually associated with the coming of sound was the shift in audience snack preferences. In February 1929, the National Theater Supply Co. introduced its peerless popcorn and peanut machines. Whereas hard candy and peanuts-in-the-shell had been the treats of choice in silent film days, talking film audiences would not tolerate the munching and shell cracking sounds. Relatively noiseless popcorn quickly replaced peanuts at the concession stand.[31]

Exhibitors also tried altering the time-tested structure of the movie program. The most controversial strategy was the double feature, running two films (usually an "A" and a "B" picture—that is, a high-low rental combination) for the price of a single admission. This practice was common with independent theaters in out-of-the-way areas where the features were short and cheap, but it had never been a serious factor in big-city exhibition. "The major producers and distributors fought the double feature vigorously until 1934 when the National Recovery Administration denied the majors the right to ban it," according to Paul Seale.[32] Exhibitors sometimes ran double features as an alternative to renting several expensive shorts to fill out the program. At its April meeting the Motion Picture Theater Owners of America pleaded with producers to make longer features because shorts cost more per minute than features. Alicoate commented on the effect of sound on the projection time of features:

> Personally we have always preferred quality to quantity but that won't suffice as an argument to an irritable and squawking customer who has been used to two hours of amusement for his two-bits and feels cheated if turned out ten minutes earlier. Formerly a small exhibitor could kid his gang along, and frequently did, by slowing his machines to sixty or seventy [feet per minute]. Now with machines timed to run ninety that simply can't be done. Today a sixty-minute feature runs just that and no more. For a two-hour show the little fellow needs plenty more film or another feature. (*Film Daily*, 20 May 1930, p. 1)

A few months later he published the running times of several new features that exceeded eighty minutes, purporting to show that producers were responding to exhibitors' complaints.[33]

Sometimes nothing worked and the manager faced the prospect of no longer showing movies. Rather than shutter the theater, many enterprising independent owners and a few national chains explored an alternative amusement, miniature golf—or as it was called then, Tom Thumb golf. In the spring of 1930 operators began ripping up the movie seats and installing putting greens. By summer even the Fox, Publix, and Warner organizations were turning their unprofitable houses into miniature golf courses. Warner Bros. refitted at least twenty-five Stanley theaters for golf. Even the Apollo on 125th Street in New York was converted to a golf house. The trade press lamented the "Tom Thumb menace" and chastised exhibitors who succumbed to it. But the craze passed with the summer; by September 1930, *Film Daily* noted with satisfaction that seventy-five courses were for sale in Los Angeles, and that "takers are few and far between."[34]

Perhaps the scariest thing about the mini-golf fad was that the industry's unshakable belief that audiences would go to the movies no matter how bad things got was badly shaken. The public *was* willing to spend its dimes and quarters on cheaper amusements. Desperate exhibitors were more than ready to abandon movies if a more lucrative use appeared for their big buildings.

The Depression's Toll

Adolph Zukor, a staunch economic Darwinist, proclaimed in an advertisement that

> to us in the motion picture business, one of the outstanding lessons which 1930 has driven home repeatedly is that the public, no matter what general conditions may be, will patronize *good* pictures. Good pictures! Nothing in this business can take their place, nothing is so absolutely necessary to the continued prosperity of all phases of the industry. Week after week, when other businesses have been languishing, when poor pictures have been starving, we have seen good pictures draw thousands of people to box-offices. The record has been so plain that the wonder is anybody ever could have been deluded with the idea that there was a substitute for good pictures. (*Film Daily*, 2 January 1931, pp. 9–11)

His optimism could not cover up a fundamental truth: in 1931 and 1932 the audience did not show up. All the good pictures could not put disposable cash into the pockets of jobless workers or prevent bankers from foreclosing on mortgages. Realizing the effect of severe unemployment on admissions revenue, exhibitors sponsored National Motion Picture Week, 18–25 November 1931. Theater patrons were urged to make donations for the national relief effort. "Give him a lift," appealed the ads. Retrenchment hit the local Bijou hard and devastated the big movie palaces and chains. The Roxy Theaters Corporation made a small profit in 1930 but lost $163,571 in 1931.[35] The Roxy itself had been sold by Fox to a consortium of investors who cried loudly when the management attempted to shut down the theater for four weeks in an effort to stop the cash outflow. A federal judge sided with the bondholders and prevented the closing.[36]

The fortune of the Warners' Theatre on Broadway is emblematic of exhibition at large. Like all Warner houses, it was reconfigured with a wide Vitascope screen in January 1931.

Maurice Chevalier lent his name to the 1931 "Give Him a Lift" campaign.

Unfortunately, this event coincided with the decision by the majors to halt all widescreen production. Soon the former flagship theater began operating as a second-run house. An event which symbolized the distance the talkies had traveled occurred in March 1931, when The Jazz Singer was re-released for a two-week exclusive engagement at the Warners'. The revival flopped so badly that the theater canceled it after three days. "Reaction to the pioneer sound film," according to the trade postmortem, "was that it appeared tremendously out of date in the face of the fast progress made by talkers." But current releases fared no better, and in April 1932 the Warners' Theatre closed. On the West Coast the newly built Hollywood Warner Bros. Theatre was also shuttered for several months. It reopened in May 1931 with Svengali (1931) but soon became a grind house (that is, giving continuous performances at popular prices).[37]

Theater managers, of course, tried to hold the profit line. They slashed ticket prices. In many regions the cost of admission, already down from around thirty-five to fifty cents in 1930, reached ten cents. Matinee prices were extended to 6:00 P.M. to draw workers into the theater. Many independents successfully renegotiated contracts which returned them to the more advantageous flat rental system except for "big situations"— pictures from which the studio expected to make more money. To reduce their taxes, most businesses used accelerated depreciation schedules. The Internal Revenue Service ruled that it would allow depreciation of theater organs only if the units were physically removed, thus providing a valuable tax incentive for the wholesale destruction of these historic instruments.

The years 1931–1933 were dismal for most business, but for show business they were particularly harsh. Construction of movie palaces halted. As *Film Daily* tersely concluded, "The day of the de luxers is virtually over."[38] In general, the more theaters they owned, the more the production companies suffered. Paramount received help from Lehman Brothers in refinancing its theater debt in 1931, but this biggest of the studio-theater combines went into receivership anyway. It emerged reorganized in 1935. The Fox Theaters Corporation and the Balaban and Katz Circuit went into receivership in 1932. Balaban and Katz, which operated thirty-five theaters in the Chicago region, claimed that Paramount had saddled it with $2.5 million in rental obligations. Sam Katz himself had been forced out of Paramount Publix. Fox's Wesco subsidiary was reorganized in 1933, eventually to became National Theaters. Harley Clarke's General Theater Equipment went into receivership after losing $900,000 in 1931. Loew's survived the Depression because it pared itself to a small chain of about 150 big-city theaters. Warner Bros. refused to go into receivership and sold 300 of its 700 theaters. RKO at first seemed to be a lucky scavenger, acquiring distressed theaters when their owners could not pay RCA for its sound systems. But these became albatrosses when RCA stopped its subsidies to the film company. RKO went bankrupt in 1933 and did not recover until 1940.[39]

This glance at exhibition illustrates that the producing and consuming functions of the film business were separate but ultimately codependent. Obviously neither component could exist without the other, but since each wanted to maximize profits, inherent conflicts erupted from time to time. The coming of sound was a period marked by a lack of harmony. Exhibitors who could afford to convert to sound seem to have done so willingly in order to satisfy their customers. But those whose revenue base was insufficient to support the investment were reluctant, and some of them spoke out against the unfairness of the talkies and their distributors. Perhaps it is here that the idea arose that audiences did not like the talkies and big studios forced them on consumers. More likely it was the owner of the local theater, who did not wish to turn over a substantial portion of revenue to convert the house, with an aversion to talkies. For all classes and locales of theater owners, however, the primary issue surrounding the coming of sound was the decreased sovereignty of the local manager.

As for the question of why audiences seemed to forsake the silents, perhaps one answer is that embracing the talkies did not necessarily imply a rejection of the films of seasons past. The talkies succeeded not because they replaced silents, which had inexplicably gone from popular to despised, but because audiences of the time looked at the sound film as an improvement on silents. They selectively evaluated the talkies against other competing forms of entertainment, such as music concerts (especially jazz) and miniature golf. Before 1930 audiences might have attended theaters to participate in several locally specialized forms of entertainments, whether stage shows, talent contests, or sing-alongs. Increasingly, the movie house showed sound movies and nothing else. The most probable reason is that live participatory events became poorly attended, while talking pictures held interest. Because of the imperative to survive the Depression, these structural changes in the program were perhaps inevitable. It may have been a sense of something lost by the local community with the passing of hometown-generated entertainment that contributed to the later nostalgia for the silent age.

Charles King and Anita Page in THE BROADWAY MELODY *(MGM, 1929).*

PART 2

Three Seasons: The Films of 1928–1931

If a revolution is a sudden event which throws over the past regime and substitutes a new oppositional rule, then the conversion to sound was certainly no revolution. The talkies were not instantaneous, although once sound film was in place, it was accepted very quickly. Part 2 presents a survey of major studio releases to look at what happened to the films themselves during the period following the signing of the ERPI and Photophone licenses and the twilight of silent exhibition.

As the talkies fanned out from the urban centers toward smaller towns, the nature of the film audience changed. The statistically average moviegoer who had access to talking pictures was increasingly likely to inhabit a small or medium-sized town. Hollywood tinkered with adjusting content to accommodate regional tastes. With more and more people experiencing the "thrill" of talking pictures, the novelty of sound for its own sake soon wore off. Fascination gave way to discrimination. The use of sound in motion pictures went through distinct—though overlapping—phases, from silent film supplement to integrated component. These changes were motivated in part by Hollywood's rapidly increasing technical mastery, but technology alone is not sufficient to explain the direction in which the industry took sound. That explanation has more to do with consumers—the movie fans who exerted economic pressure and the critics who condemned some uses of sound and praised others.

Part 2 begins in the summer of 1928, when film audiences began to taste the first fruits of the industry's experiments. It ends in the spring of 1931, more than one thousand films later, when Hollywood had definitely stopped producing silent movies, when the critical consensus had accepted that sound, rightly or wrongly, was permanent, and when only a tiny minority of moviegoers even had the option of attending a silent film.

Chapters 12, 13, and 14 present a "seasonal" review of some significant films which a moviegoer might have encountered during 1928–1931. In the 1920s the exhibition season extended from Labor Day (September) through Memorial Day (May). During the summer, the "orphan" season, theaters showed less expensive fare and often closed during the hot months of July and August. In early spring, traveling studio and distributor sales representatives sold blocks of films for the following season to independent exchanges and exhibitors. (Some of these productions had been finished before the studios' annual closing in January, some were still to be produced, and some would never be made.) A theater manager had more bargaining power if he booked films from only a few distributors (typically only two or three studios). The range of films available in a particular market depended on the number of competing theaters and on whether they were studio-affiliated or independent.

Of course, no individual moviegoer saw all of these films, nor was there an ideal audience experiencing the waves of innovations in film form and content that characterized these three seasons. Observations about audience behavior are always inferential and generalized. Most of our evidence derives from three indirect sources: box-office results, trade journal commentary, and critical accounts. These indicators, as discussed in part 3, are problematic. For now, however, they provide the best way to trace the unfolding of the talkies.

The diversity of product in circulation gave moviegoers a chance to shop, and the film industry strove to favor their preferences. When the transition began, sound was treated by the studios as a bonus, something dispensed to add value to a film or a program. Audiences seemed to respond favorably, regardless of the quality or content. It may also be that there was a tendency to think of movie sound as a new kind of electrical appliance; audiences were drawn to see what science had wrought. They were curious, and producers gave them what they wanted: sound tracks which spiced up traditional films by injecting music, noises, and perhaps an added reel or two of talking. Many producers apparently regarded sound as a way to rejuvenate old film genres. The virtual Broadway conception was also still powerful, and many of the new films adapted existing entertainment forms. The filmmakers drew freely from musical, operetta, and vaudeville material. The exploratory all-dialogue features from Warners generated public interest and long lines, confirming the suspicions of the studios that the talkies might succeed this time. The strength of the response was a surprise, but this possibility had already been taken into account in the studios' hedging strategies; the larger ones were already building or upgrading their facilities in Hollywood and New York. Critics, meanwhile, emphasized the need for high technical standards of reproduction, disliked post-synchronized sound tracks, and yelped when speech was incomprehensible.

By the second season, 1929–1930, what had passed as a novelty a year before was now criticized as too loud or ostentatious. The films handled filmed performance in different ways. One was to segregate it as a short subject, literally substituting it for the former live entertainment. Within features, performances were integrated into the larger fiction of the film story. They could be either encapsulated or contained. An *encapsulated* act was presented more or less in its entirety, but as a stage act justified by the story. SHOW BOAT (dir. James Whale, 1929), for example, shows the singing of Jerome Kern's songs as part of the show boat's routine entertainment program. A variant of encapsulation was the theme song, a musical intermezzo inserted in a film to break up the action, to show off the star's singing talent (or that of a voice double), and, incidentally, to stimulate sales of records and sheet music. *Contained* performances presented singing and dancing logically as a plot device, most commonly the backstage motif about the trials and tribulations of putting on a show, interspersed with an unfolding romance between young lovers. This motif provided plenty of opportunities for filmed performances.

The wayward tendencies of sound—evident in the part-talkie, for example, or in "static" genres like the trial film—were curbed. Broadway was still an ideal, at least for some producers, and several films appropriated legitimate theater, not only to provide ready-made sources and talent but to attract a higher class of moviegoer while exposing the masses to dramaturgic and operatic art.

The 1930–1931 season was one of consolidation. Many musicals flopped, especially those which failed to rise above the clichés of the operetta, revue, and backstage story. After more than one hundred musicals in the previous season, fewer than thirty were released in this one. There was a critical reaction against "theatricality," although what the term was understood to mean is somewhat obscure. Critics, instead, settled on keeping all the acoustic effects in balance and under control as the first principle of sound production. Acting, voice, and story values were primary. The audible part of a film was not to distract the viewer. Borrowing a term from radio, I call this approach espoused by critics and practiced by Hollywood the *modulated* sound track. The most successful films, notably the so-called realist productions, limited dialogue and effects to creating irony, pathos, or laughter and providing narrative information. There was even a call for a return to silent film practice among its most extreme advocates.

For consistency and convenience, the films are discussed according to their respective studios. This method of organization is perhaps more valid for the first half of the transition, when the studios were using sound blatantly to compete and to distinguish their product. In the second half, the industry set out to standardize sound practice, and the uses of the sound track became more uniform. Did audiences care whether their films were from a certain studio? One cannot be certain. There were definite connotations to, and genres identified with, some of the producers (Paramount's European class, MGM's constellation of stars, Universal's Westerns). But if the studio label influenced a moviegoer's selection of a film, it probably carried about as much weight as a manufacturer's label on a phonograph record or a publisher's imprint on a book. The choice of studio product depended, too, upon the size of the consumer's town; the bigger the city, the greater the selection. If film audiences could be said to have "brand-name" loyalty, it was to certain stars, not producers. Genres also played a role—given a choice, a consumer could indulge his or her inclination to see a comedy, Western, gangster, melodrama, adventure, romance, or thriller. But we must be cautious about imputing motives. Because movies offer relatively cheap entertainment, there have always been many who attend for no conscious reason at all.

During the three-season span, sound film changed from being a genre in itself to being simply generic. There is a rapid falloff in the critical literature of references to a film's use of sound. This corresponds to Hollywood's standardization of techniques and establishment of storytelling conventions that balanced voice and music. When all films had dialogue, the term *talkie* lost its descriptive power.

Short subjects, travel films, and animation changed dramatically with sound. As described in chapter 15, these forms replaced the live entertainment which had kept each theater's bill of fare distinctive and competitive. Shorts standardized the program, limited the individual theater manager's power to diversify the bill, and made movie theaters a place reserved exclusively for film projection. The sound short was also something of a laboratory for features. Many technical experiments and unconventional content approaches could be tried out with relatively low risk. The travel film partook of the newsreel's connotation of authenticity, sometimes in quite exploitative ways. Cartoons capitalized on the studios' acquisitions of music libraries. Animating to the beat of popular music, synchronizing actions with funny noises, and giving characters voices transformed this short form into a powerful new mode of film production. The example of Mickey Mouse shows the importance of character development in creating animation's illusion of life. Walt Disney's initial difficulties also demonstrate how the major studios tried to restrict independent producers' access to sound technology.

The coming of sound had the potential to open up the movies to subjects which addressed the interests of ethnic and linguistic minorities. Some filmmakers even dreamed of producing regular features outside the Hollywood institution. Chapter 16 sketches some efforts to establish nonmainstream sound cinema, as well as Hollywood's response.

The talkies bolstered Hollywood's increasingly important multinational status. Chapter 17 examines the ways in which Hollywood behaved as an international business and as a cultural influence, shifting quickly from imperialism to negotiation. For American audiences, the distribution of foreign-language productions (made in the United States and abroad) diversified urban film consumers' viewing opportunities. It is even possible that the directors of some of the imports may have influenced Hollywood's attitude toward the sound track.

It is tempting to see the process outlined in part 2 as a rebalancing, a return to the state of equilibrium represented by the "Golden Age of the Silents." But more accurately, it was a reorganization accompanying a necessary adaptation to a new technology. The talkies *were* something new and different, masquerading in some respects as something old. In 1928 sound was a new era in entertainment; in 1931 image and sound were integrated into one seamless experience: the movies, a familiar component of everyday life.

12

The New Entertainment Vitamin, 1928–1929

The talking movie is here to stay.
JACK ALICOATE, 25 APRIL 1928

For the dedicated movie fan of 1928, it must have been an exciting and perhaps bewildering year. One heard of the studios' experiments in sound, but unless one lived near a major exhibition market, the talkies were more a rumor than an actuality. The majority of the films making headlines as talkers were playing locally as silents. But all around, theaters were undergoing conversion. When they started showing sound films regularly, moviegoers came to hear what the fuss was about. Like customers looking over new-model cars, audiences wished to learn what differentiated this product from the older one. Producers were eager to put their new prototype through its paces so that fans could see and hear what the sound film could do.

In May 1928, when the major producers signed their ERPI licenses, the next season (which would run from the fall of 1928 through the summer of 1929) was already being sold. What to do about sound? What to do with these films? Blind bidding and block booking had guaranteed security to Hollywood because product was sold before it was made. But sound introduced uncertainty. What if the competition got a head start, leaving one with a supply of unwanted silents? Anxious not to be left behind, the studios announced that a total of two hundred titles for the next season would have sound of some sort. And the sound would have to be flashy, calling attention to the new marvel. This required that everyone, for the first time, give some thought to answering the basic question, *What is a sound film?* Producers tried out various hedging approaches, including synchronized music and effects, goat glands, and part-talkies. The aim was to make something that could be called a sound film in order to cash in on the widespread curiosity, to buy time in order to explore efficient ways of making talkies, and to ascertain audience preferences. As a result, the 1928–1929 season was extraordinarily diverse and is difficult to categorize. Most of the films of the introductory period, however, show off their status as sound films. There are many kinds of films discussed in this chapter, but almost all of them are distinguished by their "you can't miss this!" approach to sound.

Al Jolson in THE SINGING FOOL *(Warner Bros., 1928).*

Warner Bros. and First National

The Warners and First National studios (under the control of Warners since the 1928 Stanley chain acquisition) continued to set the pace for sound production, turning out pictures around the clock. Alexander Korda, a contract director then, recalled that "there was only one sound channel, and this was used during the day-time in Warner Brothers studio, and at night-time by First National."[1] Day-to-day production at the studio was becoming increasingly influenced by Darryl F. Zanuck, an outspoken partisan for the talkies. Zanuck had been "supervising" most of the studio's output as well as writing it. He would remain a powerful production chief at the studio until his departure to form Twentieth Century Pictures in 1933.[2]

Zanuck and Jack Warner recognized that much of their success in sound was attributable to Al Jolson's stardom. On 7 August 1928, Warners signed a contract with the entertainer to make three more pictures. In addition to star perquisites, such as approval of the story, director, and cast, Jolson was also to be paid $225,000 for each film, plus 10 percent of the gross receipts over $1 million for the second and third feature—a highly unusual instance of profit participation for that time.[3] The studio launched the 1928–1929 season with a bang: Jolson in THE SINGING FOOL (dir. Lloyd Bacon). The company spared neither expense nor publicity about the expense. It set an advertising budget at $1 million, hired Irving Berlin to write a special song, leased the Winter Garden theater (still a Broadway fixture), and equipped it with a sound projection system. Jolson plugged the film in personal appearances. A "tremendous advance campaign" for the film's theme song, "Sonny Boy," was organized by De Sylva, Brown, and Henderson, the composers and sheet music publishers. (In three months De Sylva sold 500,000 copies of the sheet music and Brunswick sold 375,000 records.)[4] On 17 September, Jolson was a guest on *Vitaphone Jubilee*, a Warner Bros. weekly radio program on CBS. *Variety*, in cooperation with Warners, published a special twenty-four-page section on the film and the studio.

The plot is as schmaltzy as the singer's first film. Jolson plays Al Stone, a singing star who is victimized by Grace, his gold-digging wife (Betty Bronson). She breaks his heart when she takes their son (played by four-year-old Davey Lee) and runs away with a gangster. After wasting a few years as a derelict, Al meets an old friend, Grace (Betty Bronson). She helps him recuperate and inspires his Broadway comeback. Meanwhile, the boy becomes terminally ill. Jolson's bathetic rendition of "Sonny Boy" after his son dies is the topper following six other song hits. Richard Barrios has calculated that Jolson is on-screen for 105 minutes.[5]

The opening of THE SINGING FOOL at the Winter Garden was brilliant, emotionally powerful, and "cluttered with notables." Maurice Kann observed that "mascara ran freely from carefully and artfully made-up eyes, but the women didn't seem to mind it particularly. Executives and hard-boiled theater operators whose tears are usually of the crocodile variety shed real ones last night." Kann, unlike most reviewers, was impressed by Jolson's acting ability and praised the sections of semi-improvised dialogue: "His two long sequences where the baby [Lee] talks to him and where he replies in conversation and in song are of permanent achievement. So natural, so charming, so simple and withal so touching, these particular stretches of footage are among the most magnificent ever recorded on celluloid."[6] Kann declared that the sound revolution was now on. "The word-of-mouth advertising is spreading fast. Maybe you don't think the public catches on in a hurry. If you were in the neighborhood of the Winter Garden yesterday afternoon, all doubt would have been removed."[7]

"Sonny Boy" sheet music from The Singing Fool *(Warner Bros., 1928).*

Most New York critics rated the film excellent. Of special interest, though, is the intensity with which Jolson's charismatic personality impressed them. Mordaunt Hall of the *Times* pinpointed the appeal of the film, "not in its transparent narrative, but in Mr. Jolson's inimitable singing. One waits after hearing a selection, hoping for another." Another commentator called the story "familiar hokum" but gushed over Jolson's "sincerity and genuine feeling." Initial reviews set the tone for the general opinion concerning the movie's significance: "The talking picture is practicable, inevitable and, in this case, at least, powerful. THE SINGING FOOL justifies the Vitaphone and all the experiments that have hitherto passed as talking pictures."[8] Although THE JAZZ SINGER (dir. Alan Crosland, 1927) has entered the history books as the film that started the sound revolution, it was the one-two punch of THE LIGHTS OF NEW YORK (dir. Bryan Foy) in July and THE SINGING FOOL in September 1928 that proved beyond doubt to producers and exhibitors that a feature sound film with a big star had the potential to make millions. Simultaneously, the popular press, which had showed little interest in talking features after THE JAZZ SINGER, now passionately embraced the concept.

Issues of quality and appropriate material entered critical discussions about sound. Aside from the Jolson vehicles, which were in a class by themselves because of his drawing power, adaptations of previously successful stage plays were controversial. For example, Vitaphone's THE HOME TOWNERS (dir. Bryan Foy, 1928), adapted from a George M. Cohan play, was lauded by some critics. Others pointed out that the dialogue was good only because it had been transposed from the stage production, and that traditional movie qualities were lacking. "Everything," according to the *Graphic,* echoing what was becoming a familiar refrain, "has been sacrificed to sound."[9] Hall, however, introduced what would grow to be an important motif in his influential criticism of sound, the issue of who was in control:

> Having been produced with a sense of restraint and an intelligent conception of the coupling of the cinematic values with the lines, it provided an agreeable entertainment. It has, it is true, mechanical defects, for sometimes the voices were a trifle explosive and on other occasions they were not a little too weak. But it was plain that with experience the players will learn to control their voices, or, perhaps the directors will eventually learn more about the control of sound. (Mordaunt Hall, *New York Times,* 24 October 1928)

Hall seems to have been disturbed by problems in scale-matching, that is, fitting the spatial presence of the voice to the space in the image of the speaker. This is an early example of what would soon become a call for a modulated sound track that kept all the parts in balance.

With seemingly bottomless resources, Zanuck converted his most elaborate spectacle to date into a part-dialogue film. NOAH'S ARK (dir. Michael Curtiz), after an arduous summer production schedule marred by setbacks, including the alleged drowning of two extras during filming of the flood scene, premiered in Los Angeles at Grauman's Chinese Theater on 1 November 1928.[10] It was Warners' first production to cost more than $1 million to complete. In the primary story set in Paris at the beginning of World War I, Mary (Dolores Costello) falls in love with Travis (George O'Brien). They lose each other during the fighting. Falsely accused of being a German spy, she is on the verge of being shot by a firing squad. Then the long story of Noah begins, with the same principals playing the lead characters. Miriam (Costello) is about to be sacrificed when the Deluge rushes

NOAH'S ARK *(Warner Bros., 1929) souvenir program.*

into the temple. Japheth (O'Brien) saves her, and they board the ark. Returning to the modern story, one of the members of the firing squad recognizes her—it's Travis! Mary and Travis learn of the armistice, and they are saved. The dialogue scenes prompted the only exceptions to the otherwise glowing reviews of the spectacle. The *Express* called them "a trivial adjunct to the silent majesty and magnitude of the major part." The talking sequences, written by Zanuck and directed by Roy Del Ruth, presented Costello speaking in a pleasant enough voice, but in an emotionless, stilted delivery.[11]

One of the few stars who rivaled Jolson was Fanny Brice, whom Warners arranged to borrow from Florenz Ziegfeld, Broadway's impresario of the Follies revue. MY MAN (written by Zanuck under the pseudonym Mark Canfield, and directed by Archie Mayo) opened as Warners' big Christmas attraction. As Fannie Brand, Brice plays a working girl in a Broadway costume shop who auditions for a Broadway show produced by Landau (André de Segurola), a promoter modeled on Ziegfeld. The film received only a lukewarm critical response. The main draw—apparently the only draw of this part-talker—was hearing Fanny Brice sing seven of her most popular songs. When the film failed to catch on nationally, critics speculated that too few non–New Yorkers knew who Brice was or why she was supposed to be the "female Jolson." Herbert Goldman also points out that Brice may have been victimized by prevailing sexist attitudes toward female performers. "Fanny was now thirty-seven in a day in which many women were considered too old for leads at thirty."[12] Although MY MAN was not considered a great success, it nonetheless reaped profits.

In fact, most Warners' sound specials performed extraordinarily well at the box office (see appendix 1). THE SINGING FOOL did good business, but nothing came close to THE LIGHTS OF NEW YORK, an astounding return on investment in any epoch. Yet the studio seemed slow to pick up the ball on the talking gangster film.

For some of the studio's subsequent efforts at serious melodrama, talking may have done more harm than good. The reviews of ON TRIAL (dir. Archie Mayo, 1928) were bland, and Pauline Frederick's voice was deplored. She plays the wife of a businessman who is accused of murdering his partner and must take the stand and expose the real killer. The Elmer Rice play had been notable for its inclusion of long, narrated flashback sequences, which were duly incorporated into the movie version. Hall blasted the sound quality:

> There is quite a good deal of lisping as the players utter their lines and frequently what they say is not spoken with adequate emphasis or thought. There are periods when the speech is slightly muffled, which seems to have been done to avoid explosive phases of the Vitaphone. In quite a number of cases the diction is peculiarly poor. In fact, one concludes toward the end of this offering that it would have been a far more exciting picture had it been presented in silent form. (Hall, *New York Times*, 15 November 1928)

The unfortunate CAUGHT IN THE FOG (dir. Howard Bretherton, 1928) was regarded as a "sickly specimen of sound film." May McAvoy again failed to impress the listeners: her "half dozen talking bits just fair." The voices in STATE STREET SADIE (dir. Archie Mayo, 1928) were felt by Hall to be laid on too thick: "So you have crooks that call each other names, laugh and say quite a number of 'Wa-als,' which must be a favorite way for a gangster to begin his interrogation of his underlings."[13] These poorly received part-talking crime films might have steered Warners away from following up quickly on the success of its all-talking drama. This was during the regimen of the "Warner Proportion" (only 75 percent talking in each film), so the studio was still playing its hunch that audiences wanted part-talkies.

When Warner Bros. took over control of First National, by far the most important talent acquisition, or so it seemed in 1928, was Colleen Moore. Probably the highest-paid star in Hollywood, she was acclaimed for her lead in the World War I drama LILAC TIME (1928).[14] It seemed certain that her charisma would grow with the talkies. But Moore came as a package deal, and the other part of the package was John McCormick, her husband and the First National producer in charge of her projects. Aside from personal problems which would lead to divorce (theirs was supposedly the marriage fictionalized in Cukor's WHAT PRICE HOLLYWOOD? [1932]), McCormick misjudged the importance of sound. He scoffed in public at the fad, then blundered in selecting SMILING IRISH EYES (dir. William A. Seiter, 1929) for Moore's vocal debut. Irish girl Moore pines for her actor boyfriend Rory (James Hall) until she saves enough money to join him in New York. But she flies into a jealous rage when she sees him performing at the theater with a female costar and returns to the homeland. Rory joins her and brings the whole clan back to the United States. The story is insipid and the ethnic characterizations so stereotypically insulting that the picture was later banned in Ireland. Worse, at its premiere Moore's talkie received many laughs, "only they weren't intended." The audience faulted "a story that wallowed unpardonably in saccharine through a long array of senile situations that passed out with horse cars."[15]

First National tried to recover by casting Moore in a "mature" role in the musical melodrama FOOTLIGHTS AND FOOLS (dir. Seiter, 1929). She plays a cabaret performer leading two lives as Betty Murphy, ordinary girl, and as Fifi D'Auray, star of "The Sins of 1930" revue. The notices were less devastating. The *Evening Journal* said, "Colleen does better work in this one than she has ever done before." But most found her Fifi character's accent unconvincing. An "embarrassing attempt to appear and sound Gallic," reported the *Morning Telegraph*. *Film Daily* advised exhibitors, "Though her French accent isn't so hot, she gets over the story to make it click as a good program offering. . . . It can be sold as something entirely different for Colleen, but don't promise too much."[16]

Warner Bros. expanded the virtual Broadway concept to feature length in THE DESERT SONG, not released nationally until May 1929. Directed by Del Ruth, it was adapted from a Sigmund Romberg–Oscar Hammerstein II operetta about the romantic exploits of a sheikh hero, the Red Shadow (John Boles) and a naive heroine (Carlotta King).[17] Myrna Loy was typecast as a generic Arab vamp. Though the film was essentially complete at the beginning of the year, Barrios argues that Warners' inflexible release schedule delayed the film until audiences were no longer excited about musicals. "The company adhered to its program so rigidly that it often botched the timing on its early talkies by keeping them on the shelf until their allotted time arrived. . . . It had been predetermined in the fall of 1928 that *The Desert Song* had a particular slot in the Warner schedule, and there it remained, waiting for its audience while the parade passed by."[18] *Film Daily* did not know what to make of the lack of precedent for this first "filmed operetta." It advised baffled exhibitors, "You'll have to decide for yourself on this one."[19] Los Angeles gave the experiment mixed reviews. The Vitaphone music was called "tonally perfect" and a "tremendous achievement of recording immense choruses." The New York reviews, on the contrary, were tepid. Although Boles and King were admired, on the whole DESERT SONG was "a ponderous and generally dull production that has the cash customer fidgeting in his pew for the greater part of the footage" (*Telegram*).[20]

FOOTLIGHTS AND FOOLS (*First National, 1929), with Colleen Moore (center).*

While the critics held back, the cash customers, however fidgety, were abundant. The healthy gross receipts helped sustain the operetta craze at Warners.

ON WITH THE SHOW (dir. Crosland) premiered in Los Angeles in May 1929 and was a big hit. Another backstage story, it is memorable for its two dynamic numbers sung by Ethel Waters. Her signature "Am I Blue?" was also the theme song. The story begins with the "Phantom Sweetheart" touring show about to close for lack of revenue before reaching Broadway. The star, Nita (Betty Compson), refuses to finish the performance until she receives her back-pay. Kitty (Sally O'Neil), a hatcheck girl, takes her place and wows the crowd, paving the way for her big break in show business and her romance with the head usher Jimmy (William Bakewell). The musical numbers are mostly encapsulated, like inserted Vitaphone shorts. Crosland did attempt to open up the frontal stage view by inserting shots from the wings, glimpses of stagehands operating the curtain, and so on. Sound is foregrounded in the characters' unusual voices: Snitz Edwards's raspy Brooklynese, the Dorsey Twins' squeaks delivered in unison ("Go sit on a tack"), a dresser jabbering in French. Sound is used for humorous counterpoint when a character onstage recites, "How calm and peaceful the old plantation is at dusk," followed by a raucous shot of the "belles" yelling and fighting backstage. The movie is something of a hybrid genre, combining elements of the musical revue, the romantic comedy, and the whodunit. (In a subplot, the box office is robbed.) Couching of the music inside a narrative, however slightly done in ON WITH THE SHOW, was presciently seen by Kann as the next trend. "It is effective, beautiful and a clear demonstration of what the sound picture of tomorrow will be," he wrote. There were some interesting dissents though:

"This film gives you a very excellent idea of a musical comedy—but a rather routine and commonplace one" (*Post*). ON WITH THE SHOW was photographed in Technicolor, and the papers frequently compared Warners' color innovation to its sound experiment in THE JAZZ SINGER. Hall, however, was impressed neither by the sound nor by Technicolor: "The dialogue, so jarring on one's nerves, sometimes comes from cherry-lips on faces in which the lily and the rose seem to be struggling for supremacy."[21]

Warners timed SAY IT WITH SONGS (dir. Lloyd Bacon) to premiere on 6 August 1929, Vitaphone's third anniversary. Jolson's appeal in this, his first all-talkie, was still universal. Critics liked young Davey Lee as much as in his previous pairing with Al. Everyone recognized that the story was very similar to THE SINGING FOOL. Joe Lane (Jolson) has to serve time in prison for accidentally killing a man in a jealous rage. Released, he runs away with his son, Little Pal (Lee). The boy is struck by a truck and loses his voice (dramatically ironic for a talkie) and his ability to walk. A doctor will cure him, but only if Little Pal returns to live with Jolson's ex-wife, now married to the doctor. Critics faulted Jolson and Warners for laziness. The story "has many loopholes and unexplained situations which will detract from its appeal," the *New York Post* commented. "As always plot and common sense are sacrificed when the possibility of producing a few more tears comes into sight."[22]

Fox Movietone

In May 1928, Fox announced that all films in the 1928–1929 season would be available with Movietone. Exchanges would receive three versions: silent with intertitles; with synchronized music; and part-dialogue.[23] For most Fox feature releases, "sound" still meant the virtual orchestra. Raoul Walsh's THE RED DANCE (1928) was all synchronized music, save for its theme song, "Angela Mia," sung by André de Segurola. Dolores Del Rio played Tashi, a Russian peasant girl who is swept up in the intrigue and excitement of czarist politics. It ran at the Globe in July along with THE FAMILY PICNIC, the first two-reel Movietone all-talking comedy. It starred Raymond McKee and Kathleen Key and contained no written titles. Again, this production is comparable to the Vitaphone two-reel playlets (or to THE LIGHTS OF NEW YORK, which was playing concurrently). George Bernard Shaw's famous Movietone News recording also debuted on this program.[24]

A momentous decision was made in July. The twenty-six films scheduled for the 1928–1929 lineup of Fox silent comedies were canceled, and the completed but unreleased silent two-reelers were junked. Fox explained that silent comedy "had outlived its usefulness." Introducing the two-director system was another important change. THE AIR CIRCUS, which opened 1 September 1928, was the first Fox part-talking feature, and its production demonstrated the new division of labor. Howard Hawks shared credit with Lewis Seiler, the director of Tom Mix's Westerns who had been hired to do the talking sequences. The dialogue was "staged" by Charles Judels, a film actor and former general stage manager for the Shubert organization.[25] Hawks directed the nontalking exterior action scenes.[26] Two aspiring aviators, Buddy (David Rollins) and Speed (Arthur Lake), enroll in flying school and vie for the attentions of Sue (Sue Carol). Buddy seems to be at a disadvantage when he discovers he fears heights. However, he triumphs over acrophobia and flies off to save Speed and Sue from certain death when their plane becomes disabled. "The dialogue is quite good most of the time, but it is a little too long," wrote Hall.[27]

MOTHER KNOWS BEST *(Fox, 1928) lobby card.*

Judels also directed the talking sequences of MOTHER KNOWS BEST (1928, codirected with John Blystone), a stage-mother story by Edna Ferber transparently based on the life of Elsie Janis. Sally Quail (Madge Bellamy) is the talented daughter whose professional and personal life is dominated by her mother (Louise Dresser). Only after having a nervous breakdown does Sally establish her independence. Fox's advertising emphasized that fans of Ferber's novel could *"Hear* and *See* the players talk their parts on Fox Movietone." In fact, the film was only a part-talkie with performances in which the actors showed off their vocal skills. Madge Bellamy, though her voice was weak, was appealingly impish doing her impersonations of Al Jolson in blackface and Harry Lauder. MOTHER KNOWS BEST received backhanded praise: "Several sequences of Movietone dialogue lift a very good production into something better."[28]

The first milestone all-talking film program was presented at the Roxy during the week of 15 November 1928. It comprised the newsreel and two Movietone comedies, including John Ford's three-reeler NAPOLEON'S BARBER. This all-dialogue film told the story of a barber who regales a customer with stories of what he would do if he met Napoleon. Needless to say, the customer *is* Napoleon. Ford later claimed that, against the wishes of the sound crew, he innovated exterior dialogue scenes. *Film Daily* took note: "Sound effects well handled, talking clear, especially in two outdoor sequences."[29] Since the Movietone trucks and the crew to operate them were readily available, and since Fox managers encouraged shooting outdoors, one wonders why Ford would have

IN OLD ARIZONA *(Fox, 1929), with Edmund Lowe and Dorothy Burgess.*

encountered so much resistance. Hall found himself forgetting "the novelty of audible productions," an important new criterion for judging sound excellence.[30]

The biggest critical success of early 1929 was Fox's IN OLD ARIZONA, the first all-talking Western feature. The project had been interrupted when the director, Raoul Walsh, was injured. While motoring on location, he collided with a jackrabbit, which smashed through the windshield and caused the director to lose an eye. The two-director system paid an unexpected dividend when the codirector, Irving Cummings, stepped in to replace him.[31] Warner Baxter gave a winsome performance as the Cisco Kid, for which he would receive an Academy Award. The treacherous Tonia Maria (Dorothy Burgess) sells the Kid out to Sergeant Dunn (Edmund Lowe), but the Kid tricks Dunn into shooting her, and off into the sunset he rides. A catchy De Sylva, Brown, and Henderson theme song ("My Tonia"), natural sounds recorded outdoors, and an engaging story captivated audiences and critics. "The microphone caught everything," bubbled Kann. "When the caballero sings as he rides out of the picture his voice grows fainter as it would in real life. When the cows moo, you hear them and when the stage coach driver cracks his whip, your ears get that, too."[32] The lively Western broke the Roxy's weekend record with a gross of $54,000. The *Daily News* found Edmund Lowe's voice thrilling and Warner Baxter's Mexican accent "simply swell." "The most interesting talking picture yet to be heard in this town," the *New York Post* declared. Hall's portentous *Times* comment again emphasized "forgetting" sound as something positive: "Often the story is so well told by the dialogue of the characters that one forgets for the moment the novelty of the Movietone."[33]

Myrna Loy and Roy D'Arcy in THE BLACK WATCH *(Fox, 1929).*

WILLIAM FOX MOVIETONE FOLLIES OF 1929 also used the two-director method. Directed by David Butler and William K. Wells, the film is a collection of musical acts strung together by a gossamer narrative about a plantation heir (John Breeden) who backs a vaudeville revue starring his belle (Lola Lane). Many critics thought Stepin Fetchit's dance number stole the show. Although the AFI catalog cites a Technicolor sequence, the trades announced that it was to be shot in Multicolor, another two-color process, underwritten by Howard Hughes, that was supposed to compete with Technicolor.

Lumsden Hare directed the dialogue (and played the Colonel) in THE BLACK WATCH (1929), while John Ford directed the action. Victor McLaglen portrayed Captain King of the Black Watch regiment. His mission is to quash a rebellion of "natives" in the Khyber region, eventually made possible through the sacrifice of the Indian girl Yasmani (Myrna Loy). "From a viewpoint of new uses for sound, John Ford's latest directorial effort for Fox reveals brilliantly clever effects in synchronization and photography," wrote the *Los Angeles Examiner.* But other reviewers sensed a clash of directorial styles, observing that the film's images, sound, and story failed to knit together: "No picture in the brief history of the talkies has approached THE BLACK WATCH for the vivid union of the art of photography with that of sound recording. Yet the new film at the Carthay Circle will go down in cinema history as a might-have-been-great production. This is due, chiefly, to John Ford's inability to tie his gorgeous mass scenes into a story" (*Los Angeles Herald*). Kann agreed. The "incidents don't piece together . . ., the resultant pattern is ragged."[34] In spite of these reviews, the show had a long run on Broadway.

LUCKY STAR (dir. Frank Borzage, 1929) was released in its part-talking version. It is a melodrama about two war veterans (Charles Farrell and Guinn "Big Boy" Williams) competing for the heart of Janet Gaynor. "Last two reels [of] dialogue, with Farrell and Gaynor voices [were] just fair," said Jack Harrower, *Film Daily's* regular reviewer.[35]

Paramount

After the fire destroyed Paramount's Hollywood soundstages in January 1928, Roy Pomeroy and the engineers relocated to the Paramount Eastern Studios in Astoria to battle numerous technical problems with sound. *Burlesque*, a drama which was to have been Paramount's first talkie, was postponed repeatedly. Edmund Goulding began shooting it at Astoria, but eventually the project was transferred to Hollywood. At the time, Pomeroy said he was experimenting with recording the sound on a separate film-strip, then transferring it to disc.[36] *Burlesque* was eventually released in 1929 as THE DANCE OF LIFE, codirected by John Cromwell and Edward Sutherland (although Victor Fleming, uncredited, had a hand in it as well).

Paramount was an especially aggressive recruiter of talent from the New York stage. In 1928 B. P. Schulberg signed the directors John Cromwell in May, Robert Milton in June, and William deMille in August. The last was described as "a stage director for fourteen years, and . . . a dramatist as well as producer." DeMille's cinematic credentials, strangely, were left unmentioned. He was Cecil B.'s older brother and a Hollywood veteran since 1916, having written the script for WHY CHANGE YOUR WIFE? (1920) and directed MISS LULU BETT (1921).

The first released Paramount sound films were hasty goat gland jobs. WARMING UP (dir. Fred Newmeyer, 1928) was a baseball story with Richard Dix, shot silent. The production head, Walter Wanger, took the negative to the Victor studios in Camden for post-synchronization. Reviewers were dissatisfied and demanded more dialogue. The *Film Daily* reviewer stated specifically that talking would have improved WARMING UP: "Synchronization . . . is good with all the familiar sounds of a ball park, but the lack of dialogue is very noticeable."[37] Hall, presumably at the same press screening, criticized the synchronization: "The smack of a ball against a bat is heard some time before Lucas has finished winding up." Of the eleven New York reviews, only four liked the ambient sound effects, with the *Daily Mirror* singling out the "wham of the bats." There were complaints about the abrupt alternation of silent sequences with sound effects. Pomeroy's team had added "wild" (nonsynchronous) dialogue in the crowd scenes (as in SUNRISE [1927] and OLD SAN FRANCISCO [1927]), but most reviewers interpreted the experiment as a botched attempt to lip-synch. In a remarkable instance of the media intervening in studio affairs, the *World* advised that WARMING UP ought to be the last such picture until Paramount "can synchronize speech and action in the films with something approaching naturalness and despatch." In another synchronized attempt, LOVES OF AN ACTRESS (dir. Rowland V. Lee, 1928), the silent star Pola Negri fared no better; critics claimed that the sound track was too loud and the effects too abundant.[38] Hall felt that the film

> demonstrates ad absurdum the potentialities of synchronization. The varied noises taking part in the action of the picture range from the squealing effect

(Left to right): (undetermined), Clive Brook, and Doris Kenyon in INTERFERENCE
(Paramount, 1928).

> when a baby is shown crying through sundry barnyard effects early one
> morning to vocal selections. An orchestra in the pit would have been better.
> (Hall, *New York Times,* 30 July 1928)

Victor Fleming's WOLF SONG, similarly, was criticized for its over-the-top acting. Audiences hooted at Lupe Velez's melodramatic performance.[39]

Roy J. Pomeroy had been the man of the hour at Paramount after WINGS began its road-show engagements with striking sound effects in January 1928. He was already justly famous for his photographic parting of the Red Sea in DeMille's THE TEN COMMANDMENTS in 1923. He was also supervising Paramount's radio experiments, chaired the technical committee of the Five-Cornered Committee, installed Western Electric gear at Astoria and thereby learned talking-picture recording techniques firsthand from the ERPI technicians. When Pomeroy returned to Hollywood, he told Lasky that sound was so complicated that only he could direct the studio's talking films. He demanded a raise from $250 to $2,500 a week and was given responsibility for INTERFERENCE, which was shot in Hollywood. "He knew he had us where he wanted us," Lasky recalled. The studio was playing it safe: its first all-talkie was a remake of an earlier silent version, which in turn was an adaptation of a successful play, and the studio shot a new silent version at the same time. Evelyn Brent played a woman who is accused of murdering her blackmailer, but the real perpetrator is revealed to be her former husband, who was believed to have been killed in the war. West Coast critics liked the film and praised its dialogue, while the ones in New York described it as "dull" and "lethargic." The quality of the recording, however, was frequently commended. Hall wrote, "One even heard a pen scratching its way over the paper as Evelyn Brent wrote a message with her left hand." Refining his idea of what we are calling a modulated sound track, he praised the "auxiliary" sounds as interesting without being "obtrusive." He liked the absence of "shouting or screaming."[40] INTERFERENCE (which opened at the Carthay Circle on 5 November 1928) set off a volley of crime-and-court stories. The trial film genre seemed tailor-made for the talkies because it was set-confined, dialogue-driven, and easily adapted from the abundant theater source material available. Among the movies capitalizing on legal drama were THE BELLAMY TRIAL (dir. Monta Bell, 1929), HIS CAPTIVE WOMAN (dir. George Fitzmaurice, 1929), THROUGH DIFFERENT EYES (dir. John Blystone, 1929), THE TRIAL OF MARY DUGAN (dir. Bayard Veillier, 1929), and MADAME X (dir. Lionel Barrymore, 1929).

INTERFERENCE proved to be the swan song for Pomeroy. His brilliant career nose-dived. Success seems to have transformed him into the archetypal tyrannical sound-man. David O. Selznick, a new hire at Paramount in 1928, recalled the story of Pomeroy's ruin:

> When he came back [from Astoria] he was treated as a thing apart. He allowed no one on the sound stage, presumably lest the secret leak out; he relaxed this rule only for short periods. He insisted on handling everything himself, which included the direction of the scene. He was as much qualified to direct as directors were qualified to head the trick department.
>
> It reached the point where one day I told him that we had cast a certain actor in the next sound picture, and he told me curtly that the sooner we executives realized that there would be no casting in sound pictures without his approval, the better off we would be. We were all terrified, particularly we who were not in charge. But after a period of a few months it became apparent that other studios were making sound pictures and maybe there were other gods that could be obtained. [Paramount's general manager B. P.] Schulberg contacted the Western Electric authorities. They sent out their technicians, who had no ambitions whatsoever other than to do a good technical job; and the new king was toppled from his throne. Within a few weeks everyone in the studio knew all they needed to know about sound, and in an amazingly short space of time the transition was made and we were making sound pictures along the same assembly-line methods that were employed for the silent pictures. (David O. Selznick, *Memo from David O. Selznick* [New York: Viking, 1972], pp. 17–18)

Pomeroy's downfall seems attributable partly to his own hubris, but it seems that he was also emulating the "ERPI-men" in their quest for secrecy and self-aggrandizement. He resigned from Paramount in January 1929. "His desire to direct is said to be the cause of controversy," reported the laconic *Film Daily*.[41]

The first feature to be completed at the upgraded Long Island facility was THE LETTER (1929), adapted from a Somerset Maugham play. It was to be the new look of Paramount Pictures: a prestigious stage property, a leading lady of Broadway (Jeanne Eagels had defined Sadie Thompson in Maugham's *Rain*), and a cosmopolitan New York director (Jean de Limur). It was mostly talking but had music-only scenes. But neither this film nor its follow-up, JEALOUSY (dir. de Limur, 1929), did good business. Eagels's career ended tragically after a heroin overdose later in 1929.[42]

THE COCOANUTS initiated full-scale sound feature production at Astoria. The rationale for locating in the East was obvious: the Marx Brothers could shoot the film by day while performing on Broadway in their play *Animal Crackers* by night. Robert Florey and Joseph Santley (a stage director) codirected, Irving Berlin wrote a song, and Morrie Ryskind prepared the script based on the 1925 Broadway vehicle. As the filming progressed, the musical component was gradually pared away, accentuating the Marx Brothers' verbal burlesque. Later Groucho told of Paramount's resistance to certain carryovers from the stage. An executive objected to Groucho's painted mustache—because it would obviously be "phony"—and to his theatrical asides.

> On the stage I frequently stepped out of character and spoke directly to the audience. After the first day's shooting on *Cocoanuts,* the producer (who has since retired from the movies for the good of the industry) said, "Groucho, you can't step out of character and talk to the audience."
>
> Like all people who are glued to tradition, he was wrong. I spoke to them in every picture I appeared in. (Sometimes they answered back. This I found rather disconcerting.) Nevertheless the movie industry went on just the same, turning out its share of good and bad pictures, and nobody seemed to care whether I stepped out of character. (Groucho Marx, *Groucho and Me* [New York: Random House, 1959], p. 225)

Groucho may have been referring to Monta Bell, the producer in charge of the Long Island studio. Bell admitted that shooting the Marx Brothers film was a six-month ordeal. Among the problems he cited were: "breaking up of dialogue with more action, the bringing of freer movement into the scenes. This will increase naturalness while it promotes interest. Talking pictures are getting more vigorous and sprightly all the time." He wanted more outdoor scenes and was working to make the soundstage, as he put it, less like a radio broadcasting station. "We learned much from the [COCOANUTS] experiment, and in some ways it represents our most difficult accomplishment."[43] Delays and retakes held the film back until June 1929. Supposedly the brothers' rapid-fire delivery—the opposite of the enunciated tones the talkies were supposed to favor—was the reason. Perhaps because critics were uncomfortable with the Marxes' mixing of stage and screen conventions, the reviews were not enthusiastic. Jack Harrower wrote, "This is another case of a musical comedy transferred almost bodily to the screen and motion picture treatment forgotten." Kann, like many others, thought that the play was not a good choice for the screen. "We found it alternately entertaining and wearisome, with a shade or two on the latter." Speaking out strongly for a different approach, he urged more unity between the music and the dialogue. "The impression grows stronger that the proper application of musical comedy to pictures must be a blending of the former with the latter. . . . Coherence is needed, but coherence is lacking."[44]

Meanwhile, back in Hollywood, the second Paramount all-talkie completed was THE DOCTOR'S SECRET (1929). It was an adaptation of James Barrie's *Half an Hour,* a play in which the action literally takes place in thirty minutes. William C. deMille, who had starred in INTERFERENCE and studiously absorbed Pomeroy's sound techniques,

"My Wild Party Girl," sheet music from THE WILD PARTY *(Paramount, 1929).*

"Louise," sheet music from INNOCENTS OF PARIS *(Paramount, 1929).*

directed the film. It was about twice as long as the play and turned the comedy into a drawing room drama—a big mistake in *Film Daily*'s view. It would have made a nice talking short, but as an all-talking feature it was an "actionless drama, slow and heavy." The voice of the veteran stage actor Ruth Chatterton, however, "is perfect"; moreover, "she screens well, and knows her acting angles."[45] This opinion was not shared by all. "Ruth's poise was almost poison in the hinterlands," Lasky wrote. "Those who had never had the opportunity of hearing a cultivated, well-modulated voice thought she was putting on airs. . . . When our audiences got the first dose of it, they complained bitterly. Our salesmen demanded, 'No more accents. The public don't like accents.'"[46]

Once the Los Angeles plant was restored, the bulk of Paramount's production was based there in the capable hands of reliable directors like Dorothy Arzner. She was responsible for easing Clara Bow into the talkies with THE WILD PARTY (1929). Bow played a coed who spars with, but ends up engaged to, her professor, Fredric March. The sound quality was uneven, but Bow's voice was intelligible, and her Brooklyn accent only occasionally detectable.

Paramount rushed its Maurice Chevalier vehicle, INNOCENTS OF PARIS (dir. Richard Wallace, 1929) into production. The film was one of the studio's top grossers for the year. Chevalier's assertive personality, his endearing Gallicisms, his almost too-French accent, and his signature tune "Louise" made the otherwise ordinary film a one-man tour de force. Chevalier had been making films in France since 1908, so he was totally at ease before the camera.[47]

THE CANARY MURDER CASE (dir. Malcolm St. Clair, 1929) was that rarity, a film with "effective talking sequences." William Powell's voice and acting were singled out. "As an all-talker, it is far more effective than the silent version." As a result of his success, Powell was officially "elevated to stardom" by Paramount.[48] The dour voice and deadpan delivery of the character actor Ned Sparks added more vocal interest to the casting.

Film Daily made one of its keenest critical assessments about two young stage players with distinctive speaking styles who were featured in THE HOLE IN THE WALL (dir. Robert Florey, 1929). "Claudette Colbert . . . and Edward G. Robinson . . . are immense, their voices register beautifully," wrote Harrower.[49]

MGM

Nicholas M. Schenck, upon signing with ERPI, issued a cautious press release:

> The application of sound to pictures will unquestionably in its final develop-ment help to make the motion picture more than ever the greatest single entertainment force in the world. But it will not be the policy of Metro-Goldwyn-Mayer to rush into print with anticipated elaborate plans for talk-ing pictures. Rather it will be our policy to proceed so that each of our films employing the use of sound may do so with the most intelligent and sympa-thetic application. (*Film Daily*, 16 May 1928, p. 1)

As many studio executives did during 1928–1929, Schenck regarded sound as a kind of spice to be sprinkled on judiciously, as needed. Irving Thalberg shared that opinion, and as a result, MGM was the most conservative studio where sound was concerned. It tested the waters in November 1928 with a short subject featuring some stars. Ernest

Monte Blue's whistling lesson with Raquel Torres in WHITE SHADOWS IN THE SOUTH SEAS *(MGM, 1928).*

Torrence is supposedly calling from London (on AT&T transatlantic equipment, naturally) to announce the opening of the Empire Theater. George K. Arthur, Joan Crawford, Norma Shearer, and John Gilbert (who keeps gushing "colossal, amazing, and wonderful") take turns at the mike.[50]

The first announced MGM feature releases were THE TRIAL OF MARY DUGAN (dir. Bayard Veillier, 1929), an all-talking adaptation of a Broadway hit, and NIZE BABY from a Milt Gross comic strip.[51] WHITE SHADOWS IN THE SOUTH SEAS was the first actual MGM sound film on Broadway. W. S. Van Dyke shot it in the Marquesas Islands, then Douglas Shearer supervised the pressing of discs at the Victor studio in Camden. It opened at the Astor Theater on Broadway with a track of synchronized music and effects—for example Leo the Lion roaring audibly for the first time—on 31 July 1928.[52] Other audio surprises included a pig that emerges from a tent and oinks when a woman swats it with a broom. New York critics were divided, one describing the experience as "for almost the entire length of the picture the rather scraping, tinny sounds of an orchestra rendering a stickily sentimental theme melody" (*New York World*).[53] Hall thought the sound was "average," "bathetic," and "unfortunate." *Motion Picture* magazine said that the synchronization was not well done and "adds nothing to the merit of the photoplay."[54] This reviewer made an exception for the scene in which Monte Blue teaches Raquel Torres how to whistle. Although the sound was post-dubbed, the effect

Norma Shearer (second from right) in THE TRIAL OF MARY DUGAN *(MGM, 1929).*

of lip-synch was satisfactory. The scene ends dramatically with the interruption by an offscreen drum. Actually, there are other rather subtle sound effects. When a young diver drowns, we hear dirge-like music overlaid with a sobbing voice. This segues to festive ukulele music. On the screen, Doc (Monte Blue) is shown looking up; then there is a shot of dancing at the saloon (ostensibly the source of the music), then of him tearing his shirt. The changing music reflects his emotional state. Later we hear a gunshot and see a close-up of his slow reaction as he realizes he has been hit. But there are also some jarring anomalies. When the native music-makers strike up their instruments, we hear the sounds of a Western orchestra.

MGM's second sound film was also a goat gland. ALIAS JIMMY VALENTINE (dir. Jack Conway, 1928) was made into a sound film after the fact at the Paramount sound laboratory (another good example of how sound encouraged the studios to cooperate). In the last two reels, Lionel Barrymore and William Haines dubbed dialogue over footage shot silent. Hall advised the studio "that they must learn, with regard to sound, that enough is as good as a feast." He thought that the sound effects and dialogue were excessive.[55]

Norma Shearer was unquestionably the most privileged actor in the talkies. Her husband, Irving Thalberg, was head of production and artistic director at MGM and personally in charge of producing her films. Her brother Douglas was the recording engineer. Thus, her three features of 1929 were designed with distinctive MGM panache. Each was an expensive Broadway property which treated "adult" subjects. THE TRIAL OF MARY DUGAN was adapted by Veillier from his play. The extremely cautious Thalberg tested scenes by having them acted out before a live audience in the studio prior to shooting. For Harrower, the technique backfired; he dismissed the film as a too

THE BROADWAY MELODY *(MGM, 1929) souvenir program.*

literal recording of the stage presentation. But he lauded the star's vocal talent. "Norma Shearer surpasses herself in name part, with superb voice range and remarkable emotional ability."[56] THE LAST OF MRS. CHEYNEY (dir. Sidney Franklin) was an English society drama in which Shearer is the unlikely leader of a gang masquerading as aristocratic "swells" in order to steal jewels. Sound is foregrounded early when a heavily accented Cockney servant observes, "Some of those charity singers 'ave 'orrible voices." It was filmed with two cameras in long static takes, except for the final shot, which is a slow track from long-shot to a close-up two-shot of Shearer and her fiancé, Basil Rathbone.

MGM's 1929 breakthrough was THE BROADWAY MELODY. Speaking from the stage of the Chinese Theater in Hollywood, the director Harry Beaumont told his audience,

> At the present time I believe we have reached a point where an entirely new creation is being perfected—a form of entertainment combining some of the best elements of stage and screen, but distinct from either. I look upon real human interest stories with a natural musical setting as the most fertile field for progress here. . . . The direction of talking pictures demands much closer attention to detail than the silent film. A sound picture is virtually "made" before its scenes are photographed, for every sequence must be rehearsed until it is perfect before the filming begins. (THE BROADWAY MELODY souvenir program, 1929, Yranski Collection)

Beaumont's casual mention of the hybrid nature of his film zeroed in on a crucial aspect of sound that would influence dozens of subsequent musicals. Integrating the musical setting "naturally" into the story produced the "coherent" musical form which would eventually replace the revue format. (Though some of the musical numbers, including "Wedding of the Painted Doll" and "The Boy Friend," are encapsulated sound shorts, introduced by close-up inserts of the turning pages of the playbill.) Beaumont carefully pointed out that the labor-intensive talking pictures demanded extra rehearsals. Bessie Love's ukulele-playing scene alone took more than three hours to film. The film was a smash and "earned the best gross since *The Big Parade* [1925], and twice as much as any other film of its season."[57]

The story of THE BROADWAY MELODY follows two sisters (played by Bessie Love and Anita Page) who take their vaudeville act to New York and fall in love with the same man (Charles King). According to Arthur Freed, the studio did not risk casting any big stars in case the film proved to be a flop.[58] Written by Edmund Goulding, the film is full of satirical touches, like the names of the Ziegfeld-like producer Francis Zanfield (reminiscent of Darryl Francis Zanuck) and the philandering playboy Jacques Warriner (which sounds on-screen just like "Jack Warner").[59] The story for about two-thirds of the film guides the romantic conflict to its inevitable happy ending. The remainder shows the backstage machinations of putting on a show called "The Broadway Melody," featuring a theme song also called "The Broadway Melody." Some of the musical numbers are "overheard" by the viewer, as when the arranger (played by the real composer James Gleason) spontaneously tries out some impromptu ideas on the piano. Uncle Jed, who speaks with a comic stutter, is a typical example of vocal foregrounding.

THE BROADWAY MELODY was praised by newspapers and the trades alike. Several picked up on Beaumont's attempt to integrate story and song. The *New York Evening Journal* said, "Talking and singing help the screen story, and the screen story helps the

Composer James Gleason's cameo in THE BROADWAY MELODY *(MGM, 1929).*

talking and singing sequences. In other words, it all goes to show what can be done with the new eye-and-ear industry; here is utilized the technique of both stage and screen, combining the good features of each." *Film Daily* proclaimed, "A picture to shout about." Bessie Love's performance, the lyrics by Arthur Freed, and the music by Nacio Herb Brown would prompt showmen to dust off the "SRO" (standing room only) sign, Kann predicted.[60] The Academy bestowed on it the second award for best picture.

As a result of its stunning success, all fifty 1929–1930 titles from MGM were announced as at least part-talking. Symptomatic of the studio's transition from Vitaphone-like shorts to feature musicals was the abandonment of New York production. Nick Grinde, who with great fanfare in the fall had opened MGM's Cosmopolitan studio, was in May 1929 suspending its operation.[61] Among the long-awaited sound debuts were DYNAMITE (1929), Cecil B. DeMille's first all-talkie, and Greta Garbo's first utterance in ANNA CHRISTIE (dir. Clarence Brown, 1930).[62] Garbo feared that her Swedish accent might impair her work in sound and wanted to delay as long as possible. Her silent films, like THE SINGLE STANDARD (dir. John S. Robertson, 1929), were still very successful.

MADAME X received a big send-off by Kann. He praised Lionel Barrymore's first effort at direction as superb, "so deft and so expert that the problem of how best to use his abilities becomes knotty." Other critics felt that this melodrama (the fourth screen version) was creaky and that Ruth Chatterton was stiff. The *Erpigram* chuckled that the maudlin story even made the engineers weep. "They've geared up the sound volume so it can be heard above the splashing of the tears."[63]

United Artists

Chaplin was preoccupied with his project CITY LIGHTS and was on a rampage against the talkies. In November 1928, he could see "little likelihood" of screen pantomime ever becoming secondary to talking pictures. His famous maxim was widely reproduced: "Motion pictures need dialogue as much as Beethoven symphonies need lyrics." Chaplin's reputation as an actor was unassailable, but his opinions apparently were not universally accepted. Wesley Stout called him "the great unreconstructed rebel of Beverly Hills." Although the actor "talks nonsense about pictures in general," Stout conceded that Chaplin's declaration never to speak was justifiable because his art was pantomime. "A resounding kick in the pants never has needed amplification in words."[64]

Of the original founders, Douglas Fairbanks and Mary Pickford were the most active UA producers during this season. Both reluctantly accepted sound. Later Douglas Fairbanks, Jr., reported that the partners "had no fear because they had been stage stars first. I don't think they gave it much thought, other than the fact they both appreciated the movies where it was better to be seen and not heard. They thought something was lost when they brought talk into it." In THE IRON MASK (dir. Allan Dwan, 1929), his first talking picture, Douglas Fairbanks, Sr., spoke only in a prologue and epilogue, but nevertheless he gave a ringing endorsement of the new trend in filmmaking while attending the Broadway premiere. In March their fans learned that Fairbanks and Pickford would costar for the first time in an adaptation of *Romeo and Juliet*. This was quickly abandoned (perhaps because the hero would have been forty-six and the teenage heroine thirty-six). Instead, their talking double-debut was the somewhat more plausible

COQUETTE *(United Artists, 1929). Herald distributed to moviegoers.*

COQUETTE (*United Artists, 1929*). *Advertising to the trade.*

THE TAMING OF THE SHREW (dir. Sam Taylor, 1929). Harrower panned the film as slap-stick. "Much of the show looks as if Mack Sennett has revived his pie-tossing days."[65]

In March 1929, Pickford proclaimed that she would never make another silent film. "The real future of the screen is in talking pictures." Boldly she announced that her next vehicle, COQUETTE (dir. Sam Taylor, 1929), adapted from George Abbott's stage hit with Helen Hayes, would be released in a talking version only.[66] Pickford bobbed her hair and studied southern accents to get the role right. The plot was lurid melodrama for America's sweetheart, climaxed when the heroine's father, having killed her lover, com-mits suicide in a courtroom scene. Kann commented, "Mary talks for the first time in her long career. Audiences will want to see and hear her primarily, perhaps in order to satisfy their curiosity. . . . Mary assumes the drawl necessary to the character she plays. She is charming and, while the accent is occasionally overdrawn, most capably does she perform. Her voice is pleasantly modulated and highly effective." The New York critics were generally thumbs-down on COQUETTE: "The sophisticated Mary Pickford is not as compelling as 'America's Sweetheart'" (Evening World); "not as good as Helen Hayes" (Graphic); "too-heavy southern accent" (Herald Tribune). The World did give the hero-ine credit: "Miss Pickford is in every way splendidly equipped for the talking films. Her voice, sweet and pleasing and with a certain individual quality which seems to coordi-nate itself to a marked degree with the visual Mary Pickford whom everybody knows is clearly a practical one."[67] Her peers agreed; Pickford won the Oscar for best actress.

D. W. Griffith's waning career waned a little more when LADY OF THE PAVEMENTS (1929) came out. It was a part-talkie, with some singing scenes. Critics liked the ener-getic star, Lupe Velez, but were indifferent to Griffith's direction. Joseph Schenck pre-viewed the film extensively around the country before its New York premiere in order to forestall the inevitable effects of the bad reviews. Part of the problem was technical. UA's disc pressing was botched, resulting in unintelligible voices. Writing in January 1929, Griffith expressed optimism:

> The pictures already made are too slow in dialogue. Imitation of stage tech-niques will kill the talking picture if it is continued. A new medium for dia-logue must be found, and I know it will be found. I believe I know how to do it; and, in another year, I believe I will be able to demonstrate it. We must continue to use motion picture technique—the technique which has made motion pictures what they are today, and add the dialogue. When this is done successfully, you will see the greatest entertainment the world has ever witnessed. But we must preserve the speed, action, swirl, life and tempo of the modern picture today. (quoted in John H. Dorr, "Griffith's Talkies," Take One 3, no. 8 [November-December 1971]: p. 8)

Thus, Griffith joined those who viewed sound primarily as an "add-on" to enhance the silent feature, not something fundamentally different. There was talk that Griffith was going to remake THE BIRTH OF A NATION (1915) in sound using much of the original cast, with dialogue and copious Negro spirituals. This was one of several Griffith ideas firmly rejected by his backer, Schenck. Instead, the filmmaker decided to make a biog-raphy of Abraham Lincoln.[68]

Goldwyn continued his successes with BULLDOG DRUMMOND (dir. F. Richard Jones, 1929), Ronald Colman's first talking picture. It was a tremendous hit. Kann raved that the dialogue of the playwright Sidney Howard was sparkling, witty, and never ponder-

ALIBI *(United Artists, 1929), with Regis Toomey and Chester Morris.*

Erich von Stroheim, Gloria Swanson, and Walter Byron (the leading man chosen on the basis of his voice) during rehearsals for QUEEN KELLY *(United Artists) in 1928.*

ous, and that the star "bridges the gap between silent and sound pictures in one leap and proves here that via the talker medium his drawing power is very considerably enhanced."[69] Newspapers also saw something new in the film's fast pace and what they perceived to be its nontheatrical language. The *New York Evening Journal* observed that the film was a departure from the use of sound as a supplement: "As to the talking, the highest praise one can—and does—offer to the film is that, unlike many other talkies, it neither gives the impression of a stage play being photographed or a movie given the addition of sound." The *New York World* wrote, "Here at last is an all-talking film which is not all talking. Here is the basic method of pure motion picture augmented . . . by speech when speech is the only thing that will suffice." Goldwyn also teamed up with Florenz Ziegfeld to produce films based on the impresario's theatrical properties. It was anticipated that these would be recorded as widescreen color films and that Eddie Cantor's WHOOPEE! would be the first of five coproductions.[70]

Another success story was ALIBI (1929), directed by Roland West, an independent releasing through UA. West also cowrote the screenplay with the veteran writer C. Gardner Sullivan. The surprisingly violent story was regarded as harsh but realistic by critics, and Chester Morris was nominated for an Oscar for his performance as a tough ex-convict. In 1929 West returned with THE BAT WHISPERS, another low-budget mystery thriller.

Howard Hughes's Caddo Productions announced in May 1928 that HELL'S ANGELS would be finished in time for a September release by United Artists. Indeed, the film

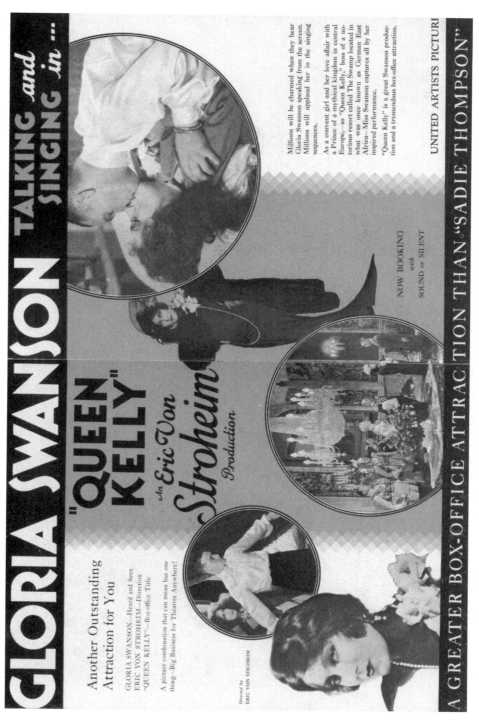

QUEEN KELLY *advertised to the trade as a talkie, February 1929.*

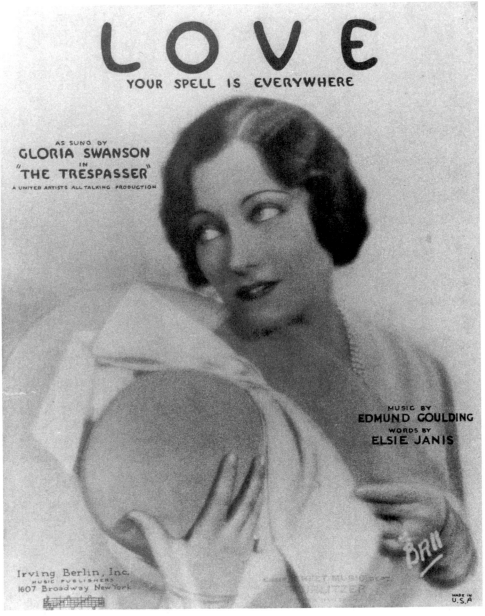

"Love," sheet music from THE TRESPASSER *(United Artists, 1929).*

had been nearly completed as a silent with synchronized effects, but Hughes realized that it would be old hat next to the new all-talkers appearing from every studio. He hired the stage director James Whale to film dialogue scenes at Christie's Metropolitan Sound Studios. He scrapped most of the silent footage except for the outstanding flying stunts. New scenes were recorded by deploying "both microphones and cameras in the air by other planes and balloons." The release was put off until November, then until 1929. Even that proved optimistic.[71]

THE QUEEN KELLY FIASCO

Gloria Swanson was responsible for the most spectacular failure in the UA roster. *The Swamp* (later retitled QUEEN KELLY) was announced in July 1928. Joseph Kennedy financed the film through the company he set up on the FBO lot, Gloria Productions. He loaned William LeBaron from FBO/Pathé to produce, and Kennedy and Swanson selected Erich von Stroheim to direct. Stroheim later gave out much incorrect information. The director's friend Herman G. Weinberg wrote in 1937 that after sound came in, Kennedy "opined that the worst talking film would make more at the box-office than the best silent film" and stopped shooting the silent version. Stroheim wrote to his biographer, Peter Noble, that "the showing of Al Jolson's first sound film stopped production."[72] Even allowing for mistakenly remembering THE SINGING FOOL as THE JAZZ SINGER, Stroheim's memory is not accurate; shooting did not begin until November 1928, two months after Jolson's second film. Yet RCA's press releases published in the summer of 1928 (which precede THE SINGING FOOL) show that Swanson was specifically recruited by FBO to make a sound film, and that the QUEEN KELLY project was envisioned from the start as at least part-talking: "Gloria Swanson's next for United Artists will have talking sequences. Voice tests are now being made and the leading man will be chosen with suitable attention to his vocal ability." Further evidence of Swanson's intentions resides in the amendments to United Artist's ERPI license agreement. Item 9 reads:

> We [ERPI] understand that you [UA] are obligated by contract to distribute the productions of Gloria Swanson, and that at the present time she is producing her pictures through a company which is not licensed by us to make sound records and that her pictures which you are required by contract to distribute may have sound records accompanying them made by others than our licensees. We have no objection to your distributing her pictures and accompanying sound records so made so long as your existing contract obligations to do so are in force. (John Otterson–Joseph Schenck agreement, 11 May 1928, box 85, United Artists Collection, Wisconsin Center for Film and Theater Research [WCFTR])

When UA mistakenly charged Swanson's company for ERPI fees, her representative wrote back in March 1929, "We cannot recognize any indebtedness to the Electrical Research Products Company because it is our intention to use the Photophone system in connection with the pictures which we shall make in which Miss Swanson appears." Thus, Swanson was the first big star to announce a talking project.[73]

Work on the script proceeded through 1928, and contrary to Stroheim's account, shooting was halted when he spent extravagantly on retakes and began filming sexually suggestive scenes that could not possibly have been approved by the Hays Office censors. Richard Koszarski doubts Swanson's innocence in these matters, pointing out that the bordello scenes had been identified as such in early scripts. "Only the cumulative effect of von Stroheim's directorial extravagance is left as an explanation."[74] But was there another reason? From November 1928 through 17 January 1929, von Stroheim had been shooting the film as just another silent. Kennedy obviously was committed, at least in a gentlemen's agreement with Sarnoff, to produce a film with RCA Photophone. Swanson admitted in her memoir that she and von Stroheim disliked sound.[75] One can conjecture that the purpose of the 17 January meeting with Swanson, described by Koszarski as "a discussion of how best to inject sound into the picture," was to relay Kennedy's insistence on incorporating dialogue into QUEEN KELLY. Kennedy's views were presented by E. B. Derr, his chief of staff. Also present was Edmund Goulding, who had just written THE BROADWAY MELODY. The changes made in the script included adding scenes with "synthetic sound," that is, post-synchronized effects and vocal dubbing, as LeBaron was doing with some FBO films. The final straw for von Stroheim has been attributed to his argument with Swanson over a disgusting scene involving tobacco juice. But it is possible that when Kennedy fired him on 21 January, the dispute over sound may have played some part. Soon, Edmund Goulding was hired to shoot talking and singing footage. The picture was still imagined as a 40 percent talkie.

Kennedy arrived in Los Angeles to confer with Swanson during February 1929. They decided to shelve the project and write off the $750,000 that Kennedy had invested. Evidently someone forgot to tell United Artists. An advertisement in *Film Daily* on 28 February 1929 featured Joseph Schenck boldly pitching sound in the doomed film: "Gloria Swanson, talking and singing in QUEEN KELLY, vitalizes the drama." Swanson and Goulding convinced Kennedy to finance a new all-talkie to be called *The Love Years*. It was written and directed quickly by Goulding and released as THE TRESPASSER in October 1929. It became one of Swanson's biggest hits. The fan magazines adored her spunkiness and the fact that she took numerous voice lessons in order to sing the theme song "Love."

The QUEEN KELLY project, meanwhile, would not die. In March 1929, Benjamin Glazer (an MGM writer and friend of Kennedy's who had collaborated with von Stroheim on THE MERRY WIDOW [1925]) wrote a new ending. In April, Swanson, on her own, hired Paul Stein to add "synthetic" dialogue.[76] Apparently Swanson planned to turn her film into a goat gland. The cast reassembled in December 1929—without Stroheim, needless to say—to make some singing inserts in another effort to salvage the movie by reincarnating it as a musical. Richard Boleslawski directed these musical numbers. *Film Daily* reported that "*Queen Kelly*, the Gloria Swanson picture shelved some time ago and lately revived for production by Pathé as an operetta, will be released through United Artists. The picture will have color treatment by Pathé's multicolor method." Kennedy thought he had commissioned Franz Lehar, the Austrian composer of *The Merry Widow*, to devise the music. But Lehar wrote only one song. Goulding, meanwhile, wanted nothing further to do with this fiasco. When Kennedy and Swanson tried to pressure him by withholding royalties for the theme song he had written for THE TRESPASSER, he sued them. Kennedy finally walked away from what was now an $800,000 debacle. Swanson, however, continued hiring writers, technicians, and consultants to save the film. In 1931 the editor Viola Lawrence cut together von Stroheim's footage and Gregg Toland shot a new ending. This "final" version had a score but no dialogue, "synthetic" or otherwise.[77]

Seena Owen bathes in QUEEN KELLY, *1929.*

Swanson was so tenacious in part because her 1925 United Artists contract prevented her from producing outside the studio until she had completed three "specials." Furthermore, a substantial payment in the form of 166 shares of UA stock had been escrowed pending completion. Early in 1932 Swanson presented her synchronized sound version of QUEEN KELLY to Schenck and demanded her stock. UA's vice president and general manager in charge of distribution, Al Lichtman, arranged a sneak preview in Stamford, Connecticut, and reported the grim event:

> When the main title was first flashed on the screen, the people seemed to settle back expectantly. As the story progressed they became very restless, and later they laughed at many spots that were intended to be serious. All in all, the general reaction was very bad.
>
> I personally interviewed a number of people in the lobby of the theatre and their remarks were all very disparaging. The exhibitor, who is one of our best customers, said he could not possibly show a picture of that kind in his theatre. . . .
>
> It is my opinion we could not gross sufficient money on the picture in the United States to even justify the cost of prints, and it would do Miss Swanson irreparable damage. Furthermore, I doubt very much if we could get the picture passed by the censor boards in New York, Chicago, Ohio and Pennsylvania, surely not without so many cuts that there would probably be no sense to the film at all with the cuts they would most likely make. (Al

Lichtman to Lloyd Wright, Gloria Productions, 10 February 1932, box 151/2, UA Collection, WCFTR)

Joe Schenck wrote to UA's corporate attorney urging that QUEEN KELLY not be accepted by the company as one of Swanson's mandatory specials. He did not mince words:

> It is entirely impossible to release that picture and it would be extremely detrimental to Gloria if the picture was released. We could not even get the price of the prints out of the distribution of the picture. Even in the days of silent pictures, that picture would be a very bad picture. Today, in my opinion, it is terrible. Furthermore, no censorboard would ever pass it. (Schenck to Dennis O'Brien, 29 February 1932, box 151/2, UA Collection, WCFTR)

Swanson released this version (with synchronized music) in Europe in 1932.[78] Some of the silent footage found its way into SUNSET BOULEVARD (dir. Billy Wilder, 1950), where it represents the glorious stardom of Swanson's Norma Desmond, watched by her icy butler played by Stroheim—one of the great casting ironies in cinema. When the fictional silent star Desmond visits the Paramount studio, she symbolically pushes an annoying mike on a boom away from her face. Later Norma damns modern films with her immortal line, "I am big. It's the pictures that got small." She conveniently ignores the fact that Swanson's QUEEN KELLY was, from the start, supposed to be a talkie.

Universal

In June 1928, UNCLE TOM'S CABIN and THE MAN WHO LAUGHS, which already had finished their big-city runs, were scored by Erno Rapee. Sound effects and some dialogue sequences were added. Exchanges were supplied with two sets of prints—regular silent and the goat gland versions.[79] It was not until the weekend of 23 June that the studio announced its decision to go into sound production, trumpeting that eighteen of the next season's films would be scored.[80] Universal began refurbishing one of its old Fort Lee, New Jersey, stages for sound short subject production.[81] Surreptitiously, it has been claimed, the studio also borrowed a Fox Movietone News truck under the pretense of doing some sound tests. Within the space of two weeks the all-talking MELODY OF LOVE (dir. A. B. Heath, 1928) and talking sequences for at least three already-shot silents were cobbled together.[82]

Photoplay quipped that MELODY OF LOVE, with Walter Pidgeon, was "valuable because it shows how not to make a talkie."[83] Its story was weak. Jack (Pidgeon) lost the use of his arm while serving in France during the war. When he encounters a girl he met over there, Madelon (Mildred Harris), who is now a showgirl in the States, the limb comes back to life and they vow to get married. Despite the film's "lung power," it was not "aided by its audible accompaniment." According to Hall, "a little of this dialogue offering goes a long way." The *Daily Mirror* mused that it was as if a gang of children playing in the backyard had said, "Let's make a talker."[84] Indeed, that's a fair description of the film's production, except that it was shot by grown-ups. The reception of this film shows that the novelty of sound was no longer sufficient to save a bad movie.

Conceiving their films as silents with sound tacked on was an increasingly old-fashioned approach which undoubtedly hurt the talking versions of Universal's pictures.

Paul Fejos, 1928.

Moreover, Universal's facilities still lagged behind the competition's. It was not until February 1929 that the studio built its first fully equipped sound screening room at Universal City so that sound tracks "might be heard as they would be played."[85]

One cannot attribute these tight economic policies only to a stingy Carl Laemmle. Universal budgeted $1 million each for BROADWAY (1929) and THE KING OF JAZZ (1930). Nor was there an abhorrence of innovation at the studio. Universal's European directors and cinematographers were known for their expressive effects. Paul Fejos, one of Hollywood's brightest talents, directed BROADWAY and was chosen for THE KING OF JAZZ (although he was eventually replaced by the Follies director John Murray Anderson).[86] The German expressionist director Paul Leni had created THE CAT AND THE CANARY (1927) and THE MAN WHO LAUGHS (1928) for Universal. The studio's halting approach toward sound is more likely traced to Laemmle's conviction that the public's affection for talkies was a brief fling and that one day silence would reign again. His decision to sell off the studio's theaters rather than invest in wiring them for sound and his pledge to always supply silent product showed his deep-seated skepticism about the future of sound.

One of the films sonorized during the bout of unauthorized sound recording was Fejos's LONESOME, the first Universal part-talkie released. When it had run in June 1928 as a silent, the film was a remarkable example of the late-twenties style of actively roaming cinematography (although the trade critics did not like it).[87] In its October 1928 talking reincarnation, Kann observed that two of its three dialogue sequences were pretty good, but the third was awful. It is a simple story of a young man (Glenn Tryon) and a girl (Barbara Kent) meeting at Coney Island, then losing each other in the crowd—only to discover at the end that they live in the same apartment building. Fejos's camera flits giddily through the silent scenes in Coney Island but freezes rock-steady in the talking ones, causing an abrupt change in visual style. The dialogue is delivered in flat, amateurish voices which brought down the reviewers' wrath. Kann wrote, "It proves that Universal, in company with other producing companies, has to ferret out a method of handling this new entertainment vitamin" [probably referring to the "goat gland" vitamin].[88]

Probably because of Carl Laemmle, Sr.'s vacillating position on sound, Universal's producers did not know whether they were in the sound or silent business. One of their most important investments was SHOW BOAT, the screen version of the Ziegfeld hit based on Edna Ferber's best-seller. Universal had purchased the film rights for a record $100,000 before the stage production opened. But Laemmle had not optioned the Jerome Kern and Oscar Hammerstein II music, because in 1927 he had not contemplated making a sound film. The studio began filming it silent in 1928, but the Broadway show's popularity threw a wrench in the works. Universal was forced to negotiate for limited musical and vocal rights. Under the terms of the deal with Flo Ziegfeld, the picture was banned from New York until at least one week after the close of the play.[89]

SHOW BOAT (dir. Harry Pollard) was shot, abandoned, and reshot so many times that the production record is like a jigsaw puzzle. Universal, early in 1929, announced a plan to shoot silent and sound footage on alternating days. This press release conflicts with another issued just five days later: "The film, just completed, is to have the dialogue and music portions inserted. These remakes will be taken at the Ziegfeld [theater]." But the Universal executive R. H. Cochrane implied there were already two separate films: "Our leading picture SHOW BOAT was not only bought as a silent one but the silent version was made complete from start to finish. Afterward a sound version was made, including the Ziegfeld hits from his stage show of the same story."[90] The film had a dual premiere in

Miami and Palm Beach. Miami's opening was disrupted "by [the] disappearance of the operators, with the sound reproducing equipment out of order." Union agitators were blamed.[91]

Though the original version disappeared soon after its release, it has been recently restored and re-released on laser disc. The 1929 product contained only traces of the original score and would not be considered a musical by most modern viewers. Most of the silent footage was retained, and two talking and singing sequences were added. Only two Kern songs were included in the film. To preserve some contact with the original production, a two-reel (eighteen-minute) prologue was filmed. In it, Carl Laemmle and Flo Ziegfeld make brief remarks. Otis Harlan, who starred in the film, introduces the stage cast members Tess Gardella, Jules Bledsoe, and Helen Morgan singing five numbers from the show. According to the *New York Evening Journal,* "Bledsoe's rendition of the ["Old Man River"] number is about the most effective yet recorded on the singing screen."[92]

SHOW BOAT received bad notices when it opened in New York in April 1929. Kann assailed the director, Harry Pollard, in a front-page editorial for letting the film grow to its 12,400-foot length. "Practically every major sequence is drawn out and made unnecessarily repetitious to the point of fatigue." Other reviews described it as a long and "draggy" melodrama. Like all Universal productions, the film was also released in a silent version.[93]

In 1929, Laemmle made his son Carl, Jr., head of production and there was a marked upturn in ambition and quality. Junior Laemmle, as he was called, started off with a magnificently produced musical extravaganza, BROADWAY (dir. Fejos). While modern viewers are impressed by the technical virtuosity of BROADWAY, almost all of the critics of the time compared the film unfavorably to its source, a nightclub melodrama directed by George Abbott with a two-year Broadway run behind it. "A good bit of a bore," groused the *Telegram.* The *Daily Mirror* and the *World* reviewers were among the few who noticed Fejos's gargantuan set and crane-mounted camera work. According to the *World,* "His treatment of the photography inside the Paradise Cafe is singularly well done. Here his camera seems to float in midair over and about the great, glistening hall, dipping now and again to pick up and emphasize by proximity the individual work of the dancers and singers."[94]

Universal's other films were not impressing the critics. The *New York Sun* called Paul Leni's THE LAST WARNING (1929) "a curious and rather dull hodgepodge of bad talking sequences and unrelated silent ones." "Too many outbursts of shrieking, merely to prove the effects of the audible screen, to cause any spine chilling," said the *Times.* And there seemed to be mechanical difficulties: "The sound effects were way off when caught at the Colony on Broadway, and the dialogue sequences were far from impressive."[95] This would be Leni's only sound film. He died of an infection shortly after its release.

Independent Producers

Powers Cinephone had limited success. The company operated out of the old Paragon Studio in Fort Lee, New Jersey. At first Pat Powers contemplated servicing the post-production sound needs of the film industry, synchronizing music to silents, as he had done with THE WEDDING MARCH (dir. Erich von Stroheim, 1928).[96] By mid-June 1928, he was advertising "to apply sound to motion picture negatives either during or after the film-

George Jessel in LUCKY BOY *(Tiffany-Stahl, 1928).*

ing of the picture."[97] Powers, like Sarnoff at RCA, called attention to his system's inter-changeability with Western Electric equipment. In December he offered a turntable unit so that exhibitors could run Vitaphone discs as well as optical tracks.[98] Powers's most illustrious customer was Walt Disney, who contracted for four cartoon sound tracks (see chapter 15).

Other small producers jumped on the sound bandwagon. Sam Sax, president of Gotham Pictures and a leading independent producer, announced the filming of *The Girl from the Argentine* in Hollywood with RCA Photophone. (Gotham and Bristol-phone would start a joint venture to wire theaters in October 1928.)[99]

Among Tiffany-Stahl's first talkies were MARRIAGE BY CONTRACT (1928), directed by James Flood, with Patsy Ruth Miller, and LUCKY BOY (1928), directed by Norman Taurog, with George Jessel. Having blown the movie role of a lifetime, he was rather pathetically billed as "The Original 'Jazz Singer.'"

This season of the goat gland must have created an impression of strangeness for movie-goers. In the silent days one had a predictable experience at the movies; during the introduction of sound, as Hollywood undertook different approaches, neither the form nor the content of the show could be reliably anticipated. Audiences must have assumed, along with many producers, that silent films were not endangered by these new talkers. The kind of movies that one saw in 1928–1929 were likely to convince few that a "revolution" was on. This was the year of the "big hedge": some of these films talked, some did not, and some looked just like the slapped-together concoctions they were. Several directors tried on sound in various sizes and shapes, looking for a crowd-pleasing fit. Meanwhile, consumers were also exposed to considerable marketing hype about the talkies.

Fundamental questions about the talkies were being posed. Some criticism was directed toward film's relationship to theater, a perennial topic. In a way this issue was a red herring because Hollywood had relied on the stage play as a source of story mate-rial for many years. Mordaunt Hall, representatively, worried about the influence of the-atricality on dialogue and acting. Would the technical limitations of sound cinematography and the influx of Broadway talent somehow turn cinema into a kind of stage play? These concerns would continue to be articulated over the next few years.

Stars and future stars of sound cinema emerged during this season. Jolson was a crossover from music and radio, but aside from the obvious lure of his singing, his abil-ity to make trite dialogue heart-rending and to extract tears from his audience suggested the talkies' dramatic potential. Other players became known primarily through their film work: Maurice Chevalier, Edward G. Robinson, Stepin Fetchit, Eugene Pallette, and even Warner Baxter, with a hokey Mexican accent, captured attention in part owing to their distinctive vocal styles. To one hearing the talkies for the first time, film must have seemed like a carnival of screen voices. Certainly the chance to experience a Broadway musical or see a famous play locally was appealing, but increasingly it was interesting human speech in "ordinary" films that people came back to hear.

While the studios were highlighting their investment with flamboyant insertions of sound effects, Hall and other journalists were reacting against this approach. Like overly garish Technicolor, they felt, sound should not call attention to itself as a supplement. Accents had to be genuine, as Mary Pickford's and Colleen Moore's were not. Story and picture had to mesh, as they apparently failed to do in THE BLACK WATCH. Rather than function as inserted musical interludes, talking and singing worked best when they were part of the fiction, told a story, and established character, as in THE BROADWAY MELODY. If dialogue was added to a picture, its usage—unlike the talking sequences of NOAH'S ARK, LONESOME, and LUCKY STAR—had to be consistent with the rest of the film. In short, reviewers and trade commentators welcomed sound and preferred talkies to silents. But they threw on the brakes when the studios exaggerated the sound track's presence. Already in 1928–1929, preferences for an integration of sound and image were being expressed by the conservative press, which wanted to preserve the "coherence" (Kann's word) typical of the late-twenties silent film.

Critics were eager to carve out a special place for foregrounded sound. Interesting effects were acceptable if "natural" (unlike the excessive shrieking in THE LAST WARNING). Crazy fake accents and loudmouth talking were acceptable (for some listeners) if confined to Marx Brothers comedies. Acoustic spectacle and flashy musical numbers were appropriate in the genre of the musical. In fact, it might be speculated that the rise of the musical comedy and operetta film during this season and the next was the result of public impatience with Hollywood showing off its sound-film prowess too expressively. While the consensus was that sound should be dispensed gradually in other genres, in the musical, on the contrary, the prevailing attitude was: anything goes.

13

Taming the Talkies, 1929–1930

Cinematographers now do everything they did in silent drama days in Hollywood.

JOHN SEITZ, *Cinematographic Annual 1930*

The obvious question to ask John Seitz is, Why was adapting sound filmmaking to "silent" practice considered desirable? This conservative impulse probably did not arise simply from practical considerations; it required skill, resourcefulness, and effort to maintain the appearance that everything was the same. Many stresses inside the industry pushed film toward systematic stability. It is also likely that external forces were at work.

The films of the 1929–1930 season approached sound in seemingly contradictory ways: they exploited it while hiding it. Audiences could still see movies which emphasized the newly discovered screen voice. They could also observe film styles which played down formal expression and novel effects to construct an illusion of unified audiovisual space. Just as the sound engineers were making their technology "inaudible," many filmmakers were subduing their techniques.

The sound film's relationship to theater continued to evolve into one of love-hate. Virtual Broadway in its older form, recording discrete performances, tended to be confined to short subjects. But some producers still regarded big-time musical revues and dramatic hits from the New York stage as movie ideals.

Superabundance: Revues and Musicals

Adapting musicals was a path of little resistance for movie producers. These proven New York successes with recognizable stars and tunes which left you humming must have seemed to producers like a quick road to riches. Now we would call these shows pre-sold packages. A studio could hire a Broadway director and performers, transform the play's book into a screenplay, record the songs, and voilà! The public would beat a path to the door to see this improvement on the virtual Broadway idea. Richard Barrios aptly characterizes the events of mid-1929 as a "musical virus infecting Hollywood."[1] Broadway was the center of the entertainment universe, and audiences evidently were

THE HOLLYWOOD REVUE OF 1929 (MGM) lobby card.

keenly interested in seeing what all the fuss was about. Many went to the movie theaters. Apparently, though, not all fans and critics liked what they found there.

In retrospect, we tend to think of all these films as "musicals" and to see their development as an evolutionary progression. But the early sound musical was not a well-defined or homogeneous film form. Barrios posits numerous examples of overlapping subgenres, and Rick Altman has criticized the standard historical account of the musical.[2] Far from being linear transitions, these early musicals were pastiches made of separate theatrical traditions—the revue, the operetta, and the musical comedy.

The film revue presents its musical and comedy numbers as discrete performance blocks, often in the form of encapsulated sound segments. The order in which these blocks appear, their length, and even their content are not crucial to the overall development of the film. The roots of this kind of filming were in the theatrical revue, a form which had flourished for about forty years. Martin Rubin has argued that the revue was one of several aggregate entertainment forms which grew out of a nineteenth-century aesthetic of *superabundance* that provided spectators with more than they could possibly absorb in a single sitting, for example, the three-ring circus. The cinema prolonged the aesthetic of superabundance by overwhelming the viewer with dense spectacle—for example, filling the screen with all-star performers from a Ziegfeld musical in sound and color, as in the closing pageant of parading showgirls in WHOOPEE! (dir. Thornton Freeland, 1930). In the early-twentieth-century stage revue, a master of ceremonies (W. C. Fields, Josephine Baker, and Maurice Chevalier are Rubin's examples) presents the show and provides coherence. In contrast to the unrelated acts of vaudeville, the revue was organized around a theme or a simple narrative progression. (The format survives vestigially in Las Vegas and touring ice shows.) This stage entertainment had lost much of its popularity when the talkies came along. "By the late 1920s," Rubin argues, "these spectacular revues, although still active, were being viewed as bloated dinosaurs by many critics and sophisticates. . . . As it had done for the melodrama earlier, the cinema gave a new lease on life to the spectacular production number and to the revue form that nurtured it."[3] Good examples are the MGM Metrotone Acts produced in 1929. Each is introduced by a well-known emcee, such as the radio personality Jack Pepper. He speaks directly to the audience, even urging them to applaud after each performance. (Pointing offscreen, Pepper warns, "And I'll be listening, from over here.") Each performance is discrete and opens and closes with a curtain. Or consider the Fox revue HAPPY DAYS (dir. Benjamin Stoloff, 1929). Shot in the 70-mm Grandeur process, the filmmakers tried to engorge the big high-resolution screen. "Three-quarters of the footage is devoted to a series of spectacular stage ensembles that are eye-openers in screen pageantry, numbers involving masses of people and bigness of backgrounds," observed *Variety.*

> There is, for instance, a whole minstrel first part, with four tiers of people in the ensemble, numbering a total of eighty-six and all of them screened in proportions that give them individuality. There are several dance ensembles, one of them with a leader and thirty-two girls in intricate maneuvers, and each separate dancing girl visible in what would otherwise be a semi-atmospheric shot. (*Variety,* 19 February 1930)

The only lack in this display of superabundance was color—which, the commentator assured his readers, was just around the corner.

The operetta was another resurgent nineteenth-century musical form. Big hits like *Rose-Marie* and *The Student Prince,* both 1924, and the landmark *Show Boat* in 1927, were prototypes for the movies' singing spectacles. (One of these, *A Connecticut Yankee* [1927], was the debut of the young choreographer Busby Berkeley.) These stories told in song were the source of many direct screen adaptations, such as RIO RITA and THE ROGUE SONG. The latter (from Lehar's *Gypsy Love*), with Lawrence Tibbett, showed the power of the virtual performance as a lure; *Variety* noted that the volume of the film's sound track eclipsed the star's real voice: "The power is tremendous, and those who go from the Astor to the Metropolitan to hear him are going to be surprised at the difference in volume on the big auditorium hearing. That's what that mike can do."[4]

Screen musical comedies were often adapted from stage predecessors. The resulting film musicals tried to cover all the entertainment bases. Filled with music and pageantry, they were conveniently symbolized by the slogan "All-Talking, All-Singing, All-Dancing." SPRING IS HERE (dir. John Francis Dillon, 1930) is a good example of the superabundant musical. It has a narrative that corresponds to the book in a stage show, but it also uses the conventions of the operetta for introducing songs. For instance, in a soliloquy the actor "thinks aloud" with musical accompaniment, and lovers' words segue into song (which expand with the addition of a chorus and dancers).

Genre boundaries were very fluid. Around 1929–1930, it was the rare movie that was *not* a musical in some sense of the term. Practically every film had a specially composed theme song. (Contrary to received opinion, the theme song written by Dorothy Parker for DeMille's DYNAMITE [1929] was "How Am I to Know," not the apocryphal

Superabundance crowds the frame in NO OTHER WOMAN *(Fox, 1928). Marion Morgan Darcos (center) performs the "Zebra Dance."*

"Dynamite, Dynamite, Blow My Sweet One Back to Me.") Most movies, even Westerns like IN OLD ARIZONA (dir. Walsh and Cummings, 1929) or flapper melodramas like THE WILD PARTY (dir. Arzner, 1929) had gratuitous songs. The showgirl in Hal Roach's first talkie, HURDY GURDY (1929), said it best. "If you can't think of anything to say, just sing." And she does. Producers finding themselves in the same quandary about how to insert their de rigueur musical sessions seem to have heeded her advice. Reviewers singled out films which did *not* contain music, including THE VIRGINIAN, DISRAELI, and MADAME X. Another factor not to be underestimated was radio. All these Hollywood musical formats were influenced by, and competing with, variety show programs on contemporary broadcasts.

Critics during the season of 1929–1930 grew tired of Hollywood's musicals. Their remarks are consistent with declining box-office revenue for these films, suggesting that their sentiments were widely shared. The harshest comments were directed toward films which failed to keep a story flowing. The *New York Herald Tribune*'s review of NO, NO, NANETTE (dir. Clarence Badger, 1929) demanded an integration of music and narrative: "Instead of mixing up the story with the songs, the screen *No, No, Nanette* insisted on placing the musical numbers at the beginning and end of the picture and on making them fit in with some fantastic plot about the production of a show. Thus, the outdated narrative, deprived of the salvation of song cues, was forced to wander on aimlessly to a tedious conclusion, and all of the frailties of its formula were cruelly exposed." By contrast, Don Carle Gillette, the *Film Daily* reviewer, found that MONTE CARLO (1930) properly mixed song and story: "Ernst Lubitsch has done it again! . . . It boasts an amusing and touching romance, witty dialogue and racy humor. The songs are comic as well as tuneful, and they don't get in the way because they are part of the plot and help to swing the story along."[5] An example is the justifiably famous "Beyond the Blue Horizon" number. As Jeanette MacDonald flees Paris, the tempo of her song is picked up from the chugging of the locomotive. The whistle becomes part of the score. The train hurtles through the South of France, and when it passes peasant grape-pickers in a vineyard, they supply the song's chorus in perfect serendipity. Though humorous, the sequence also provides the essential narrative bridge from one locale to another. Lubitsch's films showed that in an integrated musical, the music could reinforce a strong story and add star interest.

This season was in a state of flux and uncertainty as musical films were defined and refined. But the musicals did not immediately become, contrary to the message of SINGIN' IN THE RAIN, the permanent archetypes of film genres. Rather, the period was more like a shopping spree in which filmgoers selected then rejected these entertainment options.

MGM

Metro's 1929–1930 season was one of extraordinary productivity and sound innovation. Among the studio's most influential films was THE HOLLYWOOD REVUE OF 1929 (dir. Charles Reisner and Christy Cabanne [uncredited]), which set off the revue craze immediately after its June premiere. Adoring and curious fans bought tickets to ogle the studio's much-touted constellation of stars, seduced by the promise that their favorites' voices would be heard on the screen, many for the first time. Some two dozen screen personalities (minus MGM's biggest draws, Chaney and Garbo) did a stint before the camera. Each skit was interspersed with wisecracks from the masters of ceremonies, Conrad Nagel and Jack Benny. The souvenir program pitched THE HOLLYWOOD REVUE as technical wizardry and a celebration of virtual Broadway over the real thing:

> Concentration of engineering experts on the various problems of vocal and sound reproduction have eliminated minor difficulties associated with the first period of experimentation, while new camera effects and novelties have been introduced in sound, along with Technicolor and the "phantom screen."[6]
>
> Since musical productions have already proved extremely popular it is likely the production of revues and photoplays with a musical setting may prove one of the most significant phases of the current screen expansion. There are no limits for the future, and most of the handicaps which the stage faces in presenting dramatic spectacles are banished through sound film progress. (THE HOLLYWOOD REVUE souvenir program, 1929, Yranski Collection)

The film is a fascinating museum piece for many reasons—not the least of which is hearing John Gilbert speak in both his stage and "natural" voices (doing *Romeo and Juliet* in jazz talk and a little pig-Latin). THE HOLLYWOOD REVUE has become an icon of the musical by dint of its featured song, Nacio Herb Brown and Arthur Freed's "Singin' in the Rain." This production number was ambitious but not lavish. The *mise-en-scène* creates some striking visual displays when the dancers parade across rainbow-shaped risers wearing see-through raincoats.[7]

Marion Davies in "Tommy Atkins on Parade," THE HOLLYWOOD REVUE OF 1929 *(MGM).*

Marianne (*MGM, 1929*), *with Lawrence Gray and Marion Davies.*

Marion Davies's talking debut was in THE HOLLYWOOD REVUE, where she (rather awkwardly) leads a platoon of toy soldiers through some drills in "Tommy Atkins on Parade." But her first talkie was supposed to have been THE *Five O'Clock Girl*, costarring Charles King and Joel McCrea. William Randolph Hearst was not pleased with his protégée's singing or her mike fright–induced nervousness. Though publicity for the film had already circulated, in January 1929 he prevailed upon Louis B. Mayer to shelve it permanently. Davies's first released talking feature was MARIANNE (dir. Robert Z. Leonard, 1929) in which she plays a French country girl who entertains some American doughboys. To protect itself this time, MGM shot the whole film first as a silent—a very expensive hedge—then as a talkie with a different supporting cast. Her performance seems natural and unstilted, with no hint of her legendary stuttering.[8]

THE ROGUE SONG (dir. Lionel Barrymore), a high-profile showcase for the Metropolitan Opera great Lawrence Tibbett, opened in January 1930. Unfortunately, no complete print is known to survive, so his dynamic performance is lost. Although the all-Technicolor picture was proclaimed by the *New York Evening World* to be "one of the great achievements of the cinema," other reviewers had reservations. The *Post* columnist felt that it "becomes a little tedious when, after two hours of scenery and costumes, all that emerges is a program of Viennese melodies rendered by Mr. Tibbett, soloist." MGM was aware of this pitfall. The stage operetta was, as the term implies, a little opera, and the songs were sung with operatic seriousness. Laurel and Hardy were cast

America's foremost Baritone

TO bring you the new, vital figure for the further glory of your talking screen Metro-Goldwyn-Mayer has reached into the highest realm—the Metropolitan Opera From this renowned company of immortal voices has been picked the greatest, your new star

LAWRENCE TIBBETT

THE ROGUE SONG *(MGM, 1930) publicity.*

as flunkies to Tibbett's Russian rogue. (One of their scenes survives.) Though their inclusion might seem incongruous, most operettas (stage and screen) contained foils to the central romantic couple. Not only did they supply comic relief, but their presence may have been calculated to assure the public that the film was not too highbrow. The producers clearly wished to make the form popularly accessible.

Another project, *The March of Time*, was so botched it was never released. Charles Reisner shot numerous acts around a "vaudeville: old-and-new" theme. Its original title, THE HOLLYWOOD REVUE OF 1930, shows its adherence to the stage revue format. However, the studio could not settle on a satisfactory unifying story. For some reason, it was abandoned; perhaps the turning of the tide against musicals killed the film. MGM salvaged some of the ambitious musical numbers for shorts and a 1933 feature, BROADWAY TO HOLLYWOOD (dir. Willard Mack).

Possibly in an effort to perk up its musicals, the studio hired one of the highest-paid popular writers of the time, P. G. Wodehouse, author of the best-selling Jeeves series. He was at the height of his writing career, turning out novels, plays, magazine stories, and serials, and was in the limelight as a lyricist after writing "Bill" for *Show Boat*.[9] But whatever his credentials, any screenplay at MGM was committee-written. IT'S A GREAT LIFE (dir. Sam Wood, 1930), for example, ended up as another BROADWAY MELODY knockoff starring the Duncan sisters. Wodehouse did not receive a screen credit. A "substantial percentage of the footage is devoted to songs, numbers and comedy business," noted *Variety*. But it exonerated the film because "plots certainly amount to very little in most musicals, stage or screen."[10]

After returns on musicals began to fall, the studio rededicated itself to emphasizing star vehicles. MGM's biggest disappointment was in the performance of the former silent comedians under contract. Harry Langdon's one-reeler THE HEAD GUY (prod. Hal Roach, dir. Fred Guiol, 1930) gave the impression that he was "still experimenting to find out his forte in the talking line. In this comedy he is at his best when he confines himself to pantomime." In Langdon's feature SEE AMERICA THIRST (dir. William James Craft, 1930), "there is seldom anything said that is laughable."[11] The most unfortunate transition though was Buster Keaton's. FREE AND EASY (dir. Edward Sedgwick, 1930) was a fascinating failure (although not at the box office, where it did well). Keaton plays a rube who accompanies Elvira (Anita Page), elected Miss Gopher City in a beauty contest, to Hollywood. Elvira finally finds stardom, and so does Buster, as a gaudily made-up clown. One attempt to foreground sound by adapting a silent-comedy sight gag does not really work. Buster attempts to make a farewell speech at the station, but the band drowns him out each time he opens his mouth. Its fanfare also obscures the whistle of the train, which departs without him. There are some interesting behind-the-scenes shots of the MGM soundstages, revealing the studio's new blimped cameras. We see them photographing scenes two cameras at a time, a slimmed-down application of the multi-camera technique. There are detailed shots of the Western Electric mikes and giant loudspeakers onstage for the sound playback during the musical numbers. The film is also chock full of MGM cameos and fan-oriented jokes, for instance, Cecil B. DeMille wondering aloud whether Norma Shearer can sing. (This was probably also a send-up of the musical craze.) There is a long and unfunny bit where the director Fred Niblo tries to coach Buster, who constantly forgets his lines. One wonders whether the writers had Niblo and Lionel Barrymore's work with John Gilbert in mind in one scene. The director Barrymore advises the actor John Miljan, "Just do it exactly as you rehearsed it, and remember, this is really the high spot of the picture. Don't act. Just quiet and intent. This is a triangle domestic business, and the audience has so much of it in their own lives that they're apt to kid it unless you're very convincing."[12] The story screeches to a halt near the end as Buster embarks on some encapsulated musical numbers, leading to the "Free and Easy" finale. Some of Keaton's old spark remains, but not enough to distract critics from his strained performance. *Film Daily* saw a

> fair comedy with Buster Keaton getting over the laughs spottily in [a] Hollywood studio setting. . . . Where he is really supposed to be funny, the laughs fail to materialize. Here he is the king playing in a musical comedy extravaganza, and the stuff falls pretty flat. Buster seems out of his element, for his well known pantomimic ability is sacrificed to the new school of articulate gagging." (*Film Daily*, 20 April, p. 11)

While the trade reviews were bad enough, the respected critic Robert E. Sherwood published a damning critique:

> Buster Keaton, trying to imitate a standard musical comedy clown, is no longer Buster Keaton and no longer funny. It is in the field of comedy that the motion picture has reached its highest peaks of artistry and also of individuality. Indeed, the greatest excuse for its existence has always been the "chase." Not one of the greatest humorists or clowns of the printed page or the stage has ever been so gloriously funny as Charlie Chaplin, Harold Lloyd or Buster Keaton, when viewed in the act of escaping from justice. Why, then, should a member of this mighty trio consider it necessary to wear musical comedy makeup and costumes and sing silly songs for the getting of a laugh? (*Film Daily,* 14 May 1930, p. 6)

Keaton's DOUGHBOYS (dir. Sedgwick, 1930) was a box-office flop as well as a critical disaster. During World War I Buster encounters his old boss, who has become a German lieutenant. Buster naively tries to bring the German troops some sausages from the American side. He walks through his dialogue without much interest. Hall was quick to point out that Keaton's acting "by no means suffers through his voice, which is happily suited to his screen personality."[13] The film does exhibit, however, some changes in MGM's sound techniques. Notably, much of the film was shot outdoors with live recording in which background sounds sometimes obscure the dialogue. Although the standard MGM two- and (less frequently) three-camera setups are used in most of the film, some scenes are shot with a single camera using the "silent" multiple-take technique. In a shot–reverse shot sequence with Buster and the sergeant, for example, two edited-together takes had to be used, otherwise the cameras would have been visible. There are some obvious examples of acoustic foregrounding. Buster plays the ukulele and sings "You Were Meant for Me," and his girlfriend Mary speaks in an unintelligible voice because she's chewing gumdrops.

Joan Crawford's "women's pictures" seldom received strong reviews, but they made money. *Film Daily,* typically, described OUR BLUSHING BRIDES (dir. Harry Beaumont, 1930) as "another of those pretty screen stories made for the shop-girl vote. . . . A lot of the film is given up to fashion displays of lingerie, with the girls behind the counter also acting as models—and all for 20 bucks a week."[14] Despite this lack of critical enthusiasm, the film ranked among MGM's ten top-grossing films for the year.

ANNA CHRISTIE (dir. Clarence Brown, 1930), adapted from the Eugene O'Neill play, was a critical and box-office success for MGM, for Marie Dressler, and for Garbo. MGM's biggest star had been pressed into sound against her wishes by Irving Thalberg. The public, however, fanned by the studio's "Garbo Talks!" saturation advertising campaign, eagerly awaited the silent star's first words. *Film Daily* admitted that "Garbo displays a voice which is somewhat heavy and accented at times, but is mellow and understandable." After its Los Angeles premiere, the *Herald, Times,* and *Examiner* all gave ANNA CHRISTIE rave reviews, and they loved Garbo's speech. "There is no need to worry," the *Record* reassured its readers. "Garbo's voice is, I think, quite the most distinguished on the talking screen." "La Garbo's accent is nicely edged with a Norse 'yah,' but once the ear gets the pitch it's okay and the spectator is under the spell of her performance."[15] ROMANCE (dir. Clarence Brown, 1930), a summer release starring Garbo, was not as successful. Thalberg judged the star's singing voice to be inadequate, but she

Heralds for MGM talking stars, distributed in theaters in 1929–1930.

refused to have close-ups, which would have exposed any voice-doubling. So her character either sings offscreen or a double appears in long-shot. Hall, alluding to the doubling, described her voice as "peculiarly deep-toned" and inconsistent with the "bell-like tones" of her singing. *Film Daily* found that her enunciation became clearer as the film went on (or did the reviewer's comprehension get better?): "Playing an Italian opera star, [Garbo's] dialogue at times early in the story is somewhat difficult to understand but it steadily improves."[16]

MGM had another high-profile talking-film holdout, Lon Chaney. Claiming that his contract covered only pantomime services and that the talkies made films inaccessible to deaf people (such as his parents), he demanded a $150,000 bonus (later lowered to $75,000) to speak on film. Louis B. Mayer employed a devious tactic. If the star would not make a talkie, then he would force Chaney to make what would have been MGM's only silent film in 1930. Thalberg intervened, reached a compromise, and Chaney signed a five-picture contract to "remake some of his successes as talkies." For the speaking debut of "The Man with a Thousand Faces," Thalberg selected Chaney's 1925 hit in which the actor played three roles. Chaney developed distinctive dialects for each character and, as a publicity stunt, signed a notarized affidavit swearing that all the voices were his. THE UNHOLY THREE (dir. Jack Conway) opened on Broadway in July

Harry Earles and Lon Chaney (right) in THE UNHOLY THREE *(MGM, 1930).*

THE BIG HOUSE *(MGM, 1930)*.

1930 and was a smash. *Film Daily* wrote, "Now the public will get a chance to hear not only Chaney's voice for the first time but also several other voices he impersonates, and he is impressive in all of them. . . . [The story] is a bigger draw in sound, for so many of the dramatic incidents depend on audible effects, such as the ventriloquist's dummy. . . . Chaney and his varied speaking voices is the big draw in the billing." Unknown to studio executives and fans, however, Chaney had advanced lung cancer and died of a throat hemorrhage on 26 August 1930.[17]

MGM experimented with untested genres. THE BIG HOUSE (dir. George W. Hill, 1930), a hard-boiled prison story, was appreciated for its contemporary relevance by *Film Daily:* "Sensational subject, timely on account of prison disasters still fresh in the public mind, should make it a money-getter in the metropolitan lanes."[18] Kent (Robert Montgomery) is a young man guilty of a misdemeanor. Owing to prison overcrowding (message! message!), he must be placed in a cell with the hardened criminals Morgan (Chester Morris) and Butch "Machine Gun" Smith (Wallace Beery). THE BIG HOUSE still packs an emotional punch. The 1930 reviewer predicted—incorrectly—that its downbeat tone would be a box-office liability. "The heavy, depressing theme and its lack of feminine appeal will prove a handicap for the family trade."[19] Opportunities for foregrounding sound abound. The inmates sport various accents and speech impediments. Many plot points are communicated by eavesdropping on conversations. The sound of the mess hall is bleak, the machine shop is deafening, and the riot scenes are cacophonous. Solitary confinement, in contrast, was filmed with a long section of com-plete silence. When Morgan reads a letter to Butch informing him of the death of his mother, the camera (blimped) frames the tight close-up from only a few feet away, resulting in a powerfully intimate moment. In the chapel, the prisoners prepare for their escape while singing the ironic hymn "Open Thy Gates." There are elevator shots and even an astonishing zoom lens point-of-view shot—one of the earliest (if not the first) in a Hollywood movie. THE BIG HOUSE won the Oscar for sound recording. Douglas Shearer's peers evidently appreciated such effects as the stamp of the prison-ers' feet keeping time with background music (a variation on the musical technique of synching to playback), the reverberating clang of the closing prison doors, and a surre-ally incongruous bell ringing in the background as Montgomery's body measurements are recorded for eugenic classification.

A real surprise is THEIR OWN DESIRE (1930), directed by E. Mason Hopper. The story, which has more action than the star Norma Shearer's earlier verbose melodramas, takes full advantage of the possibilities of Western Electric's new mobile equipment, but unobtrusively. The first section is an exterior scene featuring a tracking shot with Shearer and Lewis Stone chatting on horseback while riding toward the moving truck–mounted camera. Later she and Robert Montgomery get acquainted while splashing in a noisy swimming pool. A dance floor provides the opportunity to demon-strate the camera's new fluidity. A scene in a canoe on a river was recorded, apparently, with the microphone disguised in a hanging tree branch. A conversation begins in the parlor and continues seamlessly as the speakers relocate onto the terrace. All these sound tours de force, which must have tested the ingenuity of Douglas Shearer's record-ing team, are accomplished with minimal showiness. *Variety* noted that the film "seems to depend less on actual conversation than the average talker," indicating how dialogue was being nudged into its modulated status.[20]

MGM was always associated with star quality. But there were exceptions. THE SEA BAT (dir. Wesley Ruggles, 1930), starring Raquel Torres, was supposed to be another WHITE SHADOWS IN THE SOUTH SEAS. Instead, this story of a love triangle interrupted by the attack of a giant stingray (hence the title) was described as a "wild meller of South Sea island filled with hooey that brings laughs in wrong places. One of the season's worst. . . . The hardboileds in the balcony of Loew's New York gave it the haw-haw, which is enough."[21] Wisely sticking to MGM's policy of making star vehicles, Nicholas Schenck praised the voices of his biggest names: "We have discovered excellent recording voices not only among the stage veterans, such as Lewis Stone and H. B. Warner, but also among players without stage experience. John Gilbert, Marion Davies, William Haines, Greta Garbo, Norma Shearer, Joan Crawford—all down the line of stars we have found remark-ably good voices."[22] This assessment turned out to be spectacularly inaccurate about the first three stars mentioned. Haines's voice was judged to be too effeminate for his fans (although one suspects homophobia at work here, since he was one of Hollywood's few openly gay actors). Davies, though a gifted comedienne, never really clicked in sound. John Gilbert, whose famous downward spiral from stardom on account of his bad voice is discussed in chapter 19, bombed with REDEMPTION (dir. Fred Niblo). Gilbert's first talkie, hastily shot in seventeen days, had been shelved in 1929 but was resuscitated in May 1930. By then, the matinee idol had lost forever his patina of stardom.

Fortunately for fans, there were relatively few such embarrassments. In October 1929, Mayer wrote a memo to Thalberg: "M-G-M is still behind the other studios in sound production, but quantity is not important. . . . What matters is that M-G-M

Warners' Theatre program for GENERAL CRACK *(Warner Bros., 1929).*

becomes identified with the quality talking picture."[23] This public relations policy is clearly reflected in the studio's "class" productions. The reputation that MGM enjoyed in the 1930s as the "Tiffany" studio was well deserved. That image was carefully planned and executed inside the colonnaded studio in Culver City. The story flops and star misfires during the transition season show clearly that these strategies usually, but not always, worked.

Warner Bros.

In order to cultivate an aura of quality (and to compete with MGM), Warners purchased many Broadway properties, including *Disraeli*. It engaged George Arliss, who had created the Benjamin Disraeli role, to reprise it for the sound cameras. Although the *Times* felt that the "tonal quality of the voices is capital," several New York reviews dismissed DISRAELI (dir. Alfred E. Green, 1929) as "snapshots of the stage play."[24] *Film Daily* concurred on the "high grade of sound recording" but, ever-attuned to the popular market, questioned the film's mass appeal and predicted that it would be limited to class houses— "speculative product for the average audience."[25] SO LONG LETTY (dir. Lloyd Bacon, 1929) was also an effort to film a stage chestnut. The title is a joke on the physique of the long-legged actress Charlotte Greenwood. She had performed the stage version for fourteen years before Warners bought the play.[26] *Variety* felt that the plot was stale and the star past her prime. Another Warner Bros. prestige picture was GENERAL CRACK (dir. Alan Crosland, 1929), John Barrymore's first all-talking feature. Reviewers criticized the lagging story, an Austrian period piece based on a 1928 novel, but adored Barrymore's famous velvet voice. Noting his distractingly tight breeches, they even commented on his sex appeal: "Barrymore is superb and certainly an eyeful for the female customers."[27]

Warner Bros.' entry into the revue race was THE SHOW OF SHOWS (dir. John G. Adolfi), which opened in November 1929. The Technicolor film was very faithful to the stage revue format. Emcee Frank Fay introduces the individual skits, which open and close behind a curtain. Warners' top stars, including Beatrice Lillie, Louise Fazenda, and Rin Tin Tin, perform brief skits. The overall effect is like a dozen Vitaphone shorts strung together for two hours. Among the high points of the revue are John Barrymore's baroque delivery of Richard III's soliloquy from *Henry VI* and Winnie Lightner's "Singin' in the Bathtub," her parody of "Singin' in the Rain." The emcee and several performers address the camera directly and look down to speak with "Lou" (Louis Silver, the Vitaphone Orchestra leader) as if they were appearing live on the movie house stage. The aesthetic of superabundance reigns; in fact, the "Lady Luck" finale has something of the feel of a three-ring circus. The curtains (festooned with a couple of dangling ladies) part to reveal a set above which hang three enormous chandeliers, each made of half a dozen live women. Showgirls in towering headdresses, acrobats, startlingly aerobic break dancers, and a pageant of barely clad chorines pull the moviegoer's attention from one hyperactive focal point to the next.

The musical comedies from Warner Bros. featured the big Technicolor musical GOLD DIGGERS OF BROADWAY (dir. Roy Del Ruth) in October 1929. It grossed more than $2.5 million and was Warners' only true blockbuster of the 1929–1930 season. The film was adapted from the play *The Gold Diggers,* which Warners had filmed as a silent in 1923. Winnie Lightner belts out songs in her raucous style, and Joe Burke's "Tip-Toe Through the Tulips with Me" became the anthem of parlor ukulele players around the world. The film apparently exists only as a nine-minute fragment, but its story, from an Avery Hopwood play, was the basis for the famous GOLD DIGGERS OF 1933. The plot is an integrated backstage musical. Judging from the surviving section, the performances appear motivated by the backstage premise. But the extended tap-dancing finale with a line of dozens of syncopated walking sticks takes us back to the superabundant revue.

For its big Christmas 1929 draw, the studio presented its adaptation of Ziegfeld's musical romance SALLY (dir. John Francis Dillon). Warner Bros. constructed inside a Burbank soundstage a faux Long Island mansion complete with an extravagant "'four-sided' set, that is, built exactly as in real life with all four sides complete." It required fifteen hundred lights, "the largest number of incandescent lamps ever used in motion pictures." Although the Vitaphone crew consisted of twenty technicians on the set and four in the recording rooms, "a single man, the 'mixer,' sat in his lone sound-proof booth and adjusted the dials that regulated the flow of sound from the many microphones."[28] The story concerns a playboy, Blair (Alexander Gray), who casts aside his society fiancée after falling for waitress–chorus girl Sally (Marilyn Miller). The ambience of her pancake-house milieu is established by her friends' native New York accents (though Miller herself "enunciates" in an unlikely slightly English accent). The revue at the Elm Tree Inn on Long Island provides the opportunity to encapsulate some musical numbers, for example, that of the Albertina Rasch Ballet. This film also uses the stage convention of commencing to sing during an intimate conversation. When Blair tries to console Sally about her lack of success in getting a dancing job, he launches into Jerome Kern's "Look for the Silver Lining." Many New York critics did not like what flowed from the screen, praising Marilyn Miller's tap dancing but finding the story boring.

In SHOW GIRL IN HOLLYWOOD *(First National, 1930), Jimmy (Jack Mulhall, inside a soundproof camera booth) hears Buelow's (John Miljan) confession through the sound system.*

SHOW GIRL IN HOLLYWOOD (dir. Mervyn LeRoy, 1930) received lukewarm reviews, but it is of interest now because its story provides a glimpse into the making of a Hollywood revue. There are some revealing shots of the Warners/First National Burbank sound facilities. We see a musical number in production, filmed by several cameras in their "ice boxes." In the story, the lecherous director Frank Buelow (John Miljan) tricks the innocent Dixie Dugan (Alice White) into joining him in Hollywood. Optimistically, she leaves behind her boyfriend Jimmy (Jack Mulhall), a talented but destitute composer who is scraping by writing musicals in New York. She does not get the promised contract from Superb Motion Picture Studios, but the studio head and his yes-men decide they must have Jimmy to write the screen version of his Broadway revue "Rainbow Girl." Misled by Buelow, Dixie almost blows her career until Jimmy, sitting in a camera booth, overhears the cad confessing his treachery over an open Vitaphone mike. The final scene is the premiere of *Rainbow Girl*—the motion picture—at the Warner Bros. theater in Hollywood. The Warner stars Al Jolson, Ruby Keeler, Loretta Young, Noah Beery, Sr., and Noah, Jr., make cameo appearances. During the musical

Crowd outside Under a Texas Moon *(Warner Bros., 1930).*

number on the screen, the film cuts freely between the space of the Warner Bros. theater and the film on its screen, conflating the two spaces.

These musical comedies lavished attention on the details of the song and dance sequences, but the stories contained the performances by establishing music as the characters' employment. Operettas like SONG OF THE WEST, SONG OF THE FLAME, BRIDE OF THE REGIMENT, and GOLDEN DAWN (all 1930), because they duplicated the middlebrow appeal of such shows on Broadway, seldom tried to integrate the songs with a believable story. These frivolous plots with the libretti sung in "operatic" voices backed by overpopulated choruses tended to be more successful on stage than on screen. "Seemingly all the weaknesses, without the strength, of stage operettas get transferred to the screen," concluded *Variety*.[29]

UNDER A TEXAS MOON (dir. Michael Curtiz, 1930) was part Western, part romantic operetta, with a smattering of a story. Don Carlos (Frank Fay) spoils a cattle rustler's operation. It earned a positive review from *Film Daily*'s Gillette: "A swell job has been done on this glorified Western in Technicolor. . . . Dialogue is ideal, direction is imaginative, outdoor scenes are beautiful, color is among the best to date, and altogether it is an unusually delightful entertainment that should get the money anywhere."[30] Although it was not released until April 1930, it had been shot in mid-1929, and was one of Warners' first to have access to the Western Electric Kearny trucks for location sound recording on discs. Thus, the camera could amble along with Don Carlos from one amorous señorita to the next, accompanied by the incessant strumming of the "Under a Texas Moon" theme song.

Paramount

THE VIRGINIAN (dir. Victor Fleming) was "distinguished from the average type of cowboy picture because of its important cast and excellent acting. . . . Action is nearly all in a deliberate, serious vein, with the few comedy touches failing to help much."[31] Its somber tone was faithful to Owen Wister's classic Western novel.[32] The film begins with titles superimposed over a vast herd of lowing steers. Audiences already knew the story of the drifter without a name (a taciturn Gary Cooper) whose friend Steve (Richard Arlen) is corrupted by the evil rustler Trampas (Walter Huston). They must have waited expectantly to hear the famous exchange:

TRAMPAS: "When I want to know anything from you I'll tell you, you long-legged son of a—"
THE VIRGINIAN: "If you wanna call me that—smile."

Sound was also foregrounded in the hilarious incident of the two buddies mixing up babies at a mass christening. The wails of the "little mavericks" fill the sound track. There was also the Virginian and Steve's quail-like secret whistle. This token of their friendship returns chillingly when a real bird calls out just after Steve's hanging. Jesse Lasky claimed optimistically that THE VIRGINIAN would bring back the genre and attract new mature audiences. The talking Western, he said, will be "designed with a view to the fact that we are now an adult people."[33] He followed up with THE TEXAN (1930), directed by John Cromwell, from an O. Henry story, also starring Cooper.

Paramount's foray into virtual Broadway was GLORIFYING THE AMERICAN GIRL (1929), adapted very literally from the Follies of 1929. The film director was Millard Webb, and the revue numbers were directed by John Harkrider. The Ziegfeld stars

Foregrounding sound in THE VIRGINIAN *(Paramount, 1929). "You long-legged son of a ———" (Walter Huston).*

A locomotive's steam blast startles a "wild" cow.

Molly (Mary Brian) is amused by the Virginian's (Gary Cooper) inarticulate speech.

The whistle that bonds the Virginian and his friend.

Rudy Vallee, Eddie Cantor, and Helen Morgan did their bits. Though expensive, and given a semblance of a backstage melodrama plot, it joined the increasing ranks of musicals panned by the critics. "Nothing . . . that has not been done in the talkies many times before," said the jaded *New York Post*. "Its plot fairly reeks with familiarity."[34] PARAMOUNT ON PARADE (1930) was a revue filmed by fifteen separate units on both coasts, using eleven directors (Arzner, Lubitsch, Goulding, et al.). Observing what by then had become a convention of the genre, the performers and hosts look into the camera and address the audience as though physically present in the theater. "Can you folks hear me out there?" asks the emcee, Richard "Skeets" Gallagher. In addition to the usual song and dance numbers, there are also encapsulated sketches. Warner Oland, Clive Brook, William Powell, and Eugene Pallette bring together their characters Fu Manchu, Sherlock Holmes, Philo Vance, and Sergeant Heath in a mystery spoof. The film not only highlights their distinctive voices but displays a bold expressionist set. Ruth Chatterton's segment is a self-contained playlet with a song and a flashback sequence. Helen Kane does her trademark boop-boop-a-doop routine. Maurice Chevalier is the revue's headline player, singing two numbers and leading the finale. After his rendition of "All I Want Is Just One Girl," nine-year-old Mitzi Green does her impression of the French crooner.[35]

Chevalier was cast in a custom-made vehicle, THE LOVE PARADE (1929), directed by Paramount's star director, Lubitsch, at Astoria. It was Lubitsch's first sound film and the first screen appearance by a newcomer from the stage, Jeanette MacDonald.[36] Sparks fly when the willful queen of Sylvania must accept an arranged marriage with Chevalier, an émigré from Paris. Lubitsch mobilized the camera. For example, during the wedding procession, it tracks backward between flanking rows of guards, creating an impression of depth. A specially constructed set enabled the director to supervise two scenes at once. The program discussed Lubitsch's meticulous care: "He rehearsed the major players in THE LOVE PARADE for weeks before he permitted a camera to be turned on them." (Of course, with all that multi-camera raw stock rolling, and with technicians hovering about, this was also a cost-effective approach.) The "Lubitsch touch" shows in every scene. Wry double entendre–laced dialogue and offscreen sound fool the audience into expecting risqué situations which never quite develop. With a wink at the censors, THE LOVE PARADE was successful indeed, receiving six Academy Award nominations.[37] The "touch" reappeared quickly in MONTE CARLO, released in August 1930.

ANIMAL CRACKERS (dir. Victor Heerman) with the four Marx Brothers, also opened on Broadway in August. As with their first film, most of the musical numbers from the comedy were cut, emphasizing the Marxes' screwball banter. Nevertheless, the opening sequences were still firmly in the Gilbert and Sullivan tradition of the comic opera parody. Singing butlers introduce Roscoe W. Chandler (a.k.a. Abie the fish peddler, Louis Morin) and Jeffrey T. Spaulding (Groucho). Groucho's appearance is heralded by his "Hooray for Captain Spaulding (the African Explorer)" theme, and he and the chorus of guests sing "Hello, I Must Be Going." The plot about a stolen painting comes in last place in importance behind Harpo's "silent" physical gags, Chico's ethnic malapropisms, and Groucho's being Groucho ("We took pictures of some native girls, but they weren't developed"). *Film Daily*'s review forgave the lack of plot: "While most of the repartee is nonsense, it gets the laughs and that's what counts."[38]

Rouben Mamoulian's APPLAUSE (1929) repelled some critics on moral grounds. An aging burlesque queen (Helen Morgan) is supporting her daughter (Joan Peers) in a Wisconsin convent, but the girl is oblivious to her mother's occupation. With Zukor's

THE LOVE PARADE *(Paramount, 1929) souvenir program.*

Foreground sound in APPLAUSE *(Paramount, 1929). As April walks the city streets, she's mistaken for a prostitute by men shown only from the waist down. The annoying dog's bark underscores her insecurity.*

The long lens creates shallow depth of field which creates psychological subjectivity in this conversation between April and Nitch.

As he describes the rewards of being a vaudeville performer, the camera racks focus to show April's attention shifting from his voice to the silhouette of her mother onstage.

Tony's skyscraper-roof proposal of marriage to April is punctuated by a fly-over by a roaring airplane.

blessing, but allegedly fighting the Astoria technicians, Mamoulian played with his sound system as though it were a new toy. Several effects had been seen in silent films but were given novel twists with sound. He split the screen, for instance, to show both sides of a phone conversation and liberated the camera by wheeling it around the set during takes. In the burlesque house scenes, he adjusted the level of background sound to create acoustic depth through scale-matching, so the dancing sounds are louder when shown in medium shot than when seen in long shot. This suggests the subjective perception of the burlesque house audience. "Confusing" was *Photoplay*'s verdict. Presumably its "depressing" story, only slightly mitigated by a tacked-on happy ending, affected word-of-mouth advertising. Mamoulian retreated back to the stage.[39]

Dorothy Arzner tried an interesting use of dialogue in SARAH AND SON (1930). Sarah Storm (Ruth Chatterton) is a German immigrant who speaks with a gutteral accent in the early scenes. To signify her rise to opera stardom and her assimilation into "society," her accent gradually becomes cosmopolitan.

Fox

SUNNY SIDE UP opened in October 1929. The immensely popular screen lovers Janet Gaynor and Charles Farrell made their singing debut in the film and were praised by the New York critics. The director David Butler opened the film with what would become an early-sound cliché, a camera tour of a neighborhood in which urban sounds produce an aleatory "noise symphony." It was claimed that the film grossed $3.5 million for Fox.[40]

Raoul Walsh's THE COCK-EYED WORLD (1929) was a sequel to his 1926 hit WHAT PRICE GLORY? Still working under the two-director system, William K. Wells directed dialogue. Victor McLaglen and Edmund Lowe reprised their roles as foul-mouthed World War I sergeants. The silent film had been something of a cause célèbre because astute viewers could read the original barracks-level dialogue on the players' lips. A talkie equivalent of this effect was impossible, of course, so the rough language was toned down in the censorable speech of the sequel. Reviewers singled out the sergeants' argument over which one of them had fathered a mutual girlfriend's child. It was vulgar, salacious, and "more ribald than rollicking" (*New York Graphic*).[41] The macho tone was tempered by several songs, including De Sylva, Brown, and Henderson's "You're the Cream in My Coffee."

There had been a well-publicized defection from Fox when F. W. Murnau, the director of SUNRISE, quit in May 1929 to join the documentarist Robert Flaherty in a venture, called Color-Art Productions, to make talking pictures in exotic lands. The first project (which became TABU [1931]) was set in the South Seas.[42] Meanwhile, Murnau's OUR DAILY BREAD, begun as a silent for Fox in 1928, was re-edited with new footage and released with sound as CITY GIRL in February 1930.[43]

RKO-Radio Pictures

RIO RITA premiered 6 October 1929. Radio's entry into the musical extravaganza derby turned out to be the studio's biggest hit. The once-popular silent film player Bebe Daniels starred. She had just made news by buying out her Paramount contract when

"*If I Had a Talking Picture of You,*" *sheet music from* SUNNY SIDE UP (*Fox, 1929*).

"So Dear to Me," sheet music from THE COCK-EYED WORLD *(Fox, 1929).*

that studio refused to test her for sound roles. She threw herself into the part of Rita with verve. Lee de Forest, a relative, would visit her on the set "doing things to the microphone, moving mikes around to better positions and that sort of thing."[44]

Following the fashion, RIO RITA had two directors. Luther Reed, formerly of Paramount, adapted the Ziegfeld stage show. Russell Mack directed the dialogue scenes. The quest of Rita (Daniels) for Texas Ranger Jimmy Stewart (John Boles) is punctuated by many interjections of operatic duets, dance numbers by a chorus line which pops out of nowhere, and the routines of Bert Wheeler and Robert Woolsey, who are Rita and Jimmy's comic foils. Wheeler is an American playboy looking for a Mexican divorce, and Woolsey is his lawyer. The film was an early effort to "open up" the operetta source, that is, to re-stage it in a "natural" setting. Exterior locations were used extensively, with flying insects and a stiff breeze often captured in the takes. Unlike, say, THE DESERT SONG, in which the staginess of the environment contributes to the stylization of the music, the (relatively) authentic-looking outdoor sets of the hacienda and village heighten the contrast when the RIO RITA troupe begins to perform. The music numbers were shot synched to a playback, making some ambitious tracking shots possible. In one, the camera moves into the village market, pans around, and tracks back to reframe the dancers. There is one overhead shot of the dancers forming a geometric pattern on the floor. Elsewhere, background music plays continuously behind the dialogue while a scene in the village dissolves to a later scene in the General's mansion. The continuous music bridges a narrative transition. It must be said, though, that RIO RITA had many technical shortcomings. The dialogue shot outdoors is poorly mixed and frequently drowned

RIO RITA (*RKO, 1929*), *with Bebe Daniels and John Boles.*

out by background sounds and by the chorus. (It improves noticeably when the shooting moves onto a soundstage.) There are discontinuities (jump cuts) mid-scene when the
dialogue turns to singing. Once this is masked by an awkward cutaway of the Rangers
riding away, but most of the jumps remain. Its roughness notwithstanding, RIO RITA was
hugely successful and made the studio a $1 million profit.[45]

The Wheeler and Woolsey team quickly moved up from the supporting cast to
become the studio's biggest talent asset. For their first showcase film, THE CUCKOOS (dir.
Paul Sloane, 1930), RKO was insecure and hired Roscoe "Fatty" Arbuckle (the wrong-
fully disgraced silent film clown) to direct—uncredited—the comedy scenes.[46] Not only
was their vaudeville physical comedy and their corny jokes typical, they brought to the
talkies their distinctive vocal qualities. Woolsey (the tall one with glasses) had Everett
Edward Horton's voice with Groucho's delivery; Wheeler had an unexpectedly high,
child-like voice. They went on to make twenty-one films before Woolsey's death in 1938.
Variety advised RKO to time their editing better so as not to cut off laughs. Some of the
jokes in THE CUCKOOS were "wholly lost" because the gags followed too quickly.[47]

THE VAGABOND LOVER (dir. Marshall Nielan, 1929) was a blatant exploitation of
RKO's connection to radio. The plot assumes an antagonism between middlebrow jazz
and high-class opera. Rudy Vallee impersonates a correspondence-school jazz orchestra
leader but is unmasked when he impetuously agrees to perform at a charity ball hosted
by Marie Dressler. She confesses to Vallee that she prefers popular music to opera
("Jazz, I just adore jazz. I don't know why. [*She shimmies.*] It does something to me")
and exits singing Fanny Brice's "I'm an Indian." The party sequence is an excuse to
encapsulate some acts, including an opera singer's "O Sole Mio" and four "singing
orphans." Rudy Vallee's conversational delivery is somewhat halting and monotonous,
but the shortcomings of his ordinary speech make his sweet crooning voice all the more
surprising in contrast. Not only does RKO showcase one of NBC's biggest stars, there
are also two plugs for the network—once when we hear a radio announcer broadcast
that Rudy has confessed his masquerade, and again at the charity ball when the NBC
logo is prominently displayed on the stage microphone.

SEVEN KEYS TO BALDPATE (dir. Reginald Barker; dialogue dir. Russell Mack, 1930)
came close to the perfect cliché of canned theater. It was a good recording of what
George M. Cohan's play must have looked and sounded like onstage, captured with
multi-camera filming. During a brief introduction we meet William (Richard Dix),
whose friend bets that he cannot complete a novel in one night at the deserted Baldpate
Inn. Variety felt that time had run out for this type of filmmaking:

> The screen hasn't availed itself of its unlimited scope in this transition [from
> the stage]. Fully 90% of the action occurs on the country hotel living room
> set, projecting with more artificiality than clumsy carpentry on the legit
> boards.
>
> The theme is brought to the film with entrances and exits as numerous and
> conventional as when producers began feeling their way with dialog. . . . What
> was illustrated a year ago is reiterated: that the average stage play cannot
> practically be transposed to the screen and hope to be anywhere near simi-
> larly successful. (*Variety,* 1 January 1930)

The studio also produced a "realist" adaptation of a best-seller, THE CASE OF SERGEANT
GRISCHA (dir. Herbert Brenon, 1930). Critics not only found the story of a Russian peas-

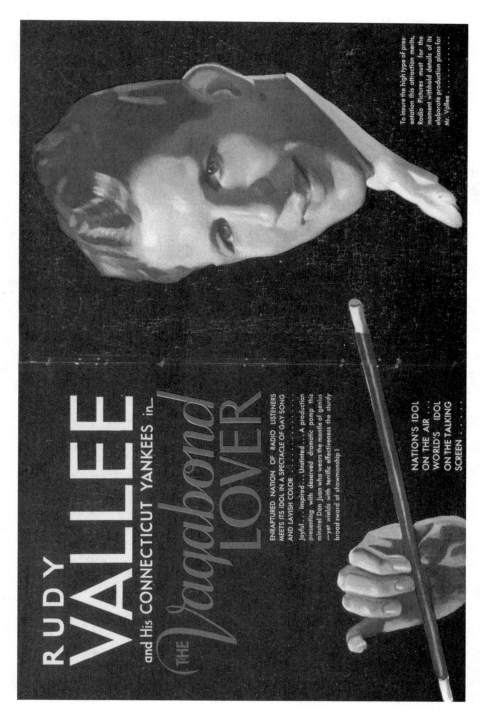

Advertising for THE VAGABOND LOVER *(RKO, 1929).*

ant (Chester Morris) who escapes from a German prisoner-of-war camp gloomy but pointed out a mismatch of character and voice. *Variety* seethed: "After watching this blundering lout with his Park Ave. dialog for about two reels, about the only regret [is that] he was not shot earlier and the picture made into a short."[48] It took a beating at the box office.

Universal

Carl Laemmle, Sr., justified Universal's reliance on remakes by arguing that there was a shortage of material upon which to base talkie plots. THE PHANTOM OF THE OPERA (1930), part remake and part goat gland, was proof that silent pictures could draw again. But critics saw the film's second success only as a sign of the fans' devotion to its stubbornly mute star. "Chaney steals the show throughout. The lovers, in the dialogue scenes, look rather weak compared with their silent version."[49]

After "Junior" Laemmle became studio head, the first venture in his bigger-is-better strategy was THE KING OF JAZZ (dir. John Murray Anderson, 1930). The white bandleader Paul Whiteman is the "king," so anointed in Walter Lantz's cartoon prologue by caricatured Africans and jungle animals. Basically a music revue with vaudeville blackout sketches interspersed, the film is organized around the theme of the origins of jazz. A narrator tells us, "America is a melting pot of music, where the melodies of all nations are fused into one great new rhythm." Various national dancers (Italians, Spanish, etc.) perform. But no Africans (or African Americans) contributed to this American melting-pot musical form, according to the message of the film. Only one black actor, a child, appears in it. Michael Rogin observes, "By the compensatory cultural logic of the jazz age, Whiteman's music has nothing to do with jazz."[50] *Variety* noted a lacuna of a different sort:

> If there is one big thing the Whiteman band is identified with besides its leader, Paul, it is George Gershwin's "Rhapsody in Blue." The millions who have never heard the great Whiteman band play this biggest of all jazz melodies won't hear it here, either. Mr. Anderson has seen fit to scramble it up with "production." It's all busted to pieces, and, while it's all there, it's not the Whiteman number it would have been had it been played simply straight as a musical composition by the jazzing orchestra that does it so well and as it should have been." (Sime, *Variety*, 7 May 1930)[51]

THE KING OF JAZZ was a $2 million flop.[52]

This failure was more than compensated for by Universal's ALL QUIET ON THE WESTERN FRONT (1930). The dramatization of Erich Maria Remarque's powerful antiwar novel produced "one of the greatest pictures in the history of films. Lewis Milestone scores a directorial triumph, with his picture sure to set a standard for war productions to attain."[53] It is a simple story. Baumer (Lew Ayres) joins the German army with his schoolmates, swept up in the patriotic furor to serve the fatherland in 1914. In one of the many foregrounded sound sequences, the audience gets a lecture on how to identify the different kinds of incoming shells according to the shrieking sounds they make. Agonized screams, shots, explosions, and general cacophony depict acoustically the danger of the battlefield. Three years later, while on leave from the front and shattered by

Universal tried to convince exhibitors that THE KING OF JAZZ *(1930) would attract new "sophisticated" audiences. The film itself contained no nudity.*

ALL QUIET ON THE WESTERN FRONT (*Universal, 1930*) *souvenir program.*

the horrors of battle, Baumer returns to his old school and denounces war's evils. Later, back in a trench during a lull in the fighting, he reaches out to catch a butterfly and is shot dead by a French sniper. We see a close-up of his hand and hear the offscreen rifle. Softly understated sounds heighten the tragic moment: someone is playing sweet harmonica music as cannons thunder in the distance. The two superimposed sounds thematically connect the themes of war and peace. The earlier noise of battle makes the tranquillity of Baumer's death all the more incongruous.

The Academy gave ALL QUIET ON THE WESTERN FRONT its best picture and best director awards. The Laemmles took the success as an affirmation of the studio's change to upscale programming. They acknowledged that the move was in response to an evolving audience:

> For a long time we watched the changing trends in the industry and made up our minds that the moment had come for greater specialization in pictures and concentration on fewer, bigger and better productions. . . . The change comes at a dramatic and psychological moment in the industry's history. No longer is it necessary, in order to supply entertainment to the millions, to spread thin over the whole country. The census now under way has already shown the increasing drift of population to the urban centers. For the first time in America, the mass of people live in communities that are preponderantly urban. This means, in film terms, that the great majority of picture-goers is found no longer in the smaller communities, but in the larger towns and cities. It is for the mass that pictures are, and always have been made; and it is the larger theaters that, more and more, are supplying the demand. It is clear that such a change calls for the production of pictures that will first of all meet the needs of the larger house, because the larger house is meeting, in its turn, the greatest needs of the public. And the logical outcome of the recognition of this fact is specialization in production—the making of bigger, better and fewer pictures. (*Film Daily*, 16 June 1930, p. 3)

Junior Laemmle's intentions were good and the praise for ALL QUIET ON THE WESTERN FRONT was welcome. But in actuality, Universal still needed the steady returns on traditional fare like Hoot Gibson's Westerns (for example, TRAILING TROUBLE and THE HIDE-OUT [both 1930]). Besides, many of the picture palaces targeted by this new urban strategy were beginning to close. The commitment to keep the dwindling small houses supplied with low-revenue silent product was becoming a burden. Despite all the promises, the studio's effort to become a prestige producer was short-lived.[54]

United Artists

The progression of sound design in CITY LIGHTS epitomizes the ambivalence shared by many producers. Though Charles Chaplin's long-lasting antipathy toward the talkies is now legendary, he was not opposed to nondialogue sound. Indeed, much like John Ford, he felt that synchronized music was essential for his films. David Robinson's research shows that Chaplin, almost from the start, had contemplated at least an orchestral sound track for CITY LIGHTS. And contrary to accepted opinion, Chaplin initially was not absolutely opposed to talking. In the summer of 1928, he was working on drafts of the filmscript and told the press that he had not decided whether the film would have sound effects, a score, or talking.[55] By the following spring, Chaplin seems to have made up his mind. He told interviewers from United Press International in March 1929 that he disapproved of talking films and would never make one. He repeated this position—"For me, it would be fatal"—in the fan magazines in May and June.

Chaplin's decision was the result not only of soul-searching but possibly of experiment. It was reported that he had shot as much as ten reels of sound test footage—longer than an average 1920s feature film. This information came out in an unverified *Photoplay* account:

> Charlie Chaplin will not talk in his next picture. There will be no fanfare of pressagentry about this. Charlie has reached his decision in his own quiet way.
>
> For almost a year he has been working on a new picture. Half way through he stopped production and gave his cast and studio staff a vacation. The next day sound technicians moved in with their equipment, and Charlie was not seen in his usual haunts for weeks.
>
> During that time he made over ten thousand feet of talking picture test film, and when he finally emerged from the privacy of his studio, he was still puzzled.
>
> Only a very few close friends have seen and heard the tests, and it is known that they have advised him to stick to the pantomime, in which he has no equal.
>
> Now he is considering a picture in which there is sound and dialogue for the other characters, but in which he will remain silent. (James R. Quirk, "Close-ups and Long-Shots," *Photoplay*, November 1929, p. 27)

Filming began in December 1929 but was delayed again and again. According to Robinson, the decision to have only synchronized music was not irrevocable until May 1930. Principal photography was concluded in December 1930.[56]

D. W. Griffith finished his ABRAHAM LINCOLN "after thirty-one days of hard work." Jack Alicoate pronounced it "a decided achievement." The *Film Daily* reviewer praised Walter Huston's portrayal, which he felt created intimacy with the president. Compared to other releases of mid-1930, Griffith's film is slow-paced and the performers drone their lines (attributable, perhaps, to the dialogue director, Harry Stubbs). The story of Lincoln's life is told in episodes illustrating turning points, somewhat reminiscent of the tableau style of narration practiced a quarter-century earlier. Sound, for the most part, is handled conventionally, that is, with a master shot and two cameras recording the medium shots. There are, however, instances of experimental sound foregrounding.[57] A prologue depicting the arrival of a slave ship in 1809 (the year of Lincoln's birth) was filmed with a swooping silent camera by the German émigré Karl Struss. The post-synched sound track begins with the work shouts of the men in the hold, blends with an African tom-tom, and climaxes with the splash of a slave's body thrown overboard. Some sequences modify Griffith's silent-editing technique by using audio effects to establish ironic contrasts. Thus, we see parallel scenes of gentlemen arguing about slavery in Boston and in Richmond. But in lieu of their voices, we hear the wail of a gathering storm. Similarly, the Civil War begins with alternating scenes of northern and southern soldiers marching away to the strains of "The Battle Hymn of the Republic" and "Dixie," respectively. The message seems to be that only the superficial differences of their uniforms and theme songs set apart the two sides, symbolically justifying Lincoln's pleas for national unity. One can view Griffith's approach to sound as old-fashioned: he was definitely using it as an ostentatious add-on; alternatively, his assertive acoustic symbolism was consonant with the calls for a nonillusionistic, asynchronous use of sound being heard from commentators outside of Hollywood, such as René Clair and Eisenstein.

The newly all-talking HELL'S ANGELS (dir. Howard Hughes, 1930) hit Los Angeles and Broadway with a blitz of ballyhoo. Greta Nissen starred in the silent version (released in Europe), but her Swedish accent cost her the role in the talkie. Her replacement was the platinum-blonde midwesterner Jean Harlow. (Though she plays a British socialite, she has no trace of an English accent.) Hughes went out of the way to highlight the $4 million expense of remaking the film with sound. But sensitive to the prevailing hard times, the program assured movie fans who might be feeling the pinch that "the tremendous cost of HELL'S ANGELS was not the result of waste or inefficiency. The story was well constructed at the outset, but the script called for scenes which were undreamed of before, and were obtainable only by an unprecedented outlay of time and money."[58] There were Technicolor sequences and six reels of flight scenes projected in the Magnascope oversized format.

Hughes personally oversaw the installation of a special six-projector system at Grauman's Chinese Theater. There were two banks of three machines each. One ran the picture only. A second interlocked projector ran the normal sound track, and the third ran a supplementary effects track. These sound effects were literally added on, playing over the regular sound track through high-powered amplifiers and a dozen mighty loud-

HELL'S ANGELS *premiere, Grauman's Chinese Theater, Hollywood, 1930.*

Douglas Gilmore, Jean Harlow, James Hall, and Ben Lyon.

speakers. They blasted the audience with roaring propellers, exploding ammo dumps, and a crashing zeppelin. The second bank of projectors was used for reel changes.[59] In New York, anticipating overflow crowds, Hughes staged a dual premiere with simultaneous screenings at the Criterion and Gaiety Theaters. The impresario Sid Grauman orchestrated the publicity and ordered twenty-eight thousand square feet of dazzling electric sign displays for Times Square.

HELL'S ANGELS is the saga of two English brothers, Roy (James Hall) and Monte (Ben Lyon). Roy is brave and enlists when the war breaks out; Monte is a coward who enlists inadvertently at a society ball. Later, after two breathtaking flying sequences, they are captured by Germans. Roy must shoot Monte when his brother is on the verge of revealing military secrets, then is himself executed by a firing squad moments before the Allies arrive. *Film Daily* advised exhibitors to abandon their usually cautious editorial restraint: "Superlatives which are ordinarily extravagant may be justly used in describing this picture, particularly the sequences made in the air." Newspaper reviewers outdid themselves in inordinate praise. Monroe Lathrop's report in the *Los Angeles Express* concluded, "The most extraordinary output ever to emerge from the motion picture studios. An achievement in picture drama that will stand for a long time as a model to aim at. A sensational success—it has virile drama linking together its spectacles, and in the variety of its appeal with suspense and humor it is electrifying."[60]

Columbia

Frank Capra was Columbia's chief asset in 1929. Besides being able to handle Harry Cohn's legendary crudeness, Capra was a proficient and resourceful director. Lacking its own sound facilities, Columbia rented Christie's Metropolitan Sound Studios. Capra recalled, "While many big shots mulled about sound, or tried exorcising it with incantations of 'fad!' 'won't sell!' some sharpie wangled priorities in sound equipment, hung horse blankets on the walls of a 'barn,' and had himself a rental sound stage with customers waiting in line."[61] Dialogue scenes for THE YOUNGER GENERATION (1929), a part-talker adapted from a Fanny Hurst story of Jewish immigrant assimilation in New York, and THE DONOVAN AFFAIR (1929), Capra's first all-talkie, were shot at Metropolitan. The latter was a whodunit adapted from a current play. The police inspector Killian (Jack Holt) solves the murder of the playboy Donovan. For once, the butler really did do it.

Columbia's first dialogue film shot at its Gower Street studio was FLIGHT, released in November 1929. *Film Daily* praised the work of the director and "dialoguer" Capra, who "put into it a lot of audience angles . . . the good old box office values that always click with the popular crowds"—an early definition of those homespun populist qualities later called "Capra-corn." The film tells the rambling story of Lefty "Wrong Way" Phelps (Ralph Graves), who joined the marines to forget the trauma of having run the wrong way to score the winning touchdown for the opposing college football team. He meets Elinor (Lila Lee), a nurse, at flying school, but his loyalty to his instructor, Panama Williams (Jack Holt), who also loves her, prevents him from showing his affection. He crashes on his solo flight and is demoted to mechanic. Panama takes him to Nicaragua when the navy calls on the fliers to avenge some marines killed there by revolutionaries. Lefty overcomes his fear, performs some stunts in his plane, and convinces Panama that Lefty and Elinor were made for each other. FLIGHT was shot on a low budget, using stock footage of football games, air circuses, and—contrary to what Capra wrote in his autobiography—rear projection for close-ups in the flight scenes.[62] Almost all the scenes were shot outdoors and were poorly miked; as a result, the dialogue is often drowned out by background noises. Graves and Holt engage in several scenes of casual repartee which come across as relaxed improvisation. These appear to have been shot using Capra's devious technique of getting around Harry Cohn's prohibition on filming more than one take. The actors would repeat the scene two or more times with the camera running continuously (therefore, one take) until the director was satisfied. Capra foregrounded sound mainly in the aerial scenes with gunshots, bomb explosions, and propeller wash. But once he introduced an innovative nondialogue passage: Lefty is shown squirming in embarrassment as Elinor, offscreen, tells Panama that she loves Lefty. Two scenes contain what surely must have been a first in the talkies: the audience is subjected to the sounds of vomiting when the protagonists get airsick.

In April 1930, Frank Capra scored again with LADIES OF LEISURE, a story about a wealthy artist (Ralph Graves) trying to reform a gold-digging model (he does). This film introduced Barbara Stanwyck, who, under Capra's attentive direction, quickly became a favorite of movie fans.

Independents

When critics noticed them at all, the releases from the independents coping with sound suffered in comparison to their larger-budgeted competitors. Tiffany Pictures' THE LOST ZEPPELIN (dir. Edward Sloman, 1930) is representative. The plot is an effort to meld a society melodrama with an adventure film, while capitalizing on Admiral Byrd's polar expedition. The South Pole explorer Commander Hall (Conway Tearle) agrees to give his wife (Virginia Valli) a divorce on the eve of departing for the hapless polar expedition. She is in love with the Commander's aeronaut partner (Ricardo Cortez). After a crash at the pole, Mrs. Hall realizes that her husband was not so bad after all. He is miraculously rescued, and they are happily reunited.

Technically, the sound recording was primitive. Many scenes on the zeppelin set are accompanied by a constant engine roar on the sound track that is supposed to convey realism but also makes the dialogue unintelligible. Some sequences appear to have been filmed with one camera using the multiple-take method, and others with two cameras. This is evident because the noisy room tone changes with every splice. Critics were not impressed. The *New York American* said, "The yarn has been woven into a picture ever since Jesse Lasky's barn first housed a clicking camera." According to the *Telegram*, "The film would have fared better as a silent production because it would not have been burdened with the stilted and unimaginative dialogue it now has." The *Times,* only slightly more generously, wrote, "It appears to have been fashioned with a view to appealing to boys from eight to ten years of age."[63]

Flirting with Theater

The 1929–1930 season was one of competing expectations for the sound film. There was no obvious formula for mastering the new medium. Some studios evidently expected a hybridization between Broadway and Hollywood to occur, hence the rush to purchase musical and dramatic properties, their authors and their personnel, lock, stock, and barrel. These purchases required the studios to underwrite actual theatrical production and contract to transpose stage revues and plays to the screen. Though the range of material went from screwball comedy to "adult" topics (for instance, adultery, divorce, prostitution, and alcoholism), there was a definite flight to theatrical quality. Especially during this time when moralists were renewing their attack on Hollywood, presenting filmed versions of serious works by Somerset Maugham and Eugene O'Neill and historical dramas like Disraeli (1929) generated respect and cultural capital (while hinting at some of those works' notoriety).

Bringing famous directors like George Abbott and Mamoulian to Hollywood was intended to take advantage of their name recognition as much as their talents. Theater-associated personnel came as producers, directors, writers (of music and lyrics as well as stories), and, of course, performers. The most notable change in production during this period was the adoption of the two-director system. Films from the studios exploiting their investment in theater tended to be talk-heavy, showing that the new "dialogue directors" were earning their pay. The new practice of introducing outside specialists (preferably from New York) who would properly rehearse actors and coax the best vocal performance from them reflects both the film industry's search for established models and the deeply ingrained notion that talking was something inherently not of cinema and in need of control.

Producers availed themselves of theatrical form in the new films. Unfortunately, the word *theatrical* as a formal description is vague and almost meaningless. Critics and trade writers seem to have been using it in two ways: attempting to mimic the structure of the Broadway source, and relying on dialogue to tell the story. Our survey shows that there were enormous variations in the "faithfulness" of the adaptations during this period.

Films like GLORIFYING THE AMERICAN GIRL (1929) retained the virtual Broadway aesthetic, while ANNA CHRISTIE (1930) might be thought of as a reconstruction of O'Neill's dramatic situations using some of his lines as inspiration. Such films were faithful if they captured the spirit of the dialogue, emotional "tone," intentions, and message (at least the noncontroversial parts) of the original. Also, if the movie actors delivered their lines in the distinctive style of the stage, that made the film "theatrical" for many commentators.

These tactics—adapting well-known stage source material, augmenting Hollywood personnel with Broadway newcomers, and making movies self-consciously theatrical—were tried out, modified, and sometimes integrated with traditional filmmaking practice during this season. For example, dialogue-free moments of backstage ambience, atmosphere, or the "noise symphony" begins several films from this time. The inspiration for such introductory segments may have come from the stage; Mamoulian's production of *Porgy* and Elmer Rice's CITY STREETS, for example, began with nondialogue noise scenes (which became the archetype for the opening of LOVE ME TONIGHT [dir. Mamoulian, 1932]).[64] The eavesdropping we hear in several films from 1929–1930 (and later) had been a typical silent film narration, of course, but it was an element of stage dramaturgy which readily transposed into the talkies.

Reviewers of these films tended to react negatively toward anything which interfered too much with narrative progression, including theatrical lines. For example, THE RACKETEER (dir. Howard Higgin, 1930) was considered "one of the talkiest talkers to date." *Variety* reported that it "becomes so immersed in dialog, much of which is superfluous, that it never has time for action."[65] Depending too much on talking became associated with excess theatricality.

Incidentally, the studios' importation of New York intellectuals to work on talking-picture dialogue had the unanticipated side effect of injecting politics into Hollywood society. Among the recruited story talent was the novelist Samuel Ornitz, who was employed to write dialogue at Paramount (e.g., THE RICHEST MAN IN THE WORLD [1930], SINS OF THE CHILDREN [1930]). The Marxist playwright John Howard Lawson was hired by MGM and co-wrote dialogue for DYNAMITE (1929), THE SEA BAT (1930), and OUR BLUSHING BRIDES (1930). Two decades later they would both be among the "Hollywood Ten" witnesses jailed for refusing to cooperate with the House Committee on Un-American Activities.[66]

The question remains, Where was the pressure coming from to maintain the Hollywood film more or less as it had been without sound? One hypothetical answer might be: from within the industry's rank and file. Filmmakers feared that so-called stage techniques were too confining. John Seitz, claiming to speak for them, argued that theatrical tendencies hindered the motion pictures' novelistic liberty: "The stage, because of certain limitations, the immobility of its settings, the necessary division of a play into acts, is restricted to the one-channel type of story. It cannot achieve the freedom of a novelist who can develop a theme through a principal and many interesting, related channels, all advancing toward a desired culmination."[67] Although perhaps on shaky ground aesthetically, Seitz's equation of the cinema's spatial mobility with the novel's liberty, as opposed to the "static" theater, exemplifies a common defense of the movies.

Theater was increasingly seen as an intruder. Established Hollywood craftspeople saw the eventual failure of musicals and canned theater as a vindication of the "old way" of filming. Jack Alicoate wrote this paean to Hollywood's *auteurs:*

> Check over the past eighteen months of hectic production activity and you cannot help but come face to face with one irresistible conclusion. The successful silent director of the days before the coming of sound is the outstanding director of the talkers today. True, we have had an invasion of directors from the legitimate [theater]. A few have made good. Many more have fallen by the wayside. Probably no collective film body has had more to contend with than the director through the coming of sound. Each day brought new changes of system as well as innovations in recording. That he has been able to emerge with flying colors, still in command of the situation is an engaging tribute to the Director, who, after all, is the keystone to the temple of production. (*Film Daily,* 4 March 1930, p. 1)

Underlying this tribute to the old-time Hollywood director was a conservative view of the unfolding influence of sound on the industry. Alicoate saw the talkies as only a temporary obstacle or disruption, not the revolution that it was formerly believed to be. Theatrical influences had been dissipated. Sound had been assimilated into the Hollywood institution. New dialogue directors (with some notable exceptions, like George Cukor) had been put in their place. The old regime, led by directors like William Wellman, John Ford, Alfred E. Green, and Lubitsch, had "regained" control.

The insistence that sound films conform to traditional styles and subjects probably can also be traced to the box office. Big-budget theatrical transpositions were not bringing in sufficient revenue to support the cost of rights and stars. When models borrowed from the stage proved less successful, filmmakers were able and willing to reinstate their silent practices. Engineers and technicians were ready to accommodate them. There were significant exceptions—HELL'S ANGELS' acoustic pyrotechnics, for instance—but generally by late 1930, Hollywood films showed that producers were responding to the critics' clamor for less foregrounding of sound effects, more narrative integration of dialogue, and less aural overstimulation. But characteristically, they responded late—in the 1930–1931 season—and they overreacted, interpreting the critics' call for less noise as a call for silence.

14

The Well-Tempered Sound Track, 1930–1931

Forget art.
CARL LAEMMLE, JR., 1931

In 1930 regular customers began attending movies less frequently and spending less money. The motion picture industry cut back on production budgets, furloughed workers, and sold theaters, all the while trying to keep America's alleged movie habit alive. The talkies had lost their allure as a technological novelty and a harbinger of scientific progress. The films of the 1930–1931 season had to succeed or fail on factors other than their use of sound.

The new filmmaking was very different. Sounds were being consolidated into the unostentatious presence which the critics had been espousing for a year or so. There was even a tendency to indulge in what producers were calling "silent" technique, though no one—except Charlie Chaplin, and even he only briefly—thought that real silent filmmaking would return. Filmmakers had the technical capacity to emphasize or diminish the sound at their disposal. It could be brought in or out, up or down, made "expressive" or "inaudible," as desired. Voices and effects could be "synthetic," the term used for dubbing and adding sounds in post-production. Music could well up and fade back to underscore action and mood. The new modulated sound track constructed a heterogeneous sensory environment, but one always dominated and unified by the voice.

The technicians' increasing control of signal-to-noise in recording and playback was driven, in large measure, by a desire to improve the comprehension of human speech. Quieter recording media and directional mikes could amplify the voice above the internal noise of the thermionic system and isolate it from the unwanted sounds of the environment. The moviegoer could hear language, even softly spoken, without straining. Fans favored those actors with distinctive voices who spoke in a wide-ranging natural style and yet could soften their articulation for a more intimate effect. The boys on the lam in PUBLIC ENEMY (dir. William Wellman, 1931) can argue stridently or whisper conspiratorially and still be understood.

As ever, acoustic presence continued to be foregrounded, but was used blatantly only in comedy scenes. So when the heroes slip on a wet street in FIFTY MILLION FRENCHMAN (dir. Lloyd Bacon, 1930) a funny note on a slide whistle can accompany them. The romantic leads in THE LOTTERY BRIDE (dir. Paul Stein, 1930) still break into an unprovoked, unintegrated love song, which may be enjoyed for its own sake. "It is a pictorial contribution that causes one to wish that the performers would sing more and talk considerably less," conceded the *Times'* Mordaunt Hall. He was still impressed by sound as punctuation in MOBY DICK (dir. Lloyd Bacon, 1930): "When one hears the man in the main top shouting 'Thar she blows!' it creates a thrill such as the screen is seldom capable of affording."[1] At the same time, but with no sense of self-contradiction, Hall espoused integrating sound as "inaudible" support for the image. The modulated sound track should only call attention to itself in a few circumscribed situations. For example, Dorothy Arzner's ANYBODY'S WOMAN (1930) used a clever device to highlight sound. An electric fan "blows" a conversation across a hotel courtyard. Hall was not impressed. "This more or less ingenious notion can be accepted in an early episode, but when it crops up again in the climactic sequence the result is emphatically disappointing."[2] For the *Times* critic, this overly assertive use of sound was old-fashioned. His review of GOOD NEWS (dir. Nick Grinde, 1930) reacted specifically against the formerly impressive aesthetic of superabundance: "With sudden flaring into moonstruck ballads, 'hot-cha-cha' dance numbers and all manner of contrivances short of a balloon ascension, the story is unfolded of a college hero who has flunked in astronomy." Even Jolson's charisma failed to redeem BIG BOY (dir. Alan Crosland, 1930) because "the ancient ideas throughout the tale scarcely atone for Mr. Jolson's gift of melody."[3] THE ROYAL FAMILY OF BROADWAY (dir. George Cukor and Cyril Gardner, 1930) exemplified Hall's insistence on sound not distracting from story development. "It moves along with such sureness and rapidity that it seems over all too soon. . . . It is evident that any extraneous dilly-dallying with cinematic stunts would have interrupted the narrative." Hall attributed the film's snappy story to the original Kaufman and Ferber play, but for creating the brisk screenplay—"possibly the fastest example of film work"—he praised the directors and writers, Herman Mankiewicz and Gertrude Purcell. He mused:

> It causes one to reflect on the difference between this current offering, which incidentally was produced at Paramount's Astoria studio, and those that were put out two years ago. Here the leading rôles are performed by experienced players [Ina Claire and Fredric March], with the consequence that there is never any hesitation in their lines and their voices are admirably recorded, so well that one can't help thinking now and again of the vast progress made in the technical end of this relatively new form of entertainment. (Hall, *New York Times,* 23 December 1930)

Hall contrasted this film to the first talkies: "It is a film without the slightest sign of the old technique."

Trying to describe the specific effects of sound, Hall occasionally used the terms "sound close-up" and "sound intrusion" to describe acoustic events which stood out from the normal level of the sound track. The first term suggests an analogy to the silent-movie inserted close-up image; the second acknowledges that such effects are artificial additions to the "normal" acoustic environment. When these effects were properly orchestrated, the result could be superior to the silent film. In the review of MOBY DICK, Hall adamantly maintained that the talkie was better than the 1927 version (THE SEA BEAST) precisely because it was "enhanced by a variety of sounds and the power of speech."[4]

The movies of 1930–1931 show the effects of Hollywood's efforts to operate under tighter fiscal controls and stabilization. There were fewer releases as well as less emphasis on blockbusters and big spectacles. The musical genre breathed its last gasp (until its revival with Busby Berkeley's extravaganzas for Warners in 1933), while studios tested the gangster and Western. The comedies of this period have in common their performers' idiosyncratic voices and delivery styles, as well as the much-appreciated zany anarchism of their plots. These films attracted viewers the way pratfalls and chases did a decade earlier. Audiences seemed to be fascinated by the likes of El Brendel, the comedian with the corny Swedish accent in JUST IMAGINE (dir. David Butler, 1930), in which he plays a "sleeper" who is killed by lightning in 1930 and revived in 1980, and in THE BIG TRAIL (dir. Raoul Walsh, 1930), in which he is a henpecked immigrant settler. Moran and Mack dazzled white audiences with their "Black Crow" dialects. Stepin Fetchit drawled. Ole Olsen convulsed himself with shrill giggling. Eddie Cantor sang and joked with a Jewish inflection. Ed Wynn's high-pitched nuttiness in FOLLOW THE LEADER (dir. , 1930) was contagious. (Hall thought that "his gags could never be pictured to such advantage in a silent film.")[5] Chevalier oozed Gallic charm in PLAYBOY OF PARIS (dir. Norman Taurog, 1930). Will Rogers's southwestern vowels were welcome. Charlotte Greenwood distinguished herself "with her ear-splitting voice and thrashing movements . . ., her steady stream of slang and wisecracks."[6] These comics' vaudeville roots were clearly showing. Their voices were their living onstage, and the talkies gave them a national audience.

More subtly, melodramas and romances benefited from the ability of the camera to move in close to hear a sad crack in the voice or billets-doux spoken by lovers. Marlene Dietrich, in MOROCCO (dir. Josef von Sternberg, 1930), enthralls the listener with her world-weary throatiness, as when she tells Gary Cooper, "There's a foreign legion of women too, but we have no uniform, no medals, no flags. But we are brave."

The Musical: Welcome as the Measles

The fate of Fox's SONG O' MY HEART demonstrates the musical genre's increasing loss of favor as early as February 1930. Frank Borzage shot the film, which starred the renowned tenor John McCormack, partly on location in Ireland using Technicolor and the Grandeur process. *Variety* liked the film as a virtual performance: "The recording on McCormack is excellent, as is the judgement evidenced in the handling of all the component parts. . . . Besides, John McCormack and eleven McCormack songs for 75 cents." Yet the plot was a trifle. Obviously, because Fox had paid McCormack $500,000, it wanted to reap as many notes as possible from him. The public apparently desired something more than a cinematic concert; the film played poorly, and McCormack's option for a second film was not picked up.[7]

The box-office failure of THE KING OF JAZZ (dir. John Murray Anderson) in early 1930 was another sign that the public was tiring of the concoction of attractions constituting the revue movie.

> What it lacks most is a little more skill in its construction, for it runs from the ultra artistic to the commonplace. It is a magnificent patch work quilt clumsily sewn together, for it has everything, including trick photography, exquisite color, a cartoon sequence, some good laughs and the most stupendous sets shown to date in a screen musical. The whole affair is rather a musical cocktail centered around King Paul himself and his merry musicians. (*Film Daily*, 4 May 1930, p. 1)[8]

Hall described Warners' SWEET KITTY BELLAIRS (dir. Alfred E. Green, 1930) as "operetta-conscious in a dull way."[9] *Variety* actually liked BRIDE OF THE REGIMENT (dir. John Francis Dillon, 1930), but to the extent that it departed from the musical norm: "Containing a nicely knit story . . . with less emphasis laid on the music than most operetta talkers, *Bride of the Regiment* has a far better chance than many of the predecessors in its class." Filmmakers, the review continued, were "realizing fans are far more concerned with story and plot." CHILDREN OF PLEASURE (dir. Harry Beaumont, 1930), because it contained so many songs, was "built for the novelty era."[10] Reviews like these clearly demonstrate the pressure which studios were receiving to integrate music within a narrative—or omit it.

Why, the trades pondered, had the musical become so prevalent? "Can it be that the mental weavers of Los Angeles-by-the-Sea can think of no other tales than those about chorines, dressing rooms, soubrettes and bum comedians or has Hollywood gone so completely Broadway that nothing else matters?" queried *Film Daily*. "Too much aqua pura," *Variety* remarked in its inimitable style, "has trickled under the trestle since the backstage formula was first promulgated by Hollywood."[11]

The rapid falloff in box-office returns for musicals that began in the summer of 1930 continued during the new season, reflecting an unmistakable popular backlash against the genre. Fan magazines and exhibitors' letters to the trade press communicated the general public's increasing boredom. Samuel Goldwyn, one who listened, predicted that 50 percent fewer films would be made in 1931, with the biggest cuts in musicals: "It is ridiculous for studios to attempt to turn out fifteen to twenty musical productions a year. The best showmen on Broadway with years of experience in the field are only able to do one or two."[12] Alicoate confirmed that Hollywood was rebalancing its genres: "Reacting to box-office experience and exhibitor pleas, producers are making another reduction in the number of musicals for next season. . . . Scenario writers have been instructed to go slow on musical material." The cuts in musical production were supposed to have precipitated an "exodus of chorines from Hollywood," along with songsmiths, musicians, and assorted Broadway talent. Paramount even laid off Jeanette MacDonald.[13]

Why the change in taste? The simplest explanation is that the public was surfeited with the glut of musical movies as a genre. But some critics and industry insiders suggested that the public was dissatisfied with the content: plotless revues and excessive singing. The composer Sigmund Romberg (*The Student Prince, Viennese Nights*) complained that music and dancing failed on Hollywood screens because the producers had not adopted what he called a graduated approach to musical content:

> Did the movie producers realize the difference between a score and a song? Did any of them stop to think that a score is a unit of melodies written after careful consideration, by graduation, to bring an audience into a certain mood, or frame of mind, as the book may require? Nobody knew, or cared, that in a score, a composer, from the opening note to the closing bar, through skillful manipulation of different tempos, with different instrumentations, through different songs, plays for two and a half hours with an audience and sells them something so satisfactory that, by the end of the evening, they go out whistling his numbers and recommending the show to their friends. (Sigmund Romberg, "What's Wrong with Musical Pictures," *Rob Wagner's Script*, 2 August 1930, reprinted in Anthony Slide, ed., *The Best of Rob Wagner's Script* [Metuchen, N.J.: Scarecrow, 1985], p. 12)

Implicit in Romberg's criticism that the musical was not being approached as a whole, structured work but rather a series of "numbers" is the neglect of the function of the "book," the narrative element. The composer and lyricist should lead an audience through the operetta's structured progression. He believed that instead of canned revues, moviegoers responded to films with a story. Alfred E. Green, the Warners director, concurred: "Music must be subordinated to action."[14] The *Wall Street Journal* reported that this was the Hollywood consensus: "Film producers in planning their new production programs will endeavor to place more emphasis on the quality of entertainment and less on the mere novelty of sound. The industry has been deluged with musical revues and operettas for the screen. This fall it seems more likely that greater importance will be given to plot."[15] Alicoate wrote in "Flops of 1930" that musicals had "committed box-office hari-kari."

> A great majority of these screen musicals that came in like a lion and went out like a lamb were beautiful, but Oh! so dumb. We believe the musical talkie still has a chance regardless of the fact that it is now as welcome as the measles in most directions. *Sunny Side Up* was a smash because it combined story and action with honest-to-goodness comedy and bright tunes that one could remember. (*Film Daily*, 1 July 1930, p. 1)

Hall liked VIENNESE NIGHTS (dir. Alan Crosland, 1930) because "its none too novel narrative often captivates one's interest."[16] After a year of complaints about their lack of originality and entertainment value, Hollywood stopped releasing musicals. Does this mean that producers were following the critics' recommendations? Not necessarily—perhaps not even likely.

While the critics may articulate (accurately or not) the reasons behind audience reaction to films, only when the trend becomes a box-office reality are studios likely to react in turn. The films of the 1930–1931 season were the first to suffer the jolt of the Depression. Superabundance was expensive. These films had to do very well just to recoup the high cost of production values (which might include Technicolor photography and release prints), royalties paid to Broadway producers, and hefty fees for stars. But contrary to the general belief that hard times generated a desire for escapist fare, audiences showed little interest in these revues and musicals. Mordaunt Hall's ten-best list of 1930 films, significantly, did not contain a single musical.[17]

Several productions with a Broadway genesis were de-tuned for their movie versions. Columbia, for instance, bought the rights to the James Gleason and Maurice Marks musical *Rain or Shine,* but Capra's 1930 screen version contained no songs (only some background music from the original). Instead, it featured the comedian Joe Cook doing his balancing act circus specialty. "There may not be much to the factual story of this musical comedy now without song," wrote Hall, "but it possesses the quality of humor that is not too strained."[18] What happened to FIFTY MILLION FRENCHMEN strikingly illustrates this retreat from musicals. Warner Bros. had underwritten the original Broadway musical, which featured songs by Cole Porter, specifically for the purpose of filming it. But when the studio shot the movie, it cut out all the songs, including the soon-to-be standard "You Do Something to Me." A few Porter melodies were used as (extremely expensive!) background music. The play's love story was transformed into a filmed farce showcasing the slapstick of the Palace Theater comedy team of Olsen and Johnson. It ends with a chase in fast-motion (silent comedy style) with post-dubbed footsteps and sound effects. "With the song and dance numbers eliminated and action being substituted in their place," said *Film Daily* with approbation, "this screen adaptation of the Broadway musical success comes off as a fairly satisfying piece of comedy entertainment."[19] The tendency to strip musicals of their music (which in these cases had already been paid for by the studios) demonstrates clearly that the genre was rejected not primarily for economic reasons but rather as a response to customers' changing tastes.

As always, however, these changes were not global. Hollywood did not suddenly decide to throw aside the earliest conception of sound as a supplement and adopt the ideal of the voice-dominated environment. The films of this season were full of contradictions. In some musicals, like the above two examples, the songs were naturalized to the point of extinction. In others, song-and-dance numbers were still conspicuously encapsulated as virtual performances. (Jules Bledsoe, for example, sings "The Toreador" from *Carmen* and "Old Man River" from *Show Boat* in REMOTE CONTROL [dir. Malcolm St. Clair, Nick Grinde, 1930]). Some movies used nonstop talk, superabundant sound effects, and background music to maximize the acoustic potential of the medium; others experimented with extended nondialogue passages for a contrast effect. Even within one film some parts flaunted vocal and audio effects and other sections used sound "inaudibly." And finally, in early 1931, CITY LIGHTS was released. Because it was the most prominent new film to buck the trend and use no dialogue whatsoever, Chaplin's film was widely viewed as a test.[20] Would it stand against the talkies? Would it, as Chaplin hoped, start a return to silent filmmaking as a minority practice within Hollywood?

The Modulated Sound Track

PARAMOUNT

A film that exemplifies the direction in which Hollywood was taking sound is Josef von Sternberg's MOROCCO, starring Adolph Menjou, Gary Cooper, and Paramount's German discovery, Marlene Dietrich. Tom Brown (Cooper) is trying to forget a woman by the usual means, a stint in the French Foreign Legion. He meets Amy Jolly (Dietrich), who is also ailing from a broken heart and has renounced men altogether. She is starting her new life as (apparently) a lesbian chanteuse in a seedy nightclub. Brown catches her eye, though, and inevitably restores her to heterosexual man-worship. In the final scene, she kicks off her high heels to trek across the Sahara behind Brown's platoon. (The film leaves room for doubt as to whether this is the right choice.)

Technically, the track is rather noisy. The splices are clearly audible because they were not altogether successfully blooped. This defect, however, enables us to hear how the different effects and music tracks were assembled. There is plenty of vocal foregrounding, exploiting the accents of the principals. (Amy Jolly is supposed to be French.) Vocal background sound occurs throughout, but especially in the nightclub scenes where conversations murmur behind the exchanges between Menjou and Dietrich. The film is punctuated by sound close-ups, sometimes associated with a gratuitous inserted source image (castanets, a flapping flag) and sometimes just added for acoustic "color" (the foghorn, the howling desert wind). Rising and falling sound levels indicate approaching or receding troops on the march. Sternberg's use of sound is perhaps analogous to his stocking every scene with ubiquitous palm-leaf fans. These acoustic atmospheric effects evoke a multi-sensory experience of the existential and erotic swelter of Morocco.

Morocco *(Paramount, 1930), with Marlene Dietrich and Gary Cooper.*

But the film is also notable for its pronounced *lack* of talking in key scenes. At the opening, when Brown is setting up a date with an Arab girl (a prostitute), they communicate by glances and finger gestures. At movie's end, Brown and Jolly stare long and longingly at each other. There are no words during the entire final scene, only the rising metaphoric wind and the fading sound of a marching drum, which continues past the Paramount "The End" logo. Arthur Carew of the *Los Angeles Express* understood the significance of Sternberg's approach: "We must use dialogue sparingly, only when lines definitely highlight the character or point up the situation. Fortunately recent developments which have produced *The Blue Angel, Morocco, Outward Bound* and other cinematic gems are leading the way into a better understanding of our future needs."[21]

WARNER BROS./FIRST NATIONAL

The musical turned around to sting Warners with big losses for BIG BOY, the Jolson vehicle, and VIENNESE NIGHTS, the last of the grand talkie operettas. (Both were directed by Crosland in 1930.) Zanuck, whose studio was the most committed to the now-unpopular stage-based musical, had a strong incentive to shift production to what he called "topical" subjects. He found his ideal in a novel by W. R. Burnett, the source for LITTLE CAESAR (dir. Mervyn LeRoy, 1930). The story was transparently based on the sensational exploits of Al Capone. "Raw meat stuff reel after reel."[22] The ambitious sound track established the ambience of the gangsters' milieu. Edward G. Robinson's gravelly-voiced performance fascinated audiences and critics. But his snarling argot was something never before heard in the movies: "Yer yella, ya dirty . . . ," and, "Yeah, I'll park it. I don't need no cannon to take care of guys like you." Dialogue is used to implicate the eavesdropping movie viewer in the narrative, as when Big Boy (Sydney Blackmer) says conspiratorially, "Listen, Rico. I'm gonna talk to you, but you're not gonna hear a word I say, see? This is inside dope." Rico (Robinson) pays close attention—and so do we. In the famous opening scene, we see a dark gas station off in the distance. Shots ring out, a cash register chings, and a door slams to depict the robbery without showing it. As Sam introduces Rico to the mob, LeRoy interpolates footage shot silent with a mobile camera, flitting from face to face. The same technique is used in the tour-de-force New Year's Eve holdup of the Bronze Peacock nightclub. The sound editors have constructed a track with several planes. Crowd noises continue as Rico bursts into the lobby (filmed silent). In a series of rapidly edited views (only two to ten seconds each, joined by dissolves), Rico executes the heist. The only dialogue is a close-up of Rico barking out, "Stay where you are," just before he shoots the crime commissioner (dubbed gunshots). Outside, the sound track blends into the street noise of the city. Hall scored LITTLE CAESAR high on its story and acting: "The production is ordinary and would rank as just one more gangster film but for two things. One is the excellence of Mr. Burnett's credible and compact story. The other is Edward G. Robinson's wonderfully effective performance."[23] The actor's voice became the icon of tragic gang leaders.

The Warner "realist" cycle was under way. SINNER'S HOLIDAY (dir. John Adolfi, 1930), a squalid story of carnival life, gave the contract player James Cagney an important role. He confesses to a murder in the last scene and is led away to his execution, his voice aching with high-strung emotions. DOORWAY TO HELL (dir. Archie Mayo, 1930) starred Lew Ayres and Cagney in a supporting part. Hall appreciated the evocation of criminal atmosphere: "a plausible screen version of the underworld which will bring the flavor of familiar things to a public that has watched with growing alarm the reckless activities of

The Bronze Peacock heist in LITTLE CAESAR *(First National, 1930). As his gang fires,
Rico's (Edward G. Robinson) face is superimposed in a lingering dissolve.*

gangland."[24] Zanuck promoted Cagney over Edward Woods to play the lead in PUBLIC
ENEMY. The new star's bravura performance included individualizing mannerisms—a
sly wink, a soft punch on the chin with the fist—as well as a voice that ranges from
sweetness with his lover to shrill vulgarity (to the waiter in a speakeasy concerning a couple of drunks: "Send those two smack-offs home to their mothers"). The director,
William Wellman, utilized the relatively portable Vitaphone recording gear to open up
his story with exterior shooting (using the Warner/First National backlot street sets and
the main street of Burbank to stand in for Chicago's Michigan Avenue). These exteriors
appear to have been filmed with a single camera, but multi-camera cinematography was
used liberally on the soundstages. The scene in which Mike (Donald Cook) confronts his
brother, Tom Powers (Cagney), about his life of crime is noteworthy. The action takes
place in Mike's bedroom in the space of about eight feet. Yet apparently five cameras
were recording simultaneously: one for a frontal long-shot, one for a frontal medium-
shot, one for an oblique medium-shot from the right, and two for over-the-shoulder
shot–reverse shot close-ups during the tensest moment of the argument. In addition, the
frontal camera tracks in close, pulls back during the confrontation, then pans and tilts to
follow Cagney as he kicks the door.[25] This use of multiple cameras has little in common
with multi-camera recording of the superabundance of a big stage number; the technique instead is used to micro-analyze the dramatic scene into its component visual
parts. In addition to providing the editor with "easy" match-action cuts, the multi-camera cinematography preserves the spontaneous intensity of the performance.
Meanwhile, the sound track keeps running uncut and the recording level is unchanged

throughout. Elsewhere there is some acoustic spotting, for example, using the staccato sound of an unloading coal truck to camouflage the rival gang's machine-gun attack. But for the most part, the effects are used to create mood and dramatic unity. There is no theme song, in the sense of an encapsulated performance; rather, "I'm Forever Blowing Bubbles" emerges as a leitmotif at key moments during the film. We hear an ominous version under the main titles, a honky-tonk piano rendition, and finally, the tune playing on a phonograph record in the Powers' parlor. It symbolically hits the final groove just as Tom's mutilated body crashes over the threshold. The horror of Tom's death is emphasized by the banality of "Bubbles." The public loved the film and idolized Cagney, despite (or because of) the scenes in which he impulsively shoots a racehorse because it killed his boss and when he crams a grapefruit into his lover's face. Robert Sherwood picked up on the misogyny which runs throughout these early gangster biopics:

> Cagney's ascent to eminence during the past year has been astounding, unaccountable. He is the type who, according to all the laws and traditions, should be a competent small part player, but never a star. . . . Cagney is the first one whose appeal is based on a sock in the jaw delivered either to the man he hates or to the woman he loves (preferably the latter). Every time Cagney clenches his little fist, the audience begins to squeal with delight, and when he lands it with audible impact upon the fair countenance of Mae Clarke or Joan Blondell or Loretta Young, or whoever the unlucky girl may be, the audience's enthusiasm is unbounded. "Hit 'er again, Jimmy!" they shout in their atavistic glee. What's the reason for this? Is it possibly a manifestation of wish-fulfillment? Have the film fans been nourishing a secret desire to bust the noses of their favorite cuties? (*Film Daily*, 7 March 1932, p. 9)

FOX

Another new performer with a quirky voice would prove to be among the most important male dramatic stars to emerge during this period—but not immediately. *Film Daily* found it somewhat remarkable that Fox had chosen for a principal role in Raoul Walsh's *The Oregon Trail* an actor whose only experience had been in bits, extra work, and assisting in the Fox prop shop. Marion Michael "Duke" Morrison became John Wayne, and the film became THE BIG TRAIL, released in October 1930. (The paper found the musical score to be even more remarkable: "Strange to say, the film won't have any theme song.") Winfield Sheehan was enthusiastic about the neophyte actor with the honey voice and was "laying out big plans for a smashing meller with all the trimmings called NO FAVORS ASKED, to star John Wayne who has done big things in THE BIG TRAIL." The actor signed a long-term contract in August.[26] The story shows Breck Coleman (Wayne) and Red Flack (Tyrone Power) locked in a bitter struggle for control of the wagon train (rather like what was happening in the Fox home office). Recorded sound overlays are used extensively to create atmosphere. A distant figure sawing logs, for example, is accompanied by sounds of her work. Most of the camp scenes have the sound of dogs barking—though not coming from any visible canines. Orchestral music is used much like that in silent films. When Coleman is telling Indian stories to the children, ersatz Native American music plays. A homey tune plays as he says good-bye to his girlfriend, Ruth (Marguerite Churchill). Sometimes the balance between the planes of sound

John Wayne in THE BIG TRAIL *(Fox, 1930).*

effects is not good. On the steamboat landing, for instance, the actors can scarcely be heard through the layers of din. Hall complained that occasionally the voices did not come from the mouths of the players. (This dislocation was probably induced by the widescreen Grandeur image.) There is vocal foregrounding as Zeke (Tully Marshall) impersonates various animal calls, and Brendel speaks in his caricatural Swede dialect.

MGM

The studio produced one of the last full-fledged operettas in December 1930. Lawrence Tibbett costarred with Grace Moore, also from the Metropolitan, in a film adaptation of NEW MOON (dir. Jack Conway). (Moore's previous solo film, A LADY'S MORALS [1930], was a musical biopic about Jenny Lind that had flopped.) They sing Oscar Hammerstein II and Sigmund Romberg's original score, sometimes motivated by the plot, but sometimes not.[27]

THE BISHOP MURDER CASE (dir. Nick Grinde, 1930) was an amusing low-budget film which explored the acoustic possibilities of the detective genre. Solving the murder mystery hinges on discovering the source of a scream heard in the first scene. As Philo Vance, Basil Rathbone uses his mellifluous voice to establish his character's Sherlockian command of any crime scene (although microphone placement problems sometimes make his speech fade in and out—this film was recorded by Donald (or Frank) MacKenzie, not Douglas Shearer).[28] Prerecorded offscreen sounds help establish a dramatic space: creaking doors, footsteps, sirens, typewriter keys, a ticking clock. The plot is conceived to maximize sound clues for establishing the serial killer's method of operation (leaving nursery rhyme clues). A radio broadcast informs us when midnight arrives. Finally, like the trial films, this one indulges in a long spoken explanation of the criminal's motives and the details of the detective's reasoning.

Cecil B. DeMille's second film for MGM was his flamboyantly campy MADAM SATAN (1930), which can perhaps be described as *Ship of Fools* set on a dirigible—with show

NEW MOON (*MGM, 1930*), *souvenir program.*

tunes. A highlight is the "electrical ballet": the guests dress as spark plugs and other symbols of electricity. A reporter visiting the soundstage recalled the experience:

> Only the property man's catalogue could describe in detail what was there. Only a colorist of the Dada school could convey an impression of it. It would have made a combination of the New Orleans Mardi Gras, a sunset over Vesuvius, Broadway at night, and the Quat'z Arts Ball seem pale and repressed. It was supposed to be a fancy dress party on board the Zeppelin. . . . At the height of the festivities the Zeppelin was to break to bits, and somehow you hardly blamed it. (Mildred Adams, *Woman's Journal,* June 1930, p. 16)

The climactic zeppelin crash, with all the principal characters getting their just desserts as they parachute into various symbolically appropriate landing spots, gave DeMille a chance to enhance his spectacle with booming sound effects. But Edwin Schallert wrote in the *Los Angeles Times,* "The superabundance of sound palls, and leaves one weary."[29]

WAY FOR A SAILOR (dir. Sam Wood, 1930) was a "weak number lacking punch and with little woman appeal. [John] Gilbert [who was said to have collaborated on the writing and direction] miscast, and entire production ordinary." *Film Daily*'s scorching continued:

> It is hard to figure out just why they took the trouble to produce this one. It is one of the weakest productions on the entire M-G-M schedule. The story is pretty sordid, detailing the routine life of sailors on a merchant ship. The lives of three sailor buddies, Gilbert, Wallace Beery and Jim Tully, are high-

WAY FOR A SAILOR *(MGM, 1930) herald.*

> spotted in trips to various foreign ports. Then arrived in London, we see
> Gilbert's love affair with a girl whom he finally induces to marry him. He has
> taken some money the sailors gave him to buy a concertina, and with it gets
> himself a suit and pays the wedding bill. Business of the sailors punishing
> him for his deception, while the girl beats it on learning he is still a sailor
> although he told her he had become a civilian. And so on and so on, a flat
> tale with no appeal to the femmes. (*Film Daily,* 14 December 1930, p. 11)

Hall was kinder, allowing that Gilbert was a little better than in REDEMPTION, but only
partly successful in delivering his British accent.[30]

Vidor directed a somber A Western, BILLY THE KID (1930), with John Mack Brown.
The film has background music motivated by the Western setting and a theme song.
Billy's rendition of "The Cattle Rustler's Song" is integrated into the narrative by fore-
telling the ending ("I know that in the Great Beyond we'll sing heigh-ho"). Gunshots and
painful screams shocked viewers with the sounds of violence ("more reports of firearms
are heard here than in any other film," observed Hall). But these are contrasted with
scenes of cowboys singing around a piano, a domestic image that suggests the carving
out of a home on the wild frontier. Narrative information is conveyed through eavesdropping, as when Billy (Brown) overhears the plot to kill his boss, Tunston (Wyndham
Standing). The tune from a music box is used in ironic counterpoint to a crackling fire
as Billy flees a burning building. The sound of sizzling bacon is spotted when Pat Garrett
(Wallace Beery) fries a batch to entice the hungry Billy from his cave hideout. Slight
continuity errors between shots within scenes reveal that Vidor did not consistently use
multi-camera shooting—if he used it at all—perhaps because the film was released in
both standard 35-mm and Realife versions. Hall thought that "the views on the wide
screen are so compelling that when one goes to see a picture on an ordinary sized screen
the standard image looks absurdly small."[31]

Marie Dressler won an Academy Award for her performance in MIN AND BILL.
George Hill, as he had done in THE BIG HOUSE, brought the camera in close for melodramatic intensity. Dressler's face graphically registers Min's warring emotions when she
says farewell to her adopted daughter Nancy (Dorothy Jordan), who is leaving the
shabby wharf to marry the scion of a wealthy Boston clan. Unknown to the daughter,
Min has just shot Nancy's biological mother (Marjorie Rambeau) to prevent her from
revealing her lower-class origins. There is noticeably less foregrounding of sound effects
than in Hill's previous work. Instead, natural sounds suggest an audible bouquet of the
seedy waterfront just offscreen. Sound also constructs screen space with architectural
precision, inviting the viewer to infer an imaginary relationship between the sets. In the
boardinghouse barroom, an unseen piano is heard. As Min goes upstairs to her room,
the piano sound fades to an intermediate level when she is in the hall outside her door,
then to a barely audible level when she enters her room. (The changes were evidently
done by mixing a prerecorded track in post-production.) When Bill (Wallace Beery)
peeps through her keyhole from outside, the piano reverts back to the louder "hall
tone." It resumes its nearly inaudible level when he enters her room, diminishes, then
disappears, ignored by all but the most acoustically attentive listeners.

The gin-soaked voices of Dressler, Beery, and Rambeau are crucial in establishing
their plebeian social status. Nancy's transformation from low-class gamine to prep-school
graduate worthy of a high-society marriage is conveyed by costume, by bearing, and
especially by the change in Jordan's voice, which goes from common to cultured.

RKO

Radio Pictures' initial box-office success quickly dissipated. DIXIANA (dir. Luther Reed, 1930) cost a fortune but was unpopular with critics and lost money. Ambitious pre-production plans for a stereoscopic, all-Technicolor extravaganza were greatly scaled back, but it remained a lavish production. Bebe Daniels is Dixiana, a singer and juggler in a New Orleans circus in the 1840s. She is courted by Carl Van Horn, the son of a Pennsylvania Dutch family which has inherited a great plantation. Dixiana leaves Carl, played by the Metropolitan Opera star Everett Marshall, to save his honor when his stepmother will not allow a déclassée actress in her house. The comedy duo Wheeler and Woolsey provide mild slapstick, including a running gag about picking up some cigars and getting a kick in the pants. The technical difficulties Reed had with sound in RIO RITA have been brought under control, but in DIXIANA there is much less creative experimentation. Some songs are encapsulated performances, as when Dixiana sings from the music-hall stage. Others develop spontaneously operetta-style in duets with Carl. Hall, who may have been contradicting his ongoing campaign for better integrated musicals, but who always liked a good song, wrote of Marshall, "His singing is a distinct asset to this production, so much so that one wishes there was more of it and less of the somewhat futile attempt at a story." Bill "Bojangles" Robinson also dances an encapsulated tap routine, his only appearance in the film. New York audiences responded to it with applause.[32]

DANGER LIGHTS (dir. George B. Seitz, 1930) contains its share of foregrounded sound effects to capture the auditory environment of its rail-yard setting. The film premiered in the Spoor-Berggren Natural Vision widescreen format, with sound on a separate track, but in most cities the film played in the normal 35-mm Photophone format. Train whistles, a rock slide, and the acoustic spectacle of a tug-of-war between two locomotives thrilled the listener. Its sound-recording engineer, Carl Dreher, designed many scenes to showcase his new parabolic microphone. Nevertheless, in the scenes shot on location in the train yard, the loud background noises frequently occlude the characters' speech. Elsewhere, ambitious and more successful attempts are made to isolate characters' dialogue as they move around the set, as in the bar scene. By holding the parabolic mike on a character and *not* following him as he left the picture—for example, in Doyle's shower scene—an effect of acoustic depth was created. Several times the camera (and sound) reframes by tracking into a close two-shot.

RKO's monumental Western CIMARRON, adapted from Edna Ferber's novel and directed by Wesley Ruggles, is a sprawling story inspired by the settling of what became Oklahoma. The saga highlights the heroism of Yancey Cravat (Richard Dix), a newspaper editor and family man who is not above shooting a bad guy in church. The film is a good example of the successfully modulated sound track: gunfights, stampedes, and land rushes are wildly raucous; the printing press operator has a comic stutter; and the intimate moments between Dix and Irene Dunne are punctuated with long silences. It was voted best picture by the Academy for 1931.

UNIVERSAL

The case of Universal, though unique, is instructive. Having ventured into the pricey domain of "quality" production, the studio executives retreated to familiar genres when the financial risk increased. The Laemmles knew from experience that the public

CIMARRON *(RKO, 1931) two-sheet poster.*

wanted to be scared by Gothic thrillers. THE CAT CREEPS (1930), directed by PHANTOM's Rupert Julian, was a talking remake of THE CAT AND THE CANARY (dir. Paul Leni, 1927). It was nondescript. DRACULA (dir. Tod Browning, 1931) was, on the contrary, a big hit. It, too, was a quasi-remake, heavily influenced by Murnau's classic NOSFERATU (1922). The sound track is rich in ambient effects (including the Count's "children of the night") that conjure a creepy atmosphere (analogous to Murnau's stock-footage inserts of weird nocturnal creatures). "As the scenes flash by," smiled Hall, "there are all sorts of queer noises, such as the cries of wolves and the hooting of owls, not to say anything of the screams of Dracula's feminine victims, who are found with twin red marks on their white throats."[33] Hungarian-born Bela Lugosi's liquid, if sepulchral, voice had just the right mixture of seduction and Transylvanian chill.

COLUMBIA

CHARLEY'S AUNT (dir. Al Christie, 1930) was a remake of the Christie brothers' 1925 production. It was canned theater, preserving the three-walled set which provided plenty of doors and windows for entrances and exits. It used sound to foreground the "Oxford" accents of the characters and their student slang. Charlie Ruggles steals the show with his unique vocalization full of stutters and verbal double takes and, of course, his falsetto when dressed in drag as the aunt from Brazil, "where the nuts come from."

UNITED ARTISTS

It was still Goldwyn and Schenck who powered United Artists. Samuel Goldwyn's 1929 partnership with Flo Ziegfeld paid off. Goldwyn had agreed to back Ziegfeld's next productions, including WHOOPEE! and *Simple Simon* (starring Ed Wynn), in exchange for the film rights.[34] In the plot—or more accurately, the excuse—for Eddie Cantor's musical mishaps in WHOOPEE! (dir. Thornton Freeland, 1930), he is a hypochondriac, Henry Williams, who goes west for his health. He resists the attentions of Miss Custer (Ethel Shutta), his passionate nurse, but seems to have more of an eye for Wanenis, the half–Native American who is in love with Sally, who is eloping with Henry to avoid marrying Sheriff Bob Wells, who is after Henry for . . . get the picture? After disguising himself in blackface and passing as a Jewish Indian, Henry somewhat reluctantly proposes to Nurse Custer. He looks into the camera and signs off with his tag line, "That's all there is." "The film is completely Technicolor, is gorgeously costumed and alluringly musical. There is no attempt at realism," said *Film Daily* approvingly, referring to the stylized Art Deco–influenced southwestern sets, flamboyant clothes, and Busby Berkeley dance routines, complete with his overhead "kaleidoscope" shots of dancers. The climax is a procession of showgirls mounted on horseback wearing increasingly outrageous headdresses—and not much else. Cantor exudes high spirits and cracks gratuitous Jewish in-jokes ("I could never be an aviator—" [rolls eyes] "Can't eat sandwiches").[35] In "My Baby Just Cares for Me," he kids his rivals in the talkies:

> My baby don't care for Lawrence Tibbetts [*sic*],
>   She'd rather have me to kibitz.
> Chuck Rogers is not her style,
>   Or even Chevalier's smiles.

The heralds for WHOOPEE! *(United Artists, 1930) emphasized the movie as virtual Broadway at bargain prices.*

Scott Berg has observed that WHOOPEE! is significant as a direct transposition of a Ziegfeld revue to the screen, "one of the most telling fossils of that extinct genre—with all its nonsensical convolutions of plot, unexplained comedic star turns, and burstings into song." Contemporary urban audiences evidently liked those aspects and liked Cantor too; the film grossed $2.6 million. However, the production cost diminished Goldwyn's profits. The film failed in smaller and regional markets, prompting Goldwyn to rethink how he marketed Cantor nationally.[36] WHOOPEE! is also an example of a film which used sound simply as a means of recording music and voice, while scarcely calling attention to itself as a means of expression.

Douglas Fairbanks announced he was remaking THE MARK OF ZORRO (1920) as a talkie—he never did. He did, however, take over REACHING FOR THE MOON (dir. Edmund Goulding, 1931), an Irving Berlin project costarring Bebe Daniels. He completed it and previewed it as a musical with five of Berlin's songs. But the genre was considered to be such box-office poison that he recut the film and released it with only one musical interlude. "It's a suave, 1930 model Doug Fairbanks who frolics through this clever piece of entertainment, set against a lavish background of Wall Street, Park Ave. and a modernistic ocean liner," said *Film Daily* appreciatively. "The dialogue is swift and sophisticated."[37]

Mary Pickford's KIKI (dir. Sam Taylor, 1931), unfortunately, was a flop: "Mary Pickford seems miscast in hoydenish and very artificial role that lacks conviction," observed

Adolphe Menjou and Pat O'Brien in THE FRONT PAGE *(United Artists, 1931).*

Film Daily. Again, accents were a problem. "Miss Pickford manages a French accent surprisingly well for the most part, though she lapses from dialect often enough to hurt any illusion she hoped to create along that line," said Hall.[38] She made one more talkie in 1933, then retired from the screen.

Lewis Milestone directed THE FRONT PAGE (1931), adapted from the hit comedy play by Ben Hecht and Charles MacArthur. Howard Hughes's Caddo Productions produced it for distribution through United Artists. Though eclipsed today by Hawks's remake HIS GIRL FRIDAY (1940), the original version is really an extraordinarily fast-paced and lively film. In many ways it is the antithesis of the stereotypical early sound movie. Milestone's camera roams the sets on its prototype Bell and Howell Rotoambulator, a three-wheeled dolly capable of tight turns. The scene in which Walter Burns (Adolphe Menjou) descends to the shipping area of his plant was shot on location in a real newspaper building using artificial lighting. As he strolled, the camera whisked along on tracks, panning to keep him framed. Meanwhile, location sound recording captured the roar of the machinery and shouts of the workers. For the most part, the construction of the film went back to silent technique—single-camera, multiple-take cinematography and fast editing. The scenes in the newspaper office, in particular, use shots of only a couple seconds' duration to build up a frenetic atmosphere. The reporters' wisecracks, punctuated by ringing telephones and the gratuitous noise of one of them plucking a banjo, show the chaos of their professional lives.

CITY LIGHTS *and* LE MILLION: *Silence Is Golden*

In the fall of 1930, Charles Chaplin was still shooting CITY LIGHTS. He stridently reassured his fans, "My own pictures will *always* be silent." Furthermore, he believed that there were enough like-minded producers to justify forming a company to satisfy what he called "a strong market for inaudible pictures." He was allocating $5–10 million for a new studio in the San Fernando Valley where he would direct two silent dramas annually and produce five silent features a year by other directors. (He did not plan to appear in these films himself.)[39]

Chaplin hoped that CITY LIGHTS would revive the silent film. His dream of starting his own studio to produce nondialogue features was still alive on the eve of the premiere. The press book heralded: "CITY LIGHTS Is Expected to Change Trend of Film World. . . . Movie Prophets Predict Avalanche of Talkless Pictures as a Result."[40] The director seized every opportunity to denounce dialogue films, but now he conceded that they were here to stay:

> I shall never speak in a film. I hate the talkies and will not produce talking films. The American industry is transformed. So much the better or worse, it leaves me indifferent. I cannot conceive of my films as other than silent. My shadow appears on the screen as in a dream, and dreams do not speak. Artists, like Will Rogers, Bebe Daniels, Gloria Swanson, Bessie Love are interested in interpreting the talking films because they are thus able to present the maximum of their talent. But they are actors; as for me, I am a mime and all the nuances of my art would be destroyed if I were to accompany them with words or with sound effects. (Quoted in *Theatre Arts Monthly*, November 1930, p. 908)

The long-awaited premiere of CITY LIGHTS took place on Friday, 30 January 1931. Los Angeles police estimated that fifty thousand fans tried to catch a glimpse of the star. Two police officers escorted Chaplin to his seat in the theater. True to his word, Chaplin released the film with a music score, but without dialogue.

The *New York Times* recognized Chaplin's intention; the headline announced, "Takes Fling at 'Talkies.'" The trade papers treated the film as a test case. Would Chaplin's reputation keep silents viable? "The lively controversy which it was predicted would be started by Charlie Chaplin's *City Lights* is now raging, following the premier of the picture Friday night at the new Los Angeles [theater]," *Film Daily* reported. "Praise of the silent comedy is enthusiastic, but opinions are sharply at variance on the point of whether it will influence any appreciable trend back to silents. The majority so far think not."[41] The *Record* gave a typical pronouncement: "*City Lights*, though it was received with whole-hearted delight and punctuated with innumerable bursts of applause from the audience, is no menace for the talkies. It is the exception that proves the rule."[42] In January 1931, the American film industry had long passed the point at which it could have reverted to silent production even had it wanted to—and it did not.

The Los Angeles reception of Chaplin's film seems to have tempered his feelings about the future of silents. He admitted as much when he was interviewed in New York upon arriving to attend the 6 February premiere at the George M. Cohan Theater. Silent pictures, he conceded, would never return, but he was still confident that a num-

CITY LIGHTS (*United Artists, 1931*).

ber of films would be made without dialogue. The new studio he had claimed to be establishing was no longer mentioned. Now he even foresaw directing a talker of his own, but never acting in one. He announced that a current project (never to materialize) would have a Spanish theme and be dialogue-free.[43]

In New York, despite a skirmish with United Artists about the publicity, rental, and admission price that caused Chaplin to take over the premiere himself, CITY LIGHTS succeeded fabulously.[44] But clearly the film failed to open the door to a new kind of "talk-less" picture, in part because it was quite old-fashioned, not only in its technique but in its story. Alexander Bakshy, in *The Nation,* derided the director's mawkishness: "Chaplin's growing seriousness, his desire to be more than a mere comedian deceived him into holding sentiment more precious than fun."[45]

CITY LIGHTS' success was not transferable, either to other films or to other actors. Most commentators saw Chaplin as a unique genius. Alicoate discussed this pyrrhic victory:

> The irresistible Mr. Chaplin paid Broadway his tri-ennial visit last evening and as usual Mr. Chaplin sent home the smartest first night audience of the season again singing his praises as the greatest pantomimist of all time. *City Lights* is all silent and typically Chaplinesque in its mixture of laughs, tears, pathos and slapstick. The story, although episodic, hits the high spots with delightful frequency. As to the question of sound vs. silent, this Chaplin affair settles nothing. Chaplin is king. He can do no cinema wrong. He could turn handsprings anywhere in filmland where others would not dare to tread. For instance, here he even gives sound the merry raspberry via travesty and it is as delicious a screen morsel as one will find. If *City Lights* does nothing else it will demonstrate that Silence is Golden, at least in this instance, and as far as *City Lights* the box-office is concerned. (*Film Daily,* 8 February 1931, p. 1)

For the New York critics, the director-star's performance eclipsed the sound issue: "Chaplin is so perfect and his comedy inventions are so distinguished," offered the *Herald-Tribune,* "that even those of us who are enthusiasts for the speechless manner will realize that [CITY LIGHTS'] success is due to its star's perfection in his medium." The *Journal's* argument was expressed as simple logic: "*City Lights* is entertaining, and entertainment is a quality that is not limited to any one medium. Therefore the absence of dialogue in this production raises no argument on the subject of speech versus silence." According to the *World*, "The fact that *City Lights* is told by pantomime rather than by spoken dialogue goes practically unnoticed in witnessing the picture."[46] *Film Daily's* commentator wrote that Chaplin's refusal to go talkie was good business sense: "And why have so many screen idols with good voices crashed since they started to talk in the talkies? So Charlie, the Wisest of 'em All, preserves his Mystery and Elusiveness in *City Lights* by not using his Voice. For Charlie knows better than anybody that his great comedy talent alone would not keep him perennially popular."[47]

CITY LIGHTS was a lucrative testament to Chaplin's incredible star power. It made millions in profits worldwide during the bleakest years of the Depression. But it was neither a turning point nor the swan song of the silent film. As an idiosyncratic vehicle for Chaplin, it did not seriously challenge sound production practices, either by showing the superiority of silent acting technique or by repudiating the aesthetic inroads made by the talkies. It should be pointed out that CITY LIGHTS is not the "pure" silent film that Chaplin and reviewers publicized. Its score was carefully arranged (by Chaplin and Arthur Johnston) to closely complement the action, exactly like the music for synchronized features circa 1928. Hall shrewdly commented, "There are times when the notes serve almost for words."[48] There are two scenes which foreground dialogue by parodying it. The now-famous opening sequence finds the Little Tramp asleep on a monumental statue during its public unveiling ceremony. The dignitaries speak, but farty squawks emanate from their mouths instead of words. Chaplin equated lip-synched speech with highbrow pomposity and flatulent bourgeois complacency. Later Chaplin swallows a whistle, and its notes substitute for his voice. "This is what I think of your dialogue film," he seems to be expostulating. One aspect of the plot of CITY LIGHTS dramatizes Chaplin's theoretical position. The Little Tramp befriends a blind flower girl (Virginia Cherrill). Through many tragicomic mishaps, he provides her with enough money to have an operation that gives her sight. The emphasis on vision as necessary to being a whole person argues for its special status relative to speech and hearing. This, of course, is also the privileged sensory mode of the silent cinema.

CITY LIGHTS did confirm that dialogue was not a strict requirement to carry a film to a great critical or popular success. A movement to go back to silent technique was already in the air. It was not that anyone wanted to make silent movies again per se. Some proponents wanted to return to the practice of single-camera cinematography, but others were usually advocating that the all-talking, all-singing film be superseded by movies with modulated techniques which would enable talkies to utilize some formal conventions of silent production, if that was the desired effect. Producers were alternating nondialogue passages with talking and limiting background music to underscoring dramatic moments. The modulated sound track concept guarded a special place for silence. Alicoate noted that audiences were finding talk boring: "Pictorially you can hold almost any audience if the action is sufficiently thrilling, enticing or entertaining. Trying to hold that self-same audience with a two-hour load of inane, stupid talk is quite another and more difficult problem. Of course, every writer of dialogue cannot be constantly brilliant, but one thing is certain, unless he is continuously entertaining his picture cannot be commercially successful."[49]

Another inspiration for the so-called silent technique was found in René Clair's Parisian comedy LE MILLION, which opened in New York in May 1931. Clair deeply admired Chaplin and may have had the implications of the theme of restored vision in CITY LIGHTS in mind when he made his famous statement, "A blind man attending a true dramatic work and a deaf man attending a real film, even though they are both losing an important part of the work being presented, would not lose the essential part"[50] Unlike Chaplin, who repudiated the talkies in CITY LIGHTS, Clair seized upon sound with a vengeance, playfully foregrounding its artificiality. In contrast to, say, WHOOPEE!, in which the acoustic dimension is subsidiary to the performance and the auditor is encouraged to ignore the sound, LE MILLION never lets us forget that the acoustic component is as much a construction as the whitewashed sets. Clair's offbeat musical romance built around the pursuit of a winning lottery ticket replaced dialogue with actors singing and talking in rhyming couplets. Clair created teasing confusions between on- and off-screen sound. He also experimented with asynchronous audio tricks, as in the famous scene in which a chase after a coat is synched to the cheers of an invisible football (or rugby) crowd. The surprisingly strong response and the enormous acclaim for Clair's film excited critics. His simplified plot, minimized dialogue, and reliance on "pantomime" revealed an economical yet pleasing way to make a sound film. Why this style was misnamed "silent" is unfathomable, but the end product was certainly differ-

René Lefevre and Annabella in LE MILLION *(Tobis-Forenfilm, 1930).*

ent from the effect of the modulated sound track. *Film Daily* advised domestic film-makers to learn from this new international style: "The tendency is toward a return of the expressive pictorial technique of the silent film, with sound, music and a limited amount of dialogue in the background, the idea being that pictures of this type have the best chance of breaking through the barriers of all countries."[51] Joseph Schnitzer, president of Radio Pictures, announced a return to silent film technique for his company's 1931–1932 season:

> Dialogue will be minimized and used only to serve a similar purpose to the printed title, namely, to motivate the action and clarify situations. This move will serve two important purposes. Firstly, the novelty of sound is wearing off. By that I mean, the American public at first was anxious to have every click and footstep recorded in sound. Those times have passed. Combining silent picture technique with sound will do away with uninteresting talking sequences where two people sit at a table and talk for five or ten minutes without any action whatever. Secondly, the picture will be more adaptable to foreign versions. (*Film Daily,* 13 July 1931, pp. 1, 11)

Everyone, including Hollywood moguls, enjoyed Chaplin's little joke and LE MILLION's creativity. These films may have influenced a few comedy productions. Keaton's PARLOR, BEDROOM AND BATH (dir. Edward Sedgwick, 1931), and Harold Lloyd's FEET FIRST (dir. Clyde Bruckman, 1930), for example, contain more "pantomime" than the previous talkies of those two actors.[52] For several industry spokespersons and popular critics as well, restoring the techniques of the past became a rallying cry. Whether these films and their commentators' favorable remarks actually had significant impact on Hollywood production is difficult to ascertain. Universal Pictures announced in June that it would remake LE MILLION in English—but it never did. Cecil B. DeMille did call for more old silent picture technique, with dialogue used as an auxiliary. There is not the slightest trace of an effort to do so in his third and final MGM production, THE SQUAW MAN (1931), a remake of his Western done previously in 1914 and 1918. Recalling the Warner Proportion of 1928–1929, Paramount announced that its new comedy formula was 90 percent action mixed with 10 percent dialogue. The *Film Daily* poll reported a more moderate exhibitor consensus that 25 percent dialogue was about right.[53]

Mass or Class?

The ideal of the modulated sound track did not develop in an economic vacuum. The Depression reached Hollywood by way of the box office in the fall, at the beginning of the 1930–1931 exhibition season. Hollywood, having no inclination to take unnecessary risks, joined other industries in reorganizing for the uncertain economic environment. In line with other aspects of production, sound had to be used as efficiently and predictably as possible, and thus producers needed to disseminate standard practices and conform to conventional styles. The directors and technicians who turned out routine weekly releases, Hollywood's bread and butter, quickly absorbed sound production as another workaday task.[54]

The use of theatrical material was discredited by critics. In Jack Alicoate's opinion,

> that a new writing technique must be cut and tailored to fit the sound screen
> is universally recognized. . . . In the present situation the re-vamping of the
> old silents into talker come-backs will help for a while but it's simply taking
> the easiest way. Lifting material bodily from the legitimate stage and trans-
> planting it on the talkative celluloid will do only in spots. Probably more than
> fifty per cent of stage material, both past and present, is utterly unfit for
> screen use. (*Film Daily,* 10 March 1930, p. 1)

Thornton Delehanty wrote in the *New York Evening Post,*

> The terrible examples of screen plays which have derived from the stage are
> those in which the content has been lifted bodily from one medium to the
> other. That was what happened with practically all of the earlier talkies, and
> it is why so many discerning people threw up their hands in horror when
> sound supplanted silence in the motion picture realm. Even today, when
> definite advances have been made toward a distinct talking picture tech-
> nique, it is seldom that a stage play successfully survives the transcription to
> the talking screen. (Quoted in *Film Daily,* 11 March 1930, p. 6)

Gilbert Seldes, writing in the *Evening Graphic,* was instrumental in popularizing the
notion that filmmakers must adapt sound to an ideal cinematic essence: "If the talkies
stop emphasizing dialogue and go in for conversation; if they discard their feeble idea of
keeping speakers in view; if they learn to use speech and other sound as active parts in
a great harmony, of which the moving picture is another part, then they will begin to
make a new art of themselves."[55] Seldes's notion of a "great harmony" provides as good
a definition as any of the modulated sound track.

There was a perception among critics (whether true or not would require a statistical survey) that fewer plays and more novels and magazine stories were being adapted.
(The "original screenplay" was still a rarity.) "The connecting link between screen and
fiction was strengthened during 1931," concluded *Film Daily.* "Reading tastes coincided with the public's taste for motion pictures as is shown by the fact that some 150
books, ranging from the classics to best-sellers of today, had been filmed."[56] Now that
the sound film had become almost universal, Alicoate warned producers of the risk of
being overintellectual:

> Each [literary source was] an artistic success and each, apparently, some-
> thing the great ninety per cent did not care particularly to see. The motion
> picture industry and its army of dependents cannot exist or carry on to the
> tune of raving critics or the approval of a decidedly intellectual minority. Its
> definite duty is to provide the great ninety per cent with the type of screen
> entertainment it prefers. [That] catering to a hundred million is naturally a
> leveling experience, is obviously rather clearly defined. Until the public,
> generally, respond to the subtle and more intellectual aspect of screen writ-
> ing, direction and production, the process of reincarnating the motion pic-
> ture to the point of intelligentsia-complex, must, of economic and financial

necessity, be at least temporarily held in abeyance. In other words, the public evidently prefers to laugh and be amused, and not to have to think. (*Film Daily,* 19 March 1931, pp. 1, 2)

Contradicting commentators like Alicoate, the public had also cultivated a dislike for comics and musicals. The trade critic Gillette aptly observed in "Another Theory Gets a Jolt" that, despite the cry from theater managers that the public wanted laughter, only three of the thirteen top-grossing films in the 1930–1931 season were comedies.[57] Social problem and gangster films performed unexpectedly well, a fact which did not go unnoticed by moralists.

Whether cinema did or should appeal to an elite or to a mass audience had always been a fundamental question of cinema. The Laemmles of Universal were characteristically blunt. Carl Senior reacted to a Sherwood column which supported the Hays Office's call for cleaned-up films and ads: "You favor advertising with the 'highest esthetic appeal,'" retorted Laemmle. "You might get by with that if you were running a theater for esthetes, Mr. Sherwood, but I hope for your sake you never experiment with it elsewhere, unless you are backed by a bank roll which can weather a permanent business depression." Carl Junior could not have said it more plainly: "Forget art. . . . Our mission is to furnish entertainment, not to educate the public or foster propaganda. Stick to the proven essential of show business—make pictures for the vast inarticulate public—stop trying to please the arty and articulate critics. The mob who made the film industry possible and prosperous always will be your best customers."[58] The flip-flop in attitude by the producer of the urbane KING OF JAZZ and Remarque's prestigious ALL QUIET ON THE WESTERN FRONT is amazing. Universal, smitten by a negative cash flow, was henceforth staking its fortune on Bela Lugosi's vampire and, soon, Boris Karloff's monster. This conception of the movie audience as a lower-class mob might explain the moguls' and exhibitors' tendency to restrain experimentation and to standardize sound. With the industry in depression, there would be little incentive to adapt properties which appealed to an elite audience or to indulge in risky ventures like unorthodox audio techniques.

The short life span of the virtual Broadway concept in feature production suggests that literal transposition from stage to film was never a viable style. The industry's efforts over the previous years had been channeled into creating a sound track which would enhance the film with dialogue without reveling in its technological origins. Hollywood had developed sound into an all-purpose mechanism. The same equipment and technicians could record and construct a sound track for screwball comedies, melodramas, or musicals. Hollywood had mastered the technical challenge of sound and was prepared to give audiences traditional movies with stories, not overt theatrical presentations such as vaudeville acts, opera selections, or upper-class melodrama. Though films would never again be silent, the production process was once again routine. And going to the movies was fundamentally the same experience it had been a few years before sound.

15

The Sound of Custard: Shorts, Travelogues, and Animated Cartoons

A tenet of the "evening's entertainment" concept of the movies was that the program had to be varied and diverting. Short subjects acted as a buffer, a curtain-raiser to prepare the audience for the feature that followed. Another important function of the one- or two-reel productions of the classic period was to ensure that the program as a whole would appeal to an audience diversified by age, gender, education, and general interest. Some viewers would like sports more than fashion shows, some would prefer travelogues to cartoons. Sound added to the novelty value of shorts, opened up a new world of verbal comedy, and provided filmmakers with a laboratory in which the new technology could be tested and fine-tuned.

Short Subjects

Vitaphone maintained the substantial lead it had established for its sound shorts by increasing the frequency of releases to four pictures a week in 1928. The schedule was divided into three categories. The Vitaphone Presentations, which included musical numbers of the sort found on the first Vitaphone programs, were heavy on opera, jazz, and comedy monologues. As the series name implies, these continued the virtual Broadway tradition and substituted for presentation acts. Vitaphone aggressively signed performers from the legitimate stage. Robert Ober, Irene Rich, Charles Ruggles, Daphne Pollard, Winnie Lightner, Jack Benny, Jay C. Flippen, and Karyl Norman ("The Creole Fashion Plate," a female impersonator appearing at the Palace) were listed as the top attractions of 1928.[1]

The Vitaphone Playlets were all-talking adaptations of theatrical pieces and original comedies. Generally, they were two reels long (about twenty minutes). Subjects ranged from "heavy melodrama" (for example, THE BEAST [1928]) to "a fair amount of comedy" (THE NIGHT COURT [1928]).[2] Vitaphone Varieties included assorted novelty series and were produced on both coasts. An advertisement emphasizes the different appeals: one promises virtual Broadway, the other the voices of Hollywood stars:

Let the diplomats parley, let the pacifists rave, but the most furious war in history wages on right under their collective nose. It's a bloodless battle, of course, but Broadway versus Hollywood is the cinema Battle of the Century.

Vitaphone Varieties, the entertaining short subjects, offer a field of honor for the struggle. Two studios, one in Hollywood and one in Brooklyn produce the Varieties. On the Western front, we find screen favorites in the casts, while the Brooklyn studio garners the cream of Broadway "names."

The movie veterans laugh as they talk of "screen personality" and "screen technique." The stage folk offer "stage presence" and "speaking voice" in rebuttal. (Reproduced in *Vitaphone News* 2, no. 11 [Winter 1993–1994]: p. 8)

Several of these forays into "screen technique" provided an opportunity to test methods and subjects not explored in features. All-talking shorts had been tried out in late December 1927, with the one-reel MY WIFE'S GONE AWAY and the two-reel SOLOMON'S CHILDREN. Bryan Foy's Flatbush unit seemed to encourage formal innovation. An unusual treatment of the sound track occurs in OVERTONES (1928), reviewed by *Photoplay:* "It's one thing to listen in on two middle-aged women, each jealous of the other, having a tea fight. But it's quite another to hear their respective inner-selves snarling at each other while honeyed words flow on the surface." The critic found the

Spencer Tracy and Katherine Alexander in THE HARD GUY *(Warner Bros., 1930).*

effect of the offscreen interior monologue voices confusing, demanding to know "just what IS the Vitaphone aiming at, anyway."[3] Among the 1929 experiments was HIGH WATERS, which played with the abstract notion of audiovisual counterpoint as it intercut shots of the singer Guy Robertson with footage of the recent Mississippi flood. Some of these films were nonsensical. TINY TOWN REVUE (1929) was "an aggregation of midgets who do several snappy jazz numbers." For some reason, *Film Daily* thought that "women, in particular, will go for this."[4] For many New York actors, these playlets were recognition of a job well done onstage. Spencer Tracy, fresh from a stint as a gangster in *The Last Mile*, appeared in THE HARD GUY (1930). For him and a few others, the one-reel drama was a stepping-stone to a film career. In CRIMES SQUARE (1931), Lil (Mary Doran) asks Marty (Pat O'Brien), "You're comin' back to me or you're gonna finish that stretch you walked out on?" Her "urban" voice goes with her floozy character, consistent with the trend in feature films (like MIN AND BILL). A cut in the middle of this sentence bridges a match-action cut from long- to medium-shot.

Among the most successful productions were the short comedies by Mr. and Mrs. Jack Norworth. The first release was THE NAGGER (1929), "a bedtime scene between a suspicious wife, who is obsessed with curiosity about 'that other woman,' and a fibbing husband who is trying to grab off some sleep. The Norworths, past masters of the variety stage in this sort of comedy, put it over with a wallop. Laughs follow each other with practically no letup." Gregory Ratoff was another favorite. In FOR SALE (1930) he demonstrated his popular shtick, a telephone monologue in which he impersonated a tenacious salesman with his humorous Yiddish accent.[5] George Burns and Gracie Allen recreated their vaudeville routine in the short LAMBCHOPS. After their dialogue, which is spiced with many asides to the camera, they end with a song and pretend to have run out of material.

GEORGE: That's funny—We're supposed to be off the screen. What'll we do?
GRACIE: I know a little story—I made it up.
GEORGE: Well that'll get us off—maybe never on again. (*He asks her to whisper the story to him. She looks at the camera, says, "Pardon me," and whispers.*)
GEORGE: That's the story?
GRACIE: Yeah.
GEORGE: Well, we finally got off—Now get outa here. (*They exit.*)

Such films disseminated New York performances (with their distinctive mannerisms and accents) around the country.

The original Vitaphone concept remained intact. Instead of packaging shorts with Warner Bros. features, the company was building a library of varied subjects which exhibitors could rent individually to play with any program, much as they previously had done with live acts.[6] Thus, during the period of increasing uniformity of filmed entertainment, the shorts on the program were almost the last bastion of the independent owner's effort to individualize his program. Not only did Vitaphone take an early commanding lead in this market, they became the artistic model for all short film production, inspiring other companies to set up shop in New York in order to tap the rich talent of Broadway, radio, and the record industry.

The Fox Movietone Entertainments are a good example. They were being turned out in New York at irregular intervals until January 1928, when they went into national distribution. These one- and two-reelers were designed specifically to compete with the

LAMBCHOPS *(Warner Bros., 1929), with George Burns and Grace (later Gracie) Allen.*

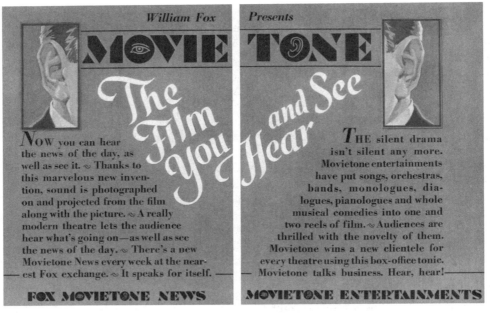

Movietone News and Entertainments advertisement, May 1928.

Vitaphone shorts, offering "vaudeville, band concert, and operatic presentations." The first number included material which had played at the Roxy for almost a year: Raquel Meller, Ben Bernie and his orchestra, and Chic Sale. Future releases were to be condensed screen versions of musical comedies.[7] Notable among the new numbers were the shorts filmed by Ruby Keeler and Robert Benchley. RUBY KEELER (1928) reproduced the nineteen-year-old dancer's tap-dance routine from her vaudeville act, "a short, but good peppy number." (In September 1928, she would marry Al Jolson.) THE TREASURER'S REPORT (1928) was Benchley's monologue as a nervous stuttering church treasurer.[8] His stand-up lecture on the SEX LIFE OF THE POLYP (1928) kept "loud guffaws of laughter coming from all over the theater." The biggest hit among audiences, however, was AT THE BALL GAME (1928), a vaudeville skit by Joe Cook. "It kept the audience in a constant spasm of laughter. . . . It's a natural for Movietone purposes, and Joe's voice gets across distinctly."[9] THE HAPPINESS BOYS (1928) featured the popular radio group performing its theme song and other numbers. Fox also produced some serious shorts to compete with the Playlets. THE LASH (1928) was a well-received melodrama with Hal Crane, William Davidson, and Richard Tucker. The scene shows the police interrogating a son, who confesses to killing his abusive father to save his mother. "It carries a great punch, and should go well where they like their drama good and heavy," *Film Daily* predicted.[10] On the other hand, the reviewer did not like THE DEATH SHIP (1928). "As a sample of how poor a talking subject can be, here it is. Look no further. It's one of those things that makes the worst sample of the silent screen look like a good picture in comparison." He thought that Mitchell Lewis ("his voice was never meant to be heard under the guise of an entertainment feature") and Jason Robards were "all pretty hopeless in this speakey." It was "directed, staged and acted as they do it out in the backwoods with the local dramatic league."[11]

MGM rivaled Warners as a supplier of shorts, but rather than investing in extensive in-house productions, the studio distributed films by independent producers. The Broadway musical and radio impresarios Gus Edwards and Major Bowes signed in October 1928.[12] Hal Roach was the most important independent producer of shorts at MGM. He heralded the renovation of his studio for sound by announcing, "The custard pie of two-reel films has been celebrated in song and story, but no one off the lot has yet been permitted to enjoy the thrill caused by sound of the impact of such a piece of pastry with a convenient physiognomy." At first Roach's "Our Gang" shorts were released with music tracks only, for instance, THE SPANKING AGE (1928). Like many producers, Roach embraced music and effects but had initial doubts about dialogue. Talking, he felt, slowed the action, which retarded the number of gags, which meant fewer laughs. "Every comedy we ship is clicked for sixty laughs," he assured his public. "Otherwise we don't ship."[13] SMALL TALK (1929), the first "Our Gang" all-talkie, was a three-reel hit. "To hear Wheezer and Mary Ann Jackson talk is cunning beyond words," *Film Daily* gushed.[14] Soon Laurel and Hardy led Roach's repertory in convincing audiences that their idiosyncratic vocal humor was every bit as funny as their physical slapstick had been. Charles Barr, writing about THE PERFECT DAY (1929), observed, "It shows them adjusting easily: in a positive way, using sound effects and dialogue wittily; in a negative way, not being inhibited by it. One needs to make no sharp separation between their silent and sound shorts."[15]

W. C. Fields, while appearing in *Ballyhoo*, an Oscar Hammerstein II musical, stopped by the Radio-Victor Gramercy Studios to make his first talking short, THE GOLF

SPECIALIST (1930). Again, sound was shown to be an asset to those comedians who had practiced verbal humor. Fields's distinctive voice established his enduring character, and the timing of his gags was perfect. The trades loved it: "A Knockout . . . Despite the length of the picture [twenty-four minutes], it maintains such a consistently amusing tempo that no audience is likely to tire of it, unless it's from too much laughing."[16]

Paramount, like Warners and Fox, used the short-subject format to test new film forms. THE SONG OF THE BUILDER (1928) was an unusual "experimental" short film, described as a "noise symphony." "As the words of [Edgar Guest's] poem are thrown on the screen, they are heard audibly from the disc record. The construction sounds familiar in skyscraper work are heard distinctly and realistically."[17]

Mack Sennett (releasing through Pathé, then through Educational Pictures) signed with RCA Photophone in August 1928 and built his own soundstage.[18] Sennett's first all-talkie, THE LION'S ROAR, was released on 27 November, the first in Educational's lineup of sound shorts. It contained a variety of sounds: "instrumental, vocal, and in animal noises the range jumps from a bird's chirp to a lion's roar."[19]

Short subjects gave a tremendous boost to independent producers. The indies stood to benefit from exhibitors' desire to cut presentation and orchestra overhead while offering their customers a well-rounded package. In fact, several small studios outpaced the majors with their conversion to sound. Educational Pictures Exchange, the leading producer of shorts and novelties, signed an exclusive contract with Vocafilm in January 1928. This sound-on-disc system imitated Vitaphone's presentation format and promised to bring name acts to small theaters everywhere.[20] E. W. Hammons, president of Educational, observed that "one needs see a comedy properly synchronized with sound but once to realize what a startling increase in audience appeal is accomplished when voices and sound effects are added to the antics of the comedy stars."[21] Appropriately, its slogan was "The Spice of the Program." Vocafilm was a failure acoustically, and Educational soon switched to RCA Photophone.

In late June 1928, Christie Studios (releasing through Paramount) committed to synchronization with ERPI. Tiffany-Stahl contracted with RCA in July to post-synchronize color shorts in the Tiffany-Tone series. The independent producer Ethelyn Gibson claimed to have made the first sound serial, FIVE CARDS (1928).[22] For the small companies, start-up cost was minimal for capital expense and employee training. Laboratories would advance loans in anticipation of later work orders. Having smaller management bureaucracies, many of the indies were capable of acting more swiftly than large companies. And perhaps because they tended to deal directly with states' rights distributors and independent exhibitors, they were a bit closer to the pulse of the public. Consequently, the silent short subject disappeared much faster than the silent feature. By 1929 talking shorts were going over like a "house afire."[23]

One way in which the short subject differentiated itself from the feature was by adopting a satirical tone toward the main part of the program. Numerous parodies of Hollywood hits appeared. Perhaps the most indicative series was the Dogville Comedies, directed by Zion Myers and Jules White and distributed by MGM in 1929–1931.[24] Their HOT DOG, a one-reel nightclub story, had a cast of fifty dogs. "Language is placed in the mouths of these animals that is perfectly suited to their every action." THE DOGWAY MELODY was a send-up of MGM's hit musical and contains a hilarious rendition of "Singin' in the Rain" performed by harmonizing and dancing pooches.

Short subjects, like these from MGM in 1930, ensured that the program offered something for everyone.

Travelogues and Exploitation Films

In the public commentary about the films of the late twenties, the theme of transporting the subject into the viewer's geographical space (as though beamed by radio) is a consistent motif. Sound contributed to this illusion of facilitating an uncanny presence. The travel film, part ethnographic documentary, part titillating attraction, had been an important component of cinema since its beginning. Producers quickly adapted it to take advantage of sound's transportive function.

Commentators and reviewers invariably mentioned the enhanced impression of imaginary presence and "realism" that sound afforded. The overt purpose of these films was to capture the ambience of exotic lands, and sound helped complete the illusion. These films traditionally were shorts, but the episodes could be strung together to create feature-length releases. The travel film still had vestigial ties to the lecturer format. Sometimes the sound track of music and effects would supplement a live lecture, but quickly its recorded narration incorporated the live speaker's function. Martin Johnson and his wife Osa Johnson had been outfitting cinematographic explorations since the teens and had toured with movies that combined education with exploitation. Their safari film SIMBA, THE KING OF THE BEASTS; A SAGA OF THE AFRICAN VELDT debuted on Broadway in January 1928 to great acclaim. A union musician played ordinary phonograph records backstage. This system was later christened Dulcetone and traveled with the film on its road-show tour of 150 cities before opening nationally on Christmas Day 1928. The action purported to show the Lumbwa tribe's defenses against a marauding pride of lions, but there were shots of various African beasts interspersed, as well as scenes of the Johnsons at work (he cranking the camera, she poised with a protective shotgun). There were also two shorts on the program, one a compilation drawn from the Johnsons' films of the previous fifteen years, the other a "Movielustration" described as "an animated song reel, synchronizing singing of the special song dedicated to the picture." The film and shorts were edited by Terry Ramsaye.[25] ACROSS THE WORLD WITH MR. AND MRS. MARTIN JOHNSON (1930) had a music-synchronized track. A talking prologue showed Osa Johnson entertaining guests in her parlor. The upper-class setting is a foil to the "ferocious-looking head-hunters in the South Seas."[26]

AFRICA SPEAKS (1930), photographed by Paul Hoefler and recorded by Walter Futter, was originally entitled UBANGI. It preserved the old-fashioned separation of the sound from the picture by advertising itself as "an exciting feature . . . accompanied by a Movietone lecture." Hoefler claimed that all the animal sounds were authentic, recorded on his own homemade equipment in the jungle, but it does not take a close listening to ascertain that the sound is all post-dubbed. Unlike the Johnsons' work, which has some anthropological interest, this film is fully in the exploitation mode. The hunters come upon some lions and send a bearer for rifles. "Before the dusky individual can get to the weapons one of the lions pounces on him and it is explained . . . that it was then too late to help the native." There are many shots of naked Africans. The Pygmies are romanticized as people of the forest and "not related to the Negro." *Film Daily* thought there was box-office appeal in the filmed safari: "As they pursue their route they meet up with strange-appearing tribes, including pygmies and duck-billed women who are distinctly a femme novelty."[27]

The Strangest Romance Ever Filmed!

COLUMBIA'S BIG-MONEY SMASH!

Filmed by Paul L. Hoeller and Walter Futter for the Colorado African Expedition

"AFRICA SPEAKS"

Sensations in AFRICA SPEAKS (Columbia, 1930).

Animation

During the sound rush of 1928, there was a four-way race between Amedée J. Van Beuren, Walt Disney, Charles Mintz, and the Fleischer Studio to get the first synchronized cartoons on the screen.

When Joseph Kennedy reorganized KAO in May 1928, he spun off the unit that produced the "Aesop's Fables" cartoon series, directed by Paul Terry. It was purchased by Van Beuren, who announced on 18 August in *Moving Picture World* that all his cartoons would be available with RCA Photophone sound. Paul Terry's DINNER TIME (1928), which had been completed as a silent, was the first one. Despite cartoonist Terry's avowed lack of interest in sound, the Van Beuren "Fables" were popular. The reason is suggested in a review of STAGE STRUCK (1928), with Farmer Al Falfa: "The sound effects are good comedy effects, and make the popular cartoon subject more entertaining than ever. Here is one place sound belongs without any arguments. No matter how poor the effects may be, the kids will always interpret it as part of the comedy and kidding."[28] In other words, because the audience was assumed to be uncritical children, quality was unimportant.

On 19 August, *Film Daily* reported that George Winkler had arrived in New York to confer with his brother-in-law and business partner Charles B. Mintz about a series of sound cartoons using a new character. "By golly, even cartoons are going to talk," commented Kann. "Wonder what a cartoon voice will sound like?"[29] Mintz was operating an animation studio in New York producing "Oswald the Rabbit" for Universal, a silent series created by Walt Disney the year before. Recently Mintz had hired the originator's staff and squeezed Disney out of the operation.[30]

Reading this front-page announcement, Disney probably felt that Mintz was once again about to preempt his new plan, a sound cartoon series starring a new character named Mickey Mouse. He arrived in New York two weeks later and met with the *Film Daily* publisher, Jack Alicoate, to find out about recording studios. He followed up by trying to meet William Fox, who refused to see him. RCA was willing to synchronize his films at the Gramercy studio, but Disney was appalled at the expense, run up by ASCAP music license fees. Disney saw DINNER TIME at the Mark Strand, where it had opened on 1 September, and was not impressed.[31] He wrote back to his brother Roy Disney and his business partner, the animator Ub Iwerks:

> Frankly speaking, the sound situation is still a big mystery to most of them yet. None of them is positive how it is all going to turn out. But I have come to this definite conclusion: sound effects and talking pictures are more than a mere novelty. They are here to stay and in time will develop into a wonderful thing. The ones that get in on the ground floor are the ones that will more likely profit by its future development. That is providing they work for quality and not quantity and quick money. Also, I am fully convinced that the sound on film is the only logical thing for the future. (Walt Disney to Roy Disney and Ub Iwerks, 14 September 1928, folder F66, John Canemaker Collection, Fales Library, New York University)

He finally recorded his synchronized score (Carl Stalling's arrangement of royalty-free public domain tunes), sound effects, and limited vocals (a squawking parrot, which he performed himself) on the Powers Cinephone system. The film was STEAMBOAT WILLIE (1928).

Unlike his competitors, who understood sound for their cartoons as an embellishment to the silent film (just as most live-action producers did), Disney planned his films with motion, composition, and character centered on sound properties.[32] The archival story sketches for STEAMBOAT WILLIE show the importance of acoustic preplanning:

> SCENE #2.
> Close up of Mickey in cabin of wheel'house, keeping time to last two measures of verse of "steamboat Bill." With gesture he starts whistleing the chorus in perfect time to music . . . his body keeping time with every other beat while his shoulders and foot keep time with each beat. At the end of every two measures he twirls wheel which makes a ratchet sound as it spins. He takes in breath at proper time according to music. When he finishes last measure he reaches up and pulls on whistle cord above his head. (Use FIFE to imitate his whistle)
> SCENE #3
> Close up of top of wheel'house with three whistles, one is tall and skinny, center one is medium size, and the last one is short and squatty. When the cord on the first one is pulled down the whistle stem squats down and then shoots up and steam with various notes mixed in shoots out. "TOOT" then the center one goes, Too-De-Loo-Doo—— The last one is asleep and doesn't make any sound. The other two whistles register surprise . . . the center one gives it a punch and wakes it up. Then it goes "Dum-Dum" in base tone. ("Supplementary Material," *Mickey Mouse: The Black-and-White Years*, laserdisc collection, Walt Disney Home Video, original spelling and punctuation)

During recording, an inked "bouncing ball" on the edge of the film stock helped the conductor keep the beat when the film was shown with the projector's aperture plate removed. Disney applied for and was granted (in 1933) a patent for this process.[33] But the hard part was for an independent cartoon producer to find a distribution outlet.

While Disney was calling on uncooperative distributors in October 1928, the Fleischers reentered the sound cartoon business. Max and Dave Fleischer, always technically curious, had synchronized a dozen or so "Song Car-Tunes" between 1924 and 1926, using De Forest Phonofilm. However, the technical limitations of that system, as well as its marketing and distribution problems, prevented any widespread success. Nevertheless, when the 1928 industry conversion to sound began, the Fleischer sing-alongs clearly were a precedent for animators. THE SIDEWALKS OF NEW YORK (1928) was the first in Paramount's "Inkwell Imps" sound series. These releases provided even more incentive for Disney.[34]

In November, Cinephone announced that sound tracks for the first four of a twenty-six-film series of cartoons by Walt Disney were being prepared: STEAMBOAT WILLIE, GALLOPIN' GAUCHO, THE BARN DANCE, and PLANE CRAZY.[35] Pat Powers used his connections to secure a two-week Broadway run for the first of the films. The screening of STEAMBOAT WILLIE made headlines in the trade press—but not because of its later historical significance as Mickey Mouse's debut. Rather, Powers openly dared ERPI to enforce the interchangeability clause. The unlicensed Powers Cinephone recording was projected on the Colony Theatre's Western Electric sound system, and "no attempt . . . [was] made to prevent showing of the picture."[36] Kann editorialized: "A Cinephone sub-

Advertisements for the "Mickey Mouse" series emphasized the character's talent as a musical performer.

ject with music and sound effects is being reproduced over Western Electric equipment at the Colony, right here in New York. No interference, no trouble and two days have gone by. We make bold to assert there will be none." While the issue of compatibility was being fought out in smaller venues across the country, STEAMBOAT WILLIE was the first non-ERPI, non-RCA film shown on Broadway. So in addition to its aesthetic contribution to the history of animation, Disney's film should also be recognized as an event in the exhibition history of the talkies because it was a successful challenge to Western Electric's legal resistance to "interchangeability."[37]

Although he did not beat Terry or Fleischer to sound, Disney must have had some satisfaction in knowing that he had scooped his enemy and former employer Charles Mintz. The same day that STEAMBOAT WILLIE opened, 18 November, Mintz announced that Universal's "Oswald" series would henceforth continue with full sound and music effects. The first, HEN FRUIT, was not released by Universal until 4 February 1929.[38] Disney had the last word—or the last squeak.

For most of the 1920s, Pat Sullivan's "Felix the Cat" was the leading cartoon series. But when the distributor, Educational, demanded sound versions for the 1929–1930 season, Sullivan refused to comply. Overnight the thriving studio disbanded. In October, Sullivan sold twelve cartoons to Copley Pictures, which made synchronized versions on disc and film. Some of these might have been new films animated by the original designer of Felix, Otto Messmer. Some had been previously released. John Canemaker describes these post-synchronized sound tracks as "sloppy, rarely matching the action on the screen."[39]

Meanwhile, in 1929, Disney's GALLOPIN' GAUCHO and THE BARN DANCE were basking in extended runs at the Strand. In March the animation studio became the first one to have its own on-premises sound system. Pat Powers's engineer William Garity traveled to Los Angeles to install the Cinephone recording apparatus and to act as the staff's technical adviser.[40] Disney was still looking for distributors for his "Mickey Mouse" cartoons and "the first print of a new series of novelty sound cartoons." This was animator Ub Iwerks's masterpiece, THE SKELETON DANCE (1929), the initial installment of the "Silly Symphonies." The film was a grotesquely witty escapade in a graveyard synchronized, beat for beat, to Grieg's "March of the Dwarves." But Disney, now a producer with a desirable product, was able to dictate his own terms. He attempted to distribute the "Mickey" series himself by states' rights, advertising unsold territories in May. The "Silly Symphonies" were available separately.[41]

THE SKELETON DANCE became the most successful cartoon of its time. Its long runs matched those of prominent studio features: four weeks at the Carthay Circle in Los Angeles, a long engagement at the Fox in San Francisco, and an unprecedented rebooking at the Roxy.[42] Critics who had studiously ignored Disney (idolizing "Felix") hailed the film for its imagery and its meticulous application of sound. (It was also Disney's first venture into the world of highbrow music.) The *Film Daily* reviewer wrote, "Here is one of the most novel cartoon subjects ever shown on a screen." After this rapture, Kann himself took the unusual step of arranging a private screening to see "why all the ravings." He found that "even frozen faces will crack under its infectious fun."[43] Based on the film's extraordinary popularity, Columbia Pictures in August acquired the distribution rights for all of the "Silly Symphonies" in the United States and Canada. However, "Mickey Mouse," billed as "A Walt Disney Comic by 'Ub' Iwerks recorded on Powers Cinephone," continued to be handled by Disney through independent exchanges. In July 1929, Disney cartoons were in lights on the marquees of five Broadway houses.[44]

Otto Messmer's ad for "Felix" tries to associate the cat with Jolson's tag line.

Disney's competitors now were hustling to catch up with him, committing outright plagiarism of Mickey and Minnie in the case of Paul Terry's WOODEN MONEY (1929). This was a "Fable" in which "Milton Mouse and his sweetie" subject Farmer Al Falfa to a "mice nightmare." Reviewers felt that there was "nothing much new in this cartoon." The third released "Mickey," PLANE CRAZY, by contrast, was greeted as "a volume of laughs that are by no means confined to the juveniles." [45]

Back in his New York studio, Mintz produced twenty-six "Krazy Kat" cartoons to compete with "Oswald" and "Mickey." Coincidentally the films of Disney's rival were also distributed by Columbia. [46] Among the numerous shoestring operations that started releasing sound animation was Kolortone Productions, formed by Leo Britton and George Jeffrey. They were especially ambitious and announced six all-talking cartoons made in Brewster Color. [47]

Walter Lantz, an animator and gagman, moved to Universal City to supervise "Oswald," the series that Disney had lost to Winkler and Mintz, who were then fired by Universal. The "Oswald" cartoons were released with synchronization and some dialogue. [48] The highest-profile animation event of 1930 was the premiere of Lantz's Technicolor prologue for Universal's THE KING OF JAZZ. The cartoon, animated by Bill Nolan, is a spoof of SIMBA. Paul Whiteman is big-game hunting for the king of beasts. A monkey hits him with a coconut, raising a bump which turns into his "crown." There are Disneyesque sound gags, as when Paul's bullets play a xylophone tune on the lion's teeth. Lantz attempted to use a "visual metronome" to guide the bandleader Paul Whiteman in the recording session. The "King of Jazz," however, eschewed Lantz's gimmick and performed ad lib—getting the beat just right. [49]

Max and Dave Fleischer continued to release (or possibly re-release) the follow-the-bouncing-ball "Song Car-Tunes" on a states' rights basis through the distributor Alfred Weiss. These included OLD BLACK JOE (1929) and MY OLD KENTUCKY HOME (1929), silent films furnished with scores by Paul Edouarde. [50] Meanwhile, Fleischer began releasing two series of eighteen "Paramount Screen Songs" and eight "Talkartoons" in June. [51] DAISY BELLS (1929) was hailed: "In the days of B.S.—before sound—Max Fleischer's song cartoons always provided diversion. Now that the ear hears while the eye sees, the entertainment qualities of this series is [*sic*] considerably enhanced." [52] The sound tracks were popular songs copied from 78-rpm records purchased at the local music store. The animators would listen to the song, then devise effects which would coincide with the drumbeats, caesurae, and so forth, on the record. Leslie Cabarga writes that THE ACE OF SPADES (1931) was pre-synchronized in this way. "The entire soundtrack, including dialogue, came from a black vaudeville record." Max Fleischer felt that his technique was original enough to deserve a patent. [53]

Hugh Harman and Rudolph Ising were two of Disney's animators who had defected from the studio when he lost the "Oswald" series. Sometime in 1929 they produced their own three-minute sample reel called BOSKO THE TALK-INK KID. Unlike other cartoons of the period—including Disney's—this one contained animated characters speaking dialogue, however crudely. They had no better luck than Disney in finding a national distributor until they met Leon Schlesinger. He operated a company, called Pacific Art and Title (still in business), which supplied title cards for silent films—a business seemingly with very poor prospects in 1929! One of Schlesinger's contracts was with Warner Bros. (It is rumored that Schlesinger was one of the backers of THE JAZZ SINGER.) He and Jack Warner agreed that the "Bosko" series had potential because it would exploit

BOSKO THE TALK-INK KID (*Looney Tunes, 1930*).

the resources of Warners' three newly acquired music publishing companies. In January 1930, Schlesinger, Harman, and Ising signed a contract in which the cartoonists agreed to produce a 600–700-foot sound motion picture by April, and Schlesinger agreed to distribute it.[54]

George Quigley, in charge of Vitaphone Varieties, announced the new series of "Looney Tunes," the name inspired by the "Silly Symphonies." The cartoons appeared in the context of other Vitaphone novelties, such as Robert L. Ripley's "Believe It or Not." Each "Looney Tune" was supposed to be based on a Warner musical property. The first, SINKIN' IN THE BATHTUB (1930), with music by Frank Marsales, was animated by Isadore "Friz" Freleng. The plot satirizes Lightner's "Singin' in the Bathtub" from THE SHOW OF SHOWS.[55] The protagonists Bosko and Honey look rather like Mickey and Minnie's cousins. Their caricatural features and costumes identify them as African-American types.

> The antics of this comic pair are presented with a burlesque background of popular tunes from Vitaphone feature picture successes—songs that have already become national hits through the showing of the productions, through radio broadcasting and the sale of sheet music, phonograph records and piano rolls. Film patrons are prepared to welcome these animated parodies of these songs with open arms. (*Film Daily*, 20 April 1930, p. 1)

Bosko and Honey's antics, accompanied by the incessant beat of Warners songs, makes each cartoon a mini-musical. The revue was becoming passé in features, but it lived on

"Looney Tunes" christened, May 1930.

in "Looney Tunes" for a decade. In 1931 Schlesinger signed Harman-Ising to make a second series, the "Merrie Melodies," and initiated the classic period of Warner Bros. animation.[56]

When Walt Disney met with Pat Powers in 1930 to renegotiate his Cinephone contract, he was stunned to hear that Powers had already lured away his partner and top animator, Iwerks, to create his own series. Suspicious of Powers's accounting practices, Disney broke away and, benefiting from Frank Capra's recommendation to Harry Cohn, received a one-year contract to deliver thirty "Mickey Mouse" cartoons to Columbia. At first the agreement was only for certain territories, but Columbia took over world rights in March. The contract was crucial, for as Gomery has observed, the "Disney [organization] needed a base on which to build its innovation of sound; it needed distribution agreements with powerful studio patrons . . . to fully exploit marketing leverage. Without these corporate sponsors to distribute its products around the world, the Disney company surely would have gone the way of any number of now-long-forgotten, marginal, Hollywood companies."[57] Disney and his character's rise to stardom were phenomenal in the early thirties. "Mickey Mouse is probably the latest screen star to break into the big bulb class. His name is now adorning electric lights on marquees throughout the country," reported *Film Daily*. A Columbia ad described Mickey as the "Darling of two continents. Lindy, Prince of Wales and Don Juan rolled into one."[58] Meanwhile, Iwerks's "Flip the Frog" began at MGM in 1931, but the frog could never emerge from the mouse's shadow.[59]

Among the innovations Walt Disney was pondering were color—inspired by Lantz's KING OF JAZZ prologue—and widescreen. "I believe that the inclusion of color in cartoon

Disney's important distribution deal with Columbia, 1930.

Ub Iwerks's self-portrait drawing Flip the Frog for MGM, 1931.

comedies offers great possibilities for pictorial effects, but would add very little so far as comedy is concerned," Disney wrote.

> There are many problems in sound yet to be worked out, and I should like to see this angle perfected before considering color. After all, in a cartoon comedy it is laughs and personality that count. Color alone will not sustain public interest unless the cartoon itself is exceptionally clever and unique—a good, clever black and white cartoon should hold its own for some time to come. As for the wide screen, its possibilities and advantages are unlimited for the feature picture, but as yet, I can see no special advantage for its use in the production of cartoon comedies. (*Film Daily*, 6 April 1930, p. 17)

Disney would sign an exclusive contract with Technicolor for its three-color process in 1932—and would make widescreen cartoons in CinemaScope twenty years later.

At the Fleischer studio, the sound people were still trying to arrive at a satisfactory process for synching the "Talkartoons." The practice of using commercial recordings was stopped because of rights problems and the insistence of the musicians' union. Instead, Disney's "bouncing ball" was modified by Lou Fleischer into a contraption called a Beater. He made a sprocketed-cam punching machine which perforated holes in the film representing the beat. The conductor used the projected bouncing light to maintain tempo.[60] A review of the "Talkartoon" THE BUM BANDIT (1931) shows that the pressure to achieve an integrated aesthetic was strong, even in animation: "The idea, art work and synchronization are excellent. However, inclusion of considerable dialogue, with a corresponding decrease in action, detracts somewhat from the effectiveness of this type of short."[61] In 1931 the studio leased an additional floor at 1600 Broadway, ostensibly to expand the "research department . . . which carries on experiments with the Fleischer method for synthetic sound."[62]

Film Daily conducted an extensive poll of exhibitors in 1930, asking the question, "What type of short feature in sound do you consider most popular and most important to your program?" The results showed that shorts were prized as audience-pleasers. Comedies ruled, with 341 votes, followed by newsreels, with 107. Significantly, animation, primarily through the influence of Disney's sound films, had risen substantially above its throwaway status in the silent period. Cartoons received 87 votes, taking third place and handily beating musicals (47), novelties (39), color subjects (19), sketches (12), and dance films (5).[63]

The mediocre showing of musicals, sketches, and dance subjects in 1930 reflects the live-action anti-musical trend. It also suggests that animation was taking over some of the musical's function. The poll clearly shows that audiences' preferences were moving away from the short subject as a recorded spectacle toward an appreciation of it as a self-contained mini-movie, with sound used, as in the feature, to combine with the image, not to slow down the story or to be the main draw. As feature films grew longer with the coming of sound, the contrast between the short subject and the multi-reel parts of the program became more distinctive. Some shorts took over functions banished from features, such as experimental foregrounding of sound effects and virtual Broadway–style canned performances. Novelty and travel genres were alternatives to Hollywood features. And like the newsreel, sound preserved (or synthesized) the acoustic dimension to generate an aura of veracity. Of all the short film forms, however, none was transformed by sound more than the cartoon. The syncopation of rhythmic motion with an assertive beat, the humorous sound effects, and the funny voices created a new comic world and the possibility for any number of charming, wacky, drawling, squeaky, lisping, or stuttering characters.

16

Outside the Mainstream

Sound opened new possibilities for bringing previously unheard voices and languages to Hollywood. The precursor was definitely radio, which was broadcasting regional songs (for example, mountain and western music on shows like *The Grand Ole Opry*) and ethnic humor (in exaggerated Jewish, Mexican, Italian, and Irish accents) to widely scattered homes where such entertainment had never before been heard. The transition to sound in film coincided with a wave of enthusiasm among white audiences for entertainment performed by African Americans. Many listeners liked traditional spirituals and minstrel acts, but the Jazz Age took its name from the most popular music of all. The motives for this admiration, the subject of considerable speculation, are far from clear. Was this interest driven by curiosity and respect for black culture—as in Rouben Mamoulian's successful Broadway staging of *Porgy?* Or was it an effort to contain or exclude minorities by erecting boundaries of representation? In his description of the melting-pot ethos of the 1920s as a "racial cross-dressing," Michael Rogin argues that it was an effort to construct a myth of American origins.[1] Whatever the stimulus, motion pictures were unarguably part of the process.

The industry commentator Arthur W. Eddy observed in 1929, "Negro sketches, which were almost an unknown quantity before this talking picture business, are now finding more and more spots on Eastern programs."[2] It is not surprising that all-talking, all-singing films would exploit these extremely popular artists, capitalize on the interest in African-American music, and perpetuate racist stereotypes and black caricatures.

Most of the filmed appearances by established African-American performers were in musical shorts. Christie Comedies, releasing through Paramount, produced a series of sketches adapted from short stories by Octavus Roy Cohen, a white southerner who for a quarter-century had specialized in stories of plantation life for *Saturday Evening Post* readers. MELANCHOLY DAME (1929) was a typical ten-minute reel. The cast included the singers and dancers Florian Slappey, Webster Dill, Ed Thomson, Roberta Hyson, Charles Olden, Evelyn Preer (who had starred in Oscar Micheaux's THE HOMESTEADER [1919]), and Spencer Williams (the veteran actor and future director). *Film Daily* thought that "the principals all deserve mention for excellent work." Other films in the series were MUSIC HATH CHARMS (1929), with Slappey, Roscoe Griggers, Bud Peagler, Professor Aleck Champagne, Sam Gin, and Willie Trout, and THE FRAMING OF THE SHREW (1929), featuring Privacy Robson, Slappey, and Lawyer Evans Chew.[3] These entertainers would already have been known to patrons of urban theater and the touring black vaudeville circuits, but not necessarily to white film audiences. Al Christie said, condescendingly,

> We discovered very early that the usual colored screen actor was practically useless because it was next to impossible for him—or her—to memorize long speeches. Of course there were exceptions, but very few of them. We went to the legitimate stage for most of our principals—the colored legitimate stage. One of our principals in the first colored talkie, THE MELANCHOLY DAME, is Evelyn Preer, of the Lafayette Players, a splendid actress. . . . The colored stage players are remarkably quick "studies" and seldom "go up" in their lines. (Al Cohn, "How Talking Pictures Are Made," *Photoplay*, December 1928, p. 110)

Other African Americans who had leading roles included George Reed, who played in MAGNOLIA (1929), adapted from Booth Tarkington's play. George Dewey Washington, a bass-baritone with a long vaudeville career, recorded at least five one-reel performances for MGM in 1928 and 1929 and appeared in two of the four Metro Movietone Revues. He performed as a "gentleman tramp" character. "Washington has oodles of personality, and is remarkable for his clear tonal quality that makes every syllable perfectly understandable."[4] Duke Ellington, who at the time was a draw at the Cotton Club and on RKO theater tours, appeared in BLACK AND TAN (dir. Dudley Murphy, 1929). ST. LOUIS BLUES (dir. Murphy, 1929) proved to be the only screen appearance of the legendary singer Bessie Smith.[5]

RKO was aggressively putting black performers under contract. "Marguerite Robinson, Negro singer," according to a press release, "is the first of her race to be signed to a long-term contract." Hall's Chorus, consisting of forty-one singers, was also signed by RKO. Their first appearance was supposed to be in DIXIANA.[6] One of the highlights of this musical is the long tap dance by Bill Robinson. Typically, it is narratively gratuitous, an encapsulated element of spectacle inserted to delight those audiences who would appreciate a performance by "Bojangles." The segment was also easily excisable for audiences who did not welcome his presence.

Jules Bledsoe was featured in OLD MAN TROUBLE, in the Columbia-Victor "Singing-Talking Gem" series. In the seven-minute film directed by Basis Smith, he talks to his "mammy" and sings two numbers from the Broadway version of *Show Boat,* in which he starred as Joe in 1927. The opera baritone had performed in roles ranging from *The Emperor Jones* to *Aida*. "One of the best things in its class that has yet been presented in sound shorts," wrote *Film Daily*. "Bledsoe's voice registers beautifully and has an appealing quality that is bound to get over with any type of audience."[7]

Many mainstream musicals relied on black entertainers. ON WITH THE SHOW (1929) is typical. Many of the musical numbers feature African Americans, including some spectacular, but uncredited, tap dancers. The film begins with fans entering the theater saying that they can't wait to hear Ethel Waters sing "Am I Blue?" As promised, Waters performs onstage, but we never see her or the other black performers offstage or mingling with the other players. It is as though they existed only as pure entertainment.

Three 1929 Hollywood feature releases showcased black players. HEARTS IN DIXIE (dir. Paul Sloane) advertised: "Negro spirituals . . . sung by a magnificent chorus—stevedores and roust-abouts croon thrilling melodies as the 'Nellie Bly' pulls into [the] wharf—cake-walks, folk dances, native jazz orchestras, the birth of the blues . . . in a breathlessly beautiful and realistic panorama of life along the levees and in the cotton fields with a cast of 200 *Native Entertainers*."[8] This cliché-ridden melodrama stars Clarence Muse as Nappus, a lazy, middle-aged sharecropper. Muse was a well-educated

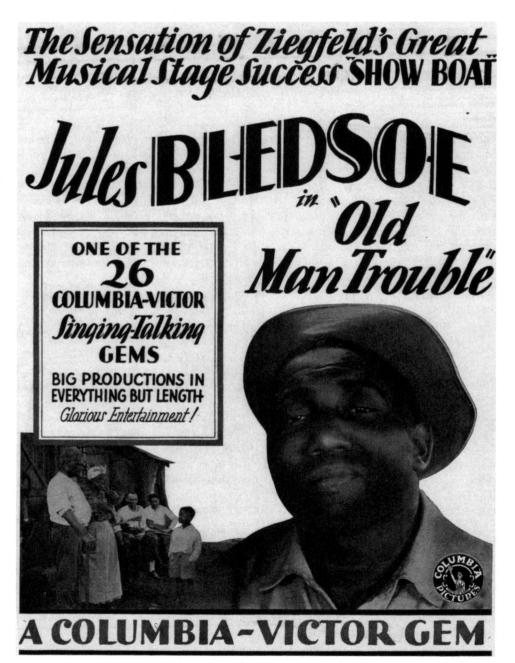

Jules Bledsoe in OLD MAN TROUBLE *(Columbia, 1929).*

(LL.B. from Dickerson University) writer and producer of plays, as well as an accomplished actor. He was one of the founders of the Lafayette Players of Harlem. Nappus's stepson is shuffling Gummy, played by Stepin Fetchit. Both would soon become important black character actors. Paul Sloane also directed a low-budget feature, NORTH OF DIXIE (1929), "in which Charles Gilpin, Negro star is at work as his initial talking picture." This feature, also with an all-black cast, was taken from Walter Weems's play *Lonesome Road.*[9]

The third and boldest project was HALLELUJAH! (1929), directed by King Vidor for MGM. Its African-American cast and interesting (though slender) plot were regarded by many as a sign of Hollywood's racial tolerance. The story (credited to Vidor), however, showed how difficult it was even for well-intentioned liberals to break away from stereotypes. Zeke (Daniel L. Haynes, Bledsoe's understudy in *Show Boat*) is a no-account cotton picker who accidentally kills his brother during a crap game. He finds redemption from his iniquities by becoming a preacher. His woman Chick (Nina Mae McKinney) dies in an accident, and Zeke hunts down and kills her lover, Hot Shot (William Fountaine), whom Zeke holds responsible. He returns home after serving on the chain gang and is reunited with his family.

MGM arranged for a Western Electric Kearny truck to meet the crew in Memphis, but when it was delayed, Vidor proceeded to shoot the exterior scenes silent, assuming he could postdub dialogue. (The interiors were shot later in Hollywood with standard recording procedures.) Without Moviolas or other precision sound-editing gear, postproduction on the location scenes dragged on for six months. The interludes of hymns and spirituals are moving, and the long sequence in which Zeke chases Hot Shot through the swamp is a magnificent sound montage (all post-synched). Vidor symbolically premiered the film at Broadway and Harlem theaters simultaneously in August 1929.[10] Kann lauded the experiment as artistically engrossing:

> The narrative and its background concern a world far removed from the standards and understanding of the white man. As you read this in impersonal type, it may seem far-fetched to comprehend how the desires and emotions of a set of black men and women can hit so closely home. When you realize, however, that those motivations are kin of all humans no matter what the color pigment of their skin may be, this reaction becomes far more clear. (*Film Daily,* 21 August 1929, p. 1)

Kann congratulated MGM for its HALLELUJAH! experiment but predicted that most audiences would not like it. His liberal comment is all the more remarkable in light of *Film Daily*'s frequently racist jokes and reviews laced with demeaning epithets.[11] Like the films themselves, the trade press simultaneously praised the performers and confined them inside a racial stereotype. *Film Daily*'s reviewer was impressed that HALLELUJAH! had been created by a southerner: "King Vidor, a Texan, here has attempted to film a cross-section of the life and mentality of the Southern Negro. As a general thing, he has succeeded admirably. His insight at all time seems to bear the stamp of authenticity. Never is the spectator inclined to doubt the director's treatment." He complained, however, that at the end the story lost its dramatic effect.[12]

The film went on to lose money at the box office. Because of the race subject, MGM had difficulty distributing it. Although it received critical praise, HALLELUJAH! apparently caused discomfort in smaller towns and was not booked at all in southern white

THE GHOST TALKS *(Fox, 1929) lobby card.*

theaters. In cities, black audiences frequently had to wait to see the film until it played at neighborhood houses. Then they laughed at the country stereotypes.[13]

Inevitably there was a backlash from some exhibitors against the surge in African-American shorts and features. At their convention in Columbus, Georgia, southeastern exhibitors objected to HALLELUJAH! and expounded on the "reaction of audiences of this section to the number of films featuring Negroes which have been released in recent months." The delegates went "strongly on record against Negro pictures and call[ed] upon producers of the industry to 'severely restrict or entirely forego' the making of pictures exploiting the Negro race."[14] What bothered the southern exhibitors was that these films were leaving the segregated theater circuits and entering mainstream cinema. The big studio features and the entertainment shorts were probably aimed at the "Cotton Club" market—whites who were attracted to black music and (imagined) lifestyles. But this approach was not tolerated in the Jim Crow South.

All three of these features, HEARTS IN DIXIE, NORTH OF DIXIE, and HALLELUJAH!, were influenced by the minstrel tradition, which had been an American vernacular in the nineteenth century. By the end of the 1920s, however, it had become nearly extinct until the talkies came along. Variety's review of MAMMY (dir. Michael Curtiz, 1930) leaves little doubt that the movies (with radio) revived the minstrel show.[15] The characterizations of blacks as contented workers and amiable, talented singers in the first two features, and imbued with "natural" religion in Vidor's film, were probably not questioned by most white moviegoers of the time. From this background emerged the one true African-American star of the period, Stepin Fetchit. The talkies brought his unique vocal performance to millions, and he was featured in no fewer than nine films in 1929. He garnered the praise of critics in THE GHOST TALKS, in which he appeared with the respected stage stars Helen Twelvetrees and Charles Eaton. "Seasoned screen players

Stepin Fetchit, June 1930.

like Stepin Fetchit in cast outdistance them," *Film Daily* reported. "First two reels tedious with artificial dialogue. . . . Pepped up in final reels with good comedy work of Stepin Fetchit from the comedy lots. This darky gets over big."[16] As Gummy in HEARTS IN DIXIE, "Stepin Fetchit gives a fine characterization of a lazy Negro highlighted by great comedy work." Fox appreciated its star's entertainment potential and hired Walter Weems to write an original screenplay for Fetchit's first feature.[17] Already in his earliest talkies Fetchit had adopted his permanent role as the dim-witted, drawling southern black man—far removed from the actor's actual offscreen personality.[18]

Of course, much of the material heard in the talkies was adapted by white performers masquerading as blacks. Al Jolson's appearance in A PLANTATION ACT and THE JAZZ SINGER merely transposed to the screen brief glimpses of his famous stage act. The press book distributed to publicize THE JAZZ SINGER gives an account of the genesis of Jolson's makeup in his vaudeville days:

> He was still a white face comedian at that time, and perhaps he would have been to this day if not for an old negro who sometimes helped him in dressing. He was not able to employ a regular dresser then.
>
> "Boss, if you skin's black, they always laugh," the darkey said.
>
> Jolson decided to try it. He blacked up with some burnt cork and rehearsed before the old negro.
>
> "You's jus' as funny as me, Mistah Jolson," chuckled the old man. (Warner Bros., THE JAZZ SINGER, Pressbook, 1927)

Whether or not it really happened, this explanation is a stunning attempt to justify the Jewish entertainer's minstrel stardom by tracing it to its "old" African-American origins.

On radio, whites starred in programs like *The Gold Dust Twins*, which featured "Negro dialect" humor and song, and *Amos 'n' Andy*. This program, which had been in distribution by disc transcription for about a year, went national on NBC in August 1929. The white comedians Freeman F. Gosden and Charles Correll played southern stereotypes transplanted to the urban working class. More than forty million listeners tuned in, many buying their first radios expressly for the purpose.[19] RKO hired Gosden and Correll for CHECK AND DOUBLE CHECK (dir. Melville Brown, 1930). The publicity claimed that they would receive $1 million for one month's work, a figure that was astronomical and apocryphal. The RKO account book gives the total cost of the production, which presumably included salaries, as $967,000.[20] The white actors re-created their vocal roles in a hokey, uninspired comedy set in Harlem, which was represented by one establishing shot. They performed their caricature Negro dialect in blackface. Many viewers would have been surprised by an unbilled appearance by Duke Ellington, suppressed in the advertising because of the "southern angle." CHECK AND DOUBLE CHECK packed in audiences and, in November 1930, was held over in 125 theaters. *Film Daily* glowed, "This is another piece of proof that the business is there and can be corralled with the right stuff, plugged with the right kind and right amount of advertising."[21] CHECK AND DOUBLE CHECK became one of RKO's most profitable films of the season. Yet remarkably, a sequel was never made. It has been said that the studio conducted a survey of patrons as they left the theaters, and few indicated that they would return for another film; they had just been curious about what "Amos 'n' Andy" would look like on the screen.[22] That this is the whole story is very unlikely. As an April 1931 press release indicated, there were probably legal and content problems, for RKO

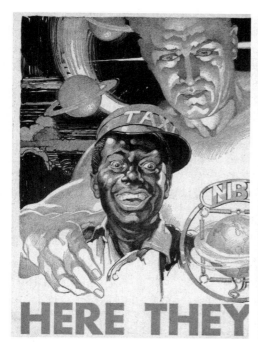

The RCA Titan introduces Gosden and Correll, radio's Amos 'n' Andy, in advertising for CHECK AND DOUBLE CHECK *(RKO, 1930).*

was then negotiating with NBC for two more "Amos 'n' Andy" pictures "along different and classier lines than their first production."[23]

The economic risk to the studios was in possibly offending not blacks, but whites. Jolson's BIG BOY (dir. Alan Crosland, 1930) presented a special problem. In the character of Gus, an African-American jockey, Jolson makes jokes at the expense of whites. According to *Variety,* the coda scene in which Jolson appears as himself and sings without blackface makeup was designed to make the film acceptable to white southern exhibitors.[24]

How African-American audiences viewed CHECK AND DOUBLE CHECK, Jolson's films (especially BIG BOY), and blackface comedies in general is difficult to know. The studios made these primarily for white audiences, welcoming any bookings from segregated black theaters as unplanned profit. But the extent of black attendance at these films is unknown. Though the representations of African Americans were frequently demeaning, Slide reports that Moran and Mack, the white radio actors who performed as "The Black Crows," for example, had many black fans. They starred in WHY BRING THAT UP? (dir. George Abbott, 1929) and ANYBODY'S WAR (dir. Richard Wallace, 1930). Similarly, Cripps has noted that while there was certainly divided opinion, most blacks seemed to enjoy the *Amos 'n' Andy* radio program. "But movies were different," he writes, "for on radio one could fancy them in the mind's eye as genuinely black rather than as greasepainted Dybbuks played by two whites."[25]

Audiences had many opportunities to see and hear black entertainers in feature film cameos and in entertainment shorts. But other dramatic roles were rare. One example is YAMAKRAW (1930), a Vitaphone short which used "expressionistic" sets and lighting to tell a SUNRISE-like story of a young black farmer who leaves his girlfriend and journeys to the big city. *Film Daily* gave the short film a relatively long notice:

> Fascinating Negro Rhapsody. Here is a musical novelty of such an unusual nature that it is bound to provoke comment both in the trade and among the public. It's an expressionistic rhapsody composed by James Johnston dealing with the Negro. Murray Roth, who directed it, has employed a wide variety of new camera angles and lighting technique, resulting in a most fascinating piece of dramatic and musical artistry. Swift flashes, mostly in gray silhouette, depict a jazz symphony of Negro life that is arresting in movement as well as dramatic in idea. The music is good and the acting and dancing are clearly descriptive. Besides being something that appreciative audiences will welcome with applause, this can be set down as a notable example of what the screen and its imaginative directors are able to do in the line of different entertainment. (*Film Daily*, 27 April 1930, p. 13)

Another example is the CIMARRON character Isaiah, played by Eugene Jackson.[26] Although he is typecast as a servant boy, he performs in a very natural style and is given conversational lines. He dies tragically in the crossfire between the hero and villain.

Conceived and directed by whites, these representations were intended to be respectful, even mythopoeic. Inevitably they repackaged patronizing stereotypes. As James Snead observed, "Film is never 'one person's story'—film is always typical, broadcasting certain codes about social status and interrelationships. Mythification can both elevate and degrade. Indeed, the two properties are interdependent."[27] Dudley Murphy's films are excellent examples of this view from outside the culture. After making some experimental "Visual Symphonies," Murphy went to Paris in 1923, according to William Moritz, wishing to take advantage of the advances in film sound there. Murphy fit right in with the "lost generation" in Paris and collaborated with the Cubist painter Fernand Léger on BALLET MÉCANIQUE (1924). Returning to New York, he tried to capture the feel of the Harlem Renaissance on film in the shorts BLACK AND TAN (1929), ostensibly about "life in the black and tan section of Harlem," and ST. LOUIS BLUES (1929), which centers on the question of how Bessie Smith got "the blues."[28] These efforts by what Cripps calls "white Negrophiles" seldom emerged from the morass of ingrained conventions of blackness and misrepresentations of the African-American experience. The limitations of mainstream producers are illustrated by a *Film Daily* anecdote: "Albert Howson, Warner scenario editor, is all a-puzzled trying to figure out the mental ratiocination of the Chicago censors who ordered the word 'darky' cut from Al Jolson's *Big Boy* because Chicago negroes might be offended by it. And Howson always thought it was an affectionate word."[29] Assuming that the last sentence was sincere, the anecdote shows that Hollywood was stuck in a plantation attitude toward blacks, far from the concerns and sensibilities of late-twenties urban African-American culture. The black voice in the Hollywood of 1930 was generally spoken in an entertainment dialect written, approved, and understood—and often performed—by whites.

GOLDEN DAWN (dir. Ray Enright, 1930) is proof enough. Seen today, the film's political incorrectness careens between shocking and hilarious. But it was made as a straightforward adaptation of Otto Harbach and Oscar Hammerstein II's stage musical, which Busby Berkeley had directed. The producers seem to have been oblivious to its humili-

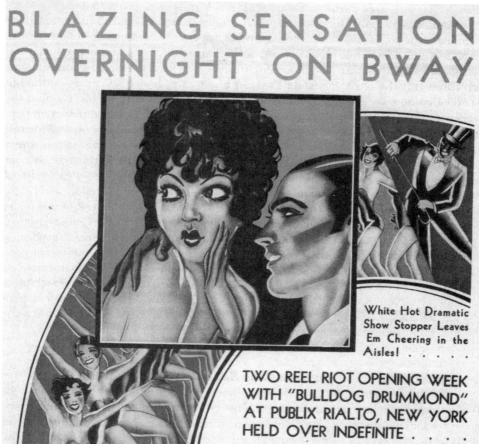

RKO used associations with jazz dance and dice to sell St. Louis Blues *(1929).*

ating racism, anti-Africanism, and implicit apartheid political message. Set during World War I in East Africa, British prisoners of war are distracted by blonde, alabaster-skinned Vivienne Segal, who has been chosen by her tribe to be a sacrificial offering.[30] An English officer prisoner-of-war (Walter Wolff) suspects that Dawn may not be black, and he falls in love with her. His commander gives him leave to rescue her, but only if it can be proven that she has some white blood. A timely appearance by her down-and-out white father does the trick. The villain Shep, played by Noah Beery in blackbody, is the cruel overlord. He sings in operatic baritone, but when he speaks, his vocabulary is peppered with "Sho' nufs" and "Massas," as though he had been dropped off in Africa by some passing minstrel show. Beery's characterization utilizes sound to reinforce every cliché about black men: his repeated "Whip Song" symbolizes his sexual terrorism; his linguistic incompetence condemns him to the underclass; and his mewling in defeat reveals his true cowardice. Dawn's voice, on the other hand, is untainted by any Negro dialect, and she sings her love song in the Jeanette MacDonald aria style when she bursts forth with "For Him I Call My Bwana." Said the reviewer for the *Herald-Tribune*, "Reason totters at the thought that any one could have conceived in seriousness such a definitive catalogue of vulgarity, witlessness, and utterly pathetic and preposterous nonsense."[31] Yet few white viewers seem to have been offended by the racism of this film. As in the blackface minstrel tradition, the transference of conventionalized black traits to white actors was seen as benign entertainment. The film seems to confirm Rogin's claim that "minstrelsy's successors, vaudeville, Tin Pan Alley, motion pictures, and radio did not so much displace as incorporate blackface."[32]

Independent Race Talkies

Where black audiences would have seen these or any other films from the major producers is another question. There had been a struggling "race cinema" exhibition circuit all through the twenties—though scarcely acknowledged by the film trade press. Many of these segregated independent houses (about half of which were black-owned) could not afford to buy or take out loans for sound. The theaters which did convert were tardy. The Plaza, for example, "the principal Negro house in Little Rock," installed an off-brand Moviephone system in late summer 1929, the first reported sound installation in a race house in Arkansas. In Montgomery, Alabama, on the other hand, a top-flight ERPI system went into the Pekin Theater, described as "one of the finest in that city . . . 'of, by and for' negroes only." All personnel, including the projectionists, were African Americans. In *Film Daily*'s national theater census, it was determined that 501 houses exhibited "pictures with all-colored casts to colored audiences." Segregated theaters existed in twenty-three states but were concentrated geographically: one-third east of the Mississippi, two-thirds south of St. Louis.[33] If Dan Streible's study of exhibition in Austin, Texas, can be generalized, it would suggest that about one-third of these houses were destined to close without ever projecting a sound film.[34] The vicious cycle here is apparent. Minority producers could not convert to sound filmmaking; exhibitors could not show sound prints. So silent films held on longer in these venues than elsewhere until eventually the owners gave up.

By early 1930 there were 455 "colored" houses, down about 10 percent in less than a year. These included 56 theaters in Texas, 42 in North Carolina, 38 in Ohio, 35 in Florida, 24 in California, 23 each in Illinois and Alabama, 21 in Georgia, and the rest dispersed among 22 states. African Americans' access to theaters in white urban areas was still restricted. The National Association for the Advancement of Colored People, for example, filed two suits against the Kenwood Theater in Chicago. The group alleged that race discrimination was practiced in at least 20 percent of the city's theaters.[35]

Sound brought difficulty for producers making movies outside industry channels. Like virtually all films produced in the twenties and early thirties, those destined for the race market were made by whites. A good example is the producer Lou Goldberg, a booking agent specializing in promoting African-American acts for stage shows. He also had supplied performers and scripts to Columbia for its musical shorts. In May 1929, he produced at least seven films in association with the RLA Talking Pictures Corporation. Typical releases were HARLEM REVUE, featuring Ralph Cooper and the Cooperettes, and WASHBOARD BLUES, the last of the series, with Mamie Smith.[36]

The marginal companies which supplied this market could only rarely afford to lease studio space. One special case was Oscar Micheaux, the flamboyant pioneer of race film-making. He announced two talkers in December 1929, one a tale of Harlem (which, presumably, became EASY STREET) and the other, DAUGHTER OF THE CONGO; both were released with synchronized tracks in 1930. With the backing of his company's board members Frank Schiffman and Leo Brecher, Micheaux leased the Metropolitan Sound Studios in Fort Lee to make talkies with ERPI disc-recording equipment. Among the first were THE EXILE, in 1931, and VEILED ARISTOCRATS the following year.[37] Micheaux also announced that he would direct an unusual project, A SOUL IN PAWN (1931). This was to be a sixteen-reel production which could be shown either as one or two films. "The pictures will include music, songs, cabaret shows and dancing."[38] Avowedly oriented toward the urban black middle class, these films use the actors' diction and dialect to convey the characters' upward mobility. But Micheaux's silent films had always been crudely made by Hollywood standards, and his use of sound was technically atrocious. There is considerable controversy about whether his work, in Thomas Cripps's words, "was in a baffling husk that made it often inaccessible to the audiences for which it was made," or whether it represented a rejection or an alternative view of Hollywood narrative and style. Charlene Regester points out that "African American filmmakers were, in the pre–Civil Rights era, operating under a completely different set of circumstances and were part of a complex set of dynamics over which they had little or no control. Ultimately this had to affect the films they produced."[39] Micheaux was hampered by his cavalier attitude toward quality, chronic lack of funds, and steadily decreasing outlets as the Depression decimated the race theaters. Recognizing the limitations of his market, Micheaux continued to release both sound and silent versions of his films throughout the decade of the thirties.[40]

Yiddish Talkies

Sound made possible the creation of films that addressed local audiences in their native languages. Like race cinema, these were primarily ultra-low-budget productions. The approximately fifty Yiddish-language films made in New York in the early 1930s are good examples.[41] These filmmakers spurned the assimilation ethos of the Jewish Hollywood moguls and made films that addressed the niche market in which Yiddish, the language of Jews from Russia and Poland, was spoken. There was irony in the development of the entertainment industry in the 1920s. As Hoberman observes, "American show business was becoming more Yiddish, as well as vice versa. Jolson, Brice, Tucker, Cantor *et al.* represented America's first generation of openly Jewish popular entertainers."[42]

Yet respect for tradition was hard to find. Many of these immigrants preferred traditional tales and religious piety to the jazz antics of Al Jolson and stories lauding the American dream of rags-to-riches success and the benefits of intermarriage. Comedians like Benny Rubin, whose dialect shtick poked fun at Jews in SEVEN MINUTES OF YOUR TIME (1928), NAUGHTY BOY (1929), MARIANNE (1929), and IT'S A GREAT LIFE (1930), were especially offensive. Independent Yiddish filmmaking activity was centered in New York's thriving Jewish theater culture. The Maurice Schwartz Yiddish Talking Pictures Corporation signed a long-term contract with Vocafilm in October 1928 and announced plans for six features.[43] Schwartz was the impresario of the Jewish Art Theater. (Its most famous graduate, Muni Weisenfreund, as Paul Muni, had just been signed by Fox to star in THE VALIANT.) The first releases were made by Sidney Goldin, an actor and film director with years of experience in the business. He had moved from New York to Vienna to establish Goldin-Film. The prospect of having talking-picture resources had drawn him back, and in May 1929, he premiered EAST SIDE SADIE, a silent with added dialogue scenes. Goldin found another ally in Max Cohen, a film producer at Metropolitan Sound Studios (where Micheaux's talkies were made.) Their first project was AD MOSAY (*The Eternal Prayer,* a.k.a. THE WAILING WALL [1929]), and they claimed that it was the "first talking picture in the Jewish language." Harry Alan Potamkin, critic for *Close-Up,* claimed it was "about the worst film ever made."[44] There was supposed to be a story based on the Hebron riots of 1929, but descriptions indicate that it was mainly static long-takes of choirs and similar performances, with blank leader separating the shots. It featured Lucy Levin and the cast of the Jewish Art Theater.[45]

Judea Films was founded in December 1929 by Joseph Seiden, another veteran producer of silents (including at least one race film, PARADISE IN HARLEM, and a Yiddish newsreel). His partners were Sam Berliner, Abe Leff, and Moe Goldman, all Bronx exhibitors. Their ambition was to produce twelve Jewish talking pictures to show in their three houses and to create a fledgling circuit in other metropolitan areas. They also used Goldin as their director and availed themselves of the RCA Photophone facility. The first releases were two-reel shorts. STYLE AND CLASS (1930) was a filmed stage revue and SHUSTER LIBE (A Shoemaker's Romance, 1930) was a comedy starring Joseph Buloff. Jennie Goldstein, known as the leading Jewish tragedienne, was signed for series of Yiddish and English talkies. She backed out, however, after disagreements with the producers.[46] Judea's features were adaptations of the popular plays *Eybike Naronim* (ETERNAL FOOLS, 1930) and *Mayne Yidishe Mame* (MY YIDDISH MAMA, 1930), and performances of great cantors in THE VOICE OF ISRAEL (1931). At this time, according to Erik Goldman, "Goldin could take credit for having directed every Yiddish narrative talking picture to date."[47] Goldin died in 1936 in the midst of a filming, but limited Yiddish production continued through the end of the decade, owing in part to circulation of these films in Poland. With only a couple of dozen theaters, the Yiddish cinema producers suffered even worse economic constraints than the African-American independents, who had a few hundred outlets. Additionally, internal destructive forces were at work, such as opposition from the Hebrew Actors Union (which thought that movies degraded the profession), internecine religious tensions, and the decline of the Yiddish-speaking audience for such films in the United States. Another factor might have been competition from Hollywood as a few studios reached out for this specialty market.

Hollywood Goes Ethnic

Sound tempted the major studios to experiment with films with minority appeal. Paramount, for instance, tested Chicago with one of its Polish-language films made in Joinville, France. French- and Spanish-language films were natural applications of sound, for they could be exhibited in Quebec, Latin America, and ethnic enclaves in U.S. cities. Most of the major studios, especially Fox, made Spanish-language films intended for domestic and Latin American distribution (see chapter 17). As Brian Taves has observed, these U.S.-made foreign-language films were "the aesthetic successors to the multi-linguals made by the major studios at the beginning of the sound era for overseas audiences."[48] Universal produced THE GREEN MILLIONAIRE (1929) from Abraham S. Schomer's play of the same name. It was shot with Yiddish dialogue but also circulated in an English version.[49] The ethnic performer George Sidney made a series of monologues for Universal, including COHEN ON THE TELEPHONE (1929). His lines were in English, but his Yiddish dialect "will hand any audience a great kick," *Film Daily* believed.[50] From 1927 to 1932, Sidney teamed with Charlie Murray in a series of "Cohen and Kelly" films. The transition to sound provided the opportunity to lay on thick their exaggerated accents. As with *Amos 'n' Andy*, the national distribution of these films coincided with an interest in ethnic material on radio. NBC, in November 1929, started airing *The Rise of the Goldbergs*, fifteen-minute monologues (in English) about everyday New York Jewish life related by the engaging Gertrude Berg.[51]

Drag Comedy

Though neither racial nor ethnic, another cinematic byway flourished briefly at this time. The female impersonator Julian Eltinge's film MAID TO ORDER (dir. Elmer Clifton, 1929) was produced at Tec-Art. Nicknamed "Mr. Lillian Russell," Eltinge was a famous beauty and had appeared in dual roles in several silent films.[52] His competitor Olyn Landick, another well-known vaudeville female impersonator, made ALL STUCK UP (dir. George Lemaire, 1929), a Pathé two-reel comedy. Anthony Slide has observed that female impersonation was indigenous to the popular stage. It was not until later in the 1930s that dressing in drag became identified with homosexuality and thereafter lost its appeal as popular entertainment.[53]

Actual representations of gay characters in early sound films invariably reduced them to stage clichés. A good example is the stage manager in THE BROADWAY MELODY (1929), who carries on an effeminate rave about lavender costumes. As with female impersonation, exploiting a man speaking in a woman's voice or with a stereotypical lisp was an easy way to arouse curiosity and elicit humor.

The Talkie Melting Pot

Hollywood promoted the melting-pot ethos with a vengeance. In films like THE KING OF JAZZ, we see Italians, Spaniards, Irish, Scots, Russians, Mexicans, Polish Jews, English, and Germans stirred into a literal pot to produce jazz. (African Americans were not ingredients in this mixture.) Eddie Cantor, in WHOOPEE!, shows the comic exploits of a Jew who goes to the Wild West. (The plot twist revolving around an Indian who turns out to have no Indian blood and can therefore marry the heroine is almost a burlesque of

The costumer in The Broadway Melody *(MGM, 1929) spoke with a stereotypical lisp.*

Golden Dawn.) The Marx Brothers, especially in Animal Crackers, squeeze laughs from the hardships and cultural dissonance of immigration.[54] It is difficult to evaluate the effect of such films. On the one hand, they may have raised the audience's consciousness of its ethnic minority constituency, but on the other hand, they may have reinforced (perhaps even created) minority prejudices. On a general level, the tendency was to dilute these groups' separateness, either by showing the minority's inevitable assimilation or by making its resistance to assimilation into a joke. Hollywood's traditional response to ethnicity has been to wipe out difference under the guise of promoting its distinctiveness. Desser has commented on this propagandistic tendency in commercial film:

> Whether [they] did so out of fear of outside censorship or control, or out of an inchoate sense of gratitude on the part of the major emerging film producers to their new American home, American movie-makers worked toward envisioning a unified society of white, middle-class citizens. One of the problems of this society, one of its contradictions, was between a vision of unified culture and the facts of difference, primarily ethnic difference. Ethnicity was a fact of American life, as was racism, sexism, and other forms of bigotry and discrimination. (David Desser, "The Cinematic Melting Pot," in Lester D. Friedman, ed., *Unspeakable Images: Ethnicity and the American Cinema* [Urbana: University of Illinois Press, 1991], p. 383)

The talkies provided a handy means for exploiting this contradiction. Ethnic voices and musical traditions could readily be expropriated, transformed into entertainment, while both cordoning off and erasing the source.

The acoustic melting pot is caricatured brilliantly in HURDY GURDY (dir. Hal Roach, 1929). The Irish cop Edgar Kennedy just wants to escape the heat wave by taking a nap on his Delancey Street tenement fire escape. All around him, though, his neighbors carry on in a Babel of ethnic New Yorkese—Spanish, Italian, Yiddish, German, and generic Brooklyn. Kennedy, ironically of course, refers to them as "foreigners" in his strong Irish brogue. (Judging from the film, no African Americans lived on Delancey Street.) The film calls attention to New York's multi-ethnicity by foregrounding these various accents. But by identifying them as non-American, it also suggests that they should be (and probably will be) assimilated.

The sound film quickly became a showdown for ethnicity. During the introductory period, performers like Rubin, Sidney, Brice, Cantor, Jolson, Edgar Kennedy, Charlie Murray, and Stepin Fetchit were admired for their ethnically specific vocal characterizations. After 1930, though, many of these differences were effaced. (Cantor's PALMY DAYS [1931], in which the star's Jewishness was soft-pedaled, is a case in point.)[55] In Hollywood, the coming of sound was a time of great opportunity for African Americans in show business, strictly in terms of employment prospects. But the roles were limited to a few categories: servant, jockey, country bumpkin, plantation worker. Characterization, expressed most often in speech, was highly conventional. Actors like Clarence Muse joked about having to learn how to speak in Hollywood Negro dialect. The producers tried (and succeeded) in molding screen blacks into their preconception (based on memories of minstrelsy) of how African Americans behaved and talked. Even when blacks were placed on pedestals as superhumanly gifted singers and dancers or shown to possess extraordinary spirituality and religion, these celebratory gestures just isolated them further as cinematic spectacle. The role of blacks on the screen during this period is analogous to the uses of jazz by society at large. The entertainers, like the musical form, were absorbed by white culture to serve its own purposes.[56]

Minority filmmaking and ethnic-language production could have continued indefinitely, with separate (but unequal) production the norm and with segregated exhibition continuing the patterns of silent film days. The Depression ended this possibility. Big studios honed their product to appeal to the largest common denominator. Minority filmmakers did not have the resources because their small markets could not support them. Both race cinema for blacks and Yiddish cinema avoided sensitive issues like whites' racism and anti-Semitism. They seldom if ever addressed external issues like segregation or discrimination. Rather, the filmmakers tended to be interested in stories that would teach and delight. Often the films were about the difficulty of coping with domestic hardships. These melodramas lend themselves to interpretation as symbolic discourses about minority culture, but it is necessary to read between the lines to see in the family crises they depict metaphors for larger and unmentionable themes of oppression.

These other voices faded after the mid-1930s. The saturation of American society by radio and the talkies undoubtedly had a leveling effect on the spread of ethnic sounds and images. At the time, social critics claimed that the media would eliminate regional differences in American speech. On a national level, that did not happen. But with ethnic minorities, assimilation gradually stirred "foreign" ways of speaking into the melting pot. Now the surviving fragments of this filmmaking are among the few artifacts of a distant era of cultural history.

17

Foreign Affairs

Sound enabled the American film industry to solidify its power as the leading exporter of entertainment. At the end of the 1920s, about two-thirds of the world's 57,341 cinemas were outside the United States and provided Hollywood with substantial distribution revenue. Though one can read again and again that producers were terrified that sound would mean the loss of overseas markets, there is little expression of such terror in the trade journals of the day. Nor do the statistics show any decreases in exports. It is more likely that producers saw the emerging technology as an opportunity to saturate European markets with their product. The challenge, as with all other aspects of sound, was how to channel it in ways that would gather new audiences.

While the studios were converting in 1928, many were not convinced that the talkies would succeed in the domestic market, let alone overseas. So they did not develop a uniform strategy for international exploitation. Fox, for instance, rejected speaking parts in foreign releases as "unfeasible for the present at least."[1] United Artists' Joseph Schenck would not consider any international distribution schemes for sound films. He doubted that the talkies would catch on regardless of the export country's language: "Even in English-speaking countries only certain pictures will permit of spoken lines as an accessory. Even with these there will be only occasional instances of success."[2] N. L. Manheim, the export manager of Universal, asserted, "I firmly believe that the silent picture will always have an important place on the screens of foreign countries." *Film Daily* polled industry executives in 1929, asking, "Does sound mean an end to internationalism in motion pictures?" Most of the responses were long-winded pronouncements about America's cinematic invincibility. Will Hays's complete reply was, "The answer is certainly not."[3] Though terse, it was right on the mark. Exports in 1929 set a new record: 282,215,480 feet (against the old record of 9,000,000 feet in 1919). "A rather engaging answer to the suggestion that the talkers have ruined our foreign film trade," mused Jack Alicoate.[4] Of course, most of this footage was silent. The slow change to sound in Europe undoubtedly prolonged the production of silent versions of Hollywood talkies. It also gave Americans a chance to make plans which, in principle, would let them tighten their grip on European and Asian commercial film.

U.S. exports had dominated world markets since World War I. At the end of the twenties, before the conversion to sound began, this commanding position showed signs of weakening. Britain successfully imposed a quota in 1927. Germany, France, Italy, and the Scandinavian countries had been trying to form a cartel to resist the Americans, a loosely defined movement called "Film Europe." American firms' market share in these countries had been decreasing since 1926. The U.S. Department of Commerce responded by strengthening its Motion Picture Division.⁵ How would sound affect this possibly shifting balance of trade?

The 1928 Department of Commerce report indicated that Great Britain provided the greatest opportunity for expansion, not only because of the shared language, but because the "advanced popularity" of the movies in Britain ensured the financial worthiness of the conversion. Next in profit potential came Germany, and then, a distant third, France. The Commerce report concluded that because of the lack of European linguistic or economic unity, no single country making films in its own language could compete with Hollywood.⁶

Some Americans realized that the talkies could give Hollywood a tremendous advantage. The problem was that linguistic differences were also difficult for the American producers to overcome. How to export sound? Kann gloomily observed, "Here is a difficulty for which they can supply no answer."⁷ The basic issues, which were linked, concerned trade and quota problems, language, cultural, and technical difficulties.

The European film industries were not unsuspecting victims of Hollywood's aggressive charge. Several European sound systems had been developing apace with American experiments.⁸ We have already seen that there might have been a murky exchange of ideas between the Tri-Ergon group and de Forest in 1921–1922. The inventors Vogt, Engl, and Massolle continued to refine their variable-density sound-on-film system. The big studio conglomerate Ufa (Universum-Film AG) purchased an option on it and began trial Tri-Ergon production with *Das Leben auf dem Dorfe* in 1923, then let the process languish. In France the Gaumont Company had pursued its prewar interest in sound-on-disc. Gaumont abandoned this line of research in 1925 and formed a partnership with Electrical Fono-Film of Denmark to exploit the system developed by Petersen and Poulsen. This one recorded the sound optically on a separate strip of film. Meanwhile, the various international branches of De Forest Phonofilm attained limited success. They filmed music-hall entertainments, wired out-of-the-way, independently owned theaters, and eked out very little appreciation for the equipment's poor quality sound reproduction.

American filmmakers automatically committed themselves to international distribution when they signed with ERPI because the Western Electric subsidiary was already licensing equipment to European and Asian producers and promising American sound movies to exhibitors. In May 1927, ERPI licensed Salabar, a music publisher, to produce short sound films of the musical variety genre in Paris using Western Electric equipment. American-made Vitaphone and Movietone pictures premiered in European capitals in 1928—with the English-spoken parts untranslated. They did "good business, but by no means phenomenal," the trade journal editor Ernest Fredman observed. But these films renewed interest on the part of European entrepreneurs. In London, Warners had leased the Piccadilly Theatre to play Vitaphone. THE JAZZ SINGER premiered on 27 September 1928. (It had already played in Europe as a silent.) It was followed by THE TERROR (1928), a big hit in the United States that took "an awful slamming" in London. ("So bad that it is almost suicidal," reported one correspondent.) THE SINGING FOOL opened at the Regal in the West End and was well received. But the initial talking-picture wave in Britain failed to produce the excitement that had marked the American reception. In January 1929, there still were only eleven Western Electric houses in the British Isles. "Very naturally the situation has been of great interest to British and Continental exhibitors," wrote Fredman. "But the fact remains that despite all the volume of talk one has listened to on this subject there is something akin to almost complete apathy evinced by exhibitors in England."[9] At RCA, David Sarnoff knew that if sound caught on in the United States, nascent European competition was poised to emerge. Determined to beat both Western Electric and the European studios, he sent J. D. Williams to London in June 1928 to negotiate British RCA Photophone sales.

The first Gaumont-Petersen-Poulsen program of musical shorts was projected in Paris on 6 October 1928. As 1929 began, though, there were only two theaters in Paris playing sound films. In Berlin, Walther Ruttmann made *Die Melodie der Welt*, a poetic documentary sponsored by the Holland-Amerika steamship line. It was mostly stock travel footage edited with post-synchronized noises and a score by Wolfgang Zeller.[10]

Italy's economy retarded the film industry's conversion to talking, but the government's involvement in sound production was direct. "Premier Mussolini has interested himself personally in films as a moulder of national habits." His Luce organization entered into an exchange agreement with Ufa that would speed up production of Italian sound films.[11] Otherwise, Europe's changeover to sound crept along.

The only serious challenge to the American sound systems was presented in 1928 by Tobis Klangfilm. Tobis, an acronym for Tonbild Syndikat, was a multinational patent pool based in Berlin that controlled the rights to Tri-Ergon (except for William Fox's North American license). In October 1928, the Dutch combine Küchenmeister bought a controlling interest. Also in October, the German electrical trust AEG (Allgemeine Elektrizitäts Gesellschaft) consolidated under the name Klangfilm a competing group of patent holders: the Polyphon phonograph company, Telefunken radio, and the electric company Siemens-Halske. As ERPI was wiring theaters briskly in Europe during the spring of 1929, Tobis claimed that Western Electric's Movietone-Fox-Case-de Forest–derived apparatus infringed on Tri-Ergon. The German rivals dropped their differences and merged to resist the Americans. Tobis Klangfilm flexed its muscles and obtained injunctions to cancel the premiere of THE SINGING FOOL in Berlin. It successfully enjoined ERPI from installing equipment in Germany and the other countries where the Tobis Klangfilm patents were recognized as valid. Outside Germany, Tobis Klangfilm set up facilities for making local-language films. Its most successful venture was establishing, in February 1929, Société Française des Films Sonores Tobis in the former Eclair studios in Epinay (near Paris). Suddenly, the U.S. companies had a powerful challenge to their right to record Europe's films and wire its theaters.

ERPI's John Otterson tried to negotiate with the Germans, but Tobis demanded high royalties. With the cooperation of the MPPDA, Hollywood producers retaliated by refusing to release their films in Germany. There was not sufficient unity among the Americans, though, to sustain the boycott. General Electric bought an interest in AEG, which gave RCA Photophone limited access to Tobis's markets. In London, Hitchcock shot BLACKMAIL (1929) on the RCA system for British International Pictures. In France, Gaumont's competitor Pathé-Nathan licensed Photophone for five years. Its international success was MON GOSSE DE PÈRE (1930), also made in English as THE PARISIAN, both directed by Jean de Limur and starring the bilingual Adolphe Menjou.[12]

Warner Bros. also bought its way into Europe. In April 1930, the company purchased a 20 percent interest in the European patents and licenses of Küchenmeister, thus becoming a partner of Tobis Klangfilm. This was a coup and an insult to Western Electric, which was still blocked by the Germans. With the boycott weakening, the U.S. majors had no choice but to negotiate. Adolph Zukor urged Will Hays to convene a conference to settle affairs.

Menjou made THE PARISIAN (MON GOSSE DE PÈRE, *Pathé-Nathan, 1930*) *in French
and English during a dispute with Paramount.*

The Yankees Invade

Will Hays's cocky attitude was apparent when he insisted that American films played in foreign countries "by invitation":

> The entire world today is in the market for pictures. . . . Ours is not a foreign invasion at all. Our pictures go abroad by invitation. The people of the world want them, despite the activities of foreign governments to lessen the effectiveness of the American film industry by practically subsidizing indigenous film production. However, by revealing the need for our films abroad, and by proving our sincerity in exhibiting worthwhile foreign productions here, amicable adjustments are being effected in foreign countries, which will lead to happier business relations in all European countries. (*Film Daily*, 21 June 1928, p. 3)

By mid-1929, the race was on between ERPI, RCA, and Tobis to wire theaters in Europe and Asia. In the United Kingdom, fifty ERPI technicians were installing equipment around-the-clock. Residents of Warsaw, like fans in many cities, saw and heard Jolson in THE SINGING FOOL in the summer of 1929.[13] American chauvinism was never more apparent than during the initial staking out of international sound markets. Far from believing that the incapacity of non-English-speakers to understand the talkies might upset the applecart, movie showmen, on the contrary, predicted that the talkies would establish English as a universal language. The film industry believed that "ten per cent of foreign audiences understand enough English to comprehend American movies."[14] William C. deMille told an Academy seminar, "In as much as the introduction of American films into Europe has resulted in Europeans wearing American hats and shoes and almost everything else, so we may be sure that in a couple of generations from now, all Europeans will be speaking English so that they may continue to see and understand American films."[15] According to Winfield Sheehan, "Talking pictures may in time make the English language known throughout the civilized world."[16]

There was a foreshadowing of trouble, though. American films were immensely popular at the box office, but the press and intellectuals in other countries resented the American executives' pushiness. When Jesse Lasky remarked during a 1928 visit to England that there would be no silent pictures in five years, he triggered an angry response in the local papers. According to one, "The British public will never submit to American-made films in which performers speak in the nasal twang of the Yankee." The British journal *Close-Up* in particular responded with vituperation against the talkies. French critics formed the "League of Silence" in noisy protest. They argued that "Americans should not imagine that in addition to having to swallow their films we will have to put up with their language or be forced to learn it if we are to understand their new movies." Even the orchestral music in synchronized prints was not exempt: "The same melody does not appeal to a French and to an American audience."[17]

The theater and film director Max Reinhardt exemplified the most common response among defenders of film art. Since the teens, motion pictures had been hailed as a kind of visual Esperanto, understandable by all peoples. Now, according to the famous dramatist, "films which are universal in appeal and really international, can only tend to be destroyed as an international art through the addition of the limitation of language." Throughout Europe, critics and filmmakers, including Rudolf Arnheim, Béla Balázs,

René Clair, Abel Gance, Fritz Lang, Eisenstein, and his Russian colleagues, denounced synchronous sound cinema.[18]

Turning a deaf ear, Americans quickly devised strategies to extend their sound monopolies. Their statements ring with the rhetoric of cultural imperialism, complete with military terminology. Words like *invasion, offensive,* and *assault* appear regularly. When Western Electric wired the Hogaku-za theater in Tokyo, for instance, the press release proclaimed: "ERPI has captured another country!"[19] Japan had utilized the *benshi,* a live commentator who supplied voices and narration alongside silent films, a practice seemingly incompatible with the showing of talkies. American sound engineers were diverted by the conflict and belittled Asian resistance:

> It was amusing during the showing of *Redskin* [1928] to hear the interpreter trying to raise his voice above the music and effects. It gave the impression of Benshi vs. ERPI. . . . He was getting rather angry, according to the manager, who explained one day that if we did not favor him he might start a general strike. There is no organization among the operators here. (J. L. Pickard, "Old and New Meet in Orient as *Benshi* and Talkies Combine to Entertain Patrons," *Erpigram,* 1 September 1929, p. 2)

The *benshi* did indeed go on strike in 1929. Though Japanese sound production began on a limited basis in 1931, silent movies generally proved to be more resistant to colonization than anticipated; the commentators were a close-knit group of workers with a strong public following and their own union. They kept performing with silent Japanese films well into the 1930s.[20]

Nathan D. Golden prefaced his Department of Commerce film export report for 1929 with a description of the "film famine" in European production induced by American talkies: "The advent of sound pictures abroad, the foreign producer's inability to produce sound pictures, his fear of producing silent ones, gave to the American producer an open field in the past year in marketing an increased number of silent pictures."[21] An unusually brazen exposition of the industry's strategic plan to take over Europe appeared in the Hollywood trade journal *Film Mercury.* The unnamed executive pressed the economic advantage: "We know already what language is being used in England, in Germany, and in France against the American invasion. And we know as well that those who clamor the loudest have been, and still are, our best clients." He mapped out the plan:

> We are following, after a few cautious steps, a campaign strategy which is very simple; we are buying theaters in the capitals and in the important big cities first; from there we will spread out everywhere. Let's leave them little respite so that our financiers can quickly force the extermination of what little remains of what used to be called the European film! We won't permit ourselves, you say, to grab their theater circuits! Aren't we doing just that right now in London, in Berlin, and in Paris?
>
> The heads of the European film industry moreover hold out their hands to the all powerful American dollar with such greediness that they don't even see opening before them the grave into which they will soon stumble.
>
> Another part of our plan consists in luring to Hollywood all European artists of any renown. When silent films were king this tactic worked mar-

velously and it should be perfectly suited to the talking film as well. In the
theaters of England, Germany, and France will resound national sound
tracks made in the U.S.A. What European producer will vie with us when
we have captured their greatest actors with our money? (*Film Mercury*,
March 1930, quoted in Dudley Andrew, "Sound in France: The Origins of a
Native School," *Yale French Studies* no. 60, 1980, pp. 97–98)

Whatever the cultural risk, Hollywood producers had little economic risk. They were
still flush with domestic revenue derived from the talkies. But they were beset with pro-
cedural, technical, marketing, and cultural questions. Should they just show American
films "straight," in their original English versions? Would some form of "voice doubling"
work—recording alternate-language versions while the English version was being shot?
Could they dub Hollywood features into foreign languages? Should different-language
versions be produced in Hollywood? In international locales? This option was clouded
by aggressive foreign governments intent on protecting their domestic film industries
from "invasion." Germany, Great Britain, Austria, France, Italy, and Hungary had quotas or "contingent" plans which restricted imports or tied American distribution to local
production. Anyway, international audiences adored Hollywood stars. Would they pay to
see films with native-speaking nonentities?

Minimal Translations and Multilingual Subjects

Reflecting the producers' confidence in their audiences' willingness to accept English,
one of the initial responses was to do as little as possible to alter the original American
versions. MGM's international success with THE BROADWAY MELODY was very influential; the film circulated in many countries in English with superimposed titles explaining
the action between songs.[22] The tendency to supply international markets with films
requiring minimal translation may have extended the life of the part-talking movie, since
it was easier to subtitle short dialogue scenes (or just delete them) while the remainder
of the film played as a synchronized silent. Kristin Thompson has hypothesized that the
abundance of revue musicals in 1929–1930 also might be attributed to Hollywood's
grappling with its language problems. "Even with no translation they proved attractive;
when subtitled they required a minimum of writing to keep the audience up with the
action. It seems likely that the vogue among the studios for this genre had partly to do
with the desire to maintain exports." The sections in revue films with big American stars
could play in the original version. Local stars could have segments in their native
tongues interspersed. In PARAMOUNT ON PARADE, for example, Chevalier did sketches in
French, Egon von Jordan regaled German audiences, and Rosita Moreno hosted GALAS
DE LA PARAMOUNT. Perhaps illustrating the "if you can't lick 'em, hire 'em" approach, the
studio brought Susei Matsui, the leading *benshi* of Paramount's Tokyo theater, to
Hollywood to host the Japanese-language version. PARAMOUNT ON PARADE was also
made with inserts in Czech, Dutch, Polish, Hungarian, Danish, and Serbian.[23] THE KING
OF JAZZ played Berlin with the popular actor Arnold Korff as the master of ceremonies.
"He did not annoy the audience at all, and that takes considerable doing in this most
thankless of all forms of dramatic tidying up." In HOLLYWOOD REVUE OF 1929, Dita
Parlo sang in French and German. The film director Sergei Eisenstein and the composer Igor Stravinsky performed a duet in the German version. The climax featured

Buster Keaton, Norma Shearer, Joan Crawford, Marion Davies, and Laurel and Hardy "all apparently breaking out in German in the finale, 'Singin' in the Rain.'"[24]

Voice doubling and dubbing had been practiced in Hollywood since 1927, but the techniques and equipment available in early 1930 were inadequate for large-scale application. Most sound tracks were still recorded with the music, effects, and dialogue mixed together on the fly. H. M. Knox of ERPI reported that "the temporary expedients of fitting foreign words to English lip movements, and other make-shifts, have been tried and hastily abandoned. The foreign language pictures of the future will be recorded in each tongue."[25] These films became known as multiple-language versions. The original Hollywood story was reshot with actors speaking different dialogue. Usually the movies were carbon copies, but sometimes the script, locale, and costumes were modified to reflect the customs and censorship demands of the destination country. (Even British exports were modified; WHOOPEE! and MAMMY, for instance, were adjusted to accommodate local taste.)[26]

Paramount led the way in multiple-language production, followed by MGM, Warner Bros., Fox, Universal, RKO, Columbia, Pathé, and a few independents. These non-English shorts and features were shot domestically using actors and stories with international appeal.

Warners was the first American producer to experiment with foreign-language production. As usual, its laboratory was the Vitaphone shorts unit. Economy was the main goal, so one important early tactic was to hire entertainers who might please North American as well as foreign audiences. Don Alberto, an Argentinean dance orchestra leader, made shorts which could be appreciated by aficionados of Latin music everywhere. They were shown in Spanish-speaking regions of the United States and exported to South America. In October 1928, Vitaphone released the playlet TWO HUNDRED AND FORTIETH STREET and Gregory Ratoff's comedy FOR SALE in English, French (CULOT AMÉRICAIN), and German (ECHTIGER AMERIKANER). Also in its Brooklyn studio, Warners produced a German talking feature, THE ROYAL BOX (DIE KÖNIGSLOGE, 1930), directed by Bryan Foy, with Alexander Moissi and Camilla Horn. Moissi was an acclaimed German actor and a pupil of Max Reinhardt whom Foy had seen on tour in 1928. The story of the nineteenth-century English actor Edmund Kean, according to *Variety,* was "nearly devoid of any action, with all interest mainly in the dialog and one or two situations."[27] The film ran at the Fifth Avenue Playhouse for six weeks in 1930, before opening in nine U.S. cities with significant German populations. It was accompanied by a program of all-German Vitaphone shorts. Warners was encouraged enough to set aside $2 million to produce forty-three multilingual features for 1930–1931 (a goal which proved wildly ambitious). To ensure a supply of multilingual actors, Jack Warner inaugurated the Vitaphone School of Language. Four Berlitz instructors came from New York to Burbank to train players to speak in foreign-language talkies.

RKO's big film of 1929, RIO RITA, was among the first to attempt a dubbed sound track. In November, distributed by United Artists, it played in eleven Spanish-speaking countries. Though there were complaints about the sound quality, this does not appear to have been the only, or even the most important, reason for the failure of dubbing. William LeBaron admitted that despite the enormous publicity attending the foreign versions of RIO RITA, these releases "did not receive [the] anticipated cordial reception in their respective countries, audiences showing a marked preference for the English original."[28] In other words, hearing the actual voice of the star was held to be more important than complete linguistic comprehension. Consequently, RKO tried two other solutions, neither of which worked. First, it dabbled in French-language production and

Gregory Ratoff (right) in FOR SALE *(Warner Bros., 1928).*

set up a unit headed by Henri de la Falaise, Gloria Swanson's husband. He had worked in Hollywood for William LeBaron (and Joseph Kennedy) since 1928. The result was three films. ECHEC AU ROI was a remake of THE ROYAL BED (1930), originally directed by Lowell Sherman. It starred Françoise Rosay and Emile Chautard, and was codirected by Léon d'Usseau and de la Falaise. Its story of a king who would rather play checkers than attend to affairs of state and the bedchamber was not particularly popular. Next came LE FILS DE L'AUTRE (from THE WOMAN BETWEEN), and, finally, NUIT D'ESPAGNE, all in 1931.[29] LeBaron formed a transatlantic alliance with Basil Dean's Associated Talking Pictures of London. Under the arrangement, RKO provided technical supervision of the films, to be made in Hollywood, in exchange for U.S. distribution rights.

RKO also concocted the most technically extravagant plan for multiple-language versions. It hired Carroll Dunning, a founder of Prizma Color, to exploit his blue-screen and traveling matte process whereby images of actors speaking their native language on a soundstage could be composited onto a prefilmed location background, thus saving exterior shooting expenses. Dunning traveled to Berlin with his son in January 1931 to demonstrate how to make German, Spanish, French, and Swedish versions of BEAU IDEAL (1931, originally directed by Herbert Brenon). But the financially ailing studio quickly abandoned these schemes and all foreign-language production. When RKO opened its prestige picture CIMARRON at the Champs-Elysées theater in Paris, it played only in the American dialogue version.[30]

Warners intended to supply its German branch, Deutsche First National Pictures (Defina), with American-made covers. The experienced actor and director William Dieterle was in charge and was allowed to recruit actors in Berlin.[31] Hall, writing on DER TANZ GEHT WEITER (1930, adapted from THOSE WHO DANCE), opined that "the German cast . . . is uniformly competent and in addition the film has the advantage of perfect recording and imaginative photography and direction." Warners' most ambitious foreign-language cover was MOBY DICK (1930). Never leaving Burbank, Michael Curtiz directed a French version and most of the German version, DÄMON DES MEERES (though Dieterle directed some scenes).[32] Dieterle played Captain Ahab, John Barrymore's part in the original. Later he reminisced:

> I was hired to make synchronizations. Sound had just come in, and Holly-wood was afraid of losing foreign markets. So they hired German, French and Spanish units to make foreign versions of important features. . . . The four films we were to make had already been completed. All the sets were still standing and dressed—we used the same costumes and everything. The big difference was that we had just ten days to make each picture. The supervisor of all this was Henry Blanke. (Quoted in Tom Flinn, "William Dieterle, the Plutarch of Hollywood," *Velvet Light Trap* 15 [Fall 1975]: p. 6)

Warner Bros. soon tested its German connections by moving into overseas coproduction. With Nero-Film, Warners planned to make trilingual versions in Berlin of THE THREEPENNY OPERA, an adaptation of the Bertolt Brecht and Kurt Weill stage production, with G. W. Pabst directing.[33] Though it seemed like a guaranteed hit, there were numerous production delays, not the least of which was caused by the famous lawsuit in which Brecht sued Pabst and the producers over their treatment of the script. He lost the case. In the German version, Rudolf Forster played Mackie Messer and Lotte Lenya played Jenny. In the French version, L'OPÉRA DE QUAT'SOUS, Albert Préjean and Margo Lion had these roles. The film was not released until February 1931. *Film Daily* described DIE DREI GROSCHENOPER as "all a wild jumble, poorly motivated and directed, with some good atmospheric scenes and acting far superior to the muddled and long-drawn-out and tiresome story." The English version was never made.[34]

MGM boasted of the quantity of stars and directors on its payroll who could speak several languages. Louis B. Mayer promised at least six multilingual films for 1929–1930 and budgeted $6 million for them. More than sixty international actors, writers, and directors were hired at a cost of $40,000 per week.[35] The former German expressionist director Arthur Robison came to Hollywood, made a German-language TRIAL OF MARY DUGAN, and returned to Europe.[36] Belgian-born Jacques Feyder was the most prestigious discovery, having made several high-quality productions in France throughout the 1920s, capped in 1928 by THÉRÈSE RAQUIN (shot in Berlin, and LES NOUVEAUX MESSIEURS), which was notorious for having sustained heavy political censorship in France. Feyder directed Garbo in MGM's last silent film, the stylish and shocking (she gets away with murder) THE KISS (1929). After this auspicious beginning, he was assigned the multilingual productions. The first Culver City French release, LE SPECTRE VERT (1930) redid THE UNHOLY NIGHT (originally shot by Lionel Barrymore in 1929) and was well received in France.[37] Feyder remade John Gilbert's HIS GLORIOUS NIGHT (1929) with different casts in German (released in Berlin under its original title, OLYMPIA) and in French (SI L'EMPEREUR SAVAIT ÇA! [1930]). The German version was a failure. The *Times'* Berlin correspondent wondered, "The same play, with John Gilbert, was already a frost in English, so why make a German version of it?" He noted, "The making of these foreign versions in Hollywood costs anywhere from $80,000 to $125,000—surely neither [OLYMPIA nor DER TANZ GEHT WEITER] will get back the money invested in them. So it is still an open question whether it is worth while trundling a complete German cast across an ocean and a continent to make a film among the hills of Hollywood."[38] The French version was better, though the stars from the Comédie Française tended to speak to the microphone rather than to each other. Françoise Rosay, the actress who was married to Feyder, won praise. THE BIG HOUSE was made by Paul Fejos in German as MENSCHEN HINTER GITTERN (1930) and in French as BIG HOUSE (1930). The Spanish version was directed by Ward Wing.

The most famous foreign version is unquestionably the German ANNA CHRISTIE (1930), starring Greta Garbo, directed by Feyder, and shot in three weeks. The American actors were replaced by Theo Shall, Hans Junkermann, and Salka Steuermann. Garbo's vocal delivery is more conversational in German, the cut of her costume less austere, and the details of Anna's sexual past less ambiguous than in the Clarence Brown–directed American version. "Her presence is if anything," said Hall when the film ran in New York, "more striking in this current work than in the English version." After MGM ceased foreign-language versions, Feyder shot two English-only features, DAYBREAK and SON OF INDIA (both 1931). Spanish-accented Ramón Novarro played an Austrian officer in the first and was outfitted with a turban for the second. Feyder returned to France in 1931 and resumed his distinguished career. The multitalented, multilingual Novarro directed, acted, and danced a tango in the French and Spanish versions of CALL OF THE FLESH (dir. Charles Brabin, 1930).[39]

Hal Roach's new MGM comedies, such as BRATS (1930), with Laurel and Hardy, were made simultaneously in French and Spanish by James Parrott, directing through interpreters. Stan and Ollie learned to pronounce their lines phonetically. Roach also produced, under Keaton's sponsorship, several two-reel remakes in Spanish of Fatty Arbuckle's old comedies. Charley Chase signed a new five-year contract with Roach, "which, due to the comedian's speed in mastering foreign languages, puts Chase in the big money class."[40] Roach also directed French, Spanish, and Italian versions of his 1930 feature MEN OF THE NORTH.[41]

Buster Keaton tried out his Spanish in DE FRENTE, MARCHEN (1930), a remake of DOUGHBOYS (1930) with Conchita Montenegro, and ESTRELLADOS (1930), from FREE AND EASY (1930). He mouthed German in CASANOVA WIDER WILLEN (dir. Edward Brophy) and tested his French in BUSTER SE MARIE (dir. Edward Brophy and Claude Autant-Lara), both 1931 remakes of PARLOR, BEDROOM AND BATH (1931).[42]

Glancy's study of MGM grosses shows that even films which did poorly in the States often did well overseas in their international versions. Foreign audiences evidently liked Buster Keaton's talkies (available in French, German, and Spanish) better than Americans did. But—instructive to executives, no doubt—films distributed overseas in their original versions, such as Novarro's musical comedies (for instance, IN GAY MADRID [1930]) and the Lawrence Tibbett–Grace Moore operettas, also did very well.[43]

Fox's spectacular Western THE BIG TRAIL (1930) was shot in five versions with different actors in John Wayne's scout role.[44] Fox produced Spanish-language shorts and feature remakes at its Movietone City plant through 1932. It also distributed German sound films in Berlin through a joint venture called Defa (Deutsche Fox-Film AG); its exploration of the idea of organizing a studio of its own in France for production of for-

"Breck Colman" in THE BIG TRAIL *(Fox, 1930) was played by Jorge Lewis in the Spanish version, Gaston Glass in French, John Wayne in English, Franco Corsaro in Italian, and Theo Schall in German.*

eign versions did not come to fruition. Fox's expansion into Europe was obviously curtailed by the company's disintegration back home.

United Artists functioned only as a distributor in Europe. Joseph Schenck did try to take advantage of Jolson's vacation in Berlin to cast him in a German- and Yiddish-language picture, SONS O' GUNS, but his proposal coincided with the ERPI-Tobis dispute over quotas and the Hollywood boycott of Germany. The project was canceled.[45]

Universal had no plans for producing abroad in May, but in July 1929 the studio reconsidered and decided to make some shorts in Berlin. Most production remained at Universal City and was bare-bones. In one rather desperate experiment, Universal resorted to the transatlantic telephone when Conrad Veidt dictated some sequences intended to transform the silent THE LAST PERFORMANCE (dir. Fejos, 1929) into a talkie. The star's voice was "projected into the microphone for recording the picture."[46] BOUDOIR DIPLOMAT (1930) was directed in English by Malcolm St. Clair at a cost of $344,000. The French and German versions both began filming on 3 November 1930 and *shared* a $146,292 budget and a twenty-four-day shooting schedule. The former was directed by Marcel de Sano, while Ernest Laemmle helmed the latter. The French version was discontinued on 17 November. The German version wrapped on 29 November, on schedule, but having consumed 80 percent of the budget for both films. The Spanish-language DRÁCULA (dir. George Melford, 1931) was filmed after-hours on the English-language set in Universal City and starred Carlos Villarías in Bela Lugosi's role.

The smaller studios were ambivalent. Pathé hired the Latin band leader Xavier Cugat, who was the top attraction at the Coconut Grove nightclub, to compose a theme song and lyrics for an all-Spanish feature. Columbia aimed to make half of its 1930–1931 product trilingual and began by casting Alla Nazimova in English, French, and Russian versions of a feature (which never materialized). Columbia did release four Spanish-language films in 1931, beginning with CARNE DE CABARET, a remake of TEN CENTS A DANCE (1931). Mack Sennett produced French, German, and Spanish versions of his comedies. Fleischer made a Spanish cartoon, *La Paloma*.

Independent companies (including the ones specializing in Yiddish) attempted to meet the needs of this specialized market. René Cardona and Rodolfo Montes founded the Cuban International Film Company in New York and produced SOMBRAS HABANERAS (1929), probably the first Spanish-language American sound feature.[47] Sono-Art World Wide adapted its film WHAT A MAN! for Spanish moviegoers as ASI ES LA VIDA (dir. George Crone, 1930). The Hollywood Spanish Pictures Company, working with Xavier Cugat, made CHARROS, GAUCHOS Y MANOLAS, a musical revue distributed in Mexico. Italotone made an Italian-language feature, SEI TU L'AMORE? (dir. Alfredo Sabato, 1930) in Hollywood, reportedly with a very high budget of $150,000. The story is somewhat similar to RKO's STREET GIRL (1929): three men save a woman from committing suicide, and she eventually becomes rich and successful. *Variety* and the *New York Times* had different takes. "American producers have a fitful warning in this first Italian dialoger made in Hollywood," forecast the trade paper. The reviewer praised the lavish sets but felt they were not well utilized. The actors spoke Italian with distracting American mannerisms. Hall, although he too dismissed the dialogue as "halting," was nevertheless impressed by the film's positive reception as the audience beamed at hearing a movie in its own language: "[It] attracted a greater throng than has ever been seen in the Eighth Street Playhouse. In fact, the place was uncomfortably crowded. . . . [T]he audience yesterday afternoon derived no end of amusement out of the film. When they were not laughing they were smiling broadly, and it was almost as interesting to watch some of the faces as to look at the screen."[48]

Paramount in Europe

The studio that made the greatest commitment to multiple-language versions was Paramount. At first, the studio hedged its bets between domestic and foreign production sites. Adolph Zukor announced that twenty foreign-language features would be shot in Hollywood and Astoria. Maurice Chevalier was hired, in part, to exploit his potential for bilingual production. He succeeded admirably. Indeed, these films revived his film career in France. He impressed Parisians in the Astoria-made LA CHANSON DE PARIS (1929) as much as he had Americans in the original version, INNOCENTS OF PARIS (1929). "His previous work for the screen—the silent screen—did him less than justice. In his sound film he is himself, free to give the whole of his art without restriction," the *Times*' Paris correspondent reported.[49] LE PETITE CAFÉ was a remake of a Max Linder silent film shot in France in 1914. This pet project of Chevalier's was considered better than the English version, PLAYBOY OF PARIS (1930). LA PARADE D'AMOUR and LA GRANDE MARE exploited Chevalier (in both) and Claudette Colbert (in the latter). These 1930 films were covers of THE LOVE PARADE (1929) and THE BIG POND (1930). Adolphe Menjou and Colbert remade SLIGHTLY SCARLET in French as L'ENIGMATIQUE MONSIEUR PARKES (1930). Reviewing it at New York's Fifty-fifth Street Playhouse, Hall concluded that "it proves that the only way to make a foreign language picture is to have a native cast or those who are as familiar with the language as Mr. Menjou is with French."[50] Soon Zukor, Lasky, and

Paramount's international executives surmised that European production was essential for European-language films. (Besides, Paramount would be able to access some of its profits which had been frozen by European governments.)

Jesse Lasky, scouting Paris, outlined how he thought multilingual production would work. Paramount's story buyers would focus on properties with international appeal. After the picture was shot in Hollywood, it would then be remade abroad with foreign directors and players, using the American film as a blueprint.[51] Zukor announced that ten foreign-language titles would be produced in France by a new subsidiary, Paramount-Continental Films (Société Ciné-Studio-Continental). Robert T. Kane supervised the five stages, originally the property of Gaumont, in Joinville-le-Pont, a village on the eastern outskirts of Paris. Paramount licensed Western Electric equipment for simultaneous production in up to six languages. Zukor wanted to form a joint venture with the other big studios. "Such an agreement," he said, "would strengthen the American position abroad and result in great economies all-around." No one signed up with him.[52]

From the ten features proposed in February, the planned number of releases by Paramount had swollen to 110 by August 1930. The reason for the shift was simple: Lasky said that the talkies being made by Kane's unit, nicknamed Babel-on-the-Marne, cost 20 percent less than they would had they been shot in Hollywood.[53] Kane recruited directors with international experience, for example, Jean de Limur. Principal actors came to Joinville from the countries where the films would be shown. Greta Garbo's brother Sven appeared in När rosorna slå ut (1930), the Swedish talker made with the same sets and costumes as Un trou dans le mur, the French version.[54] But all non-speaking roles went to French actors. While most of Kane's productions were assembly-line remakes of American films, there were also original productions. The most successful example was Marius (1930), an adaptation of Marcel Pagnol's play. The polyglot director Alexander Korda was fresh from a stint at Paramount, First National, and Fox in Hollywood, where he had not distinguished himself. He had, however, become friends with Robert Kane. He captured the authentic Marseilles dialect of Pagnol's characters by the simple expedient of hiring the original stage cast. "The soundtrack," in Andrew's opinion, "perhaps for the first time in France, made the locale palpable and the story that developed within it as natural as the sun beaming down on the provinces."[55] But he also shot German and Swedish versions of Marius—in the time it normally took to make one film.

International Films in the United States

Often missing from the discussion of the international effects of the transition to sound is any mention of the fact that American audiences for the first time had numerous opportunities to see and hear talking pictures from other countries. Frequently these were straight imports—no subtitles, no dubbing—which had been released to satisfy the exchange requirements imposed by various government quotas. The language problem was handled by distributing a written plot synopsis. Mordaunt Hall advised the patrons of Versuchen Sie Meine Schwester (dir. Carl Lamac, 1931): "Persons not understanding German will do well to take time to read the summary of the story printed on the back of the program before settling down."[56]

British companies, eager to crack the sound barrier, sent teams to the United States to learn talking-picture techniques. The producer Victor Saville and the actors Estelle Brody,

John Stuart, and Dorothy Cumming came to the RCA Gramercy studios in New York to record dialogue sequences for KITTY. This film had been completed silent in 1928 but was re-released in 1929 with its last reel talking. "For a few moments the voices are splendid and then suddenly there is an effect as if one of the characters were talking through a barrel, using it as a megaphone."[57] British and Dominions Film Corporation, which had purchased a Western Electric system in January 1929, teamed its director Herbert Wilcox with the American Marshall Nielan to shoot BLACK WATERS (1929) in Hollywood. The film about a murderous sea captain stalking passengers on his fogbound vessel starred James Kirkwood and Mary Brian and was distributed in the United States by Sono Art-World Wide. The crowd at the Arena Theater in New York jeered it. "The talkies may be in the infancy," explained Variety, "but some of the babies that are coming along are talking out of turn. And this baby is about the gabbiest that has come down the film pike."[58]

While ERPI and Tobis were disputing in Europe, imported German films played in small American theaters showing foreign and avant-garde films. The talkies uncovered an unexpected mine in the German population of America's key cities. Since these imported films played in their original languages, the appeal was obviously limited. Comprehending the plot without knowing German was a major critical point for wider release. The first all-talkie made in Germany, BECAUSE I LOVED YOU (DICH HAB' ICH GELIEBT, dir. Rudolf Walther-Fein, 1930), was easy to understand, but Alicoate commented sarcastically on the plot, which he felt showed the influence of THE SINGING FOOL: "Those clever Germans must have been opening mail from Hollywood for they have not only chosen the highly original back stage theme around which to build their production but have added the little pal angle as well." Harrower was nevertheless optimistic: "As the first German all-talker, this carries a promise of worth-while things from the Berlin market. So finely is it acted and directed, that you do not have to understand German to follow clearly every scene of the action."[59] This was not an issue with THE WHITE HELL OF PITZ PALU (dir. Arnold Fanck and G. W. Pabst, 1930). This "mountain film" starred Leni Riefenstahl and had spectacular scenes shot inside a glacial crevasse. Universal tacked on a blow-by-blow narration by the radio announcer Graham McNamee. "To have this knight of the superlative describe the wondrous views in the Alps is to gild the lily with a vengeance," twitted Hall.[60]

American audiences encountered English-language foreign films coproduced by Paramount and Ufa, whose studio head Erich Pommer had ambitious plans for trilingual production and international distribution. Twelve films came over in the 1929–1930 season. These were supervised by the American Floyd Gibson, nicknamed the "dialect doctor." The first was THE IMMORTAL VAGABOND (DER UNSTERBLICHE LUMP, dir. Gustav Ucicky, 1929).[61] A vanguard of twenty films in the Supertone series included the studio's first all-talkie, MELODY OF THE HEART (MELODIE DES HERZENS, 1930), with Dita Parlo, who had recently returned from Hollywood after disappointing English voice tests. The movie premiered in New York in August 1930 with both versions playing in separate theaters. The poor chargirl Parlo is forced into prostitution in order to save money for life with her lover Willy Fritsch after he returns from the military. But he rejects her after encountering her at the Paradise Café. Reviewing the German version, the trade again felt that most audiences could understand the film.[62] Hall, however, administered a beating to the English print. He criticized the pace, the dialogue, and the speakers' accents:

> The one in German at least has its deliberate dialogue spoken by native
> actors. The English copy, with the same players, has but one or two lines that

are not uttered with a decided foreign accent. How the recording of the voices in this production has been accomplished is of small consequence, for it might have been preferable to have had still further haphazard synchronization than to have the lines spoken as they are, with ludicrous hesitation as well as a German accent. (Hall, *New York Times*, 1 September 1930)

The nonstop orchestration underscoring especially bothered him. He concluded, "There have been many silly American productions, but none that falls as low as this." Hall liked, however, DER TIGER VON BERLIN (dir. Johannes Meyer, 1930). He felt that "it is far ahead of any other European audible production so far presented here" and singled out an example of its integrated approach to picture and sound: "The screen is dark, but the voices of two of the characters are heard and also the periodical reports of a pistol, the flashes of which serve to give an outline of the person firing the weapon."[63]

The landmark import was THE BLUE ANGEL (DER BLAUE ENGEL, 1930), with Marlene Dietrich and Emil Jannings, directed by the American Josef von Sternberg. Dietrich's erotically charged characterization of the singer Lola-Lola earned her a long-term contract with Paramount. The film is full of fascinating sound highlights. The background music and patter establish the ambience of the Blue Angel cabaret. Von Sternberg worked closely with the arranger Friedrich Holländer to create an alternative to the operetta-based formula by using sound to create narrative structure. Music is "naturalized" in the manner of APPLAUSE. Jannings whistles a chorale melody to his pet canary, which whistles back. Later its silence signals the bird's death as we hear the school bell's chimes. Eventually, Jannings's cock-a-doodle-doos show his humiliating descent into madness, creating a symbolic parallel with the caged bird. When the professor is found dead at the end of the film, "the music resolves into the Chorale tune, the main melody picked out on muffled chimes against a background of flowing strings and harp arpeggios. The film ends in a long tracking shot back through the classroom as the clock outside strikes twelve."[64]

THE BLUE ANGEL was shot simultaneously in German and English with the same principals but with different supporting casts. The English version opened in the United States in December 1930 while MOROCCO was still playing. Dietrich excels as the "English" cabaret artiste with the husky voice. Emil Jannings, who had returned to Germany because he could not or would not learn to speak English while in Hollywood, is convincing as Professor Rath in the German version, but he gives an uncommitted, obviously phonetic English performance in the export print. He begins speaking to Lola in German, but she stops him by saying in English, "You'll have to speak my language with me now." The erotic content of the Blue Angel cabaret show, the lyrics, and the double entendre of the dialogue were mostly eliminated for American audiences. *Film Daily* praised the film's narrative clarity and Marlene Dietrich: "Ufa has produced a talker in which much of the dialogue is in English and all of the story easy to follow. Much attention is paid to details of the plot, which is modest and sometimes unconvincing. . . . Miss Dietrich has plenty of beauty and sex." In a press release, Jesse Lasky raved, "Marlene Dietrich is the most promising player I have come across in seven years."[65]

Geza von Bolvary's international hit ZWEI HERZEN IM 3/4 TAKT (TWO HEARTS IN WALTZ TIME, 1930) ran for eleven months at the Fifty-fifth Street Playhouse before English titles were inserted. It revitalized interest in the schmaltzy but obviously very popular operetta film.

Americans were treated to two adaptations of DIE PRIVATSEKRETÄRIN (dir. Wilhelm Thiele, 1931). The original version circulated at the same time as its British-made ver-

ZWEI HERZEN IM 3/4 TAKT (*Associated Cinemas of America/Super-Film GmbH, 1930*) *program and synopsis.*

sion, SUNSHINE SUSIE (U.S. title: OFFICE GIRL, dir. Victor Saville). Thiele's DIE DREI VON DER TANKSTELLE played a few American art houses. It was a merry operetta built around a gas station and starred the popular duo Lilian Harvey and Willy Fritsch. Thiele loaded the sound track with "exploding gasoline, crashing thunder."[66]

René Clair's UNDER THE ROOFS OF PARIS (SOUS LES TOITS DE PARIS, 1930) was praised as a modest production in which "the director put real brains in his work, and uncovered a really new technique." *Film Daily* noted with pleasure that "dialogue has been cut to about twenty-five per cent of the usual. Pantomime gets over everything graphically. One trick is a darb, with the players talking [on] the other side of glass doors, not a word being said but everything perfectly understood by the audience. American audiences can grasp it easily."[67] The film was also shown in a German version. MURDER! (1930) was another transatlantic hit. *Film Daily* lauded the screenwriter Alma Reville but did not mention the director (and her husband), Alfred Hitchcock. "The picture should be a wonder in any house and, in this case, it is a pleasure to give our British confrères a hand."[68]

Though their financial impact on the industry was not great, these imports had significant technical and aesthetic ramifications. New ideas about sound influenced American craftsmen and eventually brought many of the filmmakers to Hollywood.

Meanwhile, small theaters across the country thrived showing foreign-language films. This unexpected niche market was the embryo of art-house exhibition. In New York City the Fifty-fifth Street Playhouse (150 West Fifty-fifth Street, 300 seats) and the Fifth Avenue Playhouse (66 Fifth Avenue, 264 seats) specialized in foreign films. Michael Mindlin's Little Carnegie Playhouse (146 West Fifty-seventh Street, 411 seats) offered to "producers throughout the world a show-window for their artistic and unusual productions." In 1928 this theater affiliated with similar ones in Buffalo, Rochester, Chicago, and the Fifth Avenue Playhouse to form the nation's first art-house mini-circuit. The exhibition of these films in the United States was facilitated by the American and German sound equipment manufacturers' adoption of a "treaty" in mid-1930.

The First Paris Agreement

The tide began to turn against the Tobis Klangfilm patent monopoly in May 1930 when Western Electric won a suit that nullified crucial Tri-Ergon Austrian patents. With both sides motivated, an international conference on sound was held in Paris in June and July. Will Hays was the chair. ERPI, RCA, the Tobis Klangfilm interests, and representatives of the affected producers—thirty delegates in all—agreed in principle to establish international marketing boundaries.

This so-called First Paris Agreement, concluded on 22 July 1930, divided the world into German, American, and unrestricted commercial zones where royalty differentials would favor the principal patent groups in each area. German-speaking countries, central Europe (including France and Italy), and Scandinavia were the territory of Tobis; the United States, Canada, Australia, New Zealand, India, and the Soviet Union (if it so chose) would benefit the Americans; and the rest of the world (including the United Kingdom) was to be shared according to agreed-upon proportions (25 percent Tobis and 75 percent American, in the case of the United Kingdom) or remain open for free competition.[69]

The First Paris Agreement temporarily suspended the underlying disputes about patents. Some differences were never resolved, and American producers finally did not sign it. (But RCA and ERPI did, so the studios' signatures were not necessary to implement the agreement.) There was plenty of territory to go around. According to the Society of Motion Picture Engineers, two-thirds of the world's theaters were yet to be wired. Canada (with its relatively small number of theaters per capita) led the world in percentage of wired theaters: 70 percent. The United States was 55 percent wired, the United Kingdom was at 47 percent, and the other countries were far behind. By voluntarily limiting power and carving out geographical boundaries, the conglomerates hoped to control what could have been a devastating trade war. The First Paris Agreement ended the stalemate, defined the rules of engagement for the principal players, and, of course, maximized potential profits for the major producers.[70]

Despite European corporate and governmental support of native-language production and exhibition, and in the face of guardians of national cultures who lamented "Americanization" and the attendant violation of class, social, and linguistic standards, Hollywood was clearly continuing to dominate the international film trade. (That is, until politically motivated restrictions in Germany and Italy began to take effect.) Though most American audiences were unaware of it, their films had become part of the expanding sphere of the country's international cultural influence. American movies dispersed regional ways of speaking and glorified Main Street values—while most of the world was listening in.

A Shadow of Class: Multilingual Versions Decline

After competing vigorously to establish their place in foreign-language production in 1929–1930, by mid-1931 the American studios were heading for the exits. The low return on their foreign-language productions made their departure from the field necessary. C. J. North's Commerce Department report on worldwide exhibition discovered that European sound cinemas were growing at a very competitive pace. The United Kingdom had awakened from its previous apathy to become the most thickly theatered country, with a movie house for every ten square miles; two-thirds of them had sound. In Germany stringent import regulations became effective 1 July 1930. The First Paris Agreement limited competition from American companies, but the severity of the worldwide depression took its toll on exhibition everywhere. As if that were not enough to discourage Hollywood, ERPI was treating each foreign version as though it were an original production and charging the studios $500 per reel. The producers refused to pay and negotiated a royalty reduction in December 1931.

"To version or not to version? That seems to be the question," began a *Film Daily* soliloquy in March 1931.

> It is rather accepted that the foreign version jaunt has proven anything but financially satisfactory and that, except in the case of Spanish editions, the present scheme may be consigned to the ashcan before another year rolls around. With the foreign sound situation being mastered locally and production in several countries abroad taking on a certain definite shadow of class, the problem becomes constantly more complicated. (*Film Daily*, 17 March 1931, p. 2)

Compare the boom of 1930 to the bust of 1931. Warner Bros. completed four Spanish, four French, and six German export versions in 1930. In February 1931, it transferred production to the Teddington Studios in England and made thirteen simultaneous

English and French features. Then, in June 1931, it abandoned the foreign production program.[71] MGM, which had shot 102 foreign-language productions (45 features and 57 shorts) in Culver City during 1930, produced 33 Spanish, French, and Italian features in the spring of 1931. After this batch, there were no more MGM multilingual versions; all international releases were dubbed American prints. Fox gradually abandoned its Spanish features unit at Movietone City.[72]

The accelerated decline of international production at Paramount is amazing. At the beginning of 1931, Paramount's ambitious schedule called for eighty features and one hundred shorts to be produced at Joinville. By June, Adolph Zukor was issuing press releases denying that the studio was closing. But already Kane, along with Korda and others, had moved to London. The French studio limped along making two or three features a month in Spanish, German, and French until October, when it shut down. Robert Kane returned from London in March 1932 to shoot three features there, but otherwise, the Joinville plant was used for dubbing.[73] The advent of noiseless recording facilitated dubbing. Music and effects were recorded on separate tracks from the vocals, so that only dialogue needed to be replaced to make a version in another language. Moviolas and sound-editing gear kept everything in synch. And the manufacture of foreign versions could be done in Hollywood where Paramount executives could keep an eye on things. For audiences who preferred films in their original language, subtitles could be superimposed at the same time—an acknowledgment that even in the same cities (then as now), some viewers strongly preferred dubbing, some subtitling.

American filmgoers were probably oblivious to these international operations, but they did experience indirect effects. For example, the Hays Office carefully monitored motion picture content for anything that would offend a prospective trading partner. The Production Code of 1930 affirmed that "the history, institutions, prominent people, and citizenry of other nations shall be represented fairly." Like other provisions of the Code, this one proved to be unenforceable, but producers could point to this theoretical restraint on unflattering representation when dealing with foreign governments.

In January 1931, Tobis opened an American office to book its films into Broadway houses. It also announced an ambitious plan for a circuit of two hundred cinemas to showcase European films. The first release on the Tobis-Forenfilm label was to be René Clair's splashy musical Le MILLION. Despite its own winning ticket in the form of Clair's film, Tobis was shut out of the keen competition for Broadway houses. In May the Germans abandoned their attempt to find a Broadway opening and booked Le MILLION into the Little Carnegie Playhouse. (Sous LES TOITS DE PARIS had played there for five weeks.) Tobis also ceased efforts to establish a national circuit. Le MILLION was very successful in its limited urban run. Though it was neither dubbed nor subtitled, there were interpretive sections not found in existing prints: The sound track was "in French dialogue that is interspersed with a most cleverly worked-in explanation in English. No one in this country who sees this production will fail to understand its goings-on, or be deprived of enjoying its theme because of the foreign tongue." These sections were "several scenes in which two Britishers on a roof, peeping in at the doings in an atelier below, tell in English of what has happened and is at the moment taking place."[74] Clair had repudiated his earlier statements condemning dialogue and was working in an "international" style that exploited sound creatively while retaining anachronistic touches from his early surrealistic silent films. Partly owing to his work (as discussed in chapter 14), the trade journals predicted a "return to silence" that would benefit international distribution of Hollywood films:

Dubbing and the use of native stars speaking the language of the respective countries have proved unsatisfactory, the foreign managers report. Importing of expensive foreign players for the production of the multilinguals in Hollywood also has failed to pan out profitably, since the Hollywood stars are preferred by the foreign audiences. As a consequence, opinion among major companies is gradually crystallizing on the fact that the best course lies in the silent technique, enabling the addition of a little music and other touches whereby the regular Hollywood productions can be adapted at low cost for exhibition abroad. (*Film Daily*, 17 July 1931, pp. 1, 8)

Manheim, in charge of Universal's exports, also favored the old ways. "If . . . we revert to the old silent technique, and tell the story with pantomime, with action scenes, with sub-titles, and add to this music and whatever sound effects are possible, and only use dialogue when it is absolutely necessary, we will then have a type of picture that can be readily and inexpensively adapted for foreign countries, and, in every probability, such a picture would be highly acceptable right here in America."[75]

The multiple-language versions often had an ersatz aura which failed to capture the spirit of the Hollywood original. Usually shot in two weeks, more or less, the perfunctory, rote quality of the performances was readily apparent. The American-made foreign films also were often insensitive to European sensibilities. The Berlin reviewer of OLYMPIA (1930), for instance, accused the author of the scenario of "totally misunderstanding sentiment in modern Germany." Dieterle's DIE MASKE FÄLLT (1930), made in Burbank for Warners, retained the sets, costumes, and Mississippi setting of the story. Indeed, everything was the same except that the actors spoke German.[76] Production values were diminished. Furthermore, European audiences were losing interest in films which emphasized talk too much. *Film Daily*'s correspondent reported that moviegoers in England and on the Continent, like their American counterparts, were also tiring of musicals. "Too much of the music has not been of the type to satisfy the tastes over here, while the lavishness of the productions seems to make no impression on the audiences. Broad comedies with more action than dialogue are the most popular of any United States product being sent to this side at present."[77] Then, too, the Depression was affecting revenue in all industrialized countries, cutting deeply into the economic base—admission receipts—necessary to subsidize this capital-intensive operation. Recent writers have suggested that multilingual production also died out because of reasons that went beyond economics. Psychological identification with Hollywood stars, concepts of national culture, political conflicts, the middle- and working-class appeal of Hollywood films, and the idea that American cinema did not represent a place as much as a state of mind are other factors that might explain the decline of these international productions. Dubbing and subtitling enabled studios to sidestep many of the cultural and political pitfalls that had made foreign-language production so risky.[78]

The European Political Situation

Besides the unfavorable balance sheet for the Americans producing in Europe, several incidents suggested that Americans were in danger of losing control over their own product. In France the right-wing actors' union threatened a strike on the grounds of preserving the linguistic identity of their national cinema. They protested the use of non-native French speakers to dub imported films.[79] In Italy, there was an exercise in cultural power consistent with Benito Mussolini's nationalist agenda. His undersecretary of state, Leandro Arpinati, issued a decree on 22 October 1930 which stated that films would no longer be authorized for exhibition if they contained any foreign-language dialogue. Despite protests that this restriction would contribute to unemployment and cut off Italy from international film circuits, the order stood. CIMARRON, THE TAMING OF THE SHREW, BROADWAY, INNOCENTS OF PARIS, HALLELUJAH!, SOUS LES TOITS DE PARIS, and HELL'S ANGELS were among the films shown in a unique format. The sound tracks were re-recorded with Italian-produced music and sound effects (suppressing all dialogue), and the spoken lines were replaced by superimposed subtitles. (Songs were allowed to stay in the original language.) One critic counted 210 subtitles in SYNTHETIC SIN (1928).[80]

Dubbing into Italian was the obvious expediency. In the spring of 1932, two studios specializing in dubbing opened in Rome. MGM started a dubbing operation there in 1933. But in October the dubbing of foreign-made films was declared illegal. Paramount reshot a few films in Rome with native casts but soon gave up. These events show how precious language was for preserving (and policing) national culture. As the 1930 decree stated,

> Foreign-language cinema cannot become a useful tool of linguistic culture, but on the contrary, functions as a pernicious vehicle. It encourages the propagation of slang expressions and artificial pronunciation. Its affected phrases disfigure our language's spontaneous maturation and development. It contradicts our mode of expression, our attention, in a word, our national traditions. (Quoted in Mario Quargnolo, "Le Cinéma bâillonné," in Christian Belaygue and Jean-Paul Gorce, eds., *Le Passage du muet au parlant* [Toulouse: Cinémathèque de Toulouse/Editions Milan, 1988], pp. 42–45)

Universal must have anticipated trouble with its European release of ALL QUIET ON THE WESTERN FRONT. The studio was more than willing to accommodate the various censorship demands of each country where it was shown. In Germany, though, the film was a lightning rod for the National Socialists. This reaction could hardly have been surprising, since the book by Erich Maria Remarque on which it was based had already sparked protests and soon would be publicly burned. It is easy to see why. The protagonist Baumer is the personification of the ideal Aryan the Nazis were recruiting for their cause. His teacher introduces him to the class as "one of Germany's iron youth. Look at him—sturdy, and bronzed, and clear-eyed. The kind of soldier every one of you should envy." But instead of glorifying sacrifice, Baumer admonishes the students, "When it comes to dying for your country, it's better not to die at all. There are millions out there dying for their country, and what good is it?" Universal made a German-dubbed, heavily cut version which passed the Berlin Censorship Board in November 1930. At its premiere in December, Nazis, led by Joseph Goebbels, took over the theater. "Stink bombs, white mice and sneeze powder were released and the cinema was vacated with members of the Nazi Party even requesting refunds on the way out."[81] Demonstrations and counterdemonstrations disrupted Berlin for about a week. Then the government banned the film as an untrue representation of Germany in World War I.

In January 1931, Universal began an all-out effort to get its film seen. Albert Einstein visited Universal City to watch it with Carl Laemmle. The famed physicist condemned

Lew Ayres as Baumer in ALL QUIET ON THE WESTERN FRONT *(Universal, 1930).*

the ban and made worldwide headlines. (Later Einstein's writings would also be burned.) Laemmle personally traveled to Berlin to negotiate with the Germans. After more cuts were made, the shortened print was passed for exhibition. The new version replaced existing prints not only in Germany but all over Europe, so that the Reich's image would not be internationally tarnished. In March 1931, the Reichstag ruled that the banning in December had been unjustified. However, when Hitler became chancellor in 1933, the film was condemned again and not screened publicly in Germany until 1952. The film buff Goebbels, however, carefully guarded his own original print of ALL QUIET ON THE WESTERN FRONT, which, with poetic justice, was utilized in the 1984 restoration of the film.[82]

The government mandated in July 1932 that dubbing had to be done in Germany with native speakers. "Paramount found out subsequently that the 'Aryan' dubbers assigned to complete the sound track for *The Sign of the Cross* (1932) substantially altered the script by revising several dialogue sequences into heavily anti-Semitic harangues."[83] Kevin Brownlow and David Gill conclude their documentary *Cinema Europe* (1995) by blaming the Depression and the rise of ultranationalism for decimating the European film industries. The talent which might otherwise have challenged the United States in mastering the art of sound cinema was forced to flee—most often to Hollywood.[84]

As the world economic situation worsened, some Americans burrowed into isolationism and xenophobia. In 1932, Representative Samuel Dickstein introduced a bill that would have imposed a heavy tax on foreign actors and noncitizens like Chaplin and Dietrich. "I do not see any reason why a 65 per cent surtax should not be imposed upon all of those aliens who come here for the sole purpose of making money, taking it right back with them or sending it away, without even a nickel having a chance to come back here."[85]

Though the Paris Agreement of 1930 had held the promise of rationalizing sound worldwide, as the Five-Cornered Agreement had consolidated the industry domestically, many issues lingered. American producers had experimented with various methods of presenting their films abroad in an effort to retain their pre-Depression profits: original versions, written synopses, superimposed subtitles, intertitles, side-titles projected on a separate screen, inserted narrational foreign-language sequences, remaking, and dubbing. Most of these were rejected by international audiences, who wanted to experience movies in their original versions, with subtitles, or dubbed. Despite their optimism in 1929, American producers did not immediately regain their dominance of Europe; indeed, sound stimulated domestic native-language production in several countries. Far from establishing English as the new universal language, the talkies were seized upon by foreign countries as an audible symbol of American cultural imperialism. As political tensions escalated in Europe, the Americans would lose many of their markets, but whether this loss was attributable to the introduction of sound is debatable. The First Paris Agreement did, however, open up the American market to foreign distributors. With exhibition limited to small theaters in a few cities, these imports had little impact nationally, but American directors and critics nevertheless had the opportunity to learn fresh approaches to sound from some of them.

A second Paris conference on sound was convened in February 1932. In fact, this would be the beginning of ongoing negotiations which lasted throughout the remainder of the decade. New agreements were reached in 1935 and 1936, but this phase ended in 1939. After the second European war began, ERPI notified Tobis that its licensees would no longer honor the contracts.[86]

PART 3

Hearing the Audience

We do not create the types of entertainment, we merely present them. People see . . . a reflection of their own average thoughts and attitudes. If the reflection is much lower or much higher than their own plane they reject it. [People] influence pictures far more than pictures influence people.

IRVING THALBERG, REMARKS BEFORE THE AMPP, 1930

Talking cinema became the new norm for Hollywood because the great majority of moviegoers accepted, perhaps even demanded, it. The wave of enthusiasm in 1928 and 1929 stimulated studio and theater conversion, and the drop in paid admissions beginning in 1930 underscored the necessity for the industry to consolidate, standardize, and retain the "masses." Parts 1 and 2 demonstrated that, by 1931, sound had reached a technical plateau in the sense that audiences would not be aware of any improvements or breakthroughs for more than a decade. Sound-film style had been nudged by critics toward the ideal of the modulated sound track; restraint and narrative underpinning prevailed—except in expressly demarcated moments, such as comedy effects. Moviegoing as a social practice had assimilated the talkies into the usual routine. The dialogue film had gone from marvel to mundane in about three and a half years.

Part 3 takes a closer look at issues related to what we can call *audienceship,* that is, the interaction between active, discriminate moviegoers, the film production system, and the external pressures affecting that dynamic. Unlike the notion of spectatorship, which in recent theoretical applications has connoted an idealized and socially or even biologically determined film viewer, audienceship encompasses the widely varied movie attenders thrown together by numerous motives at a particular time in the theater. Film audienceship constitutes a temporally fleeting socioeconomic-aesthetic moment, not a general principle of film viewing. This construction of the variegated audience is particularly apropos of the 1920s and early 1930s, when, as Gilbert Seldes recorded, many people went to "the movies" as much as to any particular film. The location of the theater may have been as much of a determinant as what was showing inside.

Nevertheless, there were many arguments among observers of films and their audiences about the talkies; among the most contentious were the struggle over the definition and control of the voice by popular critics, censors, and the film industry, and the regulation (real or imagined) of performers' lives and careers through stardom and the fan-audience. These chapters investigate how social power was asserted over cinema and how Hollywood tried to contain it; how consumers may (or may not) have acquired their own power as articulate fans; and finally, how moviegoers apparently did not really drop everything to see THE JAZZ SINGER in unprecedented droves, as legend has it.

The coming of movie sound unleashed the voice with unexpectedly strong repercussions. Chapter 18 details the lively struggle to restrict the range of vocal expression. Once again, we have an example of the public rejecting a "first offer" from Hollywood—in this case, another twist on the virtual Broadway theme. The studios tried to set aside some of their production for elite middle-class consumers and felt that casting actors from the legitimate stage in successful theatrical adaptations would raise Hollywood's cultural capital and perhaps annex a new affluent audience. While some commentators felt that exposing the masses to properly spoken English would ameliorate society, film critics and audiences (heard in Hollywood by way of exhibitors, distributors, and fan reactions) rejected stage eloquence as laughable, boring, or just plain incomprehensible. To the dismay of those who thought the movies held out hope to rescue speakers of blighted Americanese, it was the language of the urban milieu (for example, in STREET GIRL) and of Westerns (as in THE VIRGINIAN) that tended to be regarded as "natural."

The voice signified more, however, than just a way of speaking; it also denoted class. Who was in charge of the movies anyway? Prior censorship of film was legal and widely practiced. To the moralists, the movies were dangerous to vulnerable elements of society, especially children. Their fear of film as a bearer of social disruption was barely concealed. Sound easily reaffirmed it. Public fascination with stories set in gangland, brothels, waterfronts, and other liminal environments (depicted in "realistic" vocabulary and accents) disconcerted those agencies which had set for themselves the task of policing film content. Hollywood responded by agreeing to regulate itself (a tactic which had served it well in the 1920s and continues to do so in the 1990s). Though it pictured itself as artistically oppressed and lacking First Amendment protection, censorship was a boon as well as a bane for Hollywood producers.

Chapter 19 examines the problematic response to the talkies in the pages of movie fan magazines. Were these truly offering a populist reaction to Hollywood? Or were the readers and letter writers dupes of the "culture industry?" Were the columnists who pledged to articulate the concerns of the movie fan really covert extensions of the studios' publicity tentacles? Did fans affirm or reject the talkies? Here again, one finds controversy within the consensus.

Chapter 20 examines one of the most enduring legends of film culture. Through media and box-office analysis, we see how the status of THE JAZZ SINGER's Broadway premiere in 1927 was amplified by Warner Bros. and a corps of accomplice commentators and critics. The chapter raises questions about the difficulty and value of focusing on audience reception as a historical method. How do we "hear" film audiences of the past?

Chapter 21 presents a few suggestions about sound put forward by film critics of the day and concludes with thoughts on how the transition to sound changed—and did not change—American cinema.

18

The Voice Squad

Psychologically, the larger the audience, the lower the moral mass resistance to suggestion.

"REASONS SUPPORTING PREAMBLE OF
PRODUCTION CODE OF 1930"

The transition to sound in American cinema set off a struggle to control and contain the social effects of the talkies. Audiences, the media, censors, and the film industry's internal custodians were disturbed by the changes they were seeing and hearing. The new and unregulated utterances coming from the screen stirred up a simmering debate over what screen actors should say and how they should say it, over who should control the end-users' access to films, and who should monitor the movies' implicit values. During the 1920s seven states and several major cities had established boards of censorship to regulate films shown within their jurisdiction, and in 1930 legislation was pending to establish others. These agencies professed to safeguard citizens from the movies' possibly hazardous moral environment. Local boards of review also provided a bully pulpit from which the local clergy, uplifters, and police vented their opinions. Besides these officially sanctioned outlets, informal influences such as newspaper editorialists, writers in mass-circulation magazines, fan magazines, and, to a limited extent, trade journals took aim at film content and claimed both to sway and to reflect public opinion. Although the efforts of censors and the rhetoric of the popular press may at first seem to be unrelated or antagonistic, these groups had a common goal of defining and restraining the power of film to affect the attitudes and behavior of viewers. Insisting on issues of quality, propriety, decency, and taste was a strategy for channeling the new film-making into acceptable forms. And sound was the catalyst. Censors, both formal and informal, may have intended to preserve the public good or the art of cinema, but both these agendas were also heavily marked by issues of class and culture.

Criticism and censorship both tried to control the voice but were inherently different. Unlike censorship, public commentary had no statutory right to change films. Public discourse does, however, represent considerable economic influence. A critical anomaly results: public reaction, if it has any effect, influences unmade not current films. Unlike a theatrical performance, which may be revised or fine-tuned, the response of the film audience and critics can have little effect on an individual film. In this sense, films are like novels, which are not normally revised after publication. But unlike novels, movies had a finite, usually very short, shelf life in the days before videocassettes. Massive public approval could occasionally result in a holdover at the theater, but dis-

The quality voice. Ruth Chatterton and Raymond Hackett in MADAME X *(MGM, 1929).*

ruptions of the exhibition schedule had to be justified by exceptional box-office performance. Sometimes a studio recalled a film after preview screenings for repairs, fine-tun-
ing, or a major overhaul. But once a title was released, the film usually circulated
unrevised to fulfill the producers' booking contracts. Since Hollywood had few quantifi-
able means for receiving feedback from large masses, producers relied on gross receipts
as the best measure of a film's popularity. Favorable critical response and the volume of
fan mail sent by the actors were usually regarded as secondary indicators. Certainly a
rave or pan by Robert Sherwood or Mordaunt Hall might cause a noticeable shift in
attendance, but in general the correlation between critics' reviews and box-office
receipts was weak.

Producers tried to predispose customers to attend their shows. Prevue trailers enticed
moviegoers with snippets of a story and glimpses of stars. Press agents and publicity
offices supplied stills, press books, serializations, and newspaper copy. They arranged star
appearances and interviews and set up press screenings. Feature promotions, such as
comic-strip tie-ins or Sunday supplement photo sections, were available as free filler.
Criticism, especially at the level of the local reviewer, was often based on prompts found
in the studio's press kit. Sometimes studio executives got involved. At Paramount in particular, directors and managers often went public. Editorial pieces (that is, not explicit
publicity for their studio) by Jesse L. Lasky, Cecil B. DeMille, and William deMille
blurred the boundaries between producer commentary and public commentary.

Censorship boards, however, were empowered to change or to deny a license to show
a film. The majority of movies were routinely passed in toto. New York State censors

under James Wingate, for instance, viewed 2,543 subjects from 1 July 1928 through 30 June 1929 and rejected eight of them. This good rate of passage, as Lea Jacobs has shown, reflects the MPPDA's pre-release negotiations with the censors and the studios' willingness to accommodate them. Censors' cuts imposed additional expenses if they deemed it necessary to tamper with a film. The advent of sound greatly elevated the stakes for studios. An offending movie might have to be resynchronized or even partly reshot to secure a release in New York State, Pennsylvania, Ohio, or Chicago.

Of the many debates circulating around the film industry, the struggle for control over the voice was the most inclusive. Arguments ranged over two broad areas: shaping the form of the voice according to preconceived ideals, and restricting the content of language in order to protect the welfare of the listener.

Reeling in the Out-of-Control Voice

Everyone is a film critic, and this seems to always have been the case. But the attitudes among popular authors in mass-circulation publications toward the proper application of the voice underwent change as sound became established. The issues commentators confronted were not the economic realignment of the film industry, the changing international status of Hollywood production, or other trade-press concerns. Rather, they wanted to know how the new technology would change the existing movie institution. Were the filmmakers trying to fix something that was not broken? Who would determine the use, style, and social responsibilities of the speaking voice in film? Though many-faceted, the arguments progressed through distinct areas of emphasis. First was the "quality" phase, which presumed that the voice was an entity separate from the actor's body and could be molded to an ideal vocal standard derived from the legitimate stage. Then there was a reaction favoring "naturalism." The stage voice was deemed to be stilted and too artificial for the movies. Intimacy and a "natural" voice were substituted as ideals. Then came a compromise "hybrid" phase. Critics championed actors who spoke with clear diction, as onstage, but with the everyday spontaneity, ease, and colloquialism of American (not British) English. These efforts to come to grips with speech correlate roughly with the critical attitude toward the sound track from 1927 through 1931, changing from an enhancement of the picture to sound and image integrated as the modulated sound track.

Quality, Class, and "Brains"

The national excitement about electrically reproducing the voice over the radio created speculation about linking speech and images. De Forest Phonofilm showed that it was feasible that talking pictures and something like television might soon be a reality. Well before the 1926 Vitaphone premiere, the desirability of adding speech to film was already being debated in the popular press. A typical enthusiast in 1922 gave a rationale for the inevitable combination of theatrical dialogue and cinema (via radio, he thought) to replace the missing acoustic dimension:

> Man is a friendly animal and loves to hear his own voice, and for that reason
> the motion picture, wonderful as it is, has never been able to replace the
> spoken play. The rarest value of good acting is in oral expression. . . . The

sound of sobbing from the darkness, for example, stirs us more than any mere physical action. Sarah Bernhardt, speaking from the darkness of a deserted battlefield, thrills us with her voice, though we cannot understand the language she speaks.

Think of the powers of the voice combined with the powers of the motion picture! Is there any limit to its possibilities? (Butler, "Radio to Make Movies Talk," p. 673)

But others were pessimistic about the voice's recordability and wondered whether it was proper for speech to be part of the cinema experience at all. Writing in 1924 on "The Human Voice Divine," an author who identified himself as a "high-brow gentleman" argued that speech was the soul of drama, including the movies. He confessed that when he went to films, he missed hearing the voice of "Doug," and was confident that Dr. de Forest's machine would soon reproduce it. But he also foresaw a problem. Modern American speech had already degenerated, and talking films would degrade it further. "The spoken word," he claimed, "is what suffers the taint of mediocrity; or even, in the 'silent drama,' the ignominy of sheer obliteration. What wonder that we degenerate into monosyllabic grunts! Our priceless inheritance, the thing which might save us most surely from bestial oblivion, we have sold for a mess of machinery."[1]

George Jean Nathan, the outspoken conservative theater critic for the *American Mercury,* similarly felt that the talkies condemned film to the domain of the "booboisie." After viewing the first program of Vitaphone shorts, he predicted that sound would backfire:

> Aside from its commercial value in certain short-reel subjects, such as an opera-singer doing her bit, or a politician exuding the usual platitudes, or a musician making pretty sounds, it will bring to the motion-picture exactly the thing that the motion-picture should have no use for, to wit, the human voice, and that, further, once it brings it, the motion-picture will have a tough time holding its own even among the boobs who now make it the profitable institution it is. (Quoted in "The Vitaphone—Pro and Con," *Literary Digest,* 25 September 1926, p. 29)

These arguments center on preserving the voice as the property of a cultural elite and are consistent with the intelligentsia's far-flung attacks on middlebrow values in the 1920s. The addition of sound came just when critics were elevating the silent cinema to "art," and it was difficult for them to conceive how talking was conducive to the kind of filmmaking they revered in THE GOLD RUSH (1925), THE LAST LAUGH (1924), and SUNRISE (1927). Other critics had an approach-avoidance conflict with theater. They held it dear as a venue for "modern" ideas expressed in a specific linguistic style and as a metonymy for the highbrow culture to which cinema should aspire. But many also cherished film as an autonomous art with its own rules and attributes, such as dynamism, the ability to compress time and space, to alternate long-shots and close-ups, to linger on faces, and so on. These were assumed to be superior to stage techniques. Thus, some critics hated speaking films because the voice pulled the movie away from something essentially "filmic" and modern, and toward old-fashioned theatricality. But many other commentators thought that the stage was superior to cinema and that perhaps the talkies could benefit from film's new theatricality. Nathan and those like him regarded theater as a bastion of vocal correctness. He saw the "formerly mute" cinema encroaching on the prerogative of the educated class to define and enjoy film on its own terms.

As the transition to sound got under way, movie actors were revealed to possess a heretofore unnoticed flaw: they lacked both intelligence and the ability to speak proper English. Many writers felt that the latter was symptomatic of the former. One concerned critic noted that the change to sound would require the development of entirely new techniques, in part because "the stars of the screen do not know how to speak and the scenarists do not know how to write dialogue."[2] Surprisingly, some of this criticism of actors' voices emanated from the film industry itself. William Fox said in 1927, "Many of the present players who may still be popular [in five years] will have to take courses in elocution, and we will then be able to look at and listen to a motion picture without a subtitle or a spoken title." David Sarnoff of RCA also thought that film actors would have to be taught to speak, insisting that "at present no one would want to listen to the sort of speech they use."[3] These executives' comments are enlightening because of the prejudices they embody. Deriding the intelligence of actors was an old custom, of course. What was new was the implication that current film stars who did not speak *could not* speak. Their voices were inadequate. It is ironic that Fox and Sarnoff, both first-generation immigrants, should belittle the diction of movie stars. Their potshots at actors' voices suggest that, perhaps symptomatically among the film moguls, they expected the talkies to disseminate an ideal of cultural homogenization and assimilation through quality speech.

One motif in criticisms of the voice was the distinction between the silent film's emphasis on the body and the talkies' accent on the mind. Ideals of athleticism, beauty, and "it" (sex appeal) no longer sufficed in the sound film. Now the articulate would supersede the beautiful and sensuous—but dull and vocally benighted. Actors' speech signified their intelligence. Film executives at one of their conferences heard Dr. Frank Vizetelly, the editor of *Funk and Wagnall's Dictionary*, say unequivocally that speech correlated with "mental efficiency." Even a passable voice was useless if not guided by "brains." Frederick Lonsdale predicted that "the Hollywood beauty actors and actresses . . . will soon be as dead as the third and fourth rate touring companies whom the talking films will supplant."[4] The critic Waldo Walker ventured, "[It] may mean that the old type of actor, the man and woman with complete histrionic ability, will enter the new field in larger numbers, and that the 'doll-faced' and 'sheik' types of movie stars who lack ability and training to act speaking parts may disappear." The arts critic Seldes also forecast this "serious displacement of moving picture favorites" based on physical prowess or appearance. "Probably a more intelligent type of player will be required and the young woman who looks well [*sic*] in a close-up or a young man who expresses 'it' by jumping over six-foot fences, will receive less fan mail than those whose voices register warmly and clearly and who learn the new technic of acting which the talking film requires." Elocution teachers were needed "so that moderately intelligent words will be at least moderately intelligible in the new films." He noted that "intelligent people now in the moving pictures," including Chaplin and King Vidor, were extraordinarily dubious of the new medium.[5] Robert Sherwood also prioritized intelligence as a survival trait forced on Hollywood by the talkies:

> What matters infinitely more than the tonal quality of the star's voice, or the perfection of his or her articulation, is the nature of the star's cerebral functions. For every one representative of the Beverly Hills nobility who will be

sent to the guillotine in the near future because of faulty diction, there will be a dozen who are decapitated because they lack the capacity to memorize three or four sentences at a time and to retain them for as long as ten minutes. (R. E. Sherwood, "Renaissance in Hollywood," *American Mercury,* April 1929, p. 432)

Edwin Hullinger professed, "There is nothing that reveals shallowness of the soul as quickly as the voice. Sheer, undisguised shallowness tires an audience quickly. And a voice cannot be tampered with, retouched or covered over by means of clever studio lighting. At last the movies may be compelled to 'go in for brains.'"[6] Another commentator described the new acting expectations:

In the older order of things the candidate for screen honors had virtually no chance of success unless he or she had "it." . . . Sound has changed all that. "It" has been supplanted by personality. The fanciful has given way to the real. The public can no longer be fooled and so droves of heavy lovers and impassioned ladies of the premicrophone days are drifting back to the overalls of the filling station and the apron of the cafeteria. They were like strutting peacocks; beautiful to gaze upon, terrible to hear. (Maurice L. Ahern, "Hollywood Horizons," *Commonweal,* 21 May 1930, p. 72)

If the silent film actor's voice was wrong for the talkies, what was right? The legitimate stage—distinct from vaudeville and its ethnic vernacular—was problematic for those who defended the autonomy of cinema art, but it was one readily available model for quality talking performance. The widespread view was that silent players were not suited to bear this cultural responsibility. Nathan protested that movie actors' voices would always be inferior to those of their New York and London stage counterparts: "To expect a pantomimist, talented though he be, to be the possessor of a vocal organ capable of expressing all the shadings of dramatic speech is surely expecting a lot." Robert Sisk wrote, "What chance has a cinema favorite, formerly skilled in the mixing of chocolate syrup with carbonated water, of speaking lines as an actor should? Such work, obviously, will take skilled performers, and they will have to come from the stage."[7] William deMille, who divided his directing between New York and Hollywood, perceptively noted that spectators had been "imagining" screen stars' absent voices. Hearing their actual voices was apt to disappoint them. These regional, uncultured voices often were inappropriate for the sophisticated roles demanded by the theatrical material of the new cinema. "Many delightful young women," deMille believed,

lose all their charm the moment their voices are heard; stalwart "he-men" may shed their virility with the first sentence they speak; the rolling Western "r" gives the lie to an otherwise excellent "society" characterization, and uncultured enunciation destroys the illusion created by beauty. In very few cases does the voice of a screen idol satisfy "fans" who, for years, have been imagining it. (William deMille, "The Screen Speaks," *Scribner's,* April 1929, p. 369)

The columnist Rob Wagner developed this line of thought. Stage stars, he argued, are physically real people in a real world, while screen stars have a dreamlike or phantasmagorical quality. "Only so long as they maintain this dream quality does the adulation continue. The moment they come to life, either in a personal appearance or in the speakies, they are instantly reduced to the common denominator of every other pretty little girl."[8] The vitriolic Nathan scoffed at the public's naive attribution of an imaginary voice to a star's face, making veiled references to Bow, Pickford, and Garbo:

> The yokel who once imagined that the Mlle. X., were she to whisper to him "I love you," would sound like a melted mandolin, now hears his goddess speak like a gum-chewing shopgirl. The worshiper of the Mlle. Y.'s seductive girlishness now beholds her, in the grim, hard light of the talkies, to be a middle-aged woman with the voice of a middle-aged woman. The farmhand who once dreamed of the Mlle. Z. as an exotic and mysterious dose of cantharides will now see her simply as a fat immigrant with deradenoncus and over-developed laryngeal muscles assisting in the negotiation of pidgin-English. Valentino died in time. Think what would have happened to his flock of women admirers if the unsparing lighting of the talkies had betrayed his imminent baldness and the movietone his bootblack voice. (George Jean Nathan, "The Pictorial Phonograph," *American Mercury*, July 1929, p. 7)

The speech which movie stars allegedly could not enunciate was a unique dialect probably not heard on any street. In a revealing interview, Conrad Nagel discussed how it had taken years of training and mentorship to banish his "defective" Iowa-bred speech. "I had a terrible struggle to shake my mid-western twang, and developed a series of exercises for my tongue and lips that I practiced diligently, all for the purpose of breaking my drawl, and also to place my voice correctly."[9] His achievement was to be able to speak sophisticated parts in the standard language of the stage. This consisted of clipped speech with "pear-shaped" vowels and sharp consonants. Forensic aficionados found their ideal in the Movietone footage of George Bernard Shaw. "We have heard his voice," the editors of *Literary Digest* proclaimed, "and are tempted to nominate him as a model for all the Better English Clubs in existence. This exhibition seems to settle once for all the claim that the best English comes from Dublin, for the delicious Irish overtone adds a music to his perfect enunciation." A speech professor corroborated the implication that standard English was British English: "Among those familiar with modern speech pedagogy there will be, I believe, general agreement as to English phonetics being the simplest and best means to this end [good diction]. It is, of course, the basis of speech training in many of the largest universities and colleges." The American readership was also informed that British commentators were appalled by U.S. regional accents and bad grammar. The British press launched salvos against the "corrupting influences of 'American English.'"[10]

On the stage, there may have been a practical explanation for this enunciative speaking style: it helped actors project their voices so that their lines would be intelligible in the farthest rows of the theater. But there was also an ideological aspect to the preference for this style. Genteel American theater critics favored the English accent typical of London's West End theaters over "common" American English because it connoted class and culture. This mannered speaking style can be heard by listening to Norma Shearer in THE LAST OF MRS. CHEYNEY (1929) and Ruth Chatterton in MADAME X (1929). Under the direction of MGM's Sidney Franklin, one of the studio's "society" directors, and Lionel Barrymore of Broadway's "royal family" of theater, these characteristic stage voices transposed pristinely to the sound track. (One may also hear Margaret Dumont and John Barrymore parody the "quality" voice in her Marx Brothers movies and his TWENTIETH CENTURY [1934]). The enunciative style seemed to many critics to be destined for the technical characteristics of the talkies, for which lines supposedly had to be intoned slowly to minimize electrical distortion. Lasky emphasized the positive social effects of transposing stage speech onto the screen. "I look for better English and clearer enunciation as the result of dialogue films. If all of our popular feminine stars let their hair grow long, they could end the bobbed hair vogue in short order. Slip-shod speech modes can be influenced in the same manner."[11] Cecil B. DeMille predicted that sound films would have a leveling effect on the language: "The talkies have drawn toward uniformity the most ununiform and diverse tongue the world has ever known. There are scores of dialects of English, some of them very harsh and bad. There are one or two methods of speaking. It is towards a happy medium of speech that the studios of Hollywood are aiming."[12]

British actors—Boris Karloff, Ronald Colman, Victor McLaglen, Reginald Denny, and Basil Rathbone, notably—acquired an instant aura of sophistication. For native actors who did not have formal stage experience, the new filmmaking was presumed to require a vocal upgrade, precipitating anxiety about "elocution." Dorothy Manners reported that "all the girls" (i.e., actresses) are "having their voices cultivated," as though this were a passive process like having one's nails done.[13]

Led by Paramount, MGM, and Fox, the studios established vocal training departments and forced actors to "improve" their voices. Fans read about the dreaded studio voice culture expert and the sound-recording technician. According to Mayme Ober Peak, "He tells the director just how maybe May McAvoy spoke too high in the middle of that sentence about her lover, or Emil Jannings gave a grunt that sounded like a blast of dynamite. Once, Chester Conklin in *Varsity* (1928) registered an admonition for caution in a hoarse whisper to Mary Brian that rocked the stage when it came through the amplifier!"[14]

Nervous studios recorded hundreds of voice tests, short films made with actors reciting passages at varying distances from the microphone in order to rank their talking and singing abilities. Paramount's efforts to educate its voice pupils took the form of on-the-job training:

> The big studios have always had kindergartens for the kids in charge of certificated teachers furnished by the board of education but paid for by the companies. Now they are adding voice culture and English courses for their stock players under long-time contracts. At most studios the young star receives her instructions in the school-room and then makes her tests in the laboratory, but on the Paramount lot I found a unique stunt of combining the lessons and tests in one operation. I happened into the studio bungalow of little Mary Brian,[15] and there sat that bright-eyed young lady declaiming into a microphone with apparently nobody to hear her. I soon learned the answer. After doing her exercise she picked up the telephone and listened inquisitively. "This saves both time and embarrassment," she explained as she hung up the receiver. "Professor Bluett and Mr. Pomeroy, head of the technical department, both heard me over in the laboratory, and while Professor Bluett corrected my English Mr. Pomeroy listened to my recording tests." (Rob Wagner, "Photo Static," *Collier's*, 23 February 1929, p. 28)

MGM claimed to be making the largest commitment to elocution, building a two-story building for the teachers and engaging the University of Southern California to test and repair "weak spots" in voices. Weakness in the voice was almost always a female trait. Their travails when they faced the technology of the recording microphone was said to be physiological:

> Most of their [the USC experts'] effort will be concentrated on the feminine player. "Women, more than men," states one of the professors, "will be forced to [take] intensive and scientific training for talking pictures, because of a simple scientific fact. The voice of a man is naturally heavier, vibrating at between 100 and 300 vibrations a second, while woman's goes up to around 500 to 700. At this vibration the sibilant sounds, such as the 'S,' 'Z,' the hard 'O,' 'X,' and 'P' become hisses or blasts, as they are vibrated at a higher speed than the balance of the vocal sounds." That is why, he explains, "few soprano singers have succeeded in making successful phonograph records." (Mayme Ober Peak, quoted in *Literary Digest*, 20 October 1928, pp. 60, 62)

Nevertheless, because the voice could be isolated and trained, there was optimism that this limitation could be overcome by hard work and the application of science. Several studios resorted to newfangled devices for quantifying vocal properties in an effort to sidestep subjective judgment. Universal's electronic "syllable sleuth" was something called the "telegraphone." Professor Verne Knudsen brought his USC "voice detector" machine to MGM. He was "prepared to eradicate the ordinary flaws found in diction and enunciation. Players can watch the recording of their own voices and study how to eliminate the 'kinks' in the voice."[16] William deMille recounted—possibly tongue-in-cheek—an anecdote that illustrates the extent of actors' anxiety as they sought to teach themselves to speak:

> Gone are the shoutings, the music, the noises of electric lights, the hum of the cameras, and the tense directions through megaphones. Instead, a silent group of actors awaits a silent signal upon a silent stage. Between "shots" groups of quiet-voiced players bring forth dictionaries and discuss meanings of words and their pronunciation. The responsibility of the spoken word, hailed with joy by veterans from the stage, is a heavy burden to some of those actors whose whole professional career has been silent. (William deMille, "The Screen Speaks," *Scribner's*, April 1929, p. 368)

New aspirants and established actors rushed to vocal coaches in 1928 to "train" their voices. Journalists emphasized the great personal discipline and labor required to alter the voice. Dr. Vizetelly was quoted giving actors this advice: "If your lips would keep from slips, five things observe with care. Of whom you speak, to whom you speak, the manner, when and where." Even Mary Pickford claimed to be nervous about her first voice test. She told an interviewer that she "will never, never, never make a speakie." But in 1929 she flip-flopped and told another interviewer that she welcomed the talkies and was preparing to take advantage of them. She reflected the producers' hedging strategy of preserving "silent" technique: "There will be plenty of experts concentrating on the talking feature. But we mustn't forget what we already have." Gloria Swanson's singing

Joan Crawford practices the "Indian Love Call" with director Lucien Hubbard on the set of Rose-Marie *(MGM, 1928).*

in THE TRESPASSER was achieved, *Collier's* magazine confided, with the aid of fourteen voice lessons. Wagner wrote about one star, a "lisping film-favorite," whom he overheard "repeating over and over again, 'The Leith police dismisseth us.'" Phyllis Haver, Leatrice Joy, and Janet Gaynor were taking lessons. Mary Philbin, perhaps anticipating international stardom, was studying German.[17]

Several universities instituted elocution lessons for aspiring movie actors. Readers also learned that experts, such as those lampooned in SINGIN' IN THE RAIN ("Moses supposes his toeses are roses"), promised clients a fast break into the talkies but provided only disappointment. Young people had always been lured to Los Angeles by movie scams, and sound provided a golden opportunity for con artists. The Vitaphone director Bryan Foy tried to discourage young women from coming to Hollywood and signing up for voice instruction: "Elocution lessons won't do a lot of these little girls much good. They lose in naturalness as much as they gain in clearness and enunciation." Fly-by-night voice teachers, according to Hullinger, had replaced acting schools as Hollywood's "chief pest, fetching double and quadruple their former rates." Wagner remarked on the many voice culturists who were promoting themselves in newspaper ads. But he may have inadvertently encouraged neophytes when he observed that even the best voices could flop when recorded or broadcast, while the voices of untrained extras and veteran silent actors sometimes ran away with scenes.[18]

Many took for granted that the British-accented speech of the New York stage would become the norm for movies, but there were a few dissenters. Perceval Reniers, for one, pointed out that, despite some excellent legitimate voices—Otis Skinner, Walter Hampden, Margaret Anglin—"for the rest our stage is overrun with misguided young women who are imitating either Mrs. Fiske or Ethel Barrymore and with young men the source of whose inspiration I have yet to discover. It seems to lie somewhere between John Barrymore of *The Fortune Hunter* and George Cohan of *Broadway Jones.*" Similarly, Frank Wilstach (publicity director for the Hays Office) observed that theater patrons "do not go there to listen to an actor or actress hypnotized by the melody of his or her vocal cords. If this were the case, there would be schools of elocution on every corner." Many of the most popular and renowned actors of the past had in fact been tainted by bad enunciation. He doubted that few legendary thespians or currently successful Broadway actors could pass an elocution test.

An alternative vocal performance model for the talkies was the language heard on radio. There, too, like the out-of-control voices coming from the movie screen, one could hear a panoply of speaking styles derived from different classes and regions. In the case of the ventriloquist Edgar Bergen, these voices came from the same person. His own speaking voice was the refined New York stage. The playboy dummy Charlie McCarthy spoke in jazzy slang. Mortimer Snerd, the yokel dummy, spoke like the hick he was. Radio was also a medium for disseminating middlebrow gentility. "Cultured" commentators who spoke in educated voices, including Joseph Henry Jackson, the Yale professor William Lyon Phelps, and, especially, Alexander Woollcott, presented literati and social critics on radio in "living room conversation" formats. Woollcott's *Town Crier* program interspersed banter with personalities with book and theater reviews.[19] Producers of motion pictures must have been interested in trying to attract some of this "sophisticated" clientele to their highbrow stage and operatic adaptations.

The elocution vogue reveals a specific anxiety about the voice. It was the *standard* of speech and language that was the issue, not some innate acoustic property. Otherwise, ameliorating the voice would be impossible. The supposition that the voice can be isolated and altered suggests that it was something extra, apart from the personality or physical being of the actor. Like the sound track, which was at the time conceived of as a supplement to the silent film, the actor's voice was being treated as a separate commodity. The debate over who controlled the disembodied film voice had repercussions in the realm of labor, increasing the executives' anxiety about actors. The producers quickly appended riders to the Standard Agreement that legally recognized the separation of the voice from the body and established their right to exploit it. The actor's vocal capability was then marketed as a separate entity in advertising campaigns like "Lon Chaney Talks" and "Garbo Talks," where the speaking star was a selling point.

The "quality" voice sounded better as an ideal than it did on the screen. The enunciative style proved to be very unpopular with general audiences. Critics began pointing out that the delivery which might have been suitable for the theater was inappropriate for the intimacy and closed space of the cinematic medium-shot. By 1929 the call for film voices to emulate stage voices had been silenced.

The Natural Voice

By late 1929, elocution had become a Hollywood joke:

> An actress would enter a restaurant, order a cup of coffee and wonder where she could find someone to teach her how to order a cup of coffee in a restaurant scene on the screen. Even the fact that the waiter brought her the cup of coffee she had ordered did not make her conscious of the fact that without training she had managed to get the coffee, which, after all, is the main idea behind the order, either on or off the screen. No matter what degree of artistic perfection she achieved in uttering the order, the sum total of the returns it would bring her would be one cup of coffee, and she got that without even one lesson in elocution. (Welford Beaton, "High-Hatting Little Brother," *Saturday Evening Post,* 24 May 1930, p. 62)

Again, failure to adapt to the demands of sound is attributed to the actor's stupidity; she is not smart enough to realize that her way of speaking is already satisfactory. As the transition to all-talking films unfolded, there was a corresponding shift in the press's emphasis from enunciative speaking to what was called naturalism. Rather than promoting stage diction, popular writing more frequently ridiculed it as Hollywood's folly. The year 1929, according to Welford Beaton, marked the peak of "the screen's capitulation to the stage." He argued that Hollywood wanted to turn out "the kind of entertainment the country wants, but its ambition always had been to produce something of which Broadway approved." The resulting middlebrow concoction was unsatisfactory in both respects. Belatedly, the industry was realizing that stage actors "are equipped but little more to make a motion picture than they are to perform an operation for appendicitis or to fill a tooth."[20] According to Foy, "Sound is going to be a great thing for good character actors, who can talk their parts naturally as well as play them."[21] Richard Watts also came out in favor of the natural voice:

> It became noticeable that the only triumphs in the new medium were those registered by child actors [i.e., Davey Lee], who were unconscious of the microphone, Negro performers [i.e., Stepin Fetchit], who weren't interested

in the technique of acting, and such experienced stage and screen players as Lionel Barrymore. No member of these groups was interested in elocution. All of them were natural before the microphone and, as a result, gave performances possessing a quality that talking pictures had not previously provided. (Richard Watts, Jr., "All Talking," *Theatre Arts Monthly,* September 1929, p. 709)

Unusual voices and accents, which had been condemned in 1928 as unpleasant and expendable, were welcomed as distinctive if they matched the speaker's character. Fans were even appreciating players like Joe Fusio, "the talkies' first stutterer." Significantly, few of these commentators suggested that Hollywood's notion of stage diction was outdated or misguided. They largely ignored the trend in progressive drama of using everyday language and realistic situations, such as in the plays of Elmer Rice (*Street Scene*). For most critics, the stage meant traditional fare and the mass-audience appeal of Broadway's big theaters. An exceptional spokesperson for the talkies was John Meehan, a playwright, stage director, and Oscar-nominated screenwriter (THE DIVORCÉE [1930]). He came out against long rehearsals in movie acting. Though necessary for multi-camera cinematography, rehearsals tended to destroy spontaneity. Meehan pointed out that "acting as such, has been out in the theater for a long time and one of our most difficult problems in the theater was in keeping the players from acting. In talking pictures we can eliminate this difficulty very easily by limiting rehearsals. . . . Dialogue must be snappy and crisp. There is little need for long speeches in talking pictures." Jesse Lasky also distinguished between the speaking style of modern theater and the melodramatic tradition: "The old declamatory style is a hindrance rather than a help to today's actor. In the literature of the stage as elsewhere the demand is for the natural, for the truth of life, for fidelity to character and situation. I ask our actors to be natural, speak naturally. . . . None of our artists has been instructed to go in for voice culture." This last statement, as Wagner's interview with Mary Brian showed, obviously was not true; Paramount had joined the other studios in the elocution craze. But evidently it was deemed necessary to cover up the now-discredited practice of voice culture in order to promulgate the illusion of "natural" speech.[22]

The definition of naturalism included a proper match between voice, the actor's appearance, and the social milieu of the fiction. A case in point is the attack on Chester Morris in THE CASE OF SERGEANT GRISCHA (1930) by *Variety*: "To give a peasant who confesses he can neither read nor write, dialog that would fit a Belasco society drama was giving this picture a kick in the slats before the rest of the works are thrown in."[23] Wesley Stout wrote, "Nor is elocution an asset, and as for voice culture—well, the most ludicrous sound effects recorded to date have been, not the 'dese' and 'dose' of Tenth Avenue ancestry, but the phony English accents of several ladies who spoke the language serviceably until they had their voices lifted." Watts announced: "The vogue of the elocution teachers faded dismally as soon as it was discovered that either complete naturalism or technical precision gave certain stage players their feeling of ease. It became obvious that an absence of self-consciousness was the only thing to make players forget the terror of the microphone and enter into the more serious matter of characterization."[24]

The Marx Brothers, perhaps more than any other stars, persuaded critics that voice training was futile. Even articulate commentators like Sherwood strained to describe the brothers' linguistic appeal. His characterization of it as a "beautiful madness" anticipates the surrealists' love of these comedians' chatter:

The weird quality of [the four Marx Brothers'] spoken humor is precisely right for the movies. It is an insult to speak of it as "wise-cracking," for that suggests the glib, trite patter of Broadway. The Marx boys exalt their worst puns with a beautiful madness—the same form of madness that was in "Alice in Wonderland" and *Shoulder Arms.* Perhaps the greatest proof of this is that very few of the Marxian gags can be quoted and still sound funny. . . . Up to now, [the actors] have been seriously burdened with opening choruses, singing juveniles, love interest and other irrelevancies. They don't need plots—particularly such inordinately complicated plots as those which packed the librettos of *The Cocoanuts* and *Animal Crackers.* They certainly don't need musical numbers, other than those that they happen to provide for themselves. All that the Marxes do need is elbow room. (Robert E. Sherwood, *Film Daily,* 28 September 1930, p. 8)

This was the lesson for Seldes: "Everyone else I have heard from the screen enunciates painfully, to carry out the director's illusion that speech is unnatural to human beings; Groucho and Chico chatter along." Seldes was surprised that he liked the Marx Brothers so much in THE COCOANUTS. He had not anticipated that Groucho's famous high-speed vaudeville ranting would record well, yet it was almost flawless. Harpo's performance, however, was not successful. His muteness seemed unreal, and in his close-ups he seemed to be pleading to talk. Unlike Seldes and other mainstream critics who were dis-

ANIMAL CRACKERS *(Paramount, 1930), with Margaret Irving and Harpo Marx.*

turbed by Harpo Marx's screen silence, Beatrice Wilson argued that Harpo "will be perfectly at home, and the screen should be the more fitting medium for his genius."[25]

Alexander Bakshy, the editor of *The Nation* whose partisanship for the talkies developed slowly, conceded in 1929 that "the popularity of the talkies is not wholly a craze for novelty. Their success is much more due to the warmth and intimacy which has been given the picture by the human voice and which is so unmistakably missing in the silent picture as this comes from Hollywood." By 1932 he was convinced that the stage voice had no place on the screen: "No representation of life in a talking picture can ever be convincing so long as it carries the hall-mark of the stage battle of words. Even the so-called 'natural' stage dialogue is too inflated to appear natural on the screen."[26]

These writers, rather than treating the voice as disembodied, malleable, and a surplus commodity, were calling for acting which did not sound like acting. Though they praised performers whose voices were unique (even star quality), they insisted that actors' idiosyncrasies, accents, and vocal mannerisms had to be subordinated to the standard of creating believable fictional characters. Even as these critics were emphasizing authenticity as a criterion of film excellence, directors were integrating sound effects, music, and dialogue with the film image and reducing the sound track's intrusiveness.

THE HYBRID VOICE

After debating for about two years, the critics seemed to lose interest in the search for the perfect voice. Vocal style had to be intelligible and intelligent, fit the character and dramatic situation, and, most important, convey a sense of illusionistic "presence." Audiences wished to experience performers as individualized characters or stars, not as theatrical personae. Simultaneous with the channeling of recording techniques toward the modulated sound track, the public and critics were formulating a new rhetoric of vocal performance that emphasized moderation. The actor's skill at different kinds of expression in many registers became crucially important. The ideal screen style integrated the best of stage and movie acting styles. William deMille explained the reciprocity of what we can call the hybrid voice:

> In many cases the stage actor who doesn't know picture technic is no better off than the screen actor of no vocal experience; except that it is frequently easier for the stage actor to learn screen technic than for the screen actor to develop a voice which he doesn't possess. . . . At the present time the ideal actor for talking pictures seems to be the stage actor with screen experience. (deMille, "The Screen Speaks," p. 368)

Lasky, speaking of the "new order" imposed by the talkies, recognized that neither the stage actor's voice nor that of the screen actor was by itself sufficient for the sound cinema:

> The star system—that is, the system of featuring some popular star on even terms with the picture itself—will prevail in this new order of things. New faces will be seen, as a matter of course; we are always on the alert for new personalities; but the star of the legitimate stage will not supplant the silent headliners merely because of their voices. The talking pictures will present new problems to both schools of acting. The movie player will have to learn

something of the other's art and the stage star will have much to learn from
the film-wise actor. (Jesse L. Lasky, "Hearing Things in the Dark," *Collier's*,
May 1929, p. 48)

Unlike the quality voice, the hybrid style revived the ideal of photogenic beauty. Lasky
told *Film Daily*, "Some stage players will have sensational success in the new field but by
no means will the stage player supplant the screen artist because of the peculiar demands
of the new form of expression. Beauty is still an important part of screen entertainment.
A melodious voice will never take the place of physical beauty; it can add to it, but can
never supplant it." For the consumer, nothing was to detract from the direct enjoyment
of an actor's personality. Ideally, his or her speech would be unobtrusive or, if it did stand
out—for example, by exhibiting an accent—it would be pleasant. Beaton wrote in 1930,
"In not one instance did a stage player become prominent on the screen . . . until he had
substituted screen technic for stage technic, and until he had climbed his way up slowly
in the new art."[27]

ACCENTS

A sad story ran in the trades. Fox had brought seven beauty contest winners from foreign
countries to Hollywood. Because of their inability to master English, their contracts
would not be renewed and they were being sent back to their native lands. This was but
one anecdote illustrating a brief mini-crisis about the status of international speakers. A
popular writer described these actors as "immediate and spectacular victims" and predicted that soon they would be reduced to playing comic relief and French maids. "So
excellent an actor as Emil Jannings will be salvaged by plying him in such old Warfield
roles as *The Music Master* or original stories that can exploit his German English."
Contract players who were reported to be studying English included: Olga Baclanova,
Paul Lukas, Ramón Novarro, Karl Dane, Nils Asther, Renée Adorée, Raquel Torres,
Greta Garbo, Dolores Del Rio, Vilma Banky, Lili Damita, and Mona Rico. Lasky
defended his Paramount employees, stating that everyone on the payroll spoke good
English. He had specifically instructed Chevalier and Jannings not to lose their accents
because American and British actors who could play foreign parts with the proper dialect
were difficult to find. (His reasoning still reflects the older view of the voice as a detach-
able surplus value.) The Paramount production head B. P. Schulberg expressed his support for Baclanova and Jannings. The trades confirmed that dialects were not being
banished: Garbo had been cast for ANNA CHRISTIE, and Jean Hersholt's Danish-English
and Maurice Chevalier's thick French voices had proven to be charming, not alarming.[28]

No producer was more sensitive to the dialect problem than Samuel Goldwyn (who
himself, because of his accent and malapropisms, sported one of Hollywood's most infamous voices). His leading man Ronald Colman spoke beautiful British English. Vilma
Banky, his leading lady, was another matter. In 1925 Goldwyn had brought her from
Budapest to Hollywood to make her a big star—and he did. She and Colman competed
with Garbo and Gilbert as screen lovers, but the intertitles gave no hint that she spoke
barely a word of English.

BULLDOG DRUMMOND, Colman's talking debut as an English detective, was a hit
when released in May 1929. Critics agreed that his soft-spoken, lightly accented voice
was perfect. The *New York American* predicted, "The thousands of feminine fans who
have adored this silent man are going to go simply crazy about him now that he is speak-

The hybrid voice. Ronald Colman, seen here in RAFFLES *(United Artists, 1930), had what many considered the best voice for the talkies: a British accent (but not too strong), clear enunciation, unstilted delivery, a distinctive voice, and a "natural" demeanor suited to the roles he played (here, a gentleman thief).*

ing his piece. Colman has that which is known as a personality voice. It is much more colorful than his appearance or his acting, so with this new asset added to his visible attractions, Ronald Colman is in the talkies as long as he wants to stay in." But Simon Rowson, an important industry representative from London, watched BULLDOG DRUMMOND in New York and witnessed the dismay of women fans in the audience. "They could not conceal the disappointment they experienced at the discovery that he spoke a different language from their own!"[29]

Vilma Banky's first sound vehicle was a romantic comedy called THIS IS HEAVEN. As with Colman, Goldwyn chose to highlight, not hide, his star's accent. He cast her as an immigrant short-order cook at a pancake restaurant who falls for a millionaire disguised as a chauffeur. Though the film was basically finished in January 1929 and included three talking sequences, Goldwyn could not decide whether her dialogue was acceptable or not. While he vacillated, the trade press and gossip columnists had a field day disparaging Banky's allegedly incomprehensible speaking voice. *Film Daily* reported in February,

> Talking sequences of *This Is Heaven* are back in the picture, setting at rest a controversy of some proportions here at the studios. Samuel Goldwyn eliminated the dialogue because he felt the picture did not need it. This brought kicks from some exhibitors, coupled with gentle kidding from some

Goldwyn reassures exhibitors that Vilma Banky's Hungarian accent will draw fans to
THIS IS HEAVEN *(United Artists, 1929).*

> locals, who thought Miss Banky's voice would not register. Accordingly,
> Goldwyn accepted the challenge and the picture is to go out with dialogue.
> A screening here satisfied the producer that Miss Banky's voice records well,
> her accent even seeming light for the part of an immigrant girl. (*Film Daily,*
> 7 February 1929, p. 9)

When Goldwyn finally premiered the film in New York, Kann wrote, "Just why Sam
Goldwyn experienced cold shivers before deciding whether Vilma should talk or not, we
fail to see. Miss Banky has a lovely voice and an accent that is positively entrancing. . . .
The gorgeous Vilma will smite you all over again with her foreign English."[30]

But when THIS IS HEAVEN opened nationally in May, reviewers compared the film
unfavorably to BULLDOG DRUMMOND. Several picked on her heavy accent. Of course, it
did not help the film that, by mid-1929, part-talking sound tracks were passé. In the final
tally, Goldwyn lost $200,000. Banky's career was nearly over, and Goldwyn, the story
goes, tried to deduct $50 from her $5,000-a-week salary to pay for the voice lessons.[31]

Then there was the problem encountered when American actors were supposed to
be speaking the native language of their characters. The New York stage convention
was for everyone to speak English regardless of the fictional language. This had also
been the norm in silent film intertitles. But talkie adaptations using the same convention were criticized as unnatural. Kann chided the unintentional linguistic humor in
INNOCENTS OF PARIS: "And those gendarmes with their New Yorkese lingo! There'll
probably be an official protest about it." Probably referring to MARIANNE, Jerome
Beatty wrote, "The unrealistic scene is one in which a French peasant speaks to a

German. In the picture, as in the play, both talk in perfect English." He asked rhetor-ically, "What can be done in situations like that?"[32] Lubitsch poked fun at this conven-tion in THE LOVE PARADE. A courtier asks the Count (Chevalier), who is supposed to be a "Sylvanian," how he got his French accent. (Of course, the other Sylvanian speaks perfect stage English.) The Count replies by beginning to tell a raunchy farmer's daughter–type joke about a doctor's wife, but we cannot follow it because there is a cut to a long-shot with the conversation shown from the other side of glass doors. Then cut-ting back to the interior shot, the Count gives the punch line, "When I woke up I had lost my cold, but I had thees terreeble French accent."

By the time of ALL QUIET ON THE WESTERN FRONT, in which the characters are German, the actors spoke their normal English and generated few if any complaints about the lack of an accent. Indeed, the accent crisis evaporated as quickly as it had materialized after audiences began hearing their film favorites speaking. Colman, Chevalier, Garbo, and the others showed that voice differentiation by an accent was a plus—if it contributed to the integrated vocal performance style, or what the press was calling the "personality voice." Whether critics actually had any impact on what was coming out of the screen can-not be known with assurance. But certainly the voices of the new vocal stars were anything but conventional. The most memorable actors' unique speech was consonant with the clas-sical cinema's emphasis on individualized characters. Gary Cooper's flat monotone, Robinson's growl, Cagney's nasalisms, Eugene Pallette's raspy basso profundo, Garbo's sul-try guttural, Betty's "boop-boop-a-doop," Mae West's invitations to tussle—they defied all prescriptive categorization. These voices could never really be controlled. The debate turned away from how the movies talked to what they were saying.

Censorship

While sound studios claimed to be bringing the best of Broadway to the nation, motion picture detractors pointed out that they brought undesirable elements too. Raymond Moley of the Hays Office wrote:

> Execrable girl-and-music shows, heretofore seen only by the out-of-towner on an occasional trip to New York, were being brought by the talkies to every hamlet. The frenzied filming of Broadway plays without regard for the fact that a motion picture, whether talking or silent, is certainly not a play from the point of view of either art or prudence, brought the clink of highball glasses, the squeal of bedsprings, the crackle of fast conversation to a thou-sand Main Streets. (Raymond Moley, *The Hays Office* [New York: Bobbs-Merrill, 1945], p. 65)

This account, a little hysterical, captures the impression made by the talkies on those guardians of social norms who feared the movies' influence. This was the downside of film as a "democratic" art; it had the potential of spreading the opposite of the quality voice. Public watchdogs were bolstered by the Supreme Court's declaration in *Mutual Film Corporation v. Ohio Industrial Commission* that motion pictures were "capable of evil, having power for it." The 1915 ruling had legalized prior censorship of motion pic-tures and empowered state and local boards to ban them. One reason the Hays Office existed was to fend off efforts to further regulate film content. The "fast conversation" of the talkies gave those who wished to subdue cinema's social power a highly visible (and audible) excuse to rally around the banner of morality.

In September 1929, the Motion Picture Producers and Distributors of America discussed the threat of intensified censorship at its national conference. The upshot was *See and Hear,* a "textbook or community handbook," nominally authored by Will Hays, extolling the social virtues of the sound film. One might not guess from a cursory reading of the little book that the movie czar's puff piece was an image-building response to a critical situation. Hays sings the praises of the producers' good deeds, which range from filming "surgical operations by the masters, in colors," to sending movies to leper colonies in the Canal Zone. When he describes "the Formula," referring to the procedure of acquiring "recent books and plays that deal in themes and situations and topics which in previous years were discussed only in whispers," his message about censorship is unmistakable:

> The method, which is of course thoroughly legal and which has proved efficient, is not censorship in any sense of the word. No censorship could have brought about the results which have been attained. At the same time, the formula does not, by any possible interpretation, limit the production of vital or artistic pictures. Any method which did that would fail absolutely. (Will Hays, *See and Hear: A Brief History of Motion Pictures and the Development of Sound* [New York: MPPDA, 1929], p. 29)

But many people were claiming that it was the Formula, a policy in effect since 1924, and the 1927 list of "Don'ts and Be Carefuls" which had failed. The latest drive was by Senator Smith Brookhart of Iowa, a confirmed movie-hater. His bill's chief proponents were women's organizations and Protestant laymen, led by William Sheafe Chase. For years Chase had testified in favor of various bills that would have mandated national censorship. *Film Daily's* opinion of his latest crusade was openly hostile: "Rev. Canon William Sheafe Chase, generally regarded an arch foe of pictures, and world's long distance champion mudslinger, is at it again, this time circularizing members of Congress with a reprint from *Harrison's Reports,* in which that publication pans alleged filth in WEST OF ZANZIBAR and points to that picture as an argument in favor of passage of the Brookhart bill."[33]

While censorship was always annoying to the industry, the addition of sound transformed the issue into a financial one. Trouble began as early as 1926, when Chicago required scenes to be cut from four reels of DON JUAN. Warner Bros. re-scored and re-recorded the discs for those sections, about forty minutes of film. Frank Woodhull, head of the Motion Picture Theater Owners, clearly viewed the matter as one concerning money, not morals: "[Censorship] must be stopped if the public is to be properly served with synchronized film. It surely is apparent to a mind not in the least mechanically inclined, that to delete parts of scenes would destroy the accompanying melodies and in many instances force the tremendous expenditure of remaking the entire picture."[34]

In 1928 censorship boards started taking a close look at, and a listen to, the talkies. Preparing to join in the battle, Hays set up an office in Los Angeles maintained by "Colonel" Jason Joy and a staff of a half-dozen assistants. Joy's assignment was to help the industry respond to union demands, to review scripts to head off possible trouble, and to form liaisons with women's groups, social reformers, and others in positions of power who might need to be convinced that the MPPDA's self-censorship was already vigilant enough.[35]

Even before all the studios had signed with ERPI, censors were anticipating the coming of sound and securing their jurisdiction over it. In May 1928, James Wingate, director of the New York state board, requested $5,000 from the legislature to purchase sound equipment for checking dialogue. GLORIOUS BETSY was the first film to run in New York accompanied by a trailer announcing that the talking part had been passed by censors. Beginning with THE LIGHTS OF NEW YORK, producers were required to present synopses and transcripts of the dialogue to the board. Following that lead, Maryland, Virginia, and most of the other state boards also began censoring sound tracks.[36]

One of the most influential boards was Ohio's, since many midwestern states relied on its judgment. The board asked the state's attorney general to empower it to pass on film dialogue. He complied in July 1928, giving it the right to censor sound films "with the same privileges as with 'ordinary picture films.'" (The presumption was that sound was an extraordinary addition to the "ordinary" entity.) Rather than conform, Fox schemed to embarrass the board by refusing to submit a Movietone newsreel showing Herbert Hoover accepting the Republican presidential nomination. Would Ohio ban Hoover? Imagine the headlines. The board did not take the bait and, indeed, proved itself to be as clever as Fox. It passed the film without screening it, declaring that its "special nature" made it an exceptional case. Edwin Hullinger was heartened by the industry's resistance. He saw Hollywood "girding itself for a struggle against the censorship which it alone, among our agencies of expression, has been called upon to endure." He maintained that, "in moving picture headquarters in New York, no secret is made of the fact that the industry is only waiting for a favorable opening to launch a general offensive against the institution of censorship wherever it exists and to carry its case before the American people."[37] Hullinger's sources were Lewis Innerarity, representing Pathé Exchange, Carl Milliken, former governor of Maine and now secretary of the MPPDA, and Harry Warner, in his capacity as president of Vitaphone. Warner took the unusual slant that censorship "creates a tyranny of one generation over another generation the members of which possess an entirely different set of standards." His remarks were remarkably frank.

> My grandmother would have thought herself eternally damned if she did the things my wife and children do today without a second thought; and young people are openly discussing subjects that could never be mentioned in mixed society a score of years back. The everyday chatter of our modern youth would make our grandparents' hair stand on end. Everybody except the censors knows this—knows that America is throwing off the prudery of the past. . . . An examination of the personal background of the incumbent film reviewers [i.e., the censors] would tell its own story. A generation that has lived its life is trying to regulate the amusements of a world with which it is no longer in spiritual harmony. Naturally there is friction.

He added a personal note:

> When I was five years old, my parents left Poland to escape the suffocation of a rigid censorship which forbade free speech. My family had large property holdings; my father came to America for spiritual rather than economic reasons. And today I find myself obliged to struggle against an attempt to create in America another censorship slightly different in character but

Few Words
—on a big subject
By JACK ALICOATE
(Continued from Page 1)

This Is What All Newspapers Would Look Like If Theorists Were Allowed To Censor The Press As They Do Pictures

VOL. LII No. 56   Thursday, June 5, 1930   Price 5 Cents

on First Nat'l List

COMMITTEE WINS   VITAL POINTS

Directors Named

An Experiment
—*noble or otherwise*
By JACK ALICOATE

Preferred Stockholders' Committee Continuing Activity

With announcement of the names of the eight men proposed as directors on behalf of the 8 per cent preferred stockholders, the recently formed Protective Committee of Pathe yesterday issued a statement through Richard A. Rowland, chairman, denying it had any intention of
(Continued on Page 8)

Fewer Musicals

STORIN NAMED BY AS GEN. MANAGER FOR R. I.

Providence — Harry F. Storin, manager of the Victory, has assumed the general managership of the houses in Rhode Island, succeeding Foster Lardner. Lardner has been identified with the Providence theatrical field for the past 26 years. Following a vacation he will return to this state to resume activities in the theater business.
(Continued on Page 2)

Only Six Films Held O. K. for Children in Canada

Ottawa—Only six films are given complete sanction for presentation to children in the so-called "white list" of the Canadian Council on Child Welfare for 1930. They comprise "The Aviator," "The Cohens and the Kellys in Scotland," "His First Command," "Honey," "Only the Brave" and "The Vagabond King."

Storage Limit Increased and Sprinklers Eliminated

With one major issue yet to be discussed, the committee appointed by the New York Fire Commissioner for amending the present Code of Ordinances has succeeded in putting through two vital points favoring exhibitors. The one concerns increasing footage requirements five times the old figure of 5,000 feet, bringing the
(Continued on Page 8)

75 EXHIBS FIRE RULE VIOLATIONS

In order to avoid having their houses closed on grounds of failure to comply with the New York Fire Department's 10-day order to remove all inflammable material, about 75 exhibitors belonging to the Theater Owners' Chamber of Commerce are filing appeals to the fire department through their organization.

Amendments to Sections 5 and 10 of the Code of Ordinances and Rules of the Board of Standards and Appeals, now being worked out by the committee appointed by the Fire Commissioner, soon will be in the hands of the corporation counsel and then to the Board of Aldermen.

19 Counties in Nebraska Have No Picture Shows

Omaha—Nineteen of the 93 counties in Nebraska have never had picture shows, R. J. Miller, theatrical advertising man, has informed the local Chamber of Commerce following a survey by film interests.

Day Off

Columbia Names Baker Chicago Shorts Manager

Columbia announces the appointment of Will Baker, formerly branch manager for the company in St. Louis, as short subject sales manager in the Chicago territory. Baker was Chicago short subject manager for Universal before his joining Columbia.

SIX LAWRENCE HOUSES SOUGHT BY WARNER BROS.

Lawrence, Mass.—Warner Bros. are dickering for the Empire chain of six local houses. They are the Palace, Broadway, Empire, Colonial, Premiere and Star, combined seating capacities of these houses totals up to 8,880.

Film Daily *published a graphic editorial.*

equally as rigid, in its way, as the one my parents thought they were leaving behind forever! (Quoted in Edwin Hullinger, "Free Speech for Talkies?," *North American Review*, July 1929, p. 742)

Although this statement has the fragrance of a press agent's melting-pot fantasy, the executive's declaration puts a fine point on the debate over censorship as a mixture of economics and democratic principles. Warner cast the conflict as a family metaphor not unlike the theme of the tyranny of the older generation in THE JAZZ SINGER and THE FIRST AUTO. Warner's sentiments about the censors being out of touch with film audiences were echoed by a *New Republic* claim that civic leaders were usually appointed to boards as figureheads or window dressing, but the actual work was done by "sub-censors." These were "young girls, or well meaning elderly ladies with political pull, or men so incompetent that they are willing to accept small pay."[38]

Flaunting its strength, the Ohio censors ordered substantial cuts in THE WILD PARTY. But the Paramount exchange resisted by substituting black leader for the censored picture track and letting the sound on disc continue. Clara Bow kept talking while the screen went blank. Things became tricky in Boston, where "there are some lines that can be spoken on week days that are entirely improper on Sunday. Which makes it necessary to have Sunday cues and week-day cues for the operators."[39] Censorship previously had been invisible, but with the addition of the sound track, its interruption of the flow of the story was joltingly apparent. Audiences and critics were aware that something was being withheld from them.

When the Pennsylvania board announced that it would not approve sound films without reviewing their words, both Fox and Vitaphone vigorously protested. The latter sought an injunction in Philadelphia to prevent having to submit the sound track of POLLY MORAN (1928) for review, claiming that the state law which established the board mentioned only pictures. The court of common pleas denied the injunction. Fox joined Vitaphone in lodging an appeal, using SHE'S STILL MY BABY (1928) as a test case. Confusingly, Warners-Vitaphone lost its appeal to Judge Martin, while Fox won its plea to Judge McKevitt. The case was argued in the state supreme court, which affirmed, on 4 February 1929, that censors did indeed have the right to control dialogue in films.[40]

There were a few victories for producers. In Kansas the attorney general ruled that the state board of review exceeded its authority when it censored dialogue. Pathé secured a temporary restraining order enjoining New York censors from deleting sound portions of SAL OF SINGAPORE (1929). The board had already passed the silent version, but it had appended a special stamp reading, "This license is invalid when the film or any part thereof is used in conjunction with mechanical devices for the reproduction of sound or by the use of persons for the utterance of language." Pathé lawyers claimed that such power gave censors the right to prohibit lectures illustrated with films and therefore abridged freedom of speech. The board eventually won. One area which saw a loosening of censorship after the coming of sound was the newsreel. Fox attorneys argued that constitutional guarantees of press freedom extended to news reportage in films. In 1929 the governor of Pennsylvania signed a bill exempting newsreels from censorship, and most other states followed suit.[41]

The Supreme Court had sanctioned controlling motion pictures, so there seemed to be little recourse. Meanwhile, constraints against novels and theater had been for the most part removed. Hollywood wanted to annex this sophisticated market for the talkies. Also, the critical pressure to adopt the "natural" voice colloquialized film dia-

Clara Bow and Fredric March in THE WILD PARTY *(Paramount, 1929).*

logue in pursuit of everyday language. Hullinger set the tone for a lively debate: "The question still remains, why should the movies and talkies be subjected to a supervision that magazines, playwrights and comic strip artists escape?" New York Mayor Jimmy Walker observed: "We have censorship of motion pictures in six [*sic*] states. Are we to conclude from this that damnation is running rampant in the other forty-two states where there is no censorship? And even with censorship I can't find that humanity, that society, has materially changed in this country of ours." President Campbell of the University of Chicago told a meeting of the Motion Picture Theater Owners of America that censorship was "un-American in principle and resented by the majority of our population." Dr. Joseph L. Holmes, a professor of psychology at Columbia University, attacked government censorship at the 1930 National Board of Review of Motion Pictures Conference. The democratic solution, he proclaimed, resided in "a social control, expressed in a community demand for the best in motion pictures recreationally and educationally."[42] Yet Seldes, regarded as a liberal social commentator, endorsed cautious controls:

> I think it desirable that the opponents of the censor should bear always in mind the peculiar circumstances of the moving picture, instead of assuming that the movie resembles in any way a book read in solitude; they should be aware also of the dirty sexual pictures available in secret places in most large cities and be ready to answer when asked whether they want these pictures publicly shown. It seems to me that as soon as the opponents of the censorship have a positive plan, they can do something to undermine the censor's authority, and not before. (Gilbert Seldes, *An Hour with the Movies and the Talkies* [Philadelphia: Lippincott, 1929], p. 115)

Though most debate centered on First Amendment issues, there were other arguments about the economic effects of censorship. Hullinger, for instance, pointed out (quoting statistics in all likelihood furnished by Hays) that one-third of the American film audience resided in areas controlled by state or municipal censors. Even George Jean Nathan produced a curious economically oriented argument. He suggested that higher standards of dialogue censorship would be bad for movie business because of a double standard pertaining to visual and audio censorship. Suggestive poses had become tolerated, but saucy dialogue was unacceptable. He maintained that

> Clara Bow is currently allowed to display her anatomy for the incalescence of sailors, to the great profit of the Messrs. Zukor and Lasky, but the moment Clara opens her mouth and says, "Come on, boys, get a load of this!" the censors will hop on her and the Messrs. Zukor and Lasky will be out money. . . .
>
> The silent movies, with very few exceptions in the last three or four years, have prospered most greatly from the display of sex garbage. The talkies, without this sex garbage, after their novelty has worn off, will have a difficult time of it. The statistics show clearly that the movie public, save for an occasional airplane or seltzer-syphon picture, wants to spend its money on stories dealing with fornication either contemplated or achieved. . . .
>
> For a while . . . that public will get a kick from hearing its favorite dummies speak, but it will not be long before it will yearn again for the days when, censorship or no censorship, it could work itself up over the French

post-card insinuations of Hungarian, Mexican and Scandinavian houris stretched out languorously on sofas, of Brooklyn and Flatbush ex-stenographers coyly showing their backsides and of side-burned former counter-jumpers lighting the incense in their louvered bachelor apartments and licking their chops over the imminent prospect of bolting the door on one of the Talmadges. (George Jean Nathan, "The Living Corpse," *American Mercury*, September 1929, p. 505)

His argument is that dialogue is more censorable, so the talkies would be less overtly sexual than the silents were, and therefore derive fewer profits from the prurient desires of the lowbrow consumer. Other critics felt that censorship actually increased the sleaziness of movies. *The Nation* pointed out this hypocrisy, editorializing that "censorship has succeeded only in removing from the films every trace of intelligence, while it has left them dripping with every variety of implied sensuality."[43]

On the New York stage, four-letter words were increasingly heard, comedy was ribald, drama was "adult," and revues featured topless showgirls. As wired movie houses became more abundant in every region and in smaller towns by mid-1929, different standards of what constituted acceptable material inevitably became a problem. Joseph Jackson, who wrote THE SINGING FOOL and THE TERROR, said, "Audiences who have been fed on the raw beef of *What Price Glory?* and other such frank stage plays will hardly keep a straight face if they hear a top sergeant declare: 'My Goodness, I've never been so shocked in all my life.'"[44] Sherwood concurred that it was inappropriate and unrealistic to use soft language in films of war like ALL QUIET ON THE WESTERN FRONT, or in prison pictures like THE BIG HOUSE. He also savored the capricious nature of movie censorship:

> One of the many odd things about the movie business is that whereas you can have films entitled *Hell's Angels, Hell's Heroes, Hell Harbor* or *Hell's Island,* you cannot permit a character on the screen to use the word "hell." In communities where censorship laws exist the prohibitions against profanity in all its forms are strict and definite and the celluloid merchants are bound to respect them. (*Film Daily*, 26 August 1930, p. 5)

Many others, however, especially in the educational community, maintained that films harmed children. "In my judgment," said E. A. Ross, professor of sociology at the University of Wisconsin, "children under ten years of age should not be allowed to attend the movies except those shown under the auspices of schools, churches or other agencies dedicated to the promotion of child welfare. The ordinary commercial film is intended for a general audience and cannot possibly be expected to take into account the mentality of children under ten. Such children are likely to obtain the most twisted and unreal idea of life from following the ordinary commercial film." Professor Patty S. Hill, Teachers College, New York, agreed: "Personally I have always urged parents not to build up in young children a taste for movies in the early days of child life. At this period he lives in a theater of his own making. He is the actor, his playmates are fellow-actors." A judge of the New York City Children's Court, Franklin Chase Hoyt, cited the medical basis for suspecting the movies' deleterious effects: "I entertain grave doubts as to the advisability of permitting young children to be subjected frequently to the constant eye-strain of the movies at a time in life when this delicate organ is in its plastic period of formation. Nor is the foul air or the nervous tension the right sort of hygienic diet to prescribe for a ten-year-old child." These concerns echo the research programs sponsored by the Payne Fund then under way. Sound was conjectured to be a threat to public health and safety.[45]

While it consistently editorialized against "external" censorship, *Film Daily,* speaking for exhibitors, also objected to the content of some films, feeling that the studios went too far. It was the local manager who took the brunt of angry parents' and civic groups' anger. On THE WILD PARTY, for instance, Jack Alicoate commented, "The scenes are far too wild in spots for nice young girls and boys to absorb." Von Sternberg's direction of THUNDERBOLT (1929) was praised, but the death-house sequence was "hardly in good taste." Alicoate cautioned exhibitors to watch APPLAUSE first before playing it. "One of the lines regarding a couple of chorus girls and the Catholic Church must come out immediately." In retrospect, most of these opinions seem quaint. This example from HOT SHOTS (1929) illustrated a scene which was too risqué: "A boy and a girl hesitatingly approach the marriage license bureau. They enter and the clerk asks how old they are. Then a few lines about the necessity of parental consent. Whereupon the boy turns and says: 'Who do you think that guy is over there with the shotgun?'"[46]

Alicoate presented the exhibitors' view in an editorial entitled "The Public Must Be Catered To":

> All this theoretical talk of reformers about what to give them [movie cus-
> tomers] in the way of production and story fare is so much sliced liver-pud-
> ding. If this great international industry is to continue as a dominant force in
> the world's activity and progress it must continue to give its millions of
> patrons what they demand in the way of story material and what the ever
> changing demands of thought, demeanor and morals warrant.

There were limits, though: "Modernism is not smut. . . . Our thought rather is that the progressive and modern ideas of our younger thinkers must be considered if we are not to let the parade pass us by. Public demand cannot be sidetracked." Alicoate presented an analogy with the movies' hypothetical feminine audience: "If the dear ladies wish to wear their hair long and their skirts short no power on earth can stop them. So with pic-ture story material. Keep a finger on the public pulse. The answer is manifest. Give the dear old public what it wants and ninety-nine percent of the home folks will be satis-fied." He concluded with this advice for the exhibitor:

> When you are next approached by the self-esteemed local censor and told
> how much good he or she is doing by cutting the very heart and life out of
> fine, splendid pictures, ask point blank if his or her morals have, up to this
> time, been impaired by seeing so many salacious pictures in the raw, and if
> not, why not. (*Film Daily,* 24 March 1930, pp. 1–2)

The Hays Office found itself in the impossible situation of trying to appease groups with diametrically opposed notions of how film sound should be controlled. Producers wanted to score with mature adults in big cities, young audiences, flappers, and "jazz babies" keen to hear their own argot on the screen. The intelligentsia wanted films to have the intellectual dialogue and linguistic freedom of the stage. Moralists, religious leaders, and protectors of women and children wanted movies to reflect the Ten

Commandments and small-town virtues. Meanwhile, Hays still assumed that movies were made for a homogeneous audience consisting of "the family." Yet it was clear from the reactions to sound that the cinema audience was heterogeneous, composed of many different groups with incompatible standards. In the same screening, a risqué gag might amuse some and embarrass others. Getting pressure from all sides, Hays decided to bolster Hollywood's audible morality.

THE MOTION PICTURE PRODUCTION CODE OF 1930

Will Hays appealed to his association's members in January 1929 to avoid censorship by making clean films. He said, "Coincident with the full realization of the fact that the motion picture industry must resist the attempt in some places to censor speech from the screen is the renewed determination on the part of the industry to make certain that its pictures are of such quality that no reasonable person can claim any need for censorship." At the time, the industry's guidelines for self-control took the form of the "Don'ts and Be Carefuls," a list of proscribed words and situations written by a committee chaired by MGM's Irving Thalberg. The spirit of the text was ignored by Hollywood, not the least flagrantly by MGM. In A WOMAN OF AFFAIRS (1928), for example, "director Clarence Brown . . . cunningly dodged the censor stuff by treating the many-lover episodes as a series of photos with captions taken from a newspaper's files."[47] Reviewers regularly characterized current films as licentious. HOT FOR PARIS (1929), from the Fox studio, one of the consistent providers of this type of material, was described by the *New York Daily Mirror*: "The comedy is very frank. The dialogue is very stag. . . . But it's still an hilarious comedy, particularly for the men." Hall said it was "a rowdy, raw affair."[48] With the prospect of sound unleashing a torrent of expletives, cuss words, and naughty jokes, such as could be heard on the New York stage, Hays moved to forestall a trend that could become a linguistic lightning rod attracting more serious reforms.

Another impetus for changing the self-regulatory protocol was economic. Fox's takeover of Loew's had triggered the Justice Department's investigation of the industry's monopolistic practices. The October 1929 Crash made the industry skittish about any threat to the box office. There was a general need to get the house in order. The industry's dependence on stable financing and debt management meant that shareholders, banks, and investment houses wanted assurance that the product would circulate freely and that cash flow would be regular. Censorship not only threatened this stability but generated wasteful re-shooting, re-recording, and re-editing. Nearly a year before the Production Code was adopted, Lasky had urged replacing the hodgepodge of local censors with a system whereby scenarios would be submitted to a central agency and approved in advance, "before the story is filmed and before the music accompaniment has been engraved on the discs."[49]

A production code was drafted by another committee chaired by Thalberg, but this time it had a strong dose of Catholic conscience. The genesis of the 1930 Code has been traced to a surprising coalition of industry, religious, and banking interests. Early in 1929, Martin Quigley, the publisher of *Exhibitor's Herald-World*, complained to Hays that Hollywood was not suppressing adult content unless forced to do so. He was primarily concerned about the salacious advertising featuring suggestive poses and hints of female nudity that he was obliged to run in his trade paper. (The same ads ran in other periodicals.) Fox's ads featuring bare-breasted chorus girls may have been the specific ones which offended Quigley, a devout Catholic. Hays approached Father Daniel A.

Advertisement for THE FOX MOVIETONE FOLLIES OF 1930.

Lord, a Jesuit priest at St. Louis University. A traditionalist and an enemy of "modernism" in contemporary life, Lord had written numerous pamphlets about religion and the movies and had been Cecil B. DeMille's religious adviser on KING OF KINGS. (George Bernard Shaw, whose plays and philosophy he abhorred, was Lord's bête noire.) Lord was in consultation with George Cardinal Mundelein of the Chicago archdiocese, who already had been discussing movie morality with Hays, Jason Joy, and C. C. Pettijohn of the MPPDA. Mundelein approved of Lord's draft of a new production code containing theological justifications for moral content and suggested another powerful ally—Harold Stuart, of Halsey, Stuart and Company. He was the Chicago banker who then was fighting to reorganize William Fox's empire. He had strong personal and business connections to Mundelein as a friend and a creditor, and a demonstrated antipathy to Fox. The cardinal passed the draft of the code to Stuart, who in turn lobbied Zukor to get it okayed by Hays.

In February 1930, Lord made a presentation to an assembly of film industry executives. There were major differences between Quigley and Lord's draft and Thalberg's draft. The producers insisted on the freedom to adapt best-selling "frank" novels. Thalberg, Jack Warner, B. P. Schulberg, and Sol Wurtzel of Fox "argued that the advent of sound brought a wider, not a more restrictive, latitude in subject matter to the movies. With the addition of screen dialogue, they held, actors and actresses could 'speak delicately and exactly' on sensitive subjects that could not be portrayed in silent films." Yet the producers accepted the Code the next day, "without a whimper."[50] Gregory Black, wondering why the industry would adopt restrictions so clearly against its interests, offers two explanations. The Code would enable Will Hays to extend his influence over the Los Angeles studios; and accepting the Code made sense from the economic angle. Besides, producers had no intention of following its literal mandates (some of which were practically impossible to interpret anyway). According to Stephen Vaughn, the producers retreated, but they had not surrendered. "They still argued that they be allowed greater freedom in choosing subjects for stories. . . . They pledged themselves to make 'a sincere effort' to 'clean up' characterizations that might violate public taste. But the primary concern for the producers remained the box office. If a picture 'does not please its audiences,' they explained, 'it is a failure.'"[51]

Timely pressure on the producers came in March 1930 when Representative Hudson introduced a bill that would have made the motion picture industry a public utility and forced studios to pay the salaries of federal regulators. Hays's counsel Pettijohn denounced it as "so socialistic and radical as to constitute a dangerous threat to all branches of the industry." While Hudson's bill had little chance of passage—his 1928 version had failed—it was symptomatic of the type of assault the producers feared. The MPPDA adopted the Motion Picture Production Code on 31 March 1930. Soon afterward, President Frank Woods endorsed it on behalf of the Academy of Motion Picture Arts and Sciences.[52]

The final version drafted by Jason Joy (following Lord and Quigley) was a compromise document in which theological idealism mingled uncomfortably with producers' pragmatism. Our chief interest is in how the accepted draft responded to the struggle to control dialogue content.

The preamble to the Code acknowledged that sound was a motivating factor: "During the rapid transition from silent to talking pictures they [motion picture producers] realized the necessity and the opportunity of subscribing to a Code to govern the production of talking pictures and of reacknowledging this responsibility." The section that forbade obscenity was one sentence: "Obscenity in word, gesture, reference, song, joke, or by suggestion (even when likely to be understood only by part of the audience) is forbidden." However, the section banning profanity included a Rabelaisian list of taboo utterances:

> Alley cat (applied to a woman); bat (applied to a woman); broad (applied to a woman); Bronx cheer (the sound); chippie; cocotte; God, Lord, Jesus, Christ (unless used reverently); cripes; fanny; fairy (in a vulgar sense); finger (the); fire, cries of; Gawd; goose (in a vulgar sense); "hold your hat" or "hats"; hot (applied to a woman); "in your hat"; louse; lousy; Madam (relating to prostitution); nance; nerts; nuts (except when meaning crazy); pansy; razzberry [*sic*] (the sound); slut (applied to a woman); S.O.B.; son-of-a; tart; toilet gags; tom cat (applied to a man); traveling salesman and farmer's daughter jokes; whore; damn, hell (excepting when the use of said last two words shall be essential and required for portrayal, in proper historical context, of any scene or dialogue based upon historical fact or folklore, or for the presentation in proper literary context of a Biblical, or other religious quotation, or a quotation from a literary work provided that no such use shall be permitted which is intrinsically objectionable or offends good taste). (MPPDA, "A Code to Govern the Making of Talking, Synchronized and Silent Motion Pictures," 1930, reprinted in Garth Jowett, *Film: The Democratic Art* [Boston: Little, Brown, 1976], pp. 468–470)

There was also a list of specific racial epithets which, though neither profane nor banned, were "obviously offensive to the patrons of motion pictures in the United States and more particularly to the patrons of motion pictures in foreign countries." Enumerating the banned words gave screenwriters and in-house censors their "Don'ts" list, which they could use to determine whether a film was clean.

The film moralists' demands were represented by general imperatives. The philosophical rationale was contained in a separate declaration, "Reasons Supporting Preamble of Code." Recent commentators have claimed that Hays suppressed this statement until it served his purpose to release it in 1934, in order to hide the pervasive Catholic influence on the Code. The author of "Reasons," who is assumed to have been primarily Father Lord with advice from Quigley, observes that "this art of the motion picture, combining as it does the two fundamental appeals of looking at a picture and listening to a story at once reached every class of society." This view is consistent with the notion that film sound was separate from the visuals. There is an implication that these two "appeals" are unsophisticated activities, since the lower as well as upper classes may participate. The author of "Reasons" also justified restraining film's freedom in comparison to that accorded the novel and the newspaper because its audience was more diverse.[53]

Black argues that "there was a fundamental misunderstanding" between Lord, Quigley and the Catholics on one side, and the producers and Hays on the other. Contrarily, it is also possible to read the code as a victory for both sides; each left the conference thinking it had pulled a fast one on the other. For instance, Hays (or his ghostwriter) went public in *Ladies' Home Journal* in July 1930 and used the Code to reassure readers that the industry was responding to the new moral problems precipitated by the sound picture. "The work of reflecting social and community values in the production of motion-picture entertainment," he wrote, "has constantly progressed." It was the "constructive criticism" of women's clubs and similar groups that had impressed the producers with the desirability of revising the Code. "Sound brought new dramatists, new artists and new dramatic material to the motion-picture industry, and it was found necessary to formulate additional and new principles of self-regulation which would guide the making of silent, synchronized and talking motion pictures."[54] While he congratulated the women on their moral victory, a glance at many films from the 1930–1934 period shows that the Production Code was flagrantly ignored. Among the biggest offenders were sly sex comedies like Mamoulian's LOVE ME TONIGHT (1932), and Wheeler and Woolsey's lewdness is legendary. Horror films like DRACULA (1931) and crime films, including CITY STREETS (1931), THE SECRET SIX (1931), PUBLIC ENEMY (1931), and SCARFACE (1932), appalled. Women used language to express sexual knowledge—and most shockingly, desire. There were "kept woman" films like BACK STREET (1932). Hedonist Mae West's saucy dialogue in her Paramount comedies NIGHT AFTER NIGHT (1932—"Goodness had nothing to do with it"), SHE DONE HIM WRONG (1933), and I'M NO ANGEL (1933—"Beulah, peel me a grape") stunned censors. Dietrich's eroticism in THE BLUE ANGEL and MOROCCO raised eyebrows in many venues but sailed by the MPPDA watchdogs. Screenwriters grew adept at combining sexuality with platitudes and retribution. The moralists wanted cinema to be "twentieth-century morality plays that illustrated proper behavior to the masses." Richard Maltby suggests that the Code can be read as a sign of how far producers were out of touch with their consumers. "Like other Hollywood conventions, the Production Code was one of several substitutes for detailed audience research. . . . In its practical application, the Code was the mechanism by which this multiplicity of viewing positions was achieved."[55]

Self-censorship was a misnomer for what the Hays Office did. Jacobs has suggested that the "enforcement" of the Code was mainly a publicity ploy, that regulation was very unsystematic, and that negotiation still occurred case by case. If there was a potential problem, as with POSSESSED (1931), the studio might "forget" to submit the script for MPPDA review. Two genres in particular were problematic: the "fallen woman" story, with its suggestion of adultery and ungoverned female sexuality, and the gangster story, with its ambivalent idealization of Capone-like anti-heroes. These genres burgeoned in spite of the Code because the MPPDA allowed hypocritical redemptive endings. Evading the Code and detecting the run-around became a game for studios and viewers "in the know."[56]

MPPDA reviewers passed on scripts before viewing films, so the procedure made it easy to stay pure in word but to sin in deed. In MOROCCO's first scene, Gary Cooper is silently gesturing to a prostitute. His commander catches him and demands, "What are you doing with those fingers?" Cooper drawls, "Nothin'—yet." Though considerably tamed from Ben Hecht and Charles MacArthur's stage play, THE FRONT PAGE (1931) still contains its share of double entendres. A report comes into the newsroom that a Swedish masseuse has been arrested on the complaint of a lot of angry wives. She's treating their husbands with electricity "at a dollar a time." Half the stock exchange is at the police station offering to post bail. The producer Howard Hughes also defied the banned word list ("nerts"). In PUBLIC ENEMY, the gangster Putty Nose (Murray Kinnell) is singing at the piano: "Mrs. Jones, big and fat, slipped on the ice and broke her ———." At this point he is interrupted by an offscreen whistle. Since nothing has been uttered, the spectator is free to complete the rhyme. Two possibilities would be *hat* and *cat,* but both were on the taboo list because they were slang for genitalia and prostitute. A more likely possibility would be the obscene slang *twat,* which would be narratively appropriate in the lowlife beer-joint setting and consistent with the "natural" speech of such characters. In either case, the profanity has been artfully constructed to exist in the mind of the viewer-auditor, not in the censorable script or on the sound track.[57]

The frank "realistic" speech of the protagonists in PUBLIC ENEMY was both a novelty effect and a scary evocation of the characters' antisocial menace. Ironically, the Hays Office's intervention appears to have been instrumental in defining one of the eternally memorable mobster voices. Moralists had denounced DOORWAY TO HELL (1930) because the gangster star, Lew Ayres, was too charming and sympathetic. According to Robert Sklar, Hays wrote to Warners questioning whether "a young man of fine features" was right for such a role. Underlying Hays's criticism is an assumption that gangsters should be portrayed as ethnic stereotypes, not as WASPs. In the meantime, Edward Woods, a "juvenile" character actor, had been cast for the role of Tom Powers in PUBLIC ENEMY. Heeding Hays's suggestion, Darryl F. Zanuck reassigned the Tom Powers role to the actor who had played Ayres's sidekick in the earlier film, James Cagney. Instantly, Cagney's punk hero and his tough Irish-inflected speech captivated the country—and appalled censors.[58]

How effective were the standards and strictures of the press and the censors against the talkies? The question is still open. Rather than self-censorship, negotiated self-restraint might be a more accurate description of the Hays Office's work. As Mick Eaton put it, "The establishment of the Hays Code ensured the industry's freedom from outside censorship by either state or federal governments. Similarly, the establishment of the code ensured that the studios acquired a stranglehold over the outlets for distribution throughout the states. The cinema became a much safer investment than, say, the press or radio."[59]

There is no question that the Code, as accepted and interpreted, was designed to promote Christianity and enforced to benefit the industry. The producers and exhibitors supported the Code in theory and probably did not really mind self-censorship in practice because the institution potentially could spare them the onus of deciding whether each title was marketable. The need for exchanges to alter prints for different communities was alleviated. Thus, indirectly, the Code accelerated the standardization of the sound film. But since there was little respect for the Code among censors, self-regulation was not completely successful in eliminating costly editing. NUMBERED MEN, a First National prison film released in June 1930, for example, was so "drastically cut by the [New York] censors at the preview that [the] print had to be sent back to the Coast for some refilming and re-recording."[60]

There was also the problem of the independents. Without power to enforce its bans, the Hays Office could be ignored by any promoter who could find a house willing to show his film. This was the case with WHITE CARGO (1929), a British "white slavery" exploitation film. American studios had shied away from filming the story since the novel from which it was adapted had been banned by Hays according to the Formula. This action benefited MPPDA members because each producer knew that no other would compete by producing this "hot" property. When the RKO theater chain started negotiating to show the film, Hays stepped in to block the screening of the foreign interloper. He did not succeed. The promoter, Harold Auten, rented the George M. Cohan Theater, charged $2 admission, and sold the film nationally through states' rights. Audiences saw WHITE CARGO and numerous other exploitation films—but not at theaters controlled by MPPDA affiliates.[61] "Sex hygiene" movies like HER UNBORN CHILD (1929), exotic films like INGAGI (1930), and nudist films made the rounds of what *Film Daily* called "junk" houses. Frequently these were silent films of foreign origin, revitalized by adding narration and sound effects. One exception was ELYSIA, one of the most famous nudist features. It was produced and directed in 1933 by none other than Bryan Foy.[62]

The Production Code was unsatisfying to just about everyone. Hollywood did not "reform." It still saw its mission as giving the audience what it wanted. If that was to hear heart-rending cries, violent shouts, or lewd remarks, the studios were ready to provide them. If the Code could supply a framework wherein the industry could pay lip service to God-fearing morality, stave off outside intervention, satisfy its creditors that it was stable and legitimate, while continuing to make films that attracted large urban crowds, so much the better. As the trade papers, exhibitors, and influential producers like Thalberg and Zukor agreed, there was a consensus that Hollywood should observe limits. But they argued that if the box office favored sex, violence, and "fast" talk, studios had to compete to supply the demand. And in the years 1930–1933, films like these provided the industry with a few financial bright spots and audiences with thrills and diversion in an otherwise bleak era. Meanwhile, the guardians of society's values and the nascent Catholic Legion of Decency looked on in frustration and contemplated future remedies.

Despite the rhetoric of uplift from Hollywood concerning its mission of improving the nation's language and morality, what really counted was reaching out to and holding larger audiences. When the studios turned to the stage for fresh story material, new voices, and an existing pattern for speaking—the enunciative style—they no doubt envisioned a quick patch for the problem of what to do about sound. Theater was a reservoir of vocal talent and stories with proven merit. It also served the rhetorical purpose of enabling the moguls to wrap themselves in class and culture and to spread proper English to the "hamlets." But their quest for refinement encountered inherent differences between Broadway and the movies. The New York stage was characterized by highly conventional vocal style, and few social controls over vocal content. In Hollywood, on the contrary, there were no existing conventions for the movie voice, but numerous social strictures controlled the content of vocal expression.

The 1928–1929 tendency to dissociate the voice from the actor's body allowed competition among various groups for jurisdiction over the voice as a commodity: producers who contracted for it; actors who articulated it; critics who wanted to limit its range and restrict its use according to class and ethnicity; and censors who feared its potential for religious, social, and class disruption. The box-office popularity of "bad" voices, the general willingness to tolerate seemingly antisocial subjects, and the spread of vulgar language were genuinely disturbing to the gatekeepers of decency. Profound distrust of the actual filmgoing public and its "mass psychology" pervades the "Reasons Supporting the Code." The mandarins distrusted their constituents. Joseph Breen, who would become the chief industry censor in 1934, described the motion picture audience as "youngsters between 16 and 26 . . . , most of them nit-wits, dolts and imbeciles."[63]

By 1931 the critics were no longer assuming a distinction between the speaker and his or her vocals; voice had become desegregated into "personality," part of the actor's distinctive identity. Also, the provenance of a story (whether an original screenplay or adapted from a play or novel) did not really matter as long as it was a good one. As for morality, there is scant evidence that most people regarded the movies as any more deleterious than amusements like miniature golf, or that they wanted the government to prescribe entertainment for them. Censorship did not have strong grassroots support. Most municipalities did not control access to films. Numerous legislative bills strengthening censorship were regularly introduced during this period, but all failed to pass.

Because of lack of enforcement and the MPPDA's lack of jurisdiction over exhibition (especially by independents), audiences seldom were completely denied the right to see questionable films. "Sensational" subjects often attracted crowds to theaters. For example, the powerful Chicago board practiced giving "pink slips" (admission restricted to adults only) to controversial movies. The Balaban and Katz theaters reported that THE LETTER (1929) and CAREERS (1929) did land-office business under this "restriction." Critics pointed out—and producers surely took note—that more people were seeing these films than would have normally, and that the censors were providing great free publicity.[64]

The struggle to control the voice through proactive influence and external constraints failed, at least until enforcement of the Code was stepped up in 1934. By then, sound films had long become the norm, and the moralists shifted their attention from dialogue to "situations," such as adultery. Until then, Hollywood filmmakers' creativity was not seriously stifled. The movie fans looked neither to the artful use of the voice nor to whether it embodied Christian rectitude. For most of them, the stars continued to be the object of secular worship, selected according to idiosyncratic and largely unpredictable criteria. Their voices became just another ingredient added to the star mix.

Just when the end of the Jazz Age was witnessing a perceived loosening of morals and an expansion of artistic license in literature and theater, the film studios were applying their new talking capacity to themes from best-selling novels, subjects from mature plays, and language which was commonplace in conversation at home, in the workplace, and in intimate situations but unheard and unheard-of in public. Limiting speech and expression in entertainment for the public good, particularly when it is a product of unfamiliar new technology, remains controversial to this day as we debate television ratings and expression on the Internet. Then as now, the controversy centers on the question of whether language reflects harmful dystopic tendencies in society—or causes them.

19

Constructive Criticism:
The Fans' Perspective

The film is MOVIE CRAZY (1932), and Harold Lloyd is a star-struck fan who, through improbable twists of fate, finds himself making a screen test. He embraces his leading lady and emotes, "Oh, Marjorie! I love you, I love you, I love you, I love you." The joke, that nerdy Harold is replaying the talking-picture debut of the matinee idol John Gilbert, would have elicited laughter of recognition from audiences of the time. Lloyd is poking fun at early sound pictures, and perhaps also at the fans' role in making and unmaking talking stars. Harold, the fan, can do no better than the derided star when given the chance to cope with the talkies. The sequence also indicates the implicit tension over who was in control of the movie business: star, studio, or "crazy" fan. As a performer who made a difficult transition to sound and as a producer in decline, Harold Lloyd was intensely aware of the changing taste of the public and the difficulty of gauging it.

Industry organizations, including the Hays Office, theater owners' associations, and the Academy of Motion Picture Arts and Sciences, coordinated the dissemination of knowledge about sound in a systematic fashion. But as the screen found its voice, where was the voice of the consumer? There were no motion picture viewer associations; fans had no "czar" equivalent to the producers' Will Hays. Clergy, reformers, and censors looked upon moviegoers suspiciously. The popular press, articulating aesthetic and practical criteria, claimed to be mouthpieces for the general public, but the extent to which critical opinion represented popular views is unknown. Certain publications, however, claimed to speak for the consumer: movie fan magazines. What did they and their readers say about the talkies?

The late 1920s saw a proliferation of periodicals aimed at specialized markets. Originally the venerable *Photoplay* (founded in 1911) and *Motion Picture Classic* (1915), the preeminent movie fanzines, had been story digests. Gradually their orientation shifted to cultivating fan response. By 1930, *Screenland* (commencing in 1920), *Screen Play* (1925), *Screenbook* (1928), *Screen Stories* and *Screen Romances* (1929), *Modern Screen* and *Movies* (1930) were part of what had become a huge publishing industry based on Americans' movie craziness. In addition to these titles, "affinity" magazines provided fan-oriented coverage. The advertising department at Columbia Pictures assumed, in 1930, that there was 90 percent shared readership between filmgoers and consumers of *Liberty, True Story, Film Fun, Detective Magazine, Love Magazine, New Movie, Home Magazine, American Weekly, Screen Play Secrets,* and *Redbook.*

Vitaphone advertising campaigns lured moviegoers through newspapers, radio tie-ups, prevue trailers, and fan magazines.

As titles like *Screen Secrets* suggest, these movie publications had strong associations with romance and "confession" magazines. This should not be a surprise, because many had the same publisher, were frequently displayed together on newsstands, and attracted the same market. Like the confession magazines, movie fanzines sold fantasy and vicarious pleasure to an audience composed primarily of female readers under twenty-five. The periodicals "fanned" consumers' desire to learn more about movies and to become "fanatic" about their screen favorites. The media historian Theodore Peterson observed, "The fan magazines probably resulted from and helped to perpetuate the star system of the movies. They created a picture of the 'real' life of the movie stars, of the 'real' Hollywood, as synthetic as the world that the movies themselves portrayed. But for the typical reader, there was nothing artificial about such articles."[1] This picture of the engrossed movie consumer—probably young, female, and unable to distinguish fiction from reality—is deeply rooted in our conception of fandom and encouraged by wistful letters to the editor like this one:

> What a blessing the talkies are! Lonely rooms to come home to in the evening after a day of loneliness no matter if we work with hundreds and come in contact with thousands. Lonely dinners, lonely walks, and lonely nights!
>
> Now, overnight it seems, our friends have multiplied fourfold. Maurice Chevalier twinkles at us with his naughty eyes, singing his songs for us alone, Gloria Swanson shows us her beautiful gowns, Richard Dix acts as "big brother," Paul Whiteman's orchestra sets our feet tingling, John McCormack sets our hearts singing—all of them bringing us sympathy, friendship and romance. And we leave the theater, our heads high, cheered for the moment at least, and believing that perhaps happiness is waiting for us just around the corner. (B.F., "Black and White," *Motion Picture Classic*, July 1930, p. 104)

The authenticity of letters like this one is contestable. There is no assurance that "B.F." was not a staff writer. Because the fanzines often gave small prizes for published letters, there was also an incentive for freelance authors to contribute what they thought the editors wanted to read. It is even possible that males (maybe incarcerated, who knows?) were masquerading as female movie buffs. But *Photoplay*'s editor James R. Quirk strove to create a very different snapshot of his magazine's correspondents:

> Every month there pour into the editorial offices of this publication from three to five thousand letters from motion picture devotees. Most of these letters are sent in by young women to the various service departments [i.e., responding to advertisements] but at least a thousand letters a month are from readers sincerely and intelligently interested in the development of their favorite form of entertainment.
>
> College professors and stenographers, nurses, housewives, mothers, fathers, bank officers, school teachers, all real fans, all expressing their helpful opinions, paying respects to actors, actresses, directors and producers whose pictures please, or voicing kindly criticism of those who disappoint.
>
> These letters are carefully read by the editorial staff, and the editorial policies of the publication are often guided by them. They constitute an accurate barometer of the popularity of plays and players. Of late they have

been concerned with talking pictures. (James R. Quirk, "Close-ups and Long-shots," *Photoplay*, March 1929, p. 24)

Like Will Hays, Quirk tried to create the impression that his constituency was a cross-section of middle-class America. But it is difficult to take as literally true Quirk's claim that many "professors" and "bank officers" (connoting well-to-do, middle-aged white males) were writing fan letters. Evidently he was taking pains to establish that the readership of *Photoplay* consisted of more than the stereotypical "little shop girl" movie fanatic. Many of the letters to the editor printed in the correspondence section were purportedly from men. But lacking other demographic evidence, we can look at the advertising in *Photoplay* and see that the ads contradict the editor's idealized heterogeneous image. The preponderance of sales pitches were for women's clothing and health, cosmetic, and household products. The magazine's staff and advertisers definitely assumed that the readers were women consumers, consistent with the prevailing notion in the industry that the majority of filmgoers were young females. The monthly column by Carolyn Van Wyck, "Friendly Advice on Girls' Problems," and romantic fiction inviting female identification makes the magazine's gender orientation obvious.

Gaylyn Studlar, however, has rebutted the widely accepted view that the fanzines encouraged passive spectatorship. Her analysis shows that editorial content and readers' letters frequently questioned the patently manufactured quality of official Hollywood publicity and were skeptical of efforts to launch new stars by hard-sell techniques. Reading the pages of these magazines in search of attitudes about sound reveals that representations of the passive consumer and the active constructor of cinematic pleasure competed head to head. The movie fan was the escape-seeking, lonely-hearted adolescent on one page and the active proponent or opponent of sound films on another.[2]

In addition to questions of authenticity and the demographics and assertiveness of the readership, we must also wonder about fan magazines' independence from the studios' influence. The magazines of 1927–1931 were not full of smutty scandal and near-libelous innuendo, as some were in the post–World War II period. But neither were they paragons of objective journalism. Some articles are vestiges of the origins of these publications as promotions for sponsoring movie studios. Many stories were rehashes of publicists' press kits and star agents' promotions. They also included some "inside" information which could be corroborated in the trade press. Thus, on any given page, gossip, insinuation, subjective opinion, and biased fabrications might merge with competent observation and what appeared to be reliable information about production.

But the magazines definitely needed the studios. The symbiotic nature of the fanzines demanded that an editor like Quirk walk a thin line. For his subject matter—especially news items, press releases, and, most important, photographs—he relied on the industry's self-interest. At the same time, Quirk sounded a constant editorial refrain of his independence from the studios and partisanship for the fan, although, as Koszarski observed, "his own standards were too idiosyncratic for any reader to fully comprehend."[3] To serve as a spokesperson for fan power, it was essential that the editor not be perceived as a dupe of the moguls. He spoke for the "little" person and stressed that his magazine was a public service. *Photoplay*'s tag line was "The National Guide to Motion Pictures." Repeatedly Quirk lauded movie-loving readers and assured them that they collectively possessed economic and aesthetic power. He devoted pages to readers' responses and exhorted them to register complaints and compliments, "remembering that the object of these columns is to exchange thoughts that may bring about better pictures and better acting. Be constructive." It was also vital for fans to believe that their comments were effective. "Those who make pictures, those who act in them, and those who comprise the photoplay's vast audience," Quirk pledged, "may find your opinions interesting and your suggestions helpful."[4] This rather weak promise may in fact accurately describe the fans' impact on Hollywood. Certainly the studios must have paid attention to the opinions expressed in these publications (along with newspaper reviews and critical articles in mainstream publications), but the unfaltering measure of favor was always box-office revenue.

The industry was ambivalent about these publications. On the one hand, the studios courted fan magazine writers, recognizing them as a source of publicity and advertising. In 1930 the Academy invited fan editors and writers to a "free lunch" at which the famous lawyer (and film industry lobbyist) Louis Nizer was the speaker. He advised the editors to avoid too many "superlatives" in their ads and articles. On the other hand, Hollywood mistrusted the fan magazines, and several times in the 1930s pressured the Hays Office to restrict their reportage. Producers regarded fan culture and the publications that facilitated it as something else in need of concerted industry intervention.

The studios were able to call the shots. They retained contractual control over their performers' private as well as public lives and so held the power to dispense whatever knowledge they chose. Of course, some scandals were too big to contain and were written up by journalists who were outside the studios' sphere of influence. In such cases, the job fell to the fan magazine editors to explain and interpret what their titillated and/or disappointed readers were hearing "outside" the system. The studios' cooperation with the magazines was camouflaged by the authors' claims to be disseminating allegedly private information. Secrets and inside dope about pictures and stars were available "exclusively" to each magazine's loyal readership. The reporters personified themselves as espionage agents. Dorothy Manners of *Motion Picture Classic* spied on the privileged inner circle of Hollywood producers. *Photoplay*'s Cal York let it be known that he was the bane of studio managers. He boasted of illegally entering closed sets, of scooping revealing interviews with anonymous insiders, and of cultivating his special status as confidant to the stars, few of whom hesitated to bare the details of their private lives. In point of fact, Manners, York, and the other regular columnists were more like double agents, selling their knowledge of the fantastic world of Hollywood for the price of an issue but really passing on information with a wink from the cooperative studios. The columnists adopted the personae of voyeurs and tattlers to enable readers to project themselves into the presence of their most cherished film stars.

Reading these fascinating articles, it is easy to forget that the film companies were the gatekeepers of industry knowledge. Fan magazine editors and writers no doubt had the same "silent bargain" with studios that book reviewers had with publishers, tacitly recognizing that a good review or star puff piece was linked to advertising revenue. Reporters' press credentials could be revoked. York could be banned from the back lot, and *Photoplay* could lose its "favored-nation" status with studio insiders or be sued for libel. The fountain of production stills and star portraits that illustrated Manners's pieces could dry up. And, of course, studios could elect not to purchase display advertising for their new releases. Yet the studios tolerated, and sometimes colluded with, these prying, sensationalist, and often inaccurate journals. Their pages provided an important forum for presenting potential new stars, honing the careers of established stars, and channeling and blocking information about actors and productions. "Behind-the-scenes" knowledge of production circumstances and stars' lives could boost attendance. Fan magazines were also the crucible in which the paradox of stardom was concocted: movie stars are glamorous, charismatic beings we can never approach, yet they are basically just plain folks like us, with similar interests and foibles.

These magazines are clearly not reliable as historical sources in the traditional sense. They are nevertheless highly useful to read as mediators of a complex web of exchange between the industry, the commercial world, and the consumer. We cannot look at them for the "truth" about the transition to sound because that was often suppressed in an effort to write a story with a certain bias. It would be better to regard them as a parallel form of entertainment (not unlike today's TV programs which repackage publicity about stars and show business in the guise of "news"). We can read fan magazines as filters through which ideas about the movies emerged, analogous to the ways in which trade journals strained the news about sound according to what the editors believed were their constituents' interests. Thus, it is all the more surprising that remarkable differences of opinion about sound were aired in the fanzines. These differences must have reflected both the misgivings of consumers about the talkies and the tentativeness of producers about which direction they should take sound. If fan magazine coverage was an accurate barometer of public sentiment, as Quirk claimed, then the magazines' treatment of the advent of sound reflected a fragmented and confused response to the talkies by the public.

The Talkies—Pro and Con

James Quirk came out in favor of the talkies only during the summer of 1928, well after the studios had signed with ERPI and were wiring soundstages and theaters in earnest. Admitting his initial skepticism, he conceded that sound would "change the entire map" of the business within two years, introduce new stage personalities, force some favorite actors into second place, revolutionize newsreels, double the size of the audience, and put an end to "many affectations of speech."[5] Fan correspondence arriving at *Photoplay* was slow to acknowledge the talkies, possibly because it was necessary to live in or near a major city to experience them. But by early 1929, while the industry was hedging with dual versions and part-talkies, controversy raged in the mail pouch. The editors searched for a trend:

> These letters indicate that the talking picture or the sound effect picture is still regarded as a novelty, and that the public is not so sure that they will continue to be satisfied with full length, all-dialogue entertainment. Nine out of ten say they would rather have a first rate silent picture than a second rate talking picture. They complain of the mediocre photography and static quality of the acting in the talking versions, and are sensible of the greater sense exertion and brain effort demanded by them. They are unanimous in their praise of talk and sound in news reels, and there seems to be a definite acceptance of two reel talking pictures when combined with a silent feature.
>
> There are many who say they will not attend any more full length talking pictures because of the added strain, but there are many more who name several short subjects they have enjoyed hugely. (James R. Quirk, "Close-ups and Long-shots," *Photoplay*, March 1929, p. 24)

For a while the pages provided a lively forum for a divided readership as the magazines gave coverage to those for and against the talkies.

FOR THE TALKIES

Minor Horton of Okmulgee, Oklahoma, knew what he liked about the talkies and submitted a list:

a. They will give us real acting by real actors rather than a series of close-ups of pretty faces and figures.

b. They will help to Americanize movies, thus excluding "Foreign Finds," who are not even American citizens.

c. They will afford excellent musical accompaniment by good orchestras.

d. Instead of wondering what is actually said we can now hear the exact dialogue of the stars.

e. Talkies will give many fans a chance to see and hear the world's greatest stage favorites and other notables that they might never have seen otherwise.

f. They will provide a greater choice in movie entertainment as to whether it shall be silent or Talkie.

g. And last but not least, there will be no written titles for the ladies to read to the children. This will also eliminate much of the eye-strain from hurried reading. ("Brickbats and Bouquets," *Photoplay,* May 1929, p. 123)

Horton's letter is worth examining in detail because it touches on so many aspects of the talkie debate. His first point about the "reality" of actors could refer to their naturalism, their sincerity, their professionalism, or all three. It seems to imply that real actors who can speak their lines as well as pose will be from the stage. He suggests that the silent film was characterized by the camera's excessive attention to women's faces and bodies. Does this mean that real acting is more masculine and that close-ups are less interesting than long-shots—as in "action" scenes, for example? His hint that a beautiful appearance competes with the voice was addressed more specifically by Colleen Moore's manager John McCormick when he was asked about sound: "What am I doing to prepare Colleen for this change? Nothing! For picture screen personalities faces are the important things, and, up to date, few of the stage stars with trained voices have proved to have film faces."[6] Such perceived differences between face and voice reflected Hollywood's separation of image and sound, as well as a deeper schism between the viewer's confidence in the good looks of actors and the substance of their dialogue. This view paralleled the belief that sound revealed the intelligence or stupidity of actors. Several other readers pointed out that silent stars were failing in the talkies because their careers had been built on appearances. Floyd Casebolt of Waxahachie, Texas, wrote, "Too many lightweight actors and actresses have made the cinema grade because they had good looks. But now come the talkies and they are going to be a hard taskmaster. Dumb clothes-horses are going to be relegated to the scrap heap sooner or later. The talkies will bring the acid tests."[7]

Horton's sentiment about Americanizing the movies raised a divisive topic. While many hated the thought of losing certain artists, some were openly exhorting Hollywood to rid itself of alleged foreign domination. This attitude may have reflected a division between cosmopolitan production and regional exhibition tastes. The melting-pot character of early sound definitely played better before urban audiences than rural ones, to which presumably Horton belonged. His seemingly isolationist reaction may have been more, however, than Dust Belt xenophobia. Sklar has characterized the national sentiment of the period as one of "unbridgeable difference between social groups. Its ugly side was legislative restriction on immigration, based on ethnicity or national origin; its positive quality, a new recognition of the vitality of cultural variety . . . what we would now call multiculturalism."[8]

Horton's approval of musical accompaniment may refer to the synchronized or part-talking films that were circulating in early 1929. He implies that these sound tracks provided orchestras that were superior to the local live accompaniment. The importance of this criterion probably depended on the size of the listener's city and the expertise of the musicians. Like "B.F.," many readers favored the sound film because of the music.

Wondering what the stars actually were saying intrigued and frustrated many viewers. Many viewers lip-read the dialogue scenes in silent films, sometimes complaining later that the actors either were not saying what they were supposed to or were saying something profane. Also implicit in Horton's remark is a distrust of silent intertitles and their ability to convey the "real" speech of the actors. He prefers the concrete literalness of spoken dialogue, in contrast to the many fans who adored the silent movie because it allowed them to imagine their favorite stars' voices.

Horton's praise of the talkies' ability to present high-class stage performances assumes that fans wanted to experience this kind of entertainment. He seems to welcome Hollywood's virtual Broadway strategy of bringing canned talent to the local theater. Another enraptured fan, Clifton Ray, was a press agent's dream: "Didn't I recently see Fannie Brice and *hear* her, right down south? Answer is *I did.* And how? Why, talkies, of course. How else could Broadway arrive on Forsythe Street in Jacksonville [Mississippi]? *My Man* brought her right to my very door. There she was, singing all the way through it. Realized dreams." Renée Delage had grown up in Paris, where she had always dreamed of seeing Maurice Chevalier perform but could never afford the price of a music-hall ticket. "Last week I went to the United Artists Theater to see him in *Innocents of Paris.* . . . I had an idea of how he looked—but what a thrill when I heard his voice! Thanks to the movies and to the talkies. I owe them one of the happiest moments of my life."[9]

Horton's mention of being able to choose between silent and sound films refers to dual versions. He assumed that the two kinds of films would coexist and the fan would continue to have a choice. The studios encouraged this belief. Warner Bros.' *Photoplay* ads for Brice's film, for example, included the notice: "If there is not a theatre in your community equipped as yet to show *My Man* as a talking picture—be sure to see it as a silent picture."[10] Apparently Horton shared the common belief that talkies would augment, not replace, silents.

Ladies reading to children, eyestrain, other distractions, and physical discomforts were associated with silent presentation. The sound film imposed a discipline on the audience that Horton welcomed.

Horton's list comprises many of the arguments in favor of the talkies, but not all. Dorothy Pritchett of Fort Brady, Michigan, wrote: "[The talkies] have 'gotten me' to the extent that a silent picture actually bores me nowadays, and I believe that to be the general opinion of this post. When I think of the master minds and skilled workmanship that made it possible for us to HEAR our favorites—I'd like to cheer for talkies—and I do, inwardly. Even 'voice doubling' doesn't dim the attraction."[11] She was awed by the foundations of sound cinema in science and technology.

AGAINST THE TALKIES

A letter from D. H. Chapman of San Francisco opposed sound:

> At their best, talking films are only an imitation of the stage, and I have never
> been able to take the stage very seriously. In the first place, I dislike the arti-
> ficial voices affected by stage players, and then there is something so stilted
> and limited about stage technique. Pictures have always gotten into the very
> heart of personalities and situations, whereas the stage and talkies merely
> skim the surface. The silent movies, accompanied by appropriate organ
> music, were soothing to the nerves, stimulating to the imagination, often
> artistic, and a lot of fun. ("*Classic's* Readers Respond on the Talkies," *Motion
> Picture Classic,* September 1929, p. 82)

Chapman's objection is that the theatricality of dialogue films is harmful. For her (him?),
stage voices were not "real acting," but contrived. It was theater that was superficial. If
cinema adopted talking, these theatrical qualities would replace the silent film's superior
ability to develop characters, stars, and "situations." Chapman spoke for those readers
who found the ambience of the silent movie house more pleasing than that of the sound
theater. Many regretted the loss of the "soothing" or almost hypnotic state induced by
watching silent movies. The greater "strain" of concentrating on dialogue was frequently
mentioned.

One argument against the talkies accepted the inevitability of censorship. George
Kent Shuler, publisher of *Motion Picture Classic,* argued that certain subjects could not
be treated as dialogue pictures and therefore would limit film to puerile themes.

> The picture carrying the spoken word would naturally have to carry a plot
> which doesn't place its figures out of character. . . .
> With pictures that carry strong dramatic meat it would be utterly impos-
> sible to exploit the dialogue. . . . No improvement could be made over the
> pantomime revealed in the outstanding opuses of the screen. The expres-
> sions of the characters in these films offer an eloquence that makes dialogue
> or speech genuinely out of place and out of order. (George Kent Shuler,
> "Pictures and Personalities," *Motion Picture Classic,* June 1928, p. 15)

He predicted two lines of filmmaking determined by content. Hollywood would make
light romantic films in sound "and leave the heavy melodramas to pantomime and captions."[12] He also fretted about the culture gap between New York and regional movie
houses. Broadway's dialogue was acceptable for sophisticated audiences, but unsuitable
for distribution to the rest of the country. He was contradicted by one of his columnists,
Cedric Belfrage (who referred, perhaps with ironic intent, to the "innocent girlish
minds" of his readers!). Belfrage interviewed Edmund Lowe, the foul-mouthed
Sergeant Quirt in WHAT PRICE GLORY? Lowe denied that the talkies would kill adult
subjects. "Sure, there is a little problem there: this matter of making hard-swearing characters seem natural in the talkies. But we've faced much worse problems than that in
developing the movies." Belfrage suggested that audiences would feel deprived if they
did not get uncensored dialogue.[13]

The talkie-hating readers were fortunate in having Charlie Chaplin as their
spokesperson for the silent film. Chaplin's articulate and heartfelt diatribes against

sound frequently made the papers, and many comments condemning sound in the fan magazines refer to his exemplary resistance. In August 1930, *Motion Picture Classic* put silents "on trial." They were "defended" by Chaplin. The magazine did not claim that Chaplin himself wrote the piece; it appears that the arguments were fabricated by the staffer Charleson Gray from the star's public comments and from press releases promoting CITY LIGHTS, undoubtedly with Chaplin's authorization. In his defense of silents, Chaplin (via Gray) complains about the poor quality of the talkies' stories. "While I consider a good stage play far superior to a good talking picture, I consider a good silent film of the same play as superior to both." He griped about unreliable acoustic reproduction and was bothered when speaker placement caused the voice to seem disembodied: "During a tense love scene, the dialogue will appear to be proceeding from the characters' feet. . . . Rarely do words ever seem to be coming from the lips of the speakers themselves." He argued that remaking films in foreign languages was neither commercially nor linguistically acceptable. The talkies were dealing a deathblow to pantomime, an ancient art form. His final argument is humanist (and, incidentally, sums up the moral of the story in CITY LIGHTS): "The efforts of the earth to communicate with Mars are as nothing to the efforts of one human being to communicate with another." Chaplin predicted that "my future films are to have even more of a vogue than those of the past, if I am to judge public sentiment by the thousands of letters which pour into the studio, begging that I remain in the field of silent pictures."[14]

The behavior of fans at the box office reflected how torn they were in their interest in the talkies. A reporter bemoaned the confusing situation:

> A few weeks ago four hundred of you stood in line in a pouring rain at eight-fifteen on Monday morning on Broadway to buy seats for Clara Bow's first talkie, *The Wild Party*. . . . Yet a short time ago when the largest movie house in Glendale, a neighboring town to Los Angeles, flashed the announcement that its screen would soon sing and talk, the audience—which means you—burst into boos and catcalls of disapproval. . . . Fan-letter departments at the various studios report that you are writing your favorite stars more and more urgently to make a talkie, though three months ago you were writing them, begging them not to. And . . . questionnaires distributed in the biggest theater chains would seem to show that the audiences patronizing these houses wanted silent movies, while they were crowding the same theaters as never before to hear talkies. It is all very puzzling. (Dorothy Donnell, "Do You Want the Talkies?" *Motion Picture Classic*, July 1929, pp. 87, 89)

One gathers that neither the studios nor the fan magazines could ascertain the public's appetite for entertainment. On the contrary, we see those institutions scrambling to find or to influence the fickle consumer's vaguely defined and "puzzling" pleasures.

Personality and Stardom

First and always foremost, movie stars were fan magazines' stock in trade. Not surprisingly, the bulk of published material on sound concerned the adjustment that picture personalities were making to dialogue and their career changes. The debates echo the preoccupation of the general press in focusing on vocal quality but differ in their concern for how the voice affected star status.

Fanzines, before the talkies became commonplace, speculated about which stars' voices would adapt best to sound. Dorothy Manners, discussing Clara Bow's silent picture RED HAIR (1928), quipped, "Now if they would only use the Vitaphone on Clara's wisecracks the triumph would be complete."[15] There was curiosity about John Barrymore's singing debut announced for GENERAL CRACK (1929) and anticipation of Janet Gaynor and Charles Farrell's harmonizing in SUNNY SIDE UP (1929). These expectations are consistent with the disembodied-voice attitude which marked popular criticism. Shuler observed that "it behooves the boys and girls out Hollywood way to develop their vocal chords."[16] It is as though the "quality voice" was not part of the actor but part of the medium itself. The actor' job was to adjust his or her physiology to that mechanical paragon.

The fan magazines provided abundant opportunities for viewers to express their opinions concerning stars' voices. Sometimes these were conspicuously polar, as in this exchange about Mary Pickford's southern accent. Maye Higdon of Atlanta approbated, "In *Coquette* the dialogue sounded so perfectly natural it was hard to believe that all the actors were not Southern people." But Milton Hutchinson of Richmond, Virginia, castigated, "Surely Miss Pickford and the supporting cast do not think that we Southerners say 'sho' for sure, and 'luv' for love."[17] These writers were staking a linguistic claim on the talking-picture representation of their dialect.

The case of Pickford also highlights the concern of many viewers that there be a good match between a voice and a star's perceived image (which here did not include a strong accent). The general press predicted that stars' actual voices would disappoint in comparison to the "imagined" voice of the silent screen, but fan evidence suggests that the opposite was sometimes true. "I heard my first talking picture a few days ago," reported Nancy Kimball, of Jamestown, North Dakota:

> It was *The Canary Murder Case*. I thought it was great! William Powell had always been fixed in my mind as a villain of the screen until then. He will never seem the same to me again and I am glad of it, because I like him so much better this way. He has a really remarkable voice. It is so easily understood and contains such a soothing quality. Let's hear and see more of him! ("Brickbats and Bouquets," *Photoplay*, July 1929, p. 110)

With the career transitions to sound under way in 1928–1929, the magazines began itemizing those whom sound had helped or hurt. This was an irresistible opportunity for fans, authors, and editors to be authoritative. The fan magazine–composed narratives of stars' brushes with the talkies fall into four categories: silent stars whose voices were successfully recorded and who made a smooth transition; "retired" or unappreciated silent actors whose voices enabled them to make a comeback; newcomers (often from the stage) whose proficiency, it was predicted, would elevate them to stellar heights; and current film stars whose careers were suddenly terminated after failed initial appearances.

SILENT STARS WHO SUCCEEDED IN TALKIES

The introduction of voice testing gave writers the chance to personify the talkies as a demanding taskmaster. "Mike" (the microphone, of male gender) was said to love Norma Shearer, Constance Bennett, Betty Compson, and Gloria Swanson. Manners

Charles Farrell and Janet Gaynor in a not-so-private duet in SUNNY SIDE UP *(Fox, 1929).*

recounted that Shearer and Lina Basquette had excelled. Janet Gaynor sounded like a little girl but redeemed herself in SUNNY SIDE UP; the trope of the disembodied voice reappears: "Janet Gaynor turns loose her cute little singing and speaking voices in a story of high life and low in New York." Richard Watts designated as successes Bessie Love, Betty Compson, Ruth Chatterton, Anita Page, and Evelyn Brent. These lists indicate that most of the concern was for women, although some men were singled out. Hollywood insiders had predicted failure for Harold Lloyd's high-pitched voice, but it recorded "splendidly." Watts included Chester Morris, Paul Muni, and Clive Brook on his list of talkie survivors.[18]

Quirk had his own pantheon of established stars whom he deemed to have passed their trial, including Marion Davies and Corinne Griffith. Many of his comparisons evaluated the voice as an autonomous entity: Colleen Moore "came through her test with a voice that matched her sweet personality"; Clara Bow possessed "a pert echo that fitted her shadow self perfectly." He regretted the English-language training undertaken by Vilma Banky and Greta Garbo because their accents were part of their charm. (Unlike Pickford's in COQUETTE, theirs were innate, not affected.) Quirk's views either represent his own idiosyncratic opinion or parrot press agent copy; they often differ from the opinions expressed within the pages of his magazine. Of the performers he mentioned, articles typically portrayed all of them except Garbo as unsuccessful in talking pictures. This superficial difference between the editor's views and *Photoplay*'s content may reflect the magazine's attempt to straddle the competing interests of the consumers of star information (fans) and those who provided it (studios).

NEGLECTED ACTORS WHO BECAME TALKIE STARS

The sentimental favorites among fanzine readers and writers were the silent performers who had quit the film business, only to be rediscovered because of their superior voices. Dorothy Manners observed, "It's an odd outgrowth of the talkies that even the pioneer personalities of the screen are new stuff before the microphone."[19] The reporter mediated between the star and the fans when she described *Photoplay* readers as "proud of the old favorites of the screen who have come back via the talkies. Betty Compson is a good example. The fans are for you, Betty."[20] Actually, Compson was at the peak of her career when sound came in, having received kudos for THE DOCKS OF NEW YORK (1928) and having been nominated for the Academy's best actress award for THE BARKER in 1928. But her recent work as Richard Barthelmess's girlfriend in WEARY RIVER (1929) and as the star of ON WITH THE SHOW (1929) had brought her no acclaim. The situation appears to have been the opposite of Manners's reversal-of-neglect story. Helen Morgan's case was written up as another comeback scenario. She earlier had tried the movies (SIX CYLINDER LOVE [1923]), failed, and retreated to the stage to be a "sob singer." Then her lead role in APPLAUSE rewarded her with deserved film stardom. The silent star Raymond Griffith, who had failed as a stage actor after losing his voice, was having a resurgence of popularity. His "husky whisper" turned out to record wonderfully. Lloyd Hamilton, who had fallen from grace because of a life of partying and scandal, was regaining his reputation in the talkies.[21]

Lois Wilson's Paramount contract was not renewed until she "proved herself" by voice training and stage acting in Los Angeles. Antonio Moreno "had been doing a quiet fade-out until First National discovered that he has been suppressing a splendid speaking voice all these years." Edward Everett Horton ("more or less of a 'flop' in silent pictures") received a long-term contract after his success in THE TERROR.[22]

The example of Pauline Frederick, depicted by *Photoplay* as "a star who was gone [from Hollywood] but never forgotten, more in sorrow than in anger," demonstrates the magazine's apparent support of an actor who was resisting her studio and the transition to sound. In her interview with Manners, Frederick emerged as a reluctant success story who disliked submitting to the talkies. She explained that Warner Bros. did not respect her talent and was giving her bad scripts. Sound pictures were "odorous," but she was compelled to honor her two-year contract. Because of her low voice, she rationalized, she would have to study diction, "because only actors with high voices recorded properly."[23]

Bessie Love was another success story. She had been rescued from a dead-end stint in vaudeville when MGM discovered she could sing, dance, talk, and play the ukulele. According to a fan magazine account, at the beginning of her career she had

> made the mistake of going into the movies, instead of the stage. For years
> she played wistful heroines when she should have been twinkling in musical
> comedy. Came the talkies and Bessie, who had said good-bye to the studios,
> was summoned from a vaudeville tour to play in *The Broadway Melody*.
> Today, in the midst of the microphone panic, Bessie is one of the few stars
> who know where their next Rolls-Royce is coming from. (Herbert Howe,
> "The Girl Who Walked Back," *Photoplay*, May 1929, pp. 60–61, 150)

Conrad Nagel's great voice made him a star, whereas before, in silents, he had been a mere "stock leading man." According to an article by Mark Larkin, Nagel's body image and voice did not match, but he succeeded in spite of this lack of integration. The camera pictured Nagel as a man with a small, slender build. "But the microphone, by catching the intensity and sincerity of his voice, brings his real personality to talking pictures." Nagel attributed his own success to his training on the stage. In a remarkable example of the rapidly changing attitude toward the voice, Nagel described his own early performances in the talkies as overactive, artificial, and full of exaggerated theatrical emphasis. He had now progressed to the hybrid style (see chapter 18), supposedly integrating the best of the stage and movies. Shuler profiled Nagel as a Horatio Alger success story. His previous career in the "erstwhile silent drama" was ordinary; the talkies promoted Nagel to stardom:

> He came from the stage and from a successful career on the stage. Anyone who saw him as the small-town boy in *Forever After*, with Alice Brady, will remember his work as marked by both sincerity and a telling power to stir the emotions. But those same theatergoers probably were won over more by the evidence of a repression of feeling rather than a manifest and mobile expression of it. And this Nagel conveyed more by his voice than by his gestures.
>
> Hence, ever since his entrance into pictures, he has been under something of a handicap. In the words of the radio salesman, he must be heard to be appreciated.
>
> The talkies have given Nagel a chance to be heard. And appreciation of him has been emphatic. The barometer of fan mail has shown the altitude of his popularity literally zooming upward. And the manner in which those who hold his contracts are shaking hands with themselves indicates that the box-office as well as the post-office has felt the weight of his enhanced reputation.
>
> This is an instance of increased scope of effort that has already taken place with the coming of the speaking screen. It is something which has happened and which therefore is a fact. (George Kent Shuler, *Motion Picture Classic,* January 1929, p. 15)

Nagel's story is prototypical. It was assumed that his "natural" voice was defective (because of his regional accent). Through hard work and determination, he was able to change his voice to match the norms of the legitimate stage and then the talkies. The result was a hybrid movie voice, the new norm, but furthermore, his success story provided a work-ethic model to inspire fans.

Bebe Daniels was considered washed up until RKO discovered that she had a singing voice and could pick up songs by ear. In a gossipy article, Harry Lang contrasted her career with Bow's:

> Consider Bebe Daniels and Clara Bow. Envision for yourselves a see-saw. One end goes up; the other end goes down. Bebe is on the end that's going up, and Clara is—well, er, let's confine ourselves to her own admission that she's going to take a European trip by and by because she's tired. . . .
>
> When [Paramount] wouldn't give her a talkie chance, Bebe slapped down $175,000 and bought back the contract that called for her to make three more pictures. And now what?
>
> Why, just this: Bebe Daniels, as this is written, has just finished the lead in *Rio Rita* for Radio Pictures. And there isn't a doubt in the world, say the

wiseacres of Hollywood, [that] that talkie will be one of The Big Shots of the
talkie year. . . .

Strange, too. Bebe has a voice that you wouldn't think twice about, ordinarily. Nice voice, and all that, but no power—no force. Now that's just where
Mike does his stuff. He took all the nice things in Bebe's voice—and there
were plenty of 'em—and added the thing she didn't have—POWER. And
boy, what a voice it gives her on the screen!—you'd even fall in love with a
strabismic wart-hog if it had a voice like that. (Harry Lang, "The
Microphone—The Terror of the Studios," *Photoplay,* December 1929, p. 30)

Sessue Hayakawa, who "crashed back into celluloid BECAUSE of—not in spite of—the
mike!," was another for whom the talkies turned defeat into victory:

Ninety percent of the people who see and hear him will be amazed to find
out how well he speaks English! Hayakawa died in the silent pictures many
years ago because he could only do ONE kind of story—the Japanese prince
or something who married the white girl and paid for it. Or didn't, and paid
anyway! And so it's a funny thing, isn't it?—how Terrible Mike makes 'em or
breaks 'em. (Lang, "The Microphone—The Terror of the Studios," pp.
29–30, 124–26)

Actually, Hayakawa had been living in France and Japan. His first talkie was a Fu
Manchu genre picture, DAUGHTER OF THE DRAGON (1931). Mordaunt Hall thought that
"he does moderately well, even though his lines are not always spoken so that one can
understand them."[24]

Maurice Ahern celebrated Betty Compson, Bessie Love, Louise Dresser, Henry B.
Walthall, Lila Lee, Irene Rich, and Conrad Nagel. These players, "relegated almost to
the limbo of bit players long before the age of microphone have, through the suitability
of their voices, regained the eminence that once was theirs."[25] The leitmotif in Lang's
and Ahern's articles is self-determination. These performers used the heretofore-
untapped power of their voices to resist the studios' exploitation or disinterest.

Warner Baxter's story was told with the added melodramatic flair of a last-minute rescue. He had played minor film parts for years, achieving no recognition, but with the
arrival of sound he was "the most effective voice yet heard in pictures. . . . Nine months
ago he had made up his mind to give up films forever. Today he could not quit if he
would, and he wouldn't."[26] In fact, Baxter's break as the Cisco Kid came because Raoul
Walsh, who was supposed to play the lead as well as direct IN OLD ARIZONA, needed a
last-minute replacement after his eye injury. For the magazines, though, it was not this
accident but Baxter's exceptional voice which saved his career. Another actor whose
speaking and singing gifts elevated him to stardom was the heartthrob of THE DESERT
SONG, John Boles. He became an instant love object, a good example of the "woman-
made man" ideal embodied in Valentino. Evelyn M. Fess of Buffalo, New York, professed that Boles had "the most perfect screen voice so far heard. And his singing would
melt a stone. We have been looking for Rudy's successor for a long time. We needn't look
farther." Trix Shaw of Claymont, Delaware, exclaimed, "What a find! And where has he
been all the time? I never got such a kick out of screen love-making, and I've been seeing movies all my life. Oh, his expression—his voice—his singing!" In December 1929,

according to the volume of *Photoplay* fan mail, Boles displaced John Gilbert as the male favorite. (Garbo remained the leading female star.)[27]

Another fan magazine theme was the additional "job stress" inflicted on the stars by sound. Whereas acting in the silent cinema was merely posing, talking-film performers earned their millions by their sweat. H. B. Warner, a case in point, found working for the talkies to be so physically demanding that he lost eleven pounds during filming. Most of the complaints were more psychological in nature. Louise Closser Hale, who played opposite Al Jolson in BIG BOY, reported that silent screen actors and stage actors alike were afflicted with "The New Stage Fright." She confessed, "When I heard of the greatest of the women stars losing her dinner every night during the filming of a talkie I felt that I wasn't such a gump after all."[28] Peggy Wood, an actress as well as a voice teacher, explained mike fright: "The actor is worried about the irrevocability of what he is doing—the thought that every move is being photographed and recorded for all time then and there." Unlike stage work, filmmaking offered no chance to perform better the next time.[29]

The appeal of these success stories is that they propose scenarios of personal inspiration and, occasionally, resistance to Hollywood's domination. Again, their factual content may be dubious, but the messages are significant. One common theme is the success often produced by persistence and hard work. Those who persevered would eventually get their lucky break, similar to the opportunity the talkies brought to these talented but neglected actors.

The concern about stars' hard work, job stress, and mike anxiety is based on the assumption that talking-picture stars actually labored for their living, a belief that ran counter to the attitude held about silent acting. Danae Clark has argued that, "according to [Hollywood's] conventions of naturalism, stars did not work. Though some stars were distinguished for their acting ability, it was widely thought that most stars owed their success to their personalities or photogenic qualities."[30] Sound, many fan magazine correspondents agreed, forced actors to "work" and "think" by studying elocution, taking singing lessons, and rehearsing for long hours. Cal York contributed the view that the talkies had transformed Hollywood from a place of leisure and visibility to "a place where a lot of hard-working men and women live."[31] Quirk agreed, joking that sound film labor was destroying Hollywood's legendary night life: "Maybe when they [actors] get that microphonephobia, which is high hat for fear of the talkies, thoroughly out of their systems there will be some fun in Hollywood again. But right now the bootleggers are starving to death and night life ceases promptly at nine-thirty, when they all start home to spray their throats with Listerine and go beddy-bye."[32]

Did readers believe such outright prevarications? Like many of the stories of actors helped by sound, these scenarios of hardworking, stressed-out employees of demanding corporations seem designed to humanize actors, to set them up as role models, and to enhance their potential for fan identification and empathy—all of which served Hollywood quite nicely.

NEW ACTORS

Late 1928 was the peak season for recruiting talent for the 1929–1930 production period. Film players were finding that choice parts were going to those with stage experience. Pathé's Broadway import, for instance, was Ina Claire, the popular star of *The Gold Diggers*. She was hired to rekindle her stage role in THE AWFUL TRUTH (1929). Kann was impressed: "Her debut in talkers is certainly one of the events of 1929 and her picture easily one of the finest which sound has given theaters to date."[33] For fans, however, she garnered much more publicity by marrying John Gilbert after a three-week romance.

Cal York represented this trend toward Broadway recruitment as Hollywood's full-blown talking-picture panic. Beauty and "camera face" were losing out, he said, to vocal expertise. (Each was somehow autonomous from the body.) Like most who expressed opinions in the fan magazines, Dorothy Manners was skeptical from the start about the Broadway imports. She asked rhetorically, "Ever hear of Helen Twelvetrees, Dan Healy, Helen Kane, Colette D'Arville? These are but a handful of the stage people who have been cast in feature talkie productions. . . . Now, the question is, can Broadway with all her enunciation, singing and dancing, fill the places left vacant by long established idols of the screen who for some reason or other can't make the talkie grade?"[34] An anecdote was supposed to show that studio executives were out of touch with their customers:

> After six months of almost solid talkie releases with those new-fangled stars from the stage, this much has been brought to light: That the fans are not very willing to give up their old favorites for more oral, but less beautiful sweethearts. Mr. B. P. Schulberg of Paramount spent one half hour of his valuable time explaining to me that the public does not know what it wants. And yet one of the finest and most interesting productions ever put out by his organization, *The Hole in the Wall,* played to half empty houses in Los Angeles, while not far down the street America's Sweetheart was standing them in line for what many critics believed to be a mediocre picture, *Coquette.* The secret being that there wasn't a movie name in *The Hole in the Wall.* (Dorothy Manners, *Motion Picture Classic,* September 1929, p. 62)

Manners's points were that given a choice between vocally inferior but known stars (Pickford) and quality productions with (then) unknown stage stars, fans would continue supporting their erstwhile silent heroes. The audiences' preferences also showed their economic power. The failure of the imported Broadway actors was presumed to validate the wisdom of the film buff, while pillorying the moguls' mistake of ignoring the public.

Less than a year after the Broadway film rush of 1928, this crop of stage recruits was producing disappointment. "The microphone," related Quirk, "which the stage actor looked upon as a friend in need, turned out to be a tricky magician who would not tolerate the bellowings of the Shakespearean veteran or the studied affectation of the English actress from Arkansas."[35] Leonard Hall wrote in August 1929,

> The hosts of the stage and screen are gradually living down and fighting off fear and distrust, and are laboring hand in hand to the greater glory of the photoplay. The truest and finest of the theater and the studio survive, as they always have and will, whatever their medium. The incompetents and drones are perishing, as was inevitable. The great war [the talkies] has done more to shake out the wastrels and the two-for-a-nickel reputations of the film world than anything in the history of Hollywood. (Leonard Hall, "Revolution in Hollywood," *Photoplay,* August 1929, pp. 100–101)

Quirk and Hall explained the assimilation of theater actors and the disappearance of familiar players by constructing a simple Darwinist scenario. The fittest survived; the others' options were not picked up.

In September 1930, Herbert Cruikshank stated that the panic was over. The Broadway hordes were "folding their tents and silently stealing away." Some of these players had made deals for a number of pictures, and studios were paying 25 to 50 percent of their contracts to break them. (Pathé paid Ina Claire $55,000 after THE AWFUL TRUTH flopped.) "There are dozens of playwrights, song-writers, directors, technicians and others who were signed on long-term contracts, who went to Hollywood, who didn't click for one reason or another, and who were finally bought off," Lang reported. He continued, cynically, "It cost the producers thousands—for nothing. Thousands that might have been spent making fine movies; instead. And they holler about putt-putt golf courses ruining business!"[36] The moral was that, rather than waste money on Broadway talent, the producers should have listened to the fans.

These opinions about the voice parallel the critical press's definition of the right voice for the talkies. The standard evolved from the "quality" to the "natural" voice as dialogue became integrated into everyday moviegoing and the fanzines stopped paying attention to the stage and the voice. The stars would not be exorbitantly paid unfamiliar players from theater, but performers who had voices that "Terrible Mike" liked and who could act in the movies.

SILENT STARS WHO FAILED THE TEST

Even before their features were released, the fan magazine press passed judgment on stars who would *not* be hits in the talkies. *Photoplay* reported that Janet Gaynor and Sue Carol "failed to sound impressive" in their Fox tryouts. Quirk added condescendingly that a year of study and training should restore them. May McAvoy and Dolores Del Rio were judged "more effective pictorially than audibly."[37] Among others "broken" by the microphone were Mona Rico ("Terrible Mike has a Nordic superiority complex or something"), Dita Parlo ("ran afoul of Terrible Mike in Hollywood and has returned to Deutschland to do her klangfilming"), and "the sexquisite" Dolores Costello, whose career was a meteoric rise and fall. It was commonplace to lampoon Costello's delivery in GLORIOUS BETSY. The fanzine writers did not hesitate to attack her vocals: "Poor Dolores—there are two opinions in Hollywood as to what her mike voice sounded like. One clique says it sounded like the barkings of a lonesome puppy; the others claim it reminded them of the time they sang 'In the Shade of the Old Apple Tree' through tissue paper folded over a comb."[38]

Even the much-adored Constance Talmadge succumbed to mike fright. Quirk related that, "when she stepped before a camera and microphone to take a test for the lead in *The Gold Diggers*, she was ossified, and it was some few minutes before she could croak a note. She came through beautifully, and the teacher marked her A Plus, but a little iron mike had frighted this young veteran completely out of her consonants."[39]

This was the plight also of others "not born to the English language." Word that the popular Emil Jannings would probably not make any English talkies was a disappointment, but hope was held out that a story was being written for him about an immigrant struggling to become "an American." Lili Damita was notified that her contract would be canceled if she did not "learn to speak utterly without a foreign inflection." Pola Negri, Nils Asther, and Eva Von Berne were in trouble. Beatrice Wilson predicted that British Reginald Denny and Swedish Greta Garbo would have problems owing to their accented English.[40]

The fan magazines' discussion of these actors' rise to stardom or slide into oblivion was a strategy to make the transition to sound navigable for the reader. To help them understand the significance of the talkies, the magazines personalized the new medium, that is, redefined it not as an industry, economics, or technology but as an individual crisis for the star to overcome. Coping with a change in the profession gave fans, for a short time, a convenient explanation for a star's changing status. Many of the stories of the performers' adjustments to Hollywood are scenarios that mirrored the lives of "ordinary" people, but on a grander, public scale. Readers might not have known what Louis B. Mayer was like, but they knew what it was to have a mean boss. They had suffered injustice, through no fault of their own, analogous to being born with a bad voice, having an accent, coming from a low social class, or suffering other "defects." They had dreaded public embarrassment, just as some stars lost their voices before Terrible Mike. Like the established actors whose careers were struck down by the talkie nemesis, they had suffered anxiety about losing their jobs.

An excellent example of the fan magazines' propensity to refabricate events in a way that personalized them is the telling of the QUEEN KELLY debacle. Ignoring all the circumstances that contributed to the failure of this project, the magazines instead exuded compassion for Gloria Swanson's personal loss and rallied behind her plucky determination to recover:

> Nobody knows just what happened to this picture, but the rumor has been that nearly a million dollars' worth of work had to be scrapped. This series of unforeseen setbacks would have prostrated seven actresses of ordinary hardihood. But not Gloria. She picked up the scraps herself and went right ahead making another picture. What that picture is is not known. Or how good it is, or how bad. But we hope sincerely that it is good. For Gloria's perseverance and ability to stand up under fire merit reward. (George Kent Shuler, *Motion Picture Classic,* October 1929, p. 15)

This strategy personalizes the star's troubles and makes her a figure of identification. Readers could empathize with Swanson's independence and resistance, while learning an object lesson in how to cope with exploitation by a powerful system. This attitude helped define a model "new woman" who could succeed in a man's world. The magazines often praised women such as Swanson, June Mathis, Corinne Griffith, and Dorothy Arzner for their professionalism, while blaming the system for any lack of success in their careers.[41]

Accounts of talking-picture failure pointed to unsatisfactory vocals, bad acting, "sagging" narratives, professional victimization, and a somewhat xenophobic suspicion of "accents." Swanson's story of personal triumph over mismanagement and personal clashes suggests that other agendas were hiding behind such narratives. Did fan magazine–constructed scenarios of talkie crack-ups camouflage other matters not related to their voices? In two of the most famous crashes, Clara Bow and John Gilbert, external circumstances seem to have been influential.

Clara Bow. The sensational failure alluded to by Harry Lang in his "Terror of the Studio" exposé was Bow, the butt of a malicious parody called "Mother Goose in Hollywood:"

> Miss Humpty-Dumpty sat on a wall;
> Miss Humpty-Dumpty had a great fall—
> For all her "S.A." [sex appeal] and all of her "It"
> Just couldn't make her in talkies a hit!
> (Harry Lang, "The Microphone—The Terror of the
> Studios," *Photoplay*, December 1929, p. 30)

Clara Bow personified the flapper with the elusive erotic appeal "It." Eleanor Glyn coined the word for the 1927 film of that title to describe her, connoting liberated sexuality and "everything that was glamourous, mysterious, and forbidden."[42] Bow had been consistently voted a popular star throughout the late twenties, and in April 1928, she received a record amount of fan mail. Her first talkie, however, THE WILD PARTY, was lackadaisically received. Some reviewers heard an excessively sharp edge to her voice. For others, it was her Brooklyn-accented vocalization that, in the words of Lang, made her see-saw go down. The magazines typically presented her case to fans so as to induce maximum reader sympathy. They learned that she wept bitterly upon hearing her voice played back the first time. But seemingly in contradiction to her chronic mike fright, her chronic exuberance, an amiable trait in her silent pictures, was blamed for destroying the technology of the talkies:

> When Clara turned the full force of the Bow personality on the microphone and shouted "Whoopee!" her first line in *The Wild Party*, the one word caused an electrical crew an hour of work, the producers an hour's delay and the studio the price of a set of delicate sound tubes. The sensitive electrical system could not stand the shock of Clara's IT. But that was not all.
>
> The picture is an all-talkie and there is much dialogue. Whenever Clara began dialoguing, the delicate little bulbs quivered and died. The operators tried to locate the trouble, but all they could do was to replace the bulbs.
>
> Each time Clara talked the same thing happened. Any of the others could talk indefinitely and nothing would happen. But the picture was made in spite of these difficulties. (Albert Boswell, "Trials of the Talkies," *Photoplay*, July 1929, p. 114)

This treatment makes it clear that it was not Bow's vocal quality that was the problem. It was her unbridled ebullience and, implicitly, her trademark sexual vitality that was shocking the electrical system.[43]

Unlike coverage in the fanzines, the trade reviewers did not reprove Bow's vocals. *Variety*'s review of THE WILD PARTY found that, "laughing, crying or condemning, [the] Bow voice won't command as much attention as the Bow this and that, yet it's a voice. Enough of a voice to insure general belief that Clara can speak as well as look—not as well, but enough.[44] Editor Kann confirmed in *Film Daily* that nothing was inherently wrong with her speech: "Clara Bow speaks just as you'd expect she would. Her voice is hard and metallic, but she does her usual wild stuff in a way to satisfy her fans." Mordaunt Hall felt that "Miss Bow's voice is better than the narrative. It is not over-melodious in delivery, but it suits her personality. Sometimes it is distinct and during some passages it isn't. It may fail on account of technical deficiencies in the recording device."[45] These comments (which continue to segregate the voice from the actor) suggest that Bow's

manner of speaking was not exceptionally good or bad. Rather, it was her sexuality and
libertine persona which constituted her appeal. Modern critics who have evaluated Bow's
talking performances conclude that "she was a capable and charming actress."[46]

Why, then, if her voice was not a serious problem, was she represented as a vocal failure in the fan magazines? *Before* her sound films, letters to *Photoplay* from young
female readers occasionally protested that her "wild" image was not representative of
modern youth. It seems likely that some fans were turning against her because they
could not condone her behavior offscreen, and the editors substituted her alleged speaking problem for her highly visible legal problems.

Bow's private life was much more frenzied than her screen persona. Though Paramount was able to cover up many of her shenanigans, word leaked out of her alleged
misbehavior through the popular press and the tabloid *Evening Graphic.* She threw
parties, suffered a nervous breakdown, and was victimized by professional gamblers.
She did not try to hide her drinking and sexual escapades. This behavior was not an
asset in an industry that was feeling the pinch of Production Code morality. Coinciding with the advent of the talkies was her involvement in two lurid scandals. She
settled out of court with the wife of a Dallas doctor who had sued for "alienation of
affections." Then her secretary and companion, Daisy De Voe, was discovered to have
been stealing from her, tried to blackmail her, and "told all" on the witness stand. The
trial was a tabloid circus. A book, *Clara's Secret Love Life,* made the rounds. Its
dramatis personae included Gary Cooper, Bela Lugosi, and the USC football team.
Under the stewardship of B. P. Shulberg, Bow made a few more pictures for Paramount. Like Mary Pickford, she did try to change her established image. DANGEROUS
CURVES (1929), released three months after THE WILD PARTY, cast her as an ingenue
instead of a flapper. Kann reacted:

> If there is one thing Clara can't do it is trying to be coy. She's just a red hot
> flaming little baby with a sex appeal all her own, and why they can't be sat-
> isfied to let her ride that way is more than we can understand. It's a safe bet
> that there'll be such a fan holler on this one, that they'll be glad to turn Clara
> back to the hotsy totsy and let her stay there for good. She's not enough of
> an actress to ever be anything else. Just a flaming personality—that's all. But
> that's enough." (*Film Daily,* 21 July 1929, p. 12)[47]

The accounts in the fan magazines often concealed as much as they revealed and thereby
took a mediating position between the studios and other sources, such as newspaper gossip columnists like Louella Parsons and the tabloids. The stories about Bow seem to have
been composed with the aim of reinterpreting the unpleasant stories appearing in the
mainstream and tabloid press. "Events might be alluded to long after their occurrence,"
Studlar observes, "but through a strategy of indirection that relied heavily upon the
reader's preexistent knowledge of events gleaned from *other* sources, not the [fan] magazines themselves."[48] Helen Morgan is a good example. She was arrested in 1928 for operating a speakeasy, but this scandal, which would have been known by devoted movie fans,
was suppressed in her comeback stories. One reason her film career did not take off after
APPLAUSE was that her drinking made her difficult to direct, but that information was
never discussed in the fanzines. The stories drafted for Betty Compson, Sessue
Hayakawa, Warner Baxter, and others also show the tendency to rewrite facts in favor of

fiction. The coverage of Clara Bow in these publications utilized a similarly allusive style, first blaming her voice and her exuberance. Once the scandals could not be ignored, these strategies were jettisoned. Instead, the star's indiscretions, not specifically identified, were addressed in a desperate appeal to the fan. Leonard Hall's discussion of Clara Bow's personal problems was startling in its implication of the reader:

> Clara faces a crisis, and we're all involved in some measure.
> She's a woman in years, now [she was twenty-five], and not a schoolgirl thrust into an unfamiliar spotlight.
> She can't continue to gallop off the reservation, and continue to delight us too. She's stretched out her arms for understanding and help and trust—as have thousands of the rest of us. If she's failed to find them—as have thousands of the rest of us at times—she must develop resources within herself, a spiritual fortress that can defend her against all the varied and cruel assaults of life and destiny. (Leonard Hall, "What About Clara Bow?" *Photoplay*, October 1930, p. 138)

Hall identifies what that "spiritual fortress" might be—a mate. "Tasting fame and money, she galloped away—and there has never been a firm and trusted hand on the reins." Like the story of the "fallen woman" of the movies, which Bow's story is here made to resemble, there was a moral lesson for the reader. Submitting to discipline (preferably from a strong spouse) would tame her. And fans had to support her (by writing fan mail and buying tickets to her movies). Thanks to an implied common bond, consumers and the fallen star were part of the same community. Movie fans had to bring "wild" Clara back into line.

John Gilbert. "Talking Pictures? Splendid!" John Gilbert reportedly "boomed" in 1928. The story of the matinee idol's giddy decline in popularity during the transition to sound is well known; indeed, it is one of Hollywood's most enduring legends. Fan magazine readers had consistently voted him the most popular male star through 1929. MGM's romantic leading man in THE BIG PARADE, FLESH AND THE DEVIL, and LOVE had his disastrous first encounter with sound in October 1929 when HIS GLORIOUS NIGHT was released. *Variety* ran the headline, "Audiences Laughing at Gilbert." Supposedly his high-register voice sounded unsuitable for a screen lover who previously had exuded passion and prowess with costars Renée Adorée, Joan Crawford, and Greta Garbo.

The canard that Gilbert had a squeaky voice has been disputed for years. Now that viewing copies of most of his ten talking films are available, we can hear a voice that is intelligible, appropriate for his physical stature, and, though affected, by no means abnormal. Colleen Moore described it as in "the middle register—the same register as that of Douglas Fairbanks and many other male stars."[49] The voice coach Peggy Wood, writing in mid-1929, seemed unaware of any of Gilbert's speech impediments. On the contrary, she held up the screen actor's recent marriage to the Broadway star Ina Claire as symbolic of the new hybrid form: "The best that the screen has, then, combined with the best the stage can offer, will make the perfect talking picture."[50]

The bad-voice theory has been more or less replaced by a conspiracy theory: Louis B. Mayer intentionally sabotaged Gilbert's career as a vendetta for a public humiliation at the wedding of King Vidor and Eleanor Boardman in 1926. Mayer also wanted to get back at Nicholas Schenck for signing Gilbert to a contract that would pay him $500,000 annually for five years. Mayer ardently tried to break it, the legend goes, by giving Gilbert bad parts and by assigning Lionel Barrymore to direct his talking debut in REDEMPTION and HIS GLORIOUS NIGHT. Barrymore disliked Gilbert personally and was an incompetent director, a toady for Mayer, and a morphine addict. Rather than applying techniques for curing Gilbert's vocal problem, Mayer, to ensure that it recorded in an unmanly high range, ordered the bass turned down during the actor's parts. Mayer ruined his star's career and symbolically emasculated the screen's leading ladies' man by feminizing his voice.[51]

Some snippets in the press suggest that, whether or not as part of a conspiracy, rumors concerning Gilbert's voice were circulating before the release of his first feature. Reviewing the untitled 1928 MGM short (see chapter 12), Mordaunt Hall praised the voices of George Arthur, Joan Crawford, Ernest Torrence, and Norma Shearer, but was noncommittal about Gilbert's. Jesse Lasky, in his April 1929 article on sound, was probably referring to Gilbert and Garbo when he wrote, "All sorts of dire prophecies were heard. . . . For example, Cyril So-and-so, the high-salaried idol of ten million girls, would have to be retired because he could not make the vocal grade; and the beautiful Annabel Gorgeous, the greatest box-office siren in history, would have to be dropped because she had a compound lisp." Having introduced the rumor, he then disclaimed it as nonsense. "I know of no film artist who had the appearance and the intelligence to make good in the silent pictures who cannot carry on now."[52] A line in Manners's July 1929 column said that of all the major stars, Gilbert had a voice that, being too juvenile and "boyish," was the least fitting to his personality.[53] The source of this information, unfortunately (but not surprisingly), was not revealed. Conspiracy theorists would suspect that the lead was a studio plant. These comments preceded the release of HIS GLORIOUS NIGHT but were contemporary with THE HOLLYWOOD REVUE OF 1929 and the troubled production of REDEMPTION, so it is possible that these conclusions could have been arrived at independent of studio involvement.

There is hearsay evidence that audiences were already dissatisfied with Gilbert's performance. Samuel Marx recalled that the producer Irving Thalberg had been alarmed by the "wrong kind" of laughs in two previews of THE HOLLYWOOD REVUE. He removed the segment in which Lionel Barrymore directs Gilbert and Shearer in the balcony scene from *Romeo and Juliet*—only to be overruled by Nicholas Schenck. This alleged reaction to the audience's laughing response is puzzling since the scene was played for comedy. Gilbert and Shearer begin the skit speaking "serious" Shakespeare. Shearer sounds properly theatrical; Gilbert sounds like he is concentrating on remembering the lines. His voice is mellow, though somewhat nasal. This out-of-character casting of the screen lover in a high-culture role in itself might have caused Gilbert's fans to squirm. But then Barrymore intervenes (scripted), and the actors ad-lib (apparently) in their everyday voices. Shearer seems to react with real surprise when Gilbert calls her "Auntie." She objects, and he replies, "But I call Irving 'Uncle.'" His voice sounds relaxed and unexceptional, but is there a hint of slurring? They replay the scene in "jazz" talk, and it ends with Gilbert saying, "I'm nuts about you," in pig-Latin (also obviously scripted). While not hysterically funny, there is enough mirth to counteract the tension of the Shakespearean section.[54]

Contrary to popular belief, HIS GLORIOUS NIGHT, Gilbert's second talkie and his first feature release as a star, was a modest box-office success. But technically it was very crudely made. Fountain describes one seven-minute continuous take: "The camera sees

[Gilbert and Catherine Dale Owen] from the waist up. They are glued in place by the position of the microphones. There is no action at all except for a few spasmodic hand gestures. They stand in front of a painted backdrop, and on two occasions studio workmen are clearly visible walking around behind the scenery. Jack seems painfully constrained."[55] Audiences did laugh.

> A few more talker productions like this and John Gilbert will be able to change places with Harry Langdon. His prowess at lovemaking, which has held the stenos breathless, takes on a comedy aspect in HIS GLORIOUS NIGHT. The gumchewers tittered at first and then laughed outright at the very false ring of the couple of dozen "I love you" phrases designed to climax, ante and post, the thrill in the Gilbert lines. (*Variety*, 9 October 1929)[56]

The crucial question is, Were they laughing at Gilbert's voice or something else about the film?

The answer is: both. The reviews of HIS GLORIOUS NIGHT can be described as damning Gilbert's voice with faint praise. Even the superficially laudatory comments always added a qualifier. Mordaunt Hall's is typical: "[Gilbert] is to be congratulated on the manner in which he handles this speaking role. His voice is pleasant, but not one which is rich in nuance. His performance is good, but it would benefit by the suggestion of a little more wit." Owen's enunciation, in contrast, was "clear and pleasing." *Variety* observed that "Gilbert presents a voice passable when it does not have to work into a crescendo."[57] Some of the comments assembled by Fountain refer to Gilbert's apparent voice training—for example, "He can speak the English language and speak it beautifully. His diction is faultless. Obvious training has been undergone, a little too much perhaps, as yet there is no warmth in the voice." Other reviewers also noted his lack of "warmth." This seems to have been a polite way of pointing out that his speech was stilted and emotionless, but those are problems of delivery, not of pitch. Kevin Brownlow has described Gilbert's speech as, ironically, too "good":

> Gilbert's voice [in HIS GLORIOUS NIGHT] sounded no different to the other talkies in which he appears. It was quite low. The television technicians who saw it with us said he could not have been incorrectly recorded without affecting the other players in the same scene.
>
> The direction, however was lamentable. Gilbert seemed tense and his eyes constantly stared at the girl during the love scenes. The script was appalling, and worse still was Gilbert's delivery. His enunciation of every line with the correct "pear-shaped" tones was what aroused the laughter. If only he had been encouraged to relax, and to abandon that dreadful enunciation! (Kevin Brownlow, "The Rise and Fall of John Gilbert," in *Hollywood: The Pioneers* [New York: Knopf, 1979], p. 193)

The *New York Review* expressed the consensus: "His voice is neither remarkable nor displeasing but it is not that which one would associate with the Great Lover of the screen."[58]

The one passage that everyone referred to occurred during Gilbert's scene of passion with Owen: "The sound recording [is] so cavernous, so unnatural and so unpleasant that what the characters have to say matters very little," opined the *New York Post*. "Mr.

Gilbert repeatedly says, 'I love you, I love you, I love you.' It's all a lot of play acting and I don't believe a word of it. The audience did not always find it possible to take seriously the laughably stilted and affected dialogue." The *Variety* reviewer felt he was watching "an over-stressed necking party made more pronounced by the dialogue." After the "I love you" scene, "the audience knows that another and still another hugging and talking laugh combo is to go on record before the princess marries our hero."[59] King Vidor and Colleen Moore, reflecting on this famous incident, agreed that the bad script was the culprit for generating uncomfortable tension among female viewers: "[The 'I love you's'] disconcerted and embarrassed all the women in the audience, those most ordinary but still most profound words that can be spoken between a man and a woman. In their embarrassment they giggled."[60] In fact, laughter was a frequent response to love scenes in sound films (and probably to similar scenes in the silents). Billie Dove in CAREERS elicited "derisive laughter at a moment when she is using an intense barrage of histrionics." Hall cited an incident with Norma Talmadge in DU BARRY, WOMAN OF PASSION (1930) that is remarkably similar to Gilbert's repetitive "I love you's": "Miss Talmadge . . . repeats 'I Love the King' so many times that one is apt to recall Ed Wynn's amusing line: 'I love the woods.'"[61] The *Graphic* described the reaction to Frank Borzage's THE RIVER (1929): "Mary Duncan, in the feminine lead, appeared in her second film special on Broadway. And for a second time a premiere audience, Saturday afternoon, laughed at her vampire pantomime, which should teach this actress that Garboing isn't as easy as it looks from an orchestra chair." *Variety* described Duncan's love scenes as "imperative giggle material" and reported on the audience's reaction: "Having so much smouldering sexiness, it is occasionally liable to laughter. They laughed at the Gaiety [in New York], although the laughter was not altogether clear in motive. Coming from the women mostly there may have been a factor of overflowing tension expressing itself in tittering."[62] One moviegoer, Ruth Ramsay of Petersburg, Illinois, testified (before Gilbert's film was released), "Some of the love scenes [in the talkies] aren't so effective when the actors are putting their emotions in words. This is especially true when the hero pleads with the heroine for her love. While she is deciding what the answer will be, we hear nothing but the whispering, coughing audience and the suspense is terrible."[63] Shuler wrote, "An old observation has it that nothing seems so silly to a man as another man's love-letters. But there is something sillier, it would seem; not only public, but audible, love-making. It appears to be the consensus of opinion that all love scenes should be silent—unless comedy is intended." So whatever shortcomings Gilbert's voice might have had, they were compounded by the screen writers' awkward intrusion of public lovemaking in the audience's private realm. Significantly, in Berlin audiences laughed at the same scene as played by Theo Shall in the Gilbert-less German-language version, OLYMPIA. "The [scenario] author wrote in an excessively banal seduction scene in which the words 'I love you' were used again and again, each time to the accompaniment of louder titters from the audience."[64]

How did the movie fan magazines respond to this sudden misfire by one of the top international stars? There are no references to Mayer conspiracies, kissing discomfort, or overall production quality. Instead, characteristically, the pages displace Gilbert's sudden loss of popularity into three areas: lack of control over his personal life, being a victim of corporate forces (as with Swanson), and having an infirmity to overcome (the need to improve his dialogue style).

The publications energetically played up the alleged love affair between Gilbert and Greta Garbo long after the embers had cooled. The offscreen romance undeniably ended on 10 May 1929, when he married Ina Claire ("of whom there is no whomer on Broadway," according to Manners). It is evident from published mail that this wedding disappointed many of his fans who wished the star-crossed romance with Garbo to resume. It was a case of star behavior running counter to fan desires. Besides, Claire was supposed to be a snob. When a reporter asked her how it felt to be married to a great star, she quipped, "I don't know. Why don't you ask Mr. Gilbert?"[65] Fan magazines portrayed her consistently as an interloper from Broadway who had caught Gilbert, seven years her junior, on the rebound. (Many of her putative character traits seem to have been inspired by her role in THE GOLD DIGGERS.) *Motion Picture Classic* announced that the actress had become incensed when Pathé asked her to make films under the name Mrs. John Gilbert. "But think of the fan mail, Ina!" Manners advised. "What it amounts to is that the fans had rather have a look at Jack Gilbert's new wife than all the Broadway glory in the world."[66] Another gossip author implied that Claire's motives were not romantic: "I don't know that I'd go so far as to say Ina Claire made suckers of Hollywood and its gals by walking altar-ward with our leading box-office attraction, but it's worth mentioning in passing."[67] Some fans who expressed animosity toward Gilbert sounded like jilted lovers. Violet Hopwood of Flushing, New York, wrote:

> Why do motion picture actors get married? It spoils all when you know that your favorite actor, John Gilbert, has married Ina Claire! Why say that actors have a right to get married as well as other people? Don't they know when they start in pictures that they have to dance to the tune the fans play and that they can't displease their public? I wish something would be done to stop them! ("Brickbats and Bouquets," *Photoplay*, October 1929, p. 146)

Gilbert's case was aired in *Photoplay* in February 1930, before the shelved REDEMPTION was released. Katherine Albert presented scenarios to explain Gilbert's failure and alluded to the voice problem:

> What about the voice of the man who is virile as a steel mill, lusty as Walt Whitman, romantic as a June moon? . . .
> You heard it in *His Glorious Night*. It is high-pitched, tense, almost piping at times.
> His friends have known for years that it was completely unsuited to the strength and fire of the man.
> Jack's great art is pantomime. . . . It was tremendous on the silent screen. He spoke through his eyes.
> But any singer will tell you that the voice is right only when the body is relaxed. The voice, to be convincing, must flow calmly.
> Gilbert was caught unprepared for the talkies. (Katherine Albert, "Is Jack Gilbert Through?" *Photoplay*, February 1930, p. 128)

The emphasis on Gilbert's virility nips in the bud any hints of impotence or homosexuality that a "sissy" voice might convey. Downplaying the bad-voice angle, Albert's article emphasized the business aspects of Gilbert's situation, but without saying whether her information came from the Gilbert or MGM camp. He had one of the most lucrative and protective contracts in the history of the industry. Dissatisfied with his lack of independence at MGM, he had decided to accept United Artists' generous offer when his MGM contract expired. This was during a crucial phase of William Fox and Nicholas Schenck's negotiations for the former to acquire Loew's/MGM. They decided that the value of the deal would be diminished with Gilbert at another studio and so gave him the contract of a lifetime. He was to make two pictures a year at $250,000 each. He would have approval of his stories, an enormous dressing-room bungalow, and—most impressive—no options which the studio could decline to renew. "The signing of the name John Gilbert to a little piece of paper was of utmost importance to a fifty million dollar deal. Jack was more or less a pawn. He didn't realize how vital he was to the financial gods."[68]

The real villain in the piece, Katherine Albert argued, was Claire, who "distracted" the star from his work.

> While other stars were trotting to elocution teachers and voice specialists, Gilbert was flying to an obscure town in Nevada and getting married to Ina Claire. . . . All during this time, sitting across from Jack at the breakfast table, was a woman who could have taught him every *nuance* of line delivery. Ina Claire could have taught him to speak. (Albert, "Is Jack Gilbert Through?," p. 128)

But, according to Albert, it was Gilbert's proud machismo which prevented him from taking advantage of Claire's expertise, something male readers should comprehend: "If you have ever tried to learn anything from your wife, anything that she knows better than you, you will understand." Gilbert and Claire had already separated by the time the article was written. Despite the unspecified treachery of the gold-digging Claire, now that she had "left the hilltop manor" of her husband, the author was confident that Gilbert's acoustic woes were over. "I cannot believe," she exuded, "that a man who has battled life single-handed, who has taken all the hard knocks right on the chin, will let a little thing like a talkie device down him."[69] Thus, like other talking-picture failures, Gilbert was victimized by external forces, not by his own weakness.

After HIS GLORIOUS NIGHT failed to excite fans, MGM offered to buy out Gilbert's contract for $500,000. *Photoplay* applauded Gilbert's rejection of the offer as evidence of his strong character: "Jack, magnificently brave and confident insisted on making pictures. 'I'll show them!' he said, and held M-G-M to the contract."[70] Thus, his inner strength was revealed. By then the trades were openly castigating Gilbert and his dramatic failure. *Film Daily* called REDEMPTION a

> decidedly mediocre drama of Russia. Weak in nearly every department including acting and directing. Adapted from Leo Tolstoy's drama, "The Living Corpse." John Gilbert's voice fails to register well. His performance, like that of Eleanor Boardman, is unconvincing. Conrad Nagel is the only principal player who seems real. A story of recognized dramatic value has been mistreated in its adaptation and the editing job had made it a great deal worse. As it runs now it's choppy, episodic, lacks movement and attention-compelling elements. Fred Niblo is billed as the director. It is difficult to associate this incompetent piece of work with him. The plot concerns a young wastrel who marries his pal's fiancee. He dissipates his fortune and they separate, although still loving each other. He fakes suicide, his "widow" marries her old sweetheart and finally he actually kills himself to clear the way for the girl's happiness. (*Film Daily*, 4 May 1930, p. 11)

REDEMPTION *(MGM, 1930), with Renée Adorée and John Gilbert.*

Variety had no comment on the voices but predicted that when the film was released, "Gilbert will be the chief sufferer and Fred Niblo will not go unharmed in reputation."[71] Listening to Gilbert in REDEMPTION gives the impression that he is trying to speak in someone else's voice. He sounds for all the world like he is giving a bad imitation of Lionel Barrymore. (But then, so does his costar Renée Adorée.) One section is very similar to the balcony scene in THE HOLLYWOOD REVUE, with Gilbert reciting to Adorée. Taking care to speak in Shakespearean stage English (despite being a Russian), he pronounces *heart* emphatically as *hot* and repeats "tomorrow!" several times. The overall effect is very studied and declamatory.

Variety's review of WAY FOR A SAILOR specifically acknowledged the rumors about Gilbert's voice: the movie "throws John Gilbert for a loss instead of advancing him back in the talkers to the place he held in the silents. And it's not his fault. His voice is okay. Star is miscast and film seems cut to ribbons."[72]

Unlike the trade journal reviews, which indicted the overall bad quality of his films, the fan magazine accounts of Gilbert's deterioration, like those about Bow, were based on his failure to keep his voice *under control*. It is clear that the "voice" is standing in for larger issues. While their manner of speaking was not perfect, the fan magazines emphasized that Gilbert and Bow both came to ruin because of a lack of self-discipline. Gilbert's career was also sidetracked by his fling with Claire and by conniving executives, but mainly he failed by not applying himself to his craft.

How does this jibe with what we know about his real career? John Gilbert was a "difficult" actor. Fueled by alcoholism, he became an unpredictably belligerent, gun-wielding menace to those around him at home and on the set. He may well have been a pawn in the MGM power struggle between Louis B. Mayer and Nicholas Schenck, but Gilbert had ambitions of his own. It was widely known that he aspired to direct and write. In July 1927, he told an interviewer from the *Los Angeles Times* that he might quit films for five, ten, even fifteen years. He dreamed of forming his own company and making pictures to suit himself: "The star is quoted as saying he 'is not on speaking terms with his employers,' because of dissatisfaction over stories." The next day, Gilbert claimed he was misquoted.[73]

Gilbert's discontent surfaced again a year later. He published a serialized story in *Photoplay* (June–September 1928) based on his early career. This might have been a gambit for establishing his writing credentials. Quirk attested to the star's genuine authorship of the piece, and to his literary ability:

> It is interesting to note that Gilbert's ambition is to be a writer. He realizes that a star's career is short-lived—two or more years—with luck, five. With oblivion, perhaps, lurking just beyond. I would not be at all surprised if in ten years he would turn out to be a successful novelist, his closeups long forgotten.
>
> Stranger things have happened. (James R. Quirk, "Close-ups and Longshots," *Photoplay*, September 1928, p. 30)

This came during Gilbert's renegotiation of his MGM contract, so perhaps it was posturing. But the references to "oblivion" and "forgotten close-ups" suggest that someone—Quirk on behalf of Gilbert perhaps—was contemplating alternative careers for the star at the time when MGM was making its first sound film tests.

The cases of Morgan, Bow, and Gilbert demonstrate how the "voice problem" could serve everyone's interests by diverting the attention of readers away from scandal, alcoholism, bad judgment, a lack of commitment to work, and a desire for too much independence as a worker. These shortcomings were inconsistent with the mission of the movies fostered by the fanzine editors, the studio public relations teams, and the Hays Office. If, instead, the troubled performer could be represented as a victim, then his or her star quality could be prolonged and the Hollywood institution might be saved from embarrassment. The studio would salvage its investment, the fan magazine's readers would continue to follow these ups and downs, and even the star benefited if his or her personal difficulties were displaced onto outside forces, thus gaining sympathy, not condemnation. In short, the "voice problem" scenario worked well as a cover-up.

In addition to the professional and personal problems Gilbert and Bow were having, their silent film personae, the consummate lover and the flaming youth, were growing out of sync with audiences' changing expectations. These screen characters were fictions cultivated by Hollywood producers and technicians, fan magazines, and fans themselves—in the audience, in the lobby, on the telephone, in the beauty parlor, and on the job. The new image of the ideal male lover matched the voices of John Boles, Ronald Colman, William Powell, Gary Cooper, and soon, Clark Gable. Gilbert's voice was judged not to fit the visual model he had created, and his writers and directors (perhaps at his insistence) placed him in old-fashioned dramatic scenes which brought out his worst acting tendencies. Clara Bow's "flaming" exploits were no longer condoned after the quick passing of the flapper fad. Claudette Colbert, Marlene Dietrich, Norma

Shearer, Marie Dressler, and Greta Garbo, portraying "adult" women who spoke in "serious" language, were setting the new standards.

While the fanzines were speaking *for* an audience, they were also speaking *to* that audience, providing object lessons with the aim of proscribing behavior for the young fan. She needed (like Clara Bow and John Gilbert) discipline and a strong hand on the reins. Whether the consumers of these magazines accepted this implicit moral guidance is impossible to say.

Voice-Doubling

One of the earliest references to the talkies in *Motion Picture Classic* was a 1926 cartoon by Ken Chamberlain showing a muscular leading man whose voice is being "doubled" by a beefy speaker behind a curtain. The caption reads: "Warner Brothers' new Vitaphone, that records the actor's voice as the camera records the action, might be a bit disillusioning. For instance, some actors who play he-men rôles have anything but he-men voices. We suggest that Billy Evans or Hank O'Day or some other big league umpire be used to double for the voice in such cases."[74] This joke predicts the main controversy in the fan magazines in the early years of the talkies, the debate surrounding voice doubling, or using one actor's offscreen voice to substitute for another's in the recording session. The cartoon encapsulates several motifs in the "story" of the talkies. In the sound motion picture, the actor's voice is separate from his or her physical body and therefore interchangeable with the voices of other actors; the male voice denotes sexual prowess and masculinity; alternative labor (the double) can stand in for the actors being photographed; and cinematic illusionism easily tricks the spectator. Perhaps better than any other issue, voice-doubling demonstrates the rapidly changing conception of the voice from autonomous to integrated status. The practice also raised the stakes in the game of who controlled the screen voice.

Doubling had been used practically from the beginning of the talkies. Al Jolson's piano playing in THE JAZZ SINGER was performed by Bert Fiske off-camera. Cantor Josef Rosenblatt was dubbed for Warner Oland and Jolson. Though apparently common, these practices were not publicized. It was the Barthelmess scandal that raised the public's consciousness.

In January 1929, First National launched an advertising campaign for Richard Barthelmess in WEARY RIVER. He was one of the most popular and highly paid stars of the decade and had been nominated as best actor in the 1927–1928 Academy Awards. The advertisements claimed: "It's worth the money just to hear him talking and playing for the first time," and, "You'll enjoy two great stars in one when you see and hear Richard Barthelmess talking and playing in *Weary River.*" The audience's appetite was further whetted by the prevue trailer. Costar William Holden says to Barthelmess, "You know, I—I really believe that the audience out in front would like to hear you sing 'Weary River.' Wouldn't you? Eh?" asks Holden, turning to the camera and pretending to speak directly to the theater audience. Barthelmess replies, "You know, if they come to see the picture, they'll hear the song." As it turned out, the two-voices-in-one-star claim was literally true. Audiences heard the song, but Barthelmess did not sing it. The feat was accomplished by an off-camera singing double whose sounds matched Barthelmess's lip movements well, but not perfectly. Shuler pointed out to his *Classic* readers that the star's mouth moved but not his throat. According to *Photoplay*, the public "made a sound like a moribund raspberry."[75] The fanzines exposed Johnny Murray, a cornetist at the Coconut Grove nightclub whom First National had hired to sing as Barthelmess's permanent voice-double. Frank Churchill, not the star, played the piano. This news led to other revelations. *Photoplay's* Larkin revealed doubles for Corinne Griffith's operatic singing and harp playing in THE DIVINE LADY, and Laura La Plante's banjo plucking and spiritual singing in SHOW BOAT. The singer Lawford Davidson received $500 per week substituting his voice for Paul Lukas's, which was "handicapped for American pictures by a foreign accent." Margaret Livingston's dubbed voice replaced that of Louise Brooks in THE CANARY MURDER CASE. In a typical fanzine formulation designed to induce empathy, the reader learned how embarrassed she was at a chance encounter with Brooks in a restaurant.

The columnist Harry Lang illustrated a description of doubling a chorus scene with a joke:

> The cameras are trained on the beautiful chorus girls, who dance and move their lips just like Dick Barthelmess did. But they are as silent as a bill collector isn't. And down below the camera-range, or at one side, are the microphones—in front of a dozen or so lovely-voiced creatures whose loveliness often ends there.
>   "Yes, dearie; I've got a job in the pictures."
>   "You! With that pan?"
>   "No, dearie—do-re-mi-fa-sol! . . . With this VOICE! (Lang, "The Microphone—The Terror of the Studios," p. 126)

Lang alerted readers to the illusionistic combination of different voices and bodies in the talkies and tacitly promoted the notion that an actor's screen face and voice might be incompatible.

Larkin said that, "of course, every effort is made on the part of producers to guard the secret of doubling. Picture-makers feel that it spoils the illusion, that it hurts a production's box office appeal."[76] Shuler claimed that doubling would not be objectionable if the actors could pantomime it better. Appearing out-of-sync "punctures the conviction of the realness of the scene. It's bad art and bad entertainment."[77] These responses assume that the star voice was a valuable draw in its own right, that fans would want to hear their favorite performers speaking and singing in their "natural" voices, not some unknown, invisible impersonator. However, there was disagreement on this point.

The fan mail reprinted in the magazines suggests that, unlike the columnists, many viewers seemed quite willing to accept doubling simply as a component of Hollywood's trickery, not as false advertising or malicious deceit. Nina Sutton of Huntington Park, California, responded to Larkin:

> These screen people have been very satisfactory as to acting ability, so does it matter that they have doubles do their singing and playing? . . . It seems to me the most wonderful progress in the picture industry when we can see the beauty of face and form of old friends, combined with the beauty of voice we like to think theirs. After all, movies are all the romance the majority of us get out of life, so why not let the actors remain ideal in our hearts and minds? Even though the stage voice is behind the scenes, let us con-

tinue to look upon the loveliness of the screen stars. ("Brickbats and Bouquets," *Photoplay*, November 1929, p. 146)

This reader welcomed doubling because she preferred a voice that "matched" the imagined one, even if it was not the star's own voice. Voice-doubling was analogous to the practice of special effects or makeup. Because Hollywood could use technology to craft illusion, there was nothing wrong with exploiting that capability to its fullest.

The case of Lon Chaney shows even more explicitly that, for many fans, preserving the charisma of stardom counted more than enunciatory excellence. He was celebrated for his Gothic character impersonations and hideous makeup appliances. But the actor had announced that he would not speak on screen or radio. This prompted L.J.N., a *Photoplay* reader from Tulsa, to remark that Chaney was hampered by his voice: "Lon Chaney may be 'The Man of a Thousand Faces,' but with Movietone he is merely the man of one voice." Another letter writer, Esther Ford of Pittsburgh, jumped to Chaney's defense by suggesting voice-doubling:

> If he had only one voice, that would not make him lose his appeal. He could speak with an accent, lisp, or in a sing-song way. He could even have other men (and perhaps women) voice-double for him. That would give him more than one voice. There, L.J.N., you see he would be the man of more than one voice.
>
> But before he tries any of those, I sincerely hope he speaks via the talkies with his natural voice. Lon Chaney is my favorite actor and it would be the thrill of thrills to hear his voice. I'm for talkies—especially when they bring me his voice—WHEN. ("Brickbats and Bouquets," *Photoplay*, September 1929, p. 141)

Chaney's case points out how readily the screen voice was accepted as a surplus, an add-on, not unlike an extra layer of makeup or a new character role. The gist of the doubling debate was that actors possessed two or more "voices." They had their natural way of speaking, which might be unsuited for recording, and they had their professional voice, which was tailored to the needs of sound recording to fit their physical appearance and screen character. This second, constructed voice was not the actor's property. Though the studio owned the rights to it, the magazines cultivated the impression that the fans could impose their own normative demands on it.

The split between conceptions of the actor as a "real person" and as a "star" has always been part of the Hollywood star system. From around late 1928 through 1930, sound in general and voice-doubling in particular amplified this critical concern for the general press and fans alike. In the early days of the transition, during the period when the voice was considered autonomous, if a star's natural voice was unsuitable, then, instead of changing stars, it was felt that the voice should be changed. If it could not be "trained," then it was better to bring in the double. While actors' contracts explicitly gave legal control of their voice to the studio, Actors Equity was fighting to at least require the performer's consent to substitute voice-doubles. *Photoplay* sided with the studios. There was "little reason for established players to feel like self-conscious children over their bad tonsils or adenoids. It may not be necessary to operate; and, indeed, where it is, the thing may not be nearly so bad as its anticipation."[78]

STATE OF CALIFORNIA)ss
COUNTY OF LOS ANGELES)

      COLLEEN MOORE, the undersigned, first being duly sworn, deposeth and says:

      That in all talking pictures in which I have appeared, namely, "SMILING IRISH EYES" and "FOOTLIGHTS AND FOOLS", all scenes and sequences purporting to present recordations and reproductions of my speaking or singing voice, are actual recordations and reproductions of my voice; and that at no place in said talking pictures has a "double" or substitute been used for my voice.

                                                 _____
                                            (Colleen Moore)

      Subscribed and sworn to before me this fifteenth day of July, 1929.

                                          Notary Public, in and for
                                          the State of California,
                                          County of Los Angeles.

Colleen Moore published a sworn statement in Photoplay *attesting that the voice heard in* FOOTLIGHTS AND FOOLS *(First National, 1929) was her own.*

As dialogue became the norm, the emphasis in both the fanzines and the critical press switched from debating the proprietary rights of speech to judging the "naturalness" of the voice. The actual voice was now inseparable from the performer's screen personality, so doubling could no longer be used. The issue of foreign accents shows the rapidly changing attitude toward the practice and, again, parallels that of the critics. The editors of *Motion Picture* observed in mid-1929 that, for producers who had risked investing in foreign actors "who neither can sing nor speak presentably no matter how they may study and practise [*sic*]," doubling was standard practice.[79] But John J. Goodman of Los Angeles, a fan writing a year later, insisted that acting and speaking were irreducible components of a star's screen image:

> Check up on the recent talkie successes, and in the majority of cases you remember the acting and the actor. Together they make the voice. Now and then there's an exception—you recall the voice also—as Greta Garbo in *Anna Christie.* Her voice lingers because it is such a natural part of her—not the studied P's and Q's of the elocution schools. (*Motion Picture Classic*, July 1930, p. 104)

In the early days of sound, the voice had been a variable, the fitness and quality of which were readily disputed. After a while fans redefined their expectation: the speaking voice was to be an integral part of the actor.

As the voice-doubling issue illustrated, fan magazines provided viewers an outlet for expressing their opinions to their fellow fans, thus creating a feeling of solidarity and a community of film lovers. The magazine editors claimed that readers influenced stars and studios. But how real was this power to influence the status of the voice and the industry's use of sound?

Fan columnists went out of their way to address their readers directly: "The audience—which means you." The implied reader was active, but was Hollywood listening to the voices of this readership? Occasionally there were published acknowledgments that the influence of the fanzines was not all that the editors claimed. Vivian Kappner of Puyallup, Washington, lamented that her local theater did not play the recommended films: "Nine times out of ten, they show pictures that *Photoplay* warns us about. If they can't give good movies when they have the Vitaphone, then I suggest they leave the Vitaphone out."[80] Behind this complaint lurks economic reality. As film exhibition veered toward oligopolist chains during this period, neither the fans nor, increasingly, the exhibitors had direct control over which movies were presented, the transition to sound, or any other aspect of the film industry. Dorothy Manners's 1929 interview with Schulberg suggests that, in the eyes of the fanzine writer, the Paramount executive had little comprehension of what fans wanted.[81] Feisty Welford Beaton described a similar encounter in 1928, before the ERPI agreements had been signed:

> I am in a combatative mood about speaking pictures because I just have left the office of a producer who proved conclusively that such screen entertainment never would be popular, and who urged me not to advance a contrary view, because it would give my readers the idea that I am an impractical dreamer. The silly ass! I suppose that if he had been toddling about when Bell invented the telephone he would have produced proof that the public would never accept it. It is possible to tell stories on the screen better with

voices than without them, and to declare that the public never will demand the best is to combat all the history of human achievement. If I were a producer I would give sound devices my major attention and I would develop artists who can talk and directors who know color, for if there be anything certain about the future of pictures it is that in two years or less we will be making talking pictures in color and that no others will be shown in the big houses. (Welford Beaton, "Marks the Inevitable Progress of Pictures," *Film Spectator,* 4 February 1928, p. 7)

Industry gadflies like Beaton, *Harrison Reports,* and establishment critics offered responses to Hollywood. But direct communication between audiences and the producers was limited to impressionistic reports from "the field." The fan magazines provided their subscribers with an important forum for venting their opinions in the hopes of influencing film production. It was a voice. The fan magazines' reactions to sound shows that audience opinions about sound and about talking stars were too fragmented to guide producers toward or away from a distinctly fan-articulated policy. Producers paid some attention to fan magazines but may not have regarded the information in them as useful or valid, either because it was so inconsistent or because they put little merit in the opinions of the assumed authors, young females. In a television context, Ien Ang has asserted that media institutions

are generally not interested in getting to know what real people think and feel and do in their everyday dealings with television. Indeed, institutional knowledge about the television audience inevitably abstracts from the messy and confusing social world of actual audiences because this world is irritating for the institutions, whose first and foremost concern is to seize control over their own conditions of existence. (Ien Ang, *Desperately Seeking the Audience* [New York: Routledge, 1991], p. 7)

Analogously, B. P. Schulberg and Beaton's unnamed executive probably cared little about the specific involvement of fans, except for its impact on operations. They did, however, have a tangible interest in keeping up with large-scale trends that would affect the bottom line, such as a star's popularity. Understanding the pulse of the public was one way to forestall and blunt the effects of problems like scandals, and here the fan magazines were probably valuable as indicators of shifting star value.

Producers, studios, and distributors became stronger by using sound to wrest control from local managers, thereby increasing their regulation of the viewing experience. The switch to the talkies also granted the studios more authority over actors by allowing them to institute voice tests, impose restrictive contract clauses concerning speech, and threaten careers by bringing in Broadway "replacements." Doubling gave Hollywood the power to develop face and voice as separately exploitable entities. Fan response, however, had the potential of diminishing this power. By making or breaking stars, discriminating among film genres, and—the worst possible scenario—rejecting sound altogether, fandom (like unmanageable stars or independent theaters) was an economic necessity, but also a potential threat.[82]

Stars were used by fan magazines to tell the story of the transition to sound. The performers were the subjects of narratives which blended the fictional and the real, which illustrated how the talkies impinged on their personal lives. Fans' opinions were diverse, but the solidarity of fandom generated a *feeling* of participation and power over what came from the screen. As Studlar has observed, "Fan magazine readership may have given women the sense of a privileged status in reading the film text through their understanding of a 'truth' not immediately revealed on screen, beyond mere sight and visual representation."[83]

Despite the effort to promote the magazines' antagonism toward the studios, ultimately fans and Hollywood shared the same goal: to maximize cinematic pleasure for the greatest number of people. Perhaps the lack of a unified fan response explains why a cultural divide appeared in Hollywood's productions during this period. The range of film material—from international opera to girlie shows, from Westerns to ethnic comedy—can be read as an effort to address diversified viewers. Pretentious stage play adaptations like Gilbert's first talkies were aimed at a market presumed to be older, urban, better educated, and more economically upscale than the younger, rural, less-educated types who patronized William Boyd's action films or Clara Bow's flapper exploits. Hollywood's product diversification was its response to a "movie crazy" but fragmented and unknown audience. Though the actual influence of fandom on Hollywood production is not known, the fan magazines capitalized (perhaps in collusion with the studios) on the consumers' wish to control the use of sound and to fashion the talkies according to their own ideals.

20

Buying Broadway: THE JAZZ SINGER'S *Reception*

*The moving pictures are such a mixture of secret manoeuvres and false
publicity that right before your eyes an event slips into a legend out of
which is it hard to disengage a germ of truth.*

GILBERT SELDES, *Movies for the Millions,* 1937

The film that emblematizes the birth of the talkies is THE JAZZ SINGER. Jolson's blackened face, tear-jerking performance, and unabashed vocal gusto are understood to signal the end of Hollywood's silence. The 1927 film enjoys this stature not only in popular opinion but in academic discourse. An insightful article about THE JAZZ SINGER, for example, has described the musical "as a summation of those various elements which came to distinguish the musical genre." The film was an event (in Foucault's use of the term), "since it firmly established a new and promising direction in which movie narrative might turn." This scholar follows most sources in assuming that THE JAZZ SINGER was an enormous Broadway hit and that movie producers, having been burned by promoters of sound systems too often, were skeptical of its success and slow to convert to sound "despite the testimony of its box office returns."[1] But how do we know how overwhelming its profits were or what its effect on Hollywood was? Why did audiences respond with such fervor?

The research detailed in this book should make us question claims about a single film or "event" being responsible for any major change in Hollywood. But the case of THE JAZZ SINGER bears closer scrutiny because its reputation as a catalyst for the coming of sound has rested unchallenged to such a remarkable extent.

In order to check the validity of these claims concerning THE JAZZ SINGER, should we not simply read the contemporary descriptions of its Broadway premiere? Trying to reconstruct the original exhibition context has become an important method for theorizing about the reception of films. Researchers might assume that authors in the popular press speak on behalf of real audiences. Retrieving these primary documents is a welcome departure from accounts that ignore viewer-listeners altogether or, paraphrasing Janet Staiger, preconstitute their identity. The implication is that fanzine writers, trade commentators, reviewers, and mass-circulation journalists are the voice of their readers and that their writing stands in for viewers without voices. The interpretations of a few commentators become the index of the film's general reception. But to

Columbia belts Times Square with a great fist in a 1931 advertisement.

what degree can we be confident that journalists (including trade writers) represent other viewers? Or that they report the facts accurately?

The problem is, of course, that we know very little about the composition of audiences—even current ones—despite the expenditure of enormous sums by studios, investors, and networks on demographic research. As we go further back in time, evidence of original reception becomes more precious. So media analysis as a tool for understanding audiences becomes more pervasive and perhaps, as the case of THE JAZZ SINGER shows, more risky.

Our modern attitude about Jolson's film has been commonly held almost since the time of the film's release. Early published accounts of THE JAZZ SINGER's New York premiere tell of its sparkling critical triumph and its smashing unexpected success at the Broadway box office. The questions for us are, When and how was the film's status reported in the press? How accurate are the stories of the film's initial success measured against contemporary silent and sound films? And can we corroborate the stories by checking available box-office data?

Media Analysis

When we look for reports of THE JAZZ SINGER's first-night success, we immediately encounter a problem. The trade journals and major New York papers ignored the opening (although they all reported the death of Sam Warner). It was only months later that reports began to appear describing the film as a breakthrough, turn-around motion picture for Warner Bros. Curiously, the authors tended to repeat themselves in trying to express the film's importance. For example, the influential monthly *American Mercury* published in May 1928 an account of the film's accomplishment:

> Al Jolson made his appearance in *The Jazz Singer*, singing both "Mammy" and the Kol Nidre, beside conversing with his Ghetto Mamma. The celebrated Irving Berlin wept at this première and other hard-hearted gentlemen of Broadway admitted that Mr. Jolson was never better. The film coined money. At the time it was released, there were but 400 theatres wired with the talking film apparatus. It went into everyone of them and broke record after record. In New York, Chicago, Boston, Baltimore, Kansas City, and Los Angeles, it entertained the public for week after week. (Robert F. Sisk, "The Movies Try to Talk," *American Mercury*, August 1928, pp. 492–93)

This article's narrative of the premiere and its statistics were echoed in December:

> After a few of these [synchronized sound effects] feelers they [Warners] produced their great *coup*, *The Jazz Singer*, which starred Al Jolson, and which is credited with having been the biggest box office success released in 1927, even though less than four hundred theatres were then wired for sound. It was at that point that the other producers began to scratch their heads and wonder. (Helena Huntington Smith, "The Movies Speak Out," *Outlook and Independent*, 5 December 1928, p. 1270)

Another persistent story was that Jolson had aided Warner Bros. by deferring his salary:

> At the Motion Picture Club, on Broadway, which is the clearing house for news and gossip about the business, it is generally agreed that Al Jolson's picture, *The Jazz Singer*, was the turning point for sound pictures. . . .
>
> [The Warners] admitted that they didn't have enough money to pay [Jolson] what they thought he would demand, but the story was his story and he said, "I'll go out to Hollywood and see what comes of it."
>
> There are tales to the effect that during the making of the picture the Warners were so low in funds that Jolson did not draw all of his salary until weeks later. Some say that he even loaned them money to pay the other actors. So interested was he in the production that he was determined that it should be finished if he had to pay for it himself. . . .
>
> *The Jazz Singer* opened in New York, and at eleven o'clock that night the leaders of the motion picture industry, who stood cheering in the theater, knew that their business had been turned upside down. All the leaders were there. (Jerome Beatty, "The Sound Investment," *Saturday Evening Post*, 9 March 1929, p. 129)

A few months later the anecdote was retold: "As the story goes, Mr. Jolson, in his sentimental interest in the tale, even made unprecedented concessions in his price."[2] Robert L. Carringer has documented other versions of the legend of Jolson's concessions. Yet the contract with Warner Bros. is unambiguous. Jolson's pay was $75,000, to be disbursed in installments. (We assume that these terms were adhered to.) By ascribing their information to preexisting narrative forms (citing it as a "tale" and a "story"), these articles implicitly acknowledge that they are circulating fictions. Perhaps this language was believed to provide a mantle of libel protection, but it also functioned to aggrandize Jolson's stardom and the Warner brothers' business acumen.

In April 1929, Robert MacAlarney wrote:

> That October . . . [Jolson] had hoisted the infant talkie upon his blackamoor shoulder and waded across a stream every pioneer must ford. In Julius Caesar's day they called it Rubicon.
> Theater records were broken by *The Jazz Singer.* Towns where a release was doing excellent business if it ran for three days held a print for weeks. (Robert E. MacAlarney, "The Noise Movie Revolution," *World's Work,* April 1929, p. 50)

Crossing the Rubicon must have been an appealing figure of speech. Whether a coincidence or inspired by a common, as yet unidentified source, another author wrote of Jolson's first talking part:

> It wasn't much. A mere "bit"—and the picture was rolling on in its silent, sentimental way. But, to forty million movie fans, that act of Al Jolson's—his crossing the room to get at his piano—was a more important historical event than Caesar's crossing of the Rubicon. It meant that the screen had shaken off the shackles of silence. (Frederick L. Collins, "Now They Talk for Themselves," *Delineator,* April 1929, p. 21)

These articles retroactively transformed the release of THE JAZZ SINGER into a cultural, industry, and personal monument. They were not timely reports but fabrications of what happened after the fact. We can point to these elements in the journalistic construction of the film's reputation: spoken dialogue was a novelty; film executives in the audience were immediately convinced of the profitability of sound production; THE JAZZ SINGER played in all the theaters then wired; it was the big hit of 1927 and made huge sums for Warners; and Al Jolson had risked his personal funds in the film's financing.

For one thing, the repetitious tendency in the accounts suggests that the authors were either borrowing from each other—by no means an uncommon practice—or had been inspired by the same sources. Those sources might have been the journalists' rumor mills or an institutionalized source of information, such as press releases from Warner Bros.[3]

Even if we had an accurate figure for the number of people who attended the film, we still would not know who they were. Many assumptions about audiences are based on the geographical location of theaters. But in a country that takes pride in its mobility, we should not assume a demographic correlation between a theater and its locale. In fact, common sense suggests a rule of thumb: the larger the metropolitan region, the greater the diversity of the total audience. Nothing illustrates this better than Broadway. In the 1920s, the Broadway–Times Square theater district attracted a spectrum of customers ranging from upper- and middle-class patrons of the legitimate stage to itinerant moviegoers. Besides the locals, films drew tourists and businessmen from all over the country as well as military personnel.

Because of their diversity, it is risky to infer why audiences attended certain films, what they thought, or whether their reaction in the theater was uniform. Even if there were some corroboration between audience reaction and geography, the results would probably be valid for only one theater at a time. Analysts would expect significant variations in responses by time of day, day of the week, and length into the run. A film that plays well in New York might do poorly in another city, and vice versa.

Audienceship is an indeterminate activity. The film being projected was not necessarily a film attendee's main motivation for going to the movies; financial, social, and other pressures, as well as constantly changing tastes in entertainment, were also at work. Other attractions were the presentation acts, the architecture, the opportunity for romantic encounters, and the desire to enjoy leisure time by just hanging out. Cinemagoing was also an adjunct to shopping, which was facilitated by the architecture of movie palaces: arcade shops were usually incorporated into the same building—distant ancestors of today's malls.

So we should be skeptical of reports about the nature of audiences of the 1920s. Still, some empirical data about movie attendance tests the claims about what happened during the initial Broadway run of THE JAZZ SINGER.

Box-Office Analysis

The audience votes with its feet. This aphorism of stage and screen managers translates into a formula that seemingly should equate attendance with audience appreciation of a film. But the number of people going to a film tells us nothing about how they perceived its meaning or whether they even liked it. Attendance is notoriously fickle. It is affected by such factors as the appeal and penetration of the promotional campaign, the popularity of stars, and the popularity of the literary source of the story. If a film is exceptionally good or bad entertainment, then word-of-mouth advertising may be an influence. External factors also affect attendance: the opening of a strong film in a competing theater may take customers away. Other variables include transportation disruptions, the weather, and the season (moviegoing peaks during the week before Christmas).

To further complicate our analysis of THE JAZZ SINGER, attendance figures were not published at the time, only the weekly gross receipts. These might have combined two features. Houses were "scaled," that is, admissions varied according to the time of day, the place in the theater, and the age of the patron, making it difficult to estimate attendance based on the weekly gross. Certainly we can tell the hits from the flops, but using the box office as a subtle barometer of popularity has only limited usefulness. Accepting these inherent limitations, the box-office gross receipts nevertheless may be the best way to judge how many viewers attended films in the 1920s.

Even if detailed box-office records were preserved in archives, the numbers would not be totally reliable. "Hollywood accounting" practices applied to the exhibition as well as to the production end of the business. Fox, in particular, was frequently accused of padding its grosses. *Harrison's Reports,* a film rating service for independent exhibitors, warned clients that they were "at the mercy of the producer-distributors' representatives, who will no doubt present you with fictitious figures, such figures being what their Home Office will have furnished them."[4] Distributors also doubted exhibitors and resorted to audits, numbered tickets, and field observers ("checkers") to monitor their managers' honesty. The actual figures were guarded as business secrets and were probably known accurately to only a few financial insiders. Though the theaters' announced revenue must be taken with a grain of salt, it is the best available way of directly measuring a real, not hypothetical, audience.

The data in my study are *Variety's* copyrighted weekly box-office reports published for each preceding week. They were purported to be unbiased but were also clearly identified as unaudited, rounded estimates. Since the weekly receipts were transmitted by managers, the reports may have been adjusted to suit the house's own needs. Occasionally the *Variety* editor would note that the figure supplied was "generous," suggesting that his visual observations were out of line with the income reported by the management.

Because the box-office gross was an estimation, several factors may have influenced its accuracy. For example, as a run extended, the producers regularly handed out free passes in order to augment the audience. These viewers are just as important as the paying audience, of course, but their presence distorts the estimate of gross, since the producer was in effect paying for these customers in order to enhance the illusion of a competitive film. In addition, theatrical agencies sold tickets to the most popular films. There was also a thriving scalpers' market. These "ticket specs," as they were then called, resold tickets at a premium to sold-out performances. So it is difficult to know how, if at all, these non-box-office receipts were figured into the gross numbers. Finally, the published figures do not show whether the distributor made or lost money, since they do not take into account the "nut," the allowance for theater overhead and advertising expenses.

Caveats aside, by any estimation THE JAZZ SINGER was a hit. But was it the monumental success of its journalistic legend? Not quite. A comparison to the New York market shows that the film was by no means the most flourishing movie in terms of either gross or length of run.

Graph 20.1 slices four representative weeks from the 1927 run of THE JAZZ SINGER. It shows gross weekly receipts from near its opening (the two weeks ending 15 October) and from its tenth and eleventh weeks (ending 17 December). The averaged receipts of the Warners' Theatre were in the middle ranking of Broadway's fourteen important movie houses. But notice how the theater district was dominated by the three huge pictures palaces: the new Roxy (6,250 seats), the Capitol (5,450), and the Paramount (4,000). What were the popular movies competing with Warners' new sound film? In fact, they were low-budget, forgettable "programmers." The big houses drew customers seeking not only a movie but a complete entertainment experience, including the ambience of the theater, the social atmosphere, and the live stage presentations.

The summer and fall of 1927 was an especially significant period because the popularity of jazz music was just beginning to be reflected at the theaters. The Roxy had switched to a "jazz policy" shortly before THE JAZZ SINGER opened. Other theaters that had newly adopted such a policy were reporting markedly increased attendance, presumably by jazz fanatics who came for the live performances. Al Jolson was by far the most popular jazz vocalist. His chief rival as a theatrical stage act was Paul Whiteman's jazz band.

At the Warners', of course, there was no "presentation." The Vitaphone substituted virtual Broadway for these performances. *Variety's* box-office review for the week which included THE JAZZ SINGER's premiere is revealing. It was not Thursday's new talkie that the publication hailed, but rather the Capitol Theater's switch to a jazz orchestra: "Most of the excitement centered over the week-end and around the Capitol, where a new policy was inaugurated."[5] In early October the theater had been showing THE BIG PARADE (1925) in second run and taking in about $60,000 per week. After adopting its "new headline presentation act policy"—jazz acts and low-budget films—its weekly gross jumped to more than $95,000. Warners went head to head against the live jazz competition in other theaters with musical shorts like *Red Spikes and His Follies Entertainers, The Diplomats: High Hat Syncopators of Jazz, Noble*

Graph 20.1

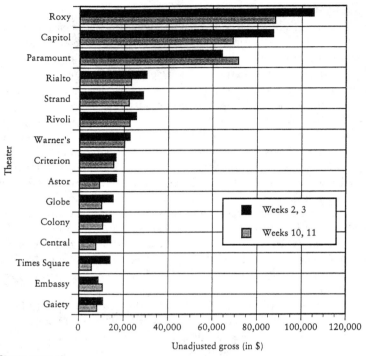

SOURCE: *Variety*, 1927–28.

Sissle and Eubie Blake in Their Original Presentation of Syncopated Ditties, and *Joe Wong, the Chinese Jazz Boy* (1927).

The gross receipts data also distort the popularity of the programs because of discrepancies in theater size. The capacity of the Roxy, for example, was more than ten times that of the Embassy. Perhaps a more meaningful comparison is based on the "seat-adjusted" gross, a ratio obtained by dividing the receipts by the capacity.

Graph 20.2 shows that by calculating the amount of money a theater was able to get for each of its seats strikingly alters our picture of the public's preferences. The Criterion, showing WINGS, flies to the head of the class, consistently taking in about $20 per week for each of its 812 seats. The Strand drops from fifth to next-to-last place (showing WHEN A MAN LOVES [1927] in third run). Despite its 2,900 seats, it was earning less than $10 for them weekly. These differences reflect the number of shows presented each week, the admission price, and the ability of the house to fill its seats to capacity. The seat-adjusted gross seems to be a better indicator of popularity than either the straight gross or simple attendance figures because it represents marketability—relative amounts people were willing to pay for a certain show expressed in terms of the demand for seats. Smaller-capacity houses tend to be favored in this calculation; indeed, like other measures, the seat-adjusted gross may be useful only for general comparisons.

Now the performance of THE JAZZ SINGER looks more impressive. It still trails the Publix stage presentation at the Paramount, but it noses out Rothapfel's extravaganza at the Roxy and the jazz band at the Capitol. No picture, however, comes close to WINGS, already running for more than ten weeks at $2 a ticket. In December the little Embassy's

Graph 20.2

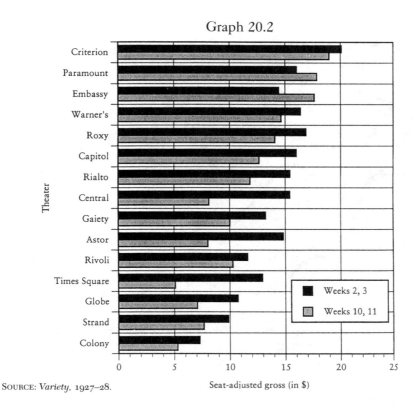

SOURCE: *Variety*, 1927–28.　　　　　Seat-adjusted gross (in $)

fortunes were elevated by the release of LOVE. Starring Garbo and Gilbert, the sensational adaptation of *Anna Karenina* immediately garnered a higher seat-adjusted gross than THE JAZZ SINGER and, for a couple of weeks, even surpassed WINGS.

A traditional measure of popularity has been how long a film plays on Broadway. Graph 20.3 compares the seat-adjusted gross of THE JAZZ SINGER's most important competitors during the length of its first-run booking at the Warners' Theatre. Again, the strength of WINGS is evident: it steadily outperformed other films and would remain at the Criterion until October 1928. The trajectories of THE KING OF KINGS and THE STUDENT PRINCE IN OLD HEIDELBERG were typical of the course of a normal run— strong films that began to fade after about six weeks. But the precipitous drop in gross receipts for SUNRISE is noteworthy and will be discussed below.

Attendance for THE JAZZ SINGER did not begin to slip until the nineteenth week, when the gross dropped below $18,000 for the first time. A month later Warner Bros. moved the film into the Roxy for a two-week run; there it took in $117,000 the first week and $109,500 the second. Much of this increased income reflects what might be called the Roxy premium. Many out-of-towners visited the mammoth picture palace just to experience the theater (it was less than a year old), and its capacity made high grosses the norm. The average weekly take was $104,000. By comparison, WHAT PRICE GLORY?, when it was bumped into the Roxy, made $144,200 and $126,000 during its two-week run. It was followed by SEVENTH HEAVEN, which grossed $123,000 and $109,000. So THE JAZZ SINGER's performance at New York's showcase movie house was a bit above average, but the film did not consistently fill the big theater to capacity. It did about the same as the silent film LOVES OF CARMEN.

Graph 20.3

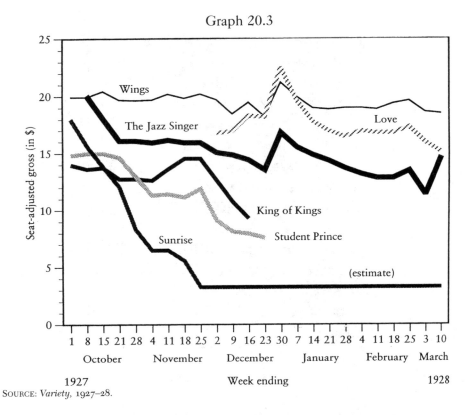

SOURCE: *Variety,* 1927–28.

While the Warners' film was among New York's top entertainment attractions, its popularity did not match Paramount's aerial saga or Garbo and Gilbert's clinches. THE JAZZ SINGER's Broadway run of twenty-three weeks was good, but not exceptional.

How did it measure up to other "sound" films? From the New York audience's perspective, seeing a film with synchronized music, sound effects, or even dialogue, as in THE JAZZ SINGER's famous singing and "talking" scenes, was no novelty. For months moviegoers had been hearing music played through phonographic systems to accompany films nonsynchronously and, not coincidentally, to eliminate the band in the orchestra pit. De Forest's Phonofilm productions had been around for years, and Fox had begun screening talking shorts with WHAT PRICE GLORY? in January 1927. In that spring, Lindbergh's takeoff and his return ceremonies had been exploited by de Forest and Fox. Although the Fox Movietone newsreel did not officially begin until December 1927, the company's talking shorts had been screened sporadically at the Roxy since 30 April and had begun playing regularly with SEVENTH HEAVEN back in June, at the Harris Theater.

The previous programs of Vitaphone features and shorts were the most important influences on the reception context of THE JAZZ SINGER. Film buffs had been entertained by Vitaphone for more than a year. Since DON JUAN, which had opened at the Warners' Theatre in August 1926, there had been three subsequent synchronized features, many one-reel musical shorts, and the two-reel playlets. Several shorts, notably WILLIE AND EUGENE HOWARD IN BETWEEN THE ACTS AT THE OPERA and AL JOLSON IN A PLANTATION ACT, were "talking" as well as "singing" pictures. A review of the seat-adjusted gross receipts for these first Vitaphone programs reveals that the first two features outperformed THE JAZZ SINGER.

Table 20.1
SEAT-ADJUSTED BOX-OFFICE GROSSES, NEW YORK, 1927

Title (Theater)	Week 1	Week 3	Week 10	Week 11
DON JUAN (Warners')	$21.48	$21.48	$18.79	$18.79
SUNRISE (Times Square)	18.01	15.65	3.24[a]	3.24[a]
THE BETTER 'OLE (Colony)	17.19	16.79	11.52	11.17
THE JAZZ SINGER (Warners')	16.67	16.09	14.86	14.42
OLD SAN FRANCISCO (Warners')	11.00	15.10	18.70	13.60
THE FIRST AUTO (Colony)	6.41	5.81	NA[b]	NA

a. Estimate.   b. No longer in first run.
SOURCES: *Variety*, weekly reports; *Film Daily Year Book*, 1927.

Analyzed at comparable moments in their first runs, we see in table 20.1 that DON JUAN ran consistently ahead of the Jolson film and that THE BETTER 'OLE began its run a little better than THE JAZZ SINGER. Less successfully, OLD SAN FRANCISCO grossed only about half as much per seat as DON JUAN; THE FIRST AUTO took in about one-third as much and was pulled after a month. Surprisingly, the gross receipts for THE JAZZ SINGER were unexceptional by Vitaphone standards.

The legend is that sound itself was such a novelty that it pulled in customers regardless of the quality of the picture. But look what happened to THE JAZZ SINGER's synchronized rival from Fox.

F. W. Murnau's SUNRISE opened with a Movietone sound track on 16 September 1927, two weeks before the Warners' film. Like the early Vitaphone features, it had no recorded dialogue. The film immediately won critical raves and several honors, including *Film Daily Year Book*'s ten-best list. Everyone agreed that it was one of the most "artistic" films ever made. But on Broadway it sank like a stone. Apparently the meaning of the film was obscure. In a front-page *Film Daily* review, Kann wrote, "It is an amazing film. It gets over to the audience an indefinite something; just what, it is difficult to describe." He singled out two positive attributes: the quality of the recorded score, and the Movietone shorts on the same program. Kann continued: "In tonal range and quality, Movietone has demonstrated its superiority in the field of synchronized sound and action films."[6]

The *Variety* reviewer also commented, "Nor should be neglected credit as a detail contributing vastly to a satisfying whole, the accompaniment of the Movietone. . . . The musical accompaniment was reproduced with flawless delicacy and under absolute control, merging into the entertainment and apparently disappearing as a separate element."[7] (That is, the sound's "inaudibility" was one of its attributes.) The two new Movietone subjects were the Vatican choir and a statement by Mussolini delivering in English what the producer Winfield R. Sheehan called "a message of friendship." *Variety* attributed much of the SUNRISE program's popularity to the shorts: "Thus far regarded as a draw. Getting all the barbers in five boroughs to hear Ben Mussolini speak his piece."[8]

But the popularity soon wore off. Though the opening seat-adjusted gross for SUNRISE was higher than that of THE JAZZ SINGER or any of the Vitaphone features (except DON JUAN), by the third week its returns had entered a strong downward trend. By the ninth week the seat-adjusted gross was around $5 per week; after that the theater no longer reported figures, although *Variety* revealed that there were days when the Times Square Theater took in less than $400.

Fox creates the impression of having cornered the Broadway exhibition market, May 1928.

Despite what must have been a huge loss to Fox, the film continued to play first-run for twenty-three weeks until 4 April 1928. Harrison used his insider sources to piece together what happened:

> It started sliding from [the fourth] day on, until the last few weeks it was pitiful. The closing week was about $3,000. The house seats 1,033. At the $2 scale, it can gross $18,000 a week. At the average of between $4,500 and $5,000, the picture must have lost a fortune. The weekly expense for advertising was not less than $3,500 and in the opening weeks more. With normal advertising in the newspapers this house cannot be run for less than $10,000 a week. The rent alone is $4,500 a week. (P. S. Harrison, "Two-Dollar 'Hits' and 'Flops,'" *Harrison's Reports*, 9 June 1928, p. 91)

An explanation for the long run might have been a policy that could be called "buying Broadway." (Harrison called it a "forced run.") Jerome Beatty described the practice:

> *Sons of Destiny* [a hypothetical movie] would run at a Broadway theater for twenty-six weeks. It would be lavishly advertised as a tremendous success. The best seats would sell for two dollars at evening performances and at Saturday, Sunday and holiday matinées. Perhaps the price would be boosted to $2.50 for Saturday and Sunday nights. Toward the end of the run free tick-

ets would be passed around liberally, so as to keep the theater well filled. . . .
"A riot on Broadway," the advertising to the trade would read, and the general impression would be that *Sons of Destiny* was making a lot of money at the [hypothetical] Columbine Theater. Yet, when the final accounting was made, the [hypothetical studio] Amalgamated would "go in the red" for $26,000. (Jerome Beatty, "The Red [*sic*] to Profits," *Saturday Evening Post,* 16 February 1929, p. 15)

Only a few pictures, according to Beatty, actually made money during their Broadway runs—THE JAZZ SINGER and WINGS were among them. Most lost thousands of dollars, but the studios wrote off the cost in their "exploitation" budgets, viewing the run as necessary to secure national audiences. "Even a flop," he reported, "will earn more money with a Broadway run back of it." Beatty also described the strategy of an unnamed producer:

He was determined that the show should have half a year on Broadway. . . .
Special salesmen were sent from house to house to sell tickets at half price.
Organizations of all kinds were solicited and offered special group rates.
School children were given slips which entitled the bearer to two tickets for the price of one. Passes by the hundreds were distributed in offices and department stores. In spite of this, some matinées played to as few as twenty-five persons, and the gross receipts one week were $2450.
    The people demonstrated with a pathetic thoroughness that they just didn't want to see this man's show. The Broadway run cost the producer nearly $100,000. When he took the picture outside of New York City, however, it played to enormous business. (Beatty, "The Red [*sic*] to Profits," p. 154)

Whether this incident involved William Fox, Cecil B. DeMille, or some other showman is unknown, but it explains the rationale for playing SUNRISE to near-empty houses for almost six months.

The movie executives learned this trick from the legitimate theater. Knowing that film producers would pay much more for a theatrical property with a long run, play producers would try to maximize a show's stay. "The custom of keeping an unsuccessful production on view long after its receipts had fallen dangerously low was often used to establish a long-run reputation," according to Robert McLaughlin. "At times everyone working with a production would work at lower salaries in a cooperative effort to keep a play open. Small and unpopular theatres were often rented for the purpose of stretching out a run and Hollywood was often duped into thinking a play was a huge popular success if the run was long enough."[9] The practice of buying Broadway, then, highlights the dangers of relying on any one measure, such as length of run, to determine a film's popularity.

Meanwhile, SUNRISE, advertised as a "Broadway Hit," opened in December 1927 at a gala $5 premiere at the Carthay Circle in Los Angeles. Its initial seat-adjusted gross was $8.84 per week, and it performed respectably for 10 weeks. Whether its West Coast success benefited from "buying Broadway" cannot be verified.

When THE JAZZ SINGER opened, it joined a cast of films which have since become legendary: THE BIG PARADE, WINGS, THE KING OF KINGS, THE STUDENT PRINCE, and

Exhibitors learn of the alleged box-office success of SUNRISE *(Fox, 1927).*

SUNRISE. Yet when judged on the basis of its actual box-office record, it was far behind the most popular films. THE BIG PARADE (1925) stayed on Broadway for two years and grossed a then-record $1.75 million, just in New York. By comparison, THE JAZZ SINGER's *total* domestic gross income was $1.97 million. (This figure includes income from the silent version and from the 1931 re-release.) WINGS had opened nine weeks before THE JAZZ SINGER and continued to sell out almost every performance through the spring of 1928. The box office reported steady income of $15,000–16,000 for the small Criterion Theater. In show-business jargon, WINGS had "legs."

Warner Bros. did not show THE JAZZ SINGER immediately in the "four hundred" wired theaters of the legend. Instead, it withheld the film from wider release until mid-November 1927, when it opened in Philadelphia at the Locust, a Fox theater with 1,800 seats. By delaying, Warner Bros. was practicing a form of buying Broadway: building up anticipation for the film outside of New York. The preview trailer that the studio prepared for THE JAZZ SINGER's national release was part of this suspense-generating strategy. It showed throngs outside the Warners' Theatre on opening night. (But the crowds were at the trade screening to see Jolson and the other invited celebrities, not to watch THE JAZZ SINGER!) The film did well in Philadelphia, opening with a $14,000 gross. But earlier in the year WHAT PRICE GLORY? had opened there with $20,000, and SEVENTH HEAVEN with $14,500, so THE JAZZ SINGER was not a blockbuster. It had an eight-week run, but the other nondialogue films had enjoyed runs of thirteen and eight weeks, respectively. The film opened New Year's Day 1928 in Los Angeles, St. Louis, Seattle, and Washington, D.C., with good, but not record, receipts.

Table 20.2
The Jazz Singer's Grosses Compared to Other Films, Chicago, San Francisco, and Los Angeles, 1928

Title	Run Ending	Unadjusted Gross (week of run)		
		Orpheum Theater, Chicago		
The Jazz Singer	3 March 1928	$12,200 (1)	$9,500 (2)	$7,300 (6)
Tenderloin	14 April 1928	13,400 (1)	11,000 (2)	8,200 (6)
		Criterion Theater, Los Angeles		
The Jazz Singer	7 January 1928	$19,600 (1)	$14,400 (2)	$8,600 (5)
Wings	9 September 1928	21,200 (1)	16,800 (2)	12,000 (5)
		Embassy Theater, San Francisco		
The Jazz Singer	18 February 1928	$20,200 (1)	$21,000 (2)	$18,000 (4)
The Lights of New York	4 August 1928	24,000 (1)	22,000 (2)	20,000 (4)

Source: *Variety*, weekly reports.

Table 20.2 characterizes the early pattern of the film's national release. At the Orpheum in Chicago, The Jazz Singer was outgrossed throughout its run by the Vitaphone talking feature Tenderloin. In Los Angeles, Wings in second run at the Criterion outperformed The Jazz Singer in its first run. The Lights of New York did better than The Jazz Singer at the Embassy in San Francisco. In summary, in its national first-run release, The Jazz Singer did well, judged by box-office receipts and the length of its runs, but it was in a distinct second or third tier of attractions compared to the most popular films of the day and even other Vitaphone talkies.[10]

If *Variety*'s data are accurate, then the "unprecedented success" of Warner Bros.' first part-talking feature was more of a retrospective creation of the media (aided by Warner publicity) than a "supreme triumph." Critics and other studios would hardly have been impressed by the film's box-office success because it was just above average. In fact, they might have been surprised that the movie did as well as it did, given Warners' reputation for low-budget program fare, such as its Rin Tin Tin films. The Jazz Singer's unexceptional opening and the Broadway failure of Sunrise in the fall of 1927 would not have convinced producers to change over to sound, especially because a good measure of the Jolson film's drawing power could be attributed to the appeal of its jazz theme and its star. It took many other stimuli, such as the subsequent Warner hits of 1928, to show executives and exhibitors that there was a growing public demand for the talkies.

Our finding that the Broadway statistics do not corroborate the story of the film's initial success does not necessarily disqualify the use of popular journalism as a source of historical documentation about audiences. It would be overly simple to say that the popular version of the story is wrong and the revisionist historian is right. Legends are also historical documents. The misleading nature of the journalistic version should make us look more closely at why The Jazz Singer legend developed the way it did.

One explanation is that historiography has its own narrative practices based on rationalizing principles such as simplicity, causality, and closure. Certainly the popular version written by the journalists tends to apply a conceptual grid to explain scattered events whose relationships might otherwise be difficult to discern. As the case of THE JAZZ SINGER illustrates, it is more "efficient" for a historical discourse to have an "event," a "turning point," a "revolution," a Rubicon to cross, than a slow, convoluted, somewhat irrational development, as was the case with the coming of sound. Rewriting events as a drama with the loose ends tied up is helpful in retelling a complicated process as a conventionalized, thus comprehensible, narrative. It is also a strategy to monumentalize phenomena: thus, the coming of sound can be collapsed onto THE JAZZ SINGER, creating a mnemonic that provides a date, a studio, a genre, and a star to epitomize a whole history. When media analysis is checked against available direct evidence, it appears that the print media were more interested in writing a "story" than reciting facts. The popular press bowdlerized certain facts (less-than-record grosses for THE JAZZ SINGER and the box-office failure of SUNRISE), while embroidering others (the former's commercial success and the latter's artistic triumph).

Classical narratives often rely on personal deeds and motives, and our media analysis of THE JAZZ SINGER's reputation shows that history too may be influenced by celebrity. Accounts of the film are intertwined with Jolson's persona. The stories personalize him by emphasizing the risks he took. The payoff was that by lending his stardom and his funding to the production, he personally guaranteed the talkies' success. For example:

> Al Jolson started the trouble. Yes, trouble is the word, unless you think it is no trouble to rebuild twenty or thirty studios, reorganize the fourth—or is it the second?—largest industry in America and equip every theatre in the country with sound-producing gadgets. A few short-reel novelties—and then *The Jazz Singer* by Warner-Vitaphone.
>
> Thousands of people had heard Jolson's songs on the phonograph, and though they enjoyed them enormously, there were many who could not understand the singer's great personal popularity in the big cities where he was known. Now, however, they heard his songs in direct contact with his own magnetic personality, and they instantly joined in the metropolitan applause. (Rob Wagner, "Silence Isn't Golden Any More," *Collier's*, 25 August 1928, p. 12)

This and similar extracts from early commentators emphasize the popularity of recorded music and the novelty of hearing it in a theater. Curiosity about new technology must have been a factor. Another one was the original audience's psychic investment in the star system and Jolson's "pull" as a performer. Increasingly throughout the 1920s, the screen personae of Chaplin, Fairbanks, Valentino, Bow, Gilbert, and Garbo were idolized by millions of adoring fans. Kindled by studio publicity, fan magazines, and numerous promotional activities, the growth of star worship appears to have been a genuine populist phenomenon of massive proportions. Parallel to cinema, the worlds of music (opera as well as jazz), sports, and current events developed indigenous fan cultures of perhaps unprecedented secular scope. Even such unlikely public figures as Lindbergh, Mussolini, and George Bernard Shaw became Movietone "stars." (One editor quipped, "Shaw 'registers' so well that one regrets a lost film actor.")[11] Radio was a catalyst for stardom. Fans had heard their voices—Jolson had been broadcast nationally several times since 1922—but the talkies imparted to the stars' images the sense of realistic presence that many felt to be the cinema's essence.[12]

◦   ◦   ◦

There are many problems with media analysis as a historical method. One is veracity: the standards of journalists generations ago were not the same as modern academic standards of accuracy and source citation. Plenty of fabrication could be introduced into the public record. Opinion and fact were not always separated.

To whom does the author answer? It would be a mistake to assume that a journalist's or a trade reviewer's audience was the movie's audience. Their constituency was made up of readers, not moviegoers. It is always possible that critical opinions have been influenced by outside editorial pressures that had little to do with film audiences. Publishers, advertisers, film producers, distributors, exhibitors, publicity departments, and press agents were instrumental in trying to shape the critical evaluations of films.

In a slightly different context, Janet Staiger has acknowledged that studying journalists' reports reveals little about social formations in general: "Such an unspoken mass [of moviegoers] deserves as much attention as does the popular press—if not more. How to do this for historical readers in a responsible scholarly way, however, is a very real problem."[13] She is referring to the representation of non-Anglo-Saxon-American viewers, but isn't the problem even more universal? Should we scrutinize our faith in the popular press to speak for all (or any) audiences? The art historian Timothy J. Clark faced somewhat the same problem in trying to analyze the reception of Manet's painting *Olympia*. His approach was to look not only at what had been written but at what critics had not said: "A close and comprehensive reading of the sixty texts of 1865," he ventured, "ought to enable us to distinguish between a rhetoric of incomprehension, produced smoothly as part of the ordinary discourse of criticism, and another rhetoric—a breaking or spoiling of the critical text's consistency—which is produced by something else, a real recalcitrance in the object of study."[14]

A fully engaged history of film reception would examine not only the institutional milieus of cinema and the interpretations of commentators but also the "recalcitrance" represented by actual audiences. Our research shows that factual information must also be provisional. "Box office," after all, is only a crude tracking system for determining the number of people moving through theaters at a given time. Retrieving numbers tells us nothing about individual or group interpretations. But we've also suggested that contemporary reviewers and later critics have had little connection with popular discourses about films.

This seems to leave us in a quandary. If we think of "historical reception" as a recoverable fact, then we will always be disappointed because we cannot know everything. Likewise, we accept the limitations of journalistic discourse, with its oblique nature. Yet if we try to anchor our findings in knowledge of actual audiences, then we are inevitably frustrated by the unattainableness of reliable direct evidence.

The case of THE JAZZ SINGER's premiere suggests that, in trying to recover historical facts about a film's place in popular reception, we must be careful to distinguish between its social context and the writing of those with vested interests in laying claim to the film for their purposes.

21

"The Great Ninety Per Cent"

*If one can lay a charge against Hollywood it will be not that it does
not know how to produce art, but that it knows almost as little about
how to make good, satisfying bilge.*

ALEXANDER BAKSHY, 1929

What's the matter?" asks Don Lockwood in SINGIN' IN THE RAIN. The head of the
studio has stormed onto the set, halted production, and sent everyone home. "*The
Jazz Singer,* that's what's the matter," the boss bellows. "It's a sensation." A spinning (fictitious) *Variety* headline confirms his prediction: "Revolution in Hollywood." But our
examination of the transition to sound between 1926 and 1931 shows that there was neither a chaotic upheaval nor, at the other extreme, a carefully executed changeover. The
transition to sound was more like an experiment that produced unexpected results.
Indeed, it seems that at no point during its development from 1926 to about 1931 did
sound behave as Hollywood hoped and expected it would. Before 1928 no one anticipated that all-sound production would mean the end of silents. Even in 1929 some executives thought that silent film exhibition would continue and that dual versions would be
around for a long time. It was felt that switching to sound would strengthen Hollywood's
hand when dealing with independent exhibitors and foreign competition. For a while
film people believed that the talkies would bring new sophisticated audiences to movie
theaters by bringing highbrow culture to the screen, all the while continuing to appeal
to the "masses." Sound production would be more profitable because expensive location
shooting would be cut back and close-up dialogue shots would increase, resulting in
smaller casts and cheaper sets. Relatively cheap Broadway talent would replace expensive Hollywood stars when the latter's lack of theatrical skills became apparent.
Audiences would reject stars who spoke in uncultured, non-American voices.

None of this happened. One function of the "revolution" scenario was to provide a
usable retelling of the incidents, omitting the complicated parts about capitalization,
expansion, competition, and the complex stylistic maneuvering that had modified cinema practice. The revolution story also saved Hollywood's face by diverting attention
from the industry's failure to appreciate audiences' initial appetite for sound films, followed by the studios' inability to anticipate the public's changing expectations about how
to utilize the new technology.

Hollywood constructed for itself a history of sound in the classical mode: the silents
were a state of equilibrium; sound rocked it; then balance was restored. The First
National director William Seiter gave a typical account in which he posited sound as a
disturbance:

In the beginning, most of the picture-makers got off on the wrong foot. "Talking pictures" became the rage, and in most cases we had nothing but talk, talk, talk. The industry went batty on the subject of dialogue, just as it did later on the subject of music. There was no dividing line, no balance. In the mad struggle to master the new medium, the motion picture was forgotten. The picture ceased to move, and after the theatre audiences became accustomed to the thrill of hearing sound, they too ceased to move—into the theatres.

Audiences became fed up with watching and listening to actors who did little but exchange interminable lines. Even the cleverest wise-cracks began to pall on jaded nerves. Theatre business began to slump. (William A. Seiter, "Motion Pictures Must Move," *Cinematographic Annual 1931,* pp. 263–64)

But now, in 1931, Seiter felt that the sound madness had been checked by the harmonious compromise achieved between action and talking. Gangster pictures and Westerns were popular because they gave fans "action and action plus." Seiter's examples were LITTLE CAESAR, PUBLIC ENEMY, THE STAR WITNESS, and CIMARRON. "In common with most directors, I have always held that we must never forget we are primarily making motion pictures. That action must have an equal place in pictures with brilliant dialogue and acting. Now that we seem to have hit upon the happy medium the picture industry ought to go places during the coming season."[1] SINGIN' IN THE RAIN replays this Hollywood view of the ontogeny of the sound film as first stopping then restoring motion. Don (Gene Kelly) is a stuntman in the days of the action-packed silent film. When sound enters the picture, his career stalls in the turgid talkies. Then he finds his true calling in the musical genre. His original knockabout silent-film athleticism has been creatively redirected into energetic (and photogenic) dancing, and the movies have been restored to a steady state.

As ERPI's Knox looked back on the recent transition, his view was more consistent with what has emerged during our survey. He told of two years filled with experiments and errors:

Silent pictures were fitted with recorded musical accompaniments. Simple stage dramas were tried on the new machine. Stars of the silent screen tried out their voices. The period might properly be characterized as one of trial, caution and conservative progress. No one knew for sure the machine, the type of picture or the audience reaction. An outdoor picture or two shook off some of the beliefs that only a sound proof stage would do. A musical comedy added color and life. The advances of 1929, so close behind us, were in reality startling in their value. (H. G. Knox, "The Ancestry of Sound Recording," *Cinematographic Annual 1930,* pp. 288–89)

His statement captures the ad hoc, tentative nature of the industry's approach to sound. A problem with the equilibrium model of historical change is that not everyone agreed that the late silent film represented a golden age. Gilbert Seldes, in the pages of the *New Republic* and *Harper's,* had routinely dismissed many silent movies as artistic failures. To him, most films were escapist mediocrities punctuated by flashes of artistic brilliance. One reason for introducing the presentation act, he maintained, was "to conceal from the movie going public the perfectly obvious fact that the movies themselves were not worth seeing." Sound only compounded the problem. "It is an instrument of enormous capacities in the hands of people who seem totally incapable of finding out to what use it should be put." Seldes confessed that the talkies induced in him "mingled emotions." It is useful to follow the internal struggle of one of the most intelligent observers of the movies as he wrestled with his warring opinions.

In "The Movies Commit Suicide" (1928), Seldes came out in favor of sound, but only after some rather tortured logic.[2] Those who had always hated the movies—he seemed to have George Jean Nathan in mind—believed that film was losing its only virtue, silence. Horrified purists and aesthetes argued that "the problem[s] of each art should be solved in the medium of that art, without calling in alien effects." Seldes parked himself firmly in the purist category by pointing out that the new form of the talking picture "needed above everything else to discover its own appropriate materials and to develop in accordance with its own capacities, cutting itself off as far as possible from the two forms of entertainment to which it is related by machinery: the stage and the silent movie." So Seldes expected, in 1928, that the talkies would add a new branch to established cinema. He praised Murnau's THE LAST LAUGH, with its sweeping camera work and silent story told without intertitles, as "the first picture which completely and exclusively expressed itself in cinematic terms. It fully exploited the technic of the camera and used for its effects only such things as the camera could legitimately record."[3] Like so many film commentators of the era, Seldes exalted motion (of the photographed subject and of the camera) as the defining characteristic of film art. Unlike most American critics, though, he attacked films which purported to be "the most accurate transcription of reality":

> The moving picture, itself an instrument which transposes reality and is capable of recording everything fantastic, has not been used by imaginative men. Speech adds another element of realism and weighs down the balance in favor of the movies' weakness. At the same time, the moment a character begins to speak from the screen his bodily unreality becomes marked—at least until one becomes accustomed to it. (Gilbert Seldes, "The Movies Commit Suicide," *Harper's*, November 1928, p. 710)

While he ridiculed the part-talkie, he also predicted that it might be possible for a director to benefit from an intrusion of dialogue "wherever [he] was willing to confess that he had to go outside of his own medium to express his ideas completely." He doubted this would happen, however, because "this would mean putting the art of the movie above the finances of the moving-picture industry—a sacrifice easily made by critics and never by producers." Because the sound film was developing as a separate form of entertainment, here was, at last, the virtue of the talkies: "The moving picture is committing suicide, but at the same time is achieving salvation." The sound film would absorb the bad elements of film and theater, leaving the silent film as an improved "art" form which would be practiced by "foreigners and amateurs, able to appreciate its values." Thus, Seldes predicted that sound would differentiate cinema according to the discrimination and class of ordinary and elite consumers. Concluding with the "salvation" theme, he drew a parallel between photography and painting and sound and silent film: "The camera made realism in painting unnecessary. The silent picture, in the same way, may be relieved of all obligation to record the actual and give itself up to fantasy and imagination."[4]

Not only did some doubt that the silents were an unqualified art form, but not every-one thought that sound was a regression to primitive stasis. Some directors accepted the talkies as a distinct improvement. In 1929, even before the camera had been "liberated" from its glass booth, the rhetorical emphasis was on cinematic motion: "Where a break in the ordinary [silent] film to allow for a close-up has been the modus operandi," Rouben Mamoulian explained, "I now guide my lens along a straight and continuous line, without breaks in continuity, without needless explanatory speeches and also sans the printed subtitle."[5] Robert Florey agreed that dialogue had actually made films more mobile:

> Speech has multiplied the movability of motion pictures a hundredfold. Whereas in the old, silent days it was possible to do only one thing at a time, now it is possible to do two. Then it was impossible to speak and move at the same time. The printed title could not be injected into too much action. How all that is changed. The camera has complete freedom to roam where it will, while the dialogue is maintained steadily throughout all necessary movement. (*Film Daily*, 4 August 1929, p. 7)

Considering the later reputation of the early talkies as motionless, Florey's final specu-lation would become ironic: "So great is the difference that we shall presently look back to the old silent picture and regard it as a comparatively stationary affair."[6]

It was not so much that silents were unbalanced and then restored by sound, but that the potentially disruptive components of early talking-film production were discontin-ued or transformed into a new style. Filmmakers, both of their own volition and at the urging of critics, stopped foregrounding sound for its own sake. Hollywood's flamboyant celebration of acoustic effects in 1928–1929—as in APPLAUSE and THE COCOANUTS—was gradually replaced by the "inaudible" tendency and the modulated sound track. Frank Capra forthrightly explained the rationale for effacing technique:

> A good cinematographer lights his picture so the audience does not realize it has been lighted; gets over the proper effect without the audience realizing he has done it. In other words, an audience should never realize that a direc-tor has directed the picture or that a cinematographer has photographed it. That is why "directorial touches" and photographic "splurges" should be kept out of a picture. They detract from the story. Excellence in direction is reached when the audience never thinks of the director's work. . . . The minute the audience becomes conscious of the "machinery" of a picture, they forget the story. (Frank Capra, "The Cinematographer's Place in the Motion Picture Industry," *Cinematographic Annual 1931*, p. 14)

Extending this logic, the sound engineer would succeed at his mission if his intervention and "splurges" went unnoticed. The modulated sound track joined other expressive ele-ments of filmmaking as part of the organic unity of the classical ensemble. Everyone in Hollywood worked mightily to produce the illusion of a regained equilibrium, but *why* did the industry take this direction rather than continue to glorify the acoustic proper-ties of the talkies?

One explanation might be that the industry always responded to technological change by trying to deemphasize it. New practices, whether in editing, camera movement, color, acting, or anything else which could call attention to itself, had to be subordinated to telling a good story. Innovations (Technicolor, camera cranes, zoom lenses) were stylistically foregrounded, then subdued as a matter of course. Meanwhile, critics would hail the new techniques, then later call for hiding them. This familiar pattern was evoked to rationalize the industry's response to sound.

Audienceship

But what of the view from the balcony? Did popular reactions exert pressure on studios to modify the direction into which they took sound? We have seen that the talkies were accepted on terms quite different from what Hollywood proposed. The "gee whiz" excitement surrounding movie applications of thermionic, telephonic, and radiophonic technology dissipated quickly. Neither the telephone nor the radio companies won the battle for the "mind share" of the talking-film consumer. By 1930 it had become apparent that the sound film would not be a radically new entertainment form. Hollywood's promised movie bridge between Broadway and Main Street had not been built, primarily because the provincials decided they were not very interested in the type of culture that the studios brought to town. A separate sound cinema which would complement, not replace, silent production withered when consumers rushed to all-talking productions. Genres and stars flitted in and out of popularity as motion picture attendance soared to new record highs in 1929–1930. The mass audience and the popular press, though by no means univocal, tested the models which Hollywood proposed. Many experiments—notably films which used dialogue intermittently, or synchronous sound effects only, and films which "canned" theater—were dismissed. (There were exceptions: newsreels, cartoons, and travel and exploitation films with sound became permanent fixtures in the movie house.) The public seemed to like best the familiar movie forms (often with stories left over from the silent days) which Hollywood had reconfigured with sound. Most talking-picture stars had already appeared in silents. This conservative trend was validated by the millions of filmgoers who returned to the talkies week after week as long as they could afford it.

The urgent need to reprocess new technology into old forms was partly due to the lack of real knowledge about film attenders. The most elusive aspect of assessing audienceship was ascertaining the consumer's preferences, the holy grail for purveyors of popular culture. People are attracted both to novelty and to sameness. In the movies this seeming paradox translates into genres (new stories in old forms) and fan culture (familiar stars in new roles, or a dynamic new performer who brings freshness to a well-known role or genre). The box office and fan magazines confirmed that, on the subject of sound, the public was not certain what it wanted. Fans relied on Hollywood to provide new movies, while the studios were trying to anticipate consumer tastes. Consequently, cyclical production and public response evolved into a circular pas de deux. As John Seitz put it, "Public demand is not expressed audibly. The producer must guess at what the public wants and endeavor to supply it. If the public reacts favorably he has guessed correctly."[7] Hollywood guessed. Audiences came or stayed away (influenced by their previous visits). From this outcome, the next educated forecast was made. The inherent instability and riskiness of this model worked to keep Hollywood stable by encouraging studios to repeat past successes, and to keep it changing by admitting fresh new ideas into the system.

The Dilemma of Democracy

The early promoters of the sound film extolled virtual Broadway as a way for ordinary people to appreciate fine music and renowned performing artists. Jack Alicoate, *Film Daily*'s publisher, had beamed in April 1928 that

> we can see a complete, extravagant musical movie comedy, à la Ziegfeld. Not the reincarnation of a successful show but [one] conceived and written expressly for the screen. Music by Berlin or Gershwin, book by Bolton or Nichols, lyrics by a Buddy De Sylva. . . . In this we will have the wedding of the two great amusement arts, the stage and screen, taking the best from each and giving the public a ten dollar attraction at one dollar prices. (*Film Daily*, 25 April 1928, p. 1)

When the "wedding" of Broadway and movies at popular prices was not consummated, *Film Daily*'s editor Maurice Kann[8] cynically reminded the industry of its promise to bring sound to nonmetropolitan regions:

> We remember there was much ado about the tone which this new agency [the talkies] would add to the institution of the motion picture by bringing to the small towns the great artists of the opera and of the stage. The roughened souls of the rustics and the rugged exteriors of the provincials were to be softened and calmed with lovely arias and beautiful symphonies carried to them from the world's musical storehouses. . . . What a mockery time has made of those verbal bouquets! For it is a singularly ironic truth that those very exhibitors and their public for whom sound was dubbed a direct gift from heaven have been unable to get within hailing distance of St. Peter." (*Film Daily*, 14 December 1928, p. 1)

Kann was speaking, of course, on behalf of silent exhibitors who wanted a piece of the talking-picture bonanza, but he was also implicitly criticizing the sound film for failing to democratize high-tone music, drama, and literature. The concept that cinema should be the bearer of egalitarian culture, however, competed with the idea that the market was an uneducated multitude incapable of comprehending fine performances. The industry was out of touch with the level of its audience. *Film Daily*'s review of Robert Benchley's THE TREASURER'S REPORT (1928) zeroed in on the difficult question of which audiences liked films of that type. Benchley was one of the Algonquin Round Table group of writers who were well known to readers of the *New Yorker*. The trade journal questioned whether Benchley's sly verbal humor would demonstrate mass appeal and described his ten-minute monologue as "a high class comedy skit that is gaited for the better class houses. The comedy is so fine in spots and is put over so quietly that in some pop [popular] houses it may fail to garner all the laughs."[9] Similarly, it was felt that Shaw's "disciples will be moved to rousing cheers over the screen of George Bernard with Movietone," but that "the mob won't get him or his stuff."[10] Kann singled out William C. deMille's THE IDLE RICH (1929) as a case of misdirected audience address:

> A perfect example of a stage play that doesn't belong on the screen. The legit theater audiences could enjoy it as a stage offering, for it kidded the great

middle White Collar class and showed them up as a bunch of nincompoops. But when you stop to figure that the big proportion of film audiences is this same White Collar class, and that they have to sit for an hour and see themselves unmercifully torn to shreds, you begin to wonder who in Hollywood decided this was good box-office material. It jus ain't. (*Film Daily*, 23 June 1929, p. 13)

The belief that Hollywood had overshot the capabilities of its customers also informed Seiter's explanation for the failure of the musical:

> We all know now what was wrong. That the motion picture public didn't understand or like musical comedies and operettas presented exactly as they were on the stage. The motion picture public, particularly in the small towns, knew nothing of stage traditions. No wonder they couldn't understand why a singer should suddenly burst into song in the middle of a scene, for no reason at all. When we get around to producing musical stories logically, then musical pictures will regain their popularity. (Seiter, "Motion Pictures Must Move," p. 264)

Alexander Bakshy, on the contrary, suspected that popularity of the sound film would dumb-down the intellectual content of the movies and alienate the remaining intelligent film viewers:

> [The talking picture's] mechanical nature makes it particularly suitable for industrial production. This does not imply that the part played by the mechanical and industrial factors in its origin disqualifies it as a medium of art. But it does unfortunately mean that because of these two factors it lends itself readily to commercial exploitation with the resultant moronisation of content. (Alexander Bakshy, "The Movie Scene," *Theatre Arts Monthly*, February 1929, p. 99)

In an effort to determine whether Broadway material, "serious" stage plays, and "heavy" novels were too elite, Alicoate went on a tour of small-town theaters. The result was a warning about regional tastes. He advised Hollywood and New York executives to ascertain the crowd's common denominator: "To a typical New Yorker it is hard to see beyond the Palisades, yet here lies that great ninety per cent, the backbone of this great country." He judged "that regardless of the modern and universal trend of progressive thought, what they'll take in the valley of bright lights won't always go in the small places," and "some gags that won't go over the pit on Broadway are good for big laughs and likewise certain sophisticated bits are entirely lost on small town minds."[11] Alicoate's journey from his Manhattan office to the hinterlands (we don't know how far he ventured) also led him to meditate on the effects of adapting too much serious drama. He wondered, "Are pictures becoming too high-brow for our great ninety per cent?"

> Here is a fair question, occasionally brought up, regarding the present swing toward too much sorrow and tragedy in pictures and too many so-called intellectual or high-brow productions. . . . The talkers have opened the way to universal presentation of the great tragedy masterpieces of the world. A

certain percentage of paying theater guests will rave over them of course. Many more, with a flare for the unusual, will be satisfied, but, it is our modest and fleeting guess that the great majority of the picture-loving public will take them only when seasoned with a proper proportion of legitimate laughs. (*Film Daily*, 31 March 1930, p. 1)

These opinions reveal that the trade valued New York entertainment as an ideal but doubted whether the rest of the country was discerning enough to appreciate it. Here is a tangible instance of trade pressure being applied to Hollywood to keep film democratic in its appeal and middlebrow in its content. Speaking for exhibitors, *Film Daily* was contributing to the leveling of the movies to sustain the interest of the largest possible audience.

The producers wanted very much to give filmgoers what "ninety per cent" of them desired (although Lasky and Thalberg and Zanuck also saw the public relations value of the "prestige picture"). The market that Hollywood imagined for most of its product was thought by many to be the same young women who purchased fan magazines. This assumption guided genre production. According to Seldes, melodramas and sentimental stories, Hollywood's routine fare, were women's pictures which did not appeal to male customers. But the new sound film, he maintained, changed the constitution of the mass audience by attracting males to action and gangster films:

> Men found the movies feminized and the great change came when Mr. Cagney in *Public Enemy* was being annoyed by Mae Clarke and rudely ground half a grapefruit into her face. From that time on it became common form for the tough guys of the picture to kick and slap their women around on the slightest provocation and roars of delight rose from the throats of men who had up to that time found nothing satisfactory in pictures except the newsreel and Mickey Mouse. (Gilbert Seldes, *Movies for the Millions* [London: B. T. Batsford, 1937], p. 51)

It is likely that the "cycles" of Hollywood early sound production (trial films, musicals, society dramas, social realist, then gangster films) were efforts to resonate with more diversified audiences—first aficionados of plays and music (not very successfully), and then men. By the time more reliable audience measurement techniques came into use in the late 1930s, it turned out that film attendees were more heterogeneous than the moguls had imagined: proportionally fewer young women, more children and males, and a more diverse socioeconomic mix. Had the film companies' assessments of their audience in the late 1920s been wrong, or had the studios really succeeded in finding films which attracted the male viewers they were aiming for? In any case, the sound gangster film seems to exemplify the industry's willingness to tailor entertainment values (in this case, misogynist pleasure) to the perceived desires of its target mass audience.

Critical Attacks and Apologies

The introduction of sound provided a few writers with the incentive to analyze films' formal properties. The canonical examples are all European, and Rudolf Arnheim is the best known. As a young critic of film and culture working in Berlin, he developed a sustained and coherent position about the new sound film. The talkies, he argued, could never be art because they mechanically reproduced reality. For example, the silent film image could be perceived either as flat or as having depth. But when a director added "real sounds,"

> the visual picture suddenly becomes three-dimensional and tangible. The acoustics perfect the illusion to such an extent that it becomes complete, and thus a theatrical space: the sound turns the film screen into a spatial stage! Now, a major and particular appeal of film lies in the fact that a film scene consists of the competition between division of the picture and movement within an area, and three-dimensional body and movement in space. Sound film does away with this aesthetically important double game almost entirely. (Rudolf Arnheim, "Sound Film [1928]," *Film Essays and Criticism* [Madison: University of Wisconsin Press, 1997], p. 30)

He professed that aesthetic form was distinguished by the *transformation* of reality, therefore film's apparent limitations (lack of color, flatness of the image, etc.) defined it as art. Restoring any of these lacks—for instance, sound—diminished the cinema's artistic status by taking it closer to other forms, such as theater, and toward realism. Such "improvements" might have made motion pictures a better reproducer of the world, but they also generated "radical aesthetic impoverishment."[12] It is apparent that Arnheim's position was very close to the one Seldes was elaborating a hemisphere away. The difference was that the German theorist was delineating a formal aesthetics of cinema art, while the American journalist was concerned with justifying film's distinction from theater and making it comprehensible to his readers.[13]

European commentators (at least those who are readily available to English-language readers), including Béla Balázs, Sergei Eisenstein, the early René Clair, Alberto Cavalcanti, and Basil Wright, emphasized that film must use sound *a*synchronously. The Russians published a famous manifesto declaring that "*only the contrapuntal use* of sound vis à vis the visual fragment of montage will open up new possibilities for the development and perfection of montage. *The first experiments in sound must aim at a sharp discord with the visual images.*"[14] Eisenstein in particular saw the image and the sound track as locked in eternal conflict, and he theorized that film derived artistry from polyphony (as in musical counterpoint) and synesthesia (using one sense to stimulate another) rather than from simply exploiting the mechanism's ability to replicate sounds.[15] Less rigorous versions of these ideas were widespread. Clair wrote in 1929 that

> if *imitation* of real noises seems limited and disappointing, it is possible that an *interpretation* of noises may have more of a future in it. Sound cartoons, using "real" noises, seem to point to interesting possibilities. Unless new sound effects are soon discovered and judiciously employed, it is to be feared that the champions of the sound film may be heading for a disappointment. We shall find ourselves left with the "hundred per cent talkie" . . . and that is not a very exhilarating prospect. (René Clair, "The Art of Sound," in Richard Dyer MacCann, ed., *Film: A Montage of Theories* [New York: E. P. Dutton, 1966], p. 40)

These filmmakers and critics opposed the Hollywood practice of constructing "bourgeois" naturalism and reproducing theatrical dialogue. Like Jean Epstein, they called for cinematography which used sound nonmimetically: "To hear everything that a perfect human ear hears is merely apprentice work for the microphone," wrote Epstein. "Now, we want to hear what the ear doesn't hear, just as through the cinema we see what eludes the eye."[16] Elizabeth Weis and John Belton comment that these detractors of the talkies were not hostile to sound per se, but to speech: "Actual language posed a threat to a figurative language that had evolved to a state of near-perfection during the silent era. The various approaches taken toward dialogue in this period reflect early attempts to disarm, undermine, or banish it entirely from the screen."[17] For many, Walt Disney's animated cartoons, in which, it was believed, sound and picture competed dynamically for the viewer's attention, were the ideal models of how movie sound should be used.[18]

This European attitude that cinema should express and interpret rather than copy "real" sounds, and divulge its trickery while so doing, were seldom expressed by American critics. (Even Seldes criticized the nonillusionism of films like THE TERROR.) In sharp contrast to the Europeans, several writers argued for precisely the kind of effacement of sound which Hollywood directors were trying to achieve. Welford Beaton, in the *Film Spectator*, was an early advocate of the talkies. In his review of THE JAZZ SINGER (which he caught during its second run at the Criterion in 1928, not at its initial Warners' Theatre booking), he took issue with those critics who favored fast-paced montage and close-ups. Beaton complained that Crosland's editing in the nondialogue portions of the film was too accelerated, and that his excessive use of close-ups fragmented space. "When Jolson returns [home] he embraces his mother, and the embrace is shown in a large close-up which effectually blots out the home and gives us only the two heads. Such treatment destroys the spirit of the scene, as so many close-ups do. The scene should have been presented in a medium shot which preserved as much of the home as its frame would have permitted." While watching HALLELUJAH!, Beaton was entranced by the singing of the spirituals. Editing them "causes too many abrupt terminations to entertaining musical numbers."[19] The critic felt uncomfortable with film practices which separated performance from its spatial and temporal continuum.

Alexander Bakshy (an editor at *The Nation* and a Maxim Gorky scholar) felt that the talkies, though imperfect, were still an "original form of drama" (significantly, not an improvement on the silent film). Sound enhanced character. His examples were THE SINGING FOOL and MY MAN: "The fact . . . that they succeed in conveying their appeal to the audience is vastly significant. Lacking as they are in color and depth, they still capture something of the personality of the artist. No doubt Al Jolson and Fannie Brice are more intimately felt and radiate more genuine warmth when one sees them on the stage. At the same time even on the screen they are unmistakably their peculiar and likable selves." Unlike Arnheim's formal position vis-à-vis film art, Bakshy was arguing that sound film succeeded as a new form of drama because the voice transmitted personality. It did not follow, however, that Hollywood would use sound for the straight recording of stage plays. Bakshy pointed out that cinema had not done so in the silents; why should sound change things? Like the Europeans, he felt that sound should be used expressively, but in contradistinction, he specifically praised speech's potential:

> Dialogue can be concentrated—reduced to a number of essential statements—as effectively as action, just as it is done now in the dialogue titles of silent pictures. Then, the talking picture will also develop the specifically cinematic method of "close up." It will be able to focus an individual utterance, and at the same time put out of focus all the other voices—a proce-

dure unquestionably in advance of the method of the "realistic" stage which, in order that certain characters may be heard, enforces a most unrealistic silence among all the other characters. And such being its technique, the spoken drama of the screen will obviously and inevitably develop into something original and non-stagy—something that will be instinct with the dynamic spirit of the movies. (Alexander Bakshy, "The 'Talkies,'" *The Nation*, 2 February 1929, pp. 236–37)

Bakshy stressed the power of character-driven cinema in his review of the opening scene of Clair's SOUS LES TOITS DE PARIS:

The length of the song, the dulness of the music, and the solemnity of the singing would have been enough to condemn this scene for any Hollywood talkie. But here comes the miracle of art. By introducing a slight action, so slight that it is almost entirely confined to an exchange of glances between the peddler and a prowling pickpocket, the artist sets off the vital force. Instantly the characters become intensely alive, the singing acquires the quality of suspense, and the whole scene begins to sparkle with humor and to throb with the pulse of human life. By vivifying touches such as this, one scene after another is transformed into a palpitating reality. (Alexander Bakshy, "*Sous les toits de Paris,*" *The Nation*, 7 January 1931)

Similarly, for LE MILLION, Bakshy counterintuitively praised Clair's individualized characters in a believable environment. His justification was that, "though his characters' behavior is at times so grotesquely fantastic, it never appears incongruous with their surroundings, or inconsistent with their normal actions." He recognized that LE MILLION was the antithesis of the Hollywood musical. "Instead of making singing and dancing more natural, more in accord with the daily life of his characters, he makes the daily life of his characters more unnatural, more in accord with stage singing and dancing." This accurate imitation of an unnatural situation, Bakshy argued, was a clever reversal but a limited solution. The only way to really solve the problem of introducing singing into a film "is to discover a cinematic form that would make dancing and singing spring as freely from the nature of the screen entertainment as they spring from the nature of the stage performance."[20] In other words, he was calling for something like the motivated plot of the American backstage musical comedy to integrate music, dance and dialogue. Bakshy repudiated the Seldes-Arnheim position:

For it has been laid down by our aestheticians that in copying the stage the talking picture would lose all claim to be regarded as a medium of art. Though why should it? A perfect copy is obviously as good as the original, and it is absurd to claim that no reproduction can be perfect. Besides, in the case of the talking picture, one does not so much copy an original stage production as imitate the stage form—which, if a sin, is certainly not a cardinal one. (Bakshy, "The 'Talkies,'" p. 236)

Seldes's influential book *The Movies Come from America* abandoned the position that art was a deformation of reality in favor of a more moderate view. In the same year in which Arnheim was writing his anti-sound diatribe, "A New Laocoön," Seldes defended the movies. But he nevertheless insisted that the cinematic essence lay, not in narrative (by implication conveyed in dialogue), but in capturing moving reality:

> People go to the moving picture to-day for precisely the same reason that they went nearly forty years ago. They went then because the moving picture moves. The only reservation that has to be made is this: if the moving picture had not learned how to tell a story, it might have vanished except in the form of the newsreel and the historical record. But this does not mean that the story is the essence of the moving picture; the essence is still the way the story is told, which is by movement, and this remains just as true to-day as it was in the time of the silent pictures. (Gilbert Seldes, *Movies for the Millions* [London: B. T. Batsford, 1937], p. 9)

As he had hoped in "The Movies Commit Suicide," Seldes still believed that dialogue was not to be shunned but to be cultivated. It had not, however, achieved the status of a separate high art: "No one has yet found a method of speech which is as appropriate to the moving picture as blank verse is to heroic drama or recitative to opera."[21]

Thus, the European and American sound debate (although the word may be misleading) had different emphases. Domestic writers tended to emphasize the affective power of film to promote identification and empathy. Though they castigated the Hollywood establishment as philistines, in fact the critics shared many ideals about the use of sound, including the modulated sound track with its balance of "essences," which included speech. The bottom line was that democratic distribution, clarity of exposition, and intelligibility were more prized than adherence to formal ideals. Some American critics—Nathan, for example—never accepted sound. But for Beaton, Bakshy, and Seldes, the talkies redeemed a silent cinema which had been foundering in repetition and complacency and was limited, not artistically elevated, by its lack of sound.

One opinion, promoted in SINGIN' IN THE RAIN and still held by many, is that sound caused a complete break with Hollywood's past. The opposite, less widely held view (argued in this book) is that sound definitely changed cinema, but not across the board, and not as a radical overthrow of film convention. Technologically, adapting to sound called for rethinking the relationship between the constructed space of the silent film image and the very different acoustic space (called theatrical by Arnheim and others) of the sound film. For a while, camera placement was sound-driven, in contrast to its placement in silent films to create a visual rhythm through editing and change of scale and to emphasize point of view and facial expression. The availability of synchronous dialogue revealed how often these visual practices in silent cinema were actually substitutes for audible language. Sound anchored the indirectness and ambiguity inherent in the silent system, bringing down the illusion of an imaginary or psychological space (especially in a part-talkie) with a thud. Quickly, though, technicians and directors eliminated such incongruities, with critics coaching from the sidelines. Film styles were adjusted or created to maximize Hollywood's traditional narrative-centered, psychologically motivated practices.

As a business, the talkies transformed the motion picture industry, but the extent to which this change was directly attributable to the introduction of sound is not clear. The tumult of the times—wild speculation and merger mania, the Fox debacle, the market crash and the Depression, the realignment of the industry—understandably contributed to the impression of chaos and revolution. In fact, the national economy, not the talkies, was the more plausible explanation for the major changes in Hollywood. For example, investing huge amounts of capital to convert studios and theaters overextended most of the major producers. But had not the Depression intervened, these expenditures in all likelihood would have been amortized ahead of schedule because the talkies were more popular than anyone anticipated.

Socially, sound actually had little overall impact on cinema-going. There was a spike in attendance during the novelty phase, then the business resumed its normal unpredictable up-and-down ways. Foreign movies left general distribution and became "art" films. Musicals went bust. But how many of these developments were attributable to popular sentiment against sound? Certainly there were superficial changes. Attendance behaviors were modified, the market realigned somewhat (perhaps attracting more men and upper-middle-class viewers), many theaters closed (again, because of the economy . . .), but in the long run, the social experience of going to the movies was remarkably unaffected by the transition to sound. (And, in 1933, the musical came back with new vigor.)

Perhaps the most important revelation of our study of American cinema's transition to sound is that sound *might* have started a revolution. If producers had followed through on their original intentions, sound films might have become something like music videos or televised plays (for example, the 1960s *Playhouse 90*–type series). Production practice in Hollywood could have been divided into what amounted to high- and middlebrow units. Different types of films could have been aimed at specific regions, demographic categories, or ethnic groups. As had happened with vaudeville and the legitimate stage, there could have evolved separate theater circuits showing various genres with proven local appeal based on class and income. (There was a movie business precedent in the way silent Westerns had been distributed to rural towns). For a brief moment in 1929–1930, there was a glimpse of the possibility that sound might make American film more responsive to its melting-pot constituents. But audiences rejected these tentative initiatives; then the Depression slammed anything that did not contribute to the bottom line, ending the budding concept of the sound film as a multivocal entertainment aimed at narrow audiences. The most revolutionary aspect of sound, suggested by the European theorist-filmmakers (usually before they had access to sound equipment of their own), was that the sound track should take off as a separate art form and interact with, rather than underlie, the pictorial component. This idea never stood a chance in the United States because it went against the grain of Hollywood production and popular criticism.

American audiences and critics also did their part to bring into line the divergent tendencies of the talkies. The disjunctive properties of sound which so intrigued the European theorists were roundly criticized when they appeared in Hollywood (even in "experimental" short subjects). The box office did not reward efforts to break out of established routines (as in HALLELUJAH! and APPLAUSE), and anything found to be jarring or disconcerting tended to be greeted with jeers or laughter, not interest or appreciation.

Apparently to everyone's relief (except perhaps a few experimental avant-garde filmmakers), the sound "revolution" fizzled out without making any elemental changes in film styles or moviegoing patterns. The industry learned how to use the technology effectively to turn out the "bilge" (Bakshy) to which audiences were accustomed and which they gladly patronized. Both before and after the coming of synchronous recorded music and dialogue, audiences appreciated humor, drama, action, spectacle, good stories, and appealing stars. They also liked novelty, which the talkies supplied for

"The Wedding of the Painted Doll," sheet music from THE BROADWAY MELODY *(MGM, 1929).*

a while. But when the thrill of the "New Era of Entertainment" had subsided, there remained the voice's psychological depth and unique capacity to define character, music's ability to sustain mood and underscore action, and acoustic verisimilitude creating an imaginary environment. These qualities were consistent with the film industry's aims and audience expectations at the turn of the 1930s, and remain so now. American cinema might possibly be art, but first and foremost it is mass entertainment.

Appendix 1

NEGATIVE COST AND DOMESTIC REVENUE
COMPARISON OF SELECTED TITLES
RELEASED 1927–1931

This table presents financial data about selected titles during the 1927–1931 transition to sound, compiled from published sources. The films are listed in order of general release date because that is when most people first would have seen them.

Warner Bros. (WB) and First National (FN) figures are from the William Schaefer ledger in the Schaefer Collection at the University of Southern California. (I am grateful to Ned Comstock, Bill Whittington, and Stuart Ng for their assistance.) Extracts from these ledgers have been published by H. Mark Glancy, "The Warner Bros. Film Grosses, 1921–1951: The William Schaefer Ledger," *Historical Journal of Film, Radio, and Television* 15, no. 1 (1995), pp. 55–73, plus microfiche appendix. For a discussion of the interpretation of the data, see also John Sedgwick, "The Warner Ledgers: A Comment," ibid., pp. 75–82.

Schaefer was a longtime WB executive under Jack Warner. The figures are based on cumulative total revenue to 1944, so they include income from re-releases. The Schaefer ledger does not specify whether these are rental or box-office grosses; I assume that they are rental grosses. Beginning with the 1929–1930 season, WB and FN grosses are not separated.

Loew's MGM data are from H. Mark Glancy, "MGM Film Grosses, 1924–1948: The Eddie Mannix Ledger," *Historical Journal of Film, Radio, and Television,* 12, no. 2 (1992), pp. 127–43, plus microfiche appendix. The original reasons for the existence of the Mannix ledger, which is in the Academy of Motion Picture Arts and Sciences Collection, are not clearly understood. Some have suggested that the executive was Louis B. Mayer's fiscal spy. The figures are rental grosses. Re-release figures are tallied separately and therefore have been excluded from my chart. Another version of this account is in appendix 1 of Samuel Marx, *Mayer and Thalberg: The Make-Believe Saints* (New York: Random House, 1975), pp. 254–64. Marx's table, without a source citation, provides profit-loss figures for selected titles for the five years after their release but omits domestic and foreign income. He includes a few titles not listed in the Mannix ledger. His cost, profit, and loss figures match the amounts in the Mannix ledger.

RKO (Radio Pictures) data are from Richard B. Jewell, "RKO Film Grosses, 1929–1951: The C. J. Tevlin Ledger," *Historical Journal of Film, Radio, and Television* 14, no. 1 (1994), pp. 37–49, plus microfiche appendix, and John Sedgwick, "Richard B. Jewell's RKO Film Grosses, 1929–1951: The C. J. Tevlin Ledger," ibid., pp. 51–58. Tevlin's figures were also cumulative—in this case, to June 1952. The ledger was compiled by the studio's General Statistics Department and signed by Tevlin, who reported to Howard Hughes, owner of RKO. Like the MGM ledger, this one contains profit/loss figures. It also details net income, so a film might seem profitable based on a positive gross (cf. ROGUE SONG) but still show a loss after expenses.

The Universal (Univ) data are very incomplete and list only "final cost." The source is "Shooting Record of Pictures," Universal Collection, USC.

In adapting this information to focus on domestic audience response, I have omitted foreign returns (supplied in all three original ledgers). (Domestic income includes the United States and Canada.) The "ratio" column is my own devising. This is not a complicated statistical operation; rather, it is simply the domestic return divided by the domestic return minus the negative cost. The resulting percentage approximates domestic return on investment and indicates box-office success. The ratio distinguishes hits from flops but should not be used for subtle distinctions between films because there are so many variable factors in the marketplace, not to mention the effects of "Hollywood accounting."

Some general disclaimers: The reliability of this data is not assured (see Ian Jarvie, "Comment [on Glancy's article]," *Historical Journal of Film, Radio, and Television,* 12, no. 2 [1992], pp. 143–44). The data seem to lump together all the versions (silent and sound, foreign) for each title. Finally, each studio used different accounting procedures, so interorganization comparisons are risky.

Title (Distributor)	Release Date¹	Negative Cost ($1,000)	Domestic Revenue ($1,000)	Ratio	Profit (Loss) ($1,000)
DON JUAN (WB)	15 Jan 27	546	1,258	130%	NA
THE BETTER 'OLE (WB)	5 Mar 27	449	955	113	NA
THE MISSING LINK (WB)	13 Aug 27	313	425	36	NA
WHEN A MAN LOVES (WB)	13 Aug 27	528	732	39	NA
OLD SAN FRANCISCO (WB)	24 Sep 27	300	466	55	NA
THE FIRST AUTO (WB)	15 Oct 27	187	169	-10	NA
THE JAZZ SINGER (WB)	17 Dec 27	422	1,974	368	NA
TENDERLOIN (WB)	14 Apr 28	188	889	373	NA
GLORIOUS BETSY (WB)	19 May 28	198	815	312	NA
THE LION AND THE MOUSE (WB)	9 Jun 28	113	869	669	NA
THE LIGHTS OF NEW YORK (WB)	7 Jul 28	23	1,160	4,943	NA
LILAC TIME (FN)	12 Aug 28	795	1,675	111	NA
OH KAY (FN)	19 Aug 28	386	475	23	NA
THE TERROR (WB)	8 Sep 28	163	1,221	649	NA
THE SINGING FOOL (WB)	22 Sep 28	388	3,821	885	NA
WHITE SHADOWS IN THE SOUTH SEAS (MGM)	10 Nov 28	365	NA	NA	450
ON TRIAL (WB)	1 Dec 28	130	1,089	738	NA
MY MAN (WB)	22 Dec 28	192	1,099	472	NA
SYNTHETIC SIN (FN)	23 Dec 28	419	496	18	NA
ALIAS JIMMY VALENTINE (MGM)	26 Jan 29	208	791	280	476
SONNY BOY (WB)	24 Mar 29	98	838	755	NA
THE VOICE OF THE CITY (MGM)	13 Apr 29	119	NA	NA	241
THE DESERT SONG (WB)	20 Apr 29	354	1,549	338	NA
ON WITH THE SHOW (WB)	1 Jun 29	493	1,741	253	NA
THE BROADWAY MELODY (MGM)	6 Jun 29	379	2,808	641	1,604
NOAH'S ARK (WB)	8 Jun 29	1,005	1,367	36	NA
THE TRIAL OF MARY DUGAN (MGM)	8 Jun 29	402	1,087	170	421

Title (Distributor)	Release Date[1]	Negative Cost ($1,000)	Domestic Revenue ($1,000)	Ratio	Profit (Loss) ($1,000)
Smiling Irish Eyes (FN)	28 Jul 29	501	614	23	NA
Madame X (MGM)	17 Aug 29	183	915	400	586
Hallelujah! (MGM)	20 Aug 29	320	NA	NA	(120)
Street Girl (RKO)	21 Aug 29	211	806	282	500
Marianne (MGM)	24 Aug 29	648	695	7	64
Say It with Songs (WB)	24 Aug 29	470	1,725	267	NA
Gold Diggers of Broadway (WB)	14 Sep 29	532	2,540	377	NA
Rio Rita (RKO)	15 Sep 29	678	1,775	162	935
His Glorious Night (MGM)	28 Sep 29	210	589	180	202
Disraeli (WB)	26 Oct 29	318	924	191	NA
Footlights and Fools (FN)	9 Nov 29	483	603	25	NA
The Hollywood Revue (MGM)	23 Nov 29	426	1,527	258	1,135
So Long Letty (WB)	23 Nov 29	293	406	39	NA
The Vagabond Lover (RKO)	1 Dec 29	204	671	229	335
Dynamite (MGM)	13 Dec 29	661	894	35	79
The Show of Shows (WB)	28 Dec 29	795	1,259	58	NA
No, No, Nanette (FN)	11 Jan 30	418	839	101	NA
Sally (FN)	11 Jan 30	647	1,219	88	NA
Seven Keys to Baldpate (RKO)	12 Jan 30	251	437	74	100
General Crack (WB)	18 Jan 30	801	919	15	NA
Son of the Gods (FN)	8 Feb 30	436	1,069	145	NA
Anna Christie (MGM)	21 Feb 30	376	1,013	169	576
The Case of Sergeant Grischa (RKO)	23 Feb 30	467	407	-13	(170)
Hit the Deck (RKO)	23 Feb 30	542	980	81	145
Free and Easy (MGM)	22 Mar 30	473	438	-7	32
Under a Texas Moon (WB)	29 Mar 30	486	667	37	NA
Hold Everything (WB)	5 Apr 30	491	1,018	107	NA

REDEMPTION (MGM)	5 Apr 30	561	398	-29	(215)
LOVIN' THE LADIES (RKO)	6 Apr 30	207	370	79	65
THE DIVORCÉE (MGM)	19 Apr 30	341	842	147	335
CHILDREN OF PLEASURE (MGM)	26 Apr 30	299	260	-13	(103)
MAMMY (WB)	3 May 30	786	789	0	NA
THE CUCKOOS (RKO)	4 May 30	407	662	63	130
THE MAN FROM BLANKLEY'S (WB)	10 May 30	422	311	-26	NA
THE ROGUE SONG (MGM)	10 May 30	646	824	28	(109)
THE BIG HOUSE (MGM)	21 Jun 30	414	1,279	209	462
FIRES OF YOUTH (Univ)	24 Jun 30	255	NA	NA	NA
THE UNHOLY THREE (MGM)	12 Jul 30	279	716	157	375
THE DAWN PATROL (FN)	19 Jul 30	729	1,061	46	NA
OUR BLUSHING BRIDES (MGM)	19 Jul 30	337	874	159	412
DIXIANA (RKO)	1 Aug 30	747	500	-33	(300)
LET US BE GAY (MGM)	9 Aug 30	257	829	223	527
ROMANCE (MGM)	26 Aug 30	496	733	48	287
DOUGHBOYS (MGM)	30 Aug 30	276	428	55	150
BIG BOY (WB)	6 Sep 30	574	437	-24	NA
MOBY DICK (WB)	6 Sep 30	604	579	-4	NA
EAST IS WEST (Univ)	12 Sep 30	422	NA	NA	NA
MADAM SATAN (MGM)	20 Sep 30	987	NA	NA	(390)
THE CAT CREEPS (Univ)	2 Oct 30	214	NA	NA	NA
HALF SHOT AT SUNRISE (RKO)	4 Oct 30	529	653	23	40
WAY FOR A SAILOR (MGM)	11 Oct 30[2]	889	NA	NA	(666)
BILLY THE KID (MGM)	18 Oct 30	605	709	17	(119)
DOORWAY TO HELL (WB)	18 Oct 30	240	613	155	NA
CHECK AND DOUBLE CHECK (RKO)	25 Oct 30	967	1,751	81	260

Title (Distributor)	Release Date[1]	Negative Cost ($1,000)	Domestic Revenue ($1,000)	Ratio	Profit (Loss) ($1,000)
Min and Bill (MGM)	29 Nov 30	327	1,223	274	731
Dracula (Univ)	9 Dec 30	341	NA	NA	NA
Hook, Line and Sinker (RKO)	26 Dec 30	287	595	107	225
Kismet (FN)	3 Jan 31	611	315	-48	NA
Viennese Nights (WB)	3 Jan 31	604	343	-43	NA
Little Caesar (FN)	17 Jan 31	281	647	130	NA
New Moon (MGM)	17 Jan 31	782	508	-35	(243)
Beau Ideal (RKO)	25 Jan 31	707	390	-45	(330)
Cimarron (RKO)	9 Feb 31	1,433	1,122	-22	(565)
Fifty Million Frenchmen (WB)	14 Feb 31	484	401	-17	NA
Gentleman's Fate (MGM)	7 Mar 31	500	375	-25	(216)
Law and Order (Univ)	23 Mar 31	156/185[3]	NA	NA	NA
Cracked Nuts (RKO)	19 Apr 31	262	595	93	150
Svengali (WB)	9 May 31	499	359	-28	NA
Public Enemy (WB)	15 May 31	230	464	102	NA
Trader Horn (MGM)	23 May 31	1,322	1,642	24	937
Everything's Rosie (RKO)	13 Jun 31	140	205	46	35

1. National release dates are as per studio records for Warner Bros. and First National. Others derive from the *AFI Catalogue.* Note that this date may vary considerably from the premiere screening. (It is usually later, but sometimes general release occurs before the premiere).

2. The *AFI Catalogue* also gives 1 November 1930 as a release date.

3. The second figure includes the cost of "added scenes."

Appendix 2

ACADEMY AWARDS RELATED
TO SOUND, 1927–1931

1927–1928 (presented 16 May 1929)

Production: WINGS (Paramount Famous Lasky)
Unique and Artistic Picture:[1] SUNRISE (Fox)
Actor: Emil Jannings, for THE LAST COMMAND and THE WAY OF ALL FLESH (both Paramount)
Actress: Janet Gaynor, for SEVENTH HEAVEN, STREET ANGEL, and SUNRISE (all Fox)
Direction—Dramatic Picture: Frank Borzage, for SEVENTH HEAVEN
Cinematography: Charles Rosher and Karl Struss, for SUNRISE
Engineering Effects:[2] Roy Pomeroy, for WINGS
Special Awards: Warner Bros., "for producing THE JAZZ SINGER, the pioneer outstanding talking picture, which has revolutionized the industry."[3]

1928–1929 (presented 30 April 1930)

Production: THE BROADWAY MELODY (MGM) (nominated: ALIBI [UA], THE HOLLYWOOD REVUE [MGM], IN OLD ARIZONA [Fox], and THE PATRIOT [Paramount Famous Lasky])
Actor: Warner Baxter, for IN OLD ARIZONA (nominated: George Bancroft, for THUNDERBOLT [Paramount Famous Lasky]; Chester Morris, for ALIBI; Paul Muni, for THE VALIANT [Fox]; and Lewis Stone, for THE PATRIOT)
Actress: Mary Pickford, for COQUETTE (UA) (nominated: Ruth Chatterton, for MADAME X [MGM]; Betty Compson, for THE BARKER [First National]; Jeanne Eagels, for THE LETTER [Paramount Famous Lasky]; Corinne Griffith, for THE DIVINE LADY [First National]; and Bessie Love, for THE BROADWAY MELODY [MGM])
Director: Frank Lloyd, for THE DIVINE LADY (nominated: Lionel Barrymore, for MADAME X; Harry Beaumont, for THE BROADWAY MELODY; Irving Cummings, for IN OLD ARIZONA; Frank Lloyd, for DRAG and WEARY RIVER [both First National]; and Ernst Lubitsch, for THE PATRIOT)
Cinematography: Clyde de Vinna, for WHITE SHADOWS IN THE SOUTH SEAS (MGM) (nominated: George Barnes, for OUR DANCING DAUGHTERS [MGM]; Arthur Edeson,

for IN OLD ARIZONA; Ernest Palmer, for FOUR DEVILS and STREET ANGEL [both Fox]; and John Seitz, for THE DIVINE LADY)

1929–1930 (presented 5 November 1930)

Production: ALL QUIET ON THE WESTERN FRONT (Universal) (nominated: THE BIG HOUSE [MGM], DISRAELI [Warner Bros.], THE DIVORCÉE [MGM], and THE LOVE PARADE [Paramount Famous Lasky])
Actor: George Arliss, for DISRAELI (nominated: George Arliss, for THE GREEN GODDESS [Warner Bros.]; Wallace Beery, for THE BIG HOUSE; Maurice Chevalier, for THE BIG POND [Paramount Famous Lasky]; Ronald Colman, for BULLDOG DRUMMOND and CONDEMNED [both UA]; and Lawrence Tibbett, for THE ROGUE SONG [MGM])
Actress: Norma Shearer, for THE DIVORCÉE (nominated: Nancy Carroll, for THE DEVIL'S HOLIDAY [Paramount Publix]; Ruth Chatterton, for SARAH AND SON [Paramount Famous Lasky]; Greta Garbo, for ANNA CHRISTIE and ROMANCE [both MGM]; Norma Shearer, for THEIR OWN DESIRE [MGM]; and Gloria Swanson, for THE TRESPASSER [UA])
Director: Lewis Milestone, for ALL QUIET ON THE WESTERN FRONT (nominated: Clarence Brown, for ANNA CHRISTIE and ROMANCE; Robert Z. Leonard, for THE DIVORCÉE; Ernst Lubitsch, for THE LOVE PARADE; and King Vidor, for HALLELUJAH! [MGM])
Cinematography: Joseph T. Rucker and Willard Van Der Veer, for WITH BYRD AT THE SOUTH POLE (Paramount Publix) (nominated: William Daniels, for ANNA CHRISTIE; Arthur Edeson, for ALL QUIET ON THE WESTERN FRONT; Gaetano Gaudio and Harry Perry, for HELL'S ANGELS [UA]; and Victor Milner, for THE LOVE PARADE)
Sound Recording:[4] Douglas Shearer, head of MGM sound department, for THE BIG HOUSE (nominated: George Groves, for SONG OF THE FLAME [First National]; Franklin Hansen, for THE LOVE PARADE; Oscar Lagerstrom, for RAFFLES [UA]; and John Tribby, for THE CASE OF SERGEANT GRISCHA [RKO Radio])

1930–1931 (presented 10 November 1931)

Production: CIMARRON (RKO Radio) (nominated: EAST LYNNE [Fox], THE FRONT PAGE [UA], SKIPPY [Paramount Publix], and TRADER HORN [MGM])
Actor: Lionel Barrymore, for A FREE SOUL (MGM) (nominated: Jackie Cooper, for SKIPPY; Richard Dix, for CIMARRON; Fredric March, for THE ROYAL FAMILY OF BROADWAY [Paramount Publix]; and Adolphe Menjou, for THE FRONT PAGE)
Actress: Marie Dressler, for MIN AND BILL (MGM) (nominated: Marlene Dietrich, for MOROCCO [Paramount Publix]; Irene Dunne, for CIMARRON; Ann Harding, for HOLIDAY; and Norma Shearer, for A FREE SOUL)
Director: Norman Taurog, for SKIPPY (nominated: Clarence Brown, for A FREE SOUL; Lewis Milestone, for THE FRONT PAGE; Wesley Ruggles, for CIMARRON; and Josef von Sternberg, for MOROCCO)
Cinematography: Floyd Crosby, for TABU (Paramount Publix) (nominated: Edward Cronjager, for CIMARRON; Lee Garmes, for MOROCCO; Charles Lang, for THE RIGHT TO LOVE [Paramount Publix]; and Barney McGill, for SVENGALI [Warner Bros.])

Sound Recording:[5] Paramount Publix Studio Sound Department (nominated: studio sound departments at MGM, RKO Radio, and Samuel Goldwyn–United Artists)
Scientific or Technical, Class 1:[6] Electrical Research Products, Inc. (ERPI) and RKO Pictures, Inc., for noise-reduction sound-recording equipment; DuPont Film Manufacturing Corporation and Eastman Kodak Company, for supersensitive panchromatic film
Scientific or Technical, Class 3:[7] Electrical Research Products, Inc. (ERPI), for moving-coil microphone transmitters; RKO Radio Pictures, Inc., for reflex-type microphone concentrators; RCA-Photophone, Inc., for ribbon microphone transmitters

SOURCES

Compiled from Charles Matthews, *Oscar A-Z: A Complete Guide to More Than 2,400 Movies Nominated for Academy Awards* (New York: Doubleday, 1995); and Richard Shales, *The Academy Awards Index* (Westport, Conn.: Greenwood, 1993).

NOTES

1. Category discontinued after this year.
2. Category discontinued after this year.
3. Charles Chaplin also received a special award "for versatility and genius in writing, acting, directing and producing THE CIRCUS." The Academy had ruled that only silent films were eligible for best-production awards.
4. First year for this category. Awards were given to the studio sound department responsible for the title.
5. The award was given for "collective achievement" by a sound department, not to individual productions.
6. First year for this category. Class 1 awards were for basic achievements which advanced the industry.
7. First year for this category. Class 2 awards were for high levels of engineering. Class 3 awards were for technical achievement.

List of Abbreviations

AEG	Allgemeine Elektrizitäts Gesellschaft
AFM	American Federation of Musicians
AMPP	Association of Motion Picture Producers
AMPAS	Academy of Motion Picture Arts and Sciences
ASCAP	American Society of Composers, Authors, and Publishers
BIP	British International Pictures
ERPI	Electrical Research Products, Inc.
FBO	Film Booking Office
FCC	Federal Communications Commission
FRC	Federal Radio Commission
FTC	Federal Trade Commission
IATSE	International Alliance of Theatrical Stage Employees
MPPA	Music Publishers Protective Association
MPPDA	Motion Picture Producers and Distributors of America
MPTOA	Motion Picture Theater Owners of America
NBC	National Broadcasting Company
NSS	National Screen Service
PDC	Producers Distributing Company
RCA	Radio Corporation of America
SMPE	Society of Motion Picture Engineers
	Tobis Tonbild Syndikat AG

Notes

CHAPTER 1. Introduction: The Uncertainty of Sound

1. Fitzhugh Green, *The Film Finds Its Tongue* (New York: Putnam's, 1929), pp. 42–43 (emphasis in the original).
2. John Douglas Gomery, *The Coming of Sound to the American Cinema* (Ph.D. dissertation, University of Wisconsin, 1975), p. 460.
3. Green, *The Film Finds Its Tongue,* p. 313.
4. David Bordwell, "The Introduction of Sound," in Bordwell, Janet Staiger, and Kristin Thompson, eds., *The Classical Hollywood Cinema: Film Style and Mode of Production to 1960* (New York: Columbia University Press, 1985), p. 306.
5. Rick Altman, ed., *Sound Theory/Sound Practice* (New York: Routledge, 1992), p. 3.
6. Unpublished survey (names withheld), Northeast Historic Film, Bucksport, Maine, 1990–1991. Courtesy of Karan Sheldon. I am grateful to Tom Gunning for bringing this survey to my attention.
7. *Photoplay,* September 1928, p. 57.
8. H. G. Knox, "The Ancestry of Sound Recording," *Cinematographic Annual 1930,* pp. 283–84.
9. Bryan Taylor, "Annual Returns on Stocks, Bonds, Bills and Inflation in the United States, 1802–1995," *Barron's,* 2 December 1996, p. 5. Meanwhile, consumer prices declined about 1 percent during the 1920s.

PART 1. A New Era in Electrical Entertainment

1. Peter Wollen, "Cinema and Technology: A Historical Overview," in Teresa de Lauretis and Stephen Heath, eds., *The Cinematic Apparatus* (London: Macmillan, 1980), p. 14.
2. Sheldon Hochheiser has pointed out that the Vitaphone "was not a single piece of equipment; it was a complex system of many interdependent parts." "AT&T and the Development of Sound Motion-Picture Technology," in Mary Lea Bandy, ed., *The Dawn of Sound* (New York: Museum of Modern Art), p. 23.
3. *Film Daily,* 1 July 1928, p. 35.
4. *Film Daily,* 5 September 1928, p. 4.

CHAPTER 2. Electric Affinities

1. George Klee, quoted in "When the Dumb Actor Speaks," *Literary Digest,* 2 June 1928, p. 29.
2. Rob Wagner, "Lend Me Your Ears," *Collier's,* 11 January 1930, p. 11.
3. Jesse L. Lasky, "Hearing Things in the Dark," *Collier's,* May 1929, p. 8.
4. Terry Ramsaye, "The Industry," *Theatre Arts Monthly,* September 1929, p. 663.
5. Rob Wagner, "Silence Isn't Golden Any More," *Collier's,* August 1928, p. 48.
6. Myron M. Stearns, "The Movies Talk!" *Ladies' Home Journal,* November 1928, p. 199; Robert E. MacAlarney, "The Noise Movie Revolution," *World's Work,* April 1929, p. 48; Peggy Wood, "See and Hear," *Saturday Evening Post,* 20 July 1929, p. 82.

7. Raymond Francis Yates, "Mr. Hoxie's Talking Film," *Literary Digest,* 9 December 1922, p. 26.

8. "Pictures That Talk," *Scientific American,* January 1923, pp. 19ff.

9. Wagner, "Silence Isn't Golden Any More," p. 12.

10. Robert E. Sherwood, "Beyond the Talkies—Television," *Scribner's,* July 1929, p. 6.

11. Gilbert Seldes, *The Great Audience* (New York: Viking, 1950).

12. D. W. Griffith, "The Movies 100 Years from Now," *Collier's,* 3 May 1924, p. 7.

13. It should be pointed out that earlier (1927–1928) Beaton had been in favor of the talkies. His later views were against the uses to which Hollywood was putting sound.

14. In her study of nineteenth-century "electrical communication," Carolyn Marvin argued that the social dimension of communication technology has been overlooked by historians. "Electrical and other media," she claims, "precipitated new kinds of social encounters long before their incarnation in fixed institutional form." Carolyn Marvin, *When Old Technologies Were New* (New York: Oxford University Press, 1988), p. 5.

15. F. H. Richardson, *Handbook of Projection: The Blue Book of Projection,* vol. 3, rev. (New York: Chalmers, 1930), pp. 989, 1016.

16. Although he was born "De Forest," throughout his adult life the inventor spelled his own name "de Forest"; James A. Hijiya, *Lee de Forest and the Fatherhood of Radio* (Bethlehem, Pa.: Lehigh University Press, 1992), p. 152. Hereafter the capitalized "De Forest" refers to corporate entities and the lower-cased "de Forest" refers to the person.

17. Susan Douglas, *Inventing American Broadcasting, 1899–1922* (Baltimore: Johns Hopkins University Press, 1987).

18. *Film Daily,* 31 July 1929, p. 1; 1 August 1929, p. 5.

19. Gerald F. J. Tyne, *Saga of the Vacuum Tube* (Indianapolis: Sams, 1977), pp. 114–15. The AT&T researchers did not believe that simply using a vacuum was patentable and did not file an application until after they learned that GE engineers were doing so. The ensuing litigation lasted until 1925, with the patent awarded to Langmuir at GE. AT&T and GE soon after exchanged patents, giving each equal access to thermionic technology. Edward W. Kellogg, "History of Sound Motion Pictures" [third installment], *JSMPTE,* July 1955, reprinted in Raymond Fielding, ed., *A Technological History of Motion Pictures and Television* (Berkeley: University of California Press, 1967), p. 218.

20. Tyne, *Saga of the Vacuum Tube,* p. 126; S. Handel, *The Electronic Revolution* (Baltimore: Penguin Books, 1967), p. 62.

21. See Alfred Chandler, *The Visible Hand: The Managerial Revolution in American Business* (Cambridge: Harvard University Press, 1977); Thomas C. Cochran, *Business in American Life: A History* (New York: McGraw-Hill, 1972).

22. William Peck Banning, *Commercial Broadcasting Pioneer: The WEAF Experiment, 1911–1926* (Cambridge: Harvard University Press, 1946), p. 280.

23. Tyne, *Saga of the Vacuum Tube,* p. 126

24. Ibid., p. 131.

25. Kellogg, "History of Sound Motion Pictures," pp. 176, 217–18; Tyne, *Saga of the Vacuum Tube,* pp. 134–43, 155.

26. GE sued de Forest for infringement of various patents in 1926.

27. A British inventor, H. Grindell-Matthews, was granted patents on a gas discharge tube design in England in 1922, and in the United States in 1926. He claimed that the Case invention infringed upon his patents and sued Fox in 1928. *Film Daily,* 27 September 1928, pp. 1, 2.

28. Handel, *The Electronic Revolution,* p. 68.

29. Kellogg, "History of Sound Motion Pictures," p. 178; *Film Daily,* 6 August 1946, p. 35. The rare earth used was thallium oxysulfide. Later Case switched to barium.

30. Lee DeForest [*sic*], Ph.D., "When Light Speaks," *Scientific American,* August 1923, p. 94.

31. Kellogg, "History of Sound Motion Pictures," pp. 176–78; Hijiya, *Lee de Forest,* pp. 102–7; Tom Lewis, *Empire of the Air: The Men Who Made Radio* (New York: HarperCollins, 1991), pp. 170–174.

32. Claude S. Fischer, *America Calling: A Social History of the Telephone to 1940* (Berkeley: University of California Press, 1992), p. 51; data from chart on p. 22. The number of phone subscriptions declined rapidly during the Depression, then recovered to about 35 percent in 1939. See also John Brooks, *Telephone: The First Hundred Years* (New York: Harper & Row, 1976), pp. 178–79.

33. Brooks, *Telephone,* p. 142.

34. Fischer, *America Calling,* p. 66.

35. Warner Bros., "Vitaphone Is Thrilling the World" [brochure], 1926, p. 3.

36. Hochheiser, "AT&T and . . . Sound Motion-Picture Technology," p. 25.

37. Richardson, *Handbook of Projection,* pp. 969–70; Barry Salt, *Film Style and Technology: History and Analysis* (London: Starword, 1983), p. 229.

38. Hochheiser, "AT&T and . . . Sound Motion-Picture Technology," p. 25.

39. Richardson, *Handbook of Projection,* pp. 1075–77. These multiple horns all delivered monophonic sound. Early projectionists were able to switch the sound track between pairs of speakers to create a directional effect, and Warners provided "fader cue" sheets for the purpose. This practice, one might say, "performance" relied on a competent, discerning, and committed operator. It did not last long.

40. De Forest had described the current emanating from microphones and photoelectric cells as "telephonic." "When Light Speaks," p. 94.

41. Julie D'Acci, "The Industrialization of U.S. Radio Culture: WEAF (1922–1926) and NBC (1926–1929) (unpublished paper, 1995), p. 2.

42. Susan Smulyan, *Selling Radio: The Commercialization of American Broadcasting, 1920–1934* (Washington, D.C.: Smithsonian Institution Press, 1994), p. 117. Robert W. McChesney has discussed the importance of studying radio *after* the implementation of the Communications Act of 1927; *Telecommunications, Mass Media, and Democracy: The Battle for the Control of U.S. Broadcasting, 1928–1935* (New York: Oxford University Press, 1993), pp. 3–6, 12–37.

43. Colin Gordon, *New Deal, Old Deck: Business, Labor, and Politics, 1920–1935* (Ph.D. dissertation, University of Wisconsin, 1990), p. 180. The United Fruit Company also had an interest in the formation of RCA: it foresaw wireless communications linking its South American offices and plantations.

44. AT&T annual report, 1921, quoted in Brooks, *Telephone,* p. 161.

45. Brooks, *Telephone,* pp. 164–65. The reference is to the Kingsbury Commitment of 1913.

46. Walter Gifford, quoted in ibid., p. 171. Banning (*Commercial Broadcasting Pioneer*) offers many details concerning the transaction.

47. Richardson, *Handbook of Projection,* p. 962.

48. Walter Davenport, "The Silent Drama Speaks," *Collier's,* 2 July 1927, p. 17; *Film Daily,* 11 December 1927, pp. 1–2.

49. *Film Daily,* 29 March 1922, p. 2. An *American Cinematographer* account of Powers's process is reproduced in Altman, "Introduction: Sound/History," *Sound Theory/Sound Practice,* pp. 118–19.

50. *Film Daily,* 7 November 1923, p. 1.

51. Joe "Danny" Dannenberg, *Film Daily,* 26 August 1925, p. 1; 27 August, p. 4. A few months later, RCA was testing its system with First National (*Film Daily,* 14 January 1926, pp. 1, 4).

52. *Film Daily,* 27 August 1925, p. 4; Bosley Crowther, *The Lion's Share* (New York: Dutton, 1957; reprint, New York: Garland, 1985), pp. 138–39. Douglas Shearer became MGM's first recording engineer, a job he still held on SINGIN' IN THE RAIN in 1952.

53. In 1924 "Roxy's Gang," carried on WEAF's network, was one of the most popular radio programs; see Smulyan, *Selling Radio,* p. 55.

54. *Film Daily,* 27 January 1924, p. 5.

55. *Film Daily,* 25 May 1927, p. 1; 20 September 1927, pp. 1, 5; Michele Hilmes, *Hollywood and Broadcasting: From Radio to Cable* (Urbana: University of Illinois Press, 1990), pp. 38–42.

56. *Film Daily,* 11 December 1927, pp. 1, 12.

57. The Fifth Avenue Playhouse was a poor choice for this experiment: as the nation's leading art house, its audience would not have been disposed to like this kind of commercial presentation. (Thanks to Kristin Thompson for this observation.)

58. *Film Daily,* 15 March 1928, pp. 1, 6; 19 March 1928, p. 1; 28 March 1928, p. 7; 3 April 1928, pp. 1, 7.

59. *Film Daily,* 20 March 1928, p. 1.

60. *Film Daily,* 26 March 1928, p. 1; 28 March 1928, pp. 1, 8.

61. "It appears that the straw that broke the patience of the audiences was the sales talk for Dodge cars which the president of the motor car company gave after Paul Whiteman had played his first selection"; *Film Daily,* 1 April 1928, pp. 1, 4. Walker begins with an account of this event, concluding, "All in all, it was a bad omen for the talkies"; Alexander Walker, *The Shattered Silents: How the Talkies Came to Stay* (New York: Morrow, 1979), pp. 1–4.

62. *Film Daily,* 1 April 1928, p. 2; 29 July 1928, p. 1. The premises vacated by KFWB were leased to Leon Schlesinger Productions for his Looney Tunes and Merrie Melodies. The building later became known among generations of animators as "Termite Terrace."

63. *Film Daily,* 7 November 1928, p. 1.

64. Hilmes, *Hollywood and Broadcasting,* p. 26.

65. W. E. Harkness to Frank Jewett, 12 December 1923, AT&T Archives. Harkness's letter also shows that the company was aware of potential music licensing problems that broadcasting performances would create. "It might also be advantageous to us to have the rights in reproductions of this class when negotiating with the various phonograph companies or musical organizations with whom we will have to deal."

66. The future ERPI would handle all three of these functions: Vitaphone movie sound, the Western Electric transcription system for radio, and music license clearance. For discussions of superpower and shortwave, see Smulyan, *Selling Radio,* pp. 44–52; for *The Amos 'n' Andy Show,* p. 114. Warner Bros. later began producing and distributing radio shows by transcription; *Film Daily,* 23 April 1931, p. 1.

67. "When Radio Answered a Call to Hollywood," *New York Times,* 10 August 1930, sect. 9, p. 12.

68. *Film Daily,* 3 May 1922, p. 3.

69. *Film Daily,* 29 April 1925, p. 6. Using a "strip of rotating film," a University of Wisconsin student, Douglas Coffey, claimed to have transmitted moving pictures by radio seven miles across Lake Mendota; *Film Daily,* 25 August 1925, p. 1. Jenkins broadcast a "radio pictures" program three nights a week in Washington, D.C., in the summer of 1928; *Film Daily,* 11 July 1928, p. 1.

70. *Film Daily,* 14 April 1924, pp. 1–2; 21 May 1924, p. 2.

71. *Film Daily,* 12 April 1927, p. 7.

72. *Film Daily,* 28 November 1927, p. 1. Presumably, Edison was filmed with the Photophone film sound system, and it was this image that was broadcast on the Kenographone.

73. Elma G. "Pem" Farnsworth, *Distant Vision* (Salt Lake City: Pemberly Kent, 1989), p. 121.

74. Lewis, *Empire of the Air,* pp. 311, 185; Handel, *The Electronic Revolution,* pp. 70, 201.

75. *Film Daily,* 9 January 1928, p. 1; 13 January 1928, p. 1; 24 August 1928, p. 8; 20 January 1931, p. 5. Film executives were impressed by a demonstration of theatrical TV at B. S. Moss's Broadway Theater. Paramount sold its interest in CBS to William Paley for $5.2 million; *Film Daily,* 23 October 1931, p. 1; 9 March 1931, p. 1. Tim White has concluded, "The failure of the studios to establish themselves as forces in television broadcasting was a result of FCC policy, not Hollywood incompetence"; "Hollywood's Attempt at Appropriating Television: The Case of Paramount Pictures," in Tino Balio, ed., *Hollywood in the Age of Television* (Boston: Unwin Hyman, 1990), p. 146.

76. For the RCA demonstration, see White, "Hollywood's Attempt at Appropriating Television," p. 150.

77. "Films That Talk," *Literary Digest,* 3 December 1921, p. 20. This article cites Ernest Rühmer in Germany, A. O. Rankine in England, Berglund in Sweden, and Grindell Matthews as predecessors.

78. Merritt Crawford, "Pioneer Experiments of Eugene Lauste in Recording Sound," *Journal of the Society of Motion Picture Engineers,* October 1931, reprinted in Fielding, *A Technological History,* pp. 71–75; Kellogg, "History of Sound Motion Pictures," pp. 176–177. Lauste letter quoted verbatim from David Robinson, *Chaplin: His Life and Art* (New York: McGraw-Hill, 1985), p. 388.

79. "Talking Films Again," *Film Daily,* 12 July 1922, p. 1; Joseph Tykocinski-Tykociner, "Photographic Recording and Photoelectric Reproduction of Sound," *Transactions of the Society of Motion Picture Engineers (SMPE)* 16, May 1923, pp. 90–119; John B. McCullough, "Joseph T. Tykociner: Pioneer in Sound Recording," *JSMPTE* 67, August 1958, reprinted in Fielding, *A Technological History,* p. 221; Joseph E. Aiken, "Technical Notes and Reminiscences on the Presentation of Tykociner's Sound Picture Contributions," *JSMPTE* 67, August 1958, reprinted in Fielding, *A Technological History,* p. 222.

80. Hijiya, *Lee de Forest,* p. 102; Lewis, *Empire of the Air,* p. 170.

81. Yates, "Mr. Hoxie's Talking Film," p. 26.

82. Gleason L. Archer, *Big Business and Radio* (New York: American Historical Co., 1939), pp. 323–25.

83. Hochheiser, "AT&T and . . . Sound Motion-Picture Technology," p. 25.

84. Kellogg, "History of Sound Motion Pictures," p. 209.

85. By 1928 the giant AEG Telefunken and BASF companies had developed Poulsen's concept into the Magnetophone. This forerunner of the tape recorder used a powdered iron emulsion on a flexible acetate band. Bell Laboratories, during the 1930s, experimented with recording on a thin

foil ribbon; Hijiya, *Lee de Forest*, p. 91; Kellogg, "History of Sound Motion Pictures," pp. 215, 176. German researchers were the acknowledged leaders in this type of high-quality recording. Their confiscated patents were made available in 1946 to American film studios; John Belton, "1950s Magnetic Sound: The Frozen Revolution," in Altman, *Sound Theory/Sound Practice*, pp. 154–55.

86. Emmanuelle Toulet, "Cinema at the Universal Exposition, Paris, 1900," *Persistence of Vision* no. 9 (1991), pp. 25–27.

87. Léon Gaumont, "Gaumont Chronochrome Process Described by the Inventor," *JSMPTE* 68, January 1959, reprinted in Fielding, *A Technological History*, pp. 65–67; Alice Guy, *Autobiographie d'une pionnière du cinéma* (Paris: Denoël/Gonthier, 1976), pp. 106–9.

88. The event described is not specifically identified as a Kinetophone presentation, but one assumes that most of these early phonographic experiments produced similar results. The incident of the running-down phonograph is questionable, however, since all known systems used electrically driven equipment.

89. Kellogg, "History of Sound Motion Pictures," p. 174; Gomery, *The Coming of Sound*, pp. 34–38; *Film Daily*, 6 August 1946, p. 35. Other phonographic systems described by Kellogg are the Synchroscope (exploited by Laemmle) and apparatuses by Georges Pomerede, E. H. Amet, and William H. Bristol. Gomery mentions the Cameraphone, the Cinephone, and Cecil Hepworth's Vivaphone.

90. Louis J. Stellum, "He Makes the Movies Talk," *Sunset*, August 1925, p. 52; Richard Schickel, *D. W. Griffith: An American Life* (New York: Simon and Schuster, 1984), pp. 451–52; Richard Barrios, *A Song in the Dark: The Birth of the Musical Film* (New York: Oxford, 1995), p. 15. The UCLA film archive holds two Kellum shorts, including one featuring the African American comedians Flourney Miller and Aubrey Lyles. They wrote the book for *Shuffle Along* (1921), "the first important all-black musical show to attract a white audience"; Anthony Slide, *The Encyclopedia of Vaudeville* (Westport, Conn.: Greenwood, 1994), p. 345.

91. Archer, *Big Business and Radio*, p. 324; Gomery, *The Coming of Sound*, p. 114.

92. W. S. Bachman et al., "Disk Recording and Reproduction," *Institute of Electrical Engineers Proceedings* 50, May 1962, pp. 738–44; J. P. Maxfield and H. C. Harrison, "Methods of High-Quality Recording and Reproducing of Music and Speech Based on Telephone Research," *American Institute of Electrical Engineers Transactions* 45, 1926, pp. 334–46; both articles reprinted in H. E. Roys, ed., *Disc Recording and Reproduction* (Stroudsburg, Pa.: Dowden, Hutchinson & Ross, 1978).

93. Edward W. Kellogg, "Electrical Reproduction from Phonograph Records," *American Institute of Electrical Engineers Transactions* 46, 1927, p. 29, reprinted in Roys, *Disc Recording and Reproduction*.

94. Richard Koszarski, "On the Record: Seeing and Hearing the Vitaphone," in Bandy, ed., *The Dawn of Sound*, p. 16.

95. W. S. Bachman et al., "Disk Recording and Reproduction," *Institute of Electrical Engineers Proceedings* 50, May 1962, pp. 738–44; J. P. Maxfield and H. C. Harrison, "Methods 1. Advertisement," *Exhibitors Herald-World*, 21 December 1929, p. 7.

96. George Kent Shuler, "Pictures and Personalities," *Motion Picture Classic*, August 1928, p. 15.

97. Lee de Forest, "Tomorrow—Who Knows?" *Saturday Evening Post*, 10 August 1929, p. 51.

CHAPTER 3. Virtual Broadway, Virtual Orchestra: De Forest and Vitaphone

1. *Film Daily*, 24 April and 19 September 1922; Lewis, *Empire of the Air*, pp. 171–72. In 1925 Tri-Ergon, Ltd., opened an office as a Swiss-chartered company at 200 Fifth Avenue to introduce talking films to American markets. The announcement cited seven years of research by J. Masselle [*sic*], H. Vogt, and J. Engl and claimed that UFA had purchased the rights to use the process in German-speaking countries; *Film Daily*, 10 August 1926; 11 August 1925, pp. 1–2; "Fox-Tri-Ergon Defeat in U.S. Was No Surprise to Europe," *Hollywood Reporter*, 16 March 1935. On American Tri-Ergon's claim, see *Film Daily*, 9 February 1932, pp. 1, 7; Kevin Brownlow, *The Parade's Gone By* (New York: Knopf, 1968), p. 657.

2. "Dr. DeForest's Talking Film," *Literary Digest*, 16 September 1922, pp. 28–29; "The Talking Movies," *Radio Broadcast*, December 1922, pp. 95–96.

3. Hijiya, *Lee de Forest,* p. 105. According to Hijiya, in 1924 William Fox learned of Phonofilm installations in six of his theaters and ordered their removal.

4. *Film Daily,* 23 September and 21 October 1922.

5. *New York Times,* quoted in *Film Daily,* 17 April 1923, p. 2; Betty Lasky, *RKO: The Biggest Little Major of Them All* (Santa Monica, Calif.: Roundtable, 1989), p. 20.

6. Fred E. Baer, "An Innovation for the Program," *Film Daily,* 3 June 1923, p. 41. For early cinema exhibition practices, see Charles Musser, *The Emergence of Cinema: The American Screen to 1907* (New York: Charles Scribner's Sons, 1990); and *Before the Nickelodeon: Edwin S. Porter and the Edison Manufacturing Company* (Berkeley: University of California Press, 1991).

7. *Film Daily,* 24 February 1924, pp. 1–2. Edward H. Jewett (Jewett-Page Automobile Company), Frederick W. Peck (a manufacturer), Rhinelander Waldo (a former New York police commissioner), and William E. Waddell (former manager of the American Talking Picture Company) were on the board.

8. *Film Daily,* 6 February 1924, pp. 1, 6; 17 February 1924, pp. 9, 33.

9. *Film Daily,* 12 March 1924, p. 11.

10. THE COVERED WAGON and SIEGFRIED were exhibited with Phonofilm scores only at the Rivoli, and then only during hours when the orchestra was off; Gomery, *The Coming of Sound,* pp. 44–45.

11. Charles Musser, in collaboration with Carol Nelson, *High-class Moving Pictures: Lyman H. Howe and the Forgotten Era of Traveling Exhibition, 1880–1920* (Princeton, N.J.: Princeton University Press, 1991).

12. Hijiya, *Lee de Forest,* pp. 103–4; Gomery, *The Coming of Sound,* pp. 40–42.

13. One investor, Julius Burns, sued de Forest for $882,000, claiming that the company had reneged on a contract option for $40 per share. *Film Daily,* 27 June 1924, pp. 1–2.

14. *Film Daily,* 30 November 1924, p. 4.

15. *Film Daily,* 19 December 1924, p. 1. De Forest had set up a British subsidiary and sold the rights to C. F. Elwell in July 1923. At its initial London demonstration, the sound was described as "throaty." Rachel Low, *The History of the British Film, 1918–1929* (London: Allen & Unwin, 1971), p. 202.

16. Bert Ennis, "Sophie Goes Talkie," *Motion Picture Classic,* May 1929, pp. 43, 74, 94.

17. Hochheiser, "AT&T and . . . Sound Motion-Picture Technology," pp. 26–27.

18. "Vitaphone Expected to Boost Earnings," *Wall Street News,* reprinted in *Film Daily,* 27 September 1926, p. 4; *Film Daily,* 5 November 1926, p. 1; 6 August 1946, p. 35.

19. Margot Peters, *The House of Barrymore* (New York: Knopf, 1990), pp. 264–65.

20. *Film Daily,* 25 September 1925, p. 4; 13 January 1926, p. 2. DON JUAN was ready to be screened in February 1926 at a Broadway theater (not the Warner) to coincide with Harry Warner's return from Europe; *Film Daily,* 28 January 1926, p. 1. In April it was announced that the film was being held back until fall; *Film Daily,* 5 April 1926, p. 2.

21. The spelling of the name of the theater varies, even in Warners' advertising. It appeared as "Warners' Theatre" on the marquee at 1664 Broadway. The Warner Bros. corporate headquarters was at 1600 Broadway.

22. *Film Daily,* 27 April 1926, pp. 1, 4; Hochheiser, "AT&T and . . . Sound Motion-Picture Technology," p. 28.

23. *Film Daily,* 3 May 1926, p. 1.

24. *Film Daily,* 17 May 1926, p. 1.

25. *Film Daily,* 25 June 1926, pp. 1, 4.

26. *Film Daily,* 25 June 1926, p. 1.

27. *Film Daily,* 22 June 1926, pp. 1, 2.

28. "Audible Pictures," *New York Times,* 8 August 1926, quoted in Barrios, *A Song in the Dark,* p. 25. The editorial also picked up on the millennial theme when the writer exclaimed, apocalyptically, "The eloquent dead will hereafter still speak."

29. "Vitaphone Is Thrilling the World," pp. 3, 8.

30. Richard Koszarski, *An Evening's Entertainment: The Age of the Silent Feature Picture 1915–1928* (New York: Scribner's, 1990), pp. 50–56.

31. Interestingly, Ford's formula describes the treatment of the sound tracks of his first synchronized films at Fox, as well as those of F. W. Murnau and Frank Borzage.

32. *Film Daily,* 27 June 1926, p. 29.
33. Richard Barrios's suggestion that Will Hays' presence on the first Vitaphone program was a sign of film producers' resistance to radio's "encroachment" is intriguing. See Barrios, *A Song in the Dark,* p. 21.
34. *Motion Picture Classic,* December 1929 (reprinted in *Vitaphone News* 3, no 1 [summer–fall 1995], p. 8.
35. Vitaphone advertisement, *Film Daily,* 30 July 1926, p. 2a.
36. *Film Daily,* 8 August 1926, p. 1.
37. Ibid., p. 3.
38. Barrios, *A Song in the Dark,* p. 24; *Photoplay,* October 1926, quoted in Walker, *The Shattered Silents,* p. 12.
39. "Audible Pictures," *New York Times,* 8 August 1926; Barrios, *A Song in the Dark,* p. 24.
40. *Film Daily,* 8 August 1926, p. 3.
41. *Film Daily,* 9 August 1926, p. 3.
42. *Film Daily,* 8 August 1926, p. 12. "[I]t may be only a relatively short time before a talking photoplay is produced"; Mordaunt Hall, *New York Times,* 15 August 1926.
43. Review summaries in *Film Daily,* 9 August 1926, pp. 1, 3.
44. Peters, *The House of Barrymore,* pp. 281–83. The final release footage was 10,018 feet (ten reels).
45. "Vitaphone Expected to Boost Earnings," *Wall Street News,* reprinted in *Film Daily,* 27 September 1926, p. 4. The sound effects during the sword-fighting scenes were obviously recorded with the orchestration, and apparently no great effort was made to achieve true synchronization with the image.
46. *Film Daily,* 23 July 1926, p. 2; 29 August 1926, p. 1.
47. *Film Daily,* 1 October 1926; 3 October 1926, pp. 1, 2; Walker, *The Shattered Silents,* p. 22.
48. *Film Daily,* 9 August 1926, p. 1; 20 August 1926, p. 1. That is, Warners intended to provide synchronized tracks for all its silent features as an option for exhibitors. The films could still be shown silent. Note that the all-sound policy had been announced earlier as well.
49. *Film Daily,* 2 November 1926, pp. 1, 6.
50. *Film Daily,* 29 August 1926, p. 1; 30 August 1926, pp. 1, 5.
51. "Vitaphone Expected to Boost Earnings," p. 4.
52. According to Hijiya, "Although at first dismayed by Vitaphone's success, de Forest soon cheered, believing it would waken Warner Brothers' rivals to the possibilities of Phonofilm"; *Lee de Forest,* p. 111. Walker cites 5 October 1926 as the premiere date of THE BETTER 'OLE; *The Shattered Silents,* p. 16. The second Vitaphone program was re-presented complete at the 1996 silent film festival in Pordenone, Italy.
53. Syd Chaplin quit Warners and made some undistinguished films for British National Pictures, then signed with MGM for the 1927–1928 season. *Film Daily,* 28 June 1927, p. 3.
54. *Film Daily,* 11 October 1926, pp. 1, 7.
55. Slide, *The Encyclopedia of Vaudeville,* pp. 253–55.
56. Al Jolson in A PLANTATION ACT was restored by Robert Gitt of the UCLA film archive in 1995. Ron Hutchinson, coordinator of the Vitaphone Project, reported that the 13 April 1995 audience "responded to this short much in the same way the October 6 [*sic*], 1926 audience did. Gasps of disbelief . . . led to rousing applause. Jolson's three filmed curtain calls which followed his performance in this short fit the audience's response perfectly." *Vitaphone News* 3, no. 1 (Summer-Fall 1995), p. 1.
57. *Film Daily,* 9 November 1926, p. 1.
58. *Film Daily,* 24 October 1926, pp. 1, 15.
59. *Film Daily,* 19 November 1926, p. 1; 23 December 1926, p. 1. Albert Warner had originally claimed forty installations; *Film Daily,* 30 December 1926, pp. 1, 8.
60. *Film Daily,* 21 December 1926, pp. 1, 6. The figure includes revenue from the silent versions; Gomery, *The Coming of Sound,* pp. 148–53.
61. *Film Daily,* 21 November 1927, pp. 1, 4.
62. *Film Daily,* 28 October, 1926, p. 1.
63. *Film Daily,* 28 November 1926, pp. 1, 16.
64. Charles F. Hynes, "The Onrush of Sound," *Film Daily Year Book 1929,* p. 487.
65. "Talking Movies for the Home," *Photo-Era,* January 1929, p. 53.
66. *Film Daily,* 3 January 1927, p. 1.

CHAPTER **4. Fox-Case, Movietone, and the Talking Newsreel**

1. Hijiya, *Lee de Forest,* p. 110.
2. Gomery, *The Coming of Sound,* p. 179; Walker, *The Shattered Silents,* p. 23. Visor's film is preserved at the Library of Congress.
3. Courtland Smith had been a journalist, former president of the American Press Association, and secretary of the Hays Office. Fox would assign him, in 1926, to develop Movietone News. *Film Daily,* 18 June 1929, p. 6.
4. Slide, *The Encyclopedia of Vaudeville,* pp. 343–44; 447–48; Barrios, *A Song in the Dark,* p. 28. Barrios notes that Ruby Keeler's Movietone test was distributed without her permission.
5. *Film Daily,* 20 September 1926, pp. 1, 7; "Prediction for 1926: Fox's Biggest Year," *Wall Street News,* reprinted in *Film Daily,* 27 September 1926, p. 6.
6. Hijiya, *Lee de Forest,* p. 111; Gomery, *The Coming of Sound,* pp. 176–78; *Film Daily,* 22 May 1927, pp. 1, 12; 11 October 1926, pp. 1, 5; 7 November 1930, pp. 1, 2.
7. Upton Sinclair, *Upton Sinclair Presents William Fox* (Los Angeles: Sinclair, 1933), pp. 107–8.
8. *Film Daily,* 30 August 1926, p. 1; 26 October 1926, pp. 1, 2.
9. Gomery, *The Coming of Sound,* pp. 178–80.
10. *Film Daily,* 5 January 1927, p. 1.
11. *Film Daily,* 28 October 1926, pp. 1, 3; 29 October 1926, pp. 1, 8. The so-called Reis patent, which would loom large in many infringement cases, was basically the process of recording the sound track on a strip of the film next to the picture by means of a slit. De Forest had purchased the slit patent from Reis and claimed to be submitting new improvements within weeks.
12. *Film Daily,* 22 December 1926, pp. 1, 4.
13. *Film Daily,* 8 April 1927, p. 1; 12 April 1927, pp. 1, 7; Lewis, *Empire of the Air,* pp. 172–74.
14. *Film Daily,* 22 May 1927, pp. 1, 12.
15. Hijiya, *Lee de Forest,* p. 111. This information conflicts with Sponable's statement that the U.S. district court dismissed de Forest's claims against Fox. Earl I. Sponable, "Historical Development of Sound Films," *Journal of the Society of Motion Picture Engineers* 48, April 1947.
16. *Film Daily,* 8 December 1926, p. 1.
17. *Film Daily,* 1 April 1927, pp. 1, 4; 24 April 1927, pp. 1, 4.
18. *Film Daily,* 24 April 1927, pp. 1, 4; Gomery, *The Coming of Sound,* p. 287. Powers was an erstwhile partner with—and litigant against—the fledgling Warner brothers in their distribution business, the United Film Service; Gertrude Jobes, *Motion Picture Empire* (Hamden, Conn.: Archon Books, 1966), p. 181.
19. *Film Daily,* 29 November 1927, p. 2. Max Schlesinger was elected president of De Forest Phonofilm Company; *Film Daily,* 13 December 1927, p. 1.
20. *Film Daily,* 17 June 1927, p. 2.
21. Tyne, *Saga of the Vacuum Tube,* pp. 300–301.
22. *Film Daily,* 22 January 1928, p. 8; 3 February 1928, p. 8.
23. *Film Daily,* 2 June 1927, p. 1. Refinancing was accomplished by finding an investor; Rudolph Spreckles, *Film Daily,* 17 June 1927, p. 1; 9 October 1927, p. 5; 2 November 1927, pp. 1, 2; 31 August 1928, p. 2; Rachel Low, *The History of the British Film, 1918–1929* (London: George Allen & Unwin, 1971), pp. 177, 186, 202–3.
24. *Film Daily,* 15 January 1928, p. 5.
25. *Film Daily,* 19 September 1928, pp. 1, 4.
26. *Film Daily,* 5 May 1929, p. 5; 2 September 1928, pp. 1, 7. The original De Forest system sound head, which read the track above the projector lens, had been relocated to the Western Electric displacement of twenty frames (14.5 inches) below the lens. The De Forest sound track width had always been 80 mils, equivalent to Western Electric Movietone.
27. *Film Daily,* 30 April 1929, p. 1; 22 May 1929, p. 1.
28. The building is currently a music recording studio. The original Fox Film studios building is around the corner at 444 West Fifty-sixth Street and now houses the High School for Environmental Studies.
29. *Film Daily,* 6 January 1927, pp. 1, 4; 23 February 1927, p. 1; 25 February 1927, pp. 1, 5, 8; Charles F. Hynes, "The Onrush of Sound," *Film Daily Year Book 1929,* p. 484.
30. *Film Daily,* 4 February 1927, p. 1. The Roxy, it should be said, was covering all the bases. It installed not one but three theater organ consoles and maintained a $30,000 music library—obviously betting on the viability of the silent film. It was also the first theater to permanently install a widescreen projection system, the Spoor process; *Film Daily,* 7 February 1927, p. 1. Sometime

during the year Roxy removed the Vitaphone disc system, for by November the theater was mentioned as having Movietone equipment only; *Film Daily*, 27 November 1927, p. 1; Koszarski, *An Evening's Entertainment*, pp. 23–25. Roxy's name is frequently given as Rothafel; I have used Rothapfel, as printed on the programs of the Rivoli and Roxy Theaters. Live stage presentations continued at the Roxy until shortly before its demolition in 1960.

31. *Film Daily*, 15 June 1927, p. 5; 6 August 1946, p. 35.

32. *Film Daily*, 9 May 1927, p. 1; 8 September 1927, p. 2. John Ford's MOTHER MACHREE, released 22 January 1928, had been completed at the time of the SUNRISE premiere but was delayed, presumably for music synchronization. Only a fragment of the film survives; Tag Gallagher, *John Ford: The Man and His Films* (Berkeley: University of California Press, 1986), p. 518.

33. *Film Daily*, 17 May 1927, pp. 1, 2; 12 September 1927, pp. 1, 7. Fox's claim was disingenuous because the Movietone fee was in addition to the Western Electric base fee. The first installation of Movietone in London was in the New Gallery Cinema in October. Again there was a clash with de Forest, who sued, claiming he and Phonofilm controlled British rights to the Case patents; *Film Daily*, 2 October 1927, p. 8.

34. *Film Daily*, 25 September 1927, pp. 1, 4, 12; 16 October 1927, p. 5; 28 October 1927, p. 7; 11 December 1927, p. 10.

35. *Film Daily*, 29 January 1928, p. 11; 5 February 1928, p. 2; 24 June 1928, p. 6; Gallagher, *John Ford*, pp. 49, 518. Gallagher refers to the FOUR SONS score as "an insipid thing" (p. 56). He credits Ford's "expressionistic" approach to music as deriving from Murnau, but it is not clear that this conception was different from the prevailing norms of film accompaniment by large orchestras. It also seems likely that Erno Rapee's background in opera and German music would have been the primary influence on the sound tracks of all the Fox films of this period.

36. *Film Daily*, 26 June 1928, p. 8.

37. *Film Daily*, 28 December 1927, p. 2. I can find no record of BLOSSOM TIME; perhaps this notice is a reference to THE RED DANCE (1927).

38. *Film Daily*, 1 May 1927, p. 1.

39. *Film Daily*, 25 April 1927, p. 1.

40. *Film Daily*, 5 June 1927, p. 15.

41. Jerome Beatty, "Shooting the Big Shots," *American Magazine*, February 1931, p. 141; *Film Daily*, 25 August 1927, p. 4; *Variety*, 19 October 1927, p. 23. So impressed with cinema was he that Mussolini set up the Luce organization (with himself as head) to produce films celebrating Italian culture. Dante's DIVINE COMEDY, produced with government funds, was to be the first venture; *Film Daily*, 15 January 1928, p. 5. Mussolini recorded a 900-foot address for Fox Movietone that he intended to be shown throughout Italy immediately following his death. In it he urged the people of Italy to "carry on the nationalistic spirit" he had fostered in them during his regime; *Film Daily*, 19 May 1931, p. 8.

42. Beatty, "Shooting the Big Shots," p. 144. Some of these stories sound suspiciously like the work of press agents.

43. *Film Daily*, 25 April 1927, pp. 1, 2.

44. *Film Daily*, 24 May 1927, p. 1.

45. *Film Daily*, 19 June 1927, p. 1.

46. Beatty, "Shooting the Big Shots," p. 69.

47. Russell Merritt and J. B. Kaufman, *Walt in Wonderland: The Silent Films of Walt Disney* (Baltimore: Johns Hopkins University Press, 1993), p. 120.

48. *Film Daily*, 6 November 1927, pp. 1, 4; 4 December 1927, p. 8.

49. *Film Daily*, 30 November 1927, p. 2.

50. *Film Daily*, 8 December 1927, p. 2.

51. *Film Daily*, 27 October 1927, pp. 1, 2; 27 November 1927, p. 12; 29 December 1927, p. 9.

52. *Variety*, 27 June 1928.

53. *Film Daily*, 15 August 1927, p. 6.

54. *Film Daily*, 12 April 1928, p. 1; 17 August 1928, p. 1.

55. Winfield Sheehan, *Los Angeles Times* interview, quoted in *Film Daily*, 22 May 1928, pp. 1, 3; Sinclair, *Upton Sinclair Presents William Fox*, pp. 104–5.

56. *Film Daily*, 23 January 1929, p. 1; 29 April 1929, pp. 1, 5; 27 March 1929, p. 1; 29 September 1929, p. 1.

57. *Film Daily*, 9 January 1930, pp. 1, 11; 11 February 1930, p. 1; 15 May 1930, p. 1; 18 April 1930, p. 2; 2 May 1930, p. 1.

CHAPTER **5. Enticing the Audience: Warner Bros. and Vitaphone**

1. *Film Daily,* 9 March 1927, p. 1; 20 December 1927, pp. 1, 12.
2. *Film Daily,* 22 March 1927, p. 1.
3. *Film Daily,* 23 May 1927, pp. 1, 2; 24 May 1927, p. 2; 9 June 1927, p. 1; 18 July 1927, p. 2; 26 July 1927, pp. 1, 10.
4. *Film Daily,* 6 January 1927, pp. 1, 4; 17 February 1927, pp. 1, 4.
5. *Film Daily,* 6 February 1927, p. 12; *Variety,* 9 February 1927.
6. *Film Daily,* 6 February 1927, p. 1, 12; 8 February 1927, p. 2; 14 August 1927, p. 7; 3 July 1927, p. 1; Mordaunt Hall, *New York Times,* 22 June 1927. Alan Crosland, in March 1927, enjoyed the distinction of having four of his films on Broadway: A MILLION BID, DON JUAN, WHEN A MAN LOVES, and THE BELOVED ROGUE. Nevertheless, he was not regarded as a gifted director. In *Film Daily's* annual poll of newspaper reviewers, Crosland's name appeared on the list of those receiving fewer than twenty-five votes; 12 June 1927, pp. 6–7. His contract expired in December, and he quit the studio. After leaving Warners, he slipped back into his pre-1926 obscurity. He died in a car accident in 1936; Ephraim Katz, *The Film Encyclopedia* (New York: Putnam, 1979), p. 288.
7. *Film Daily,* 9 February 1927, p. 1; 11 February 1927, p. 7; 9 March 1927, p. 7; 13 March 1927, p. 9.
8. Charles Wolfe, "On the Track of the Vitaphone Short," in Mary /Lea Bandy, ed., *The Dawn of Sound* (New York: Museum of Modern Art, 1989), pp. 38, 40 n.7.
9. Nobel Sissle (1889–1975) and Eubie Blake (1883–1983) were among the most important African-American musical artists of the early twentieth century. As a vaudeville team, they were noted for their dignified demeanor, avoiding race stereotyping and minstrel humor. Among their accomplishments, Sissle wrote many song lyrics and founded the Negro Actors' Guild. Blake wrote "You Were Meant for Me" and many other standards. He enjoyed an enthusiastic revival when he performed in clubs and at festivals in the 1970s as a ninety-something. Slide, *The Encyclopedia of Vaudeville,* pp. 469–70.
10. *Film Daily,* 24 April 1927, p. 9.
11. *Film Daily,* 11 February 1927, p. 2; 24 April 1927, p. 10; 3 May 1927, p. 7; Robert L. Carringer, ed., *The Jazz Singer* (Madison: University of Wisconsin Press, 1979), pp. 14–15; Gomery, *The Coming of Sound,* p. 164.
12. *Film Daily,* 24 May 1927, p. 1. Jessel signed a two-picture contract with First National; *Film Daily,* 4 August 1927, p. 2. On 12 September, he reopened *The Jazz Singer* play in Newark. Jessel had completed the second film on his Warners contract, SAILOR IZZY MURPHY, which was a flop. *Film Daily* said he failed to contribute any comedy and "looks like the goat in an impossible story" (30 October 1927, p. 13). In January 1928, he signed a contract with Tiffany-Stahl Pictures for three films, none of which was successful; *Film Daily,* 27 January 1928, p. 6. Jack Warner claimed that Jessel would have received the extra $10,000 he requested had he trusted Warner's verbal promise instead of demanding a confirming letter from Harry Warner; Kupferberg, *Take One,* January 1978, p. 29. The source of the non-Jewish personnel anecdote is "Inside Films," *Variety,* 29 June 1927, quoted in Walker, *The Shattered Silents,* p. 31.
13. Edwin Schallert, "Vitaphone Activity in Hollywood," *Motion Picture News,* 8 July 1927, p. 35, reprinted in Carringer, *The Jazz Singer,* p. 175.
14. Alfred A. Cohn, The Jazz Singer: *Adaptation and Continuity,* reprinted in Carringer, *The Jazz Singer,* p. 122.
15. Walker, *The Shattered Silents,* p. 36.
16. Herbert G. Goldman, *Jolson: The Legend Comes to Life* (New York: Oxford University Press, 1988), p. 151; Walker, *The Shattered Silents,* pp. 36–37; Jolson interviewed by Francis Gilmore, *Motion Picture Classic,* November 1927, quoted in Walker, *The Shattered Silents,* p. 35; Green, *The Film Finds Its Tongue,* p. 207.
17. *Film Daily,* 6 October 1927, pp. 1, 2. Doris Warner, Harry's young daughter, attended the New York premiere of THE JAZZ SINGER. She recalled in 1978 the applause of the audience after each Jolson number. "The excitement mounted as the film progressed, and when Jolson ad libbed the first line of dialogue to be uttered in a motion picture, the audience literally became hysterical. . . . [B]y the film's end, people were on their feet cheering and yelling"; Doris Warner Vidor, quoted in George Morris, "Opening Night: A Memoir from the Only Warner Who Was There," *Take One,* January 1978, p. 32.
18. Robert Sherwood, "The Silent Drama," *Life,* 27 October 1927, p. 124; Mordaunt Hall, *New York Times,* 7 October 1927; Barrios, *A Song in the Dark,* p. 38; *Film Daily,* 23 October 1927, p. 6.

19. Barrios, *A Song in the Dark,* p. 38, n.22. Warner Bros. ended fiscal 1926–1927 with a deficit of $1,234,413—$30,000 less than the deficit for 1925–1926. Because the accounting year ended on 27 August, the effects of THE JAZZ SINGER would not appear until the next balance sheet.

20. Frances Goldwyn to George Cukor, quoted in Scott Berg, *Goldwyn: A Biography* (London: Hamish Hamilton, 1989), p. 173.

21. "Warner Bros. Pictures, Inc., Comparison of Negative Costs and Gross Income on 1926–27 Productions to August 31, 1944," Warner Bros. Archives (WBA), William Schaeffer College, University of Southern California (see appendix 1).

22. *Film Daily,* 7 February 1928, pp. 1, 4. The unusual clause stipulated that the run would be extended on a week-to-week basis if the first four days' gross reached a certain level. For Fox, *Film Daily,* 29 March 1928, p. 2.

23. *Film Daily,* 21 March 1928, pp. 1, 3. Kann called the film a "real smash" and observed that it "is literally knocking 'em out of their seats." (Perhaps this was a reference to the volume level?) Managers were dusting off their "standing room only" signs; *Film Daily,* 6 April 1928, p. 1.

24. *Film Daily,* 1 April 1928, p. 4; 11 November 1928, p. 6.

25. *Film Daily,* 16 August 1927, p. 9.

26. *Film Daily,* 16 February 1928, p. 6; 23 February 1928, p. 4; 28 March 1928, p. 4. Exteriors were completed on 30 June; *Film Daily,* 7 July 1928, p. 11. Barrios has speculated that, "[w]ithout Sam Warner as a guiding force, Vitaphone seemed to lose the finer part of its bearings"; *A Song in the Dark,* p. 39. While these factors undoubtedly contributed to what might have been a longer-than-usual break in 1928, Warners' slowdown was not abnormal, but part of the typical Hollywood business cycle, a pause while executives planned the next season.

27. *Film Daily,* 8 May 1928; 21 May 1928, p. 7; 1 June 1928, p. 7.

28. Slide, *The Encyclopedia of Vaudeville,* p. 440.

29. *Film Daily,* 18 March 1928, p. 12.

30. *Film Daily,* 25 March 1928, p. 7; 18 September 1928, p. 2; Slide, *The Encyclopedia of Vaudeville,* pp. 510–13. Tucker appeared in the feature HONKY TONK in 1929.

31. Walker, *The Shattered Silents,* pp. 48–49; Barrios, *A Song in the Dark,* pp. 42–43. The scene containing the famous line, according to Walker, was removed by the New York state censors.

32. *Film Daily,* 27 March 1928, p. 1; 28 March 1928, p. 4; 20 April 1928, p. 7; 21 October 1928, p. 4.

33. *Film Daily,* 1 June 1928, p. 7; 21 August 1928, p. 6. The filming in Brooklyn, supervised by Bryan Foy, began in December; *Film Daily,* 12 December 1928, p. 8.

34. *Film Daily,* 27 June 1928, p. 4; Mordaunt Hall, *New York Times,* 16 June 1928; Welford Beaton, *The Film Spectator,* 28 April 1928, quoted in Walker, *The Shattered Silents,* p. 59.

35. *Variety,* 11 July 1928. THE LIGHTS OF NEW YORK cost $21,000, grossed $75,000 during its first week at the Strand, and had made $3 million by 1937; Mel Gussow, *Don't Say Yes Until I Finish Talking* (New York: Doubleday, 1971), p. 42.

36. *Film Daily,* 18 June 1928, p. 1; 19 June 1928, p. 10; Bandy, *The Dawn of Sound,* p. 51.

37. Barrios, *A Song in the Dark,* p. 47.

38. Warner Bros., "*Lights of New York* Supplementary Press Sheet," 1928. The film was also serialized to run in newspapers. Four scenes a day were published in the *New York Daily Mirror,* 9–17 July 1928, coinciding with the film's run at the Mark Strand Theater; New York Public Library clippings file.

39. Mordaunt Hall, *New York Times,* 9 July 1928.

40. *Film Daily,* 9 July 1928, p. 3; 16 July 1928, p. 1.

41. Griffith's film is referred to by its pre-release title, THE LOVE SONG; "As We Go to Press," *Photoplay,* December 1928, p. 6. Bordwell's remarks are apropos of the "sound fade-out": "Throughout the practices and discourses of the technical agencies from 1927 to 1932, one finds a highly coherent set of analogies between image and sound, between the visual and the auditory construction of the narrative space and time. In these analogies, the recording of speech is modeled upon the way cinematography records visible material, and the treatment of music and sound effects is modeled upon the editing and laboratory work applied to the visual track"; Bordwell, Staiger, and Thompson, *The Classical Hollywood Cinema,* p. 301.

42. *Film Daily,* 16 July 1928, p. 1.

43. *Film Daily,* November 1928, p. 66.

44. *Film Daily,* 16 August 1928, p. 1; 19 August 1928, p. 6. See "2 Negatives / One with Vitaphone / One without Vitaphone," Warner Bros. advertisement, *Film Daily,* 21 August 1928, p. 3.
45. *Film Daily,* 22 August 1928, p. 4; Mordaunt Hall, *New York Times,* 16 August 1928.
46. *Film Daily Year Book 1929,* pp. 860–62.
47. *Film Daily,* 2 February 1930, p. 1. I have not determined whether these trailers were actually made.
48. *Variety,* 23 March 1927; Wolfe, "On the Track of the Vitaphone Short," pp. 38–39.
49. *Film Daily,* 14 June 1927, p. 4.
50. Unlike some other trailers, this one, directed by Bryan Foy, used one camera which was "moved up for c.u." (that is, made in two takes, moving closer for the close-up take of Nagel).
51. Howard Heffernan, *Detroit News,* 21 May 1928, clipping file, New York Public Library.
52. THE TERROR trailer, continuity, WBA.
53. The studio log of music clearance registrations belies the claim that all the songs were original.
54. LOVE AND THE DEVIL trailer, continuity, box 1077, WBA.
55. LILIES OF THE FIELD trailer, continuity, WBA.
56. NO, NO, NANETTE trailer, file 1079a, continuity, WBA.

CHAPTER 6. Battle of the Giants: ERPI and RCA Consolidate Sound

1. Gomery, *The Coming of Sound,* p. 208.
2. *Film Daily,* 20 February 1927, p. 1.
3. *Film Daily,* 25 May 1927, pp. 1, 7.
4. *Film Daily,* 10 February 1927, pp. 1, 2; Gomery, *The Coming of Sound,* pp. 208–12.
5. Quoted in "Company Has Amazing Growth," *Erpigram,* 20 December 1928, p. 4.
6. *Film Daily,* 25 December 1927, p. 1; Russell Sanjek and David Sanjek, *American Popular Music Business in the Twentieth Century* (New York: Oxford University Press, 1991), pp. 34–35. The Sanjek account has minor dating errors.
7. "ERPI's Music Rights Department Is Operated on a Non-Profit Basis as Service to Producers," *Erpigram,* 15 April 1930, pp. 4–5.
8. "Revised Authorization Report," 17 September 1927, file 41 05 01 03, AT&T Archives. The request was for $29,500, about double the budgeted amount.
9. The ten licensees were Vitaphone, Paramount, MGM, Universal, Columbia, United Artists, Hal Roach, Christie, First National, and Victor Talking Machine; *Film Daily,* 27 June 1928, pp. 1, 6; 3 July 1928, p. 11; 19 July 1928, p. 1; 1 October 1928, p. 1. A listing of KAO was either incorrect or premature, since the company was in the process of becoming part of RKO and therefore in RCA's bailiwick. Al and Charles Christie owned Metropolitan Sound Studios, which sublicensed the Harold Lloyd, Caddo (Howard Hughes), and Pathé units. Fox-Case signed a license agreement on 14 November 1930, retroactive to 11 May 1928; Gomery, *The Coming of Sound,* p. 234. Harold Lloyd Productions signed its own license agreement in February 1929.
10. Electrical Research Products, Inc., Recording License Agreement, United Artists Collection, Wisconsin Center for Film and Theater Research, p. 5.
11. O. M. Glunt to R. R. Ireland, 1 February 1927, file 419 05 01 02, AT&T Archives.
12. *Film Daily,* 26 August 1928, p. 1.
13. *Film Daily,* 2 August 1928, p. 1.
14. Winfield Sheehan, *Los Angeles Times* interview, quoted in *Film Daily,* 22 May 1928, pp. 1, 3. Sheehan later denied claiming that Fox was benefiting.
15. "Closing Year Banner One for ERPI," *Erpigram* 2, 1 January 1930, p. 1.
16. *Erpigram,* 20 December 1928, p. 3.
17. GE envisioned a specialization in education. "Professors from abroad" would disseminate recorded lectures; schools would show educational films in the classroom. "Talking Motion Pictures," *Scientific Monthly,* March 1927, p. 289.
18. Charles F. Hynes, "The Onrush of Sound," *Film Daily Year Book 1929,* p. 489.
19. Mordaunt Hall, *New York Times,* 13 August 1927.
20. *Film Daily,* 24 April 1928, p. 4.
21. *Film Daily,* 6 March 1927, p. 1; 7 April 1927, p. 1. Kann editorialized, "On several occasions we have listened to long dissertations on the qualities which go to make up this individual." LeBaron shared his position at FBO with Edwin King; *Film Daily Year Book 1928,* p. 209.
22. *Film Daily,* 6 January 1928, p. 8.

23. *Film Daily*, 11 May 1928, p. 1.
24. Donald Crafton, *Emile Cohl, Caricature, and Film* (Princeton: Princeton University Press, 1990), pp. 158–59.
25. *Film Daily*, 17 June 1928, p. 1; 25 June 1928, p. 7; 3 July 1928, p. 2; 30 July 1928, p. 6. The sound version of THE KING OF KINGS opened at the Rivoli in July, and nationally on 1 October 1928. Rumors had circulated that DeMille was to join United Artists as an independent producer with backing from Joseph Schenck and Kennedy.
26. *Film Daily*, 26 March 1928, p. 1; 28 March 1928, p. 8; 17 December 1928, p. 1; 6 January 1929, p. 1.
27. *Film Daily*, 21 August 1928, pp. 1, 2. Kane was Kennedy's liaison with RCA. Kennedy's companies apparently were using the Photophone apparatus without a formal license from RCA. For the MPPA arrangement, see Gomery, *The Coming of Sound*, p. 244; for Kane, see Swanson, *Swanson on Swanson* (New York: Random House, 1968), pp. 327–31.
28. *Film Daily*, 19 August 1928, p. 3.
29. *Film Daily*, 12 August 1928, p. 1.
30. Lasky, *RKO*, p. 29.
31. *Film Daily*, 23 October 1928, p. 1; 23 November 1928, pp. 1, 7; 6 January 1929, p. 3; Betty Lasky, *RKO: The Biggest Little Major of Them All* (Englewood Cliffs, N.J.: Prentice Hall, 1984), p. 33.
32. *Film Daily*, 10 August 1928, p. 1; 15 July 1929, p. 4.
33. RCA Photophone advertisement, *Film Daily*, 3 June 1928.
34. RCA Photophone advertisement, *Film Daily*, 25 June 1928.
35. *Film Daily*, 27 May 1928, pp. 1, 9.
36. *Film Daily*, 5 June 1928, p. 12; 27 June, pp. 1, 2.
37. *Film Daily*, 18 July 1928, p. 1.
38. *Film Daily*, July 1928, pp. 1, 3. Walker's account of this incident (*The Shattered Silents*, pp. 96–97) is misleading; both Western Electric and RCA films were 35-mm, so the projector gates were the same. Only the widths of the optical tracks were different.
39. Gomery, *The Coming of Sound*, pp. 293–94, 389.
40. *Film Daily*, 30 December 1928, p. 1.
41. "As We Go to Press," *Photoplay*, December 1928, p. 6. The film is referred to as *Love Song*.
42. *Film Daily*, 1 February 1929, p. 1.
43. *Film Daily*, 18 June 1929, p. 3.
44. *Film Daily*, 17 February 1929, p. 8; 6 March 1929, p. 1.
45. *Film Daily*, 3 February 1929, p. 1; 5 February 1929, p. 14; 31 October 1929, p. 12.
46. Hochheiser, "AT&T and the Development of Sound Motion-Pictures," p. 32.
47. Merritt Crawford, "Sound-on-Film or Sound-on-Disc, Which Shall It Be?," *Film Daily*, 15 March 1929, p. 12.
48. *Film Daily*, 17 February 1929, p. 8; 21 May 1929, p. 1.
49. On DOUGHBOYS (1930) and BILLY THE KID (1930), for example, the leader states: "Synchronized Sound Print. This print must be kept in its original length. Footage numbers must be continuous and consecutive. All footage numbers must be 16 frames apart. This print must conform to continuity sheet line. An error of one frame will destroy synchronism. Footage numbers start at picture mark. Picture line start mark is numbered zero. Footage numbers end at finish mark. Check footage to finish mark on a footage counter. Check all footage to exact frame. Read your bulletin. Be exact."
50. *Film Daily*, 22 November 1931, p. 6.
51. *Film Daily*, 8 May 1930, p. 7.
52. "A year ago there was practically little demand for sound-on-film apparatus," pointed out the surprised editor. *Film Daily*, 20 August 1930, p. 1.
53. Analogous circumstances come to mind: the continued availability of 8-mm and super-8 film stock in the age of video; music in three formats (CD, cassette, and vinyl disc); video in VHS, Beta, laserdisc, and CD-ROM; and competing computer operating systems and platforms.
54. *Film Daily* (2 March 1932, p. 1) reported that 1,400 theaters dropped disc in favor of sound-on-film in 1931. There were 6,360 houses using optical tracks only, 3,542 using disc only, and 4,836 using both.
55. *Film Daily*, 24 January 1929, pp. 1, 11. For more on the Motion Picture Patents Company, see Eileen Bowser, *The Transformation of Cinema 1907–1915* (New York: Charles Scribner's Sons, 1990), pp. 217–18.

56. *Film Daily Year Book 1929*, p. 505.
57. *Film Daily*, 8 September 1929, p. 5; *Erpigram*, 1 October 1929, p. 7.
58. Fischer, *America Calling*, p. 53.
59. *Film Daily*, 4 December 1929, p. 4; *Erpigram*, 20 July 1929, p. 1; 15 March 1930, p. 5.
60. *Erpigram*, 15 October 1929, p. 1.
61. *Film Daily*, 8 December 1929, p. 1; 9 March 1930, p. 15; *Erpigram*, 15 June 1930, p. 4; 15 October 1930, p. 5.
62. *Film Daily*, 24 September 1930, pp. 1, 5; *Erpigram*, 1 January 1931, p. 1; 1 October 1930, p. 5. "In making the surveys, engineers are required to determine the exact volume and seating capacity, nature and thickness of all surfaces in the theatre, type, thickness and amount of draping and decorating material used in the theatre, exact nature of all seats, furniture, etc. Also included is a noise survey and recommendations for eliminating all noises in the house; *Erpigram*, 15 December 1929, p. 3.
63. *Film Daily*, 26 January 1930, pp. 1, 4, also advertisement; 7 July 1930, pp. 1, 2. Western Electric announced a new reproducer for small theaters at $2,950, or $42.28 per week, with no down payment; *Film Daily*, 13 April 1930, p. 1; *Erpigram*, 15 April 1930, p. 1; *Film Daily*, 11 August 1930, p. 2; 14 March 1930, p. 1. There were also many private installations, as in movie stars' homes, universities, corporations, and the screening rooms of censors. For Lyng, see *Film Daily*, 12 August 1930, pp. 1, 11; *Erpigram*, 15 August 1930, p. 1.
64. *Film Daily*, 21 December 1930, p. 10; 5 December 1930, pp. 1, 2; Mordaunt Hall, *New York Times*, 2 January 1931.
65. Erpigram, 15 January 1931, p. 5; 1 January 1931, p. 1; 1 June 1931, p. 8. The next major improvement was Western Electric Wide Range Recording and Reproducing. This delivered 40–8,000 cycles of frequency response. 42ND STREET (1933) was among the first productions to use it; Barrios, *A Song in the Dark*, p. 344.
66. *Film Daily*, 9 June 1931, p. 1; Edward W. Kellogg, "History of Sound Motion Pictures," part 2, *JSMPTE*, July 1955, reprinted in Fielding, *A Technological History*, pp. 196–97.
67. *Film Daily*, 31 December 1930, p. 6.
68. "Report of [SMPE] Sound Committee," quoted in Jean-Pierre Verscheure, "The Challenge of Sound Restoration from 1927 to Digital," *Film History* 7, no. 3 (1995), 267.
69. *Film Daily*, 16 January 1931, p. 1; 13 February 1931, p. 1; 16 March 1931, pp. 1, 8; 17 June 1931, p. 1.
70. *Film Daily*, 28 June 1932, pp. 1, 4; 29 June 1932, pp. 1, 3; Gomery, *The Coming of Sound*, pp. 277–85, 393–94.
71. *Film Daily*, 31 July 1930, pp. 1, 10. The General Talking Pictures suit would continue until 1935.
72. Gomery, *The Coming of Sound*, pp. 403–7.
73. *Film Daily*, 27 November 1931; 11 December 1931, pp. 1, 11; Gomery, *The Coming of Sound*, pp. 399–400.
74. Gomery, *The Coming of Sound*, pp. 402–3; Kellogg, "History of Sound Motion Pictures," pp. 190, 193.
75. Gomery, *The Coming of Sound*, pp. 395–96.
76. Ibid., pp. 411–14.
77. *Film Daily*, 6 August 1946, p. 22; Gomery, *The Coming of Sound*, pp. 427–28; Slide, *The American Film Industry*, pp. 109–10.
78. *Film Daily*, 3 February 1929, p. 5; 4 June 1929, p. 1; Lewis, *Empire of the Air*, p. 180. The Young Plan "scarcely got off the ground before the Hoover moratorium put an end to reparations"; Derek H. Aldcroft, *From Versailles to Wall Street 1919–1929* (Berkeley: University of California Press, 1981), pp. 85–86.
79. *Film Daily*, 19 February 1929, p. 10; 20 February 1929, p. 6.
80. *Film Daily*, 5 February 1929, p. 1; 12 February 1929, p. 2; James L. Neibaur, *The RKO Features* (Jefferson, N.C.: McFarland, 1994).
81. *Film Daily*, 24 February 1929, p. 1.
82. Seale, "'A Host of Others,'" pp. 87–88.
83. Richard B. Jewell, "RKO Film Grosses 1929–1951: The C. J. Tevlin Ledger," *Historical Journal of Film, Radio, and Television* 14, no. 1 (1994), pp. 42–43; Douglas Gomery, *The Hollywood Studio System* (New York: St. Martin's Press, 1986), p. 127.
84. Erik Barnouw, *A Tower in Babel: A History of Broadcasting in the United States*, vol. 1, *To 1933* (New York: Oxford University Press, 1966), p. 233.

85. C. E. Kenneth Mees, "History of Professional Black-and-White Motion-Picture Film," *JSMPTE*, October 1954, reprinted in Fielding, *A Technological History*, p. 137. The 16-mm standard was not adopted by the SMPE until 1932.
86. *Film Daily*, 8 June 1931, p. 1; 20 March 1931, p. 1; 9 January 1931, p. 3.
87. *Film Daily*, 10 January 1931, pp. 1, 12.
88. *Film Daily*, 8 March 1931, p. 7; 26 January 1932, p. 2.
89. *Film Daily*, 27 October 1929, p. 1.
90. *Film Daily*, 17 June 1930, pp. 1, 8; 27 October 1930, p. 2. William Fox briefly held up construction because he owned a 110-foot frontage on Sixth Avenue between Forty-eighth and Forty-ninth. He held out for $10 million; RCA offered $3 million; *Film Daily*, 22 October 1931, p. 1. Though Sarnoff hoped the complex would be called Radio City, Rockefeller Center was adopted as the official title. Besides the RCA Building hub, the thirty-one-story office building on Sixth Avenue between Fiftieth and Fifty-first was to be named the RKO Building; *Film Daily*, 24 February 1932, p. 2.

CHAPTER 7. The Big Hedge: Hollywood's Defensive Strategies

1. *Film Daily*, 3 June 1928, p. 11.
2. Harry Carr, *Los Angeles Times*, quoted in *Film Daily*, 29 January 1929, p. 1.
3. *Film Daily*, 26 August 1928, p. 9.
4. *Film Daily*, 2 August 1928, p. 1.
5. Mordaunt Hall, "Hollywood and Sound," *New York Times*, 22 July 1928.
6. *Film Daily*, 18 May 1928, p. 1; 6 July 1928, p. 1.
7. *Film Daily*, 6 September 1928, p. 2.
8. *Film Daily*, 16 September 1928, p. 9. One of MGM's star directors of the 1920s, Niblo said he liked acoustic special effects and would have used them in BEN-HUR (1926). Niblo's career stalled after his botched work on REDEMPTION, John Gilbert's talking fiasco. He tried directing in England and also did some acting, notably in FREE AND EASY (1930).
9. *Film Daily*, 27 December 1928, p. 6.
10. *Film Daily*, 25 February 1930, p. 6.
11. *Film Daily*, 22 July 1928, p. 30.
12. *Film Daily*, 23 July 1928, p. 11.
13. Herbert Cruikshank, "Doing as He Doesn't Like: Monta Bell Detests Talkies and Makes Them in Batches of Sixteen," *Motion Picture Classic*, October 1929, p. 33.
14. *Film Daily*, 28 March 1929, p. 1.
15. *Film Daily*, 3 October 1929, p. 8.
16. *Film Daily*, 13 November 1929, p. 7; 17 November 1929, p. 10. This part-talkie version, released in February 1930, has caused great confusion among film collectors and buffs. It circulates in prints which are copies of the sound version, minus the sound track. Besides a truncated story line, these prints feature extended scenes of characters mutely mouthing dialogue. The 1930 film occasionally has been revived in theaters and presented with live music as a tribute to the silent cinema.
17. Seldes, "The Movies Commit Suicide," p. 71.
18. *Film Daily*, 31 July 1928, p. 2.
19. *Film Daily*, 19 June 1929, p. 2.
20. *Film Daily*, 31 December 1928, p. 3.
21. *Film Daily*, 20 May 1929, p. 6.
22. *Film Daily*, 3 August 1928, p. 1.
23. *Film Daily*, 17 February 1929, p. 1.
24. *Film Daily*, 30 January 1929, p. 12; 4 April 1929, p. 1; 1 August 1929, p. 1.
25. *Film Daily*, 15 January 1929, p. 1.
26. *Photoplay*, September 1929, p. 127.
27. *Variety*, 19 December 1928.
28. *Film Daily*, 20 May 1929, pp. 6–7.
29. Based on data in *Film Daily Year Book 1929*, pp. 35–89.
30. *Film Daily*, 1 June 1928, p. 6.

31. Mordaunt Hall, *New York Times,* 27 December 1928, p. .
32. *Film Daily,* 30 July 1928, p. 7; Mordaunt Hall, *New York Times,* 16 July 1928; *Film Daily,* 5 August, p. 9.
33. Mordaunt Hall, *New York Times,* 30 July 1928.
34. *Film Daily,* 3 March 1929, p. 6.
35. *Film Daily,* 13 January 1929, pp. 6, 8.
36. *Film Daily,* 20 March 1928, p. 1.
37. *Film Daily,* 10 April 1929, p. 1.
38. *Film Daily,* 10 April 1929, p. 1; 21 April 1929, p. 1.
39. "Eight Leaders Give Their Views on the Future of the Silent Picture in the U.S.," *Film Daily,* 20 May 1929, pp. 6–7.

CHAPTER 8. Boom to Bust

1. *Film Daily,* 17 July 1928, p. 1.
2. Tino Balio, *Grand Design: Hollywood as a Modern Business Enterprise, 1930–1939* (New York: Scribner's, 1993), pp. 98–107; Gomery, *The Hollywood Studio System,* p. 86.
3. *Erpigram,* 20 April 1929, p. 2; Colin Gordon, *New Deals: Business, Labor, and Politics in America, 1920–1935* (New York: Cambridge University Press, 1994).
4. Thomas C. Cochran and William Miller, *The Age of Enterprise: A Social History of Industrial America* (New York: Macmillan, 1942; reprint, New York: Harper & Row, 1961), pp. 326, 346.
5. *Film Daily,* 19 November 1929, p. 1; 6 December 1929, p. 14.
6. *Film Daily,* 10 June 1929, p. 1.
7. *Film Daily,* 20 January, p. 1.
8. *Film Daily,* 30 April 1929, p. 6; 17 June 1929, p. 8. According to the *Erpigram,* the White House installation was difficult. The banks of amplifiers had to be located in the basement (20 May 1929, p. 1).
9. *Film Daily,* 28 October 1929, p. 1; 29 November 1929, pp. 1, 3; Gomery, *The Coming of Sound,* p. 345.
10. David Bordwell, "The Mazda Tests of 1928," and "The Introduction of Sound," in Bordwell, Staiger, and Thompson, *The Classical Hollywood Cinema,* pp. 294–308.
11. *Film Daily,* 4 February 1930, p. 7; David Bordwell and Kristin Thompson, "Technological Change and Classical Film Style," in Balio, *Grand Design,* p. 121.
12. *Film Daily,* 12 May 1930, p. 1; 23 July 1930, pp. 1, 4; 31 December 1930, p. 5; John Belton, *Widescreen Cinema* (Cambridge: Harvard University Press, 1992), p. 54.
13. Slide, *The American Film Industry,* pp. 8, 60.
14. *Film Daily,* 13 July 1930, p. 1. Fox features would also be booked into Warner houses for a $3 million rental fee.; *Film Daily,* 27 July 1930, p. 1; 1 August 1930, p. 1; 3 August 1930, p. 1; 7 September 1930, p. 1; 19 October 1930, p. 1; 27 October 1930, p. 1.
15. Tino Balio, *United Artists: The Company Built by the Stars* (Madison: University of Wisconsin Press, 1976), pp. 112–13.
16. *Film Daily,* 7 November 1930, pp. 1, 12.
17. *Film Daily,* 23 February 1930, pp. 1, 12; 26 November 1930, p. 1. This was paragraph 18 on credit and arbitration.
18. *Film Daily,* 6 February 1929, p. 1.
19. *Film Daily,* 26 August 1929, p. 8.
20. John Kenneth Galbraith, *The Great Crash, 1929* (1954; reprint, Boston: Houghton Mifflin, 1988), p. 169.
21. Ned Davis, "Market Watch," *Barron's,* 5 June 1995, p. 50.
22. *Film Daily,* 28 October 1929, p. 1.
23. *Film Daily,* 1 November 1929, p. 1; 30 December 1929, p. 1.
24. *Film Daily,* 6 December 1929, p. 14.
25. *Film Daily,* 30 October 1929, pp. 1, 10.
26. *Film Daily,* 19 February 1930, p. 1; 16 May 1930, p. 1. The bankers were misled by a December rally in stocks that offset some heavier losses. Paramount, for example, was down only net four points. Their assessment also did not take into account the smaller producers and the independent theaters, all of whom were affected disproportionately during the Depression's first stages.

27. *Film Daily*, 2 February 1930, p. 1; 21 April 1930, pp. 1, 7; 19 January 1930, p. 1.

28. *Film Daily*, 2 September 1930, p. 1.

29. *Film Daily*, 2 September 1930, p. 1; 3 September 1930, pp. 1, 10; 28 August 1930, p. 10; 5 November 1930, p. 1.

30. *Film Daily*, 18 July 1930, p. 1.

31. *Film Daily*, 16 July 1930, p. 1; 30 April 1930, pp. 1, 6; 28 May 1930, p. 1.

32. *Film Daily*, 21 February 1930, pp. 1, 8; 4 June 1930, pp. 1, 4; 27 June 1930, p. 6; 23 July 1930, p. 1; 29 July 1930, p. 1; 14 November 1930, p. 7; 19 December 1930, p. 1.

33. *Film Daily*, 17 September 1930, p. 1.

34. *Film Daily*, 12 January 1930, p. 4; 19 January 1930, p. 1; 6 July 1930, p. 5. The eastern studios also bred new movie talent. Paramount boasted of discovering Frank Morgan and Kay Francis; Winnie Lightner and Joan Blondell were Warner finds.

35. *Film Daily*, 20 October 1930, p. 2; 29 October 1930, p. 1.

36. *Film Daily*, 8 September 1930, p. 6; 26 November 1930, pp. 1, 6; 17 July 1930, p. 11; 18 November 1930, p. 1; Hilmes, *Hollywood and Broadcasting*, pp. 50–54.

37. *Film Daily*, 27 September 1928, p. 1.

38. *Film Daily*, 19 April 1928, pp. 1, 6.

39. *Film Daily*, 7 June 1928, p. 8.

40. *Film Daily*, 29 July 1928, p. 7. The Carthay Circle, an ERPI licensee, was also equipped with an RCA Photophone projection system.

41. Part of Warners' haste to consummate this deal was to take advantage of Kennedy's absence from the country; His KAO was one of the First National franchise holders. *Film Daily*, 21 June 1929, p. 4.

42. Although now once again called the Warner Bros. Studios, in 1972 the name was changed to the Burbank Studios when Columbia and Warners operated the lot as a joint venture, subleasing to numerous independents. The "VIP Tour" provides visitors a rare opportunity to visit a historic working studio.

43. Sanjek and Sanjek, *American Popular Music Business in the Twentieth Century*, pp. 34–40.

44. *Film Daily*, 6 April 1930, p. 42; 10 April 1930, p. 1; 13 April 1930, pp. 1, 12.

45. *Film Daily*, 23 April 1929, p. 1; 28 April 1929, p. 1; 17 May 1929, p. 1; Balio, *United Artists*, pp. 72–74.

46. *Film Daily*, 5 June 1929, p. 1.

47. *Film Daily*, 1 May 1929, p. 1.

48. *Film Daily*, 23 April 1930, pp. 1, 9.

49. *Film Daily*, 28 July 1929, p. 1; 27 July 1931, p. 1; 2 August 1931, p. 1; Douglas Gomery, *Shared Pleasures: A History of Movie Presentation in the United States* (Madison: University of Wisconsin Press, 1992), p. 224; Gomery, *The Coming of Sound*, p. 409.

50. H. Mark Glancy, "Warner Bros. Film Grosses, 1921–1951: The William Schaefer Ledger," *Historical Journal of Film, Radio, and Television* 15, no. 1 (1995), p. 59.

51. Gomery, *The Hollywood Studio System*, pp. 101–2.

52. *Film Daily*, 5 January 1930, p. 1; 27 February 1930, p. 1; 26 January 1930, p. 11; 30 January 1930, pp. 1, 7.

53. *Film Daily*, 31 August 1930, pp. 1, 9; 13 August 1930, pp. 1, 7; 14 August 1930, pp. 1, 5; 30 January 1930, pp. 1, 7; 26 May 1930, p. 1; Gomery, *The Hollywood Studio System*, p. 102.

54. *Film Daily*, 14 April 1930, p. 3.

55. *Film Daily*, 15 March 1931, p. 5; 21 April 1931, pp. 1, 6.

56. *Film Daily*, 6 April 1930, p. 24; 30 November 1930, p. 1. Overtures and trailers had already been supplied on twelve-inchers; *Film Daily*, 9 June 1930, p. 1; 13 June 1930, p. 1.

57. *Film Daily*, 19 May 1931, p. 1. Hal Wallis and Lucien Hubbard became associate executives.

58. *Film Daily*, 9 September 1931, pp. 1, 3.

59. *Film Daily*, 10 January 1929, p. 1; 27 February 1929, p. 1; Walker, *The Shattered Silents*, p. 125.

60. *Film Daily*, 2 June 1929, p. 6; 18 June 1929, p. 95; Robert C. Allen, "William Fox Presents *Sunrise*," in Janet Staiger, ed., *The Studio System* (New Brunswick, N.J.: Rutgers University Press, 1995), p. 132.

61. Lew Brown, Ray Henderson, and George Gard "Buddy" De Sylva were responsible for the lyrics and music for THE SINGING FOOL, SAY IT WITH SONGS, and SUNNY SIDE UP (1929); and FOLLOW THE LEADER, GOOD NEWS, FOLLOW THROUGH, and JUST IMAGINE (1930). Alain Lacombe and Claude Rocle, *De Broadway à Hollywood: l'Amérique et sa comedie musicale* (Paris: Cinéma, 1980), pp. 148–49.

62. *Film Daily*, 21 January 1929, p. 4. Sanjek and Sanjek, *American Popular Music Business in the Twentieth Century*, p. 40.
63. *Film Daily*, 25 August 1929, p. 1.
64. *Film Daily*, 18 July 1929, p. 1.
65. *Film Daily*, 3 January 1930, p. 1.
66. *Film Daily*, 20 February 1930, p. 7. The full text of Fox's lengthy letter was reprinted in *Film Daily*, 21 February 1930, pp. 1, 7.
67. *Film Daily*, 6 March 1930, pp. 1, 7; 28 January 1930, pp. 1, 4; 12 February 1930, pp. 1, 12; 1 April 1930, p. 1.
68. *Film Daily*, 7 April 1930, pp. 1, 8; 19 February 1930, pp. 1, 8; 8 April 1930, pp. 1, 4; 7 December 1930, p. 1; Gomery, *The Hollywood Studio System*, pp. 85–86.
69. *Film Daily*, 26 January 1930, p. 11; 6 February 1930, pp. 1, 2; 8 April 1930, p. 1; 15 April 1930, p. 1.
70. *Film Daily*, 16 April 1931, pp. 1, 11; 12 July 1931, pp. 1, 9; 1 April 1932, p. 1; 28 June 1932, pp. 1, 3.
71. *Film Daily*, 21 June 1928, p. 4; 19 December 1928, p. 2; 20 April 1930, p. 4. John W. Butler was executive manager of the studio.
72. *Film Daily*, 17 May 1928, pp. 1, 2.
73. *Film Daily*, 14 June 1928, p. 1. The film was cut down by Paramount and the sound added without the director's permission, resulting in Stroheim's lengthy lawsuit against Powers, Lasky, and Paramount.
74. *Film Daily*, 18 January 1929, pp. 6–7; 20 January 1929, p. 4; *Erpigram*, 20 January 1929, p. 5; 20 February 1929, p. 1.
75. *Film Daily*, 9 January 1929, p. 1; 3 January 1929, p. 2; 15 September 1929, p. 11; 20 April 1930, p. 4.
76. *Film Daily*, 15 March 1929, p. 2; 28 April 1929, p. 7. Mamoulian divided his time between Rochester, New York, and Broadway, producing classical opera as well as light operettas. Beginning in 1926, he collaborated on several productions for the Theater Guild. Following APPLAUSE, he directed CITY STREETS (1931) and DR. JEKYLL AND MR. HYDE (1932); Lacombe and Rocle, *De Broadway à Hollywood*, p. 222.
77. *Film Daily*, 6 February 1930, p. 1; Gomery, *The Hollywood Studio System*, pp. 30–31.
78. Gomery, *The Hollywood Studio System*, pp. 30–31.
79. *Film Daily*, 29 August 1930, pp. 1, 6; 26 January 1930, p. 11; 9 February 1930, p. 6; 3 August 1930, p. 11. See also William Paul, *Ernst Lubitsch's American Comedy* (New York: Columbia University Press, 1983); and Leland A. Poague, *The Cinema of Ernst Lubitsch* (New York: Barnes, 1978).
80. *Film Daily*, 29 August 1930, pp. 1, 6. See also *Film Daily*, 21 September 1930, p. 1; Judith Mayne, *Directed by Dorothy Arzner* (Bloomington: Indiana University Press, 1994), pp. 56–57.
81. J. I. Crabtree, "The Motion Picture Laboratory," in Fielding, *A Technological History*, p. 161.
82. *Film Daily*, 14 October 1930, pp. 1, 2; 14 March 1930, p. 1. The early sound classics THE LOVE PARADE (1929), MOROCCO (1930), and APPLAUSE (1929) were produced during Selznick's term, but his biographer points out that "David had little to do with these projects directly"; David Thomson, *Showman: The Life of David O. Selznick* (New York: Knopf, 1992), p. 91. A few memos published in Rudy Behlmer, ed., *Memo from David O. Selznick* (New York: Viking, 1972), indicate that Selznick, as head of the writers' department, routinely made story suggestions, some of which made it to the screen; see PARAMOUNT ON PARADE memos, pp. 23–24.
83. *Film Daily*, 5 June 1928, p. 2; 7 June 1928, p. 11; 20 June 1928, p. 1; 24 July 1928, p. 11; 27 July 1928, pp. 1, 3. Roach had signed a separate fifteen-year contract with Western Electric; *Film Daily*, 26 June 1928, p. 3. Some MGM films were released on the Victor Talking Machine disc system.
84. THE HOLLYWOOD REVUE souvenir program, 1929, Yranski Collection.
85. Gomery, *The Hollywood Studio System*, pp. 55–56.
86. *Film Daily*, 15 April 1930, p. 1; Glancy, "MGM Film Grosses, 1924–1948," p. 130; Gomery, *The Hollywood Studio System*, p. 52. Gomery observes that "each [of the Big Five] mirrored the entire industry, with the bulk of invested corporate capital in theaters, not production. With most corporate assets held in, and revenues coming through, the theater division, corporate decisions were aimed in that direction" (p. 8).

87. Gomery, *The Hollywood Studio System,* p. 56.

88. *Film Daily,* 24 February 1930, p. 8; 24 March 1930, pp. 1, 8; 6 April 1930, p. 38; Gomery, *The Hollywood Studio System,* pp. 127–30.

89. *Film Daily,* 6 January 1930, pp. 1, 4; 12 January 1930, pp. 1, 2, 14; 5 February 1930, p. 8.

90. *Film Daily,* 30 July 1930, p. 1; Gomery, *The Hollywood Studio System,* p. 125.

91. *Film Daily,* 1 May 1929, pp. 1, 11.

92. *Film Daily,* 26 April 1929, p. 4.

93. *Film Daily,* 25 August 1929, p. 8.

94. *Film Daily,* 13 December 1929, p. 1; 11 December 1929, pp. 1, 9.

95. *Film Daily,* 9 May 1930, p. 1; 22 April 1930, pp. 1, 7; 10 December 1929, p. 2; 28 March 1930, pp. 1, 4; 7 May 1930, p. 1; 8 May 1930, p. 2. J. J. Murdock resigned as president of Pathé, ending a connection with the film industry that went back almost to its beginning. Kennedy produced no more films for United Artists.

96. *Film Daily,* 11 June 1930, p. 1.

97. *Film Daily,* 20 November 1930, p. 1; 5 December 1930, pp. 1, 2; 1 February 1931, p. 1; 1 January 1931, pp. 1, 3; 9 January 1931, p. 4; 18 January 1931, p. 1; 20 January 1931, p. 1; 29 January 1931, p. 1.

98. *Film Daily,* 11 June 1930, p. 2; 21 February 1930, pp. 1, 8; 20 October 1930, pp. 1, 2.

99. Jewell, "RKO Film Grosses," pp. 42–43; John Sedgwick, "Richard Jewell's RKO Grosses . . . : A Comment," *Historical Journal of Film, Radio, and Television* 14, no. 1 (1994), pp. 51–58.

100. Danger Lights was released in RKO's Natural Vision widescreen in Chicago. Belton, *Widescreen Cinema,* p. 47.

101. *Film Daily,* 17 July 1931, p. 1; Behlmer, *Memo from David O. Selznick,* p. 45.

102. Lasky, *RKO,* pp. 70–72.

103. *Film Daily,* 14 December 1930, p. 10; Sedgwick, "Richard B. Jewell's RKO Film Grosses," p. 54.

104. Although the producing company had been affiliated with the United Artists Studio and the United Artists Theatre Circuit since 1926, the three organizations were separate corporate entities. Griffith, though a founder, was no longer a partner but rather worked for Joseph Schenck's Art Cinema and released through UA.

105. *Film Daily,* 26 July 1928, p. 5.

106. *Film Daily,* 6 August 1928, p. 5; 22 August 1928, pp. 1, 12.

107. *Film Daily,* 31 May 1928, p. 4; 25 June 1928, p. 6; 13 August 1928, p. 3.

108. *Film Daily,* 10 June 1928, p. 1; Fairbanks quoted in Stearns, "The Movies Talk!," p. 199.

109. Gomery, *The Hollywood Studio System,* p. 178.

110. Ibid., p. 175.

111. Balio, *United Artists,* pp. 80–94.

112. Gomery, *The Hollywood Studio System,* pp. 162–63. The area is now called Columbia Square.

113. *Film Daily,* 23 September 1930, pp. 1, 4; Gomery, *The Hollywood Studio System,* p. 162.

114. *Film Daily,* 16 March 1931 p. 3.

115. Metropolitan in Hollywood, for example, rented to Harold Lloyd, Caddo (Howard Hughes), Christie, Sono Art, Rogell, Weil Productions, Brown and Nagel, Halperin Productions, Broughton Productions, and Triangle Pictures. *Erpigram,* 1 September 1930, p. 5; Seale, "'A Host of Others,'" pp. 83, 90–98.

116. Seale, "'A Host of Others,'" pp. 89, 93; Barrios, *A Song in the Dark,* p. 203.

117. Richard Koszarski, *The Man You Love to Hate* (New York: Oxford University Press, 1983); Barrios, *A Song in the Dark,* pp. 147, 159, 219.

118. *Film Daily,* 3 January 1932, pp. 1, 11.

119. The figures were: 1926, 740 features; 1927, 743; 1928, 834; 1929, 707; 1930, 595; 1931, 396 (estimated); *Film Daily,* 3 January 1932, pp. 1, 3. The figures are somewhat misleading because, though fewer features were made, their length had been increasing since 1929.

120. Al Lichtman, *Film Daily,* 11 May 1932, p. 1.

CHAPTER 9. Labor Troubles

1. Danae Clark, *Negotiating Hollywood: The Cultural Politics of Actors' Labor* (Minneapolis: University of Minnesota Press, 1995).

2. Nancy Lynn Schwartz, *The Hollywood Writers' Wars* (New York: Knopf, 1982), pp. 8–9; Gordon, *New Deals*, pp. 299–301, 304.

3. *Film Daily*, 12 April 1927, p. 1. For a general discussion of IATSE, including its connection to organized crime, see Denise Hartsough, "Crime Pays: The Studios' Labor Deals in the 1930s," in Staiger, ed., *The Studio System*, pp. 226–48.

4. *Film Daily*, 2 August 1928, pp. 1, 6; 5 August 1928, p. 1. IATSE denied that a dispute occurred.

5. *Film Daily*, 12 August 1927, p. 1.

6. *Film Daily*, 10 November 1927, p. 2. Skouras, with his brothers Charles and George, owned all the theaters in St. Louis. Sons of a Greek shepherd, they had arrived in the United States in 1910. They seemed to have more than their share of labor trouble. Eventually Skouras would become the powerful president of 20th Century–Fox.

7. *Film Daily*, 8 February 1928, p. 1; 29 March 1928, p. 2.

8. *Film Daily*, 12 March 1928, p. 2; 7 June 1928, p. 11.

9. *Film Daily*, 19 July 1928, pp. 1, 7.

10. *Film Daily*, 13 June 1928, p. 1; 17 August 1928, pp. 1, 2.

11. Gomery, *The Coming of Sound*, pp. 303–4.

12. *Film Daily*, 23 February 1928, pp. 1, 4.

13. *Film Daily*, 7 June 1928, p. 1. The figure, upped to $10 million, was to be raised by a 2 percent levy on the wages of the members, said to number 75,000.

14. *Film Daily*, 20 May 1928, pp. 1, 2; 5 June 1928, p. 1.

15. *Film Daily*, 23 July 1928, p. 9; 19 December 1928, pp. 1, 3.

16. *Film Daily*, 16 August 1928, p. 1; 30 August 1928, p. 1; 2 September 1928, p. 1; Gomery, *The Coming of Sound*, p. 305.

17. *Film Daily*, 20 March 1929, p. 1; 21 March 1929, p. 1; 22 May 1929, pp. 1, 2; 7 November 1929, p. 1; 19 December 1929, p. 1.

18. *Film Daily*, 26 July 1928, p. 1.

19. THE SQUALL file, Warner Bros. Collection, University of Southern California.

20. Alfred Harding, *The Revolt of the Actors* (New York: Morrow, 1929).

21. Murray Ross, *Stars and Strikes: Unionization of Hollywood* (New York: Columbia University Press, 1941), p. 30.

22. "Effect of 'Talking Movies' upon Employment of Musicians and of Actors," *Monthly Labor Review*, November 1928, p. 160.

23. *Film Daily*, 5 June 1929, p. 1; 6 June 1929, p. 10; for Lewis, see Michael G. Ankerich, *Broken Silence: Conversations with Twenty-three Silent Film Stars* (Jefferson, N.C.: McFarland, 1992), pp. 176–77.

24. *Film Daily*, 7 July 1929, p. 2; 22 August 1929, pp. 1, 2.

25. *Film Daily*, 14 June 1929, pp. 1, 3.

26. *Film Daily*, 30 January 1930, pp. 1, 7; 5 February 1930, pp. 1, 6; 9 April 1930, p. 1; 10 June 1930, pp. 1, 4.

27. *Film Daily*, 20 January 1929, p. 6.

28. *Film Daily*, 20 October 1929, pp. 1–2.

29. *Film Daily*, 31 August 1930, p. 1.

30. *Film Daily*, 4 March 1931, pp. 1, 6; 18 September 1931, p. 1; 1 August 1931, p. 1; 30 March 1931, p. 1; 8 March 1931, p. 1; 24 April 1931, p. 1; 12 June 1931, p. 1.

31. *Film Daily*, 3 March 1930, p. 2; 9 June 1930, p. 1; 12 August 1930, pp. 1, 11.

32. "Effects of Technological Changes upon Employment in the Motion-Picture Theaters of Washington, D.C.," *Monthly Labor Review*, November 1931, p. 1013.

CHAPTER 10. Inaudible Technology

1. R. E. Farnham, "Motion Picture Studio Lighting with Incandescent lamps," *Cinematographic Annual 1930*, p. 253; *Film Daily*, 29 April 1928, p. 25. GE also introduced a new Mazda lamp for De Forest and RCA Photophone projectors, an important step in making film projection portable; *Film Daily*, 10 February 1929, p. 8.

2. *Film Daily*, 29 January 28, p. 10.

3. David Bordwell, "The Mazda Tests of 1928," in Bordwell, Staiger, and Thompson, *The Classical Hollywood Cinema*, pp. 294–97.

4. *Film Daily*, 16 May 1928, p. 5; 13 June 1928, p. 6.

5. Bordwell, "The Mazda Tests of 1928," pp. 294–97.

6. *Film Daily,* 8 February 1931 p. 4; 16 March 1931, p. 7; Barry Salt, *Film Style and Technology: History and Analysis* (London: Starword, 1983), pp. 126, 256.

7. *Film Daily,* 12 March 1929, p. 8; 17 March 1929, p. 17; C. E. Kenneth Mees, "History of Professional Black-and-White Motion-Picture Film," *JSMPTE,* October 1954, in Fielding, *A Technological History,* p. 127.

8. Nugent H. Slaughter, "Recording Sound on Disc," *Cinematographic Annual 1930,* pp. 435–36.

9. "Using Noiseless Camera," *Film Daily,* 21 January 1927, p. 1.

10. Practical zoom lenses were not available until 1932. Bell and Howell's initial model was sold to the army, not Hollywood. *Film Daily,* 8 May 1932, p. 6.

11. *Film Daily,* 29 April 1930, p. 8.

12. *Film Daily,* 1 March 1931 p. 8.

13. *Film Daily,* 18 June 1929, p. 3.

14. John O. Aalberg, "Reproduction in the Theatre by RCA Photophone System," *Cinematographic Annual 1930,* pp. 407–8; Salt, *Film Style and Technology,* p. 273.

15. *Film Daily,* 16 September 1929, p. 1; Paul Allen, "Wide Film Development," *Cinematographic Annual 1930,* pp. 183–95.

16. John Belton, *Widescreen Cinema* (Cambridge, Mass.: Harvard University Press, 1992), p. 56; Hall, *New York Times,* 15 December 1930.

17. Belton, *Widescreen Cinema,* p. 55.

18. Edward W. Kellogg, "History of Sound Motion Pictures," part 2, *JSMPTE,* July 1955, in Fielding, *A Technological History,* p. 194; *Film Daily,* 16 December 1928, p. 6; 26 January 1930, p. 12. Da-Lite claimed that 4,400 of its sound screens were in use; *Film Daily,* 29 January 1930, pp. 1, 2.

19. *Film Daily,* 1 July 1929, p. 6.

20. John Douglas Eames, *The MGM Story* (New York: Crown, 1977), p. 49. Shearer's solution was not particularly original since lip-synching to prerecorded sound had been standard in the Edison Kinetophone and the Gaumont Chronophone systems. The transcription process used in radio programs would have been another source of inspiration.

21. Eddie Cantor with Jane Kesner Ardmore, *Take My Life* (New York: Doubleday, 1957), p. 154.

22. *Film Daily,* 17 December 1928, p. 3. See the 1929 photograph of an MGM soundstage with "Quiet Please" on the roof in Koszarski, *An Evening's Entertainment,* p. 325.

23. *Film Daily,* 9 December 1928, p. 6.

24. *Variety,* 5 February 1930.

25. *Film Daily,* 27 May 1931, p. 1; 7 October 1931, p. 1.

26. *Film Daily,* 22 May 1930, p. 8.

27. *Film Daily,* 16 February 1930, p. 3.

28. *Film Daily,* 21 January 1931, p. 8.

29. *Film Daily,* 23 August 1931, pp. 1, 4.

30. *Film Daily,* 22 May 1931, p. 8; 3 July 1931, p. 2; Salt, *Film Style and Technology,* pp. 199, 280.

31. *Film Daily,* 22 August 1928, p. 4.

32. *Film Daily,* 16 November 1928, p. 11.

33. *Film Daily,* 1 April 1929, p. 6; 24 August 1930, pp. 6, 7.

34. *Film Daily,* 20 April 1930, p. 6; 12 July 1931, p. 13. For a discussion of the implications of these processes, see Mary Ann Doane, "Ideology and the Process of Sound Editing and Mixing," in Elizabeth Weis and John Belton, eds., *Film Sound: Theory and Practice* (New York: Columbia University Press, 1985), pp. 54–62.

35. *Film Daily,* 6 February 1930, p. 15.

36. *Cinematographic Annual 1930,* p. 427.

37. THE JAZZ SINGER file, WBA.

38. William Stull, A.S.C., "Sound Film Processes," *Photo-Era,* August 1929, p. 70.

39. *Film Daily,* 2 December 1928, p. 6.

40. K. F. Morgan, "Dubbing Sound Pictures," *Cinematographic Annual 1930,* pp. 425–31.

41. *Film Daily,* 17 October 1930, p. 11.

42. J. P. Maxfield, "Technic of Recording Control for Sound Pictures," *Cinematographic Annual 1930,* pp. 422–23.

43. Samuel Marx, *Mayer and Thalberg: The Make-Believe Saints* (New York: Warner Books, 1975), p. 146; Crowther, *The Lion's Share,* p. 149; Ally Acker, *Reel Women* (New York: Continuum, 1991), pp. 166–69.

44. *Film Daily,* 8 May 1932, p. 6.

45. Kevin Brownlow, *The Parade's Gone By* (New York: Ballantine, 1968), p. 246.
46. Watching the films indicates that inserts and cutaway shots were made separately and edited in, just as in silent film practice.
47. *Film Daily,* 13 March 1930, p. 8.
48. *Film Daily,* 16 June 1929, p. 7.
49. Mordaunt Hall, *New York Times,* 15 November 1928; 22 December 1928.
50. Rick Altman, "Sound Space," in Altman, *Sound Theory/Sound Practice,* pp. 46–64.
51. Maxfield, "Technic of Recording Control for Sound Pictures," p. 415.
52. James Lastra, "Standards and Practices: Aesthetic Norm and Technological Innovation in the American Cinema," in Staiger, *The Studio System,* pp. 200–225.
53. Altman, "Sound Space," pp. 46–64.
54. These guidelines define the limits of camera reframing. For example, moving the camera over an imaginary 180-degree axis produces a continuity "error" because screen direction is perceived to change without narrative motivation. One kind of jump cut results when the second shot in a sequence is taken from an angle less than 30 degrees from the first. A match-cut continues the motion of an object or person in the first shot at the beginning of the second shot, creating the impression of moving from one space to another.
55. Bordwell has analyzed the stylistic changes associated with multiple-camera cinematography. See Bordwell, Staiger, and Thompson, *The Classical Hollywood Cinema,* pp. 304–8.
56. Multi-camera cinematography never really ceased. An example of a late musical which uses at least three cameras running simultaneously in some of the dance numbers is TOM THUMB (1958). Today complicated stunts are routinely shot from many angles at once.
57. Prince et al., "Lee Garmes," p. 74. Print-viewing, however, shows plenty of multi-camera work in the crowd scenes, and the Burbank soundstages were set up for multi-camera shooting through the early 1930s. Garmes's memory is also hazy about magnetic recording tape, which he erroneously recalled having used during this period. Bordwell notes that recording a master scene became a permanent feature of Hollywood *mise-en-scène* and later easily made the transition to television shooting.
58. Roland Barthes, *Image—Music—Text,* trans. Stephen Heath (New York: Hill and Wang, 1977), p. 46.
59. James Frederick Lastra, "Standards and Practices: Technology and Representation in the American Cinema" (Ph.D. dissertation, University of Iowa, 1992), pp. 325–50.
60. *Film Daily,* 12 August 1930, pp. 1, 12.
61. For detailed discussions of "realism" and "invisibility," see Lastra, "Standards and Practices," pp. 77–79; Kristin Thompson, *Breaking the Glass Armor: Neoformalist Film Analysis* (Princeton: Princeton University Press, 1988), pp. 195–245.
62. André Bazin, "The Myth of Total Cinema," *What Is Cinema?* (Berkeley: University of California Press, 1967), pp. 17–22; John Seitz, "Introduction," *Cinematographic Annual 1930* (New York: Arno Press, 1972), p. 17; *Film Daily,* 30 December 1928, p. 4.

CHAPTER 11. Exhibition: Talkies Change the Bijou

1. Alan Williams, "Historical and Theoretical Issues in the Coming of Recorded Sound to the Cinema," in Altman, *Sound Theory/Sound Practice,* p. 129.
2. See also Tino Balio, "Feeding the Maw of Exhibition," in *Grand Design,* pp. 73–108; Gomery, *Shared Pleasures: A History of Movie Presentation in the United States* (Madison: University of Wisconsin Press, 1992).
3. *Film Daily,* 10 June 1928, p. 11.
4. *Film Daily,* 3 June 1928, p. 7; 27 May 1928, pp. 1, 4.
5. *Film Daily,* 4 January 1928, p. 3; Schenck quoted in UA advertisement, *Film Daily,* 7 June 1928.
6. *Film Daily,* 16 April 1929, p. 1.
7. *Erpigram,* 20 April 1929, p. 5.
8. *Erpigram,* 20 July 1929, p. 8.
9. *Film Daily,* 11 January 1929, p. 1; 18 February 1929, p. 2.
10. *Film Daily,* 28 January 1929, p. 7; 29 March 1929, p. 6.
11. *Film Daily,* 4 January 1929, p. 1; 10 February 1929, p. 8.
12. *Film Daily,* 26 March 1929, p. 1.

13. *Film Daily,* 3 July 1929, p. 1; "As We Go to Press," *Photoplay,* October 1929, p. 6; *Film Daily,* 24 May 1929, p. 1; 11 June 1929, p. 1.
14. *Film Daily,* 15 November 1929, pp. 1, 3.
15. *Film Daily,* 10 February 1929, p. 8.
16. *Film Daily,* 10 February 1929, p. 8. Soriero concluded that "selling the picture to the public, as far as the producer is concerned, has been entirely a problem of the exhibitor or theater manager."
17. *Film Daily,* 9 July 1930, pp. 1, 2; 25 February 1930, pp. 1, 5. Weekly attendance at all Publix houses in the spring and summer of 1930 was 35 million weekly, compared to 29 million for the same period ending in 1929; *Film Daily,* 7 March 1930, p. 1.
18. *Film Daily,* 13 August 1930, p. 2. Midnight shows started at the Roxy and spread around the country; *Film Daily,* 8 September 1930, p. 1; 28 July 1930, p. 1; 23 July 1930, p. 1.
19. *Film Daily,* 9 April 1930, p. 5; 10 April 1930, pp. 1–2; 17 January 1930, p. 1; 16 June 1930, pp. 1, 42.
20. *Film Daily,* 21 September 1930, p. 4; 23 September 1930, p. 3.
21. *Film Daily,* 5 March 1931, p. 8; 12 April 1931, p. 23; 23 April 1931, p. 1.
22. *Film Daily,* 6 May 1931, pp. 1, 10; 6 June 1931, pp. 1, 8.
23. Mordaunt Hall, *New York Times,* 4 October 1930; 8 November 1930.
24. RKO was said to have tried out double-system sound in its theaters earlier but dropped it because it was impractical for the trade at large. The Broadway Paramount Theater switched to double-system projection in November. *Film Daily,* 10 February 1930, p. 11; 23 November 1930, pp. 1, 2.
25. *Film Daily,* 9 February 1930, p. 1.
26. *Film Daily,* 21 December 1930, p. 6; April 1930, p. 3.
27. *Film Daily,* 10 February 1929, p. 16.
28. *Film Daily,* 6 May 1929, p. 1.
29. *Film Daily,* 25 September 1929, p. 1.
30. *Film Daily,* 6 February 1930, p. 1.
31. *Film Daily,* 17 February 1929, p. 7. Of course sound was not the only determinant; Gomery provides an economic context for the introduction of popcorn in *Shared Pleasures,* pp. 79–81.
32. Seale, "'A Host of Others,'" p. 77; *Film Daily,* 8 April 1930, p. 8; 5 May 1930, p. 6; 21 November 1930, pp. 1, 2.
33. The examples of longer films were ANIMAL CRACKERS (1930), 100 minutes; THE DAWN PATROL (1930), 95; ALL QUIET ON THE WESTERN FRONT (1930), 135; and DIXIANA (1930), 98. *Film Daily,* 15 September 1930, pp. 1, 8.
34. *Film Daily,* 25 July 1930, pp. 1, 2; 3 June 1930, p. 1; 22 July 1930, p. 1; 17 August 1930, pp. 1, 2; 18 September 1930, pp. 1, 4.
35. *Film Daily,* 29 January 1932, p. 1.
36. *Film Daily,* 11 November 1931, p. 9; 16 June 1932, pp. 1, 7; 23 June 1932, p. 1.
37. *Film Daily,* 4 January 1931, p. 1; 17 March 1931, p. 2; 2 April 1931, p. 8; 13 April 1932, p. 7; 20 April 1931, p. 1.
38. *Film Daily,* 3 January 1932, pp. 1, 3.
39. Gomery, *Shared Pleasures,* pp. 61–65; *Film Daily,* 23 June 1932, pp. 1, 8; 28 June 1932, pp. 1, 4.

CHAPTER 12. The New Entertainment Vitamin: 1928–1929

1. Karol Kulik, *Alexander Korda: The Man Who Could Work Miracles* (London: Virgin Books, 1990), p. 51.
2. The company merged with 20th Century-Fox in 1934, with Zanuck as chief of production.
3. Al Jolson–Albert Warner agreement, 7 August 1928, Warner Bros. contract file, United Artists Collection, Wisconsin Center for Film and Theater Research (WCFTR). Jolson's contract was not as lucrative as reported (up to $500,000 per film in some published sources). Furthermore, he lost about $100,000 by receiving no profit participation on SAY IT WITH SONGS. Since neither BIG BOY nor MAMMY grossed over $1 million, he earned no profit points.
4. *Film Daily,* 8 May 1928, p. 1; 2 December 1928, p. 6. The Winter Garden had been the site of Jolson's first Broadway stage appearance in 1911.
5. Barrios, *A Song in the Dark,* p. 50.
6. *Film Daily,* 20 September 1928, p. 1.
7. *Film Daily,* 21 September 1928, p. 1.

8. Goldman, *Jolson,* pp. 163–64; *Film Daily,* 23 September 1928, p. 4.

9. *Film Daily,* 28 October 1928, p. 4.

10. Bandy, *The Dawn of Sound,* p. 52. The general release was not until 15 June 1929.

11. *Film Daily,* 5 November 1928, p. 5.

12. *Film Daily,* 30 December 1928, p. 8; Walker, *The Shattered Silents,* pp. 109–11; Herbert Goldman, *Fanny Brice: The Original Funny Girl* (New York: Oxford University Press, 1992), p. 140. Flo Ziegfeld preferred spelling her name "Fannie," so it is usually billed that way during this period. She also appeared in *Be Yourself!* (1930). Brice was the subject of the play and movie FUNNY GIRL (1968).

13. *Film Daily,* 20 November 1928, p. 6; 9 December 1928, p. 10; Mordaunt Hall, *New York Times,* 3 September 1928.

14. Nick Roddick, *A New Deal in Entertainment: Warner Brothers in the 1930s* (London: BFI, 1983), pp. 18–19.

15. *Film Daily,* 24 July 1929, p. 1.

16. *Film Daily,* 17 November 1929, p. 8; 18 November 1929, p. 14.

17. Oscar Hammerstein II was a Broadway legend, having contributed in some capacity to twenty-three shows between 1920 and 1932. Hollywood adaptations of his operettas include THE DESERT SONG, SHOW BOAT (1929); NEW MOON, SUNNY, GOLDEN DAWN, SONG OF THE FLAME, SONG OF THE WEST, THREE SISTERS, and VIENNESE NIGHTS (1930); and CHILDREN OF DREAMS (1931). Sigmund Romberg taught himself music and was launched in a career by J. J. Shubert. Producing on Broadway for nearly half a century, beginning in 1914, he left a permanent mark on that style of musical entertainment. His distinctive style mixed light Viennese airs with the syncopated beat of Harlem. The Stanley Donen film DEEP IN MY HEART (1954) is a biography of Romberg. Lacombe and Rocle, *De Broadway à Hollywood,* pp. 196–97; 245–46.

18. Barrios, *A Song in the Dark,* p. 81. It may also have been the rights dispute between Lillian Albertson and Warners that was responsible for the delay.

19. *Film Daily,* 16 April 1929, p. 4; 5 May 1929, p. 9.

20. *Film Daily,* 16 April 1929, p. 4.

21. *Film Daily,* 16 July 1929, p. 4.

22. *Film Daily,* 28 August 1929, p. 8.

23. As of October, Fox reported that six talking shorts (including NAPOLEON'S BARBER) and six dialogue features were done or nearly so. The features were THE VALIANT (1928) ("in which Paul Muni . . . makes his talking picture debut"), NORTH OF DIXIE (1929), FRIENDSHIP (1929), THROUGH DIFFERENT EYES, THE GHOST TALKS (1929), and IN OLD ARIZONA (1929). *Film Daily,* 30 October 1928, p. 6.

24. *Variety,* 27 June 1928.

25. Judels enjoyed a prolific career as a character actor through the 1940s (including the voice of Stromboli in PINOCCHIO [1940]).

26. *Film Daily,* 16 September 1928, p. 6.

27. Mordaunt Hall, *New York Times,* 3 September 1928.

28. Mordaunt Hall, *New York Times,* 17 September 1928; *Film Daily,* 23 September 1928, p. 6.

29. *Film Daily,* 15 November 1928, p. 5; 2 December 1928, p. 9. Ford's retelling of his efforts to record Josephine crossing a bridge are from his interview with Peter Bogdanovich, quoted in Walker, *The Shattered Silents,* p. 113. According to Tag Gallagher, NAPOLEON'S BARBER is a lost film; *John Ford,* pp. 54, 519.

30. Mordaunt Hall, *New York Times,* 26 November 1928.

31. *Film Daily,* 22 October 1928, p. 6.

32. *Film Daily,* 8 January 1929, p. 1.

33. *Film Daily,* 22 January 1929, p. 1.

34. *Film Daily,* 16 May 1929, p. 6; 23 May 1929, p. 1.

35. *Film Daily,* 28 July 1929, p. 9.

36. *Film Daily,* 8 July 1928, p. 4; 29 July 1928, p. 7.

37. *Film Daily,* 22 July 1928, p. 31.

38. *Film Daily,* 30 July 1928, p. 7; Mordaunt Hall, *New York Times,* 16 July 1928; *Film Daily,* 5 August 1928, p. 9.

39. *Film Daily,* 3 March 1929, p. 6.

40. Mordaunt Hall, *New York Times,* 17 November 1928.

41. Pomeroy directed BEHIND THE LINES for RKO in 1930, then became a freelance consultant, exploiting his many technical patents.
42. Kim Novak portrayed the actress in JEANNE EAGELS (dir. George Sidney, 1957).
43. Herbert Cruikshank, "Doing as He Doesn't Like," *Motion Picture Classic,* October 1929, p. 33.
44. *Film Daily,* 24 May 1929, p. 1; 2 June 1929, p. 9.
45. *Film Daily,* 10 February 1929, p. 18.
46. Jessie L. Lasky with Don Weldon, *I Blow My Own Horn* (1937), pp. 217–18.
47. Chevalier was the quintessential Frenchman for American moviegoers. French critics, however, regarded him as something of a caricature of a national type, and his many films made in France were not received as well as those he made in America. "This is the paradox that assures the posterity of Maurice Chevalier." Lacombe and Rocle, *De Broadway à Hollywood,* pp. 162–63.
48. *Film Daily,* 17 March 1929, p. 5; 28 April 1929, p. 1.
49. *Film Daily,* 21 April 1929, p. 8. This film was the talkie debut of Colbert and Robinson, but each had appeared in silents.
50. Mordaunt Hall, *New York Times,* 16 November 1928.
51. *Film Daily,* 13 July 1928, p. 1. As a publicity stunt, the producers of NIZE BABY assembled amateur actors at New York's station WPAP to audition their lines over the air. The film was not released under this title.
52. Crowther, *The Lion's Share,* pp. 146–47. Leo also roared in the MGM opening logo in THE HOLLYWOOD REVUE OF 1929, but not consistently in every film until sometime in 1931.
53. *Film Daily,* 5 August 1928, p. 9.
54. Mordaunt Hall, *New York Times,* 1 August 1928; *Motion Picture,* November 1928, p. 66.
55. Mordaunt Hall, *New York Times,* 16 November 1928.
56. *Film Daily,* 31 March 1929, p. 28; Crowther, *The Lion's Share,* pp. 152–53.
57. Glancy, "MGM Film Grosses, 1924–1948," p. 133.
58. Freed, cited in Barrios, *A Song in the Dark,* p. 63, n.3.
59. In the credits, the Kenneth Thompson character is identified as Jock, but the card he presents to Queenie reads "Jacques."
60. *Film Daily,* 17 February 1929, p. 10; 28 February 1929, p. 4. Nacio Herb Brown, a self-taught amateur musician, fascinated Irving Thalberg, who hired him to write the music for THE BROADWAY MELODY, teamed with Arthur Freed. Freed came to Hollywood as a song-plugger. He opened his own theater in Los Angeles in 1924 and began writing lyrics for movies in 1928, eventually becoming one of MGM's star producers. The "Freed Unit" launched Judy Garland, Cyd Charisse, Gene Kelly, and many more; Lacombe and Rocle, *De Broadway à Hollywood,* pp. 147, 185.
61. *Film Daily,* 6 May 1929, p. 1.
62. *Film Daily,* 13 January 1929, p. 7; 19 March 1929, p. 1; 26 March 1929, p. 1; 5 August 1929, p. 7.
63. *Film Daily,* 25 April 1929, pp. 1, 2; 28 April 1929, p. 8; 29 April 1929, p. 1; *Erpigram,* 20 June 1929, p. 5.
64. Stearns, "The Movies Talk!," p. 199; Chaplin quoted in Gilbert Seldes, "The Movies Commit Suicide," *Harper's,* November 1928, p. 711; Wesley Stout, "Beautiful, but No Longer Dumb," *Saturday Evening Post,* 8 June 1929, p. 48.
65. Michael G. Ankerich, *Broken Silence: Conversations with Twenty-three Silent Film Stars* (Jefferson, N.C.: McFarland, 1992), p. 129; *Film Daily,* 25 February 1929, p. 1; 6 February 1929, p. 2; 11 March 1929, p. 1; 17 March 1929, p. 1; 8 December 1929, p. 8. "It must be added, though, that some historians now believe [Fairbanks] used a voice double"; Walker, *The Shattered Silents,* p. 148.
66. *Film Daily,* 26 March 1929, p. 1; 5 April 1929, p. 1. This title seems to have been the only exception to UA's dual-release policy. According to Balio, a silent version was eventually circulated; *United Artists,* p. 80.
67. *Film Daily,* 8 April 1929, p. 1; 14 April 1929, p. 6.
68. Walker, *The Shattered Silents,* p. 126; *Film Daily,* 19 March 1929, p. 10; Schickel, *D. W. Griffith,* pp. 545–51.
69. *Film Daily,* 3 May 1929, p. 1.
70. *Film Daily,* 13 January 1929, p. 7; 4 June 1929, p. 4; 14 June 1929, pp. 1, 3; 17 June 1929, p. 1.
71. HELL'S ANGELS souvenir booklet, 1930, Yranski Collection; *Film Daily,* 25 May 1928; 20 July 1928, p. 3.

72. Herman G. Weinberg, "Erich von Stroheim," *Saint Cinema,* 2d ed. rev. (New York: Dover, 1973), p. 47; Peter Noble, *Hollywood Scapegoat: The Biography of Erich von Stroheim* (London: Fortune Press, 1950), p. 75.

73. C. E. Sullivan (vice president, Gloria Productions) to F. A. Beach (UA), 1 March 1929, box 150/7, UA Collection, WCFTR; *Film Daily,* 12 July 1928, p. 7; 28 August 1928, pp. 1, 2; Walker, *The Shattered Silents,* p. 80.

74. Koszarski, *The Man You Love to Hate,* p. 218.

75. Swanson, *Swanson on Swanson,* p. 367.

76. *Film Daily,* 25 January 1929, p. 6; 7 February 1929, p. 1; 28 February 1929, p. 5; 10 April 1929, p. 6; 26 April 1929, p. 1; Walker, *The Shattered Silents,* pp. 153–54.

77. Koszarski, *The Man You Love to Hate,* pp. 223–24.

78. *Film Daily,* 20 December 1929, pp. 1, 8; 7 January 1930, p. 2; 23 February 1930, pp. 1, 12.

79. *Film Daily,* 22 June 1928, p. 8; 20 June 1928, pp. 1, 8.

80. *Film Daily,* 26 June 1928, p. 1.

81. *Film Daily,* 27 July 1928, p. 1.

82. These were THE LAST WARNING (dir. Paul Leni, 1929), IT CAN BE DONE (dir. Fred Newmeyer, A. B. Heath, 1929), and LONESOME (dir. Paul Fejos, 1928). Walker, *The Shattered Silents,* p. 101.

83. The fan magazine reviewed the film under the title MADELON, November 1928, p. 57.

84. *Film Daily,* 30 October 1928, p. 8; Mordaunt Hall, *New York Times,* 22 October 1928.

85. *Film Daily,* 8 February 1929, p. 8.

86. *Film Daily,* 23 April 1929, p. 6. John Murray Anderson was a Broadway musical stalwart. He directed the annual Greenwich Village Follies from 1919 through 1924, and his own revue, the John Murray Anderson Almanac, in 1929; Lacombe and Rocle, *De Broadway à Hollywood,* p. 133.

87. When reviewed during its first release, Kann thought that LONESOME was "the most violent instance of the floating camera we have yet witnessed"; *Film Daily,* 13 June 1928, p. 1. The staff reviewer wrote: "One weakness is the director's failure to keep his camera stationary more often in frequent shifting which often makes it trying for the eye"; 24 June 1928, p. 5.

88. *Film Daily,* 2 October 1928, p. 1.

89. Roy Hemming, *The Melody Lingers On: The Great Songwriters and Their Movie Musicals* (New York: Newmarket, 1986), pp. 88–89. The compositions of Jerome Kern had been appearing on Broadway since 1912, but *Show Boat* would be his all-time most successful musical. In addition to the Universal adaptation, other film versions of musicals from the period to which he contributed included SALLY (1929) and THREE SISTERS and SUNNY (1930); Lacombe and Rocle, *De Broadway à Hollywood,* pp. 209–10.

90. *Film Daily,* 22 January 1929, pp. 1, 3.

91. *Film Daily,* 17 January 1929, p. 14; 18 March 1929, p. 1.

92. Dick May, "The Restoration of *Show Boat* [1929]," *Vitaphone News* 3, no. 1 (Summer–Fall 1995), p. 3; *Film Daily,* 30 April 1929, p. 6.

93. *Film Daily,* 18 April 1929, p. 1.

94. *Film Daily,* 21 July 1929, p. 3.

95. *Film Daily,* 13 January 1929, pp. 6, 8.

96. *Film Daily,* 14 June 1928, p. 6.

97. Powers Cinephone advertisement, *Film Daily,* 19 June 1928.

98. *Film Daily,* 14 December 1928, p. 13.

99. Seale, "A Host of Others," pp. 84–86. I can find no record of release for THE GIRL FROM THE ARGENTINE.

CHAPTER 13. Taming the Talkies: 1929–1930

1. Barrios, *A Song in the Dark,* pp. 190–92, 220.

2. Ibid.; Rick Altman, *The American Film Musical* (Bloomington: Indiana University Press, 1987), p. 111. See also Jane Feuer, *The Hollywood Musical,* 2nd ed. (Bloomington: Indiana University Press, 1993).

3. Martin Rubin, *Showstoppers: Busby Berkeley and the Tradition of Spectacle* (New York: Columbia University Press, 1993), pp. 15–30.

4. *Variety,* 5 February 1930.

5. *Film Daily,* 3 February 1930, p. 5; 25 August 1930, p. 1.

6. What the "phantom screen" refers to is unclear. Perhaps it refers to a blue screen (like the Dunning process), the variable-size Magnascope screen, or widescreen formats in general.

7. "Singin' in the Rain" had appeared first in the *Music Box Revue*, a 1928 Ziegfeld show with lyrics by Freed.

8. Barrios, *A Song in the Dark*, p. 225.

9. *Film Daily*, 5 May 1930 p. 8; 6 February 1930, p. 11. Wodehouse had two careers as a screen-writer, 1930–1931, and 1935–1937; Kristin Thompson, *Wooster Proposes, Jeeves Disposes, or Le Mot Juste* (New York: Heinemann, 1992), pp. 30–31; Hemming, *The Melody Lingers On*, p. 88.

10. *Variety*, 22 January 1930.

11. *Film Daily*, 22 June 1930, p. 15; Mordaunt Hall, *New York Times*, 12 December 1930.

12. In the early train station scene, an extra hoists a placard reading: "Let us know all about Jack Gilbert."

13. Mordaunt Hall, *New York Times*, 30 September 1930.

14. *Film Daily*, 3 August 1930, p. 10.

15. *Film Daily*, 9 February 1930, p. 12; 23 February 1930, p. 3; *Variety*, 19 March 1930.

16. Mordaunt Hall, *New York Times*, 23 August 1930; *Film Daily*, 24 August 1930, p. 10.

17. *Film Daily*, 26 January 1930, p. 1; 19 May 1930, p. 1; 6 July 1930, p. 10; 27 August 1930, p. 1; Michael F. Blake, *Lon Chaney: The Man Behind the Thousand Faces* (Vestal, N.Y.: Vestal Press, 1990), p. 257.

18. *Film Daily*, 29 June 1930, p. 10.

19. Ibid.

20. *Variety*, 29 January 1930.

21. *Film Daily*, 29 June 1930, p. 10; 16 February 1930, p. 12.

22. *Film Daily*, 20 May 1929, pp. 6–7.

23. Roland Flamini, *Thalberg: The Last Tycoon and the World of MGM* (New York: Crown, 1994), p. 115.

24. *Film Daily*, 8 October 1929, p. 9.

25. *Film Daily*, 10 October 1929, p. 1.

26. *Variety*, 12 February 1930.

27. *Film Daily*, 8 December 1929, p. 8.

28. SALLY souvenir program, 1930, Yranski Collection; *Film Daily*, 25 February 1930, p. 4.

29. SONG OF THE WEST review, *Variety*, 5 March 1930.

30. *Film Daily*, 4 April 1930, p. 1.

31. *Film Daily*, 29 December 1929, p. 8.

32. The actual source was the four-act play adaptation by Kirk La Shelle in 1923.

33. *Film Daily*, 24 November 1929, p. 6.

34. *Film Daily*, 9 February 1930, p. 6.

35. When it opened in New York, PARAMOUNT ON PARADE ran 101 minutes and contained 20 numbers (11 in Technicolor). This is longer than existing prints. The film is currently under restoration by the UCLA archives.

36. Jeanette MacDonald was an established star on Broadway at the time of Lubitsch's film, having sung in ten shows since 1920.

37. THE LOVE PARADE souvenir program, 1929, Yranski Collection. The text defines "the inimitable Lubitsch touch":
There is an atmosphere about a Lubitsch picture that you find nowhere else. His players live their parts. They are flesh-and-blood, civilized people. They do nothing that does not seem utterly natural. They have a slyly humorous outlook on life. If they are indiscreet—and they very frequently are—they are delicately so. They sin with polish and a smile. They are supremely, gorgeously alive!

38. *Film Daily*, 3 August, p. 11.

39. "'It Does Something to a Girl. I Don't Know What': The Problem of Female Sexuality in *Applause*," *Cinema Journal* 30, no. 2 (winter 1991): 47–60; Barrios, *A Song in the Dark*, p. 357. Paramount recalled Mamoulian a year later to make CITY STREETS (1931).

40. *Film Daily*, 11 October 1929, p. 3; Barrios, *A Song in the Dark*, pp. 245–49.

41. *Film Daily*, 29 August 1929, p. 11.

42. *Film Daily*, 18 April 1929, p. 1; 22 May 1929, p. 8; Mark J. Langer, "*Tabu*: The Making of a Film," *Cinema Journal* 24, no. 3 (spring 1985): 43–64.

43. *Variety*, 16 April 1930.

44. Hijiya, *Lee de Forest,* p. 114; Kobal, *Gotta Sing, Gotta Dance,* p. 31.

45. Jewell, "RKO Film Grosses," pp. 42–43.

46. Barrios, *A Song in the Dark,* pp. 268–69; Slide, *The Encyclopedia of Vaudeville,* pp. 548–50.

47. *Variety,* 30 April 1930.

48. Sime, *Variety,* 12 March 1930.

49. *Film Daily,* 13 January 1930, pp. 1, 2; 16 February 1930, p. 8.

50. Michael Rogin, "Making America Home: Radical Masquerade and Ethnic Assimilation in the Transition to Talking Pictures," *Journal of American History* 79, no. 3 (December 1992): 1063–68.

51. The author also noted that Whiteman always supervised his phonograph studio sessions, and "the recording here may go to the Whiteman credit"; see also Richard Koszarski, *Universal Pictures.*

52. Richard Koszarski, *Universal Pictures: 75 Years* (New York: Museum of Modern Art, 1977), p. 17.

53. *Film Daily,* 27 April 1930, p. 12.

54. Gomery, *The Hollywood Studio System,* p. 148.

55. *Film Daily,* 2 July 1928, p. 3.

56. *Film Daily,* 3 April 1929, p. 1; *Motion Picture,* May 1929; *Motion Picture Classic,* June 1929; October 1929, p. 15; Robinson, *Chaplin,* pp. 394–95, 401, 410.

57. *Film Daily,* 29 January 1930, p. 8; Barrios, *A Song in the Dark,* pp. 335–36; *Film Daily,* 20 April 1930, p. 5; 26 August 1930, p. 1; Vlada Petric, "Two Lincoln Assassinations by D. W. Griffith," *Quarterly Review of Film Studies* 3 no. 3, (1978), pp. 345–370.

58. HELL'S ANGELS souvenir booklet. The cost figure should be taken with the proverbial grain of salt. *Variety* guessed $3 million, which still would have made it the most expensive film to date.

59. E. E. Spicer, "Special Reproducing Equipment Provides for Showing of Caddo's Epic War Film," *Erpigram,* 15 July 1930, p. 5; *Film Daily,* 18 July 1930, p. 7.

60. *Film Daily,* 5 August 1930, p. 3; 19 August 1930, p. 3; 24 August 1930, p. 10. UA distributed a silent version in Europe. It is worth noting that Hughes's arrangement with UA for distributing his film was complicated. After some months of dickering, he closed a deal to buy an interest in Art Cinema Finance Corporation for $3 million. This was the company established in 1926 by Joseph Schenck to finance his pictures for UA distribution. It was not until after Hughes was duly elected to the board of directors of Art Cinema Finance, in October, that UA took over HELL'S ANGELS for release; *Film Daily,* 15 October 1930, p. 1; 25 October 1930, pp. 1, 8; Balio, *United Artists,* pp. 67–68, 110–11.

   In November 1930, there was a power shift behind the scenes at UA when Samuel Goldwyn was put in charge of all production activity of Art Cinema. Goldwyn continued his own production separately, while controlling the UA purse strings. Joseph Schenck, the founder and former president, concentrated on distribution, the UA Theaters chain, and feuding with the Fox West Coast chain; *Film Daily,* 25 November 1930, p. 1.

61. Frank Capra, *The Name Above the Title* (New York: Macmillan, 1971), pp. 101–4; Bernard F. Dick, *The Merchant Prince of Poverty Row: Harry Cohn of Columbia Pictures* (Lexington: University Press of Kentucky, 1993), p. 45; Len D. Martin, *The Columbia Checklist* (Jefferson, N.C.: McFarland, 1991). The Christie brothers went bankrupt in 1932. Eventually the premises at 1040 North Las Palmas became Francis Ford Coppola's Zoetrope Studios.

62. Viewing the film confirms that Capra's memory was faulty when he wrote, "We had no 'process shots' then, no trick photography in which actors are photographed in studio against aerial backgrounds." Capra, *The Name Above the Title,* p. 109.

63. *Film Daily,* 31 July 1930, advertisement; 12 February 1930, p. 4.

64. SUNRISE begins with a short "summertime" montage section accompanied by the sound of raucous klaxon horns, and so forth.

65. *Variety,* 8 January 1930.

66. *Film Daily,* 14 May 1928, p. 3; 10 June 1928, p. 3; 8 August 1928, p. 7; 25 November 1928, p. 6. Another member of the Ten was Edward Dmytryk, during this period an editor at Paramount (e.g., THE ROYAL FAMILY OF BROADWAY [dir. George Cukor, 1930]).

67. Seitz, *Cinematographic Annual 1930,* p. 19.

CHAPTER 14. The Well-Tempered Sound Track: 1930–1931

1. Mordaunt Hall, *New York Times,* 29 November 1930; 15 August 1930.

2. Mordaunt Hall, *New York Times,* 16 August 1930.

3. Mordaunt Hall, *New York Times,* 6 September 1930; 13 September 1930.

4. Mordaunt Hall, *New York Times,* 15 August 1930.

5. Mordaunt Hall, *New York Times,* 6 December 1930.

6. Jenkins, *What Made Pistachio Nuts?,* pp. 245–46.

7. *Variety,* 19 March 1930; Barrios, *A Song in the Dark,* pp. 282–83.

8. Among its charms is the first screen appearance of Bing Crosby in a feature film.

9. Mordaunt Hall, *New York Times,* 6 September 1930.

10. *Variety,* 28 May 1930; 6 August 1930.

11. *Film Daily,* 10 October 1929, p. 1; review of GLORIFYING THE AMERICAN GIRL, *Variety,* 15 January 1930.

12. *Film Daily,* 5 August 1930, p. 1.

13. *Film Daily,* 3 April 1930, p. 2; 25 September 1930, p. 6; 28 September 1930, p. 1; Barrios, *A Song in the Dark,* p. 329.

14. *Film Daily,* 3 April 1930, p. 2.

15. *Film Daily,* 9 June 1930, p. 6.

16. Mordaunt Hall, *New York Times,* 28 November 1930.

17. Mordaunt Hall, *New York Times,* 4 January 1931.

18. Mordaunt Hall, *New York Times,* 8 August 1930.

19. Barrios, *A Song in the Dark,* p. 331; *Film Daily,* 29 March 1931, p. 10.

20. Actually, Murnau's TABU, released in March 1931, might be considered the last major American feature released as a silent. It contained intertitles and a synchronized music score.

21. *Film Daily,* 8 March 1931, p. 6.

22. *Film Daily,* 16 November 1930, p. 11.

23. Mordaunt Hall, *New York Times,* 10 January 1931. Reviewing THE WIDOW FROM CHICAGO, Hall had praised "the endless variety of Edward G. Robinson's particular world of make-believe"; *New York Times,* 20 December 1930.

24. Mordaunt Hall, *New York Times,* 1 November 1930.

25. My conclusions are drawn from viewing the film. It is possible that either one of the cameras shifted position (hence angle of view) or substituted longer lenses (altering the field), but I think this is unlikely. The Burbank stages routinely had six cameras available, so setting up five would not have been extraordinary. What is remarkable is training them on such a concentrated space.

26. *Film Daily,* 20 April 1930, p. 5; 12 August 1930, p. 11; 28 August 1930, p. 9.

27. Barrios, *A Song in the Dark,* p. 287.

28. The credit reads Donald MacKenzie, and is so reported in *Film Daily Year Book 1931,* p. 499. The *American Film Institute Catalogue,* however, states without explanation that the correct attribution is to Frank MacKenzie.

29. Barrios, *A Song in the Dark,* pp. 258–60; Gene Ringgold and DeWitt Bodeen, *The Films of Cecil B. DeMille* (Secaucus, N.J.: Cadillac, 1969), p. 269.

30. Mordaunt Hall, *New York Times,* 13 December 1930.

31. Mordaunt Hall, *New York Times,* 18 October 1930.

32. Mordaunt Hall, *New York Times,* 5 September 1930.

33. Mordaunt Hall, *New York Times,* 13 February 1931. Lugosi had played the Count in the stage version on Broadway in 1927, but the first choice for the movie part was Lon Chaney.

34. Jenkins, *What Made Pistachio Nuts?,* p. 164. The deal fell through, and Goldwyn did not produce *Simple Simon.*

35. The joke plays on Henry's hypochondria and on Charles Lindbergh's diet of (non-kosher) ham sandwiches during his transatlantic flight.

36. *Film Daily,* 18 September 1930, p. 1; Berg, *Goldwyn,* p. 203; Balio, *Grand Design,* p. 212; Jenkins, *What Made Pistachio Nuts?,* pp. 162–84. The strategies for Cantor's later films included "de-Semitizing" his character and advertising them as zany comedies, not as Broadway musicals.

37. *Film Daily,* 21 December 1930, p. 10. Rouben Mamoulian remade THE MARK OF ZORRO in 1940 with Tyrone Power.

38. *Film Daily,* 8 March 1931, p. 1; Mordaunt Hall, *New York Times,* 6 March 1931.

39. *Film Daily,* 7 March 1930, p. 1; 9 March 1930, p. 1; 24 June 1930, p. 3.

40. Charles Maland, *Chaplin and American Culture* (Princeton: Princeton University Press, 1989), p. 115.

41. *Film Daily,* 2 February 1931, p. 1; 1 February 1931, p. 4.

42. Quoted in Robinson, *Chaplin,* pp. 413–13; *Film Daily,* 3 February 1931, p. 1.

43. *Film Daily,* 5 February 1931, p. 1. Chaplin's next project was MODERN TIMES; production began in 1933, and it was released in 1936.

44. United Artists raised its rental to 50 percent of the box-office gross on CITY LIGHTS; *Film Daily,* 22 January 1931, p. 1. According to Balio (*United Artists,* p. 91) and Robinson (*Chaplin,* p. 415), this was done at Chaplin's insistence, against the wishes of the distributor, which feared that theaters would not book it. By March, however, CITY LIGHTS was playing in Chicago and elsewhere with a 60–40 split, the long end going to Chaplin; *Film Daily,* 1 March 1931, p. 1.
45. Quoted in Maland, *Chaplin and American Culture,* p. 123.
46. *Film Daily,* 9 February 1931, p. 1.
47. *Film Daily,* 6 January 1931, p. 7.
48. Mordaunt Hall, *New York Times,* 7 February 1931.
49. *Film Daily,* 17 March 1931, p. 1.
50. René Clair, *Le Temps,* July 1932, in R. C. Dale, ed., *René Clair: Cinema Yesterday and Today* (New York: Dover, 1972), p. 160.
51. Gomery, *The Coming of Sound,* pp. 385–86; *Film Daily,* 26 April 1931, p. 1; 11 May 1931, p. 1; 14 May 1931, p. 2; 24 May 1931, p. 10; 23 June 1931, p. 8.
52. "At the Capitol in New York it had the audiences in a continuous round of laughter every time Buster Keaton appeared, and that is most of the time"; *Film Daily,* 5 April 1931, p. 10. "There is little talking during these sequences [of FEET FIRST], for none is necessary"; Mordaunt Hall, *New York Times,* 31 October 1930.
53. *Film Daily,* 19 June 1931, p. 1; 23 June 1931, p. 8; 30 June 1931, p. 1; 28 July 1931, p. 1.
54. Because the producers were successful in standardizing sound technique, the studio-by-studio survey method of the previous chapters is less meaningful in this one but has been retained for consistency.
55. *Film Daily,* 18 April 1930, p. 4.
56. *Film Daily,* 13 July 1931, p. 11; 3 August 1931, pp. 1, 6; 24 December 1931, p. 9.
57. *Film Daily,* 1 November 1931, pp. 1, 2.
58. *Film Daily,* 1 April 1931, p. 4; 29 December 1931, p. 7.

CHAPTER 15. The Sound of Custard: Shorts, Travelogues, and Animated Cartoons

1. *Film Daily,* 17 June 1928, p. 7.
2. *Film Daily,* 17 June 1928, p. 4. THE BEAST starred Irene Rich and John Miljan; THE NIGHT COURT featured William Demarest.
3. *Photoplay,* November 1928, p. 84.
4. *Film Daily,* 5 June 1929, p. 1; 9 June 1929, p. 10.
5. *Film Daily,* 1 June 1930, p. 11; 15 June 1930, pp. 1, 11.
6. *Film Daily,* 3 June 1928, p. 5. Indeed, Vitaphone shorts continued to circulate to theaters until the 1950s.
7. *Film Daily,* 29 December 1927, pp. 1, 10.
8. Benchley's routine, originally presented as part of a revue, was reenacted in MRS. PARKER AND THE VICIOUS CIRCLE (1995). See also Alan Rudolph, *Mrs. Parker and the Vicious Circle: The Book of the Film* (New York: Applause Theatre Books, 1995).
9. *Film Daily,* 10 June 1928, p. 7; 29 July 1928, p. 9.
10. *Film Daily,* 24 June 1928, p. 7.
11. *Film Daily,* 22 July 1928, p. 31.
12. Gomery, *The Coming of Sound,* p. 261.
13. *Film Daily,* 2 August 1928, p. 1.
14. *Film Daily,* 26 May 1929, p. 9.
15. Charles Barr, *Laurel and Hardy* (London: Studio Vista, 1967), p. 39.
16. Lacombe and Rocle, *De Broadway à Hollywood,* p. 183; *Film Daily,* 6 April 1930, p. 38; 6 July 1930, p. 11.
17. *Film Daily,* 5 August 1928, p. 7. The film was copyrighted in July by George Matthews Adams.
18. *Film Daily,* 5 July 1928, p. 3; 28 August 1928, p. 1.
19. *Film Daily,* 9 December 1928, p. 14.
20. *Film Daily,* 10 January 1928, pp. 1, 8. See also advertisement, 23 January 1928.
21. *Film Daily,* 3 June 1928, pp. 1, 5.
22. *Film Daily,* 15 June 1928, p. 3.
23. *Film Daily,* 29 March 1929, p. 1; 31 March 1929, pp. 1, 3.

24. Among other titles: Big Dog House (1931), Love-Tails of Morocco (1931), So Quiet on the Canine Front (1930), and Trader Hound (1931).

25. *Film Daily*, 25 January 1928, p. 8; 12 December 1929, p. 2; Mordaunt Hall, *New York Times*, 24 January 1928. The *AFI Catalogue* gives Brunswick credit for the sound system.

26. *Film Daily*, 26 January 1930, p. 8.

27. *Film Daily*, 23 June 1930, p. 2; Mordaunt Hall, *New York Times*, 20 September 1930; *Film Daily*, 21 September 1930, p. 31.

28. *Film Daily*, 16 December 1928, p. 10.

29. *Film Daily*, 19 August 1928, pp. 1, 2, 3.

30. *Film Daily*, 3 June 1928, pp. 1, 16.

31. *Film Daily*, 2 September 1928, pp. 1, 9. "The sound effects were concocted by Max H. Manne, the incidental music conducted by Josiah Zuro and the RCA Photophone system used. A good job was done by all" (p. 9). See also Donald Crafton, *Before Mickey: The Animated Film 1898–1928* (Chicago: University of Chicago Press, 1993), pp. 211–14; Bob Thomas, *Walt Disney: An American Original* (New York: Simon & Schuster, 1976), pp. 90–98.

32. Because *Gallopin' Gaucho* and Plane Crazy had been completed as silents, they would be post-synchronized like the competitors' (basically goat gland cartoons). The fourth title, *The Barn Dance*, was, like *Willie*, intricately preplanned with music; J. B. Kaufman, "The Transcontinental Making of *The Barn Dance*," *Animation Journal* 5, no. 2 (Spring 1997), pp. 36–44.

33. Ibid., p. 38.

34. Leslie Cabarga, *The Fleischer Story* (New York: DaCapo, 1988), p. 50.

35. *Film Daily*, 13 November 1928, pp. 1, 4.

36. *Film Daily*, 19 November 1928, p. 1.

37. The *Film Daily* reviewer characterized the cartoon as "a real tidbit of diversion. The maximum has been gotten from the sound effects"; 25 November 1928, p. 9. The Cinephone-recorded sound track for The Wedding March (1928) had not been presented on Broadway. Until discs became obsolete, Disney, like other producers, transferred his sound tracks to discs for houses not equipped with optical sound.

38. *Film Daily*, 19 November 1928, p. 1; 11 January 1929, p. 6.

39. *Film Daily*, 10 October 1929, p. 2; John Canemaker, *Felix: The Twisted Tale of the World's Most Famous Cat* (New York: Pantheon, 1991), p. 129.

40. *Film Daily*, 7 March 1929, p. 8. Garity remained at the studio, collaborating in 1940 on Fantasia.

41. *Film Daily*, 3 January 1929, p. 1; 3 February 1929, p. 2; 13 May 1929, p. 3.

42. *Film Daily*, 7 July 1929, p. 9; 6 August 1929, p. 2.

43. *Film Daily*, 21 July 1929, p. 13; 25 July 1929, p. 1.

44. *Film Daily*, 6 August 1929, p. 2. Rights to eighteen proposed Mickey Mouse cartoons were obtained by Celebrity Productions for the New York territory; *Film Daily*, 4 September 1929, pp. 10–11; 16 July 1929, p. 5.

45. *Film Daily*, 10 February 1929, p. 19; 4 August 1929, p. 10; 24 March 1929, p. 12. Disney obtained an injunction against Pathé and the Van Beuren Corporation to prevent Terry from further pla-giarism, claiming that the knockoff character was "doing all sorts of things Mickey wouldn't think of doing and has brought down a flood of irate letters and complaints"; *Film Daily*, 1 April 1931, pp. 1, 7. Amedée J. Van Beuren replied, "Aesop's Fables created the characters Milton and Mary Mouse at the inception of the company in 1921 and the company has been using them. If there has been any imitation, it would appear to be at the door of Walt Disney Productions, whose char-acters of Mickey Mouse and Minnie Mouse are so similar to ours." Disney won his preliminary injunction; *Film Daily*, 3 April 1931, p. 2; 30 April 1931, p. 1.

46. *Film Daily*, 25 June 1929, pp. 1, 2.

47. *Film Daily*, 23 May 1929, p. 2.

48. *Film Daily*, 14 February 1929, p. 2.

49. *Film Daily*, 18 March 1930, p. 8; Leonard Maltin, *Of Mice and Magic: A History of American Animated Cartoons* (New York: McGraw-Hill, 1980), p. 158.

50. *Film Daily*, 10 March 1929, p. 11.

51. *Film Daily*, 23 June 1929, p. 3.

52. *Film Daily*, 9 June 1929, p. 10.

53. Cabarga, *The Fleischer Story*, pp. 50–51. In May 1930, Max Fleischer demonstrated his pre-synchronizing process, in which the "effects are recorded first and the drawings then are made in synchronization," to the patents commissioner; *Film Daily*, 19 May 1930, p. 1.

54. Memorandum of agreement, 28 January 1930, AT&T Archives, reproduced in Steve Schneider, *That's All Folks: The Art of Warner Bros. Animation* (New York: Henry Holt, 1988), p. 35.

55. "Looney Tunes #1," *Vitaphone Release Index* [n.d.], pp. 177–78, AT&T Archives. Bosko's name is spelled "Bosco" in the index.

56. *Film Daily,* 8 April 1931, p. 2.

57. *Film Daily,* 11 February 1930, p. 1; 10 March 1930, p. 1; Douglas Gomery, "Disney's Business History: A Reinterpretation," in Eric Smoodin, ed., *Disney Discourse: Producing the Magic Kingdom* (New York: Routledge, 1994), p. 72; Thomas, *Walt Disney,* pp. 100–106.

58. *Film Daily,* 9 January 1931, p. 1; 16 January 1931, p. 3.

59. *Film Daily,* 12 April 1931, p. 13, advertisement.

60. Cabarga, *The Fleischer Story,* pp. 50–52.

61. *Film Daily,* 10 May 1931, p. 11.

62. *Film Daily,* 22 March 1931, p. 2.

63. *Film Daily,* 6 April 1930, p. 3.

CHAPTER 16. Outside the Mainstream

1. Michael Rogin, *Blackface, White Noise: Jewish Immigrants in the Hollywood Melting Pot* (Berkeley: University of California Press, 1996).

2. Arthur W. Eddy, "Short Shots from New York Studios," *Film Daily,* 29 August 1929, p. 10.

3. *Film Daily,* 3 February 1929, p. 9; 10 April 1929, p. 7.

4. *Film Daily,* 1 May 1929, p. 9; 1 September 1929, p. 14; Slide, *The Encyclopedia of Vaudeville,* p. 535. According to copyright records, MGM released these titles in the "Metro Movietone Revues" series: "Chloe"/"Just a Melody from out of the Sky" (October 1928); "King for a Day"/"Half Way to Heaven" (December 1928); "Lonely Vagabond" (January 1929); "George Dewey, the Golden Voiced Son of the South" (June 1929); and "Just Be a Builder of Dreams"/"Down Among the Sugar Cane" (July 1929). Washington performed "On the Road to Mandalay," his vaudeville signature tune, in the "Metro Movietone Revue" no. 2. He sang "Ready for the River" in "Revue" no. 4. Both are included on the DAWN OF SOUND laserdisc, vol. 1.

5. Murphy's films were shot at the RCA Gramercy studio (supervised by Dick Currier); *Film Daily,* 17 November 1929, p. 9; William Moritz, "Americans in Paris: Man Ray and Dudley Murphy," in Jan-Christopher Horak, ed., *Lovers of Cinema: The First American Film Avant-Garde, 1919–1945* (Madison: University of Wisconsin Press, 1995), pp. 118–36.

6. *Film Daily,* 9 December 1929, p. 12; 15 December 1929, p. 7. Neither Johnson nor Hall's Chorus receives a screen credit in DIXIANA, nor are they readily recognizable in the recent UCLA restoration. Perhaps the chorus's voices remain in the "slave song" opening credit sequence.

7. *Film Daily,* 25 April 1929, p. 3; 9 June 1929, p. 9.

8. *Film Daily,* 24 February 1929, p. 14.

9. *Film Daily,* 30 October 1928, p. 6; Daniel J. Leab, *From Sambo to Superspade: The Black Experience in Motion Pictures* (Boston: Houghton Mifflin, 1975), pp. 86–88. Gilpin had originally been cast as Nappus.

10. Raymond Durgnat and Scott Simmon, *King Vidor, American* (Berkeley: University of California Press, 1988), p. 101. The dual premiere was symbolic both because of Vidor's well-intended acknowledgment of his African-American audience and because of its emblematic "separate but equal" implications. Blacks were turned away from the Times Square Theater and sent to Harlem; Leab, *From Sambo to Superspade,* pp. 94–95.

11. An example is Harrower's synopsis of George Dewey Washington's second "Metro Movietone Revue": "Type of production—Colored warbler. This boy, George Dewey Washington, was standing them up for three weeks in a row at the Paramount on Broadway. He's a colored Al Jolson and has that same knack of throwing himself completely into the mood of his song until it gets contagious. Dressed as a tramp, he sings 'King for a Day' and encores with 'Half Way to Heaven,' a crooning coon song that is a pip"; *Film Daily,* 18 November 1928, p. 9. These remarks were intended as compliments, and the comparison to the blackfaced Jolson was made without irony.

12. *Film Daily,* 25 August 1929, p. 18; Walker, *The Shattered Silents,* pp. 190–91; Barrios, *A Song in the Dark,* pp. 312–14.

13. *Film Daily,* 21 August 1929, p. 1. Leab gives a summary of the reaction, mostly negative, from the African-American press; *From Sambo to Superspade,* pp. 93–94.

14. *Film Daily,* 27 September 1929, pp. 1, 2.
15. "As a stage ensemble, minstrelsy has about died out; it may be a circus to the kiddies to let them see what their folks have seen—the minstrel show" (*Variety,* 2 April 1930).
16. *Film Daily,* 24 February 1929, p. 1.
17. *Film Daily,* 15 March 1929, p. 9.
18. Lincoln Theodore Monroe Andrew Perry, who took the name Stepin Fetchit, was a remarkable star. According to Charlene Register, "His painful portrayals were so scarring that African Americans have practically removed his image from the history of motion pictures"; "Stepin Fetchit: The Man, the Image, and the African American Press," *Film History* 6, no. 4 (Winter 1994), pp. 502–21.
19. Smulyan, *Selling Radio,* pp. 114–15.
20. *Film Daily,* 9 April 1930, p. 1; 13 April 1930, p. 1; 18 May 1930, p. 4.
21. Thomas Cripps, *Slow Fade to Black* (New York: Oxford University Press, 1977), p. 269; *Film Daily,* 3 November 1930, p. 1.
22. Jewell, "RKO Film Grosses," p. 43; Sedgwick, "Richard B. Jewell's RKO Film Grosses," p. 56. Bing Crosby also sang in CHECK AND DOUBLE CHECK.
23. *Film Daily,* 14 April 1931, p. 1.
24. *Variety,* 17 September 1930.
25. Slide, "Moran and Mack," *The Encyclopedia of Vaudeville,* pp. 355–57; Cripps, *Slow Fade to Black,* pp. 269–70.
26. A veteran actor despite his age, he also appeared in HEARTS IN DIXIE (as Chinquapin), DIXIANA, SPORTING BLOOD (1931), and SPORTING CHANCE (1931). According to Leab, Jackson had acted in the "Our Gang" series and appeared on television in the 1960s; *From Sambo to Superspade,* p. 88.
27. James Snead, *White Screens Black Images: Hollywood from the Dark Side* (New York: Routledge, 1994), p. 143.
28. Moritz, "Americans in Paris," pp. 130–33. Moritz (p. 130) argues that Murphy, not Léger, was the primary creator of BALLET MÉCANIQUE. The film premiered in New York with a black percussionist accompanying it.
29. *Film Daily,* 10 September 1930, p. 1.
30. Though forgotten today, Segal was about as well known as Jeanette MacDonald during her stage years. Lacombe and Rocle call her the queen of the operetta. Her career began in 1917 and she starred in numerous revues. *Desert Song,* in 1926, was her most successful performance. Her film career ended, but she continued to sing and act, making a comeback in *Pal Joey* in 1940; Lacombe and Rocle, *De Broadway à Hollywood,* pp. 292–93.
31. *New York Herald-Tribune,* 14 June 1930.
32. Michael Rogin, *Blackface, White Noise,* p. 29.
33. *Erpigram,* 20 July 1929, p. 8; *Film Daily,* 30 July 1929, p. 10; 26 November 1929, p. 1.
34. Dan Streible, "The Harlem Theater: Black Film Exhibition in Austin, Texas: 1920–1973," in Manthia Diawara, ed., *Black American Cinema* (New York: Routledge, 1993), pp. 221–24.
35. *Film Daily,* 1 December 1930, p. 1; 13 April 1930, p. 2.
36. *Film Daily,* 5 May 1929, p. 11; 19 May 1929, p. 10.
37. *Film Daily,* 6 January 1931, p. 2.
38. *Film Daily,* 8 January 1931, p. 2.
39. Charlene Regester, "The Misreading and Rereading of African-American Filmmaker Oscar Micheaux," *Film History* 7, no. 4 (Winter 1995), p. 426.
40. *Film Daily,* 18 December 1929, p. 14; Brian Taves, "The B Film: Hollywood's Other Half," in Balio, *Grand Design,* p. 345. For a lively debate on Micheaux's significance, see the articles by J. Ronald Green ("'Twoness' in the Style of Oscar Micheaux"), Jane Gaines ("Fire and Desire: Race, Melodrama, and Oscar Micheaux"), and Thomas Cripps ("Oscar Micheaux: The Story Continues") in Diawara, *Black American Cinema,* pp. 26–70. For a thorough survey of Micheaux scholarship by a co-editor of the *Oscar Micheaux Society Newsletter,* see Regester, "The Misreading and Rereading of . . . Oscar Micheaux," pp. 426–49. See also the television program produced by Pamela A. Thomas and Bestor Cram, "Midnight Ramble: Oscar Micheaux and the Story of Race Movies" (Northern Light Productions, 1994, distributed by PBS Video).

41. Besides the trade journals, the information in this section is from J. Hoberman, *Bridge of Light: Yiddish Film Between Two Worlds* (Philadelphia: Temple University Press, 1995); Eric A. Goldman, *Visions, Images, and Dreams: Yiddish Film Past and Present* (Ann Arbor: UMI Research, 1983); and Judith N. Goldberg, *Laughter Through Tears: The Yiddish Cinema* (East Brunswick, N.J.: Associated University Presses, 1983).

42. Hoberman, *Bridge of Light*, p. 114.

43. *Film Daily*, 3 June 1928, p. 11; 11 November 1928, pp. 1, 12; 10 December 1928, p. 3.

44. Harry Potamkin, "Movie: New York Notes," *Close-Up* 6, no. 2 (February 1930), p. 96.

45. *Film Daily*, 17 September 1929, p. 2. I am assuming that the picture discussed as THE WAILING WALL was AD MOSAY.

46. *Film Daily*, 24 February 1930, pp. 1, 2; 10 March 1930, p. 2; 18 March 1930, pp. 1, 8; 23 May 1930, pp. 1, 6.

47. Goldman, *Visions, Images, and Dreams*, p. 67.

48. Taves, "The B Film," p. 342.

49. *Film Daily*, 7 February 1929, p. 9.

50. *Film Daily*, 11 August 1929, p. 9.

51. Smulyan, *Selling Radio*, pp. 115–16. NBC was nervous about listener response and hesitated in releasing photographs of the Jewish cast. But a survey by Pepsodent showed that "the vast majority . . . of appeals to keep it on the air came from Gentiles"; 1932 NBC memo, quoted by Smulyan, *Selling Radio*, p. 116.

52. Eltinge's fame is suggested by a gag in Keaton's SEVEN CHANCES (1925). Buster is looking for a bride—almost any woman will do—and sees a poster for Eltinge. He enters the stage door and returns rubbing a slapped face. The viewer is left to imagine the nature of the transgression.

53. *Film Daily*, 7 October 1929, p. 3; 6 December 1929, p. 14; Anthony Slide, *Great Pretenders: A History of Female and Male Impersonation in the Performing Arts* (Lombard, Ill.: Wallace-Homestead, 1986).

54. Several essays assembled by Lester D. Friedman, ed., *Unspeakable Images: Ethnicity and the American Cinema* (Urbana: University of Illinois Press, 1991), address these social issues. In particular, see Charles Musser, "Ethnicity, Role-Playing, and American Film Comedy," on Cantor and the Marx brothers (pp. 39–81); Mark Winokur, "Black Is White/White Is Black: 'Passing' as a Strategy of Racial Compatibility in Contemporary Hollywood Comedy" (pp. 190–211); on THE KING OF JAZZ, Ella Shohat, "Ethnicities-in-Relation: Toward a Multicultural Reading of American Cinema" (pp. 215–50); and David Desser, "The Cinematic Melting Pot: Ethnicity, Jews, and Psychoanalysis" (pp. 353–78).

55. Henry Jenkins, "'Shall We Make It for New York or for Distribution?:' Eddie Cantor, *Whoopee!*, and Regional Resistance to the Talkies," in Jenkins, *What Made Pistachio Nuts*, pp. 153–84.

56. And, Rogin (*Blackface, White Noise*) argues, blacks and Native Americans were also expropriated by American Jews in entertainment for their own agenda.

CHAPTER 17. Foreign Affairs

1. *Film Daily*, 5 June 1928, p. 12.

2. *Film Daily*, 2 July 1928, p. 1.

3. *Film Daily*, 21 May 1929, pp. 6–7.

4. *Film Daily*, 5 February 1930, p. 1.

5. Kristin Thompson, *Exporting Entertainment: America in the World Film Market 1907–1934* (London: BFI, 1985), pp. 117–18, 128.

6. *Film Daily*, 29 July 1928, p. 11.

7. *Film Daily*, 2 January 1929, p. 1.

8. Thompson supplies several charts illustrating the extensive horizontal integration of the various multinational companies exploiting sound in Europe. *Exporting Entertainment*, pp. 151–53.

9. John MacCormac, "Talkers in Britain," *New York Times*, 18 November 1928; Ernest W. Fredman, *Erpigram*, 20 February 1929, p. 1.

10. Roger Manvell and Heinrich Fraenkel, *The German Cinema* (New York: Praeger, 1971), p. 51.

11. *Film Daily Year Book 1929*, pp. 1032–33.

12. *Film Daily*, 12 February 1930, pp. 1, 11; 17 December 1930, p. 1; 23 March 1930, pp. 1, 12.

13. Alicja Kisielewska, paper presented at the One Hundred Years of Cinema Conference, Lodz, Poland, 25 October 1996.

14. *Film Daily*, 7 January 1930, pp. 1, 3.

15. William C. deMille, *Variety*, 16 May 1928, quoted in Walker, *The Shattered Silents*, p. 66.

16. *Film Daily*, 3 October 1929, p. 11.

17. *Film Daily*, 25 June 1928, p. 6.

18. Some exceptions among the avant-garde jumped into sound with glee during 1929–1930. In France, Luis Buñuel made L'AGE D'OR (THE GOLDEN AGE, 1930) and Jean Cocteau began *Le Sang d'un poète* (*Blood of a Poet*, 1930). In Germany, Oskar Fischinger, an artist specializing in abstract animated films, energetically began composing visual "studies" of moving shapes closely synchronized to classical music. In the Netherlands, Joris Ivens made his thirty-six-minute "industrial symphony," PHILIPS RADIO. In the Soviet Union, Dziga Vertov welcomed sound and started writing about its possibilities well before he was actually able to make his innovative ENTHUSIASM (1929–1931); see the thumbnail summary in Kristin Thompson and David Bordwell, *Film History: An Introduction*, pp. 222–32. Many of the detractors quickly modified their attitude.

19. *Erpigram*, 20 June 1929, p. 2.

20. A. A. Gerow, "The Benshi's New Face: Defining Cinema in Taishô Japan," *Iconics* 3, 1994, pp. 69–86; David Bordwell, *Ozu and the Poetics of Cinema* (Princeton, N.J.: Princeton University Press, 1988), pp. 18–19.

21. *Film Daily*, 5 February 1930, pp. 1, 6.

22. Morris Gilbert, "*Broadway Melody* Attracts Huge Crowds, the Dialogue Being Translated by the Now Despised Subtitle," *New York Times*, 1 December 1929.

23. Henry Waldman, *Hollywood and the Foreign Touch* (Lanham, Md.: Scarecrow, 1996), p. 115.

24. Subtitles were used in Shanghai, China, where there was no *benshi*-like commentator. The text was projected onto a separate screen. J. L. Pickard, "Old and New Meet in Orient," *Erpigram*, 1 September 1929, p. 2; *Film Daily*, 9 May 1929, p. 1; Thompson, *Exporting Entertainment*, p. 159; Barrios, *A Song in the Dark*, p. 69; C. Hooper Trask, "Audible Films Inspire German Producers," *New York Times*, 23 October 1930; Alfred Bauer, *Deutscher Spielfilm Almanache, 1929–1950* (Munich: Filmladen Christoph Winterberg, 1976), p. 113; Waldman, *Hollywood and the Foreign Touch*, p. 309.

25. H. G. Knox, "English Gives Way to Babel of Tongues as Foreign Language Film Demand Grows," *Erpigram*, 1 July 1930, p. 1. He notes that THE LOVE PARADE opened in Paris in English only (p. 4). This seems strange, because Paramount made a simultaneous version in French, LA PARADE D'AMOUR. Roy Pomeroy had experimented with recording dialogue (Emil Jannings's) on a separate track; *Variety*, 6 June 1928.

26. *Vitaphone News* 2, no. 11 (Winter 1993–1994), p. 7.

27. *Variety*, 1 January 1930. The film received a mixed reaction in Berlin. Both Moissi and Vitaphone were debated; "Critics Clash over Moissi," *New York Times*, 15 December 1929.

28. *Film Daily*, 2 January 1930, pp. 1, 2; 12 June 1930, pp. 1, 2; Jewell, "RKO Film Grosses," p. 42.

29. ECHEC AU ROI played in the United States under its original title, *Le Roi s'ennuie*. *Variety*'s review of the Paris premiere described it as the "first Hollywood made talker released here [France]"; 25 March 1931. Henri de la Falaise, according to Swanson's autobiography, was living in Paris during this period, so the degree of his involvement in producing these films was probably minimal. Swanson and de la Falaise's divorce proceedings began in 1930; *Swanson on Swanson*, pp. 403–4.

30. *Film Daily*, 2 January 1931, p. 1; 11 March 1931, p. 10. Dunning advertised, "You can 'Double In' outdoor shots on indoor sound stages behind any intimate dialogue shot using a Dunning process plate. You shoot today, screen tomorrow"; *Cinematographic Annual 1930* [advertising section], p. 7. Though the process was a zealously guarded secret, Barry Salt makes an educated guess about it in *Film Style and Technology*, p. 234.

31. His 1930–1931 German-language filmography included DER TANZ GEHT WEITER, DIE MASKE FÄLLT (THE WAY FOR ALL MEN), KISMET, and DIE HEILIGE FLAMME (THE SACRED FLAME). Each of Dieterle's films was also shot in French and Spanish versions.

32. Mordaunt Hall, *New York Times*, 6 January 1931; Hervé Dumont, *William Dieterle: Antifascismo y compromiso romántico* (San Sebastian-Madrid: Festival Internacional de Cine de San Sebastián, 1994), pp. 43–45, 235–36.

33. Bertolt Brecht had an abiding interest in the cinema as well as the theater. His book *On Cinema* was published in 1930.

34. Ben Brewster, "Brecht and the Film Industry," *Screen* 16, no. 4 (Winter 1975–1976), pp. 16–29; Thomas Elsaesser, "Transparent Duplicities: *The Threepenny Opera* (1931)," in Eric Rentschler, ed., *The Films of G. W. Pabst* (New Brunswick, N.J.: Rutgers University Press, 1990), pp. 104–5; "*L'Opéra de quat'sous*," in Christian Belaygue and Jean-Paul Gorce, eds., *Le Passage du muet au parlant* (Toulouse: Cinémathèque de Toulouse/Editions Milan, 1988), pp. 96–97; *Film Daily*, 10 August 1930, p. 8; 24 May 1931, p. 11.

35. Ginette Vincendeau, "Les Films en versions multiples: Un échec édifiant," in Belaygue and Gorce, *Le Passage du muet au parlant*, p. 31.

36. The French and Spanish versions were directed by Marcel de Sano, who committed suicide soon after their completion.

37. Morris Gilbert, "Parisian Film Chatter," *New York Times*, 8 June 1930.

38. "Berlin Film Chatter," *New York Times*, 7 December 1930. HIS GLORIOUS NIGHT was also made in Spanish as OLYMPIA (dir. Juan de Homs and Chester Franklin).

39. Mordaunt Hall, *New York Times*, 6 January 1931. The *AFI Catalogue* refers to a Swedish version of ANNA CHRISTIE, but according to Waldman, this was the German version with Swedish subtitles; *Hollywood and the Foreign Touch*, p. 12; *Film Daily*, 1 May 1930, pp. 1, 8; 9 January 1930, p. 2.

40. *Film Daily*, 2 May 1930, p. 1; 31 July 1930, p. 1; 17 February 1930, p. 1; 21 January 1930, pp. 1, 8; *Erpigram*, 15 March 1930, pp. 1, 5; *Film Daily*, 6 May 1930, p. 8; 25 April 1930, p. 12; 24 February 1930, p. 1.

41. Waldman, *Hollywood and the Foreign Touch*, p. 197.

42. *AFI Catalogue*. Some sources list these films as remakes of SPITE MARRIAGE (1929). The French version of FREE AND EASY was LE METTEUR EN SCÈNE. Claude Autant-Lara, the director who would be known for his respectable literary adaptations (pilloried by the New Wave critics as "papa's cinema"), was hired by MGM as a foreign-language version director in 1930. He switched briefly to Warner Bros. in 1932, then returned to France; Waldman, *Hollywood and the Foreign Touch*, pp. 19, 77.

43. Glancy, "MGM Film Grosses, 1924–1948," p. 133.

44. IL GRANDE SENTIERO (Italian); LA GRAN JORNADA (Spanish); DIE GROßE FAHRT (German); and LA PISTE DE GÉANTS (French).

45. *Film Daily*, 30 September 1930, p. 1; Goldman, *Jolson*, pp. 195–96; Maltby and Vasey, "The International Language Problem," p. 87; Thompson, *Exporting Entertainment*, p. 156. One wonders whether rising German anti-Semitism also played a role in the abandonment of a "Yiddish" film by a performer who, at the time, was the world's most conspicuous Jewish actor. Korda, who was also Jewish, had left Berlin shortly before Jolson arrived in 1930, fearful of the open hostility he witnessed. The National Socialists won 150 seats in the September 1930 Reichstag elections; Kulik, *Alexander Korda*, p. 60.

46. *Film Daily*, 13 October 1929, p. 1. The film's working title was ILLUSION, probably changed because of a conflict with a Paramount film of that title. The German-language version retained the original title. THE LAST PERFORMANCE premiered in New York as a silent; whether Veidt's phoned-in dialogue was ever used has not been determined.

47. The film, also distributed as BAJO EL CIELO DE LA HABANA, was directed by Cliff Wheeler and edited (post-synchronized?) at Tec-Art in Hollywood; Waldman, *Hollywood and the Foreign Touch*. Cardona's career as a prolific actor and director extended through the 1940s.

48. *Variety*, 19 November 1930; Mordaunt Hall, *New York Times*, 18 November 1930.

49. W. L. Middleton, "Paris Screen News," *New York Times*, 25 August 1929. He noted also that "a considerable part of the dialogue, in English, has been cut out of the American version of the film on its transference to France."

50. Mordaunt Hall, *New York Times*, 2 September 1930.

51. Walker, *The Shattered Silents*, p. 125.

52. *Film Daily*, 18 July 1930, p. 6; 22 April 1930, p. 7; 13 February 1930, p. 9; Gomery, *The Coming of Sound*, pp. 376–78.

53. For example, THE LADY LIES (dir. Hobart Henley, 1929) was originally shot at Astoria. At Joinville it was redone as SEINE FREUNDIN ANNETTE (dir. Felix Basch, in German), VI TVÅ (John Brunius, Swedish), UNE FEMME A MENTI (Charles de Rochefort, French), PERCHÉ NO? (Amleto Palermi,

Italian), and DOÑA MENTIRAS (Adelqui Millar, Spanish). For a detailed comparison of the Swedish with the American version, see Nataša Ďurovičová, "Translating America: The Hollywood Multilinguals, 1929–1933," in Altman, ed., *Sound Theory/Sound Practice*, pp. 144–47.

54. UN TROU DANS LE MUR was the first film completed at Joinville. The Swedish version premiered in Stockholm on 30 July 1930 and played in New York; "the emphasis is on dialogue rather than action," according to Hall (*New York Times*, 10 February 1931).

55. *Film Daily*, 7 April 1930, p. 1; 13 May 1930, pp. 1, 6; 26 August 1930, pp. 1, 6; 26 February 1930, p. 15; Michael Korda, *Charmed Lives: A Family Romance* (New York: Random House, 1979), pp. 86–87; Andrew, "Sound in France," *Yale French Studies*, no. 60 (1980): 101–2.

56. Mordaunt Hall, *New York Times*, 20 June 1931. According to *Variety*, fewer than 100 people attended the opening of this film (in an 1,100-seat theater). Hot weather was the reason given (30 June 1931).

57. Mordaunt Hall, *New York Times*, 11 June 1929.

58. *Variety*, 10 July 1929.

59. *Film Daily*, 30 January 1930, p. 1; 2 February 1930, p. 8. Earlier Tobis part-talkies had run in New York. DAS LAND OHNE FRAUEN (LAND WITHOUT WOMEN) was "25% dialog"; *Variety*, 30 October 1929.

60. Mordaunt Hall, *New York Times*, 27 September 1930.

61. *Film Daily*, 7 July 1929, p. 1; 5 September 1929, p. 7. The title listed in *Film Daily* was *Immortal Rogue*. Ufa also made a French-language version. Reviewing the film in Berlin, *Variety* reported that Ufa had acknowledged that "the sound is on the whole a disappointment"; 26 March 1930.

62. *Film Daily*, 9 January 1930, pp. 1, 11; 2 March 1930, p. 1. Parlo had appeared in the German versions (made in Hollywood) of HOLLYWOOD REVUE OF 1929 and THE BIG HOUSE; *Film Daily*, 31 August 1930, p. 11; 17 September 1930, pp. 4, 5.

63. Mordaunt Hall, *New York Times*, 15 September 1930.

64. Roger Manvell and John Huntley, *The Technique of Film Music* (London and New York: Focal Press, 1957), p. 42.

65. *Film Daily*, 14 August 1930, p. 1; 16 November 1930, p. 11.

66. Mordaunt Hall, *New York Times*, 20 June 1931; Thompson and Bordwell, *Film History: An Introduction*, p. 221. The English title was *Three from the Gas Station*, and the French was *Le Chemin du Paradis*.

67. *Film Daily*, 28 December 1930, p. 11.

68. *Film Daily*, 26 October 1930, p. 10. Hitchcock also directed the German version, MARY!, at the Elstree Studio.

69. *Film Daily*, 15 May 1930, p. 2; 18 June 1930, p. 1; 23 July 1930, pp. 1, 4; Gomery, *The Coming of Sound*, p. 386.

70. *Film Daily*, 21 October 1930, p. 11; Thompson, *Exporting Entertainment*, pp. 156–57.

71. *Film Daily*, 16 January 1931, p. 1; 19 February 1932, pp. 1, 4; 9 June 1931, p. 1.

72. *Film Daily*, 17 March 1931, p. 1. Gomery states that Fox made its Spanish films in New York. Several titles are glossed in the *AFI Catalogue; The Coming of Sound*, p. 378.

73. *Film Daily*, 16 February 1931, p. 1; 23 June 1931, p. 1; 21 October 1931, p. 1; 25 March 1932, p. 12.

74. Gomery, *The Coming of Sound*, pp. 385–86; *Film Daily*, 26 April 1931, p. 1; 11 May 1931, p. 1; 14 May 1931, p. 2; 24 May 1931, p. 10; 9 March 1931, p. 1; Mordaunt Hall, *New York Times*, 21 May 1931.

75. Balio, *United Artists*, p. 95; Barrios, *A Song in the Dark*, p. 344; *Film Daily*, 20 July 1931, pp. 1, 7.

76. "Berlin Film Chatter," *New York Times*, 7 December 1930; Waldman, *Hollywood and the Foreign Touch*, p. 182.

77. *Film Daily*, 20 July 1930, p. 1.

78. Maltby and Vasey, "The International Language Problem," pp. 69, 91; Ďurovičová, "Translating America," p. 141; Ginette Vincendeau, "Hollywood Babel: The Multiple Language Version," *Screen* 29, no. 2 (spring 1988).

79. Ďurovičová, "Translating America," pp. 150–51.

80. Mario Quargnolo, "Le Cinéma bâillonné," in Belaygue and Gorce, *Le Passage du muet au parlant*, p. 44.

81. Andrew Kelly, "*All Quiet on the Western Front*: 'Brutal Cutting, Stupid Censors and Bigoted Politicos' (1930–1984)," *Historical Journal of Film, Radio, and Television* 9, no. 2 (1989), p. 139.

82. *Film Daily*, 11 January 1931, p. 12; 12 January 1931, p. 2; 15 January 1931, p. 1; 9 March 1931, pp. 1, 8; Kelly, "*All Quiet on the Western Front*," p. 149.
83. Ďurovičová, "Translating America," pp. 150–51. It should be noted that Jewish groups in the United States previously had protested alleged anti-Semitism in the original version of the film.
84. David Gill and Kevin Brownlow, *Cinema Europe*, six-part television series, 1995.
85. *Film Daily*, 1 February 1932, pp. 1, 9.
86. Gomery, *The Coming of Sound*, pp. 421–22.

CHAPTER 18. The Voice Squad

1. [The Pedestrian], "Footpath and Highway: The Human Voice Divine," *Forum*, October 1924, p. 551.
2. [Anonymous, but attributed to Alexander Bakshy], "Hollywood Speaks," *The Nation*, 26 September 1928, p. 286.
3. Fox quoted in *Film Daily*, 6 April 1927, p. 3; Sarnoff quoted in "Improvements in Talking Pictures," *Literary Digest*, March 1927, p. 20.
4. *Film Daily*, 8 November 1927, p. 6; Lonsdale quoted in *Literary Digest*, 27 October 1928, p. 29.
5. Walker quoted in "Colored Films, Talking Pictures," *Literary Digest*, 11 August 1928, p. 9; Gilbert Seldes, "The Movies Commit Suicide," *Harper's*, November 1928, pp. 709–11.
6. Edwin W. Hullinger, "'Talkies'—Transforming Light into Sound," *Current History*, September 1929, p. 1040.
7. Nathan quoted in "The Vitaphone—Pro and Con," *Literary Digest*, 25 September 1926, p. 29; Robert F. Sisk, "The Movies Try to Talk," *American Mercury*, August 1928, p. 494.
8. Rob Wagner, "Photo Static," *Collier's*, 23 February 1929, p. 28.
9. Mark Larkin, "Conrad in Quest of a Voice," *Photoplay*, January 1929, pp. 58–59, 113–14.
10. Francis T. S. Powell, "Radio and the Language," *Commonweal*, 10 April 1929, p. 653; [Anonymous], "American Debut of G.B.S.," *Literary Digest*, 18 July 1928, p. 21. Some of these British responses are extracted in "The Talkie as a Reformer," *Literary Digest*, 17 August, 1929, pp. 19–20.
11. *Film Daily*, 14 April 1929, p. 7.
12. C. B. DeMille, "Talking of Talkies," *Photoplay*, December 1930, p. 135.
13. *Film Daily*, 9 April 1929, p. 4; Dorothy Manners, *Motion Picture Classic*, October 1928, p. 88.
14. Quoted in *Literary Digest*, 20 October 1928, p. 58. Fox hired Alice Kelly to teach diction to its contract players; *Film Daily*, 29 March 1929, p. 3.
15. "Little" Mary Brian was twenty-one. She played the schoolmarm in THE VIRGINIAN.
16. Mayme Ober Peak, quoted in *Literary Digest*, 20 October 1928, p. 58; "A New Era in Sound Films," *Hollywood Revue* program, 1929, Yranski Collection.
17. Stearns, "The Movies Talk!," p. 199; Pickford quoted in Rob Wagner, "Photo Static," *Collier's*, February 1929, pp. 17, 53; Pickford quoted in Frederick L. Collins, "Now They Talk for Themselves," *Delineator*, April 1929, p. 57; William A. Johnston, "Air Follies," *Saturday Evening Post*, 31 May 1930, p. 146; *Film Daily*, 8 November 1927, p. 6.
18. Foy quoted in Stearns, "The Movies Talk!," p. 198; Hullinger, "'Talkies'—Transforming Light into Sound," p. 1040; Wagner, "Photo Static," p. 28.
19. Joan Shelley Rubin, *The Making of Middlebrow Culture* (Chapel Hill: University of North Carolina Press, 1992), pp. 276–99. One may still experience this format of a genteel erudite conversation during the entr'actes of Saturday afternoon Metropolitan Opera radio broadcasts.
20. Welford Beaton, "High-Hatting Little Brother," *Saturday Evening Post*, 24 May 1930, p. 65.
21. Quoted in Stearns, "The Movies Talk!," p. 198.
22. Herbert Cruikshank, "D-D-Doing H-H-His S-S-Stuff," *Motion Picture Classic*, August 1930, pp. 63, 94; *Film Daily*, 7 July 1929, p. 7; Jesse L. Lasky, "Hearing Things in the Dark," *Collier's*, May 1929, p. 9.
23. *Variety*, 12 March 1930.
24. Wesley Stout, "Lend Us Your Ears," *Saturday Evening Post*, 15 June 1929, p. 10; Richard Watts, Jr., "All Talking," *Theatre Arts Monthly*, September 1929, p. 709.
25. Gilbert Seldes, "Talkies' Progress," *Harper's*, September 1929, p. 457; B. F. Wilson, *Motion Picture Classic*, February 1928, pp. 48, 78.

26. Alexander Bakshy, "The Movie Scene: Notes on Sound and Silence," *Theatre Arts Monthly*, February 1925, p. 102; Bakshy, "Concerning Dialogue," *The Nation*, 17 August 1932, p. 152.

27. *Film Daily*, 7 March 1929, p. 7; Beaton, "High-Hatting Little Brother," p. 65.

28. *Film Daily*, 29 March 1929, p. 3; Lasky, "Hearing Things in the Dark," p. 9; Stout, "Lend Us Your Ears," p. 10; *Film Daily*, 7 May 1929, p. 3; 9 April 1929, p. 4; Beaton, "High-Hatting Little Brother," p. 65.

29. *Film Daily*, 4 June 1929, p. 4; Rowson quoted in "The Talkie Bone of Contention, Anglo-American," *Literary Digest*, 31 August 1929, p. 21. Rowson was described as "an entrepreneur with Ideal films" and "a leading academic figure within the British film industry during the late 1920s and 1930s"; Ian Jarvie, *Hollywood's Overseas Campaign*, p. 145; John Sedgwick, "The Market for Feature Films in Britain, 1934: A Viable National Cinema," *Historical Journal of Film, Radio, and Television* 14, no. 1 (1994), p. 15.

30. *Film Daily*, 29 March 1929, p. 1.

31. Berg, *Goldwyn*, pp. 182–85. Banky made a bilingual Hollywood film, *A Lady to Love/Die Sehnsucht jeder Frau*, in 1929, and a film in Germany, DER REBELL, in 1932.

32. *Film Daily*, 28 April, 1929, p. 1; Jerome Beatty, "The Sound Investment," *Saturday Evening Post*, 9 March 1929, p. 132.

33. Garth Jowett, *Film: The Democratic Art* (Boston: Little, Brown, 1976), pp. 166–78; *Film Daily*, 5 February 1929, p. 1.

34. *Film Daily*, 17 October 1928, p. 10.

35. Lea Jacobs, *The Wages of Sin: Censorship and the Fallen Woman Film* (Madison: University of Wisconsin Press, 1991), p. 170, n. 8.

36. *Film Daily*, 6 May 1928, p. 1; 7 May 1928, p. 1; 24 July 1928, p. 11; 1 August 1928, pp. 1, 3.

37. Edwin Hullinger, "Free Speech for Talkies?," *North American Review*, July 1929, p. 738.

38. Clements, "Censoring the Talkies," *The New Republic*, 5 June 1929, p. 64.

39. Jerome Beatty, "The Red [*sic*] to Profits," *Saturday Evening Post*, 16 February 1929, p. 157.

40. *Film Daily*, 1 May 1928, p. 1; 13 May 1928, p. 1; 3 July 1928, pp. 1, 12; 6 February 1929, p. 1. Virginia was also enacting legislation to ensure that its censors could judge sound films; *Film Daily*, 14 February 1930, p. 1.

41. *Film Daily*, 9 May 1929, p. 1.

42. Hullinger, "Free Speech for Talkies?," p. 743; *Film Daily*, 26 November 1929, p. 4; 24 September 1929, p. 11; 26 January 1930, pp. 1, 10.

43. [Anonymous, but attributed to Alexander Bakshy], "The Talkies' Future," *The Nation*, 15 January 1930, p. 62.

44. *Film Daily*, 2 December 1928, p. 5.

45. *Film Daily*, 5 February 1930, p. 7; 11 February 1930, p. 6; 14 February 1930, p. 3; Jowett, *Film: The Democratic Art*, pp. 231–232.

46. *Film Daily*, 7 April 1929, p. 5; 8 October 1929, p. 1; 30 June 1929, p. 12; 7 April 1929, p. 10. The same joke appears in THE KING OF JAZZ.

47. *Film Daily*, 20 January 1929, p. 4; 27 January 1929, p. 4.

48. *Film Daily*, 29 January 1930, p. 6; Mordaunt Hall, *New York Times*, 4 January 1930.

49. Lasky, "Hearing Things in the Dark," p. 48.

50. Black, *Hollywood Censored*, p. 42.

51. Stephen Vaughn, "Morality and Entertainment," *Journal of American History* 77, no. 1 (June 1990), p. 55.

52. *Film Daily*, 5 March 1930, pp. 1, 5; 8 April 1930, pp. 1, 12. In June, nineteen film companies adopted a separate code of ethics for advertising and publicity; *Film Daily*, 23 June 1930 pp. 1, 8.

53. MPPDA, "Reasons Supporting Preamble of Code," reprinted in Jowett, *Film: The Democratic Art*, pp. 471–72.

54. Will H. Hays, "The Cinema of Tomorrow," *Ladies' Home Journal*, July 1930, pp. 52–53.

55. Gregory Black, *Hollywood Censored: Morality Codes, Catholics, and the Movies* (New York: Cambridge University Press, 1994), pp. 39, 43; Richard Maltby, "The Production Code and the Hays Office," in Balio, ed., *Grand Design*, pp. 40–45.

56. Jacobs, *The Wages of Sin*, pp. 50–51.

57. Later when Putty Nose sings the tune again, the offensive rhyme is avoided when he receives a bullet. Strictly, such ploys violated the Code because they were "obscene by suggestion (even

when likely to be understood only by part of the audience)." Of course, whether any of the MPPDA censors got the joke (or would admit it if they did) will never be known.

58. Robert Sklar, *City Boys: Cagney, Bogart, Garfield* (Princeton, N.J.: Princeton University Press, 1992), pp. 30–31.

59. Mick Eaton, "Taste of the Past in Cinema History on Television," *Screen* 21, no. 1 (Spring 1980), pp. 12–13.

60. *Film Daily,* 6 June 1930, p. 8.

61. Renting the Cohan was a precedent followed by Chaplin six months later with CITY LIGHTS.

62. *Film Daily,* 9 March, pp. 1, 16. For a detailed discussion of the important history of the exploitation film during this period, see Eric Paul Schaefer, "Bold! Daring! Shocking! True!": A History of Exploitation Films, 1919–1959" (Ph.D. dissertation, University of Texas at Austin, 1994), pp. 624, 638, 645, 674.

63. Black, *Hollywood Censored,* p. 39. Breen was also notoriously anti-Semitic.

64. *Film Daily,* 20 June 1929, pp. 2, 3; 28 June 1929, p. 7. There was another embarrassment when the Chicago police commissioner closed THE TRIAL OF MARY DUGAN for one week in June 1929. The ban was lifted after MGM demonstrated that the film dialogue differed little from that of the play, which had enjoyed a long run in the city.

CHAPTER 19. Constructive Criticism: The Fans' Perspective

1. Theodore Peterson, *Magazines in the Twentieth Century* (Urbana: University of Illinois Press, 1956), p. 282.

2. Gaylyn Studlar, "The Perils of Pleasure? Fan Magazine Discourse as Women's Commodified Culture in the 1920s," *Wide Angle* 13, no. 1 (January 1991): 7.

3. Koszarski, *An Evening's Entertainment,* p. 193.

4. "Brickbats and Bouquets," *Photoplay,* September 1929, p. 10. Quirk's position is consistent with that of publishers of newspaper book reviews at the time, 80 percent of whom described their goal as "to serve as a guide to selection"; Rubin, *The Making of Middlebrow Culture,* p. 41.

5. James R. Quirk, "Close-ups and Long-shots," *Photoplay,* August 1928, p. 29.

6. Quoted in Dorothy Calhoun, "The Great Talkie Panic," *Motion Picture Classic,* September 1928, p. 68.

7. "Brickbats and Bouquets," *Photoplay,* December 1928, p. 10.

8. Sklar, *City Boys,* p. 6.

9. "Brickbats and Bouquets," *Photoplay,* June 1929, p. 8; September 1929, p. 142.

10. "Brickbats and Bouquets," *Photoplay,* June 1929.

11. "*Classic's* Readers Respond on the Talkies," *Motion Picture Classic,* September 1929, p. 82.

12. Shuler, "Pictures and Personalities," *Motion Picture Classic,* August 1928, p. 15.

13. Cedric Belfrage, "What Price Profanity Now?" *Motion Picture Classic,* April 1929, p. 82.

14. Charleson Gray, "*Classic* Holds Open Court," *Motion Picture Classic,* August 1930, pp. 36–37, 87.

15. Dorothy Manners, *Motion Picture Classic,* March 1928, p. 60.

16. George Kent Shuler, *Motion Picture Classic,* June 1928, p. 15.

17. "Brickbats and Bouquets," *Photoplay,* August 1929, p. 94.

18. Dorothy Manners, *Motion Picture Classic,* March 1929, p. 9; "The Shadow Stage," *Photoplay,* December 1929, p. 53; James R. Quirk, "Close-ups and Long-shots," *Photoplay,* March 1929, p. 23; November 1928, p. 30; Harry Lang, "The Microphone—The Terror of the Studios," *Photoplay,* December 1929, pp. 29–30, 124–26; Al Cohn, "How Talkies Are Made," *Photoplay,* April 1929, p. 28; Watts, "All Talking," p. 710.

19. Dorothy Manners, *Motion Picture Classic,* July 1929, p. 60.

20. "Brickbats and Bouquets," *Photoplay,* June 1929, p. 8.

21. James R. Quirk, "Close-ups and Long-shots," *Photoplay,* April 1929, p. 78; Charleson Gray, "Comeback," *Motion Picture Classic,* November 1929, p. 39.

22. Cohn, "How Talkies Are Made," p. 29.

23. Beatrice Wilson, *Motion Picture Classic,* March 1929, pp. 40, 74.

24. Mordaunt Hall, *New York Times,* 22 August 1931.

25. Maurice L. Ahern, "Hollywood Horizons," *Commonweal,* 21 May 1930, p. 72.

26. Wesley Stout, "Lend Us Your Ears," *Saturday Evening Post,* 15 June 1929, p. 10.

27. "Brickbats and Bouquets," *Photoplay*, August 1929, p. 103. *Photoplay* noted that "Johnny's fan mail in *Photoplay*'s office is enormous. There are evidently a hundred million others like Trix"; November 1929, p. 146; December 1929, p. 10.

28. Louise Closser Hale, "The New Stage Fright: Talking Pictures," *Harper's*, September 1930, p. 423.

29. Wood, "See and Hear," pp. 20–21.

30. Clark, *Negotiating Hollywood*, p. 25.

31. Cal York, "Announcing the Monthly Broadcast of Hollywood Goings-on!," *Photoplay*, June 1931.

32. James R. Quirk, "Close-ups and Long-shots," *Photoplay*, November 1929, p. 28.

33. *Film Daily*, 5 May 1929, p. 6; 4 August 1929, p. 8.

34. Dorothy Manners, *Motion Picture Classic*, March 1929, p. 60.

35. James R. Quirk, "Close-ups and Long-shots," *Photoplay*, March 1929, p. 23.

36. Herbert Cruikshank, "The Panic Is Over," *Motion Picture Classic*, September 1930, pp. 63, 106; Harry Lang, "Would You Quit Work for $250,000?" *Photoplay*, December 1930, p. 130.

37. James R. Quirk, "Close-Ups and Long-Shots," *Photoplay*, August 1928, p. 29; George Kent Shuler, *Motion Picture Classic*, March 1929, p. 15.

38. Lang, "The Microphone—The Terror of the Studios," pp. 124–26.

39. James R. Quirk, "Close-ups and Long-shots," *Photoplay*, June 1929, p. 30.

40. Helen Louise Walker, "Emil the Great," *Motion Picture Classic*, March 1929, p. 84; Constance Moran, "Pronounce or Renounce," *Motion Picture Classic*, May 1929, p. 59; B. F. Wilson, *Motion Picture Classic*, February 1928, pp. 48, 78.

41. Studlar, "The Perils of Pleasure?" p. 23.

42. Ally Acker, *Reel Women* (New York: Continuum, 1991), pp. 166–69.

43. Incidentally, Bow's actual first line is, "Just a working gal." It may be that the "Whoopee!" line was changed for the technical reasons Boswell cites, or that his anecdote is a fabrication.

44. *Variety*, 3 April 1929.

45. *Film Daily;* Mordaunt Hall, *New York Times,* 2 April 1929.

46. David Robinson, "The Mute Idols," in Anthony Curtis, ed., *The Rise and Fall of the Matinée Idol* (New York: St. Martin's Press, 1974), p. 152.

47. Paramount exercised a two-year option on the star's contract, through October 1931, scotching rumors that she was leaving. *Film Daily*, 30 July 1929, p. 8.

48. Studlar, "The Perils of Pleasure?," p. 11.

49. Colleen Moore, *Silent Star* (New York: Doubleday, 1968), p. 206.

50. Wood, "See and Hear," p. 82.

51. This is a synopsis of the version (derived from several sources) presented by Peters, *The House of Barrymore*, pp. 317–18, 580–81. Leatrice Gilbert Fountain, *Dark Star: The Untold Story of the Meteoric Rise and Fall of John Gilbert* (New York: St. Martin's Press, 1985), is the primary proponent of the conspiracy theory. REDEMPTION was directed by Fred Niblo, but some accounts say that Barrymore had started the film; others state that he was brought in for retakes. Samuel Marx, who had just joined MGM as a story editor in 1930, has taken a stand against the conspiracy theory, noting that a pair of initial Gilbert films were based on valuable properties which had been successful on Broadway. MGM's top scenarists worked on the plot and dialogue, and the best technicians shot the films; Samuel Marx, *Mayer and Thalberg: The Make-Believe Saints* (New York: Random House, 1975), pp. 109–18.

52. Mordaunt Hall, *New York Times,* 16 November 1928; Lasky, "Hearing Things in the Dark," p. 8. Of course, Lasky's wily caveats "appearance" and "intelligence" might exclude quite a few actors.

53. Dorothy Manners, "Looking Them Over," *Motion Picture Classic*, July 1929, p. 78.

54. Other factors to be considered are that Thalberg may not have liked the reaction to the performance of his wife, Norma Shearer, or that Gilbert referred to the Thalbergs without propriety as "Auntie" and "Uncle." *Variety* had a mixed review of Gilbert's delivery: "Both principals look great and play well. Gilbert appearing a bit nervous on the straight interpretation, but hopping to the slang phrasing"; 26 June 1929.

55. Fountain, *Dark Star,* p. 181.

56. Fountain, who culled dozens of reviews, insisted that she was "unable to find a single suggestion that the laughter was directed specifically at Jack or that his career in talking pictures was in any danger at all"; *Dark Star,* p. 178. As her own reprinted extracts demonstrate, though, this is not an objective interpretation.

57. Mordaunt Hall, *New York Times,* 5 October 1929; *Variety,* 9 October 1929.
58. Quotes from reviews extracted in Fountain, *Dark Star,* pp. 179–80. Regrettably, few sources of these clippings are cited.
59. *New York Post* quoted in Fountain, *Dark Star,* p. 180; *Variety,* 10 September 1929.
60. Moore, *Silent Star,* pp. 205–9.
61. Mordaunt Hall, *New York Times,* 10 June 1929; 3 November 1930.
62. *Film Daily,* 6 January 1929, p. 4; *Variety,* 26 December 1928.
63. "*Classic's* Readers Respond on the Talkies," *Motion Picture Classic,* September 1929, p. 82.
64. George Kent Shuler, "Pictures and Personalities," *Motion Picture Classic,* March 1930, p. 23; Walker, *The Shattered Silents,* pp. 169–72; "Berlin Film Chatter," *New York Times,* 7 December 1930. *Variety's* Berlin correspondent gave a different account of the premiere: "The fluent dialog is spoken by [Jacques Feyder's] actors in an easy and unconstrained manner, with charm and spirit"; 26 November 1930. Alexander Moissi in Warners' THE ROYAL BOX suffered Gilbert's fate: "His love scene with the Countess drew frequent giggles from the audience"; *Variety,* 1 January 1930.
65. Fountain, *Dark Star,* p. 171.
66. Dorothy Manners, *Motion Picture Classic,* September 1929, p. 62.
67. Walter Ramsey, "Sucker Eat Sucker," *Motion Picture Classic,* December 1929, p. 25.
68. Katherine Albert, "Is Jack Gilbert Through?" *Photoplay,* February 1930, p. 128.
69. Ibid.
70. Lang, "Would You Quit Work for $250,000?," p. 130.
71. *Variety,* 7 May 1930.
72. *Variety,* 17 December 1930.
73. *Film Daily,* 21 July 1927, p. 1.
74. *Motion Picture Classic,* December 1926, p. 29.
75. Lang, "The Microphone—The Terror of the Studios," pp. 29–30, 124–26.
76. Mark Larkin, "The Truth About Voice Doubling," *Photoplay,* July 1929, pp. 32–33, 108–10. But speaking from his twelve years' experience in exploitation (publicity), Larkin disagreed and felt that letting the public in on a secret stimulated business. He also predicted that doubling would disappear because stars were quickly learning to sing and play their own instruments and foreign accents were beginning to be regarded as assets, not liabilities.
77. George Kent Shuler, *Motion Picture Classic,* July 1929, p. 15.
78. Laurence Reid, "Camera!" *Motion Picture,* August 1928, p. 27.
79. George K. Shuler, "Camera," *Motion Picture,* August 1928, p. 1.
80. "Brickbats and Bouquets," *Photoplay,* March 1928, p. 114.
81. Dorothy Manners, *Motion Picture Classic,* September 1929, p. 62.
82. Clark summarizes the attitude of the studios toward the press: "The most beneficial policy for the major studios, however, was the active dissemination of an entertainment discourse that emphasized temperament, individuality, and a privatized notion of stardom. Under normal conditions, and with the help of their Hollywood correspondents, the studios were able to maintain this discursive and ideological upper hand—leaving actors and fanzine editors to duke it out on the sidelines." *Negotiating Hollywood,* p. 78.
83. Studlar, "The Perils of Pleasure?," p. 28.

CHAPTER 20. Buying Broadway: THE JAZZ SINGER's Reception

1. J. P. Telotte, "The Movie Musical and What We 'Ain't Heard' Yet," *Genre* 14 (Winter 1981), p. 506.
2. Stout, "Lend Us Your Ears," p. 50.
3. THE JAZZ SINGER press book does not mention the sound treatment of the film. Obviously it was intended for use by the great majority of theaters which would play the movie silent. (There may have been a press kit specifically for the Vitaphone version, but I have not located one.) The angle emphasized throughout is "Al Jolson Re-Lives His Own Life: America's Greatest Entertainer Reveals a Chapter of His Autobiography in His Moving Picture Role as 'The Jazz Singer.'" *Warner Bros. Press Books,* reel 5.
4. P. S. Harrison, "Two-Dollar 'Hits' and 'Flops,'" *Harrison's Reports,* 9 June 1928, p. 91. Harrison was so skeptical of Fox's statements that he wrote, "The next figures that I shall accept [from] the Fox organization will be those of my accountant . . . provided they allow him to examine their

books, without any restrictions. No other figures will do" (p. 92). Thanks to Richard Koszarski for bringing this article to my attention.

5. *Variety,* 12 October 1927, p. 7.
6. *Film Daily,* 25 September 1927, p. 1.
7. *Variety,* 28 September 1927, p. 21.
8. *Variety,* 19 October 1927, p. 23.
9. Robert McLaughlin, "Broadway and Hollywood: A History of Economic Interaction" (Ph.D. dissertation, University of Wisconsin, 1970), p. 59.
10. Robert C. Allen and Douglas Gomery report that THE JAZZ SINGER's greatest success came later in 1928, and that it played best in medium-size towns; *Film History: Theory and Practice* (New York: Knopf, 1985), p. 121. I have not researched the film's box office for this later period.
11. "American Debut of G.B.S.," *Literary Digest,* 28 July 1928, p. 21.
12. In his extensive "Radiography," Herbert G. Goldman cites four broadcasts before THE JAZZ SINGER's premiere (*Jolson,* pp. 372–74). Jolson's own program ran on NBC in 1932–1933 (fifteen broadcasts), and he was a frequent guest on other programs throughout the 1930s and 1940s. An adaptation of THE JAZZ SINGER, starring Jolson, was aired on the CBS *Lux Radio Theatre* on 2 June 1947.
13. Staiger, "Epilogue," *Interpreting Films,* p. 211.
14. Timothy J. Clark, "Preliminaries to a Possible Treatment of 'Olympia,'" *Screen* 21, no. 1 (Spring 1980), p. 22.

CHAPTER 21. "The Great Ninety Per Cent"

1. William A. Seiter, "Motion Pictures Must Move," *Cinematographic Annual 1931,* pp. 263–64.
2. Gilbert Seldes, "The Movies Commit Suicide," *Harper's,* November 1928, pp. 706–8.
3. Ibid.
4. Ibid., pp. 706–12. See also Seldes's "Theory About 'Talkies,'" *New Republic,* 8 August 1928, pp. 305–6.
5. *Film Daily,* 29 September 1929, p. 10.
6. *Film Daily,* 4 August 1929, p. 7.
7. John Seitz, "Introduction," *Cinematographic Annual 1930* (Hollywood: Hartwell, 1930; reprint, New York: Arno, 1972), p. 17.
8. On 1 July 1930, Maurice "Red" Kann left the staff of *Film Daily* to become editor of the *Motion Picture Daily,* a Martin Quigley publication.
9. *Film Daily,* 10 June 1928, p. 7.
10. *Film Daily,* 28 June 1928, p. 1.
11. *Film Daily,* 12 March 1930, pp. 1–2.
12. Rudolf Arnheim, *Film as Art* (Berkeley: University of California Press, 1957), p. 188. *Film als Kunst* was published in Germany in 1932 and contains many excursuses into sound. See also *Film Essays and Criticism,* especially the chapter on sound, pp. 29–51, and his *Weltbühne* reviews (1928–1933), pp. 140–78.
13. For an overview of Seldes's film criticism, which he practiced for forty years, see the chapter "'The Movies Come from America'" in Michael Kammen, *The Lively Arts: Gilbert Seldes and the Transformation of Cultural Criticism in the United States* (New York: Oxford University Press, 1996), pp. 209–44.
14. Sergei Eisenstein, Vsevolod Pudovkin, and Grigori Alexandrov, "Statement on Sound," in Richard Taylor, ed. and trans., *S. M. Eisenstein: Selected Works,* vol. 1: *Writings, 1922–1934* (London: BFI, 1988), pp. 113–14; Ian Christie, "Soviet Cinema: Making Sense of Sound: A Revised Historiography," *Screen* 23, no. 2 (July-August 1982), pp. 34–39; Kristin Thompson, "Early Sound Counterpoint," *Yale French Studies* 60 (1980), pp. 115–40.
15. David Bordwell, *The Cinema of Eisenstein* (Cambridge, Mass.: Harvard University Press, 1993), pp. 184–90.
16. Jean Epstein, "The Cinema Continues," in Abel, ed., *French Film Theory and Criticism,* vol. 2, p. 67.
17. Weis and Belton, *Film Sound,* p. 75.
18. Richard Abel, "The Transition to Sound," pp. 24–25. Does this mean that the European filmmakers wanted to make live-action equivalents of cartoons? The concert scenes in Clair's LE MILLION bear a passing resemblance to *Mickey's Follies* (1929). Eisenstein's affection for Disney

and Mickey was well founded; see Jay Leyda, ed., Alan Upchurch, trans., *Eisenstein on Disney* (London: Methuen, 1988).

19. Welford Beaton, *"The Jazz Singer,"* *Film Spectator,* 4 February 1928, and *"Hallelujah!,"* *Film Spectator,* 2 November 1929, both reprinted in Stanley Kauffmann and Bruce Henstell, eds., *American Film Criticism: From Its Beginnings to* Citizen Kane (New York: Liveright, 1972), pp. 199, 229. Beaton's insistence on long-shots and complete takes is similar to the emphasis on mise-en-scène usually associated with the French theorist André Bazin to montage practice.

20. Bakshy, "The Talkies,'" p. 236; *"Le Million," The Nation,* 10 June 1931.

21. Gilbert Seldes, *Movies for the Millions* (London: B. T. Batsford, 1937), pp. 94, 82.

Selected Bibliography

Abel, Richard, ed. *French Film Theory and Criticism: A History/Anthology, 1907–1939.* Princeton, N.J.: Princeton University Press, 1988.

Acker, Ally. *Reel Women.* New York: Continuum, 1991.

Aldcroft, Derek H. *From Versailles to Wall Street 1919–1929.* Berkeley: University of California Press, 1981.

Allen, Robert C., and Douglas Gomery. *Film History: Theory and Practice.* New York: Knopf, 1985.

Allvine, Glendon. *The Greatest Fox of Them All.* New York: Lyle Stuart, 1969.

Altman, Rick. *The American Film Musical.* Bloomington: Indiana University Press, 1987.

———. "The Technology of the Voice." Part 1: *Iris* 3, no. 1 (1985): 3–20; Part 2: *Iris* 4, no. 1 (1986): 107–119.

———, ed. *Sound Theory/Sound Practice.* New York: Routledge, 1992.

American Film Institute. *The American Film Institute Catalogue of Motion Pictures Produced in the United States.* New York: Bowker, 1971– .

Andrew, Dudley. *Mists of Regret: Culture and Sensibility in Classic French Film.* Princeton, N.J.: Princeton University Press, 1995.

Ankerich, Michael G. *Broken Silence: Conversations with Twenty-three Silent Film Stars.* Jefferson, N.C.: McFarland, 1992.

Archer, Gleason L. *Big Business and Radio.* New York: American Historical Co., 1939.

Arnheim, Rudolf. *Film Essays and Criticism.* Madison: University of Wisconsin Press, 1997.

———. *Film as Art.* Berkeley: University of California Press, 1957.

Balio, Tino. *United Artists: The Company Built by the Stars.* Madison: University of Wisconsin Press, 1976.

———, ed. *Hollywood in the Age of Television.* Boston: Unwin Hyman, 1990.

Bandy, Mary Lea, ed. *The Dawn of Sound.* New York: Museum of Modern Art, 1989.

Banning, William Peck. *Commercial Broadcasting Pioneer: The WEAF Experiment, 1911–1926.* Cambridge: Harvard University Press, 1946.

Barnouw, Erik. *Documentary: A History of the Non-Fiction Film.* New York: Oxford University Press, 1974.

———. *A Tower in Babel: A History of Broadcasting in the United States,* vol. 1, *To 1933.* New York: Oxford University Press, 1966.

Barr, Charles. *Laurel and Hardy.* London: Studio Vista, 1967.

Barrios, Richard. *A Song in the Dark: The Birth of the Musical Film.* New York: Oxford University Press, 1995.

Barthes, Roland. *Image—Music—Text.* Trans. Stephen Heath. New York: Hill and Wang, 1977.

Bazin, André. *What Is Cinema?* Trans. Hugh Gray. Berkeley: University of California Press, 1967.

Behlmer, Rudy, ed. *Inside Warner Bros.* New York: Viking, 1985.

———, ed. *Memo from David O. Selznick.* New York: Viking, 1972.

Belaygue, Christian, and Jean-Paul Gorce, eds. *Le Passage du muet au parlant.* Toulouse: Cinémathèque de Toulouse/Editions Milan, 1988.

Belton, John. *Widescreen Cinema*. Cambridge: Harvard University Press, 1992.

Berg, Scott. *Goldwyn: A Biography*. London: Hamish Hamilton, 1989.

Bernstein, Matthew. *Walter Wanger: Hollywood Independent*. Berkeley: University of California Press, 1994.

Black, Gregory. *Hollywood Censored: Morality Codes, Catholics, and the Movies*. New York: Cambridge University Press, 1994.

Blake, Michael F. *Lon Chaney: The Man Behind the Thousand Faces*. Vestal, N.Y.: Vestal Press, 1990.

Bordwell, David. *The Cinema of Eisenstein*. Cambridge, Mass.: Harvard University Press, 1993.

———. *Ozu and the Poetics of Cinema*. Princeton, N.J.: Princeton University Press, 1988.

Bordwell, David, Janet Staiger, and Kristin Thompson, eds. *The Classical Hollywood Cinema: Film Style and Mode of Production to 1960*. New York: Columbia University Press, 1985.

Bowser, Eileen. *The Transformation of Cinema 1907–1915*. New York: Charles Scribner's Sons, 1990.

Brooks, John. *Telephone: The First Hundred Years*. New York: Harper & Row, 1976.

Brown, Bernard. *Talking Pictures*. London: Pitman & Sons, 1933.

Brown, Royal S. *Overtones and Undertones*. Berkeley: University of California Press, 1994.

Brownlow, Kevin. *The Parade's Gone By*. New York: Knopf, 1968.

Cabarga, Leslie. *The Fleischer Story*. New York: DaCapo, 1988.

Cameron, Evan William, ed. *Sound and the Cinema: The Coming of Sound to American Film*. Pleasantville, N.Y.: Redgrave, 1980.

Canemaker, John. *Felix: The Twisted Tale of the World's Most Famous Cat*. New York: Pantheon, 1991.

Cantor, Eddie, with Jane Kesner Ardmore. *Take My Life*. New York: Doubleday, 1957.

Capra, Frank. *The Name Above the Title*. New York: Macmillan, 1971.

Carringer, Robert L., ed. *The Jazz Singer*. Madison: University of Wisconsin Press, 1979.

Chandler, Alfred. *The Visible Hand: The Managerial Revolution in American Business*. Cambridge: Harvard University Press, 1977.

Chion, Michel. *Audio-Vision: Sound on Screen*. New York: Columbia University Press, 1994.

Cinematographic Annual 1930, 1931. Hollywood: Hartwell, 1930, 1931; reprint, New York: Arno, 1972.

Clair, René. *Cinema Yesterday and Today*. Ed. R. C. Dale. New York: Dover, 1972.

Clark, Danae. *Negotiating Hollywood: The Cultural Politics of Actors' Labor*. Minneapolis: University of Minnesota Press, 1995.

Clarke, Charles Galloway. *Highlights and Shadows: The Memoirs of a Hollywood Cameraman*. Ed. Anthony Slide. Metuchen, N.J.: Scarecrow Press, 1989.

Cochran, Thomas C. *Business in American Life: A History*. New York: McGraw-Hill, 1972.

Cochran, Thomas C., and William Miller. *The Age of Enterprise: A Social History of Industrial America*. New York: Macmillan, 1942; reprint, New York: Harper & Row, 1961.

Cohn, Lawrence. *Movietone Presents the 20th Century*. New York: St. Martin's Press, 1976.

Crafton, Donald. *Before Mickey: The Animated Film 1898–1928*. Chicago: University of Chicago Press, 1993.

———. *Emile Cohl, Caricature, and Film*. Princeton, N.J.: Princeton University Press, 1990.

Cripps, Thomas. *Slow Fade to Black*. New York: Oxford University Press, 1977.

Crowther, Bosley. *The Lion's Share*. New York: Dutton, 1957; reprint, New York: Garland, 1985.

Curtis, Anthony, ed. *The Rise and Fall of the Matinée Idol*. New York: St. Martin's Press, 1974.

DeCordova, Richard. *Picture Personalities: The Emergence of the Star System in America*. Urbana: University of Illinois Press, 1990.

Diawara, Manthia, ed. *Black American Cinema*. New York: Routledge, 1993.

Dick, Bernard F. *The Merchant Prince of Poverty Row: Harry Cohn of Columbia Pictures*. Lexington: University Press of Kentucky, 1993.

Douglas, Susan. *Inventing American Broadcasting, 1899–1922*. Baltimore, Md.: Johns Hopkins University Press, 1987.

Dowd, Nancy, and David Shepard. *King Vidor*. Metuchen, N.J.: Scarecrow Press, 1988.

Dumont, Hervé. *William Dieterle: Antifascismo y compromiso romántico*. San Sebastian-Madrid: Festival Internacional de Cine de San Sebastián, 1994.

Durgnat, Raymond, and Scott Simmon. *King Vidor, American*. Berkeley: University of California Press, 1988.

Eames, John Douglas. *The MGM Story.* New York: Crown, 1977.

Ellwood, David, and Rob Kroes, eds. *Hollywood in Europe: Experiences of a Cultural Hegemony.* Amsterdam: VU University Press, 1994.

Eyman, Scott. *The Speed of Sound: Hollywood and the Talkie Revolution.* New York: Simon & Schuster, 1997.

Farnsworth, Elma G. "Pem." *Distant Vision.* Salt Lake City, Utah: Pemberly Kent, 1989.

Feuer, Jane. *The Hollywood Musical.* 2nd ed. Bloomington: Indiana University Press, 1993.

Fielding, Raymond. *The American Newsreel, 1922–1967.* Norman: University of Oklahoma Press, 1972.

Fielding, Raymond, ed. *A Technological History of Motion Pictures and Television.* Berkeley: University of California Press, 1967.

Fischer, Claude S. *America Calling: A Social History of the Telephone to 1940.* Berkeley: University of California Press, 1992.

Flamini, Roland. *Thalberg: The Last Tycoon and the World of MGM.* New York: Crown, 1994.

Fountain, Leatrice Gilbert. *Dark Star: The Untold Story of the Meteoric Rise and Fall of John Gilbert.* New York: St. Martin's Press, 1985.

Freedland, Michael. *The Warner Brothers.* London: Harrap, 1983.

Friedman, Lester D., ed. *Unspeakable Images: Ethnicity and the American Cinema.* Urbana: University of Illinois Press, 1991.

Gabler, Neal. *An Empire of Their Own: How the Jews Invented Hollywood.* New York: Crown, 1988.

Galbraith, John Kenneth. *The Great Crash, 1929.* Reprint, Boston: Houghton Mifflin, 1988.

Gallagher, Tag. *John Ford: The Man and His Films.* Berkeley: University of California Press, 1986.

Gardner, Gerald C. *The Censorship Papers: Movie Censorship Letters from the Hays Office, 1934–1968.* New York: Dodd, Mead, 1987.

Geduld, Harry M. *The Birth of the Talkies: From Edison to Jolson.* Bloomington: Indiana University Press, 1975.

Goldberg, Judith N. *Laughter Through Tears: The Yiddish Cinema.* East Brunswick, N.J.: Associated University Presses, 1983.

Goldman, Eric A. *Visions, Images, and Dreams: Yiddish Film Past and Present.* Ann Arbor, Mich.: UMI Research, 1983.

Goldman, Herbert. *Fanny Brice: The Original Funny Girl.* New York: Oxford University Press, 1992.

———. *Jolson: The Legend Comes to Life.* New York: Oxford University Press, 1988.

Gomery, Douglas. *Shared Pleasures: A History of Movie Presentation in the United States.* Madison: University of Wisconsin Press, 1992.

———. *The Hollywood Studio System.* New York: St. Martin's Press, 1986.

———. "The Coming of Sound to the American Cinema." Ph.D. dissertation, University of Wisconsin, 1975.

Gorbman, Claudia. *Unheard Melodies: Narrative Film Music.* Bloomington: Indiana University Press, 1988.

Gordon, Colin. *New Deals: Business, Labor, and Politics in America, 1920–1935.* New York: Cambridge University Press, 1994.

———. "New Deal, Old Deck: Business, Labor, and Politics, 1920–1935." Ph.D. dissertation, University of Wisconsin, 1990.

Green, Fitzhugh. *The Film Finds Its Tongue.* New York: Putnam's, 1929.

Griffith, Richard, ed. *The Talkies: Articles and Illustrations from a Great Fan Magazine, 1928–1940.* New York: Dover Publications, 1971.

Gussow, Mel. *Don't Say Yes Until I Finish Talking.* New York: Doubleday, 1991.

Guy, Alice. *Autobiographie d'une pionnière du cinéma.* Paris: Denoël/Gonthier, 1976.

Harding, Alfred. *The Revolt of the Actors.* New York: Wm. Morrow & Company, 1929.

Hays, Will. *See and Hear.* New York: Motion Picture Producers and Distributors of America, 1929.

Hemming, Roy. *The Melody Lingers On: The Great Songwriters and Their Movie Musicals.* New York: Newmarket, 1986.

Higham, Charles. *Warner Brothers.* New York: Charles Scribner's Sons, 1975.

Hijiya, James A. *Lee de Forest and the Fatherhood of Radio.* Bethlehem, Pa.: Lehigh University Press, 1992.

Hilmes, Michele. *Hollywood and Broadcasting: From Radio to Cable.* Urbana: University of Illinois Press, 1990.

Hoberman, J. *Bridge of Light: Yiddish Film Between Two Worlds*. Philadelphia: Temple University Press, 1995.

Horak, Jan-Christopher, ed. *Lovers of Cinema: The First American Film Avant-Garde, 1919–1945*. Madison: University of Wisconsin Press, 1995.

Izod, John. *Hollywood and the Box Office: 1895–1986*. New York: Columbia University Press, 1988.

Jacobs, Lea. *The Wages of Sin: Censorship and the Fallen Woman Film*. Madison: University of Wisconsin Press, 1991.

Jarvie, Ian. *Hollywood's Overseas Campaign: The North Atlantic Movie Trade*. Cambridge: Cambridge University Press, 1992.

Jenkins, Henry. *What Made Pistachio Nuts?* New York: Columbia University Press, 1992.

Jessel, George. *So Help Me: The Autobiography of George Jessel*. Cleveland, Ohio: World, 1943.

Jobes, Gertrude. *Motion Picture Empire*. Hamden, Conn.: Archon Books, 1966.

Jowett, Garth. *Film: The Democratic Art*. Boston: Little, Brown, 1976.

Kammen, Michael. *The Lively Arts: Gilbert Seldes and the Transformation of Cultural Criticism in the United States*. New York: Oxford University Press, 1996.

Katz, Ephraim. *The Film Encyclopedia*. New York: Putnam, 1979; Harper Collins, 1994.

Kauffmann, Stanley, and Bruce Henstell, eds. *American Film Criticism: From Its Beginnings to Citizen Kane*. New York: Liveright, 1972.

Kennedy, Joseph P. *The Story of the Films*. Chicago: Shaw, 1927.

Kobal, John. *Gotta Sing, Gotta Dance: A Pictorial History of Film Musicals*. London: Hamlyn, 1971.

Korda, Michael. *Charmed Lives: A Family Romance*. New York: Random House, 1979.

Koszarski, Richard. *An Evening's Entertainment: The Age of the Silent Feature Picture 1915–1928*. New York: Scribner's, 1990.

———. *The Astoria Studio and Its Fabulous Films*. New York: Dover, 1983.

———. *The Man You Love to Hate*. New York: Oxford University Press, 1983.

———. *Universal Pictures: 75 Years*. New York: Museum of Modern Art, 1977.

Kreuger, Miles. *The Movie Musical from Vitaphone to 42nd Street, as Reported in a Great Fan Magazine*. New York: Dover Publications, 1975.

Kulik, Karol. *Alexander Korda: The Man Who Could Work Miracles*. London: Virgin Books, 1990.

Lacombe, Alain, and Claude Rocle. *De Broadway à Hollywood: l'Amérique et sa comedie musicale*. Paris: Cinéma, 1980.

Lasky, Betty. *RKO: The Biggest Little Major of Them All*. Englewood Cliffs, N.J.: Prentice Hall, 1984.

Lasky, Jesse L., with Don Weldon. *I Blow My Own Horn*. Garden City, N.Y.: Doubleday, 1957.

Lastra, James Frederick. "Standards and Practices: Technology and Representation in the American Cinema." Ph.D. dissertation, University of Iowa, 1992.

Lauretis, Teresa de, and Stephen Heath, eds. *The Cinematic Apparatus*. London: Macmillan, 1980.

Leab, Daniel J. *From Sambo to Superspade: The Black Experience in Motion Pictures*. Boston: Houghton Mifflin, 1975.

Levin, Martin, comp. *Hollywood and the Great Fan Magazines*. New York: Arbor House, 1970.

Levin, Thomas Y. "The Acoustic Dimension: Notes on Film Sound." *Screen* 25, no. 3 (May–June 1984): 55–68.

Levy, Emmanuel. *George Cukor: Master of Elegance*. New York: Wm. Morrow, 1994.

Lewis, Lisa A., ed. *The Adoring Audience: Fan Culture and Popular Media*. New York: Routledge, 1992.

Lewis, Tom. *Empire of the Air: The Men Who Made Radio*. New York: Harper Collins, 1991.

Leyda, Jay, ed. *Eisenstein on Disney*. Trans. Alan Upchurch. London: Methuen, 1988.

Low, Rachel. *The History of the British Film, 1918–1929*. London: Allen & Unwin, 1971.

Madsen, Axel. *William Wyler*. New York: Thomas Crowell, 1973.

Maland, Charles. *Chaplin and American Culture*. Princeton, N.J.: Princeton University Press, 1989.

Maltin, Leonard. *Of Mice and Magic: A History of American Animated Cartoons*. New York: McGraw-Hill, 1980.

Manvell, Roger, and Heinrich Fraenkel. *The German Cinema.* New York: Praeger, 1971.

Manvell, Roger, and John Huntley. *The Technique of Film Music.* London and New York: Focal Press, 1957.

Marsden, Michael T., John G. Nachbar, and Sam L. Grogg, Jr., eds. *Movies as Artifacts.* Chicago: Nelson-Hall, 1982.

Martin, Len D. *The Columbia Checklist.* Jefferson, N.C.: McFarland, 1991.

Marvin, Carolyn. *When Old Technologies Were New.* New York: Oxford University Press, 1988.

Marx, Samuel. *Mayer and Thalberg: The Make-Believe Saints.* New York: Warner Books, 1975.

Mayne, Judith. *Directed by Dorothy Arzner.* Bloomington: Indiana University Press, 1994.

McChesney, Robert W. *Telecommunications, Mass Media, and Democracy: The Battle for the Control of U.S. Broadcasting, 1928–1935.* New York: Oxford University Press, 1993.

McLaughlin, Robert. "Broadway and Hollywood: A History of Economic Interaction." Ph.D. dissertation, University of Wisconsin, 1970.

Merritt, Russell, and J. B. Kaufman. *Walt in Wonderland: The Silent Films of Walt Disney.* Baltimore, Md.: Johns Hopkins University Press, 1993.

Moley, Raymond. *The Hays Office.* Indianapolis: The Bobbs-Merrill Company, 1945.

Moore, Colleen. *Silent Star.* Garden City, N.Y.: Doubleday, 1968.

Musser, Charles. *Before the Nickelodeon: Edwin S. Porter and the Edison Manufacturing Company.* Berkeley: University of California, Press, 1991.

———. *The Emergence of Cinema: The American Screen to 1907.* New York: Charles Scribner's Sons, 1990.

Neale, Steve. *Cinema and Technology: Image, Sound, Color.* Bloomington: University of Indiana Press, 1985.

Neibaur, James L. *The RKO Features.* Jefferson, N.C.: McFarland, 1994.

New York Times. New York Times Film Reviews.

Paul, William. *Ernst Lubitsch's American Comedy.* New York: Columbia University Press, 1983.

Perry, Louis B. *A History of the Los Angeles Labor Movement, 1911-1941.* Berkeley: University of California Press, 1963.

Peters, Margot. *The House of Barrymore.* New York: Knopf, 1990.

Peterson, Theodore. *Magazines in the Twentieth Century.* Urbana: University of Illinois Press, 1956.

Poague, Leland A. *The Cinema of Ernst Lubitsch.* New York: Barnes, 1978.

Prindle, David F. *Risky Business: The Political Economy of Hollywood.* Boulder, Colo.: Westview Press, 1993.

———. *The Politics of Glamour: Ideology and Democracy in the Screen Actors Guild.* Madison: University of Wisconsin Press, 1988.

Rentschler, Eric, ed. *The Films of G. W. Pabst.* New Brunswick, N.J.: Rutgers University Press, 1990.

Richardson, F. H. *Handbook of Projection: The Blue Book of Projection.* Vol. 3. New York: Chalmers, 1930.

Ringgold, Gene, and DeWitt Bodeen. *The Films of Cecil B. DeMille.* Seacaucus, N.J.: Cadillac, 1969.

Robinson, David. *Chaplin: His Life and Art.* New York: McGraw-Hill, 1985.

Roddick, Nick. *A New Deal in Entertainment: Warner Brothers in the 1930s.* London: BFI, 1983.

Rogin, Michael. *Blackface, White Noise: Jewish Immigrants in the Hollywood Melting Pot.* Berkeley: University of California Press, 1996.

Ross, Murray. *Stars and Strikes: Unionization of Hollywood.* New York: Columbia University Press, 1941.

Roys, H. E., ed. *Disc Recording and Reproduction.* Stroudsburg, Pa.: Dowden, Hutchinson & Ross, 1978.

Rubin, Joan Shelley. *The Making of Middlebrow Culture.* Chapel Hill: University of North Carolina Press, 1992.

Rubin, Martin. *Showstoppers: Busby Berkeley and the Tradition of Spectacle.* New York: Columbia University Press, 1993.

Rudolph, Alan. *Mrs. Parker and the Vicious Circle: The Book of the Film.* New York: Applause Theatre Books, 1995.

Salt, Barry. *Film Style and Technology: History and Analysis.* London: Starword, 1983.

Sanjek, Russell, and David Sanjek. *American Popular Music Business in the Twentieth Century.* New York: Oxford University Press, 1991.

Schaefer, Eric Paul. "'Bold! Daring! Shocking! True!': A History of Exploitation Films, 1919–1959." Ph.D. dissertation, University of Texas at Austin, 1994.

Schickel, Richard. *D. W. Griffith: An American Life.* New York: Simon and Schuster, 1984.

Schneider, Steve. *That's All Folks: The Art of Warner Bros. Animation.* New York: Henry Holt, 1988.

Schwartz, Nancy Lynn. *The Hollywood Writers' Wars.* New York: Knopf, 1982.

Seldes, Gilbert. *Movies for the Millions.* London: B. T. Batsford, 1937.

———. *An Hour with the Movies and the Talkies.* Philadelphia: Lippincott, 1929.

Sinclair, Upton. *Upton Sinclair Presents William Fox.* Los Angeles: Sinclair, 1933.

Sklar, Robert. *City Boys: Cagney, Bogart, Garfield.* Princeton, N.J.: Princeton University Press, 1992.

Slide, Anthony. *The Encyclopedia of Vaudeville.* Westport, Conn.: Greenwood Press, 1994.

———. *The American Film Industry: A Historical Dictionary.* Westport, Conn.: Greenwood Press, 1986.

———. *Great Pretenders: A History of Female and Male Impersonation in the Performing Arts.* Lombard, Ill.: Wallace-Homestead, 1986.

———, ed. *They Also Wrote For the Fan Magazines: Film Articles by Literary Giants From e. e. cummings to Eleanor Roosevelt, 1920–1939.* Jefferson, N.C.: McFarland, 1992.

Smoodin, Eric, ed. *Disney Discourse: Producing the Magic Kingdom.* New York: Routledge, 1994.

Smulyan, Susan. *Selling Radio: The Commercialization of American Broadcasting, 1920–1934.* Washington, D.C.: Smithsonian Institution Press, 1994.

Snead, James. *White Screens Black Images: Hollywood from the Dark Side.* New York: Routledge, 1994.

Sperling, Cass Warner, with Cork Millner and Jack Warner, Jr. *Hollywood Be Thy Name.* Rocklin, Calif.: Prima Publishing, 1994.

Staiger, Janet. *Interpreting Films: Studies in the Historical Reception of American Cinema.* Princeton, N.J.: Princeton University Press.

Staiger, Janet, ed. *The Studio System.* New Brunswick, N.J.: Rutgers University Press, 1995.

Stenn, David. *Clara Bow: Runnin' Wild.* New York: Doubleday, 1988.

Studlar, Gaylyn. *This Mad Masquerade: Stardom and Masculinity in the Jazz Age.* New York: Columbia University Press, 1996.

Swanson, Gloria. *Swanson on Swanson.* New York: Random House, 1980.

Taylor, Richard, ed. and trans. *S. M. Eisenstein: Selected Works,* vol. 1: *Writings, 1922–1934.* London: BFI, 1988.

Thomas, Bob. *Walt Disney: An American Original.* New York: Simon & Schuster, 1976.

Thompson, Kristin. *Wooster Proposes, Jeeves Disposes, or Le Mot Juste.* New York: Heinemann, 1992.

———. *Breaking the Glass Armor: Neoformalist Film Analysis.* Princeton, N.J.: Princeton University Press, 1988.

———. *Exporting Entertainment: America in the World Film Market 1907–1934.* London: BFI, 1985.

Thompson, Kristin, and David Bordwell. *Film History: An Introduction.* New York: McGraw-Hill, 1994.

Thomson, David. *Showman: The Life of David O. Selznick.* New York: Knopf, 1992.

Thrasher, Frederic M., ed. *Okay For Sound!* New York: Duell, Sloan and Pearce, 1946.

Tyne, Gerald F. J. *Saga of the Vacuum Tube.* Indianapolis: Sams, 1977.

Variety. Variety Film Reviews. New York: Garland, 1983– .

Waldman, Harry. *Hollywood and the Foreign Touch: A Dictionary of Foreign Filmmakers and Their Films from America, 1910–1995.* Lanham, Md.: Scarecrow Press, 1996.

Walker, Alexander. *The Shattered Silents: How the Talkies Came to Stay.* New York: Wm. Morrow, 1979.

———. *Stardom: The Hollywood Phenomenon.* New York: Stein and Day, 1970.

Warner, Jack L. *My First Hundred Years in Hollywood.* New York: Random House, 1964.

Weinberg, Herman G. *Saint Cinema.* 2nd ed. rev. New York: Dover, 1973.

Weis, Elisabeth, and John Belton, eds. *Film Sound: Theory and Practice.* New York: Columbia University Press, 1985.

Wilkerson, Tichi, and Marcia Borie. *The Hollywood Reporter: The Golden Years.* New York: Coward, McCann, 1984.

Zukor, Adolph, with Dale Kramer. *The Public Is Never Wrong.* New York: Putnam, 1953.

Picture Sources

Illustrations are from issues of *Film Daily* or the author's collection, with the following exceptions (used by permission):

Joseph Yranski Collection. Cover photo; pages: ii, 20, 35, 46, 62, 73, 77, 78, 79, 80, 84, 102, 105, 114, 197, 232, 237, 243, 266, 274, 276, 279, 282, 283, 285, 288, 289, 292, 293, 297, 299, 300, 302, 305, 314, 316, 318, 319, 320, 323, 324, 325, 327, 335, 339, 340, 341, 346, 349, 350, 361, 365, 366, 367, 372, 373, 406, 434, 440, 446, 454, 458, 461, 468, 491, 507, 512, 545.

Wisconsin Center for Film and Theater Research. Pages: 36, 90, 97, 185, 226, 228, 229, 252, 370, 377, 429.

Electronics, July 1930. Page: 180.

University of Wisconsin Press. Pages: 522, 523, 524.

The Vitaphone Project. Page: 67.

General Index

Italic numerals signify illustrations.

Index of Films

Italic numerals signify Illustrations.